the
LIONS
of JULY

THE
LIONS
OF JULY

Prelude to War, 1914

William Jannen Jr.

PRESIDIO

Published by Presidio Press
505 B San Marin Dr., Suite 300
Novato, CA 94945-1340

Library of Congress Cataloging-in-Publication Data

Jannen, William, 1930–
    Lions of July : Prelude to War, 1914 / by William Jannen, Jr.
        p. cm.
    Includes bibliographical references and index.
    ISBN 0-89141-569-6 (hardcover)
    ISBN 0-89141-637-4 (paperback)
1. World War, 1914–1918—Causes. 2. World War, 1914–1918—Diplomatic history. 3. Europe—Politics and government—1871–1910. 4. Nationalism—Europe. I. Title.
D5 11.J34 1996
940.3' 1—dc20   95-9454
                                                       CIP

Typography by ProImage
Printed in the United States of America

THE LIONS OF JULY

Prelude to War, 1914

William Jannen Jr.

PRESIDIO

Published by Presidio Press
505 B San Marin Dr., Suite 300
Novato, CA 94945-1340

Library of Congress Cataloging-in-Publication Data

Jannen, William, 1930–
    Lions of July : Prelude to War, 1914 / by William Jannen, Jr.
      p. cm.
    Includes bibliographical references and index.
    ISBN 0-89141-569-6 (hardcover)
    ISBN 0-89141-637-4 (paperback)
1. World War, 1914–1918—Causes. 2. World War, 1914–1918—Diplomatic
history. 3. Europe—Politics and government—1871–1910. 4. Nationalism—
Europe. I. Title.
D5 11.J34 1996
940.3' 1—dc20   95-9454
                                                                    CIP

Typography by ProImage
Printed in the United States of America

To Lynn

To Lynn

CONTENTS

ACKNOWLEDGMENTS

I would like to thank Gale Weesner, for giving up time from her own writing to put my manuscript in shape, my agent Fifi Oscard, for finding me Presidio Press, Presidio's publisher Bob Kane, and editors Dale Wilson and E. J. McCarthy, for their professionalism and intelligence.

ACKNOWLEDGMENTS

I would like to thank Gale Weesner, for giving up time from her own writing to put my manuscript in shape, my agent Fifi Oscard, for finding me Presidio Press, Presidio's publisher Bob Kane, and editors Dale Wilson and E. J. McCarthy, for their professionalism and intelligence.

PARTICIPANTS

Crown Prince Alexander of Serbia. Becomes regent on 24 June 1914 when his father, King Peter, steps down.

Herbert Henry Asquith, British prime minister.

Nicolai Alexandrovich Basili, assistant chief of chancellery in Russian foreign ministry.

Count Alexander Benckendorff, Russian ambassador in London.

Count Leopold von Berchtold, Austro-Hungarian minister to the imperial household and for foreign affairs.

Philippe J. L. Berthelot, French foreign ministry official.

Sir Francis Bertie, British ambassador in Paris.

Theobald von Bethmann-Hollweg, German imperial chancellor.

Jean-Baptiste Bienvenu-Martin, French minister of justice and acting minister for foreign affairs in Viviani's absence, 15-29 July 1914.

Arkadi Nikolaievich Bronevski, Russian chargé d'affaires in Berlin.

Sir George William Buchanan, British ambassador in St. Petersburg.

Sir Maurice de Bunsen, British ambassador in Vienna.

Jules Cambon, French ambassador in Berlin, younger brother of Paul Cambon.

Paul Cambon, French ambassador in London, older brother of Jules.

General von Chelius, German kaiser's personal representative to the tsar.

Winston S. Churchill, British first lord of the admiralty.

Field Marshal Baron Franz Conrad von Hötzendorf, Austro-Hungarian chief of the army general staff.

Sir Eyre Crowe, British assistant undersecretary in the foreign office.

Gen. Juri Nikiforovich Danilov, Russian quartermaster general.

Gen. Sergei K. Dobrolski, chief of the mobilization section of the Russian army general staff.

Alfred Dumaine, French ambassador in Vienna.

Maj. Bernard von Eggeling, German military attaché in St. Petersburg.

Gen. Erich von Falkenhayn, German minister for war.

Abel Ferry, French undersecretary for foreign affairs.

Hans von Flotow, German ambassador in Rome.

Count Johann Forgách von Gymes und Gaes, chief of section in Austro-Hungarian ministry for foreign affairs.

Franz Joseph, emperor of Austria and king of Hungary.

George V, king of England.

Baron Giesl von Gieslingen, Austro-Hungarian minister in Belgrade.

Sir William Edward Goschen, British ambassador in Berlin.

Sir Edward Grey, British foreign secretary.

Slavko Gruic, secretary-general of Serbian foreign ministry.

Richard Burdon Haldane, British secretary of state for war, mentor and political ally of Asquith and Grey.

Nikolai H. de Hartwig, Russian minister at Belgrade, dies of massive heart attack in Austrian legation in Belgrade on 10 July.

Henry, prince of Prussia, brother of Kaiser Wihelm II.

Count Alexander Hoyos, chief secretary to Count Berchtold at Austro-Hungarian foreign ministry.

Alexander Izvolsky, Russian ambassador in Paris.

Gottlieb von Jagow, German state secretary for foreign affairs.

Gen. Joseph J. Joffre, chief of the French general staff.

Jean Jaurès, deputy in French Chamber of Deputies, influential Socialist, editor of leading French Socialist paper.

Alexander Vasilievich Krivoshein, Russian minister for agriculture.

Gen. Alexander von Krobatin, Austro-Hungarian minister for war.

Richard von Kühlmann, Prince Lichnowsky's embassy first secretary.

Gen. Marquis de Laguiche, French military attache in St. Petersburg.

Prince Karl Max Lichnowsky, German ambassador in London.

David Lloyd George, British chancellor of the exchequer and leading antiwar radical.

Baron Karl von Macchio, spokesman for Count Berchtold in the Austro-Hungarian foreign ministry.

Bruno Jacquin de Margerie, political director in French foreign ministry.

Count Albert von Mensdorff-Pouilly-Dietrichstein, Austro-Hungarian ambassador in London.

Kajetan Mérey von Kapos-Mére, Austro-Hungarian ambassador in Rome.

Adolphe Messimy, French minister for war.

Gen. Helmuth von Moltke, German chief of the great general staff.

Adm. Georg Alexander von Müller, head of the kaiser's naval cabinet in the kaiser's personal entourage.

Nicholas II, tsar of Russia.

Sir Arthur Nicolson, permanent undersecretary of state in British foreign office.

Laza Pacu, Serbian finance minister.

Maurice Paléologue, French ambassador in St. Petersburg.

Nicholas Pasic, Serbian prime minister.

Raymond Poincaré, president of the French Republic.

Count Friedrich von Pourtalès, German ambassador in St. Petersburg.

Kurt Riezler, adviser to Bethmann Hollweg.

Sir Horace Rumbold, British chargé d'affaires in Berlin.

The Marchese Antonino di San Giuliano, Italian foreign minister.

Sergei Dmitrievich Sazonov, Russian foreign minister.

Nikolai Nikolaievich Schebeko, Russian ambassador in Vienna.

Baron Moritz Fabianovich von Schilling, head of the chancellery in Russian foreign ministry.

Freiherr Wilhelm von Schoen, German ambassador in Paris.

Vasili Nikolaievich Strandtmann, counselor of the Russian legation in Belgrade and acting minister after death of Hartwig on 10 July 1914.

Wilhelm von Stumm, political director in German foreign ministry.

Gen. Vladimir Alexandrovich Sukhomlinov, Russian minister for war.

Sergei Nikolaievich Sverbejev, Russian ambassador in Berlin.

Count Friedrich Szápáry von Szápár, Austro-Hungarian ambassador in St. Petersburg.

Count Nikolaus Szécsen von Temerin, Austro-Hungarian ambassador in Paris.

Count Ladislaus Szögyény-Marich, Austro-Hungarian ambassador in Berlin.

Admiral Alfred von Tirpitz, naval minister for the German imperial navy and creator of the Imperial High Seas Fleet.

Count Stephan Tisza de Boros-Jenti, Hungarian prime minister.

Count Heinrich Leopold von Tschirschky und Bögendorff, German ambassador in Vienna.

Sir William G. Tyrrell, private secretary to Sir Edward Grey.

Rene Viviani, French prime minister and foreign minister.

Wilhelm II, German kaiser and king of Prussia, grandson to Queen Victoria of England, nephew to King Edward VII of England, cousin to King George V of England, second cousin to Tsar Nicholas II of Russia, cousin to Tsaritsa Alexandra of Russia.

Theodor Wolff, editor of the *Berliner Tageblatt*.

Gen. Nikolai Nikolaievich Yanushkevich, chief of the Russian general staff.

Arthur Zimmermann, German under state secretary for foreign affairs.

Kaiser Wilhelm II

Emperor Franz Joseph

Tsar Nicholas II and King George V (to left of Nicholas II)

Theodor von Bethmann-Hollweg, German Imperial Chancellor

Count Berchtold, Austro-Hungarian foreign minister (left), *and Count Tisza, Hungarian prime minister* (right)

Sergei Sazonov, Russian foreign minister

Raymond Poincaré, President of France

Nikolas Pasic, Serbian prime minister

Herbert Henry Asquith, British prime minister

Sir Edward Grey, British foreign secretary

Count Alexander Benckendorff, Russian ambassador in London (left), *and Paul Cambon, French ambassador in London* (right)

*Sir Arthurd Nicolson, permanent
undersecretary of state, British
foreign office*

*Prince Max von Lichnowsky, German
ambassador in London*

General Helmuth von Moltke, German army chief of staff (left), *and
Gottlieb von Jagow, German Undersecretary for foreign affairs* (right)

Jules Cambon, French ambassa-
dor in Berlin

Maurice Paléologue, French ambassador in St. Petersburg (left), *and count*
Friedrich von Pourtalès, German ambassador in St. Petersburg (right)

North Sea

Baltic Sea

RUSSIAN ARMY
30+ DIVS.

EAST
PRUSSIA

GERMAN
8TH ARMY
13 DIVS.

NETHERLANDS

GERMANY

RUSSIA

BELGIUM

Berlin

Warsaw

BEF
5 DIVS

Liege

GERMAN ARMY
RIGHT WING
54 DIVS.

LUX

RUSSIAN ARMY 50+ DIVS.

Paris

FRENCH ARMY
62 DIVS.

GERMAN ARMY
LEFT WING
20 DIVS.

GALICA

AUSTRIAN ARMY
A GROUP 28 DIVS

Danube River

AUSTRO-HUNGARIAN
EMPIRE

FRANCE

Vienna

Budapest

AUSTRIAN ARMY
B GROUP 12 DIVS

Sava R

MINIMUM GROUP
SERBIA 8 DIVS

ROMANIA

Mediterranean Sea

Adriatic Sea

Belgrade

Danube River

Nish

ROMANIA

SERBIA

BULGARIA

Black Sea

Agean Sea

STRATEGIC MAP
OF
EUROPE 1914

EACH ARROW ➤ REPRESENTS 10 DIVISONS

C.G.S.

THE BALKANS 1914

NEW SERBIA SINCE 1912

AUSTRIA-HUNGARY'S
SOUTH SLAV PROVINCES

RUSSIA

AUSTRIA-HUNGARY

TRANSYLVANIA

ROMANIA

CROATIA

SLAVONIA

Sava

BOSNIA

Belgrade

Danube   River

Bucharest

Sarajevo

HERZEGOVINA

SERBIA

Nish

BULGARIA

BLACK SEA

SANJAK

MONTENEGRO

Cetinje

Scutari

Sophia

Maritia   R

Constantinople

Drin R.

Vardar

Strunia   R.

Monastir   MACEDONIA

Durazzo

ALBANIA

ADRIATIC SEA

GREECE

AGEAN SEA

TURKEY

Athens

held by Italy since 1913

DODECANESE

CRETE

C.G.S.

PREFACE
Encounter in Meran, 1926

In the summer of 1926, Prince Karl Max Lichnowsky, Germany's former ambassador to Great Britain, was walking on the promenade of the Tyrolian resort town of Meran when he saw a tall, elegant figure coming toward him. It was Count Leopold von Berchtold, Austria-Hungary's former foreign minister and the man widely regarded as the irresponsible grand seigneur who had set Europe aflame by declaring war on Serbia twelve years earlier. The prince pretended not to see Berchtold, but the count bore down on him; a meeting was unavoidable.

In his own country, Prince Lichnowsky was almost as despised as Count Berchtold because he had publicly declared that Germany's handling of the July crisis in 1914 had been a disaster. Lichnowsky never forgave the "criminal idiocy" of his government's stubborn support of Austria-Hungary, and he regarded Berchtold as the man who had dragged Germany into the Great War. The prince walked steadily on.

Berchtold could see that Lichnowsky was trying to avoid him. Nonetheless, with grave courtesy, Berchtold presented himself to the hapless prince. "I know that you might not want to speak to me," Berchtold said, "but I have something important to tell you." What Berchtold said, Lichnowsky later wrote a friend, was that he "never would have taken so hard a line on Serbia if he had not been constantly pressured to do so by Berlin." Berlin's actions, Berchtold insisted, gave him no reason to suppose that Germany opposed a general war.[1]

Having unburdened himself, Berchtold continued on his way. The postwar recriminations among the survivors were in full swing.

PART I: ANOTHER ROYAL MURDER

1: ASSASSINATION SUNDAY

Sarajevo and Vienna, 28 June 1914

Count Berchtold was enjoying a country fair near his Buchlau estate when a telegram was delivered to him. He opened it, read it, and remained absolutely still, standing in the brilliant summer sunshine and staring at the piece of paper. After what seemed a very long time, he turned suddenly and announced that he must take the next train to Vienna. The Archduke Francis Ferdinand, heir apparent to the imperial throne, and his wife had just been murdered in Sarajevo, the provincial capital of the Austro-Hungarian province of Bosnia.

The murdered archduke and the Austro-Hungarian foreign minister had been lifelong friends. Their wives, too, had been friends since childhood, and only a few weeks earlier the two couples had spent a lovely weekend at the archduke's summer palace. The brutal murder of his friend was horror enough, but the death of the forceful Francis Ferdinand meant that a twenty-nine-year-old archduke with no political experience was now in line for the throne. The Hapsburg Empire of Austria-Hungary was a bewildering complex of 51 million people divided into something like thirteen nationalities, sixteen languages, seventeen constitutionally separate "lands," twenty parliamentary bodies, five major religions, and at least seven national separatist movements. The empire had evolved over the centuries as a series of dynastic acquisitions; now it faced a wholly different world of states built on the principle of nationality. It could not survive without a strong center, and the powerful personality of the murdered archduke would have provided such a center. "However one looks at him," Berchtold wrote years later, "he was . . . a man the Monarchy needed."[1] And now the archduke was dead.

As Berchtold rode the train to Vienna, he knew that if Serbia were involved in the assassination, there would be overwhelming pressure to do something about that troublesome kingdom. Doing something about Serbia was not a problem; the problem was to do something without a war with Russia, which Berchtold dreaded above all things. He had said repeatedly

that no matter who won, such a war would end in revolution and the fall of
both the Hapsburg and the Romanov dynasties.

The man mulling those dismal thoughts was an elegant aristocrat of great
wealth, master of the magnificent Schloss Buchlau, owner of tens of thousands of acres and whole villages, and minister to the royal and imperial
household and of foreign affairs of the Austro-Hungarian Empire—also
known as the Dual Monarchy or the Hapsburg Empire or simply Austria.
The blood of generations of Czech, Hungarian, and Austro-German nobles
flowed through his veins, and he could speak Czech, Slovak, and Hungarian
as well as French and German. Like most great aristocrats in public service,
Count Berchtold started young and rose rapidly. His father had launched
him by presenting him directly to the head of the government, who was of
course an old friend. In the upper levels of imperial service, Berchtold was
almost always among relatives or old family friends, aristocrats all. He was
the Austro-Hungarian ambassador to Russia at the age of forty-three and
became foreign minister in 1912 at forty-eight.

The Austro-Hungarian foreign minister was an exceptionally cultivated
and intelligent man who presented the world with a blend of effortless grace
and unfailing courtesy that was peculiar to himself. Almost everyone who
knew him agreed that Berchtold was a man of great charm who had an appealing, self-deprecating sense of humor. A French reporter once asked him
whether he considered himself German, Czech, or Magyar. Berchtold, who
probably thought the question a little silly, answered: "I am Viennese." The
reporter then asked him what side he would choose if there were trouble
between the many nationalities of the Hapsburg Empire. Berchtold gave the
only answer that made any sense to him: "The side of the Emperor." The
reporter, a man of the new age, persisted: What if the empire came to an
end? The answer was pure Berchtold: "I would remain an aristocrat; it is not
much, but it is always something."[2]

Europe was still very much an aristocratic society before the First World
War, and no one was surprised that the new foreign minister was a member
of the old aristocracy. But quite a few were surprised that the new foreign
minister was Count Leopold von Berchtold. He had been a first-rate ambassador and was obviously intelligent, but his courtly elegance, his languid
style, and his reputation as a connoisseur of art, women, and horses led
people to regard him as frivolous. Count Heinrich von Lützow, an older
colleague and fellow aristocrat, conceded that Berchtold had a fine mind
and exceptional taste in art. He agreed with all who knew Berchtold that the
count was an extraordinary charmer with an unconquerable joie de vivre.
But, Lützow added, "in no other country in the world would one have entertained the idea of making him foreign minister."[3]

Although the British ambassador at Vienna remarked that Berchtold seemed "overburdened by his office,"[4] Berchtold worked hard and had a clear policy. He believed that the three conservative eastern monarchies—Austria-Hungary, Imperial Germany, and tsarist Russia—should live in peace and friendship and cooperate in defending themselves against liberal subversion from the west. This meant coming to an agreement with Russia to maintain the status quo in the Balkans, where rising nationalism threatened the empire's integrity. Berchtold especially feared the expansive South Slav nationalism of the Kingdom of Serbia. Unfortunately, Serbia had become a client of Russia—and Russia regarded any attempt to contain Serbia as a threat to its own position in the Balkans. Berchtold did what he could to win over the Russians while he tried to build up Bulgaria as a check on Serbia. During his twenty-eight months as foreign minister, however, he had been frustrated at every turn.

The First Balkan War broke out in October 1912 when tiny Montenegro —followed by Serbia, Greece, and Bulgaria—drove the Turks out of most of the Balkan Peninsula. Serbia nearly doubled its size while increasing its population from 3 million people to nearly 4.5 million. Serbia's army, once a negligible military factor, became a battle-tested force of 500,000 men, equipped by France and trained by French military missions. That France was the ally of Russia only made matters worse.

The Bulgarians, who had fought alongside the Serbs, believed they had been cheated out of Macedonia. At the end of June 1913, Bulgaria sparked the Second Balkan War by launching a surprise attack on Serbian and Greek positions in Macedonia. The attack was a disaster. The Romanians joined the Serbs and the Greeks to annex long-coveted Bulgarian territory, and the Turks seized the opportunity to regain some of the areas lost to the Bulgarians in 1912. In a matter of weeks, Berchtold's counterweight to Serbia was overrun. The subsequent peace treaty stripped Bulgaria of much of its new territory, while Serbia emerged larger and more triumphant than ever. Serb patriots began saying openly that the Hapsburg provinces of Bosnia and Herzegovina were next. The Serbian war ministry in Belgrade even hung wall panels showing Bosnia and Herzegovina as part of the Kingdom of Serbia.[5]

Austria-Hungary was always wrestling with nationality problems. Germans and Czechs fought bitterly in Bohemia; the Romanians of Transylvania and the Croats of Croatia resisted the rule of the Hungarian Magyars in Hungary; Italians rioted in Trieste; and Ukrainians demanded a Ukrainian-language university. Only the Poles seemed reasonably loyal. Romania coveted the Romanian-speaking areas of Hungarian Transylvania, and the Italians longed for the Italian-speaking Tyrol. In the Hungarian half of the monarchy, extreme Magyar nationalists always sounded as if they wanted to tear Hungary right out of the empire.

As far as Austrians were concerned, however, the Serbs were by far the worst. Great Serb activists were connected with a seemingly endless series of assassinations and assassination attempts; they had been making trouble ever since the Serb military coup of 1903. In that year, a group of Serbian army officers horrified monarchical Europe by murdering Serbia's pro-Austrian king and queen, the queen's brothers, and several cabinet ministers. They replaced the murdered monarch with King Peter Karadjordjevic, who was pro-Russian. Under King Peter, it was hoped, Russia would support Serbia in reclaiming its "unredeemed territories" from Turkey and from Austria-Hungary.[6]

In 1908 Austria-Hungary annexed Bosnia and Herzegovina, which it had been governing under international agreement since 1878. Serb patriots protested the rape of the Serb national destiny to anyone who would listen and pleaded with Tsar Nicholas II for help. Only a German ultimatum forced Russia to drop its support for Serbia's claims. Berchtold had opposed the annexation, which he knew would anger Russia, but his predecessor had insisted and the emperor approved the action. Now Berchtold found his foreign policy saddled with an implacably hostile and pro-Serbian Russia.

All through the first half of 1914, Berchtold received reports from Serbia that newspapers, politicians, and army officers were predicting the imminent disintegration of the Austro-Hungarian Empire. "The Serbs," remarked the British minister in Belgrade, "already see themselves before Vienna."[7] Berchtold thought it was only a matter of time before Russia's Balkan policy, French arms for Serbia, and Serbian subversion in the South Slav provinces would make the monarchy's position untenable. German diplomats reported that Berchtold seemed unduly nervous, haunted by the fear of a new Russian-sponsored Balkan League that would now turn on Austria-Hungary.[8]

When Berchtold arrived in Vienna on Sunday afternoon, his worst fears were realized: the assassins were Bosnian Serbs who had come up from Belgrade for the express purpose of executing the archduke. He spent Sunday and Monday trying to find out exactly what had happened and listening to his colleagues urging him to act. Prince Gottfried zu Hohenlohe-Schillingfürst, who was scheduled to replace Austria-Hungary's aging ambassador in Berlin, warned Berchtold that he would refuse the Berlin embassy if serious action were not taken. Berchtold replied that he had no intention of taking the assassination lying down, but first he had to find out what had happened. Conferences ran continuously as Berchtold and his colleagues assessed the latest reports from Sarajevo, worried about the impact of the assassination on the empire's internal stability, tried to find a clear line of action, and

worked out ways to prepare an inexperienced, twenty-nine-year-old arch-duke to be the heir apparent and future emperor.

All this was taking place in an intense and angry atmosphere. On Sunday night, Joseph Redlich, a political figure who knew almost everyone who mattered in the Austrian political establishment, wrote in his diary, "It must now be clear to everyone that peaceful coexistence is impossible to achieve between this half-German Monarchy with its sister-relationship with Germany, and a Balkan nationalism roused to a fanatical lust for murder."[9] Redlich, like most of his fellow Austrians, did not mention Russia.

2: BELGRADE AND VIENNA

28 June–4 July

Serbian army officers and nationalists had always regarded their government's surrender of Bosnia and Herzegovina as a betrayal of the national cause. In 1911 a group of officers founded a new organization to promote Serbian expansion. Declaring pointedly that they would rely on "action," they named the new organization Union or Death, but it was soon known as the Black Hand. Most of the founders had participated in the bloody military coup of 1903 and were suspicious of the civilians in government, particularly Prime Minister Nicholas Pašić.

Pašić was sixty-eight years old in 1914 and, at the time of the assassination, in the midst of a critical election campaign. He had been active in Serbian politics since 1875. He carefully disappeared during the 1903 coup, then returned to make himself and his Old Radical Party the dominant force in Serbian politics. A few weeks before the assassination, the army, the nationalist opposition, and King Peter combined to force his resignation. Pašić, however, was a tough old man. He had the Russian minister remind King Peter that Russia would not be sympathetic to a government not headed by Pašić. He had the French minister mention that French money and French guns might not be as available if Pašić were not there. On 11 June he forced King Peter to reappoint him, and on 24, June 1914 King Peter, old, sick, and defeated, "temporarily" stepped aside on account of illness and named his son, Prince Alexander, prince regent. Once back in power, Pašić dissolved the legislature and prepared for new elections in which he hoped to improve his working majority and undermine the army's political base.[1]

In the midst of this struggle, Pašić learned that Black Hand activists had sent three armed Bosnian Serbs into Sarajevo. The report available to Pašić, from one of the agents used by the government to keep watch on the army, made no mention of assassination or the archduke, but it was not hard to guess what young, armed Bosnian Serbs might be up to.[2] Black Hand militants had set up the assassination attempt without informing their executive committee. When the government started looking into the mission of the three armed Serbs, the militants confessed to the executive committee that they had acted on their own. The committee ordered them to call off the assassination. The assassins refused to obey.

There was not much Pašić could do. If he publicly exposed a Black Hand operation, he might well be the victim of the next one. If he quietly warned the Austrian government, he risked revealing the involvement of Serbian army officers and border guards, and there was no telling how the Austrians might react. The Serbian military attaché in Vienna had reported just a few months earlier that Austrian leaders were "extraordinarily nervous and irritable" and might, in their present state, "engage in actions which in normal circumstances they would never consider." The attaché particularly warned his superiors to avoid provocations "with our national work" on the Austrian side of the border.[3] Finally, Pašić was fighting an election in which he was accused of not doing all he could to further Serbia's national destiny. He could hardly put himself in the position of delivering Serb heroes to the Austrians. Pašić went on with his electioneering, and Serbian diplomats continued their usual warnings that the archduke's scheduled visit to Sarajevo would be dangerously provocative, without specifying anything more precise.[4]

Photographs of Pašić show an intelligent face with a large white beard and dark, deep-set eyes, brooding unsmilingly over the ferocious politics of Serbia and the Balkans. He was a man of notoriously few words, and his cunning and his ability to lie with complete sincerity were famous—much admired by his friends but leaving him with no credibility in Vienna. No one there believed anything he said, and the Austro-Hungarian chargé d'affaires in Belgrade, who regarded all Serbs as liars, said of Pašić that "he only lies less because he talks less."[5]

Liar or not, Pašić knew that a war with the Hapsburg monarchy was the last thing Serbia needed. Serbia had been fighting more or less continuously since 1912, first against the Turks, then against the Bulgarians, and again and again with Bulgarian nationalist guerrillas in Macedonia and with tribal insurgents in Albania. The army was exhausted, the peasants were resisting new calls for conscripts, munitions were short, and the national treasury was almost empty.

Serbia had only eleven divisions to face the forty-eight divisions of Austria-Hungary and would never survive an Austrian invasion without Russian help. But Russia did not want a war. When the Russian minister to Serbia heard of the assassination, his reaction was succinct: "Let us hope he is not a Serb!" When he and Pašić learned that the assassin was indeed a Serb, they agreed that the best policy would be an attitude of dignified sympathy and unprovocative calm.

The Serbian government did what it could to restrain public celebration of the murder of an Austrian archduke, and most newspapers cooperated, but *Piemont,* the newspaper of the Black Hand, hailed the assassin as a martyr to Austrian oppression in Bosnia and Herzegovina. Serbian police promptly seized every available issue of *Piemont,* but not before the worst passages had been noted and sent to their governments by resident diplomats.[6] The Austro-Hungarian chargé d'affaires reported that Belgraders were falling "into one another's arms in delight."[7]

The government's attempts to control anti-Austrian outbursts collapsed completely in the next few days. In Sarajevo, the Croat and Muslim population knew within hours that the assassin had been a Bosnian Serb. On Monday morning, 29 June, swarms of shouting, singing, chanting Muslims and Croats roiled through the streets of Sarajevo with black-draped imperial flags and black-draped pictures of the emperor and of the late archduke and his duchess. They attacked all the Serb property they could lay hands on, sacking a Serb-owned hotel, smashing the windows in the residence of the Eastern Orthodox metropolitan, and destroying all the Serb-language schools and two Serb-language newspaper offices. A conservative Vienna paper reported the next day that "Sarajevo looks like the scene of a pogrom."[8] Over the next few days anti-Serb riots spread throughout the monarchy.

When news of the riots reached Serbia, the Serb newspapers abandoned all restraint. On Tuesday night a series of special flyers appeared on Belgrade streets announcing the "Extirpation of Serbs in Bosnia!" and the "Mass Arrest of Serbs." Casualties were estimated at ten thousand. There were, in fact, almost no casualties; most of the attacks were directed at Serb-owned shops and properties. The Muslim-Croat rioters were described as "paid mobs." Austrian authorities reportedly stood by quietly while Serbs were killed and their houses burned to the ground. Spectacular and salacious atrocities, particularly against women, were hinted at. Austro-Hungarian officials were described as tyrants and oppressors, the "worm-eaten" empire as tottering on its last legs, its "day of reckoning will soon come." Maurice de Bunsen, Great Britain's new ambassador in Vienna, wrote privately to Sir Arthur Nicolson, the permanent undersecretary at the British foreign office, that "the Servian press is behaving shamefully."[9]

Austro-Hungarian newspapers responded in kind. They were confident that Europe would support an Austrian punishment of Serbia. On 29 June the *Neue Freie Presse,* an aggressively patriotic middle-class paper, assured its readers: "The princes and rulers of the Great Powers know that tomorrow can be inflicted on them what today happened to the heir of the Monarchy."

The next day the *Neues Wiener Journal* began a series of articles urging "decisive action" against Serbia, and on 2 July it asked: "What expiation is to be made for the monstrous crime of Sarajevo?" In general, the theme was that if the multinational Empire was to survive, it had to "do something."

On 1 July Belgrade's *Politika* complained that not a half hour had passed from the arrest of the assassins when "the Jewish-Austrian press were flooding the world with their reports of bombs and money from Serbia." The *Politika,* which was regarded by the French foreign ministry as having close ties to the Russian legation, always referred to Austrian newspapers as the "Austro-Jewish press." The Belgrade government did what it could. On 2 July the semiofficial *Samouprava* wrote optimistically that the "occurrence" at Sarajevo could not be made into a cause of strife between Belgrade and Vienna because neither Serbia nor Austria-Hungary could fail to accept the judgment of the civilized world.

That same day Pašić sent a memorandum to his diplomats, pointing out that "both assassins were Austrian subjects." Serbia, he continued, would do all in its power to restrain "ill-balanced people within her frontiers," but it could "on no account permit Vienna and the Hungarian press to mislead European public opinion, and lay the heavy responsibility . . . at the door of the whole Serbian nation."[10] On 4 July Vienna's *Deutsches Volksblatt* replied to *Samouprava*'s appeal to the judgment of the civilized world: Sarajevo was "a matter that will have to be settled solely between ourselves and Serbia . . . and we shall settle it as our honor and the vital interests of the Monarchy shall dictate."[11]

Meanwhile, the father-in-law of the Serbian minister to Russia, a wealthy Sarajevo banker who was known locally as the "King of the Serbs," had suffered the destruction of several of his properties during the riots; he was arrested after the assassination in a general roundup of known Great Serb nationalists. His outraged son-in-law began leaking a series of interviews to St. Petersburg newspapers. "This arrest speaks for open war," he said, and is a "provocation for the entire Bosnian population, since Jeftanovic [the father-in-law] is the most popular person in the province." The Austrian embassy in St. Petersburg lodged a sharp protest at the Russian foreign ministry. The Russian foreign minister instructed his minister to Serbia to urge restraint upon the Serbian government. The Russian minister to Serbia dutifully warned his old friend Pasic, who assured the minister that he was trying to cooperate with Austria and would avoid all provocative statements. They would have to wait and see how Vienna responded to the assassination.[12]

3: Are We Covered by the Germans?

Vienna, 1–4 July

A six-man killing team had been in place in Sarajevo on 28 June, assisted by the Black Hand's resident agent. Three of the team members were nineteen-year-old Bosnian Serbs who had come up from Belgrade; one threw a grenade that missed and a second fired the shots that killed the archduke and the duchess. All three men had been expelled from Sarajevo schools or had dropped out. All three were longtime activists who had been in trouble with the Sarajevo police. All three had found their way to Belgrade, where they spent endless hours in coffeehouses talking of revolution and Serbdom and national liberation. They had come to Sarajevo to strike a blow for freedom by killing the archduke. The Black Hand agent had also recruited two local Serb schoolboys, one seventeen and one eighteen years old. The final member of the team, and the only non-Serb, was a thirtyish Muslim who had been drifting around terrorist plots for years. He had been recruited to keep the assassination from being an all-Serb affair.[1]

The nineteen year old who threw the grenade and the nineteen year old who killed the archduke were arrested immediately. The local Black Hand agent was arrested within hours. The two schoolboys and the third nineteen year old were apprehended a few days later. Every one of them was an Eastern Orthodox Bosnian Serb. The Muslim was the only one to escape. On 2 July the killer, the grenade thrower, and the Black Hand agent agreed to make a full and detailed confession to prevent, as they said, the arrest and torture of innocent people. They admitted being armed and trained by Serbian guerrilla fighters in Belgrade, and they betrayed the entire network of contact men and Serbian border guards who had brought them and their weapons across the Serbian frontier and north to Sarajevo.

For anyone who hoped for peace, those confessions were the worst possible news.

Baron Franz Conrad von Hötzendorf, field marshal and army chief of staff, had sung the same tune for years: unless something was done about

Serbia, the monarchy would disappear. During the annexation crisis of 1908–09, he had pleaded for war, arguing that "the Monarchy will hardly have so fortunate a chance again." When that crisis was settled peacefully, Conrad predicted that "in ten years the Monarchy will have shrunk to the size of Switzerland."[2] When the monarchy failed to limit Serbia's gains in 1912 and 1913, Conrad wrote: "I know very well that behind all this [passivity] lies the fear of war with Russia, but I believe that if we constantly let ourselves be influenced by this fear . . . it will be like digging our own graves." When this argument got him nowhere, Conrad tried another: "Finally, I would like to raise the question whether an attack by the Monarchy upon Serbia at present would necessarily bring on the intervention of Russia."

Berchtold tried Conrad's argument on the German ambassador, Heinrich von Tschirschky, who dismissed it as nonsense. Berchtold had to tell Conrad that there was no political support for a war on Serbia.[3]

When the archduke was murdered, Conrad predictably insisted that the assassination "could only be answered by war."[4] This time Berchtold was ready to agree. Even before the confessions, on 30 June, he had told Ambassador Tschirschky that "everything points to the fact that the threads of the conspiracy to which the archduke fell a sacrifice run together at Belgrade." The phrase "the threads of the conspiracy . . . run together at Belgrade" was to be repeated over and over again in the following days and weeks. Tschirschky advised against hasty steps. He told Berchtold that Austria-Hungary "must make sure what they want to do; up to now all I have heard are vague expressions of emotion." He also warned that Austria would have to consider the attitude of Russia.[5]

Later that same day, in an audience with Emperor Franz Joseph, Berchtold lamented that the monarchy, the most conservative power in Europe, was being forced to make war by the expansive policies of neighboring states. The old emperor sadly agreed. Franz Joseph had been losing wars with the forces of national self-determination for much of his reign. He surrendered most of his Italian provinces to a newly created Italy in a war with France and Piedmont in 1859. He was driven out of Germany in the war with Prussia in 1866. He had stood helplessly on the sidelines as Prussia crushed France in 1870, and he watched while his ancient Hohenzollern rivals united all of non-Austrian Germany under the Prussian crown. He again watched passively as the Balkan States drove the Turks out of the Balkans in 1912 and crushed Bulgaria in 1913. The only success in his long and troubled reign had been the annexation of Bosnia and Herzegovina in 1908. Although he was understandably wary of war and dearly wanted to end his days in peace, he was not prepared to lose those two provinces to the barbarous Serbs. The emperor, however, had just talked to Count Stephan Tisza, the Hungarian prime minister, and Tisza was of the opinion that military action was not necessary. The emperor told Berchtold that he would have to get Tisza's agreement before taking any action.[6] He was not going to fight a war if the Hungarians were opposed.

Berchtold and Tisza were as different as they could be. Berchtold was elegant, Tisza was sober. Berchtold was a charmer, Tisza alienated people— a fact that bothered him not at all. Berchtold sought accommodation, Tisza held out tenaciously for what he wanted. Berchtold was a pleasure-loving and worldy Catholic whose deepest loyalty was to the dynasty. Tisza was a Magyar and an earnest Calvinist whose father had been Hungarian prime minister before him. Stephan Tisza's loyalty to the dynasty depended entirely upon the interests of the Magyar nation. He believed that sharing power with the Austrian Germans in a monarchy that was regarded as a Great Power was the best the outnumbered Magyars could expect, hemmed in as they were by Slavs on the one side and Germans on the other. If it was God's will to preserve the Magyar nation, then it was his duty to carry out God's will—and he brought enormous energy, great intelligence, and a Calvinist sense of mission to that task.[7]

Tisza was convinced that time was on the monarchy's side, that sound administration, more money for the army, and patient diplomacy would soon put an end to nationalist unrest and would eventually isolate Serbia. For Tisza, sound administration did not mean fundamental reform. He was adamantly opposed to proposals such as trialism, by which the Slavs would share power with the Magyars and the Germans in governing the monarchy. He had once warned the murdered archduke that if he tampered with the constitutional basis of Magyar-German dualism, he would face a civil war.[8]

Most Austrian Germans, on the other hand, were convinced that trialism was the only hope for keeping the South Slavs loyal to the empire. Many thought that if the monarchy were once victorious over Serbia, with the subject nations rallying to the dynasty against the common enemy, then, in the enthusiasm and fellow-feeling of the common struggle, the emperor would have more than enough prestige to break Magyar obstruction and impose trialism by the sheer impetus of a glorious military victory.

Berchtold, with lands in Hungary and a Magyar wife, was no fan of trialism; but most members of the government were, and they regarded the Magyars as the major obstacle. Joseph Baernreither, a politically active Bohemian German, noted in his diary in 1912 that whenever he asked what possible benefit there could be in a war with Serbia, he always got the "stereotyped" answer: annexation of Serbia, trialism, and "straightening out" relations with Hungary. Early in 1913 the Austro-Hungarian minister for war told Baernreither that after a successful war they would ram trialism down the Hungarians' throats![9]

That kind of talk was no secret to Tisza; assassination or no assassination, he was not going to risk a war with Serbia that could destroy Magyar rule, and he did not expect trouble when Berchtold came to see him after his audience with the emperor. He liked Berchtold. Berchtold was sensitive to Magyar interests; although he had always been close to the late archduke, he was never enthusiastic about trialism. Nor was Berchtold one of those who were forever calling for war on Serbia. Moreover, Tisza and Berchtold and the foreign ministry had just completed months of talks on a new diplomatic initiative in the Balkans, which had been finalized in a 24 June memorandum intended for the Germans. To Tisza, the assassination made that initiative more urgent than ever.

The 24 June memorandum was designed to convince the Germans that an alliance with Bulgaria was necessary. The Romanians had long been secretly allied with Austria and Germany; the Germans trusted them, the Austrians did not. The memorandum therefore proposed that Austria and Germany ask Romania to make the alliance public. Berchtold and Tisza were sure that Romania would refuse: Romanian nationalists longed for union with the Romanian-speaking portions of Hungarian Transylvania, and the Romanian monarchy would not dare to challenge them. In that case, Germany would have no choice but to let Austria seek alliances with Bulgaria and Turkey, both of whom were hostile to Serbia. If that effort were successful, the balance of power in the Balkans would continue to favor Austria and Germany; Romania, with hostile states on three sides, would find it too dangerous to turn to Russia.[10] Serbia would be isolated and contained.

What Tisza expected to discuss with Berchtold, therefore, was the prompt implementation of the 24 June memorandum. Since then, however, Berchtold had received a long, private letter from his minister to Romania. The letter warned that everyone in Bucharest believed that the monarchy was "headed for decline and dissolution"; the French and the Russians were telling the Romanians "to leave the sinking ship while there was still time." It was clear, the letter went on, that the French and Russians were working to form a new Balkan League in order to complete the encirclement of the monarchy and, when the time came, to crush it.[11] The letter, combined with the assassination and the despairing outrage of almost everyone with whom Berchtold spoke, convinced him that the monarchy could not work out the new diplomatic alignment so long as a hostile Serbia, supported by Russia, was active on the monarchy's southern frontier.

Berchtold had always opposed any risk of war with Russia. After the assassination he seems to have persuaded himself that Tsar Nicholas II, whose grandfather had been killed by a terrorist bomb, whose prime minister had been murdered by a terrorist in 1911, and whose nation was visited almost daily by assassinations and terrorist attacks, was unlikely to fight a

war to prevent the punishment of regicides. Moreover, Berchtold expected
Field Marshal Conrad to make a swift, annihilating attack on Serbia. Since
Russian mobilization was notoriously slow, Berchtold and most Austrians
believed that, faced with an already defeated Serbia and confronted by the
entire Austro-Hungarian army waiting on the defensive along its frontier,
Russia would prefer negotiation to war. This was the program that Berchtold put to Tisza.

Tisza must have been stunned to hear the usually sensible and amiable
Berchtold speak of using the Sarajevo murders to "settle" with Serbia. The
foreign minister was now talking about a surprise attack that would present
Russia with a fait accompli. Tisza held fast to the 24 June memorandum:
Austria-Hungary would be in a much better position to deal with Serbia
after entering alliances with Bulgaria and with Turkey. Berchtold, who had
spent the last two days hearing that the monarchy would collapse unless he
took "firm measures," replied that the situation could only get worse.
Repeating the arguments of his senior advisers and generals, he added that
a timid or passive response to the assassination would undermine the basis
of the 24 June memorandum: Bulgaria might then regard the monarchy as
weak and doubt its desirability as an ally.

Tisza was not used to opposition from Berchtold. It did not help that
Tisza had never liked the archduke and made no secret of it, whereas
Berchtold grieved deeply.[12] Berchtold was a different man after the assassination. The imperial finance minister wrote that Berchtold became "unshak-
ably strong" and determined to settle with Serbia.[13] When Tisza realized that
Berchtold was adamant, he insisted that no action be taken until the emperor had considered his objections, which he would submit in a written
memorandum.[14] That, for all practical purposes, put an end to the strategy of
an immediate attack on Serbia.

Meanwhile, two German newspapermen in Vienna were suggesting that
Berlin might not be as cautious as Ambassador Tschirschky's comments
seemed to indicate. On 1 July, Viktor Nauman, who was regarded as having
excellent connections in the German government, told one of Berchtold's
top aides that in German military and foreign office circles "the idea of a
preventive war against Russia was regarded with less disfavor than a year
ago," and that "it was a question of life or death for the Monarchy not to
leave this crime unpunished, but to annihilate Serbia." Nauman also thought
that the German kaiser would support a decisive action if approached in the
right way, "because he perceives the dangers for the monarchical principle."[15]

On Saturday, 4 July, a second German journalist named Hugo Ganz
showed up at the foreign ministry. Ganz, who was regarded as a particular
confidant of Ambassador Tschirschky, spoke to a foreign ministry section

chief. Ganz quoted Tschirschky as declaring that Germany would support Austria "through thick and thin, whatever it might decide to do with Serbia." According to Ganz, Tschirschky also said that "yesterday would have been better than today, but today would be better than tomorrow."[16] Though Tschirschky was officially urging moderation, Berchtold's section chief suspected that the ambassador meant his words to be repeated to the foreign ministry.

Between these interviews, Berchtold had his usual talks with Tschirschky and told him that only "ruthless action" would put an end to their troubles with Serbia. He added that although Germany always assured the monarchy of its support, in practice such support did not always materialize. Tschirschky answered "quite privately"—meaning that he was speaking for himself, not his government—that the Austrians' problem was that they never came up with a concrete plan of action. If such a plan were forthcoming, Tschirschky said, "Berlin would intervene unreservedly."[17]

Tschirschky then went off for an audience with Emperor Franz Joseph, who also complained that Serbia's intrigues "were intolerable" and that the Russians were behind them. The Serbs would never dare to carry on against a neighboring Great Power without Russian support. The emperor hoped that Berlin would appreciate the danger that threatened the monarchy from Serbia. Tschirschky reaffirmed his belief that Germany would stand "solidly behind the Monarchy," but he repeated the advice he had just given Berchtold: the monarchy needed to consider where it wanted to go and how it wanted to get there.[18]

From the moment the blunt-spoken German ambassador heard of the assassination, he had been warning the Austrians to be careful and not to act hastily, that his government would support them only if they came up with a well-thought-out plan of action. At the same time, well-connected German journalists were telling foreign ministry officials that Berlin was eager for Austria to act against the Serbs. What was going on?

Heinrich von Tschirschky was fifty-six years old and an East Prussian Junker. He was a large and bulky man with blond hair, a red face, and a brusque, assertive way about him. Tact was not his long suit. An Austrian diplomat remembered him as a man who believed that a war with France and Russia was inevitable and whose mood was usually "now or never."[19] The French ambassador wrote that he and other diplomats found Tschirschky unpleasant to deal with, overbearing, and always speaking in a manner that brooked no disagreement.[20]

Tschirschky had a desperate view of the world: Germany was in decline, monarchy was in decline, democracy was on the rise, the Slavs were on the rise, and revolution threatened from every corner. The army, he firmly believed, was all that stood between Germany and the revolutionary wave, safety was "only to be found in the constant efforts of Germany to present an irresistible armed front to the promotors of disorder."[21] Like many Prussians, Tschirschky often wondered out loud why the Austrians did not keep the Slavs in their place, and he once wrote his foreign secretary in Berlin: "How often have I asked myself whether it really is worthwhile to commit ourselves to this state, creaking in all its joints, and to continue the dreary work of dragging it along."[22] But he could see no alternative to the alliance with Austria, and he hoped against hope that the monarchy would pull itself together and once more stand as a Great Power on the European scene.

Tschirschky expressed this hope more than once, and he was as convinced as any Austrian about the need to do something about Serbia. His superiors in Berlin, however, had called for restraint during the Balkan wars of 1912 and 1913, and Tschirschky was probably still acting on that policy while leaking his real feelings to German reporters.

After talking with Tschirschky, the emperor summoned Berchtold, informed him of the ambassador's latest comments, and again urged him to reach an agreement with Tisza. Berchtold replied that if investigation tied Serbia to the assassination, the monarchy would have to take decisive action or lose its status as a Great Power. The emperor agreed that military steps were unavoidable, but, echoing Tschirschky, he insisted that they wait and see and consider future steps very carefully. Berchtold had no choice but to obey.[23] He had been pressing for a swift strike for days, but the element of speed was slipping steadily away.

Frustrated by repeated demands that he settle with Serbia "once and for all," Berchtold told his top aides that he could not lead a war against the will of both the emperor and Tisza—especially when the signals from the German ambassador were so mixed. Count Alexander Hoyos, who headed Berchtold's secretariat and who was never shy about making his views known, suggested that perhaps he should personally deliver the 24 June policy memorandum to Berlin instead of sending it by courier. If Berlin agreed to a war with Serbia, Tisza, who never wanted to appear weak before the Germans, would have to yield.

Berchtold promptly agreed; he had to be sure of Germany in any event. He wired the Austro-Hungarian ambassador in Berlin, Count Ladislaus Szögyény-Marich, to obtain appointments with both the kaiser and the imperial chancellor for the next day, Sunday, 5 July, and then made several changes in the 24 June policy statement.[24]

That memorandum made no mention of an action against Serbia; on the contrary, it accepted the possibility of conciliation. Berchtold's 4 July amendments called the differences between Serbia and the monarchy "unrecon-cilable" and concluded by declaring the "imperious . . . necessity for the Monarchy to destroy with a determined hand the net which its enemies are attempting to draw over its head." Hoyos drafted a cover letter for the em-peror's signature, arguing that "the Sarajevo affair . . . was the result of a well-organized conspiracy, the threads of which can be traced to Belgrade." Both documents continued to emphasize the necessity of an alliance with Bulgaria, but Hoyos's letter insisted that Serbia, "the pivot of the Panslavic policy," must be "eliminated as a power factor in the Balkans."[25]

To make sure that the Germans understood the seriousness of the situa-tion, Berchtold gave Hoyos a set of verbal instructions. Hoyos was to make it clear to Ambassador Szögyény and to officials in the German foreign of-fice that the time had come for a "reckoning" with Serbia. Vienna would ask the Belgrade government to give certain guarantees for the future; if these were refused, military action would follow. The monarchy wanted to know how the German government would respond to this program.[26]

By first asking for guarantees, Berchtold abandoned whatever was left of a quick-strike strategy. He appears to have decided that if he could not move fast, a German warning might force Russia to abandon Serbia as it had dur-ing the 1909 annexation crisis. In any event, Berchtold was not going to give up a reckoning with Serbia.

Meanwhile, Tisza had returned to Hungary, where he received copies of the papers Hoyos was taking to Berlin. When he saw Berchtold's amend-ments to the 24 June memorandum, he knew that Berchtold was going to use the Germans against him, and he wired Vienna on Sunday. The language of Hoyos's cover letter, he warned, would scare off the kaiser, who for all his public bluster was known to be afraid of war.

Tisza called for several changes. In the last sentence of the letter, the clause that read, "a reconciliation . . . is no longer to be thought of" was to be deleted. The same sentence ended with the words, "the peace policy of all European Monarchs is threatened so long as this center of criminal agi-tation at Belgrade continues unpunished." The word *unpunished* was to be deleted. Tisza wanted to avoid any suggestion of asking Germany to agree to a war on Serbia. Instead of being eliminated "as a power factor in the Balkans," Serbia was to be "required to give up its aggressive tendencies."

Tisza's changes arrived too late. Hoyos was already in Berlin with his oral instructions, and Berchtold was spending the day at his splendid coun-try estate at Buchlau. Tisza was a powerful man, but Berchtold controlled the diplomatic machinery.

4: THE EMPEROR AND THE FIELD MARSHAL

5 July

Seven days after the assassination, while Count Hoyos and Ambassador Szögyény were carrying out their mission in Berlin and Berchtold was enjoying a little rest at Buchlau, the eighty-three-year-old Emperor Franz Joseph was talking with one of those harsh activists of the modern age, his army chief of staff. Field Marshal Conrad used the occasion to once again remind the emperor that war with Serbia was inescapable.

What was unreal about Conrad's calls for war was that Austria-Hungary had fallen hopelessly behind in the European arms race and did not come close to matching the colossal increases in defense spending in neighboring Russia. In 1914, Austria-Hungary's forty-eight divisions were facing fifty Russian divisions to the north and eleven Serbian divisions to the south. Since the Russians had another thirty-eight divisions along their frontier with Germany, it was clear that Austria could not fight Russia, much less Russia and Serbia, without Germany.[1] Conrad had done what he could to modernize the army, bringing in new tactics, new field gray uniforms, new artillery, and a new organization; he worked constantly, taking no holidays, and new regulations flew out of his office at the rate of more than two per month.

The warlike field marshal did not project a military bearing. He was short, slight, and somewhat desiccated looking. He seemed more comical than martial in military coats that were far too large and caps that came halfway down his face; a nervous twitch in his cheek did not make things any better. But he was intensely, passionately loyal to the monarchy and to the army, and he could not bear to see the ancient Hapsburg Empire fall into decline. His father had been an army officer before him, and Conrad had been enrolled in a cadet school at the age of eleven. The army and the empire were his life.

On more than one occasion, Conrad's intensity had provoked the emperor's anger because the field marshal was always pushing the emperor where the emperor did not want to go. Not only was Conrad always demanding more money for the army, he was always proposing war. When he protested that the foreign minister had been too pacific in settling the annexation crisis in 1908–9, the emperor reminded him sharply that "I make policy; that policy is *my* policy."[2] In 1913, Conrad complained that the German kaiser seemed unwilling to support Austria in a war against Russia. The emperor had to point out that "it is the duty of rulers to keep the peace."[3]

Now they were at it again, with Conrad insisting that war with Serbia was unavoidable. Franz Joseph did not disagree, but it was a painful, reluctant conclusion forced upon him by his duty to preserve the empire he had inherited and despite the disastrous luck he had always had in war.

In July 1914, Emperor Franz Joseph was only one month short of eighty-four and had been on the throne for sixty-six years. He liked to say that he was "the last European Monarch of the old school,"[4] and he was still, as he had been when he first became emperor at the age of eighteen, a regal presence: calm, commanding, and apparently utterly assured. "He was and remained," recalled his military aide-de-camp, "a monument of self-control."[5] Political diarist Joseph Redlich was less impressed. He thought the emperor's only answer to revolution and democracy was a "rigid calm" and an "almost somnambulistic assurance."[6] But Redlich was a parliamentary liberal, and the emperor's aide-de-camp was a devoted monarchist.

The modern world was not a comfortable place for the aging emperor. "To find the right way in this land, with the prevailing unbelievable chaos of ideas and the want of even halfway capable men, is a barely soluble task."[7] He did not like typewritten documents, although he eventually got used to them. It was all King Edward VII of England could do to get the old emperor into an automobile. When the emperor learned, in 1913, that a homosexual colonel in his beloved army had been blackmailed into selling strategic plans to the Russians, the emperor could hardly believe it. "And this is the modern era? These are the creatures it brings forth? In our old days such a thing would not even have been thinkable."[8] He wrote a friend in 1911, when he was eighty-one, "I am very tired and the weakness is getting worse; I am sad and bored."[9] He would have liked to end his days in peace, but the Serbs and this dreadful assassination made the situation very difficult; his army commander was not making it any easier.

"How will you fight the war," the emperor asked, "when everyone falls upon us, especially the Russians?"

"But we are covered by the Germans," Conrad replied.

The emperor eyed him reflectively. "Are you sure of the Germans?"

"Your Majesty, we have to know where we stand."

Franz Joseph then told Conrad that a note had just been sent to Germany asking for a clear answer.

"And if the answer is that Germany will stand by us, will we make war on Serbia?" Conrad countered.

Whatever it may have cost him, the emperor was firm: "Then, yes." After a moment's pause the emperor asked, "If Germany does not give us this answer, what then?"

Conrad evaded a clear reply. "Then we stand alone. But we must have an answer soon, for the great decision depends upon it."

The emperor seemed uncertain. "The German kaiser is going on his North Sea trip. In any case, we must wait for the answer."[10]

When Berchtold came back from Buchlau on Monday, Conrad reported on his talk with the emperor. Berchtold reminded him that Tisza opposed a war with Serbia. Conrad ignored that. The critical question was whether they could be sure of Germany. Berchtold assured him that they would soon have an answer but added: "The Germans will ask us what will happen after the war."

Conrad, exasperated by the constant worries of the civilians, replied, "Then tell the Germans that we don't know ourselves."[11]

PART II: A CALCULATED RISK

5: KAISER WILHELM II

All-Highest Warlord

The assassination of the archduke was a terrible shock to Europe, but out-side of Vienna it brought no sense of crisis. Royalty and ministers were being assassinated almost every year for as long as anyone could remember. No one saw any reason to interrupt vacations, and many of the early decisions were made in the absence of senior officials.

In Germany Kaiser Wilhelm II canceled the rest of his schedule at the annual Kiel Regatta and returned to Berlin, telling his guests and the visiting British naval squadron to continue their festivities. Officials in the German foreign office did not anticipate serious consequences; their main concern was that Austria-Hungary not overreact and drag Germany into a confrontation with Russia. According to the Saxon military attaché in Berlin, however, the Prussian army general staff seemed to feel that, given Austria-Hungary's steady decline and the growth of the Russian army, Germany might prefer to fight a war now rather than later.[1]

Prince Karl Max Lichnowsky, ambassador to Great Britain, had come over from London to welcome the British squadron to the regatta. He followed the kaiser to Berlin and had a long talk with the imperial chancellor and with the assistant undersecretary for foreign affairs, but not about the assassination. The chancellor was much more interested in how the British visit was going.[2]

Lichnowsky and the imperial chancellor, Theobald von Bethmann-Hollweg, had both worked hard to secure friendship with Great Britain, but Bethmann was frustrated by his inability to wean the British from their close diplomatic ties with France and Russia. Bethmann was particularly upset by a secret report that the British foreign secretary, Sir Edward Grey, had recently agreed to talks with Russia concerning naval cooperation in time of war. Such an agreement would strike at the very heart of Bethmann's policy, and the German foreign office was convinced that Lichnowsky was naive to accept Grey's assurances of friendship at face value.

They knew that Grey was lying when he denied that he was negotiating a naval agreement, and they asked Bethmann to have a talk with Lichnowsky before he returned to London.

Prince Lichnowsky, as a great aristocrat of ancient family and a favorite of the kaiser, was not intimidated either by his foreign office superiors or by the imperial chancellor. He insisted that England needed Germany as a counterweight to the Franco-Russian alliance and would never be hostile to Germany unless Germany attempted to crush France. Bethmann, who did not like Lichnowsky and had opposed his appointment as ambassador, replied that he did not share the ambassador's optimism. The Russians were adding 900,000 men to their army and, according to secret and reliable reports, England and Russia were drawing up a naval agreement providing that "in case of war English freight steamers were to transport Russian troops to the coast of Pomerania."[3]

Lichnowsky did not believe for a moment that the British would ever commit ships to the narrow waters of the Baltic Sea and the Danish straits. He had been hearing scare stories about Russian armaments for thirty years, and the Russian guns had never gone off. The exchange was irritating for both men. Lichnowsky had an equally irritating talk with Arthur Zimmermann, the assistant undersecretary for foreign affairs, who complained that the Russians were "everywhere in our way." After those talks the prince left Berlin for his estate in Silesia; he was still on leave and saw no reason to hurry back to London.[4]

These events took place on Sunday or Monday. On Friday, 3 July, after five days of relative calm, the kaiser read Ambassador Tschirschky's report that he was taking every occasion to warn the Austrians against hasty action. The cultivation of the late archduke had been a major project of the kaiser and one of his few personal successes; the two men shared the same autocratic outlook and genuinely liked each other. Now the archduke was dead and the kaiser would have to start all over again with a new archduke, one who was completely unknown to him. Reading Tschirschky's dispatch, the kaiser underlined the ambassador's cautious warnings and exploded, as he often did, all over the margin. "Who authorized him to act that way?" "Serbia must be disposed of, *and* that right *soon!*" He underlined the words *and* and *soon*.[5]

The German foreign office received the kaiser's comments on Tschirschky's report on the afternoon of Saturday, 4 July. Word spread rapidly that Tschirschky had been reprimanded for counseling the Austrians to moderation.[6] Later, Count Szögyény, the Austro-Hungarian ambassador, asked for appointments with the kaiser and the chancellor for the next day, a Sunday. Count Berchtold was sending a special emissary with a personal letter from

Emperor Franz Joseph to the kaiser, and an important policy statement. The kaiser was scheduled to begin his annual North Sea cruise the following Monday, and the Germans were anxious to hear what the Austrians had to say; there was no difficulty about the Sunday appointments.

Count Hoyos arrived on the night train from Vienna early Sunday morning and went straight to the Austro-Hungarian embassy to meet Szögyény. Count Szögyény had been the Hapsburg ambassador to Germany for twenty-two years. He was seventy-three years old and about to be retired. He had suffered through the great Prussian victories of 1866 and 1870 and had been a pained witness to the steady decline of Hapsburg fortunes. He was distressed by Serbia's sudden rise. The kaiser, who usually had nothing but contempt for the Balkan Slavs, had regarded the 1912 defeat of the Turks as a great victory for Christendom over Islam. He had stubbornly refused Austrian requests to help Bulgaria when that nation was overrun by Serbia and its allies in 1913. "The victors dictate the terms," he had written, and "H.M. declines to intervene to restrain them."[7] The kaiser was even more unsettling when he occasionally proposed that Austria should make its peace with Serbia. Szögyény worried about the kaiser's changeability. He worried more about the increasing German contempt for Hapsburg weakness and reported resignedly, "Nothing influences political events more than a great military victory."[8] Now he would have to persuade the kaiser that Germany must permit its only reliable ally to take action before it was too late.

Dealing with Wilhelm II von Hohenzollern, Prussian king and German kaiser, was always an uncertain enterprise. From one moment to the next, an intelligent, well-informed, and lucid head of state could suddenly become a blustering buffoon who issued orders of stunning unreality. It was well known in Berlin society that "the kaiser says things that can only be explained pathologically,"[9] and most diplomats and governments were sure that the kaiser was "not quite sane."[10] Wilhelm loved to boast of the bright German sword and Germany's irresistible might. When his foreign office tried to restrain him, he would tell them, "You diplomats have your pants full, the whole Wilhelmstrasse stinks of shit," or remind them that he, Wilhelm II, "was a successor to the Great Elector and Frederick the Great."[11]

The most recent glories of the Hohenzollern dynasty fed the kaiser's delusions. In 1864, when Wilhelm was five, Prussia took Schleswig-Holstein from Denmark. In 1866, when he was seven, Prussia drove Austria-Hungary out of Germany. In 1867, when he was eight, Prussia united northern Germany in a North German Confederation. In 1870, when he was eleven, France declared war on Prussia, and the new confederation defeated France and annexed the ancient border provinces of Alsace and Lorraine.

In 1871, when he was twelve, the confederation was transformed into the German Empire, uniting all non-Austrian Germany under his grandfather, Wilhelm I, king of Prussia. The Hohenzollerns of Prussia replaced the Hapsburgs of Austria as German kaisers. Wilhelm II spent his life trying to live up to those deeds, and his reign was filled with blustering speeches and fine poses.

Wilhelm II sat at his desk in Potsdam on a mounted saddle because, he claimed, he was more comfortable in the saddle than on a chair. He believed that he was an autocrat by divine right and once told army recruits, "If I order it, you must shoot your fathers, your mothers, your brothers, your sisters."[12] His ministers promptly arranged to have the newspapers delete that passage from their reports. After a street demonstration in Berlin, Wilhelm said that the next time he would personally take command of the Berlin garrison and clear the streets. The commander called his officers together and pleaded, "Gentlemen, I beg you, you must above everything prevent the kaiser from going out at the head of one of our units. It is unforeseeable what might happen." The regimental officers, however, were used to the kaiser. "Excellence," one of them replied, "the kaiser is always saying things like that, but he never does it."[13]

Wilhelm had a withered left arm, and it is hard to be a warrior king with a withered arm. He knew that people laughed at him, and that some of the more fanatic conservatives wanted to replace him with his oldest son, which only fueled his need to assert his martial qualities. Finally, Wilhelm had strong, if suppressed, homosexual tendencies. He could not resist physical contact with men and was addicted to cruel pranks and rough physical horseplay. He would grab the British ambassador by the pants to talk with him, or pat the French ambassador on his backside.[14] King Ferdinand of Bulgaria left Berlin "white-hot with hatred" when the kaiser refused to apologize after publicly slapping his royal fanny.[15] Wilhelm could not get enough of soldiers and visited his regiment in Potsdam whenever he could. There, "one feels free with beautiful nature around you and soldiers as much as you like, for I love my dear regiment very much, those kind nice young men in it."[16] The kaiser had no idea why he was so comfortable with men.

Wilhelm sometimes gave way under the strain of being a martial Hohen—zollern; he suffered nervous breakdowns in 1908, in 1911, and during the winter of 1913–14. The 1908 breakdown followed a scandal over homosexuals in his entourage and an embarrassing interview in an English newspaper, which brought on a national outcry for the end of "personal government." The 1911 breakdown followed what Germans regarded as a humiliating retreat in a confrontation with France over Morocco, when newspapers ran headlines such as, "Here fell a king, but not fighting."[17] His wife complained bitterly at the time that "they will force him to make war, when he passionately wants peace."[18]

The most recent breakdown occurred after the Germans announced a military mission headed by Lt. Gen. Liman von Sanders to restore the shattered Turkish army. When it turned out that General Sanders was to have all the powers of a commanding general—and, more seriously, that he was to personally command the Turkish I Army Corps in Constantinople, which effectively put him in control of the city—the Russians objected publicly and vehemently.

The city of Constantinople commanded the straits through which more than half of Russia's exports passed to get to the Mediterranean and world markets. The Russians regarded the new German military mission, together with Austria-Hungary's earlier annexation of Bosnia-Herzegovina, as part of an Austro-German campaign to drive Russia out of the Balkans, control the straits, and strangle the Russian economy. When the Russians demanded General Sanders's dismissal, the kaiser reacted by playing All-Highest Warlord: "It is a question of our standing in the world. So, a stiff back and the hand on the hilt!"[19] The nationalist press screamed that Russia was bullying Germany. Russian papers declared that they could not yield. Bethmann and the foreign office wanted a way out. It was all too much for the kaiser, and he suffered another nervous collapse.

Bethmann and the foreign office finally arranged for General Sanders's promotion to field marshal and appointment as virtual commander in chief of the Turkish army. Sanders had substantial powers, but he no longer directly controlled I Army Corps in Constantinople. With the city once again under Turkish command, the Russians reluctantly accepted the change, while German nationalists raged at the "abject surrender" and painted the Triple Entente of England, France, and Russia as "the most powerful and fearful combination of states known to history."[20] The kaiser believed that once again he was being accused of weakness. By the spring of 1914 he had lost a great deal of his former exuberance, but he was still unpredictable, and no one could foresee when or how he might erupt into German policy.

6: THE BLANK CHECK

Berlin, 5–6 July

After twenty-two years in Berlin, Ambassador Szögyény knew the kaiser as well as anyone, but even he could not be sure how the interview would go. He was certain that Wilhelm would not like the idea of allying with Bulgaria. The kaiser detested King Ferdinand, whom officials in the German foreign office would often call "that drunken king." The kaiser could easily respond with another lecture on the need for a modus vivendi with Serbia, which would put Austria in an impossible position. Or he could say, as he sometimes did, that Emperor Franz Joseph had but to ask, and he, Wilhelm II, would draw the shining German sword to fight Austria's enemies. That would be perfect. However, the kaiser might also take the line followed by his foreign office during the Balkan wars of 1912 and 1913: there was no popular support in Germany for a war over Serbia. Or he could engage the ambassador in a perfectly sensible discussion of Austria's options. One just never knew.

Szögyény began by telling Wilhelm how much the late archduke had admired him, and lamented the archduke's tragic death. The Serbs, he said, were perfect savages and posed a real threat to monarchs and to the Hapsburg Empire. After further preliminaries along these lines, Szögyény asked the kaiser to read the letter from his emperor and the accompanying memorandum. The thrust of the documents was that if Bulgaria were firmly in the camp of the Central Powers (Austria, Germany, and Italy), Romania would be forced to give up its flirtation with Russia and once again become a loyal ally. However, a stable realignment in the Balkans would "only be possible . . . if Serbia . . . is eliminated as a political power in the Balkans."[1] The kaiser and Bethmann had already abandoned any hope for an Austro-Serbian rapprochement. Nonetheless, when the kaiser finished reading, his initial reaction was cautious. He would have to consult with his imperial chancellor before giving a definite answer; from what he had just read, there could be "a serious European complication."[2]

Wilhelm saw himself as the Hohenzollern protector of the once-mighty Hapsburgs and as the loyal friend of "the old emperor." Szögyény played on these feelings, and by the end of their lunch the kaiser had authorized the ambassador to inform Emperor Franz Joseph that Austria-Hungary could "rely upon Germany's full support." Of course, Wilhelm would still have to consult his imperial chancellor, but he had no doubt that Herr von Bethmann-Hollweg would concur.

Growing more belligerent as he talked, the kaiser told Szögyény that if the Austrians were truly convinced of the need for action against Serbia, he would be sorry if they failed to take advantage of the present favorable moment. They could rest assured that Germany would remain a faithful ally even if the Russians came in, but the kaiser thought that Russia would think twice before appealing to arms. As expected, he did not think much of an alliance with Bulgaria; he had never trusted King Ferdinand. But since a rapprochement with Serbia was now unthinkable, he would not object to an Austrian alliance with Bulgaria—provided it was not directed against Romania. From Szögyény's point of view, the interview could not have gone better. He wired a summary to Berchtold as soon as he got back to the embassy.[3]

While Szögyény was lunching with the kaiser, Count Hoyos was talking with his old friend Arthur Zimmermann, the under state secretary for foreign affairs. Zimmermann's superior, state secretary Gottlieb von Jagow, was away on his honeymoon. Within the German foreign office, Zimmermann was one of the tough-talking hard-liners who already thought it "extraordinarily desirable that Austria rap Serbia's knuckles with a few army corps."[4]

Count Hoyos entirely agreed. He was an aristocrat haunted by the modern age, with fantastic ideas for a return to a feudal order where only well-born aristocrats served the monarch in high office. He detested the "revolutionary movement of the bourgeois intellectuals" and their democratic nonsense, and he believed that the Hapsburg monarchy was in danger of imminent collapse. By 1914 he was telling people that the monarchy should go down fighting rather than become the "sick man" of Europe. "When I recall the spirit and atmosphere of that period," he wrote five years later, "I do not believe I would be wrong in saying that I regarded a war with Serbia as an absolute necessity." Nonetheless, "I was not clear that this was the right occasion for war." He was prepared to wait for the alliance with Bulgaria, the original purpose of the memorandum he carried to Berlin.[5] Hoyos wrote those words in 1919; Redlich's diary entries for 1914 describe Count Hoyos as eager to settle with Serbia without delay.

Whereas Szögyény had to be careful not to frighten the kaiser, Hoyos felt he must convince Zimmermann that Vienna was really going to act. Hoyos knew that the Prussians had no great respect for their Austrian ally. They often joked about Austrian *schlamperei*—a sort of messy ineptitude. Hoyos also knew that Zimmermann was a typically no-nonsense East Prussian, a blunt man who liked to project an aggressive, active posture. According to Hoyos, Zimmermann's "outspoken and decisive manner . . . impressed every German."

With a man like Zimmermann, Hoyos could not be tentative: not only was Serbia to be invaded, it was to be dismembered and distributed among the surrounding states, including Austria-Hungary. Zimmermann did not flinch. He had just received two general staff studies from army headquarters, one entitled "The Completion of the Russian Railroad Network," the other "The Growing Power of Russia,"[6] and he undoubtedly shared the general feeling that time was not on Germany's side. If Austria took that kind of action against Serbia, he told Hoyos, then "sure, there is a 90 percent probability of a European war." Zimmermann bragged that the German army was ready for anything. He even said that if Austrian forces were tied up in the Balkans, "Germany was strong enough to fight a war on both fronts alone." When Hoyos later repeated those remarks to Field Marshal Conrad, who had spent years listening to German pleas for Austrian support against Russia in the event of a two-front war, Conrad responded, "Zimmermann does not know what he is talking about."

Zimmermann, in any event, was no voice of caution. He had a reputation for being hard-nosed,[7] and Hoyos came away with the impression that the Germans expected Austria-Hungary to act forcefully. As Hoyos took his leave, he said to Zimmermann, "You could not have believed that Austria-Hungary would quietly accept the murder of the heir apparent and do nothing about it." Zimmermann's reply was almost insulting: "No, but we were a little afraid you might."[8]

For the rest of Sunday afternoon, Kaiser Wilhelm II reveled in the role of All-Highest Warlord. He called in senior military men who were not on leave and summarized his talk with Szögyény. Austria was not going to put up with Serbian plots any longer and would, if necessary, march on Serbia. If "the Russians refused to tolerate this, Austria would not be disposed to give way," and he himself had assured Austria-Hungary of German support. The war minister, Gen. Erich von Falkenhayn, asked whether any preparatory measures should be taken. The kaiser was clear and decisive: no preparations were necessary; a war with France and Russia was unlikely—although, of course, it was something to keep in mind.[9]

German imperial chancellor Bethmann-Hollweg cut short his weekend in the country to be at the kaiser's palace in Potsdam by six o'clock Sunday evening. Bethmann had already concluded that the best way to keep Romania loyal to its commitments would be to allow the Austrians to make alliances with Bulgaria and Turkey. As long as Germany continued to maintain close ties with Greece, Romania would be completely isolated if it turned to Russia and the Triple Entente. Bethmann had apparently also concluded that the Austro-Hungarian monarchy could not afford to let the assassination go unanswered, and that the present situation offered Austria an opportunity to weaken the Serbs while Europe was still angry.

Bethmann read the Austrian memorandum and the emperor's letter, and Zimmermann briefed him on his talk with Hoyos. Bethmann could not have been in any doubt about the aggressive mood in Vienna. Zimmermann, and possibly Bethmann as well, consulted with foreign office political director Wilhelm von Stumm, who was firmly of the opinion that England would remain neutral in any war over Serbia, and dismissed Lichnowsky's warnings that Russia could not leave Serbia to the tender mercies of the Austrians.[10]

The kaiser's conference with his generals was just breaking up as the two civilian advisers arrived. After summarizing the Austrian request, the kaiser declared that "Emperor Franz Joseph must be assured that even in this critical hour we shall not abandon him." The preservation of the Hapsburg monarchy, undiminished, was a vital interest to Germany. Nonetheless, Germany could not tell the Austrians what to do; in this matter "Austria-Hungary must decide for itself." Testifying before the German postwar inquiry into the origins of the war, Zimmermann said that the kaiser announced his commitment to Austria before the chancellor had an opportunity to make recommendations.[11]

If Bethmann had any doubts about the commitment, he did not express them. His relations with the kaiser were not conducive to a searching discussion in any event, and once the kaiser had taken a belligerent position before his generals it was almost impossible to budge him. Bethmann had already suffered through several serious disagreements with him and told a friend that the kaiser "found my manner of conducting policy more and more irritating every day." The Bavarian minister in Berlin reported: "They keep inventing new chancellors here . . . but for the time being Bethmann's dismissal is unthinkable." Bethmann, as usual, did considerable private agonizing, but he wrote after the war that "the views of the kaiser conformed to my own."[12]

The next morning, Monday, 6 July, the kaiser again briefed a series of military men and repeated that he did not expect Russia or France to interfere.[13] No military measures of any kind were ordered, and neither the army chief of staff nor the secretary of the navy were ordered to return from leave. When the kaiser had finished his briefings, he stepped into a waiting car and went off to begin his annual North Sea cruise.

Waiting at the dock was the industrialist Krupp von Holbach und Halbach, who wanted to see the kaiser off. Casual, as always, about discussing policy with people outside the government, the kaiser told Krupp about his commitment to Austria-Hungary. He assured Krupp over and over again, "This time I will not give in." Krupp recalled later that "the repeated imperial assurances that this time no one would again reproach him with indecisiveness had an almost comical effect." When Krupp asked about Russia, the kaiser answered forcefully that a Russian mobilization would be answered by war.[14] It was a typical imperial performance and flatly contradicted both Bethmann's and Berchtold's assumption that the onus of the decision for war could be forced on Russia.

That afternoon, as the kaiser sailed off on his cruise, Bethmann met with his state secretary for foreign affairs, Gottlieb von Jagow (who had just returned from his honeymoon), Zimmermann, Szögyény, and Hoyos to go over everything that had been said. Bethmann affirmed the kaiser's promise to give Austria-Hungary full support in any action against Serbia, and repeated that Austria-Hungary must decide the nature of that action.

When Hoyos was asked what Austria-Hungary would do when Serbia was defeated, he replied that Serbia would be divided among Austria-Hungary, Romania, and Bulgaria. Hoyos, who had no authority to make such a declaration, later explained that he had wanted to convince the Germans that the monarchy knew what it wanted. Throughout the two Balkan wars the Germans had excused their lack of support by the absence of a clear policy in Vienna. This time, Hoyos said, "I took the responsibility for giving them the sharpest and most precise goals." When Tisza heard about Hoyos's statement of war aims, however, he forced Berchtold to disavow it.

In his memoirs, Hoyos stressed that although he never hesitated to say that he, personally, thought a "passage of arms with Serbia" was inevitable, he always emphasized that his government was prepared to wait until the alliance with Bulgaria was concluded if Germany thought that, from a European point of view, a war with Serbia should be postponed. According to both Hoyos and Szögyény, Bethmann replied that although Germany could not tell Austria-Hungary what to do, it was his personal opinion "that if war was unavoidable, then the present time is more favorable than later." Hoyos and Szögyény reported Bethmann's "better now than later" comment to Vienna, and Berchtold promptly passed it on to Tisza.[15]

*   *   *

By any measure, the German commitment to Austria was remarkable. Bethmann and the kaiser had promised to support Austria in whatever action it might take against Serbia, even if it led to war with Russia—which they insisted was unlikely. It was, of course, a commonplace in court and government circles that the kaiser played All-Highest Warlord only when he was fairly certain no war was in sight, and on that Sunday and Monday in Berlin, this was exactly how everyone behaved. It was all very casual, almost cavalier.

General von Falkenhayn was skeptical about the whole business. He wrote the army chief of staff, Gen. Helmuth von Moltke, who remained on leave, that despite some fairly strong language, Vienna was not talking about a "need for war" but about a need for "energetic" political action. Falkenhayn thought the main point of the Austrian message was the alliance with Bulgaria: "The next few weeks won't see a decision in any event. It will take some time before the treaty with Bulgaria can be concluded." He added that Bethmann "appears to have as little faith as I do that the Austrian government is really in earnest."[16]

Even if the Austrians did act, the risk of a Great Power war seemed minimal. Like Berchtold, the Germans expected a swift Austro-Hungarian success against a minor Balkan power—if the Austrians ever roused themselves to action. The Russian mobilization was notoriously slow; even if St. Petersburg decided to respond, the Austrian army could be through with Serbia and back on the Russian frontier before the Russians were ready. Then the Russians would have to decide whether to attack Austria or to negotiate. Under those circumstances, Bethmann and the foreign office were almost certain that Russia would negotiate.

Under the Austro-German alliance, a Russian attack on Austria would oblige Germany to come to the aid of Austria, and all Europe knew that the Russians did not want a war with Germany, at least not for the next several years. If Russia *did* attack, forcing Germany to defend Austria, France would probably have to aid its Russian ally by attacking Germany. But if France were to attack a Germany that was simply defending its Austrian ally against Russia, Great Britain would almost certainly remain on the sidelines—and France would never attack Germany unless it were sure of Great Britain. Under these circumstances, the kaiser, Bethmann, and the foreign office felt confident that London and Paris would pressure St. Petersburg to negotiate rather than fight.

That analysis was based on a number of assumptions, none of which seem to have been made explicit during the discussions of 5 and 6 July. The kaiser, Bethmann, and the foreign office expected a swift military strike from Austria-Hungary; the entire strategy depended on the Austro-Hungarian army being back on the Russian frontier before Russian mobilization was completed. Despite the critical need for speed, there is no record of any attempt by Germany to ascertain or to impose a deadline for military action. There was no attempt to coordinate Austro-German diplomatic steps or military preparations. There was not even a discussion of what settlement the Austrians would accept to keep Russia from mobilizing or fighting. Worst of all, there was confusion among the Germans themselves. It is clear from the kaiser's comment to Krupp that he and his generals thought a Russian mobilization would be answered by war, whereas Bethmann and the German foreign office thought that they could safely allow a mobilization in order to force on Russia the onus of declaring war.[17]

Even Prince Lichnowsky was lulled by the absence of serious discussion. Stopping in Berlin on his way back to London, he learned that Count Tschirschky had been reprimanded for urging caution on Vienna, that Austria was going to take steps on Serbia, and that Germany was going to support Austria in whatever it might do. Nevertheless, the ambassador did not start to worry until later, when he was back in London. The carelessness of the Germans that Sunday and Monday would come back to haunt them later in July.

7: SECOND THOUGHTS

Theobald von Bethmann-Hollweg, 7–8 July

By 1914, Germany's imperial chancellor was an exhausted man. Ever since he had assumed the post in 1909, Bethmann-Hollweg had been under attack from the left because his reforms were too cautious, and from the right because he even considered reform. In foreign policy, Bethmann was as convinced as any chauvinist that Germany had to find markets and colonies overseas to survive. The naval program and the diplomatic moves that would enable Germany to compete in the international arena were referred to collectively as *Weltpolitik*. That slogan had enormous allure for patriotic Germans, but it made other powers uneasy: what did the Germans want? Bethmann thought that Germany could make *Weltpolitik* without war so long as it was friendly with England and careful with Russia. Many conservatives and pan-Germans thought a war would cure Germany's malaise and rally conservative forces to the crown; Bethmann regarded such thinking as idiotic. He believed that a Great Power war would bring revolution, not restoration; it would mean the collapse of Europe as they knew it and the end of monarchy. With the patriotic right bellowing for a foreign policy worthy of German power, Bethmann complained, "with these idiots, no one can conduct a sane policy."[1]

The kaiser in particular was a great burden for the chancellor. Except among intimate friends, Bethmann was not an engaging man; his propensity to lecture and his air of pensive melancholy were not likely to suit a monarch who preferred to do all the talking himself and who insisted that "I will not tolerate pessimists!"[2] When Bethmann's name was first submitted for chancellor, the kaiser objected. "I know him well; he is always lecturing and pretends to know everything better." But other men refused the appointment, or the kaiser liked them even less, and he finally, grudgingly, agreed to Bethmann's appointment. Bethmann's wife warned him, saying, "Dear Theo, you cannot do that."[3] She was right.

Apart from his uncontrollable rages, which could roar on for hours, or his nervous breakdowns, whose outcomes were utterly unforeseeable, the kaiser was inveterately rude to all his ministers. He either ignored governing altogether or, stung by some event, would suddenly intervene to insist on a "firm" policy, complaining and lashing out at his ministers' lack of vigor and courage. He was at his worst with Bethmann. It unsettled Wilhelm II that Bethmann was always under attack from nationalists and conservatives. The kaiser could tolerate opposition from the left—that was only to be expected—but not from the traditional pillars of the monarchy. He made matters worse by petulantly refusing to offer the gestures of support that would enable Bethmann to be more effective.

Bethmann, for his part, was particularly annoyed that the conservatives, the very people whose interests he was trying to protect, "make things as difficult as they can." His foreign policy seemed to be going nowhere. *Weltpolitik* without war depended entirely on colonial agreements with Great Britain, and Bethmann was convinced that only Anglo-German cooperation could prevent a future Balkan crisis from exploding into armed conflict. Despite Ambassador Lichnowsky's social success in London and four years of patient wooing, Great Britain was as close as ever to France and Russia.

Like imperialists in England, France, Russia, and the United States, Bethmann believed that without a colonial empire, a nation could not be a Great Power. He was afraid that the last chance for colonial expansion was slipping away.[4]

There was no reason for Bethmann to entertain such fears. Militarily and economically, the German Empire of 1914 was a colossus, with the most formidable army and the second-largest navy in the world. The empire's population stood at 65 million compared to France's 39 million and Great Britain's 45 million, but Bethmann saw only that Russia's population exceeded 100 million. Germany was the second-largest trading and shipping nation in the world after Great Britain, and the second-largest industrial nation after the United States. Its exports were growing steadily, and in the years before World War I its trade deficit shrank by half.[5]

Bethmann never seemed to have understood the significance of these data. He thought that Germany's economic and population growth demanded overseas expansion[6] and that Germany could acquire the necessary colonies only in agreement with Great Britain.[7]

Bethmann was therefore stunned to learn that Great Britain was engaged in secret talks with Russia for a naval agreement paralleling Britain's naval arrangements with France.[8] Worse, with such an agreement, Great Britain would no longer be free to oppose Russia in a crisis; Germany and Great

Britain would no longer be partners for peace. Germany, to avoid isolation, would be forced to defend the Great Power status of its ally, Austria-Hungary, even at the risk of "unforeseeable consequences."[9]

Bethmann had been suffering from bad dreams. People noticed that he was overweight, nervous, and unhappy with the way things were going.[10] In January 1914 he had written a friend that the constant, "shameless persecution" from all sides was ruining his nerves.[11] In May his wife died after a long and lingering illness, a personal tragedy that completely drained him. He took a leave of absence; when he returned to Berlin in June, he was said to have lost what little optimism he had.[12] Then came the assassination and the Austro-Hungarian request for German support. The Hapsburg dynasty seemed to be stumbling from catastrophe to catastrophe,[13] the Serbs were determined to create Great Serbia at Austrian expense, and England was talking about a naval pact with Russia. For Bethmann, one point was clear: Germany had no choice but to support its only reliable ally.

When the conferences ended on 6 July, Bethmann went back to the beautiful quiet of his estate at Hohenfinow; its seventy-five hundred acres were an island of peace after the storms of Berlin. He took with him a young aide from the foreign office press bureau, Kurt Riezler, who acted as his private secretary. As Bethmann told Riezler about the decisions made that weekend, the young man recorded Bethmann's forebodings in his diary.[14]

The naval talks between England and Russia were the last link in a chain that could lead to a Russian invasion of Germany's Baltic coast, covered by the British fleet. Austria was subverted from the north by Russia and from the south by Serbia, and was becoming ever weaker and more immobile. The assassination might, in the end, be useful. Bethmann was not sure that Austria would ever go to war for Germany, but if Germany fought in defense of Austria, the two nations might fight effectively as allies.

It was the Balkan dilemma all over again. If Germany encouraged the Austrians to action, they would say Germany pushed them into war. If Germany discouraged action, they would say Germany had left them in the lurch and turn to the open arms of the western powers. Germany would lose its only reliable ally. That was a completely unrealistic fear, but in the early years of the twentieth century, Europe's upper classes were obsessed by a sense of decline and fall that left them prone to an almost endless array of anxieties.

Bethmann was no exception. He believed, for example, that modern democracy would lead to political barbarism. He thought that political leadership was in decline, that no one spoke with greatness anymore, that individuals were smaller and more insignificant, and that the future belonged to

Russia, whose growing strength weighed on him. If Germany did nothing and Austria-Hungary collapsed, Germany would be isolated and surrounded by its enemies. If it supported Austria, a war with Serbia could lead to a European war. A European war would mean the fall of monarchy and the overthrow of the entire existing social order. Still, there was the hope that a frightened France would hold Russia back and that the tsar would not fight. If France held back Russia, Germany would have broken the encircling entente of England, France, and Russia. And maybe, in the end, there would be no crisis; maybe "the old emperor won't decide [on war] after all."[15]

In any event, it was up to Austria-Hungary to decide what it must do about Serbia.

8: A NOTE WITH A TIME LIMIT

Vienna, 7–19 July

A meeting of the Austro-Hungarian Imperial Council of Ministers was scheduled for Tuesday morning, 7 July, to consider emergency measures in Bosnia. Count Berchtold opened the meeting by saying that before dealing with the emergency measures, the council should decide "whether the moment had not come when a show of force might put an end to Serbia's intrigues once and for all."[1] Germany had solemnly promised its support even if events led to war with Russia, but, Berchtold went on, he was by no means convinced that an expedition against Serbia would lead to war with Russia. Furthermore, if Austria did not act promptly, "our own South Slavs and Romanians will interpret our attitude as weakness," and become even more susceptible to nationalist agitation from neighboring states. Berchtold wanted prompt military action.

Tisza had faced these arguments many times before, but he had always had Berchtold's support. Tisza knew it would be futile to oppose an attack on Serbia. Instead, he insisted that any action be preceded by a note with demands, which, however hard, would be demands that Serbia could accept. If Serbia yielded, the monarchy would have a brilliant diplomatic victory that would give it the weapons to deal with Serbian subversion and greatly ease the Balkan realignment it had just proposed to Berlin. If Serbia rejected the note, Tisza would agree to an ultimatum followed by war. He insisted, however, that there must be no annexations. Russia would fight to the death before it would allow Serbia to be annihilated.

Berchtold pointed out that the monarchy had already won a whole series of diplomatic victories, beginning with the annexation of Bosnia and Herzegovina in 1908—a victory that included a treaty of friendship with Serbia. Austrian diplomacy had created an Albanian buffer state to keep Serbia from the Adriatic; a year earlier, an Austrian ultimatum had forced Serbia to withdraw its troops from Albania. None of these diplomatic victories had solved anything. Only "a forceful intervention" would put a stop to Great Serb propaganda and subversion.

The rest of the council, which included the prime minister of Austria and the imperial ministers of war and finance, agreed. A weak response would only encourage their South Slavs "to agitation against us." The council wanted an immediate ultimatum and war. Tisza maintained his insistence on the note to Serbia; only if the note were rejected would he risk a war. Tisza was consistently outvoted, but he was the prime minister of Hungary and forced Berchtold to delay his report to the emperor until 9 July so that he could submit in writing his opposition to the majority view. That settled, Tisza angrily left the meeting.

Berchtold had no choice but to wait—the emperor would not move without Tisza's agreement—but the next morning he sent Baron Giesl von Gieslingen, his minister to Serbia, to try and bring Tisza around. Tisza repeated that there must first be a note, adding that if the note consisted of unfulfillable demands, the monarchy would have to find a new prime minister for Hungary.[2]

On Thursday, 9 July, Berchtold received Tisza's memorandum. He read it out to the emperor as part of his report on the council meeting. The emperor agreed that Vienna could not afford to appear weak, but he accepted Tisza's demand that any ultimatum to Serbia be preceded by a note. Berchtold afterward complained to Ambassador Tschirschky that Tisza was opposing energetic measures. Now Austria would have to start with a note, and Berchtold would have to find demands that would "be wholly impossible for Serbia to accept." With or without Tisza, he did not want just another diplomatic victory. If Serbia yielded all along the line, they would be right back where they started.[3]

Berchtold, however, had the Germans in his pocket, and Tisza, with no support for a diplomatic solution, retreated steadily. By Sunday, 12 July, two weeks after the assassination, the gap between Tisza and his colleagues had come down to a note followed by an ultimatum versus a note with a time limit. On 13 July, Ambassador Szögyény reported that Berlin was getting nervous and expected Vienna to move energetically.[4] Berchtold called in Tschirschky and assured him that they were moving as quickly as possible and that he hoped to reach an agreement with Tisza the next day.[5]

While Berchtold was meeting with Tschirschky, Count Heinrich von Lützow, a retired career diplomat and former ambassador to Italy, stopped by. Count Lützow warned them that if Austria made demands that Serbia could not meet, they would have a world war on their hands. It was "sheer fantasy" to think that the monarchy could localize a war with Serbia and keep out Russia. One of Berchtold's aides who was present, probably Count Johann Forgách, dismissed the danger by saying, "What can happen to us? If it goes wrong, so we lose Bosnia and a piece of East Galicia." The Hapsburgs, after all, had been picking up and losing pieces of Europe for centuries.

Tschirschky, whose earlier caution had been reprimanded by the kaiser, brusquely declared that Austria would have to decide for itself whether or not it wanted to remain a Great Power. "If you cannot screw up the courage for a decision, that is the end of your Great Power status and for us in Germany the question will arise whether we remain with our present policy or take a different line. That you can count on us if matters get serious, you have long known."[6] The Germans had a peculiar way of not telling the Austrians what to do.

The next day Tisza arrived in Vienna for a final round of talks. By then he was prepared to accept a note with a time limit, but he wanted that limit to be as long as possible so as to leave time for a negotiated settlement. Using a letter from Field Marshal Conrad, Berchtold argued that the army wanted the Serbs to have as little warning as possible. He assured Tisza that a peaceful settlement would be possible even after Austria-Hungary mobilized because the army would require sixteen days to go into action. Tisza hesitated. It was true that the army needed at least sixteen days to launch an attack; he also knew he was completely alone in his opposition, even in Hungary. He finally agreed to a note with a time limit of only forty-eight hours—for all practical purposes accepting the ultimatum he had rejected on 7 July. The conferees then approved a list of demands to be included in the note and scheduled a council meeting for Sunday, 19 July, for a final review.

Meanwhile, the Germans were getting nervous. Ever since 5 and 6 July, they had been urging the Austrians to move fast. It was now 14 July. The final conference on the note would not be held until 19 July, and Berchtold was saying that the note would not be delivered until 25 July—almost a month after the assassination! Berchtold and Tisza attempted to explain the situation to Tschirschky: Raymond Poincaré, the president of France, would be on a state visit to Russia from 20 July to 25 July, and the Austrians did not want to deliver the note while Poincaré was with the tsar. They wanted to avoid a Franco-Russian reaction that was inspired by champagne, patriotic toasts, and promises of undying support. Berchtold and Tisza assured Tschirschky that he need not have "the slightest doubt that the presence of Poincaré in St. Petersburg was the sole reason for the delay . . . they could feel absolutely assured in Berlin that there was not a thought of hesitation or uncertainty in existence here."[7]

The situation was, in fact, worse than Tschirschky was told. The Austro-Hungarian army had mobilized twice against the Serbs, once in 1909 and again in 1912. Conrad was insisting that the army not be mobilized a third time unless they were sure that war was coming because it was too expensive and too demoralizing to keep mobilizing and not fight.[8] If Conrad did not mobilize until after Serbia rejected the note and Austria declared war, there would be at least another eighteen days from the delivery of the note to the first action against Serbia. That would be almost the middle of August! The Germans had expected action long before then.

Finally, on 18 July, the note was ready. It was approved the next day by the Imperial Council, subject to final approval by the emperor. There was one last hitch: Tisza asked for a resolution stating categorically that no Serbian territory be annexed. As far as the Magyars were concerned, there were already too many Slavs in the monarchy. Berchtold replied that since no one could foresee a war's outcome, they should leave open the possibility of at least minor border changes. After a somewhat irritated debate, the Imperial Council unanimously agreed that, although they contemplated no annexations, there might be: (1) "strategically necessary corrections of the frontier lines," (2) "the reduction of Serbia's territory to the advantage of other states," or (3) an "unavoidable temporary occupation of Serbian territory." That settled, Berchtold closed the meeting.

The Imperial Council's note was a formidable document. Berchtold had rejected earlier drafts, saying he wanted conditions that, if accepted, would give the monarchy guarantees for the future. Tisza in the end had to agree to this principle. The note began by reminding the Serbian government of its 1909 treaty of friendship with Austria-Hungary. Instead of acting in friendship, the Serbian government had encouraged a subversive movement "whose object is to separate certain portions of its territory from the Austro-Hungarian Monarchy." After reciting Serbia's "criminal activities" and its participation in the assassination, the note demanded that the Royal Serbian Government publish a declaration on the front page of its official newspaper, and that the king of Serbia publish an order of the day to the army, condemning all propaganda whose object was to separate portions of Austro-Hungarian territories from the monarchy. The Serbs were also to declare that their government would proceed rigorously against anyone guilty of such activities.

The note then made ten further enumerated demands: (1) to suppress all propaganda against the monarchy; (2) to dissolve all organizations engaging in such propaganda; (3) to eliminate such propaganda from school instruction; (4) to remove all officers and officials guilty of such propaganda (the Austro-Hungarian government reserving the right to make known the names of those to be removed); (5) to cooperate with organs of the Austro-

Hungarian government on Serbian territory to suppress subversive movements "directed against the integrity of the Monarchy"; (6) to institute a judicial inquiry against every participant in the 28 June assassination (organs of the Austro-Hungarian government would be designated to take part in these judicial proceedings); (7) "with all haste" to arrest Maj. Voislav Tankositch and Milan Ciganovitch, who had been identified as the men who equipped and trained the assassins; (8) to prevent further smuggling of weapons and explosives across the frontier and to dismiss and "punish severely" those members of the Serbian Frontier Service who assisted the assassins across the frontier; (9) "to make explanations to the Imperial and Royal Government concerning the unjustifiable utterances of high Serbian functionaries in Serbia and abroad"; and, finally, (10) "to inform the Imperial and Royal Government without delay of the execution of the measures comprised in the foregoing points." The Austrians also attached a memorandum outlining the evidence against Ciganovitch, Tankositch, and the frontier guards. The Serbian government was given forty-eight hours to reply.[9]

Berchtold learned that President Poincaré was scheduled to leave Russia on Thursday night, 23 July, and he proposed that the note be delivered at 5:00 P.M. that day. He did not want to delay any longer. "Berlin was beginning to get nervous and news of our intentions had already leaked to Rome." The council agreed. The forty-eight hours would expire on the afternoon of Saturday, 25 July.[10]

The note was a clear victory for Berchtold and a substantial defeat for Tisza. The Magyar knew they were launched on a dangerous gamble. "The matter could end without a war," Tisza wrote to his daughter two days after the 19 July meeting. "God grant that it happens. Nonetheless, I cannot completely reassure you that it will not under any circumstances come to war."[11]

Meanwhile, there was nothing to do but wait.

PART III: THE DREAMWORLD OF JULY

9: LICHNOWSKY AND GREY

London, 6–9 July

Prince Karl Max Lichnowsky considered himself a liberal. He liked to say that merit was all that mattered, but at the age of fifty-four he was an aristocrat to his fingertips. Like most of his colleagues he believed that entrée into "the best circles" was an essential element of diplomacy. On this level, the prince was an enormous success. His dinner parties were brilliant, King George V enjoyed his company, and the wife of the British prime minister admired the prince's wife "in spite of black socks, white boots and crazy tiaras." The British prime minister, Herbert Henry Asquith, found the Lichnowskys "rather trying guests,"[1] but that was the only sour note. "Never," recalled a young foreign office clerk, "has any foreign ambassador achieved such rapid or resounding popularity."[2] In the spring of 1914 it seemed as if the Lichnowskys would restore the old friendship between England and Germany if anyone could.

The prince, with his elegant London suits, dark mustache, and graying temples, was a distinguished figure and, by every measure of the day, an ideal candidate for diplomatic service. He was a wealthy man with substantial properties in the Hapsburg Empire and in Prussian Silesia. And he was an aristocrat. An uncle was an officer in the Austro-Hungarian army, two aunts were married to Austro-Hungarian noblemen, and a younger sister was married to an Austro-Polish magnate and had been lady-in-waiting to Emperor Franz Joseph's late wife, Austria-Hungary's murdered empress. The Russian ambassador to Great Britain was his cousin, and the Austro-Hungarian ambassador was a distant relative whom the prince had known since childhood.[3]

But Bethmann and the German foreign office did not trust Lichnowsky. Like most great aristocrats, he was hard to control; he thought Berlin relied too much on the Austrian alliance and said so. Worse, Lichnowsky had direct access to the kaiser, and Bethmann did not want an ambassador who opposed his policies and could take his opposition directly to the kaiser.

In 1911, prior to his appointment, Prince Lichnowsky resigned from the foreign office, having waited in vain for a major embassy. The very next year, the London embassy became vacant.

Bethmann and the foreign office had wanted almost anyone but Lichnowsky. Their preferred candidate was Wilhelm von Stumm, the political director of the foreign office who had served several years in the London embassy and who was regarded as an expert on England. The kaiser, however, wanted Lichnowsky, and Bethmann's clumsy and long-winded attempts to avoid appointing the prince brought on one of the kaiser's explosions. "I will send only *My* ambassador to London, who has *My* trust, obeys *My* orders, and with *My* instructions!"[4] Within a week it was settled that Lichnowsky would be ambassador to Great Britain, and the prince departed triumphantly for his long-awaited embassy, full of the dream of constructing an enduring Anglo-German friendship.

Great Britain's foreign secretary, Sir Edward Grey, was one of Europe's many cultural pessimists who hated cities and had a horror of modernity. He believed that God might well destroy the new world of industrial factories. This "boasted civilization that has defiled beautiful country, made hideous cities, been built up and is being maintained by ghastly competition and pressure, makes men swarm together and multiply horribly." If God agreed with his view, "then the great industrial countries will perish in catastrophe."[5]

Despite an affair with a married woman and a lifetime in politics, Grey was not a worldly man. When he learned that Prince Lichnowsky was to be the new German ambassador, he asked Richard von Kühlmann, first secretary at the German embassy, what the prince was like. Kühlmann replied that although Lichnowsky had never been a specialist on Anglo-German problems, he was in high favor with the kaiser and bought his entire wardrobe from London. Grey was astonished. "You do not mean to tell me that men on the continent have their wardrobes done by London tailors the way women get their clothes from Paris?" Kühlmann was delighted. Almost anyone but Grey would have known that the whole world, at least the whole fashionable world, followed English men's fashions.[6]

Grey was no longer at his best. Since losing his wife in a carriage accident in 1906, he had lived a quiet, orderly, lonely life and struck people as being unhappy in office. Although he was only fifty-two in 1914, he had been foreign secretary since 1909 and was exhausted by the seemingly endless series of domestic crises that tormented the government—particularly the furor over home rule for Ireland. His friends began to notice that he was not keeping up with his diplomatic work. "Grey is absorbed, not unnaturally, with domestic politics and leaves things [perhaps a great deal too much] in Willie Tyrrell's hands, who is over-worked and over-wrought."[7] Tyrrell was Grey's private secretary.

Early in 1914 Grey began to notice that his eyesight was failing. In May he was told the disease was probably irreversible; when the archduke was assassinated, Gray had been planning to see an eye specialist in Germany. For a man such as Grey, who had been tennis champion at Oxford and who prided himself on keeping fit, failing eyesight was a terrible affliction. He loved the outdoors and often went to the country to watch birds and to fish his favorite streams. He even wrote a book on fly-fishing that went through several editions. Richard von Kühlmann marveled at the endless hours Grey devoted to fishing and to birds, a behavior he regarded as typically English.[8]

Grey shared the general English view that Great Britain was the most honest and the most moral of the Great Powers. "Not one of the other Powers was disinterested," he wrote, "not one of them believed that Britain was disinterested." He described his memoirs as the "meditations of a moralist."[9] He was therefore very much embarrassed when German newspapers leaked his secret naval talks with Russia in late May and early June. Count Alexander Benckendorff, the Russian ambassador, sympathized: "It will be hard for him to negotiate and deny negotiating. . . ."[10]

For years French and British army and naval staffs had been planning how to fight a war with Germany—just in case such a catastrophe should arise. The Russians learned of the talks from their French allies, and the Germans learned about them through a spy, Baron Benno von Siebert, a Russian Baltic German who was second secretary in Russia's London embassy. In April 1914 the Russians, through the French, suggested that England hold similar talks with Russia. Grey refused. First, the talks would be useless: Britain and Russia were too far apart to coordinate operations. Second, Grey wanted no more attacks in Parliament or the press for making secret engagements that might drag Great Britain into war.

The French and the Russians persisted. Grey's foreign office staff and his ambassador to Russia warned that Russia might turn to Germany if not reassured.[11] Sir Arthur Nicolson, Grey's senior career official and a perennial pessimist, anxiously agreed: "I do fear—and I know the French are haunted with the same apprehension—that if we do not try to tighten up the ties with Russia she may become weary of us and throw us overboard."[12] Grey gave in, but he insisted on absolute secrecy.

Berlin learned of the talks almost immediately. They confirmed Bethmann's worst fears: Great Britain was advancing the encirclement of Germany; the English navy would cover a Russian invasion. Bethmann, who knew that British Liberals detested entangling alliances on the Continent, arranged for a Berlin newspaper to leak the talks, claiming a source in Paris and suggesting that secret agreements might drag England into a continental war.[13] Grey was asked in the House of Commons whether the government was negotiating a naval agreement with Russia. Grey replied that there were no negotiations and that none were contemplated.[14]

Bethmann then instructed Lichnowsky to inform Grey that if there were any truth to the story of an Anglo-Russian naval agreement, relations between their countries would be severely strained. Unfortunately, Bethmann and the foreign office could not tell Lichnowsky about their spy. Russia's ambassador was Lichnowsky's cousin, and Lichnowsky talked too much. Count Benckendorff, of course, reported his conversations with Lichnowsky to St. Petersburg while Siebert passed them on to Berlin. Not knowing that Germany had a spy in the Russian embassy, Lichnowsky thought the rumors of an Anglo-Russian naval agreement were just another symptom of Berlin's unreasoning fear of Russia.

Nonetheless, Lichnowsky delivered Bethmann's warning a few days before the assassination, on 24 June, and Grey again denied that any negotiations were taking place. But Grey and the foreign office were uneasy at the extent of Berlin's information, so Grey cautiously added that he "wished to be quite frank," that his relations with France and Russia "were today, as always, most intimate," and that he "stood in permanent close touch with the Governments concerned on all matters." Lichnowsky thanked Grey for his explanation, which, he said, "offered us no ground for objection."[15]

When Zimmermann read Lichnowsky's report in Berlin on 27 June, he wrote Bethmann that their ambassador had been duped by "his conviction that he was dealing with an honorable and truth-loving statesman." They would have to give Lichnowsky "some naturally very cautious hints concerning the secret but absolutely reliable reports we are getting. . . ."[16]

Bethmann had a talk with Lichnowsky in Berlin after the assassination. Armed with Bethmann's assurances of "absolutely reliable reports," Lichnowsky returned to London. There he called on Lord Richard Burdon Haldane, a close friend of Grey's, a former Liberal minister of war, and a member of the House of Lords. Lichnowsky mentioned persistent "rumors" of a naval treaty with Russia; Haldane dismissed the rumors as nonsense. Lichnowsky then said he was worried about Austria and Serbia. He told Haldane that Berlin believed it would have to support any Austria action against Serbia. Haldane urged Lichnowsky to see Grey right away.

When Lichnowsky saw him on Monday, 6 July, Grey was a good deal more worried about the Irish question than he was about Austria. He was even more worried about what to say if Lichnowsky pressed him on the naval talks with Russia. But Lichnowsky wanted to talk about Austria. After years of being passed over, he loved being ambassador in London, and he wanted nothing so much as friendship between England and Germany. That the blundering Austrians might drag Germany into a European war in which his English friends would fight on the side of France and Russia was almost more than he could bear.

Lichnowsky began by saying that Berlin was worried. Anti-Serb feeling in Austria was so strong that Vienna might take military action. That caught Grey's attention. He said he was ready to accept military action but not annexations; Russia would never tolerate the destruction of Serbia. Lichnowsky replied that there would be some humiliation of Serbia but probably no annexations. The situation was very difficult for Berlin: if Germany tried to restrain the Austrians, they would complain that Germany never supported them. Grey could sympathize with that; he faced the same complaints from France and Russia all the time. Lichnowsky asked Grey to do what he could "to mitigate feeling in St. Petersburg," that is, to keep Russia from intervening.

Lichnowsky then turned smoothly to the naval talks and said, with great earnestness, that he wanted to speak "quite privately." When a diplomat wanted to talk privately, he was saying that he was not speaking for his government. That might or might not be true; private comments were very useful tools. They could be used to give an impression of disarming frankness. Or they could be used to deliver a threat that could not be made officially. The prince's private comment was that although he did not share the fears in Berlin, they were real, and Bethmann was very pessimistic. The Russian arms buildup, combined with rumors of an Anglo-Russian naval pact, had brought about "some feeling in Germany" that if trouble was bound to come, it might be better not to restrain Austria and let the trouble come now rather than later. Lichnowsky was warning Grey that unless Great Britain disavowed a naval agreement with Russia, Berlin—far from trying to restrain Austria—might encourage an attack on Serbia now rather than face Russia at some later, more unfavorable date.

Grey did not protest. He expressed no dismay that Austria might attack Serbia with German support. Instead, he assured Lichnowsky that he would do what he could in St. Petersburg. The fact was that neither Grey nor the English liked the Serbs, whom they referred to as orientals. English newspapers were blaming the assassination on the Great Serb movement, and even Conservative papers were speculating that the plot was "hatched in Belgrade."[17] "Everybody," recalled a young foreign office clerk, "expected Austria to take strong action."[18]

For Grey, the only question was whether France would be involved, and the answer to that question depended upon Russia. Grey was not prepared to see France defeated, but he was very much afraid that the British public, and certainly the Liberal government whose foreign minister he was, would never agree to come to the aid of France if France attacked Germany because Germany was defending its ally against Russia. The main thing, therefore, was to prevent an irreparable Russian action.

Berchtold and Bethmann were counting on that analysis.

Grey and Lichnowsky promptly sent reports—Grey to his ambassador in Berlin, Lichnowsky to Bethmann. Lichnowsky, of course, did not report his "very private" fears of the "better now than later" atmosphere in Berlin, but Grey reported them fully. Grey did not tell his ambassador anything about the naval talks with Russia other than to report German suspicions. Lichnowsky reported that Grey wanted to talk with him again about the rumors of negotiations with Russia, and noted that Grey "did not directly deny that the two fleets would be in touch in case of a common war." Bethmann's press campaign seemed to be forcing Grey into the open. On the Austro-Serbian problem, Lichnowsky reported that Grey "did not fail to recognize the danger that the situation might bring about." Grey, however, "appeared to comprehend that it would be difficult for any Austro-Hungarian states-man . . . to refrain for any length of time from the adoption of all severe measures," and had promised to do what he could in St. Petersburg.[19]

On Wednesday, 8 July, Grey, as promised, talked to the Russian ambassador, Count Alexander Benckendorff, and warned him that the atmosphere in Vienna and the provocations of the Serbian press might force Berchtold to take serious action against Serbia. Benckendorff did not think that Emperor Franz Joseph, "with one foot in the grave," would go to war, but if Austria-Hungary did try to take advantage of the "abominable" assassination, Russian public opinion would be just as aroused as that in Vienna. "That," Grey replied, "is why I take the situation so seriously." Russia's armaments, Grey added, were making Germany nervous. He made the perceptive comment that the more confident the Germans felt, the less dependent they would be on Austria. If the Germans were afraid, however, they might feel compelled to support Austria, which could be dangerous.

Benckendorff was alarmed. "Do you really regard the situation as that serious?" Grey replied with obvious feeling that the thought that "this terrible crime" could lead to war "makes my hair stand on end." Grey convinced Benckendorff that the Germans should be reassured; Benckendorff accordingly asked his foreign minister to decide how best to do so.[20] Grey next talked to the French ambassador, Paul Cambon. He told Cambon he was worried about what Serbia and Russia might do if Austria took action against Serbia. France must help him persuade St. Petersburg to be patient.

Cambon did not think Austria would hold Serbia responsible for the assassination but agreed to forward Grey's concerns to Paris. Grey then wired his ambassadors in St. Petersburg and Paris "that we must do all we [can] to encourage patience in St. Petersburg."[21]

When Grey saw Lichnowsky again the next day, he finally confessed that military authorities in England, France, and Russia had been talking to one another since 1906, but "everything has been on the footing that the hands of the Government were quite free." Grey even made the extraordinary statement—extraordinary because he sincerely believed it—that so long as the government's hands were free, "it was not necessary for me to know what passed."

In fairness to Grey, it must be said that his civilian counterparts in Berlin, Paris, Rome, St. Petersburg, and Vienna were equally uninterested in the kind of war their military leaders had planned for them.

With the military talks off his chest, Grey hastened to reassure the German ambassador. He reported that the Russian ambassador had said that St. Petersburg had no hostility toward Germany; if Austria kept its action against Serbia within bounds, it would be "comparatively easy to encourage patience in St. Petersburg." However, Austria must not provoke pan-Slav feeling in Russia because that could force the Russian government into action. Meanwhile, Grey would do his "utmost to prevent the outbreak of war between the Great Powers."

Lichnowsky reported Grey's statements to Berlin: everything would depend on what measures Austria had in mind. But, by taking the position that Berlin could not tell Vienna what to do, the Germans abandoned whatever influence they might have had on Austrian measures. Lichnowsky concluded by saying that Grey was cheerful and "saw no reason for a pessimistic view of the situation."[22] So far, the European diplomatic machinery seemed to be working just as Bethmann had anticipated.

10: JAGOW

Berlin, 9–20 July

Gottlieb von Jagow was not yet fifty when he became German state secretary for foreign affairs in 1913. Though he had been ambassador to Rome and was well liked, he was not very experienced or ambitious, and the position he now held was a man-killing job. The state secretary not only executed foreign policy, he had to deal with the German national Reichstag, the Prussian Landtag, the Prussian army, the governments of the twenty-odd German states, and sudden thunderbolts from the kaiser. Count Tschirschky had quit the job to preserve his health and took the embassy in Vienna. Wilhelm von Schoen had resigned to become ambassador to France in 1910. And Jagow's immediate predecessor had died of a heart attack. Zimmermann had doggedly refused to be his replacement, which left Jagow. Short, shy, and burdened with bad health, Jagow had also refused the job—until faced with a direct command from the kaiser. "Nothing has helped," he lamented. "I am appointed."[1]

Jagow was soon as embattled as Bethmann. Edward Goschen, Great Britain's ambassador to Germany, likened the new state secretary to "a man who is besought, and compelled against his will, to make a fourth at Bridge and then sworn at for playing badly."

Goschen, however, liked Jagow. "It is a pleasure to have to deal with such an un-Prussian, pleasant mannered man, and, moreover, with one who is obviously so well disposed towards England," he wrote.[2] Jagow was always telling Englishmen that good Anglo-German relations were essential, that a war with the Slavs was inevitable, and that France was a decadent country[3]—a judgment most Englishmen were quite prepared to believe. Jagow's great fear was that the Austro-Hungarian Empire would disintegrate. Then the Slavs of south central Europe would so outnumber the Magyars and the Germans that the German element would "go to the wall."[4] Jagow often irritated Berchtold by opposing any alliance with Slavic Bulgaria and insisting on a non-Slavic combination of Romania, Greece, and

Turkey to stand "against the advance of the Slavic flood and of Russian influence."[5] Jagow was one of the targets of Vienna's 24 June memorandum to Berlin.

Jagow, therefore, was not the man to oppose the commitments that Bethmann and the kaiser had made to Austria. He was back from his honeymoon on 6 July and was brought up to date. He, like everyone else, expected Austria to move quickly. By 11 July, Berlin knew that speed was out of the question. Both Jagow and Zimmermann complained that the "government in Vienna appears to have great difficulty in getting up the necessary energy for a demarch and has delayed the delivery of the note."[6] Riezler wrote in his diary: "Apparently they need a fearful amount of time to mobilize, sixteen days. . . . That is very dangerous."[7] It *was* very dangerous, but Berlin insisted that it could not tell the Austrians what to do.

By the third week of July the German foreign office knew in fair detail the substance of the Austrian demands. Zimmermann, in his usual blunt way, explained to ministers of several German states that it was "perfectly plain that Serbia cannot accept any such demands. . . . Thus the result would be war."[8] The war that was anticipated, if the Austrians ever got around to doing anything, was a little war with Serbia.

All through those early weeks, Lichnowsky kept warning Berlin that the great gamble was not going to work, that the outcome would not be just a little war with Serbia. On 16 July he collected all his arguments in a long letter to Bethmann. The problem was, he said, that the Austrians had no comprehensive plan that would be furthered by war. Moreover, both his cousin the Russian ambassador and Sir Edward Grey had assured him that Russia had no hostile intentions toward Germany. The Russians, however, detested the Austrians, who were their major rivals in the Balkans. If Austria attacked Serbia, Lichnowsky doubted that the Russians would be able to remain passive.[9]

Unfortunately, the German foreign office was following the advice of its political director, Wilhelm von Stumm, who insisted that Russia would not intervene and that England would remain neutral. Lichnowsky and Stumm irritated each other. Stumm did not like being passed over for the London embassy and shared the foreign office view that Lichnowsky was unreliable. Lichnowsky, who was touchy and suspicious in any event, saw Stumm as a jealous rival who begrudged his success in London and opposed his advice.[10]

It was nearly midnight on 18 July when a weary Jagow composed a long, private letter to Lichnowsky. He conceded that there could be a legitimate difference of opinion "whether we will get our money's worth from an alliance with that ever increasingly disintegrating composition of nations on the Danube." However, given England's growing intimacy with Russia, where could they turn? "You will undoubtedly agree with me that the absolute establishment of Russian hegemony in the Balkans is . . . not permissible." Therefore, "the maintenance of Austria and, in fact, the most powerful Austria possible, is a necessity for us. . . . The more determined Austria shows herself, the more energetically we support her, so much more quiet will Russia remain."

Jagow agreed that St. Petersburg did not want a war with Germany at present, but, he warned, in a few years Russia would be ready. "Then she will crush us by the number of her soldiers; then she will have built her Baltic Sea fleet and her strategic railroads." He hoped and believed that an Austro-Serbian war could be localized. If Grey, who was always talking about the balance of power, was serious, he must recognize that the balance of power would be destroyed if Germany permitted Austria to be "demolished" by Russia. Jagow concluded with an appeal: "If these arguments in favor of our policy are, perhaps, not sufficient to convince you, I know, nevertheless, that you will stand behind them."[11]

Lichnowsky found this impossible. On the weekend of 18 and 19 July, he and his cousin Benckendorff were included in a large party in the country. As soon as Lichnowsky saw his kinsman, he went to him and said, "For God's sake, don't use my name." The prince then proceeded to tell him that in the present crisis he did not expect Bethmann to be the powerful moderating force he had once been. Ignoring his cousin's plea for anonymity, Benckendorff reported to his government that Lichnowsky was "genuinely uneasy. . . . he is afraid Austria will blunder in a manner unacceptable in Belgrade."

Lichnowsky sought out his cousin again the next day. What if St. Petersburg were to offer its good services? If Emperor Franz Joseph were engaged in talks with Tsar Nicholas II, he would not permit rash measures against Belgrade. Would a letter from the tsar to the emperor be impossible? Benckendorff replied that St. Petersburg could not possibly take the first step toward Vienna for any number of reasons, a major one being that the tsar could not be perceived as increasing Austrian influence in Belgrade. Benckendorff concluded by saying that although the situation was critical, he thought his cousin's fears were exaggerated.[12]

Lichnowsky returned to the charge when he got back to London on Monday, 20 July. He wrote Berlin again, saying that "nobody in Russia is thinking of war" and urging his government to be frank with the Russians.[13]

The only other voice of caution in Berlin was that of the Italians. Although Italy was the third member of the Triple Alliance—along with

Austria and Germany—it had no interest in an Austrian triumph in the Balkans, and even less interest in a European war. The Italian wars of liberation in the 1850s had been fought in the name of Italian nationalism to drive the Hapsburgs out of Italy. The Italian foreign minister, the Marchese Antonino di San Giuliano, warned Berlin repeatedly that Italy "could never take up arms against the principle of nationality" on the side of the Hapsburgs.[14] What the Italians were interested in was completing the unification of Italy by acquiring the Italian Irredente in the Trentino, Trieste, and Dalmatia, which San Giuliano referred to as the "Italian lands within the Habsburg Empire."

The Austro-German diplomatic strategy in July was to keep Italy in the dark, deal with Serbia swiftly, and then negotiate with Russia while ignoring Italy. If Russia attacked, Italy would be obliged by the terms of the alliance to join in defending Austria and Germany.

Jagow handled Italy's ambassador, Riccardo Bollati, accordingly. On 9 July he confirmed Zimmermann's earlier assurances that Germany "always gave and will continue to give counsels of moderation to Austria-Hungary with respect to her action toward Serbia." Bollati was not reassured when Jagow added that, in his opinion, "a really energetic and coherent action by Austria-Hungary would not lead to a conflict."[15] Bollati promptly reported this comment to Rome, and San Giuliano, by far the cleverest of Europe's foreign ministers, was immediately suspicious. Jagow warned his good friend Hans von Flotow, Germany's ambassador to Italy, not to tell San Giuliano of Austria's intentions or of Germany's commitment to Austria, "on account of [San Giuliano's] predisposition for Serbia."[16]

San Giuliano was a dying man and would be dead by October, but sick as he was, he was more than a match for Jagow and Flotow. He made Italy's position clear to his ambassadors. "All our policy must aim to hinder again on this occasion Austrian territorial aggrandisement without corresponding adequate territorial compensation in our favor." He was referring to the fact that Italy had gained nothing from Austria's earlier annexation of Bosnia-Herzegovina. But San Giuliano was not ready to break with either Austria or Germany. Paris was not likely to treat Italy with respect once it was separated from its powerful allies. Time, San Giuliano knew, was on Italy's side. "I believe it therefore necessary and urgent that Germany work to make compatible both the defense of our interests and our loyalty to the Triple Alliance." He meant, of course, that Berlin should pressure Vienna to offer suitable compensation to Italy if the Italians did not stand in Austria's way.

Flotow, who was himself nervous and sickly, joined San Giuliano at an Italian spa, where the two men took the waters together. San Giuliano kept pumping Flotow on German and Austrian intentions. He also had his ambassadors make inquiries in all the major capitals until, by 17 July, San Giuliano was fairly certain that Austria "supported by Germany intended to pose unacceptable conditions on Serbia and then use the pretext to attack her." He informed his ambassadors in Berlin, St. Petersburg, Vienna, and Belgrade that Italy opposed any Austrian territorial aggrandizement.[17] Count Kajetan Mérey von Kapos-Mére, Austria's irascible ambassador to Italy, complained bitterly that Flotow was leaking Austria's plans, which could only complicate matters.[18]

On 16 July, San Giuliano instructed his ambassador in St. Petersburg to suggest to the Russian foreign ministry that it warn Vienna that, in the event of any excessive Austrian action, Russia intended to support Serbia.[19] At about the same time, Count von Lützow was telling Berchtold it was "sheer fantasy" to expect Russia to stand aside. Lützow also warned his friend Maurice de Bunsen, the British ambassador, what was in the wind. Bunsen passed the warning along to the Russian ambassador, who immediately advised St. Petersburg that Vienna was counting on the "non-intervention of Russia" and suggested that Vienna be warned against making unacceptable demands.[20] Bunsen reported all this to Grey in London, together with an analysis of the aggressive tone of the Vienna press, but added in a private letter to his friend Nicolson that he could not "yet believe Austria will resort to extreme measures."[21]

On 19 July, Jagow opened the German press campaign for "localization" with an article in the Sunday edition of the *Norddeutsche Allgemeine Zeitung:* ". . . more and more voices are heard admitting that the desire of Austria-Hungary to bring about a clarification of her relations with Serbia is justified." To maintain the European peace, Jagow wrote, "the settlement of differences which may arise between Austria-Hungary and Serbia should remain localized."[22] Everyone now understood that Germany was prepared to back Austria in Serbia. The question was, how far?

By this time, the long delay was beginning to get on Jagow's nerves. On 20 July, following a conference on naval matters with the commander of the 3d Naval Squadron, Jagow rambled nervously on the diplomatic situation for more than an hour. He was clearly worried about England, first saying that English warnings were just bluff and then making the "amazing proposal" of threatening to invade Holland if England sided with France and Russia. The army, Jagow was told, would not give a single soldier for such an enterprise.

The navy men offered Jagow little comfort. They did not like the commitment to Austria, and they were certain that England would come in on the side of France and Russia. They were not at all anxious to risk their precious fleet against the British navy. Unlike Zimmermann, whom they regarded as "certain and clear," Jagow was "uncertain, changeable, nervous, and fearful." They thought Jagow's nervousness arose from his "healthy respect for England." "How is it possible," one of them wondered, "that such a person is entrusted with the leadership of Germany's foreign policy?"[23]

11: POINCARÉ AND THE RUSSIANS

16–23 July

"My first memories of school are shadowed by lines of Prussian helmets," wrote Raymond Poincaré, who was ten years old when Prussia defeated France in 1870.[1] A Prussian officer was quartered in his home, troops were quartered in his school, and his hometown was occupied by the Prussians for four more years. For patriots such as Poincaré, the goal of life was to restore the greatness of France after its terrible defeat; there was "no other reason for existence than the hope of recovering the lost provinces."[2] There was a persistent "neither/nor" in men such as Poincaré: they neither wanted war with Germany nor would they give up hope for the two lost provinces of Alsace and Lorraine.

Poincaré became prime minister of France in January 1912, in the flood tide of French outrage over what the French regarded as Germany's bullying opposition to the French colonization of Morocco. He was elected president in 1913 on a platform of greater armaments, a longer period of service for conscripts, firmness with Germany, and close ties with Russia. "It is not possible," he declared, "for a people to be truly peaceful unless it is always ready for war."[3] Most of Europe's leaders were of the same opinion.

In the summer of 1912, Poincaré learned that the Russians were organizing the Balkan States into a league with the obvious purpose of driving the Turks out of the Balkan Peninsula. Both angry and frightened that the Russians would so expose France to the risk of war without consultation, Poincaré asked his army chief of staff, Gen. Joseph J. Joffre, what the situation would be if Austria, alarmed by a Serbian expansion, attacked Serbia, and Russia defended the Serbs. In September Joffre reported that if Austria tied up a substantial portion of its ground forces in the south, against Serbia, and if, as was likely, Italy defected from the Triple Alliance, then the Austrians and the Germans would expose themselves to giving either Russia or France a decisive military superiority, depending upon where Germany concentrated its forces. "Under these conditions," concluded the general, "the Triple Entente would have great chances of success that could bring it a victory that would permit it to redraw the map of Europe."[4]

Here, for the first time since 1870, a French general optimistically assessed France's chances in a war with Germany. Joffre's assessment depended upon three conditions: (1) that a substantial portion of Austro-Hungarian forces be tied up by Serbia, (2) that the Russian alliance remain in effect, and (3) that Great Britain fight alongside France and Russia. Poincaré never lost sight of Joffre's analysis. Great Britain and Russia must fight with France, and Serbia must be strong, because "every advantage in preparedness achieved by Austria-Hungary could, in fact, cause Germany to transfer to our frontier some of the army corps stationed on the eastern frontier."[5]

Alexander Izvolsky, the Russian ambassador to France, did not know about Joffre's analysis, but he did sense a change in French policy. The French had always maintained that they had no interests in the Balkans and would not fight a war for Russia's Balkan policy. Now, however, "the French government . . . appears to admit that an acquisition of territory on the part of Austria in the Balkans would affect the general European equilibrium and consequently also the special interests of France."[6] Under Poincaré, a powerful Serbia had become a French national interest.

When the Balkan War of 1912 ended with a newly expanded and increasingly aggressive Serbia, Germany's army chief of staff, Gen. Helmuth von Moltke, independently reached the same conclusion as General Joffre: England would fight alongside France and Russia, leaving Germany "surrounded on three sides by its enemies." Austria-Hungary had been weakened by the Balkan wars, Russia was growing stronger every year, and France was calling up an astounding 85 percent of its young men for military service whereas Germany was calling only 50 percent. Germany's larger population, therefore, was not translating into numerical superiority for its forces on the western frontier. Despite successive army increases in 1911 and 1912, Moltke urged yet another increase that, after a savage debate, passed in 1913. The increase would give Germany a peacetime army of 800,000 men and translate into a wartime army of 2.4 million upon mobilization.[7]

When the French general staff learned that Germany was going to launch a third army increase, it pointed out that France had no new manpower to call up and demanded that the term of military service for French conscripts be increased from two years to three. Poincaré agreed. Until the outbreak of war, French politics was dominated by debate over the three-year law.

After decades of bemoaning their defeat, their weakness, and their decadence, the French enjoyed a resurgence of patriotic fervor and confidence in the early years of the twentieth century. Princess Marie Dorothea Elizabeth Radziwill, born in France and married to a Prussian, visited Paris every April. During her 1912 visit, she wrote that "everyone" said they could no longer "tolerate being treated with the disdain which Germany shows us . . . if necessary, we will march."[8] For the princess, of course, "everyone" meant the world of Paris society: aristocrats, diplomats, top government officials, and army officers. It was this patriotic wave that brought Poincaré to the presidency of France.

Nonetheless, he did not have an easy time of it. He fought a bruising political battle for three years of service for conscripts in 1913. A new center-left coalition immediately formed, headed by the finance minister, Joseph Caillaux, and the leader of the Socialist Party, Jean Juarès. The repeal of the three-year-service law was the centerpiece of their election campaign, and all signs pointed to a victory for the new coalition. The right counterattacked with a ferocious assault on the private life of Joseph Caillaux, including revelations of his adulterous affair with his present wife, Henriette, when each was married to another person. When Gaston Calmette, editor of a right-wing journal, acquired and began publishing embarrassingly intimate letters from Joseph to Henriette, Mme. Caillaux was frantic. Her poor father! Her nineteen-year-old daughter!

Despite pleas from Henriette's lawyers, Calmette would not stop publishing the letters. He saw it as his patriotic duty because "Caillaux will imperil the three-year law, our alliances, and our Ententes."[9] On the morning of 16 March 1914, Henriette Caillaux dressed carefully, left a note for her husband, and went to a gun shop to purchase an automatic pistol. She had the clerk show her how to load and fire the weapon, then went to Calmette's offices and asked to see him. He was not in; she would wait. After waiting patiently for an hour or more, Henriette Caillaux was shown into Calmette's office, where she fired six shots, four of which hit the editor. Calmette collapsed to the floor. Those who rushed in claimed to hear him murmur, "I have done my duty. What I did I did without hate."[10] He died on the operating table a few hours later.

It was a truly enormous scandal. Joseph Caillaux had to resign as finance minister. Conservatives roared with outrage, but the elections in April and May resulted in a major triumph for the left. Joseph Caillaux was easily reelected to his seat and the Socialists made spectacular gains. Even with these gains, the Socialists had only 16 percent of the popular vote, but Conservatives were frightened and Poincaré wrote nervously in his diary that "Jaurés already speaks as master."[11]

The elections left France without a government for two weeks in June. Caillaux would normally have formed a new government of the left, and

Poincaré could not have stopped him. But Caillaux could not take office until after his wife's trial. Jaurés, the Socialist leader, was an impossible candidate, and no other man of the left had Caillaux's stature. Poincaré, as president, stubbornly refused any man as prime minister who would not support the three-year law. The French president was a narrow, stubborn, pettifogging lawyer devoted to hard work, order, and private property. Socialists, anarchists, and revolution threatened the fabric of society, and the enormous victory of the left distressed him greatly. The thought of an opponent of the three-year law becoming prime minister was pure pain.

After a series of unsuccessful compromise candidates, René Viviani was finally forced on Poincaré. A man of the left, an ex-Socialist, a brilliant parliamentary orator, and one of the stars of the French Chamber of Deputies, Viviani had voted against the three-year-service law, but he promised Poincaré that he would defend it as prime minister. Poincaré did not trust this promise, but no one else was available and France needed to have a functioning government for the upcoming state visit to Russia. Reluctantly and under great pressure, Poincaré summoned Viviani to form a cabinet. Viviani succeeded brilliantly. On 16 June, twelve days before the Sarajevo assassination, France once more had a government.

It was a bad time for Poincaré. The national movement that had brought him to power was, he thought, "smashed."[12] The French government was now headed by Viviani, who, following Poincaré's example, made himself foreign minister as well as prime minister. But all was not lost. Bruno Jacquin de Margerie, a career diplomat whose judgment Poincaré valued, remained political director of the foreign ministry. Maurice Paléologue, a longtime friend and political ally, was still ambassador to Russia. Alfred Dumaine, another Poincaré appointee, stayed on as ambassador to Austria-Hungary. No one dared touch France's two senior ambassadors, the Cambon brothers in Berlin and London, whom Poincaré had always found reliable. Viviani, however, was a problem.

Few recollections of Viviani are favorable to him. He was an extraordinarily volatile man whose moods could swing dizzily from deep despair to radiant enthusiasm and back again. He was a brilliant speaker, powerful and persuasive, but he was widely regarded by his opponents as an overwrought phrasemonger, "high-strung, almost ill." At the first sign of opposition, he would throw up his hands and shout and swear, or walk away muttering to himself until he calmed down.[13]

Because Viviani was a man of the left and had voted against the three-year law, Poincaré and Paléologue never lost an opportunity to warn him of the German menace and the imminent danger of war. Paléologue, who was always predicting that war was just around the corner, warned Viviani that on the day the tsar came to believe he could not count on France, he would turn to Germany and leave France to face the Germans alone. Viviani, according to Paléologue, was terrified. Without Russia, France would lose her national independence! It could mean the loss of the Republic![14] Even for Viviani, the prospect of facing Germany without Russia was unthinkable.

Poincaré had never been happy with the Russians. They were secretive, they were unpredictable, and they did not have regard for French interests. Poincaré worried that their diplomacy in the Balkans would provoke Austria-Hungary and drag France into a war with Germany. Sergei Sazonov, the Russian foreign minister, was a particular source of anxiety. He was excitable, not trustworthy, and overwhelmed by Russia's many problems. Sazonov seemed to wake up every morning with a new policy, and he did not always consult his French ally about them—the league of Balkan states that launched the First Balkan War, for instance. But France could not face Germany without the Russians, and the Germans were everywhere.

German economic and political influence was encircling France's African colonies, growing in Turkey, and threatening French Syria. German banks were gaining control of the Italian economy. Germans were investing in the Russian arms industry. German armaments firms were even getting orders from the Russian and Serbian governments, who were paying for their purchases with the proceeds from French loans![15] Belgium was pro-German and would let the German army march through its territories without a fight. The Russians were complaining that the French and English had not given Russia adequate support in the fight over the German general in Constantinople, and there was powerful support in the tsar's court for a pro-German alignment.[16] There was no end to French worries. The French chargé d'affaires in St. Petersburg could only hope that Poincaré's state visit would "demonstrate the true nature of things" and convince the Russians "of our military power."[17] Poincaré was determined that when he got to Russia he would deal with these problems.[18]

The leaders of the French government set sail for Russia on 16 July, and during the trip Poincaré did his best to brief Viviani. He emphasized the importance of the three-year-service law and of being "very firm" with the Germans.[19] Viviani nonetheless continued to make Poincaré nervous because "he is extraordinarily ignorant of foreign affairs, which do not interest him at all and which he does not even appear to understand." Poincaré was also annoyed that Viviani seemed more preoccupied with the trial of Henriette Caillaux, which was to begin on 20 July, than he was with the upcoming state visit.[20] Viviani had not wanted to go to Russia. He would rather have stayed in Paris, where the political balance hung on the outcome of the Caillaux trial. The first question he asked Paléologue on landing was for news from Paris and reports on the trial. Viviani seemed obsessed by the trial and asked repeatedly, "What are we doing here?"[21] As Poincaré and Paléologue describe the state visit, Viviani might as well have stayed at home.

The French wanted the Russians to realize that France was a power to be reckoned with despite being a republic, despite its constantly changing governments, despite the electoral gains of the Socialists, and despite the continuing controversy over the three-year law. The Russians wanted to demonstrate the power and loyalty of their army, particularly after the 1905 revolution. Political assassination was endemic in Russia; strikes and violence tore up Russian cities all through the spring and early summer of 1914 and continued through the French visit. Russian officials took pains to assure Poincaré and Paléologue that the Germans were provoking the violence in order to turn the state visit into a fiasco. Several "notorious" German agents, they said, had been identified.[22]

Nevertheless, the visit went well. Almost four days of talks were jammed into a merciless calendar of military reviews, religious services, luncheons, formal dinners, diplomatic receptions, and a visit to the grave of Alexander III, father of Tsar Nicholas II and originator of the French alliance. The Russians were determined to awe the French with the power and loyalty of Russia's huge army, and there were several beautifully orchestrated military reviews, including one in which the tsar received thunderous cheers from each regiment as he rode by. The French warned the Russians that any flirtation with Germany would be dangerous for both their nations. If war came, only prompt and simultaneous attacks by both armies could split the powerful German army and keep the Germans from overrunning France. If France fell, Russia was lost. The Sarajevo assassination was not a major item on either government's agenda.

During the course of a diplomatic reception, Poincaré found an occasion to mention the Serbian problem to Count Friedrich Szápáry von Szápár, the Austro-Hungarian ambassador. As Szápáry came through the receiving line, Poincaré, flanked by Viviani and Ambassador Paléologue, expressed his sorrow over the assassination. Noting that the Serbians were very uneasy, he asked what Vienna thought about the matter. Szápáry told Poincaré exactly what he had told the Russian foreign minister a few days earlier: Vienna viewed the situation calmly, convinced that Serbia could not refuse Vienna's just demands. Asked whether Austrian investigations had come up with any evidence of Serbian complicity, Szápáry gave the same answer he had given Sazonov: the investigation was still in progress and he had not yet been informed of its results.

An exchange followed, with Poincaré at his legalistic worst and Szápáry answering with dry dignity. Poincaré thought Szápáry needed a warning. "Serbia has some warm friends in the Russian people," he said. "And Russia has an ally, France. There are plenty of complications to be feared!" Paléologue thought that Poincaré spoke in "a more than conciliatory tone,"[23] but Szápáry was outraged to be addressed in such a manner in public and at a formal reception. He reported angrily to Vienna that Poincaré was anything but a calming influence in St. Petersburg, and that his argumentative tone differed markedly from "the reserved, circumspect bearing of Sazonov."[24] After receiving this report early on the morning of 22 July, Berchtold could only have felt confirmed in his decision to wait until Poincaré left Russia.

There was a major embarrassment when Viviani, prime minister and foreign minister of France, suffered what appeared to be a mild nervous breakdown. He had been distracted all through the visit, often talking to himself, sometimes swearing loudly, ignoring his hosts, and finally becoming so uncontrollable that Paléologue had to order a doctor from the French hospital to take Viviani away. The French explained to their hosts that Viviani had a severe liver ailment. The Russians politely accepted that explanation, but it was all terribly embarrassing.[25]

Viviani had recovered sufficiently by the morning of 23 July to consult with Sazonov on instructions for the French and Russian ambassadors in Vienna. By this time, it was widely expected that Vienna would soon be delivering a note or demand of some kind in Belgrade. Sazonov wired his ambassador at 4:00 A.M. on the twenty-third, instructing him to "cordially but firmly" bring to Berchtold's attention the dangers of an unacceptable note to Serbia; even Viviani was "not inclined to tolerate a humiliation of Serbia unwarranted by circumstances."[26] Poincaré and Viviani sent a similar instruction to Ambassador Dumaine at 2:00 A.M. the next day, by which time the Austrian note had long been delivered to Serbia.[27]

On the evening of 23 July, there was a farewell banquet on the deck under the looming guns of the battleship *La France*. During coffee, Paléologue, after consulting with Viviani and Sazonov, hastily drafted a final communiqué on the back of a menu. Following the usual platitudes on unity and loyalty, the draft concluded that "the two governments have discovered that their views and intentions for the maintenance of the European balance of power, especially in the Balkan Peninsula, are absolutely identical." Viviani was upset by the absence of any mention of peace and, like many French politicians, was wary of committing France too closely to Russia's Balkan policy. He had Paléologue revise the language to read that the two governments "are in entire agreement in their views on various problems which concern for peace and the balance of power in Europe has laid before the Powers, particularly in the East." Poincaré after the war described the communiqué as "a witness to our spirit of moderation and of our desire for peace."[28]

The final toasts by Poincaré and Tsar Nicholas II were ringing affirmations of the strength of the alliance and of peace through strength. A confidential summary of the four days of talks prepared by Sazonov for Sir George Buchanan, the British ambassador, emphasized the "perfect community of views" between the two allies, their agreement to dissuade Vienna from taking action that Serbia "would be justified in regarding as an attack on her sovereignty," and, finally, their "solemn affirmation of obligations imposed by the alliances of the two countries."[29]

The tsar and his entourage returned to the imperial yacht *Alexandria*. As the yacht raised anchor, the two French warships *La France* and *Jean Bart,* strung with lights and brilliant in the warm Baltic night, unleashed deafening twenty-one-gun salutes. At 11:00 P.M. they too raised anchor and turned slowly away—just as the first news of the Austrian ultimatum came over the wires to St. Petersburg.

12: No Serious Complications Are to Be Feared

Europe, 28 June–23 July

Vienna had gulled almost everyone. Only San Giuliano in Rome seemed to suspect what was coming. Though German newspapers expected Austria to take some kind of action with Germany's support, they did not anticipate anything that could lead to war. The British, French, Italian, and Russian ambassadors in Vienna all believed that Austria would not attack Serbia because "an isolated combat with Serbia would be impossible." Russia would be compelled to defend Serbia. Even the Serbian minister in Vienna did not think his country would be attacked.[1]

For the French man in the street, there was no July crisis—unless it was the murder trial of Henriette Caillaux, which began on 20 July. There were a few disturbing intelligence reports to the effect that Vienna regarded Serbia as the Italian question all over again and was going to take serious action,[2] but before the early-morning hours of 24 July, there was no sense of crisis either in Paris or onboard *La France*. Indeed, as late as Thursday, 23 July, when even Sir Edward Grey, the British foreign secretary, was getting nervous, French ambassador Alfred Dumaine reported from Vienna that the elderly Emperor Franz Joseph was unlikely to let threats pass into action.[3]

The press war between Austria and Serbia, however, went on unabated. On 10 July the Russian minister to Serbia, who enjoyed an almost mythic stature among the Serbs as the personification of Russian support for the Great Serb dream, died of a heart attack in the Austrian legation. The English minister in Belgrade reported that "sinister reports at once circulated that M. Hartwig had taken 'a cup of tea' at the Austrian legation. I merely mention this as affording an indication of the somewhat medieval morals prevailing in this city."[4] Serbian newspapers demanded vengeance, and for a while the Austro-Hungarian minister to Serbia was afraid that armed bands might attack his legation. But nothing happened, the fear passed, the press war continued, and Europe went on regarding the Serbs as only slightly better than barbarians.

In Austria and Hungary, there were sensational press reports of Serbian plans to annihilate the Austrian community in Belgrade in revenge for the death of the Russian minister. These reports provoked repeated queries about the government's intentions. Tisza responded with a fairly sharp speech in the Hungarian parliament on 15 July. "Our relations with Serbia must in any event be clarified," he said. He refused to be more specific, other than to say that a "clarification" did not necessarily mean war. War, he insisted, was "a sad last resort," but "every state, every nation, must be in a position to make war and must, as a last resort, desire war, if the state and nation are to continue to exist."[5]

The Russian chargé d'affaires in Belgrade, acting in place of the deceased minister, wrote that Tisza's speech made Serbian Prime Minister Nicholas Pašić very nervous, adding that "he has received information of Austrian troop movements . . ."[6] But Europe did not share Pašić's fears. On 19 July, as the Austrians and Tisza were putting the final touches on their note to Serbia, Pašić was still worried about the ominous silence from Vienna. He instructed his diplomats that Serbia wanted good relations with Austria-Hungary and was prepared to help in every way in apprehending the assassins, but as yet the Austro-Hungarian government had made no request for such assistance.[7]

There was a ripple of concern in Russia when Count Szápáry, the Austro-Hungarian ambassador, returned from leave earlier than expected—just as the Russian foreign ministry received the Italian warning that Vienna expected to deal with Serbia unopposed. The Russian foreign minister, Sergei Sazonov, decided to have a talk with Szápáry to tell him that Russia could not be indifferent to Serbia's fate. When the two men met on 18 July, Szápáry told the Russian that his government was interested only in putting an end to terrorism; moreover, Vienna was convinced "that the Serbian government would prove itself to be accommodating with respect to our demands." Szápáry, Sazonov told his section chief, "was gentle as a lamb."[8] There was no need to deliver a warning.

For most of July, Grey was more concerned about the Irish and the Germans than about the Austrians. He warned his ambassador to France that Germany "is now really frightened of the growing strength of the Russian Army." He feared the Germans might seek yet another army increase "or bring on a conflict with Russia at an early date before the increases in the Russian Army have their full effect and before the completion of the Russian strategic railways to be constructed with French money."[9] Paul Cambon,

France's ambassador in London, reported after almost two weeks of silence that Grey was beginning to worry about Austrian intentions. However, Cambon added, Sir Arthur Nicolson, Grey's permanent undersecretary, thought Grey was being unduly nervous.[10]

Eyre Crowe, a senior clerk in the British foreign office and the reigning German expert, read Gottlieb von Jagow's 19 July article and began to doubt that Germany would really restrain Austria.[11] When Grey read Jagow's article,[12] and a report from Ambassador Bunsen that Count Lützow had warned him that the Austro-Hungarian government is "in no mood to parley," Grey decided he had better talk to the Austro-Hungarian ambassador. He made an appointment for the next day, 23 July.[13]

During all this time, Austro-Hungarian diplomats were assuring everyone that there was no need to fear "serious complications with Serbia."[14] Most professionals were looking forward to a quiet summer.

PART IV: You Have Forty-Eight Hours

13: BELGRADE

23–24 July

Baron Giesl von Gieslingen, the Austro-Hungarian minister to Serbia, was instructed to deliver his government's note to the Serbian foreign ministry at 6:00 P.M. Belgrade time on Thursday, 23 July.[1]

The men of Baron Giesl's family had served the Hapsburgs as army officers since the eighteenth century, and he himself had enrolled in a military academy at the age of fourteen. Most of his army career, however, was spent on quasi-diplomatic assignments as a military attaché, as a member of military missions, or as the military adviser on negotiating teams. He decided that he might as well transfer to the diplomatic service; in November 1913, after a brief stint in Montenegro, he was appointed minister to Serbia.[2]

Giesl firmly believed that the Serbs were only waiting for the Hapsburg Empire to fall "like a worn-out corpse into the lap of the soon to be created Great Serb Empire." He also believed that "a reckoning with Serbia, a war for the Great Power status of the Monarchy, indeed, for its existence, cannot in the long run be avoided."[3] He was not at all surprised that the day of reckoning was at hand.

At precisely 6:00 P.M., Giesl arrived at the Serbian foreign ministry. He was received by Laza Pacu, the foreign minister, and by Slavko Gruic, the secretary-general of the foreign ministry, who acted as interpreter, since Pacu spoke neither French nor German. Giesl announced that he had come to present a note and began reading, slowly so that Gruic could translate. Pacu nervously interrupted to say that, in the absence of the prime minister, he could not assume responsibility for receiving such a note. Giesl replied that the Serbs had been given ample notice that an important message would be arriving. Pasic could have been available. As Gruic translated, Pacu listened, shaken, and kept repeating that he could not receive such a note. In that case, said Giesl, he would leave the note on the table and they could do with it as they liked, but he warned that the only acceptable reply would be unconditional acceptance of the note within forty-eight hours—that is, by 6:00 P.M. Saturday. Giesl then put the documents on the table and left.[4]

Ever since learning that an important message was coming, Pacu had been trying to reach Pasic, but the sixty-eight-year-old prime minister had just decided to take a long weekend and would not come back. After Giesl left, Pacu and Gruic again tried to reach Pasic, whose aide then called to find out about the note. Pasic's train, however, continued south—away from Belgrade. Perhaps Pasic just wanted time to think. In any event, sometime during the night, Pasic ordered the train back to Belgrade. He arrived at five o'clock Friday morning and called a Council of Ministers for 10:00 A.M.

Pasic was very pessimistic. Accepting the note would be political suicide. It would also be suicide to go to war with Austria-Hungary without Russia's help, and Russia showed no sign of wanting to fight. It had declined to give armed assistance when Austria annexed Bosnia-Herzegovina in 1908; it had refused to help Serbia gain an outlet to the Adriatic across Albania in 1912; it had stood aside when Austria-Hungary demanded the withdrawal of Serbian troops from Albania in 1913. Why would Russia act differently now?

When Pasic saw his ministers, they were exhausted and frightened. They had spent the night going over the note and looking for a way out. There was some blustering talk about fighting rather than accepting the note, but Serbia could not seriously contemplate a war with the Austro-Hungarian Empire without allies, and on Friday, 24 July, Serbia seemed utterly alone. There was no word from Russia. Grey's reply to an appeal from Pasic was that "the Servian government must reply as they consider the interests of Servia require"; Grey recommended that Serbia respond favorably to as many points as possible.[5] France's acting foreign minister in Paris (Viviani was still at sea) also advised the Serbs to reply as positively as possible.[6] Until early Saturday afternoon, it appeared that an isolated Serbia would have to accept the entire Austrian note, or with only minor reservations.

Prince Regent Alexander of Serbia wired appeals to his uncle, the king of Italy, and to Tsar Nicholas II of Russia.[7] Until Russia made a decision, the only way to gain time and escape invasion was to accept the note and then try to evade its more onerous provisions through diplomacy. That was exactly what Count Berchtold expected and the reason he wanted to place Austrian officials in Serbia to supervise compliance. On Saturday morning the English and the French legations in Belgrade reported that the Serbian government was prepared to agree to all ten points of the note, except for the very point that Berchtold regarded as crucial: the participation of Austrian officials in any investigation or judicial process. On this issue, Serbia would ask for an explanation as to just what Austria-Hungary had in mind.[8]

*   *   *

The Austrians had told everyone that their demands would be acceptable and that a peaceful solution was possible if Serbia acted in good faith. Foreign ministries awoke on 24 July to discover that Vienna had delivered a note that no sovereign state could accept. The Austrians were so convinced of the righteousness of their cause, and so absorbed in the substance and the timing of the note, that they never considered its impact on Europe and had barely kept their German ally informed. Ministers of the German states in Berlin had reported on Thursday, 23 July, that Berlin was completely in the dark. It still did not have a complete text of the note, it did not know what Austria would do if Serbia rejected the note, and it did not know what would happen when the Serbs were defeated.[9]

Communication among Entente governments was not much better. Poincaré and Viviani were sailing to Stockholm from Russia as planned, and wireless reports were often garbled. The Bavarian minister to Austria reported that the Entente ambassadors in Vienna had no idea what was happening. "The Englishman is in the country, the Russian went on leave day before yesterday and [the French ambassador] tried yesterday to tell [an Austro-Hungarian foreign ministry official] not to stretch the bow too tight."[10] In Belgrade, the French minister had suffered a mental breakdown, his replacement had only just arrived, and the English minister was ill. "With [the Russian minister] dead," reported Giesl, "[the French minister] apparently crazy, and the English envoy so sickly he takes virtually no part in political affairs, the Triple Entente is at present barely represented in Belgrade."[11]

Sir Edward Grey saw the Austro-Hungarian ambassador, Count Albert von Mensdorff-Pouilly-Dietrichstein, on Thursday morning. Count Mensdorff informed Grey that Austria would be delivering a note to Serbia that afternoon and that Grey would receive the text the next day. Grey replied that everything depended on convincing Russia of the justice of Austria's demands and on whether the demands could be accepted by Serbia.[12]

When the text of the note was published, German and Austrian spadework with the London editors was rewarded by a relatively mild press reaction. Even Conservative papers gave Serbia short shrift, and the Conservative stalwart, *Pall Mall Gazette,* went so far as to say that Austria's note was "conspicuous for its union of firmness and restraint."[13]

With even Conservative papers reacting mildly, and his own Liberal Party adamantly opposed to participation in a continental war, Grey's diplomacy was severely restricted. He made it clear to the Austrian, French, and German ambassadors that Great Britain was not concerned with an Austro-Serbian quarrel, or even with an Austro-Russian quarrel; Great Britain would be concerned only if France and Germany were involved.

Most diplomats believed that a Russian mobilization would facilitate negotiations by putting pressure on Austria-Hungary. Grey thought that if Austria attacked Serbia, Russia would certainly mobilize, and this, he said, would be the appropriate moment for England, France, Germany, and Italy to offer to mediate between Russia and Austria.[14]

Grey pressed both Mensdorff and Lichnowsky for an extension of the forty-eight-hour time limit and warned of the terrible consequences of a war between the four continental powers. Lichnowsky and Mensdorff both noted that Grey "expressly emphasized the number four," which meant that Grey did not think England would be involved. Grey told Lichnowsky that if the tension between Austria and Russia became dangerous, England, Germany, France, and Italy should mediate between the two nations. He did not challenge the Austrian position that it would accept no mediation between itself and Serbia. He asked Lichnowsky to submit to Berlin both his four-power mediation proposal and a proposal that England, France, and Germany ask Vienna to extend the time limit. Lichnowsky urged his government to accept both requests.[15]

On Friday evening, Grey met with the cabinet in the prime minister's room at the House of Commons; Grey listened patiently as cabinet members discussed the dangerous constitutional impasse over Irish home rule. At the end of the discussion, as the cabinet members rose to disperse for the weekend, Grey asked them to wait a moment. He had important news on the situation in Europe. Wearily and probably impatiently, the ministers resumed their seats while Grey read them the Austrian note to Serbia.

This was the first time in a month that the cabinet had considered foreign policy. The situation, said Grey, was grave, but he was hopeful that talks between Russia and Austria might lead to a peaceful settlement. Thus reassured, the cabinet members scattered into the English countryside.[16] Grey, too, left for a weekend of fishing. "Things were not yet so critical that it was unsafe to be out of town."[17]

Count Berchtold had instructed Giesl that the note was not to be referred to as an ultimatum, because Austria-Hungary would not automatically declare war when the time was up.[18] Mensdorff went to the foreign office to make sure that the British government understood this. The foreign office then wired Grey at his fishing lodge late that night: an unsatisfactory answer by Serbia would lead only to the severing of diplomatic relations and military "preparations," not to war. Grey was greatly relieved. He wired his ambassador in St. Petersburg: that "makes the immediate situation rather less acute."[19]

14: WHAT DO THE RUSSIANS THINK?

24–25 July

The Russians were furious. After the assurances given by Berchtold and Szápáry, they had not expected a crisis. Their ambassadors to France and Germany were on leave, their ambassador to Austria-Hungary had just gone on leave, the deceased minister to Serbia had not been replaced, and senior army officers were on leave or on tours of inspection. Baron Moritz Fabianovich von Schilling, director of the chancellery in the Russian foreign ministry, immediately ordered his ambassadors back to their posts and got ready to brief his foreign minister, Sergei Sazonov, who was due back from the country at 10:00 A.M. on Friday, 24 July.

When Schilling finished his report, Sazonov exploded. *"C'est la guerre européenne!"* He told Schilling to summon the Austro-Hungarian ambassador immediately. Sazonov was an excitable man who had been terrified by the 1905 revolution. He frequently lectured the diplomatic community on the rising wave of terrorism and revolution that was engulfing Russia and the thrones of Europe. He feared that Austria's annexation of Bosnia and Herzegovina and Germany's military mission in Turkey were the start of an Austro-German campaign to drive a weakened Russia out of the Balkans. He was perfectly aware that war would be a disaster for Russia, but he had long been afraid that Russia might have to take, or at least threaten to take, military action to deter Austria-Hungary from moving against Serbia. The Austrian note convinced him that the time had come.

For the first time in his life, Sazonov reported to the tsar by telephone. He told the tsar that Austria's brutal ultimatum could not have been sent without German consent. Russia had to assume that Austria and Germany were intending to use their present military superiority to start a European war. Sazonov worked himself into a considerable state, but the tsar maintained his usual remote calm. He agreed that the Austrian demands were "outrageous" and ordered Sazonov to convene the Council of Ministers as soon as possible. The tsar told Sazonov to keep him informed, but Nicholas thought his foreign minister was in an unreasonable panic. Nicholas and his cousin Willy had known each other for more than twenty years; he knew that Willy wanted peace. If the kaiser had wanted to make war on Russia, why didn't Germany attack during the Russo-Japanese war in 1904–5? Or during the 1905 revolution? Germany could have had an easy victory then; why would it want to fight now?[1]

Ambassador Szápáry arrived at the foreign ministry with two documents—the note itself and an appendix summarizing the evidence linking Serbia to the assassination. There was also to have been a lengthy dossier of evidence demonstrating Serbian participation in subversive actions against the Hapsburg monarchy, but the dossier was not quite ready. Szápáry had barely begun to read the note aloud when Sazonov interrupted. "I know what it is," he said. "You mean to make war on Serbia and this is just a pretext." Szápáry replied sharply that over the years his government had shown sufficient restraint in the face of Serbian provocations to prove that it neither sought nor required pretexts.

The discussion became exceptionally heated. Sazonov insisted that "what you want is war and you have burnt your bridges." Szápáry replied, "We are the most pacific power in the world; what we want is to preserve our territory from revolution and our dynasty from bombs." All Sazonov could see was a Germanic march through the Balkans to the straits. All Szápáry could see was the threat to the Hapsburg monarchy, and he pleaded for the understanding of a fellow monarchist. They got nowhere. Szápáry's report to Berchtold was somewhat contradictory. He noted "the relative calm of the minister" but also that Sazonov "was from first to last hostile and unyielding." Observing that Sazonov always spoke of England, France, and Europe, and never of Russia, Slavdom, and Orthodoxy, Szápáry concluded that Sazonov was not yet ready to commit himself.[2]

Immediately after this, Sazonov called in the army chief of staff, Maj. Gen. Nikolai N. Yanushkevich, to suggest a partial mobilization against Austria alone, in order not to threaten Germany. Sazonov thought a partial mobilization might induce Vienna to moderate its position and negotiate. General Yanushkevich agreed. Unfortunately, he had been chief of staff only a few months, and Gen. Yuri N. Danilov, his quartermaster general and mobilization expert, was away on an inspection tour.[3] Yanushkevich therefore ordered Gen. Sergei K. Dobrolski, chief of the mobilization section, to prepare a proclamation of partial mobilization against Austria-Hungary. Yanushkevich warned that "nothing must give Germany occasion to perceive . . . any hostile intentions to herself."

Dobrolski was astounded. Russian military doctrine assumed that any war with Austria-Hungary would mean war with Germany as well. The Russians had no plan for a partial mobilization against Austria alone, and if they improvised one and later had to go to full mobilization against Austria and Germany, they would face long delays as trains were rerouted and men and equipment reshipped. The Germans, who could mobilize very quickly, would attack into that confusion with devastating effect. Dobrolski tried to explain these difficulties to his chief, but Yanushkevich was not prepared to go back to Sazonov and tell him that the partial mobilization to which he had just agreed was impossible. Yanushkevich brusquely ordered Dobrolski to have the necessary papers for partial mobilization on his desk within the hour.[4]

Sazonov, meanwhile, was lunching at the French embassy with the British and French ambassadors, Sir George Buchanan and Maurice Paléologue. Buchanan was a solid if unimaginative career diplomat who believed that Russia was only fulfilling "her historic mission as the protector of the Balkan states" in supporting Serbia; he also thought there was "a good deal of truth" in Sazonov's argument that "if Germany knew beforehand that France and Russia could count on English support, she would never face the risks which such a war would entail." Buchanan was therefore inclined to agree with those in his foreign office who wanted to turn Russian friendship into an alliance. But he was a professional, and after the Austrian note was delivered, he was, he claimed, "determined to say not one word that could be interpreted as encouragement to Russia to declare war on Austria."[5] By and large, the documents confirm his statement.

The French ambassador, Maurice Paléologue, was another matter entirely. He and Poincaré had been friends since their school days, and both were committed to the Russian alliance, to firmness toward Germany, and to the three-year-service law. When Poincaré took office he appointed Paléologue political director of the foreign ministry, and when the ambassadorship to Russia became vacant late in 1913, he appointed Paléologue to that post.

It was not a happy choice. Paléologue was notorious for his fantastic fears and self-dramatizing lies. One French politician dubbed him "the Black Prince" because of his pessimism.[6] The British ambassador to France thought Paléologue was an excitable rumormonger whose "indiscretions were almost incredible." Buchanan regarded the appointment as a "calamity," and the Austro-Hungarian chargé d'affaires in St. Petersburg agreed, saying Paléologue had a "tireless fantasy" and a talent "for making elephants out of gnats."[7]

The Russians were not pleased. The Russian ambassador to France thought Paléologue was a windbag and a liar, and he voiced his government's reservations about the appointment. French officials conceded that Paléologue tended to imagine all kinds of intrigues, that he was nervous, and that his fantastic pessimism was a joke among his colleagues. But, they emphasized, the new ambassador was a powerful supporter of the alliance and a very close friend of Poincaré. Resigning himself, Sazonov told the tsar that in view of Paléologue's friendship with the French president, Russia could not appear to be unfriendly with regard to the appointment.[8]

In many respects, Sazonov and Paléologue were remarkably alike. They were both excitable, moody, fearful, and not always reliable. Paléologue, who was the more consistently pessimistic of the two, did not enjoy the sudden surges of optimism that sometimes swept away Sazonov's worries. The two men were in complete agreement in their awe of the German army. Both believed in the need to divide that army with simultaneous attacks in case of war, and both were convinced that the Austrian note meant war unless the Entente powers firmly resisted Austrian demands. Paléologue thought that the Austrian note was the beginning of a major Austro-German offensive aimed at the Triple Entente, and he admitted freely after the war that he "had no hesitation in advocating a policy of firmness."[9] Moreover, he did not trust his foreign minister, Viviani, whom he regarded as a weakling, a Socialist, and a pacifist who would weaken the Russian alliance by causing St. Petersburg to doubt French support.

At the luncheon with Sazonov and Buchanan that Friday, Paléologue immediately announced the need for solidarity and firmness. He took a very hard line and he made no attempt to calm Sazonov. He did this entirely on his own since he had no instructions from Paris or from Viviani, who was still at sea with Poincaré.

Paléologue and Sazonov wanted England to declare its support. Buchanan said his government desired to remain neutral. Sazonov replied that "England's neutrality would be tantamount to her suicide." Buchanan personally agreed with this assessment, as did his foreign office and his foreign minister, Sir Edward Grey, but English diplomats also knew that neither the cabinet nor Parliament nor the public would support a war in defense of Serbia. Buchanan had to reply that his government "had no direct interest in Servia, and public opinion in England would never sanction a war on her behalf."

Sazonov argued that the present crisis was not a question of Serbia, but a general European question that England could not ignore. Again, as a personal opinion, Buchanan agreed that England would be in great danger if France and Russia were crushed by the Triple Alliance, but officially he could say only that England was not prepared to commit itself. To deflect the pressure from his two colleagues, Buchanan asked what would happen if England joined France and Russia in warning Austria against interfering in Serbia's internal affairs; what if Austria ignored the warnings and took military action against Serbia? Did Russia propose to declare war?

That brought Sazonov up short. He said that the Council of Ministers was going to discuss the entire matter that afternoon and that no decision would be made until a second council met with the tsar. Personally and unofficially, Sazonov thought that "Russia would at any rate have to mobilize."

Buchanan reported to Grey that Paléologue gave him to understand "that France would not only give Russia strong diplomatic support, but would, if necessary, fulfill all the obligations imposed on her by the alliance." In other words, France was prepared to go to war. "From the French ambassador's language," wrote Buchanan, "it almost looked as if France and Russia were determined to make a strong stand even if we declined to join them."[10]

Unlike Buchanan, Paléologue did not warn his government that the Russians were considering a mobilization. Nor does he appear to have reminded Sazonov that by the terms of their military agreement, Russia was obliged to consult with France before mobilizing. Paléologue was a very dangerous ambassador.

The Russian Council of Ministers met at 3:00 P.M. on Friday, 24 July, to formulate recommendations to the tsar. The meeting laid down the basic policy Russia was to follow in the coming days: they would not abandon Serbia, and if necessary they would go to war to defend Serbia. The council made this decision knowing that Russian military forces were unlikely "ever . . . to compete with those of Germany or Austro-Hungary [sic] as regards modern technical efficiency" because Russia was culturally and industrially backward compared to those two nations.[11] But the Russians felt they had no choice.

The growing power of Russia was a nightmare to the Germans, but educated Russians saw themselves blocked and defeated everywhere while other powers advanced. The annexation of Bosnia and Herzegovina, Russia's inability to help Serbia attain its aims in the two Balkan wars, and the German military mission in Turkey all rankled. Trade statistics for 1913 showed that 45 percent of Russia's exports went to Germany and 50 percent of its imports came from Germany. "Germany," argued the nationalist *Novoye Vremya,* is "economically plundering us . . . threatening not only further economic destruction, but also military defeat."[12] In May and June of 1914 Russian stock prices and the ruble both fell, which educated Russians saw as a further sign of weakness. Russian officials regarded the brutal Austrian note to Serbia as an Austro-German challenge designed to exploit Russian weakness. *Novoye Vremya* announced that "it is time to put an end to these lusts for pillage."

Sazonov, who knew as well as anyone that Russia could not afford a war, nonetheless argued that if Russia allowed Serbia to become a protectorate of the Central Powers, Russian prestige in the Balkans would "collapse utterly." Concessions, moreover, would not ensure a peaceful settlement;

Germany would simply mount further challenges to Russian interests. A firm stand, however, meant a real risk of war, which was particularly dangerous because Russia did not know "what attitude Great Britain would take in the matter." Nonetheless, Sazonov argued, the risk had to be taken.

A. V. Krivoshein, the minister of agriculture and the man generally regarded as the most powerful and influential member of the council, gave Sazonov his full support. Like many in the government, Krivoshein believed that recent Russian history had been one of retreat and humiliation; the time had come to assert Russia's dignity as a Great Power before it was too late. War held a real risk of defeat and revolution; there was an equally real risk of revolution if the government suffered further humiliation in foreign policy. Krivoshein agreed with Sazonov that Russia's "exaggeratedly prudent attitudes" had failed to appease Germany and Austria-Hungary. Therefore, their best hope of influencing Germany and saving the peace was to show that they had made all the concessions they were going to make.

Krivoshein's speech to the council was decisive. For the next eight days Sazonov insisted on firmness, military demonstrations, and Entente solidarity. At the same time he offered one compromise proposal after another in a desperate attempt to avoid the looming choice between a disastrous war or humiliating retreat. The council made several recommendations:

1. Russia would ask Austria-Hungary to extend the time limit on the note.

2. Serbia would be asked to accept as much of the note as it could; if Austria nonetheless invaded and the Serbs were unable to defend themselves, they should withdraw into the interior and ask Europe to protect Serbian independence.

3. If the need arose, the council would ask for the partial mobilization of the Odessa, Kiev, Kazan, and Moscow military districts bordering Austria. Under no circumstances would Russia take any measures aimed at Germany. General Vladimir A. Sukhomlinov, the Russian minister for war, made no objection to a partial mobilization.

4. Military stores and military units were to be brought to full readiness levels.

5. The finance minister was to take immediate steps to reduce financial holdings in Germany and Austria.[13]

Back at the foreign ministry, Sazonov talked to Serbia's angry ambassador, Miroslav Spalajkovic, whose father-in-law had been arrested with other Great Serb activists in Sarajevo. Spalajkovic's Great Serb fervor would not permit him to believe or to accept that the Tsar of All Russia would abandon his brother Slavs, and he sent several wires to Belgrade on Friday saying that Russia would not abandon them.[14] Unfortunately, Sazonov's only official communication had been to wire his acting minister to Serbia, Vasili N. Strandtmann, saying that if Serbia was really in no condition to fight, perhaps "the Serbs for the time being should make no attempt whatever to offer resistance, but should withdraw, leaving the enemy to occupy the land without fighting while making a solemn appeal to the Powers."[15] The Council of Ministers had just confirmed that recommendation.

Sazonov assured Spalajkovic that Serbia could count on Russia; the precise form of Russian support would depend on the next day's meeting with the tsar and on consultations with Russia's ally, France. Sazonov repeated his advice that Serbia retreat without fighting, which suggested that Russia might give only diplomatic support. Spalajkovic rejected this out of hand: "We cannot allow Austria-Hungary to destroy the entire country." The only way to avoid war, he argued, was for Russia to announce that it would mobilize unless Austria agreed to negotiate its dispute with Serbia.[16] Sazonov was not ready to go that far, but when Spalajkovic ran into Count Friedrich von Pourtalès, the German ambassador, in Sazonov's waiting room, he warned the German that "this was not a question merely between Serbia and Austria, but a European question."[17]

It was seven o'clock when the ambassador was shown into Sazonov's office. Pourtalès had been trying to see the foreign minister since noon, and he immediately launched into the case for nonintervention in the Austro-Serbian dispute. Sazonov, the ambassador reported, was "very much excited." When he read those words, the kaiser underlined them and childishly wrote "good" in the margin.[18]

Sazonov was angry and afraid and let his emotions get the better of him. He poured out contempt for Austria and declared that Russia would never accept that "the Austro-Serb quarrel could be settled only between the two parties concerned." After several blunt exchanges, Sazonov skillfully pointed out that Serbia's promises in the 1909 treaty of friendship had been made to Europe, not just to Austria, and that Europe must decide the extent to which the agreement had been breached. He proposed that the six Great Powers study the question. Pourtalès assured him that neither Germany nor Austria would agree to such a humiliation. If Austria submitted its vital interests to the judgment of the Great Powers, it would mean that Austria was prepared "to dispense with her status as a Great Power." Sazonov, in his anger, was a lot more explicit with the German than he had been with Spalajkovic: "If Austria-Hungary devours Serbia, we will go to war with her."

Pourtalès interpreted Sazonov's outburst to mean that Russia "will only take up arms in the event of Austria's attempting to acquire territory at the expense of Serbia." From this point forward, German diplomacy stressed that Austria would make no annexations. Moreover, Pourtalès concluded from Sazonov's six-power mediation proposal that "immediate intervention on the part of Russia is not to be anticipated." The next day, Pourtalès wrote that the great danger was Sazonov's "passionately nationalistic and also particularly religious [Russians were Orthodox, Austrians were Roman Catholic] hatred . . . for Austria-Hungary." Nonetheless, he thought that Sazonov wanted "to temporize above all things" and "bring the matter before the judgement-seat of Europe." Several witnesses declared that Pourtalès appeared shaken by Sazonov's strong talk.[19]

It had been a long day, but Sazonov was still not done. When he had finished with Pourtalès, Paléologue was waiting, and Sazonov told the French ambassador about his angry exchange with the German. Paléologue, who was severely criticized for his aggressive diplomacy after the war, wrote in his memoir that he then warned Sazonov to be calm and to exhaust every possibility of compromise. Paléologue also claimed in his memoir that he asked Sazonov, "Can I give my government an assurance that you have not yet ordered any military preparations?" According to Paléologue, Sazonov replied, "None whatever." Nor, according to Paléologue, did Sazonov tell him that the ministers had discussed the possibility of mobilizing. However, it is clear from Buchanan's report that Sazonov had revealed that possibility to both Buchanan and Paléologue at lunch.[20] Paléologue in any event never reported the assurances he claims he asked for.

In fact, when Paléologue wired his report to his government that evening, he took a very hard line. He warned that Russia was in no mood to tolerate Austrian violence toward Serbia, and he insisted that England, France, and Russia demonstrate their solidarity. "The Triple Entente disposes of sufficient power to save the peace," he wrote. "Ergo it is necessary to make that power manifest." A few hours later, at midnight, Paléologue sent another wire, this time to *La France* as well as to Paris, to say that Sazonov was going to try and get an extension of the forty-eight-hour time limit. He added that Sazonov had begged Pourtalès to warn his government of the danger of the situation, but he still did not mention that the Russians were considering mobilization.[21]

Diplomats in St. Petersburg had begun the day early in the morning, and were still filing dispatches at midnight and the early hours of Saturday. Once the Austrian note was delivered, the pressure never let up. Diplomats and political leaders worked around the clock. There was never enough time; they snatched meals and rest as they could, looking frantically for a way out under conditions of confusion, fear, anxiety, and exhaustion. Those conditions continued until they lost the peace.

15: What Is Going On?

Paris and London, 23–25 July

Sazonov and the Russian government recognized immediately that the Austro-Hungarian note to Serbia was a serious matter. France and England, however, were distracted by domestic affairs. The French assessment, in particular, was hampered by the fact that Poincaré, Viviani, and the political director of the foreign ministry, Bruno Jacquin de Margerie, were all away. Visits had been scheduled for Sweden, Denmark, and Norway, as well as Russia, and French leaders did not at first think that the Austrian note required a change in plans. The French public was wholly absorbed by the murder trial of Henriette Caillaux, which dominated the newspapers.[1]

In Paris, Count Nikolaus Szécsen von Temerin, the Austro-Hungarian ambassador, and Baron Wilhelm von Schoen, the German ambassador, were instructed to explain the position of their governments to Jean-Baptiste Bienvenu-Martin, the minister of justice, who was acting as foreign minister while Viviani was away.[2] Szécsen explained that his government's note was an act of self-defense against a neighboring state that was trying to dismember the ancient Hapsburg monarchy. Bienvenu-Martin had no diplomatic experience and apparently did not make himself clear to Szécsen. He wrote Viviani that he had called the note "virtually an ultimatum" containing several demands that would probably be unacceptable to Serbia. Szécsen, however, understood him to say that a forceful note was understandable under the circumstances, and that "it was the duty of Serbia to take strong measures against any accomplices in the Sarajevo murder." Szécsen, in fact, was very pleased with the interview and reported that Bienvenu-Martin hoped for a peaceful solution satisfactory to Austria.[3]

Schoen, the German ambassador, saw Bienvenu-Martin next, and this time Bienvenu-Martin was joined by an experienced foreign ministry official, Philippe Berthelot. Franco-German diplomatic exchanges tended to be blunt and tense; this was not an arena for amateurs. Schoen made it clear that Germany backed the Austrian demands and that Germany desired to limit or "localize" the conflict to the two immediate participants, Austria and Serbia. Because of Europe's alliance obligations, he said, the intervention of any other power would "bring about inestimable consequences." This was a scarcely veiled threat: localization was the sine qua non of peace, and Franco-Russian intervention could lead to war with Germany.

Bienvenu-Martin repeated that Austria-Hungary could legitimately demand that Serbia punish those involved in the assassination and give guarantees for the repression of anti-Austrian propaganda; the French government was advising the Serbians to make all possible concessions, but Austria-Hungary must not ask the Serbian government to do the impossible and "risk being swept away by revolution." Berthelot added that if Austria attacked, Russia might be unable to resist the pressure to defend Serbia; he hoped that Austria would be prepared to discuss those demands to which Serbia could not agree.[4]

Count Berchtold had insisted upon an unconditional acceptance of the note. Schoen, however, seemed to have given the impression to the French government and the Russian chargé d'affaires that a negotiated settlement was possible.[5]

On the day after these interviews, Saturday, 25 July, *Echo de Paris* headlined that Schoen's message amounted to a threat: "Let Austria crush Serbia, otherwise you must deal with Germany." Under the pretext of localizing the conflict, the paper went on, lies the "threat of a collective humiliation of the Triple Entente or the prospect of a general war."[6] Sir Francis Bertie, the British ambassador to France, thought differently. He sent a copy of the article to London with the comment that *Echo de Paris* had close relations with the Russian embassy.[7] Bertie was extremely suspicious that the Russians were trying to draw Britain and France into a war to support their Balkan ambitions.

Schoen immediately protested to Bienvenu-Martin that the article was a distortion of their talk. He also reported to Berlin that the French thought Germany was trying to take advantage of the Irish crisis in England, labor troubles in Russia, and recent disclosures of arms deficiencies in France.[8] He was right; that was exactly what the French thought.

For Paris, the real nightmare was a premature Russian attack that would force Germany to defend Austria. The Franco-Russian alliance would then require France to attack Germany. Such a sequence would make it impossible for Great Britain to fight on the side of France and Russia. Bienvenu-Martin therefore instructed Paléologue to keep him informed of Russian intentions.[9] But in three telegrams sent during the course of Friday, 24 July, Paléologue never mentioned that Sazonov had raised the possibility of a Russian mobilization. In his last dispatch of the day, which went out at

12:45 Saturday morning, Paléologue said only that Sazonov had agreed "to avoid everything which might precipitate a crisis."[10]

That Sazonov was considering a mobilization Bienvenu-Martin had to learn from the French chargé d'affaires in London, to whom Nicolson read Buchanan's report of his luncheon conversation with Sazonov and Paléologue. By this route Bienvenu-Martin also learned that Paléologue was urging Sazonov to be firm and promising that "France would conform to the conditions of her treaty of alliance."[11] Bienvenu-Martin began to perceive that France might be in danger. Poincaré, Viviani, and Margerie were still in Stockholm. Bienvenu-Martin wired Paul Cambon in London to come to Paris to assist him, and Cambon left immediately.

While Paul Cambon was rushing to Paris, his younger brother Jules was trying to find out what the Germans were up to. The Cambon brothers were France's senior diplomats, and Jules, at the age of sixty-nine, was by far the most engaging personality among the Great Power diplomats. Photographs show his colleagues full of earnest dignity; those of Jules Cambon reveal a man of wit. He was shaggy, and somewhat disheveled, with an intelligent face. His interviews and diplomatic papers reveal an amused tolerance for the frailties of mankind, an only modestly hopeful world weariness, and a very, very sharp mind.

Jules and his older brother were raised in the circles of the liberal republican opposition to the France of Napoleon III. When war came in 1870, Jules fought in all the combats around the walls of Paris during the Prussian siege. Jules regarded France's 1870 declaration of war on Prussia as a dreadful mistake, brought on by the desire of the imperial government to restore its sagging prestige.[12] This was not the usual French position. Poincaré, who was both younger and more rigid than Jules Cambon, regarded the conflict as a terrible Prussian aggression.

Jules Cambon was an active diplomat and had been France's ambassador to Germany since 1907. He was tireless in his efforts to explain the Germans to his government. At the same time he made his embassy a showcase for French culture in Germany. He and his wife organized concerts, plays, and lectures featuring French artists and cultural figures. They gave a regular afternoon tea for diplomats, high officials, and important society figures. Jules enjoyed Berlin salon society and particularly favored the soirees of Princess Radziwill, whose great Berlin house was across from the French embassy. Jules often crossed the street to the Radziwill establishment after dinner for an evening of political gossip and a glass of sweet currant *sirop*.

Sir Edward Goschen, the British ambassador, also frequented the salon of the "redoubtable Princess Radziwill." Goschen knew and liked Cambon immensely, declaring that "we get on excellently together." But Cambon never lost sight of what he was paid to do, and Goschen had to add that "I always have the feeling that he has got an axe of his own to grind."[13] Jules Cambon and Goschen collaborated closely throughout their tour in Berlin, just as, in London, Cambon's brother Paul took pains to see Sir Arthur Nicolson every day.

Despite his great intelligence, Jules Cambon shared the general tendency to exaggerate Austro-Hungarian intentions. Like Sazonov in St. Petersburg and Nicolson in London, he thought Austria-Hungary had ambitions to dominate the Balkans and to challenge Russia in the straits. The Hapsburgs had been expansionist for centuries; why should they change now?

Concerning Germany, Jules was more astute. As a great and powerful industrial nation with a growing population, Germany would naturally seek influence and markets around the world.[14] Jules regarded Great Power competition as a fact of life and warned Paris in 1913 that it was shortsighted and pointless to oppose the Germans in every corner of the globe. On the contrary, it might be helpful to have German armed forces and resources scattered around the world instead of concentrating on France. France, he counseled, should focus on those areas in which it had real and substantial interests—and in those areas, France must be firm.[15]

Cambon dismissed the French fear that the 1913 German army increase constituted an imminent threat of war. Unlike Poincaré, who worried about every German advance, or his brother Paul, who entertained wild fears of Austro-German intentions, or Paléologue, who was always expecting war, Jules did not believe that German armaments were necessarily aimed at immediate aggression. Lying between a hostile France and a huge Russia, Germany always had to face in two directions and measure its strength accordingly. The Germans, moreover, were trying to make up for their retreat in the 1911 Moroccan crisis and for the obvious weakness of Austria-Hungary after the Balkan wars.[16] "Some of our compatriots," Jules wrote, "imagine that when it hails on our vineyards it is Germany's doing, but she does not yet play the role of the political almighty God that is too easily attributed to her."[17]

Jules was also far more prepared than his colleagues to defy Russian pressure. He dismissed the notion that without French support Russia would turn to Germany, saying, "It is time to put an end to the legend that without us, Berlin, St. Petersburg, and London will come to an agreement."[18]

When the Austrian note became known on Friday, Jules dropped in on Jagow for what he called a "strictly personal" exchange of views to see what he could learn about German intentions. Jules Cambon was a great believer in informal chats, and he was in any case more than a match for

Jagow. When Jagow assured him that the German government had played no role in drafting the Austrian note, Cambon expressed surprise "at seeing him thus undertake to support claims, of whose limit and scope he was ignorant." Jagow was stung. "It is only because we are having a personal conversation that I allow you to say that to me."

"Do you know where you will be led by Vienna?" Cambon asked. Jagow replied that he expected Serbia's friends to be a "little emotional," but he was counting on them to give Serbia good advice. Cambon immediately countered that Berlin could give Vienna good advice as well. Could not Germany advise moderation? Jagow's reply was weak: "That would depend on circumstances." Jagow then said that the conflict had to be localized and asked Cambon if he really thought the situation was serious. "Certainly," Cambon responded, "because if what is happening is the result of due reflection, I do not understand why all means of retreat have been cut off."[19]

Cambon talked with everyone he could find that Friday, and in a series of dispatches concluded that the Austrians were going to use the assassination to try to salvage their position in the Balkans and that Berlin would support them because Germany did not want Austria-Hungary weakened any further. Cambon forwarded an article from the Berlin *Lokal–Anzeiger,* which he described as an official paper. The article stated that "the German people feel a great relief at the prospect of having affairs in the Balkans finally cleared up."[20] Whatever Jagow and Bethmann might say, neither Jules Cambon nor any other European diplomat believed that Germany was an innocent bystander.

Buchanan's report of his luncheon with Sazonov and Paléologue got to London at 8 P.M. on Friday. Incoming dispatches were reviewed by senior clerks and department heads, who attached their comments and sent the documents on. When Buchanan's report reached Grey's fishing cottage on the Itchen the next day, it came with a lengthy analysis by Eyre Crowe, a senior foreign office clerk who was head of the Eastern Department and one of the most articulate of the anti-Germans. Having read that Paléologue was promising firm French backing and demanding that Britain publicly support France and Russia, Crowe commented, "The moment has passed when it might have been possible to enlist French support in an effort to hold back Russia."

Crowe added that this was not just another Austro-Serbian quarrel, but a struggle "between Germany aiming at a political dictatorship in Europe and the powers who desire to retain individual freedom." Crowe had always accepted the inevitability of war with Germany for the hegemony of Europe; the critical question was "whether Germany is or is not absolutely determined to have this war now. There is still a chance that she can be made to hesitate, if she can be induced to apprehend that the war will find England by the side of France and Russia."

Buchanan, Crowe, and most foreign office professionals believed that a public declaration of support for France and Russia would force Germany to restrain Austria. French and Russian diplomats made that argument all through July. But Crowe knew as well as Grey that the cabinet would never approve such a declaration. Even if war came, public opinion might well force Great Britain to remain neutral.

What worried men such as Crowe was that the ententes with France and Russia had been made to prevent French and Russian challenges to the British colonial empire. The implied quid pro quo was that Britain would support France and Russia against Germany. If that support were not forthcoming, not only might Germany dominate the Continent, but France and Russia would tear up the colonial agreements with the British and again challenge them in India, the Mediterranean, and Asia.

Crowe outlined the problem of British neutrality in a continental war with his usual lucidity: "(a). Either Germany and Austria win, crush France, and humiliate Russia. With the French fleet gone, Germany in occupation of the Channel, with the willing or unwilling cooperation of Holland and Belgium, what will be the position of friendless England? (b). Or France and Russia win. What would then be their attitude towards England? What about India and the Mediterranean?"[21]

Grey saw the problem as well as Crowe, but he did not think there was anything he could do. During the course of Saturday, 25 July, Grey received reports that Austria was ignoring the possibility of a Russian intervention, that Serbia would not attempt to defend Belgrade if war broke out, and that Russia had declared that it could not "remain indifferent" to a Serbo-Austrian conflict.[22] Faced with overwhelming antiwar sentiment in England, Grey wired Bertie in Paris and Buchanan in St. Petersburg that "I do not consider that public opinion would or ought to sanction our going to war in the Servian quarrel."[23]

Grey's inaction was almost more than Nicolson could bear. Nicolson had been ambassador to Russia from 1906 to 1910 and had played a major role in negotiating the colonial agreements that constituted the 1907 Anglo-Russian Entente. He was a fearful man and always worried that Great Britain would lose Russia's friendship. In 1912, when Grey was exploring the possibility of a naval agreement with the Germans, Nicolson was afraid that the Germans would use the talks to undermine British friendship with Russia. "Our people are so blind. We are not very strong props on which to lean and

I always fear that some day we will be left alone."[24] On 25 July Nicolson wrote Grey: "Our attitude during the crisis will be regarded by Russia as a test and we must be most careful not to alienate her."[25]

When Nicolson became Grey's permanent undersecretary in the foreign office in 1910, he was sixty-one and looked and acted much older. He was bald with a fringe of white hair and a mustache whose sides were turning white. He was terribly bent with arthritis and very unhappy. His pedantic insistence on proper English usage made him something of a joke among the younger foreign office clerks. They were amused by his "puny frame bent halfway to earth beneath his topper as it fought its way across the gravel" of the Horseguards Parade. Nicolson hated his job, loathed the Liberals, and longed to be back in the field as an ambassador. He kept pressing Grey to turn the ententes with France and Russia into alliances—which both he and Grey knew perfectly well was politically impossible.[26] Grey grew tired of Nicolson's complaints, and Nicolson was increasingly frustrated as his influence grew less and less and his relations with Grey became more distant.

Nicolson was an ardent Conservative, and his in-laws were Ulster Protestants who detested the Liberal policy of home rule for Ireland. A journalist who knew both men wrote, "For some reason—perhaps because he talks too much of Ulster, his wife still more—he has absolutely lost Grey's confidence and he does not conceal the fact that he is sick of it all."[27] William Tyrrell, Grey's private secretary, steadily displaced Nicolson as a major foreign policy adviser and had a serious quarrel with the testy Nicolson, who, according to the journalist, "wanted to leave the Russians to pipe the tune and us to dance to it whatever it may be."[28] Nicolson was promised the next available ambassadorship, but this prospect died with the war.

One of the treaties making up the entente with Russia was an agreement defining the Russian and British spheres of interest in Persia (modern Iran). When Eyre Crowe took over the Eastern Department in 1913, he was shocked at the extent to which the Russians simply ignored that treaty. In June 1914, Crowe composed a memorandum arguing for a complete renegotiation of the Persian agreement and a reassessment of British policy toward Russia. Nicolson might be ready to write off Persia for the sake of the Russians, but Crowe was not. Crowe delivered a sharp protest to the Russian chargé d'affaires on 3 June, and Grey endorsed the new policy toward Russia: blunt talk and a firm assertion of British interests.[29]

By June 1914, Sazonov was complaining that he was "sick to death" of Grey's complaints about North Persia, and Nicolson found himself the only unquestioning supporter of Russian actions.[30] Even Bertie, one of the original anti-Germans, was critical of Nicolson's willingness to sacrifice everything to the entente with Russia.

*   *   *

Bertie also worried that French chauvinism and Sazonov's flirtation with a new anti-Austrian Balkan League would drag Europe into war. On 25 July, he warned Bienvenu-Martin that "public opinion in England would not sanction a war in support of Russia if she, as protector of Slavs, picked a quarrel with Austria over Austro-Servian difficulty." Later that same day Bertie wrote privately to Grey that French public opinion would not support a war to aid Russia if Russia intervened in the Austro-Serbian quarrel. Consequently, "the French Government will probably advise the Russian Government to moderate any excessive zeal that they may be inclined to display to protect their Servian client."[31]

Neither Paris nor London nor Bertie knew that Paléologue was something of a loose cannon in St. Petersburg. However, they did know that they did not want the Russians to take any irrevocable step, and they were prepared to ask Russia to use restraint. In that respect, Bethmann and Jagow were right and Lichnowsky was wrong. On the other hand, Germany's aggressively pro-Austrian stance may have been unnecessary; with a little coolness and patience, the "encirclement" of Germany might have dissolved under the weight of England's growing disenchantment with Russia. In that respect, Lichnowsky saw farther and better than Bethmann and Jagow.

But the intimate and friendly collaboration between French and British diplomats—Jules Cambon and Goschen in Berlin, Paul Cambon and Nicolson in London—never ceased to worry the Germans. Bethmann and Jagow could not get rid of the feeling that there was something sinister about the persistent anti-German tendencies of British diplomacy because they knew that Germany was not the problem; the problem was the Franco-Russian threat to the British Empire. Why didn't the British look to Germany for help?

A large part of the answer was that Germany would never risk war with France and Russia to defend British imperial interests, and the British knew it. Moreover, British imperialists believed that "as long as we rule India, we are the greatest power in the world. If we lose it, we shall drop straight away to a third-rate power."[32] Crowe had pointed out in a 1907 memorandum that the ententes with France and Russia were based on agreements settling a number of colonial disputes because Great Britain simply did not have the resources to defend its empire all over the world. This stark reality, wrote a Liberal imperialist, "is the fundamental argument for the Convention [with Russia] for we have not got the men to spare and that's the plain truth of it."[33]

For France and Russia and for British imperialists, the ententes came to mean that Britain ought not make any settlement with Germany that would upset France and Russia. If Great Britain were to ally itself with Germany, "we shall never be on decent terms with France . . . or with Russia whose frontiers are coterminous with ours or nearly so over a large portion of Asia."[34]

Such arguments never made any sense to Grey's Liberal critics, who believed that secret understandings with France would commit England to a war on the continent of Europe. To the Liberal mind, moreover, ties with an oppressive tsarist regime were immoral. "If our statesmen had the wit to make friends with France, and even with Russia," asked the Liberal-radical *Manchester Guardian* in 1909, "with both of whom our political quarrels were far older and more difficult of adjustment, then why not have Germany as a friend rather than an enemy?"[35] Grey thought this kind of talk was so much "gush";[36] it made the French uneasy, the Russians suspicious, and the Germans harder to deal with.

For Grey, therefore, a Balkan war was a nightmare: he could not go in and he could not stay out. "I do not think we could . . . intervene on the Russian side of a Balkan war; and yet our abstention would prove a danger to the maintenance of the present grouping of European powers."[37]

The Germans, however, thought that the balance of power in Europe required Great Britain to side with Germany. They knew that the real threat to British interests lay in imperial competition from France and Russia, and they could never understand why the British kept siding with their imperial rivals and against Germany. Bethmann in particular feared that the jealous British were planning to remove Germany from the ranks of the Great Powers. All of these factors were in full play once Austria-Hungary delivered its note to Serbia.

Prince Lichnowsky and Ambassador Schoen both warned Berlin that London and Paris believed that the German government was behind the Austrian note to Serbia. On Friday evening Jagow instructed Zimmermann to send telegrams to Paris, London, and St. Petersburg declaring that Germany had nothing to do with the note and knew nothing of its contents; moreover, Germany could not ask Vienna to modify its demands because "Austria-Hungary's prestige, both internal and external, would be completely lost."[38]

When Lichnowsky read this, he was beside himself. On Saturday morning he wired back that the general belief in London was that "without our encouragement such a note would have been unthinkable . . . if we do not participate in mediatory action, confidence in us and in our peaceable sentiments will be destroyed for good and all."[39]

Berlin decided that it had to make some show of cooperating with

London. Lichnowsky had reported that Grey wanted Berlin to join Great Britain in asking Vienna to extend the time limit on its note. Late Saturday morning, Sir Horace Rumbold, the British chargé d'affaires, formally delivered this request. Jagow proceeded to engage in a deception that fooled no one.

He told Rumbold that he had not received Lichnowsky's report of Grey's request until "10 this morning," but that he had "immediately" instructed his ambassador at Vienna to pass on Grey's suggestion and to speak to Berchtold about it. Unfortunately, Jagow explained, Berchtold was spending the day at Ischl, the emperor's summer residence, to await the Serbian answer, and there might be some delay in getting the time limit extended. Jagow went on to emphasize the main line of German diplomacy: "A reassuring feature of the situation was . . . that Austria-Hungary had no intention of seizing Servian territory."[40]

In fact, Jagow had not sent any instruction to Count Tschirschky in Vienna and did not do so until four o'clock that afternoon, when it would arrive far too late to extend the 6:00 P.M. deadline. Even then, Jagow simply forwarded the relevant extract from Lichnowsky's report with a note reading, "Have replied to London that I would communicate Sir E. Grey's proposals to Vienna. But as the ultimatum expired today and Count Berchtold was at Ischl, I did not believe that an extension of time-limit would be possible."[41] Tschirschky understood perfectly that he was not to press the matter.

Arkadi Nikolaievich Bronevski, the Russian chargé d'affairs, also asked for an interview. Jagow said he could not see him until 4:50 that afternoon, which would again be too late. When the two men finally met, Bronevski asked Jagow to support the Russian request for a time extension. Jagow replied that he had just wired a similar British request to Vienna and that he would send on the Russian request as well, but it might not get there in time. Jagow added that he thought Russia should be satisfied with Vienna's assurances that it would take no Serbian territory.[42] It was a silly performance and it seriously undermined German credibility.

PART V: Negotiations

16: THE SERBIAN ANSWER IS UNACCEPTABLE

25 July

On Saturday morning, 25 July, Sazonov wrote a memorandum for the tsar declaring that the real purpose of the Austrian action, "which is apparently supported by Germany," was to "annihilate Serbia completely and to upset the balance of power in the Balkans."[1] At 11:00 A.M. the Council of Ministers met with Tsar Nicholas II at his residence at Tsarskoe Selo. The tsar still did not believe that Germany was working in collusion with Austria, but he approved all the decisions made the previous day. He was not prepared to order a partial mobilization just yet but agreed to declare immediately the "Period Preparatory to War." With that declaration, the military was free to take all the steps necessary to get ready for mobilization.

Ambassador Spalajkovic enthusiastically wired Belgrade that "the military council showed the greatest warlike spirit and decided to go to the limit in defense of Serbia. The tsar especially surprised everyone by his decisiveness."[2] Spalajkovic was right about the mood at Tsarskoe Selo; it was ferocious, especially when the news arrived that Austria had refused to extend the time limit for a Serbian reply. Lieutenant General von Chelius, the kaiser's personal representative at the court of the tsar, had an uncomfortable time of it. The war minister, Gen. Vladimir Sukhomlinov, told him that Russia would have to stand by Serbia. "What will come of it is entirely immaterial to us; we should be breaking faith with our history if we did nothing but look indifferently on." Austria, said another Russian official, had "treated us as if we did not exist." An indiscreet general told Chelius that Russian troops were "to be mobilized."

As the hour of the deadline came and went, another general told Chelius, "The guns along the Danube have probably already commenced their fire, for one only sends a note like that one after the cannon have been loaded."[3] Chelius reported these comments in a long letter to the kaiser. He also sent a short wire to the Berlin foreign office reporting that maneuvers had been canceled, regiments sent back to their garrisons, and cadets commissioned early. "I have the impression," he reported, "that all preparations are being made for mobilization against Austria."[4]

Spalajkovic's report on the "decisiveness and enthusiasm" at Tsarskoe Selo arrived in Belgrade in the course of the afternoon. Saturday was an oppressively hot day in Belgrade, and the ministers were sweaty, generally uncomfortable, and constantly changing their minds. When they had absorbed Spalajkovic's latest report, they decided that instead of agreeing to all ten demands with "minor reservations," they would risk a firmer reply.

Baron Giesl described the change in mood. The hours passed with "leaden slowness" while he waited at his legation for the Serbian answer. According to Giesl:

> A number of foreign journalists had chosen my legation as the best observation post. From them I learned at noon that they had talked with Pašić and that he had confidently held out prospects for a peaceful solution. . . . But in the early hours of the afternoon, the situation took a thorough turn for the worse. It was being stated that Serbia had been strengthened in her resistance by the assurance that she had the backing of the entire strength of Russia. It was further said that Crown Prince Alexander had gone with the telegram to the officers' club where it was read aloud and gave rise to tumultuous demonstrations in favor of war.[5]

The chaotic course of the day was later described to the Italian newspaperman Luigi Albertini by Slavko Gruic, the secretary-general of the Serbian foreign ministry. Gruic did not have a complete draft of the reply in his hands until eleven o'clock that morning. There were so many sentences crossed out and so many insertions that in some places the text was almost illegible. Several times between noon and 5:00 P.M., as he was getting a translation typed (the ministers drafted in Serb but the official reply would be presented in French), pages were taken back for further changes. By four o'clock a "final" text was ready, but the typist was nervous and inexperienced and the typewriter broke down. It was as bad as it could be.

Toward five o'clock, when the translation was nearly finished, Gruic was told of further changes to reflect the latest enthusiastic report from Spalajkovic. Now the Serbs were going to accept only three demands without reservation: they would agree to prevent Serbian officials from participating in the smuggling of arms and explosives into Austria-Hungary, to punish those involved in getting the assassins across the frontier, and to report "without delay" on their compliance with Austrian demands.

The Serbs rejected point six, which called for the participation of Austrian officials in the investigation of the assassination on Serbian territory. They partially accepted points one, two, and three, which required the suppression of anti-Hapsburg propaganda and the dissolution of the Great Serb propaganda organization Noradna Odbrana. Not rejected but made subject to conditions that would give Serbia room to maneuver were point four, requiring the removal of officers and officials participating in anti-Austrian propaganda; point five, allowing Austrian officials to come to Serbia to assist in suppressing subversive activities directed against Austria-Hungary; and point nine, demanding explanations for the "unjustifiable utterances of high Serbian functionaries" since the 28 June assassination.

Gruic complained that he could not possibly make these new corrections and finish on time. He was told to do it anyway. The last half hour was a madhouse. The final document, even as delivered, looked a mess. It was covered with corrections; whole phrases were crossed out in ink. Diplomatically, the document turned out to be a first-rate note, appearing to yield to Austrian demands while actually yielding little or nothing. By 5:45 P.M. it was ready.

The time was nearly up. Then, Gruic recalled, Pašić "turned his gaze meaningly on me and asked: 'Well, who will take it?' I felt not the slightest desire to be the messenger. I had barely time to get to the station and if I had first to take the note to the Austrian minister, I might lose my train, which would have waited for the prime minister or a cabinet minister, but not for me." Gruic, like everyone else, expected an Austro-Hungarian army to march on Belgrade as soon as the answer was declared unacceptable. The ministers, therefore, were packed and ready to get on the government train. Gruic had no intention of being left behind. "So I felt relieved when, amid general silence, Pašić said: 'Very well, then I will take it myself.' He put the envelope with our reply under his arm and descended the stair . . . followed in silence by the ministers and officials who hastened off to the station to catch the train which soon after 6 P.M. was due to leave for Nish."[6]

Baron Giesl continued the story:

At 5:55 in the afternoon the Serbian prime minister appeared in my office and gave me the answer of his government. . . . Pašić—a tall man, already near seventy, with heavily greyed hair and beard—was obviously conscious of the significance of the moment. His exceptionally intelligent eyes reflected a melancholy earnestness. When I asked him what the answer was Pašić replied in German, of which he had a full command: "We accepted some of your demands . . . for the rest, we place our hopes on your loyalty and chivalry as an Austrian general. We have always been very satisfied with you." Naturally he could not know that the decision was not in my hands; an error, more-over, which later had wide circulation.[7]

Giesl, who often complained that people blamed him personally for re-jecting the Serbian answer, promised Pašić a prompt reply. The two men shook hands, and Pašić left.

A quick reading told Giesl that the Serbian answer did not constitute an unconditional acceptance. He had already prepared the note announcing his departure, which he immediately sent to the foreign ministry, where it ar-rived at almost the same time that Pašić returned. Giesl's note stated: "As the time limit stipulated in the note . . . has now expired, and as I have received no satisfactory reply, I have the honour to inform Your Excellency that I am leaving Belgrade tonight with the staff of the Imperial and Royal Legation."[8]

Giesl had been instructed that in the event of an unsatisfactory answer, he was to catch the 6:30 P.M. train out of Belgrade, which would get him into Semlin, a Hungarian border town, at 6:40.[9] Giesl, as always, carried out his instructions to the letter. He had ordered his entire staff to be at the le-gation with no more than one suitcase per person. Codebooks and other papers were burned. Cars were waiting to drive them to the station.

The street outside the legation was full of people, and Serbian police stood guard. There were a few shouted insults, but that was all. The route to the station and the station itself were heavily guarded. The station presented an extraordinary scene. The Serbian government had ordered mobilization at four o'clock that afternoon, and the platforms were jammed with soldiers. Most of the diplomatic community was there, either to accompany the gov-ernment south to its temporary capital in the city of Nish, or to see the Austrians off. Two trains were waiting—one to take the Serbian government south, the other to take the Austro-Hungarian legation and its members' families north. High-spirited Serbian officers shouted to the Austro-Hungar-ian military attaché, "*Au revoir á Budapest.*" The legation personnel hurried onto the train, the engine gave a long shriek, and at 6:30 P.M. precisely the train rolled out of the station.

"In just thirty-two minutes," an Austrian journalist caustically wrote, "Baron Giesl reviewed the four printed pages of the Serbian answer, which treated each of the ten demands of the ultimatum separately and in addition made new proposals, found it 'unsatisfactory,' informed the Serbian govern-ment that relations were broken off, assembled his entire personnel and their baggage, and still caught the express at 6:30. A record in the diplomatic arena. . . . The war, the long-sought war, was there. . . ."[10] But the war was not there—not yet.

Tisza telephoned Giesl at the station at Semlin and immediately asked, "Did it have to be?" "Yes," Giesl said. Tisza said they would talk when Giesl got to Budapest. Giesl also wired from Semlin to Ischl—where Count Berchtold and the emperor were waiting—and to the foreign ministry in Vienna that he had left Belgrade. He then continued on his way.

Waiting was terrible. Berchtold arrived at the imperial headquarters at Ischl at 5:30 P.M. and waited in Lt. Gen. Albert von Margutti's office, where the telephone had a direct line to the war ministry in Vienna. "He was pale as death," wrote Margutti, the emperor's longtime military aide-de-camp. Berchtold sat in an armchair, waiting, not saying a word. There was no sound except for the clock chiming the quarter hours: 5:30, 5:45, 6:00. At the stroke of six, Berchtold jumped up and said, "It is hardly likely that anything will come now. I am going out for a breath of air."

Berchtold had just left when the war ministry rang to say that Giesl had left Belgrade. Margutti sent someone after Berchtold while he, as he later recalled it, "flew rather than ran to the imperial villa." The old emperor got up from his desk without a word as Margutti gave him the message, which he had written out. Franz Joseph's hands shook so badly he could hardly get his glasses on. The silence lasted for several minutes after the emperor finished reading. Finally he said, "Well, the breaking of diplomatic relations still does not mean war."

Franz Joseph comforted himself with this hope for several days. When Berchtold finally arrived, the emperor said softly, "At least, now, we know where we stand."[11]

Berchtold informed the Serbian minister at Vienna that relations between their two governments were broken and sent him his passports.[12] Vienna was jubilant. Political diarest Joseph Redlich wrote in his diary that he waited all day at his telephone until a friend called to say, "He has left!" Redlich gave a loud "Hurrah!" and went out on the streets to watch the chanting, singing, and patriotic crowds and to celebrate with his friends the monarchy's long-awaited decisive action.[13]

Giesl did not report to Berchtold until Sunday afternoon, but Berchtold's staff immediately began an analysis of the Serbian reply. Berchtold repeated the emperor's declaration that breaking off relations by no means meant war. He thought that Serbia might still give an unconditional acceptance once Austria began mobilizing. The fear of a European war, he thought, would cause England and France to restrain Russia, and without Russia,

Serbia could not resist. Berchtold also had hopes that the German kaiser would exercise a restraining influence on the tsar.[14] Berchtold had insisted all along that only a military victory would solve the Serbian question; now, with a Great Power war staring him in the face, he sometimes seemed ready to accept the diplomatic victory he had earlier scorned as worthless.

The Serbian reply put Austria-Hungary hopelessly on the defensive. Most governments thought that the Austrians had gotten all they could reasonably expect and ignored the Austrian complaint that the Serbian note was not a good-faith response.

The Austrians had demanded that the Serbian government "suppress every publication . . . the general tendency of which shall be directed against the territorial integrity of the [monarchy]." Serbia promised to introduce legislation that would enable it to provide "the most severe punishment" of those engaged in such publications, and to seek a constitutional amendment making the confiscation of such publications valid. The Austrians foresaw that this commitment would be stalled in endless legislative and judicial procedures.

The Austrians had called for the dismissal of all civil and military personnel guilty of propaganda against Austria-Hungary "whose names the Imperial and Royal Government reserves the right to make known." The Serbian response agreed to dismiss "such persons as the judicial inquiry may have proved guilty of acts directed against the integrity of the territory of the Austro-Hungarian Monarchy." The Austrians spoke of "propaganda" whereas the Serbs spoke of "acts"; the Austrians wanted these people dismissed, whereas the Serbs first wanted them "proved to be guilty." The Austrians knew how far such concessions would get them.

To the Austrian demand that Serbia accept "the cooperation in Serbia of organs of the Imperial and Royal Government in the suppression of the subversive movement directed against the integrity of the Monarchy," Serbia replied that it "did not clearly grasp the meaning or the scope of the demand," but it would be willing to accept such collaboration "as agrees with the principles of international law, with criminal procedure, and with good neighborly relations."[15] And so it went. Italian journalist Albertini, who was certainly no partisan of Austria, concluded that the Serbian reponse "sounded a lot and meant nothing at all."[16]

The Austrians recognized the problems posed by the Serbian reply and took a long time deciding how to deal with it. They were very slow getting texts to their ambassadors, who asked how they were supposed to deal with critics without the full text of the Serb note. The Germans did not get a copy from Vienna until 27 July.

*   *   *

In Germany, the news from Belgrade produced an explosion of martial enthusiasm all over the country. According to Theodor Wolff, editor of the *Berliner Tageblatt,* military bands marched about Berlin playing patriotic hymns, men made impassioned speeches, and portraits of the kaiser and Emperor Franz Joseph were mounted on a motorcar and driven through the streets. In Munich, Serb students were beaten and the cafe they frequented was wrecked. French consuls reported an "almost joyous atmosphere" in Mannheim and Hamburg. After all the tension of the preceding years, the bursting of the storm seemed almost a relief.[17]

Only the Württemberg minister to Berlin came close to raising a serious question. Why was Germany backing so harsh a note? he asked Stumm at the foreign office. Stumm repeated what was to become the constant refrain of official Germany: "Germany was no longer prepared to watch the Austro-Hungarian state be devoured by Serbdom, and if there was going to be any change at all, it could be achieved only in an absolutely unequivocal manner." Stumm added the usual line that the incompleteness of Russian preparations and deficiencies in French armaments would keep Russia quiet.[18]

Despite foreign office assurances, the Russian menace was always in the background. General Chelius and army intelligence sent a stream of reports on measures "which seem to point to the commencement of mobilization in Russia."[19] Ambassador Pourtalès reported from St. Petersburg on the "deep hatred of Austria-Hungary" in Russia. Russian newspapers fairly screamed with hostility. The nationalist *Novoye Vremya* declared insistently that Russia would stand by Serbia. The *Petersbourgski Kuryer* said that the "sole response worthy of Russia would be to mobilize on the Austrian frontier."[20]

French newspapers were more staunch than ever in their defense of Serbia. *La Matin,* a conservative, nationalist paper with a large circulation, wrote on 27 July: "Never had a people gone further along the path of concessions and even, let us use the proper expression, along that of humiliation. . . . In truth, the attitude of Austria passes understanding. She achieves a diplomatic victory, total, unhoped for, almost terrifying. And she is not content with it. She wishes to go still further."[21]

The London press continued to reflect the government's worried detachment. On 25 July the Conservative *The Pall Mall Gazette* warned Austria that it would lose the sympathy of Europe if its demands appeared to make war inevitable. On 27 July, sounding almost like Grey, the paper pointed out that there were two issues: the narrow one of the Austro-Serbian quarrel, where Austria seemed to be in the right; and the broader issue of testing the firmness of the Triple Entente by making war on Serbia no matter what

Serbia promised. On 28 July *The Pall Mall Gazette* continued the balancing act that guided most London papers and British diplomacy. Though Serbia's answer seemed "to teem with endless possibilities of evasion," Austria must not impair the sovereignty of Serbia, and it must give strong guarantees that it was not seeking territorial expansion.[22]

17: The View from the *Hohenzollern*

Norway and the North Sea, 7–27 July

Kaiser Wilhelm and his entourage immediately settled into their usual routine onboard the *Hohenzollern*. They exercised and walked on deck, and
they went ashore for excursions. They held boat races, they gave afternoon
dances onboard for the society of the towns off which the *Hohenzollern*
anchored, they gathered regularly and enjoyably at mealtimes, and they re-
assembled in the smoking salon for long evenings of drinking, smoking,
conversation, and cards. During Sunday services the kaiser read aloud ser-
mons or uplifting stories. In bad weather a staff general gave lectures on
military history. It was all exactly as it always was.[1]

There were no women, and the only civilians onboard were a liaison officer from the foreign office and the kaiser's head of the civilian chancery,
which supervised all civil service appointments. The rest of the entourage
consisted of senior officers attached to the kaiser's staff and the usual array
of tall, vigorous, good-looking military aides-de-camp.

The officers of the kaiser's military entourage can only be described as
appallingly ignorant, frightened men.[2] The old Lutheran, agrarian Prussia
that they thought they knew and loved was passing away. They foresaw
an inevitable revolution by a subversive proletariat, joined in a final Armageddon by Jews, Catholics, nonconservatives, and non-Prussians at home,
and by the Slavs, France, and Russia abroad. They saw themselves surrounded by hostile nations that were only waiting for the right moment to
strike them down. They regularly told the kaiser that it would be better to
bring on the final battle as soon as possible, to clear the air and put an end
to social ruin and moral decay before the forces of civilization and order
collapsed completely.

This was not a good environment for the kaiser. The entourage pandered
to his vision of himself as Supreme Autocrat and All-Highest Warlord, and
they all agreed that the Serbs ought to be taught a lesson. The only semblance of reason onboard was Adm. Georg Alexander von Müller, head of

the kaiser's naval chancellery. Müller was no dove but rather a nineteenth-century imperialist who believed that "world history is now dominated by economic struggle."

Müller, like Bethmann, believed that if Germany remained simply a continental power, it would grow weaker as its exports and its economy declined. To be a Great Power, a nation must be a world power with world markets, which meant *Weltpolitik* and having a world-class fleet. Like most Great Power statesmen of his time, Müller was prepared to risk war rather than face inevitable decline, and he once told the kaiser that war with England was unavoidable. But where the entourage was visceral, Müller was intellectual. He thought strategically and knew that one had to pick and choose the time and place of confrontation. He detested the "idiocy" of the army men who were forever urging the kaiser to be *forsch*—firm, outspoken, and taking no nonsense.

The kaiser's entourage did not care for Müller. He was religious, he did not drink or smoke, and he was always fussily lecturing the kaiser's young aides on the blessings of marriage. Müller was also scrupulously conscientious and far better informed than the men around the kaiser, and was regarded by them as an interfering *Besserwissen* (know-it-all) and a loner.[3] Unfortunately, even with Müller on board, there was no one on the *Hohenzollern* who was likely to try to persuade the kaiser to reconsider the promises he had made to Austria.

If anything, the kaiser's mood grew more fierce as the trip went on. Berlin forwarded diplomatic dispatches by wire—but not all of them, and many of these were modified so that the volatile kaiser would not get upset. For example, none of Prince Lichnowsky's dispatches arguing against supporting an Austrian attack were forwarded, but when Lichnowsky reported a pro-Austrian article in the Liberal *Westminster Gazette,* that dispatch was sent.[4] From another dispatch, Jagow deleted Lichnowsky's report of an English warning that Austria was underestimating Serbia, that Austria would be "bled white," and that Romania would oppose an Austrian attack on Serbia.[5]

On the dispatches he did receive, the kaiser's marginal comments gave free rein to his emotions. They reveal an irritated determination to "get" the Serbs once and for all. Kaiser Wilhelm may not have meant everything he wrote, but his comments were wired back to the foreign office and left no doubt that the kaiser was determined to be firm.

When Tschirschky, for example, described the long struggle between Berchtold and Tisza over the note, the kaiser scrawled that "it is taking a long time!" and called for sharp and unambiguous demands on Serbia.[6] When Pourtalès warned of the intense hatred and "boundless contempt" for

Austria in Russia, the kaiser wrote, "Pride comes before a fall."[7] When Turkey balked at entering into an alliance with Austria and Germany, he wrote, "The thing to do now is to get every gun in readiness in the Balkans to shoot against the Slavs and *for* Austria."[8] Reading that Great Britain expected Germany to influence Vienna's demands on Serbia, the kaiser exploded: "That is a tremendous piece of British insolence. I am not called upon to prescribe *á la Grey* to His Majesty the Emperor how to preserve his honor! . . . Grey must be told this plainly and seriously! So that he will see that I am not fooling. . . . Serbia is nothing but a band of robbers that must be seized for crimes!"[9]

The mood was very tense onboard the *Hohenzollern* on 23 July as the kaiser and his party awaited word on the Austrian note. But all they got from Berlin was a report from Jagow enclosing a memorandum of Lichnowsky's talk with Grey. The next day there was still no word from Berlin, but the kaiser did learn from a commercial wire service report that the Austrian note had been delivered. He did not get a text of the Austrian note until 25 July, and again the information arrived via a commercial wire service.

As Müller stood on deck reading the text of the note, Count Georg von Wedel, the foreign office liaison, came by. Müller said he was worried by the unprecedented sharpness of the note. Wedel echoed the sentiments of the military entourage and the foreign office, saying, "Our only worry is that Serbia will swallow the note." The captain of the *Hohenzollern* also approved the note, declaring, "After all, one does not have to put up with everything."

"That is all very fine," Müller replied, "but with the present political constellation so unfavorable for us, we don't have to be so provocative."

Then came the kaiser on his customary walk before breakfast. "Well, that is really a powerful note," he announced.

"The note is powerful, but it means war," said Müller glumly.

The kaiser dismissed such fears. The Serbs would never think of risking war.

"I stood," recalled Müller, "alone with my fears."[10]

After breakfast, the kaiser had a sudden change of heart. As he was climbing into a small boat for an excursion on shore, he was handed another wire service telegram reporting Russia's declaration that it could not remain indifferent to an Austro-Hungarian attack on Serbia. An excited kaiser gave orders to have the fleet hasten its coaling in Norway and to hold itself in readiness for immediate departure. The cadet training ships in the Norwegian fjords received orders to steam for their home ports immediately. Later that afternoon, as Giesl was breaking relations with Serbia in Belgrade, the kaiser ordered the *Hohenzollern* to raise anchor and head for home. The High Seas Fleet also received orders to break off maneuvers and to return home.

The kaiser's angry commentary on dispatches from Berlin continued. When Bienvenu-Martin voiced the hope that Austria would not reject the Serbian reply out of hand, the kaiser wrote angrily, "*Ultimata* are accepted or not! But one does not *discuss* any longer. Thence the name!"[11] "Austria," he wrote elsewhere, "must become preponderant in the Balkans, as compared to the little ones, and at Russia's expense; otherwise there will be no peace."[12] When he learned that the Serbian government was moving south to Nish after Austria severed relations, his contempt for the Slavs knew no bounds: "How hollow the whole so-called Serbian problem is proving itself to be; thus it is seen to be with all Slav nations! Just tread hard on the heels of that rabble!"[13]

Just as suddenly, there would be moments of reason and calm. As the *Hohenzollern* steamed home Saturday evening, Müller and the kaiser stood on the bridge in the stillness of the soft northern light, enjoying the serene Norwegian coastline as mountain, field, wood, and quiet rural villages glided slowly by. Müller was moved and saddened by it all. "In such times of political tension," he said, "one could almost look with envy upon this land, whose inhabitants live outside the great struggles of world history." But for the nineteenth-century Great Power player, there was a dark side to the peaceful life, and Müller added, "True, there are dangers for the development of a people in a struggle-free existence, for then they are all too easily governed by material interests."

Europe in 1914 was full of men who believed that struggle and war somehow lifted mankind out of the crass materialism of everyday life and onto a higher moral plane. But Müller did not want war then. "Given the whole nature of modern war I nonetheless hope that the war clouds that darken the heavens before us will pass away just as they did in 1911." The kaiser, in that quiet moment away from his entourage, agreed. He thought that at the last moment the leaders of the opposing nations would shrink before the colossal responsibility of war.[14]

The kaiser's mood changed again on Sunday morning when he got a wire from Bethmann. The chancellor urged Wilhelm not to order the High Seas Fleet home, since Grey was "trying to work for the localization of the Austro-Hungarian-Serbian conflict. . . ." The kaiser was outraged that a civilian would question his military orders. He had heard from Belgrade—not Berlin—that the Serbian answer was likely to be unfavorable, which could lead to Russian mobilization, which in turn could result in Austrian mobilization. "When Russia mobilizes, my fleet must be ready in the Baltic, so it is going home." When Bethmann tried to argue in a further telegram, he only made matters worse. "My fleet has orders to sail for Kiel, and to Kiel it is going to sail!" the kaiser wrote at the bottom of the telegram.[15]

Twenty-four hours after the kaiser decided to go home, Poincaré and Viviani decided that they should also return. Poincaré knew by then that Austria had rejected the Serbian answer and broken relations, but he could not make up his mind. He wrote in his diary, "We are anxious and impotent, but, even at Paris, what more could we know and what more could we do?"[16] Not many politicians would make such an admission. On Sunday, Paris was informed by the French chargé d'affaires in London that Grey, Nicolson, and the Russian ambassador wanted Paul Cambon back in London. Bienvenu-Martin then decided that he needed Poincaré and Viviani back in Paris, and his wire reached *La France* sometime during the night of 26–27 July. Viviani replied on Monday morning that they would return "without delay."[17]

18: There Must Be a Way

Europe, 26–27 July

Warnings, threats, advice, encouragement—it was all one to Berchtold. Either Serbia yielded unconditionally, or the monarchy would take military action. But he wanted no war with Russia; what he wanted was to keep Russia talking while Field Marshal Conrad destroyed the Serbian army and got back to the Russian frontier before Russia had time to mobilize. Under those conditions, Berchtold did not think Russia would fight.

The problem was that Conrad had no plans for a swift strike on Serbia. For years, whenever Berchtold had proposed a quick strike or a limited action as a means of coercing the Serbs, Conrad would reject such "half-measures" in favor of a full-scale invasion. A full-scale invasion meant mobilization and concentration at the point of attack, which required time: thirteen to sixteen days in the case of Serbia, and as many as twenty-one days in the case of Russia. An exasperated Berchtold complained in 1913, "If the war could only begin right away; but it takes three weeks! How can one get over that?" Conrad's only advice, then as it was in 1914, was to have "the necessary firmness."[1] Berchtold, therefore, worried about what the Russians would do while Vienna waited for Conrad to move.

The Russians seemed eager to talk. Pourtalès and Sazonov, who both had summer places near Tsarskoe Selo, ran into each other at the train station Sunday morning on the way to St. Petersburg. Sazonov, relieved that Austria had not yet attacked Serbia, overflowed with assurances of Russia's need for peace. Pourtalès suggested that he talk with Szápáry, who might be authorized to explain his government's note to Serbia. Sazonov eagerly accepted the suggestion, and on arriving at the foreign ministry he learned that, in fact, Szápáry had asked for an appointment.[2]

It was a much calmer meeting than their previous encounter, when Szápáry delivered a copy of his government's note. Sazonov apologized for his anger on Friday and said it was time for frank talk. Szápáry also apologized. He had been upset by the anger in Russia; he was sure it had arisen from a misunderstanding. "No one in Austria-Hungary," he said, "has the least intention of threatening Russian interests or even of entering into a quarrel with her." His government wanted peace, but it was determined to put an end to Serbian subversion. Szápáry described the horrendous consequences of a great war: it would put the entire religious, moral, and social order of Europe at risk.

Sazonov agreed entirely. With an air of great confidentiality he confessed that he had "no feelings at all with regard to the Balkan Slavs." The Austrians could have no idea how Russia "had already suffered on their account." Austria's aims were "perfectly legitimate," but, Sazonov wondered, had Austria-Hungary chosen the most practical means? Would Austria consider mediation by its ally, the king of Italy, or perhaps the king of England? Szápáry said he had no instructions but would forward the suggestion to his government. Sazonov then observed that Austria's note seemed unduly harsh; he would like to review it with the ambassador. Szápáry said he was at the minister's disposal but reminded Sazonov that he had no specific instructions to go beyond his government's note. The two men reviewed the note anyway, clause by clause. Szápáry kept repeating that he had no instructions, but Sazonov persisted. "Take back the note; modify its form and I will guarantee the result," he pleaded.[3]

It was almost a love feast. Szápáry reported that Russian policy had come a long way from its first sharp rejection of Austrian claims two days earlier. The two men parted warmly, Sazonov promising to talk to the tsar and Szápáry promising to report Sazonov's overtures to his government. Szápáry warned Berchtold, however, that "we cannot overlook that along with this diplomatic improvement a vigorous military activity continues by which Russia's military, along with its diplomatic position, will change to our disadvantage."[4]

The Period Preparatory to War had been decreed for the whole of European Russia and permitted virtually any measure short of formal mobilization at the discretion of the war minister, General Sukhomlinov. In threatened areas, Sukhomlinov could call up the three youngest classes of reserves, and early Sunday morning orders went out to call up all three so as to strengthen frontier units. Orders also went out to place fortresses in Poland and western Russia in a "state of war," to man frontier posts to wartime levels, to tighten censorship and security measures, to mine harbors, to assemble horses and wagons for army baggage trains, and to prepare depots for the reception of reservists.[5] These "preparatory measures" were not limited to areas bordering Austria; they went on all over European Russia—including the frontier facing East Prussia.

With the Period Preparatory to War in full swing, Vienna and Berlin received a flood of reports on Russian military measures. Particularly disturbing was the news that some reserves had been called up; the entire Austro-German strategy depended upon the Russian army not being ready in time. Bethmann asked Lichnowsky and Schoen to warn London and Paris that Russia's military preparations were dangerous. He also instructed Pourtalès to warn Sazonov that a continuation of such measures would force Germany to mobilize, which "would mean war." Bethmann again emphasized that Austria wanted no Serbian territory; surely they could come to some understanding.[6]

Pourtalès delivered the German warning late Sunday evening. According to his diary, he addressed Sazonov in fairly dramatic terms: "In God's name, don't give the word to your general staff!" Sazonov, startled, asked, "But mobilization does not mean the same thing by you as war?" Pourtalès replied that given their geographic situation, the Germans would have to move fast with "a blitz-like offensive" once the button was pushed.[7] He reported to Berlin, however, that he had simply warned Sazonov that the reported Russian military measures "might easily call forth countermeasures."[8]

Sazonov gave his word of honor that no mobilization was taking place. He sent war minister Sukhomlinov to the German military attaché, Maj. Bernard von Eggeling, to give further assurances, also on his word of honor, that there was no mobilization, only some "preparatory measures" along the Austrian frontier, certainly nothing that could threaten Germany. Major Eggeling reported that if Sukhomlinov called on him to reinforce Sazonov's assurances, the Russians must be nervous. The major accepted that no mobilization was taking place, but he warned that Russia's "preparatory measures are very far-reaching."[9]

Sazonov tried to reassure Pourtalès further by telling him of his highly satisfactory talk with Szápáry. He pleaded urgently with the German diplomat to suggest some way to get serious negotiations started. Pourtalès, like Schoen in Paris, believed that his government would be interested in a negotiated settlement short of complete capitulation by Serbia. He replied that he was not authorized to make any proposals, but that he personally thought Vienna might modify some of its demands. If the changes were then agreeable to Russia, Russia could advise Serbia to accept them.[10] Sazonov instructed his ambassador in Vienna to ask that Szápáry be authorized to negotiate with him with a view to modifying the Austrian note.[11] He solemnly declared to Paléologue that "I shall be prepared to negotiate until the last moment."[12]

When Szápáry got a copy of Eggeling's report, he forwarded it to Vienna, saying he was not sure whether the Russians were just trying to put pressure on Austria through military measures, or whether they were trying to get a head start on mobilization.[13] Pourtalès was more optimistic. He concluded that "Sazonov, perhaps as the result of information from Paris and London, has lost some of his nerve and is now looking for a way out."[14] Berlin got Pourtalès's assessment early Monday morning and sent a copy to Vienna. Count Tschirschky, meanwhile, reported Szápáry's impression that Russia would not go beyond diplomatic action so long as Austria-Hungary did not "devour" Serbia.[15] Schoen, from Paris, had the "distinct impression" that Viviani would "exert a pacifying influence at St. Petersburg if we are willing to counsel Vienna to moderation, since Serbia has agreed to almost all the demands."[16]

Bethmann and Jagow, who saw all these reports late on Sunday or first thing Monday morning, interpreted them to mean that England and France would pressure Russia to avoid war and that Russia would accept a diplomatic solution if Austria promised to take no Serbian territory. The kaiser was due to arrive at Kiel on Monday morning, and Bethmann sent the accumulated dispatches for the kaiser to read as he traveled from Kiel to his residence in Potsdam. Bethmann concluded his cover letter to Wilhelm by saying that "Russia does not seem to be mobilizing as yet, and seems to be willing to open negotiations with Vienna. . . . Vienna's attitude as to this so far unknown." He added that Russia had been warned against "military measures of preparation in any way directed against ourselves."[17]

The kaiser read the material and called a 3:10 P.M. meeting with Bethmann and the army chiefs. The Serbian answer was still not available, but no one seemed terribly interested. The news was good: Pourtalès and Tschirschky were optimistic. It was reported that the Serbians intended to withdraw and remain on the defensive. Austria could not complete its mobilization before 12 August. Sazonov had declared that Russia would not mobilize unless and until Austrian troops crossed the Serbian frontier. All this information produced a feeling that the crisis was going to drag on and that localization and a negotiated settlement were possible. One participant at the meeting wrote in his diary, "I have the impression it will all blow over."[18] Admiral Müller agreed. Even if it began to look like war, Berlin would have to remain quiet; let Russia declare war on Austria and put itself in the wrong.[19] If war came—if it had to come—they would not back down.[20]

Count Berchtold also got a series of optimistic reports on Monday: the Germans thought the threatening language coming out of France and Russia was just bluff; England and France were working to prevent a Russian mobilization; Jagow thought that, if worse came to worst, England would stay out; the French government was intent on avoiding a major war; the British ambassador in Paris believed that Russia would not go to war for

Serbia; and reports that the Russians had already called up reservists seemed not to be true.[21] Berchtold could see no reason to soften his stand. Instead, he sent Szápáry a wire instructing him not to mention Austria's "territorial disinterest for the time being."[22] The Germans were making Austria's "territorial disinterest" the center of their diplomatic campaign, but Berchtold was not yet ready to commit himself.

Sir Arthur Nicolson arrived at his desk at the foreign office on Sunday morning to find a series of unsettling wires, among them one from Bunsen in Vienna. "War is thought to be imminent," it read. "Wildest enthusiasm prevails in Vienna."[23] The British chargé d'affaires in Berlin reported that the Austrian embassy there believed that whether Austria would have a free hand in Serbia would depend on whether "Russia and France think that they can reckon on active support of His Majesty's Government."[24] Nicolson feared the worst, but a flicker of hope arrived in the form of a wire from Buchanan: Sazonov had suggested that if Serbia were to appeal to the powers, Russia would stand aside and leave the question to England, France, Italy, and Germany.[25]

The Russian suggestion seemed to parallel Grey's proposal for four-power mediation, so Nicolson wired Grey at his fishing cottage for permission to ask Berlin, Paris, and Rome to "authorise their Ambassadors here to join you in a conference." Nicolson was not hopeful, because he had seen what Jagow had done with their request for a time extension on the Austrian note. "Jagow did not really adopt your proposal to intervene at Vienna . . . but simply 'passed on' your suggestion and told his ambassador to speak about it. Still, no chance should be neglected." Grey agreed and the telegrams went out that afternoon while Grey headed back to London.[26]

In England, that same Sunday morning, Prince Henry of Prussia—the kaiser's brother—had breakfast with his cousin, King George V. "Georgie," according to Prince Henry, assured him that he and his government were doing all they could "to localize the struggle between Austria and Serbia" and therefore had proposed "that Germany, Italy, France and England . . . should intervene to hold Russia in check." Grey's four-power mediation became, to Prince Henry's ears, a means of restraining Russia. The prince was also convinced that George V intended that "England would remain neutral at the start; but whether she will be able to keep so permanently, I am not able to judge, but doubt it on account of her relations to France."[27]

The kaiser did not get Prince Henry's letter for several days, but Lichnowsky wired Berlin immediately that Prince Henry had reported the king's "intense desire that British-German joint participation, with the assistance of France and Italy, may be successful in mastering in the interest of peace the present extremely dangerous situation." The German naval attaché in London, however, wired that "King of Great Britain said to Prince Henry of Prussia, England would maintain neutrality in case war should break out between Continental Powers."[28] Since the naval attaché was not in the habit of clearing his dispatches through Lichnowsky, whom he regarded as anti-navy and too pro-British, Lichnowsky had no chance to comment.

Lichnowsky was also reviewing his dispatches on Sunday morning. There was a wire from Jagow saying that Germany would be ready to join in mediating an Austro-Russian quarrel—but not the Austro-Serbian quarrel—subject to "our known obligations" as an ally of Austria.[29] An instruction from Bethmann emphasized that Austria-Hungary was not seeking Serbian territory. Bethmann added that Russia might be calling up several classes of reserves without actually declaring a mobilization. "We therefore request Sir Edward Grey to use his influence at Petersburg." Schoen in Paris was asked to do the same.[30]

Prince Lichnowsky promptly wrote a note for Grey saying that if Russia called up reserves, Germany would have to mobilize. "My Government . . . instructs me to request you to use your influence in St. Petersburg." He added, "My government accepts your suggested mediation *à quatre*."[31] He did not mention Jagow's qualification that the mediation be restricted to Austro-Russian differences.

Lichnowsky was no longer the assured aristocrat who had arrived in London twenty months earlier. He dreaded a war in which England would be among Germany's enemies and was noticeably nervous, excitable, and alarmed, giving vague hints that something terrible might happen. He begged the Romanian ambassador to have his government induce the Serbs to yield; once the danger of war had passed, the terms could be revised in Serbia's favor. Nicolson noted that the German ambassador was "exceedingly anxious and perturbed," warning people mysteriously "that if they knew all that he did they would be equally disquieted."[32] Berlin was aware of the problem. "Lichnowski," complained young Riezler, "has completely lost his composure."[33]

Arriving at the foreign office, Lichnowsky found only Nicolson and William Tyrrell. He told them that his government had learned that "Russia was calling in 'classes of reserves,' which meant mobilization. If this mobilization took place on the German frontier, Germany would be compelled to mobilize—and France would naturally follow suit." His government therefore requested that Great Britain urge Russia not to mobilize.[34]

Nicolson—who was himself fearful, immensely distrustful of the Germans, and frustrated by Britain's inability to show solidarity with France and Russia—replied that the foreign office had no news of any mobilization. Moreover, it would be "difficult and delicate for us to ask Petersburg not to mobilize at all when Austria was contemplating such a measure." Nicolson, like Grey, Sazonov, Bethmann, Jagow, and everyone else, believed that Russia could mobilize against Austria without threatening Germany and that negotiations could then take place. Only the day before, Grey had told Lichnowsky that the time for mediation would not be ripe until Austria and Russia had both mobilized. Lichnowsky now told Nicolson, "The Germans would not mind a partial mobilization say at Odessa or Kieff—but could not view indifferently a mobilization on the German frontier."[35]

The German foreign office theory was that the Russians might very well bluff with a partial mobilization without ever going to war. Sazonov also thought a partial mobilization against Austria was a safe form of pressure, and Jagow confirmed this assumption several times during the course of Monday, 27 July. Buchanan, on the other hand, feared that any mobilization by Russia could unleash a war.[36]

"The main thing," Nicolson told Lichnowsky, "was to prevent, if possible, active military operations." Nicolson outlined the British proposal for a conference of French, German, and Italian ambassadors with Grey in London, along the lines of the London Ambassadors' Conference of 1912–13, which had resolved the disputes of the Balkan wars. The British proposal was offered "on the condition that Russia, Austria and Servia should suspend active military *operations* pending results of Conference." Nicolson stressed the word *operations* because Serbia had already mobilized, Austria was almost certainly going to mobilize, and Russia and Germany might follow suit. But in the British view, mobilization did not have to be followed by operations.

Lichnowsky, Nicolson noted, liked the British proposal, and added that the prince "was very excited."[37]

Lichnowsky did like the proposal. It would avert war and would again put Germany in the position of cooperating with England for peace. He wired Berlin that according to reports in London, the Russians were thinking only of a partial mobilization against Austria, "far from our frontiers." He argued passionately to Jagow to cooperate in the proposed four-power mediation. Sir William Tyrrell had told him that Grey believed that "localization of the conflict . . . was wholly impossible" once Austria crossed the Serbian border. If Germany and England succeeded in keeping the peace, however, "German-English relations would be placed on a firm foundation for time everlasting."[38]

Jagow had told Lichnowsky that Germany would "be ready" to join in mediation only between Austria and Russia,[39] but Lichnowsky ignored that restriction. Jagow, moreover, had apparently neglected to inform Bethmann of Grey's mediation proposal. When Bethmann read Lichnowsky's report, he wired his ambassador that he had heard nothing of Grey's four-power conference and reminded him again that although Germany was prepared to help mediate an Austro-Russian dispute, "we would not be able to summon Austria before a European court of justice in her case with Serbia." On that problem, direct talks between Vienna and St. Petersburg might be feasible.[40] It was Bethmann at his inflexible worst: grumpy, irritable, annoyed with Lichnowsky, and not prepared to explore the possibilities.

After Lichnowsky finally left the foreign office, his cousin Count Benckendorff, the Russian ambassador, dropped by. Nicolson read Benckendorff the 25 July dispatch from Buchanan reporting the irrepressible Paléologue's remark that "he could not believe that England would not stand by her two friends, who were acting as one in this matter."[41] Nicolson also read aloud Buchanan's warning to Sazonov: "If Russia mobilizes, Germany would not be content with mere mobilization, or give Russia time to carry out hers, but would probably declare war at once."

Jules Cambon had come to the same conclusion. Buchanan and Cambon seemed to be the only diplomats who understood how Europe's military machinery would work once Russian mobilization began. Sazonov had assured Buchanan that he had no desire to start a war, but Russia could not let Austria crush Serbia and dominate the Balkans. Since Paléologue had assured Sazonov of France's full support, Russia would face "all the risks of war."[42]

When he reported to Sazonov, Benckendorff made no comment on Buchanan's warning that Russia must not mobilize. The Russian ambassador's primary concern was England's apparent detachment. Benckendorff correctly reported that "the decisive factor is that Grey is not sure of his public opinion and is worried about not finding any support if he commits himself too far." Moreover, "what frightens England is not Austrian hegemony in the Balkans, but German hegemony in the world."[43] If Germany limited its actions to supporting Austria against a Russian attack, France and Russia might have to fight alone.

19: THE ENGLISH MEDIATION PROPOSAL

27 July

As Poincaré and Viviani steamed home aboard *La France,* they finally learned of Russia's warning that if Austria threatened "armed pressure" against Serbia, Russia would order a partial mobilization against Austria. The message from Paléologue assured them that Russia would do nothing "likely to be regarded as directed against Germany." Nonetheless, "secret preparations" were under way, and Russia's military leaders were determined "not to let Serbia be attacked."[1] Paléologue's reports were not notably precise; he gave no hint, for example, about the nature of the secret preparations. Poincaré and Viviani also learned that Benckendorff was complaining that London had no interest in a purely Austro-Serbian quarrel.

Russian complaints tended to worry Poincaré. He therefore asked Margerie to draft an instruction for Paléologue to assure Russia that France was ready to second any Russian action. Viviani objected. He insisted that the instruction read that France "is ready in the interests of peace whole heartedly to second the action of the Imperial Government."[2]

The insertion of the phrase "in the interests of peace" seems to have annoyed Poincaré. He complained to his diary that Viviani "is nervous and agitated and unceasingly mouths imprudent words or phrases which reveal a black ignorance of matters of foreign policy." Viviani, he thought, "is only comfortable when he is talking with a congress of socialists."[3]

Neither Poincaré nor Viviani nor Margerie expressed any alarm at the prospect of a Russian mobilization at this stage of the crisis. The wires sent to Paléologue that Monday contain no reminder that, under their military agreements, Russia could not mobilize without first consulting France. Nor did the French ask about the precise extent of Russia's secret preparations, or about precisely what events would trigger a Russian mobilization. No one asked Paléologue to urge Sazonov to be careful.

It is worth comparing French nonchalance with the comments of two British diplomats, Buchanan and Eyre Crowe. Buchanan repeatedly warned

Sazonov to defer any order to mobilize as long as possible. If the Russians did mobilize, he warned, they had to keep their troops from crossing the frontier. On Monday afternoon, 27 July, Crowe wrote, "If Russia mobilizes, we have been warned Germany will do the same, and as German mobilization is directed almost entirely against France, the latter cannot possibly delay her own mobilization for even the fraction of a day." Then, Crowe continued, "within twenty-four hours His Majesty's Government will be faced with the question" of whether to "stand idly aside, or take sides."[4] Since neither Crowe nor Nicolson nor Grey believed that Great Britain could afford to stand aside, and since none of them was sure that Parliament or the public would support a war, they were all eager to prevent an irrevocable Russian action. Poincaré, Viviani, and Margerie showed no such sense of urgency.

Sazonov was afraid of war, any war, and he was desperate for a way out. On Saturday, 25 July, he had told Buchanan that Russia would be ready to stand aside if Serbia asked other powers to mediate. On the basis of this remark, Nicolson had suggested a four-power ambassadors' conference to Grey. On Sunday, after his promising talk with Szápáry, Sazonov had told Buchanan that England and Italy might intervene in Vienna to ease the tension.[5] On Monday, 27 July, Buchanan learned that Sazonov was asking Berchtold to authorize Szápáry to discuss possible "modifications to be introduced into Austrian demands."[6]

Later on Monday Buchanan got Grey's proposal for the four-power ambassadors' conference in London. When he saw Sazonov again, Buchanan asked him which he would prefer: direct talks with Szápáry or an ambassadors' conference in London. Sazonov replied that he was perfectly agreeable to a conference if other powers agreed, but went on to make several other proposals and told his ambassadors that although he had not yet heard from Vienna, direct talks seemed promising. If direct talks did not work out, he said, "I am ready to accept the English proposal, or any other of a nature to resolve the conflict favorably."[7]

As he talked, Sazonov had still another idea. They might induce Vienna to negotiate by offering to have the Great Power ministers in Belgrade keep an eye on Serbian activities and to exchange information "with regard to any Serbian machinations or plots against Austria." If the ministers obtained information on Serbian subversion of Austria, the ministers "should be empowered to exercise pressure on Serbian Government with a view to preventing such plots from maturing." When Buchanan reminded him of Grey's proposal for an ambassadors' conference in London, Sazonov again said he would be ready to stand aside if the conference was accepted by the other powers.

Grey was baffled. He was pleased at the prospect of direct talks between Russia and Austria, but he was not sure just what the Great Power ministers in Belgrade were supposed to do under Sazonov's latest proposal. Perhaps if Sazonov were to present his scheme directly to the Austrians "it might then take on more concrete shape."[8] It was hard to keep up with Sazonov's diplomacy.

Nicolson was angry. "In three consecutive days," he wrote, "M. Sazonov has made one suggestion and two proposals. . . . One really does not know where one is with M. Sazonov and I told Count Benckendorff so this afternoon."[9]

Grey, meanwhile, thought that the Serbs had conceded everything that Austria-Hungary could reasonably expect. He told Lichnowsky and Mensdorff that if Austria could not accept Serbia's answer as a basis for negotiation, "then it would be absolutely evident that Austria is only seeking an excuse for crushing Serbia," which Russia would never accept. Grey reminded Lichnowsky that Germany had often asked him to use his influence in St. Petersburg; now he was asking Germany to use its influence in Vienna, "either to get them to accept the reply from Belgrade as satisfactory or as the basis for conferences." Lichnowsky closed his report with his usual warning: if it came to war, "we should no longer be able to count on British sympathy or British support." Mensdorff, however, told Berchtold that although Grey was troubled, he was not as irritable as Lichnowsky seemed to think.[10]

When Grey told Benckendorff about this exchange with the German and Austrian ambassadors, Benckendorff replied that he hoped Grey's warnings would open the eyes of the German government, which appeared to believe that England would in all circumstances remain neutral. Grey was careful; he was not in a position to make any commitments, but he was sure he had been sufficiently direct with Lichnowsky to dispel German confidence in British neutrality. Benckendorff suggested that Grey should warn Austria as well; Vienna, he cautioned, also had "too much confidence in English neutrality." Grey promised to talk to Mensdorff again, and Benckendorff wrote Sazonov, "Berlin and Vienna's confidence in British neutrality no longer has any foundation."[11]

Benckendorff was wrong. He and Lichnowsky tended to assume that Grey's lack of sympathy for Austro-German policy on Serbia was inconsistent with British neutrality. Jagow thought differently: "It is a long road from either sympathy or antipathy to the fanning of the flames of a world-conflagration."[12]

Sir Francis Bertie, Grey's ambassador in Paris, wanted no part of a war over Serbia, but France was a problem. "It seems incredible," he wrote in his diary, "that the Russian Government should plunge Europe into war in order to make themselves the protectors of the Servians. . . . Public opinion in England would never sanction such a policy, but unfortunately we might be dragged into a war through reverses to French arms and the necessity to prevent the annihilation of France."[13] That, in a nutshell, was the British dilemma.

Bertie had been Great Britain's ambassador to France for nine years. He was a great aristocrat in the mold of Berchtold and Lichnowsky but without a shred of the self-doubt that sometimes plagued those two diplomats. Bertie's ancestors had served British diplomacy for generations. Secure, proud, and seventy years old in 1914, he went his own way by his own lights and was not inclined to play second fiddle to the young snots at the foreign office. His lean, top-hatted figure and serene self-assurance were a formidable combination; he was not the man to tolerate much nonsense where his dignity or British interests were concerned—which meant making sure that the damn French did not do anything foolish. He had a reputation for regarding anyone who disagreed with him as a "bloody fool," and he was perfectly capable of telling Paléologue in 1913 that he hoped France would pass the three-year-service law quickly because "we don't want to aid people who won't fight."[14]

Bertie flatly opposed any kind of commitment to stand by France and Russia in case of war. The whole point of the ententes with France and Russia was to protect British imperial interests and to preserve the peace by containing Germany. By July 1914, Russia's disregard of British treaty rights in Persia was a serious problem, and France's penchant for supporting the Russians in the Balkans did not appear to Bertie as conducive to peace. He wanted it clearly understood that France should restrain Russia and that Great Britain was not going to war over Serbia. He was not at all happy when Alexander Izvolsky, the Russian ambassador, finally returned from Russia. "Izvolsky is expected here to-day or to-morrow," he wrote, "and he is not an element of peace."[15]

On Monday afternoon Bertie reported that the French had agreed to an ambassadors' conference.[16] He wrote Grey privately that the French "should be encouraged to put pressure on Russian Government not to assume the absurd and obsolete attitude of Russia being the protectress of all Slav States whatever their conduct, for that will lead to war."[17] Izvolsky, on the other hand, was pleased by the firm support for Russia he found at all levels of government.[18] None of his dispatches show any hint of French concern about Russian military measures. Bertie had reason to be unhappy with him.

*   *   *

That same day, Jules Cambon asked Jagow what he thought of the British mediation proposal. Jagow said he was perfectly willing to do all he could for peace, but if England wanted mediation, London must keep Russia from mobilizing.[19] Jagow also told Cambon and Goschen that Germany would not agree to hauling Austria "before a court of arbitration" and that it would not interfere in the Austro-Serbian quarrel. Germany was only willing to mediate an Austro-Russian conflict.[20] Goschen and Cambon argued that Grey was not thinking of a "tribunal" or a "court" or even anything so formal as a "conference"; all that was wanted were talks, and if the Germans and the Austrians did not like the idea of a "conference," the talks could take any number of forms. Meanwhile, Russia and Vienna should refrain from any steps that might lead to fighting.[21] Jagow replied that since Sazonov was proposing direct talks with Vienna, it might be best "to await the outcome of the exchange of views between the Austrian and Russian Governments."

In London, Eyre Crowe regarded Jagow's remarks as so much shadow boxing. "So far as we know, the German Government has up to now said not a single word at Vienna in the direction of restraint and moderation." Moreover, Sazonov was no help because "the rapid succession of fresh proposals and suggestions coming from St. Petersburg made it easier for Germany to find fresh excuses for her inactivity."[22]

The Russian chargé d'affaires also talked to Jagow on Monday and asked him to urge Vienna to empower Szápáry to negotiate directly with Sazonov. Jagow replied with what was to become his standard response: "He could not advise Austria to make concessions, but the mere transmission of Pourtalès' telegram to Vienna signified that he preferred such a solution to the situation."[23] The fact was that although Bethmann and Jagow were prepared to report that Sazonov wanted direct talks with Vienna, they were not prepared to ask Vienna to agree to them. When they sent copies of Pourtalès's report to the kaiser and to Tschirschky in Vienna, they deleted Pourtalès's suggestion that if St. Petersburg and Vienna reached agreement on revisions to the Austrian note and Belgrade accepted them, Belgrade's acceptance could be transmitted to Vienna by some third power.[24] Jules Cambon was struck by Germany's "lack of good will . . . in supporting the efforts of England. . . . We must be ready."[25]

Like most diplomats, Cambon knew that German military planning depended on Germany's ability to mobilize far more rapidly than Russia. Germany would not abandon that advantage; once it mobilized, it would fight. Cambon and Goschen therefore asked Jagow to name the conditions under which Germany might feel compelled to mobilize. Jagow replied that

Germany would not mobilize if Russia mobilized only in the south, against Austria, and he formally authorized the two ambassadors to inform their governments of that fact. Jagow added, however, that "if Russia attacked Austria, Germany would have to attack as well." That made Jagow's assurances all but worthless: if Germany was going to defend Austria against Russia, it certainly would not wait for very long while Russia mobilized against Austria.[26]

Reflecting on Jagow's words, and reviewing the military intelligence that he and every other diplomat was gathering, Cambon sent an analysis to Paris: "I think that Germany will wait until Russia attacks Austria before going into action, and will respond to the Russian attack with an attack of its own, but, if Russian mobilization appears to threaten her . . . the Germans will not shilly-shally but . . . will direct a smashing blow against us." Everyone knew that in a war with Russia, Germany would first seek to crush France in order to dispose of the threat of a French army at its rear. So long as France was allied to Russia, its peaceful intentions were irrelevant. There was hope only "if Germany were clearly informed that we will not be without effective help from England."[27]

Help was just what Grey could not offer. He could warn that a general war would be the "greatest catastrophe," the consequences of which "would be incalculable,"[28] but he could not say that Great Britain would fight.

When Berchtold learned of Grey's mediation proposal and of Sazonov's desire for direct talks, his response was brutal. "They have decided here," Tschirschky wired, "to send out the declaration of war tomorrow, or the day after tomorrow at the latest, to frustrate any attempt at intervention."[29] Berchtold was not going to submit the vital interests of Austria-Hungary to a Great Power conference where Italy was unreliable and even Germany sided with the English because Bethmann and Lichnowsky were eager for closer ties with Britain. The Entente powers had agreed in 1913 that the Serbs must get out of Albania, but they had made no move to enforce the agreement; only an Austrian ultimatum had forced the Serbs out. No one in Vienna was prepared to submit the Serbian problem to another ambassadors' conference.

Jagow's petty duplicities continued. Tschirschky's wire arrived in Berlin at 4:37 P.M. When Jagow was professing Germany's desire for peace to Cambon, to Goschen, and to the Russian envoy, he knew that Austria would declare war on Serbia in the next day or two.

Lichnowsky, who did not like the way things were going, sent a series of wires on Monday evening. The first reported that Grey was irritated over

Austria's rejection of the Serbian answer.[30] The second warned that Berlin must understand that the British regarded as a vital interest the maintenance of the peace of Europe on the basis of the existing balance of power. Berlin, however, believed that to maintain parity with the Triple Entente, Austria-Hungary would have to regain its prestige as a Great Power. When Zimmermann read Lichnowsky's report, he wrote, "Where will the balance of power be, if Austria gives in!"[31] In his third wire, Lichnowsky asked, "How can I argue for localization of the conflict, when nobody here has any doubt that by Austria's procedure important Russian interests are in jeopardy?"[32]

Grey's proposed four-power conference was uncomfortable for the Germans. The intimate and friendly collaboration of French and British diplomats—Jules Cambon and Sir W. E. Goschen in Berlin, Paul Cambon and Nicolson in London—never ceased to worry them, particularly after the experience of a solid Entente front at the London Ambassadors' Conference in 1912–13. Berlin did not want a four-power mediation—and it did not want to offend London. What to do?

Late Monday night, Bethmann wired Grey's mediation proposal to Tschirschky.[33] Although the proposal stipulated that Austria and Russia abstain from "military operations," Bethmann said nothing about halting or delaying Austria's declaration of war. However, he explained to Tschirschky, if Berlin refused "every proposal for mediation, we should be held responsible for the conflagration before the whole world. . . . Therefore we cannot refuse the mediator's role, and must submit the English proposal to the consideration of the Vienna Cabinet, especially as London and Paris continue to make their influence felt in St. Petersburg." Having said all that, Bethmann's precise instruction was: "I request Count Berchtold's opinion on the English suggestion, as likewise his views on Mr. Sazonov's desire to negotiate directly with Vienna."

Bethmann then wired Lichnowsky. "We have at once inaugurated a move for mediation at Vienna along the lines desired by Sir Edward Grey. Apart from this English suggestion we have furthermore submitted to Count Berchtold Sazonov's desire for a direct discussion with Vienna."[34] Bethmann did not tell Lichnowsky that Austria was about to declare war on Serbia. Berlin's unwillingness to take Lichnowsky fully into its confidence was undermining the ambassador's effectiveness. Grey and the foreign office knew that Lichnowsky's urgent representations did not reflect policy in Berlin. Worse, they no longer trusted Jagow.

On 25 July Jagow had agreed to "pass on" to Vienna English and Russian requests for an extension of time, making sure in each case that they arrived too late. Later that day, upon receiving a "forecast" of the Serbian answer, Grey asked the German government "to influence the Austrian Government to take a favorable view of it."[35] At the end of the day on Sunday, 26 July, Jagow called in the British chargé d'affaires to say that Tschirschky had been "instructed to pass on to Austro-Hungarian Government your hopes that they may take a favorable view of a Serbian reply." Jagow assured him that by passing on Grey's request, the German government "associated themselves to a certain extent with your hope." Crowe thought this "very insidious," and Nicolson pointed out that "this is the second occasion on which Herr von Jagow has acted similarly."[36]

Jagow now went much further. He assured Austria's ambassador, Count Szögyény, that he "was not in the slightest degree in favor of consideration being given to the English wish." He had in the past and might in the future "pass on" English proposals, but he did so because "it is of the greatest importance that England at the present moment should not make common cause with Russia and France." Germany had to be able to say to Grey that his proposals were being forwarded to Vienna.[37]

The only result of this stupid charade was that the British lost all faith in German assurances.

When Belgrade received Grey's mediation proposal, Pašić and his ministers were hesitant. A positive response from Serbia might give the English an excuse to avoid being firm with Austria and Germany. Moreover, an agreement to mediate might indicate Serbia's readiness to make further concessions. Strandtmann, Russia's acting minister in Belgrade, thought Pašić was being influenced by Spalajkovic's reports, which painted a Russia ablaze with pro-Serb enthusiasm. Strandtmann also suspected that Pašić was reluctant to have talks in London or some other European capital away from the favorable atmosphere of St. Petersburg.[38] Grey therefore found the Russians and the Serbs, as well as the Germans, dragging their feet on mediation.

PART VI: The Iron Dice Begin to Roll

20: Austria-Hungary Declares War on Serbia

Vienna, 28 July

When they spoke in Berlin on 5 and 6 July, Count Alexander Hoyos and Ambassador Szögyény had led the Germans to believe that Austria would act swiftly, but it was four long weeks after the assassination before Austria finally delivered its note to Serbia. Then, Berlin learned, an unsatisfactory answer would mean only the severing of diplomatic relations, not war. "Here," Szögyény warned, "it is universally taken for granted that an eventual negative reply by Serbia will be followed by a declaration of war from us and military operations."[1]

When Berchtold saw Szögyény's warning on 26 July, he summoned Conrad and told him that speed was essential. "When do you want the declaration of war?" Conrad countered, as always, that he wanted more time. The army chief did not want to declare war "until we are ready to begin operations—say about August 12." Berchtold could barely contain his frustration and told Conrad "the diplomatic situation will not hold that long." Conrad replied that they must be absolutely certain of Russian intentions, and the sooner the better. He would have to know by 4 August, certainly no later than the fifth, whether or not he would have to fight Russia.

Conrad wanted to know Russian intentions before he invaded Serbia, but Berchtold wanted to move fast and keep the Russians talking while the Austrian army reduced Serbia. He did not want to force Russia to an early decision, so he told Conrad, "That won't work."

Conrad then explained the Austro-Hungarian military situation. They had a total of forty-eight divisions available for mobilization. He had already ordered a partial mobilization for war against Serbia—Plan B (Balkans)— on the night of Saturday, 25 July. Plan B would send twenty of those forty-eight divisions south to invade Serbia. Tuesday, 28 July, was designated as the first day of mobilization and, since the first day was a so-called free day to give reservists a chance to put their affairs in order, not a single man would report until the next day.[2]

In a war with Russia, Plan R (Russia) would go into effect, meaning a full general mobilization that would call up the remaining twenty-eight divisions. In that case, forty divisions would concentrate on the northern frontier, in Galicia, facing Russia, leaving only eight divisions to form a defensive screen against Serbia. Under Plan R, twelve of the twenty divisions then heading south—the so-called B Group—would have to be diverted north to fight Russia. Conrad needed to know if those divisions would be required in the north before committing them to battle in Serbia.[3] With only eight divisions in the south, they would have to call off the invasion of Serbia, and that was something that no one in the government was prepared to consider.

Berchtold had already confided to Count Mérey von Kapos-Mére, his ambassador to Italy, that he saw no alternative to war with Serbia. He had always regarded himself as a man of peace and he had always wanted friendship with Russia, but fate seemed to have singled him out for war. The kind of diplomatic victory that Tisza was looking for was not enough; Berchtold wanted "a practical result—either by a fundamental cleanup in Serbia through acceptance of our demands with our cooperation, or a clash of arms which would, to the greatest extent possible, paralyze Serbia."[4] Mérey agreed, adding that they should have acted when the Serbs murdered their king and queen in 1903.[5]

To put an end to the talk of Great Power mediation between Austria and Serbia, Berchtold wanted a declaration of war as soon as possible. Hostilities had already begun in a minor way on Sunday, 26 July. A boatload of Serbian reservists was steaming up the Sava River, which marked the frontier between Hungary and Serbia, and passed too close to the Hungarian shore. Hungarian border units fired on the boat, and it swung back toward the Serbian side of the river. That was all, but the reports to Vienna said that Serbian soldiers had fired on Hungarian forces. On Monday and Tuesday Berchtold consistently spoke as if the Serbians had already opened hostilities.

Ambassador Mensdorff had told Grey that the Serbian answer was unsatisfactory and that Austria would take "severe measures."[6] Ambassador Bunsen was then instructed to try to soften Berchtold's position, and he tried all day Monday to get an appointment. Berchtold, however, was not seeing anyone until the declaration of war was on its way, so he did not see Bunsen until eleven o'clock Tuesday morning. When the two men finally met, the British diplomat said that England had no wish to interfere in Austria-Hungary's quarrel with Serbia—the English "had no very great regard for

Serbia"—but they could not help but observe that an Austro-Serbian war could lead to a wider conflict, and Grey was primarily concerned with the peace of Europe.

Berchtold replied that this was precisely the point: Great Britain was not directly threatened by Serbia; Austria-Hungary was. Moreover, it was too late to avoid hostilities. Serbian soldiers had already fired on Hungarian border troops. Berchtold was calm and spoke quietly, but he was unyielding. There would be no discussion on the basis of the Serbian note. War would be declared that day.[7]

Nikolai Schebeko, the Russian ambassador, also tried to see Berchtold on Monday and would not be put off; he finally saw Baron Karl von Macchio, who usually conducted diplomatic conversations that Berchtold did not handle himself. Schebeko warned Macchio that Russia would not yield as it had during the 1909 annexation crisis. However, if there was any hope for useful talks, he would advise his government to induce the Serbs to fall back so there would be time for negotiations before fighting actually started. He could see no other way out. If Szápáry were authorized to discuss a modification of the Austrian note, Russia was prepared to have Serbia yield much of what Austria asked and Serbia could then give an unconditional acceptance.[8]

When Schebeko finally saw Berchtold on Tuesday, a serious misunderstanding occurred. Berchtold, in the excitement and tension of declaring war, keeping an eye on Russia, and dealing with the Entente ambassadors, apparently confused Sazonov's proposal that he and Szápáry review the original Austrian note to make it unconditionally acceptable to Serbia, and Grey's proposal that the Serbian answer serve as a basis for negotiation. Schebeko, in any event, reported to Sazonov that Austria-Hungary "could not retreat and enter into a discussion of its note."[9] Berchtold, however, thought he had rejected negotiations "on the text of the note of reply that we had described as unsatisfactory."[10] That was Grey's proposal, not Sazonov's. Berchtold also thought he had rejected only direct talks with Serbia; he did not intend to reject direct talks between Sazonov and Szápáry, as Schebeko reported.[11] This was not a good time for confusion.

Spalajkovic's telegrams to Pašić were full of fight but contained no precise Russian commitment. Pašić, who was trying to find his way through the crisis with an exhausted army and an empty treasury, had told Strandtmann, "If war is unavoidable—we will fight." But he also said that he did not propose to defend Belgrade. The "foreign legations will be asked to follow the

Government into the interior of the country."[12] When he instructed Spalaj-kovic to find out what Sazonov was prepared to do, Pašić repeated that if war was unavoidable, Serbia would fight.[13]

When talking to governments other than Russia, Pašić never went that far. He said only that Serbia would do all in its power to satisfy Austria-Hungary. His approach to Sazonov was different. He wanted Sazonov to know that, if they had to, the Serbs would fight the hopeless battle—and fight alone if Russia abandoned them. His hope was that neither Sazonov nor the tsar could withstand such pressure.

Sazonov, in turn, kept his promises vague. If Serbia yielded, Russia would not have to fight. Having heard from Strandtmann that Pašić did not intend to defend Belgrade, Sazonov accepted the abandonment of the capital and a peaceful withdrawal into the interior. Serbia could then call upon the Great Powers to protect it. Spalajkovic, as we have seen, rejected the idea out of hand. For him, a historic opportunity was at hand to realize the Great Serb dream with Russian arms; he was not prepared to have Sazonov buy peace at Serbia's expense.

On 25 July, Russia's Council of Ministers had decided to go to war to defend Serbia if necessary. On the twenty-sixth they had authorized the Period Preparatory to War. Nonetheless, the only official promise to Serbia was a wire from Tsar Nicholas II to Prince Alexander of Serbia stating, "So long as the slightest hope exists of avoiding bloodshed, all our efforts must be directed to that end; but if in spite of our earnest wish we are not successful, your Highness may rest assured that Russia will in no case disinterest herself in the fate of Serbia."[14]

Pašić and Spalajkovic had been making every effort to obtain a firm Russian commitment, but all they had received were promises that Russia would not be "indifferent" to or "disinterested" in Serbia's fate. By the time the tsar's wire arrived in Nish on 28 July, Pašić was expecting Austrian troops to march into Belgrade at any hour—and he was looking for some sign, any sign, that Russia would not abandon Serbia. The tsar's wire still made no promises, but at least it was something. Pašić, who did not see how Serbia could face the Austro-Hungarian army alone, was overcome as Strandtmann read him the tsar's wire. "What a comfort!" Pašić cried. "Almighty God, great and gracious is the Russian tsar." With tears streaming down his cheeks, he threw his arms around the Russian envoy.[15]

By 28 July, the Austrian and German intelligence services were receiving regular reports on the rising state of Russian readiness, and Pourtalès kept warning Sazonov that Russia's military measures were dangerous.[16] Unfortunately, neither Sazonov nor Tsar Nicholas fully understood the implications of the Period Preparatory to War. They regarded its measures as routine preliminaries to mobilization, but Austrian and German observers saw an undeclared mobilization taking place. They were probably right.

Australian historian L. C. F. Turner made a close study of the Russian mobilization and concluded that, for all practical purposes, an undeclared Russian general mobilization began on 26 July with the Period Preparatory to War, and that Paléologue and key French officials, including the minister of war and the army chief of staff, knew what was happening and encouraged it.[17] For example, Gen. Marquis de Laguiche—the French military attaché in St. Petersburg—informed Paris on the twenty-sixth that although the Russians would avoid measures that might provoke the Germans, "nonetheless, the military districts of Warsaw, Vilna, and St. Petersburg were taking secret preparatory measures." These were northern military districts bordering on Germany. The French general staff report of 28 July confirmed this information.[18]

The Franco-Russian military convention of 1892 had originally provided that any mobilization by any member of the Triple Alliance, even if Italy or Austria mobilized without Germany, would immediately and without further notice trigger the simultaneous mobilization of the French and Russian armies. Subsequent discussion and amendments provided that unless Germany mobilized or attacked, there must be prior consultation before either France or Russia mobilized. But the alliance was secret. Not many civilians knew about it, and for a long time both governments ignored it. However, the generals who had worked out the details continued to operate on the original assumption that mobilization by any member of the Triple Alliance would trigger an automatic Russian mobilization.[19] When Austria mobilized against Serbia on 25 July, most Russian field officers regarded Austria's mobilization as a declaration of war on Russia requiring general mobilization. When the Period Preparatory to War was declared, they acted accordingly.

The question for Austria and Germany, therefore, was whether St. Petersburg sincerely wanted to negotiate and was taking military measures to put pressure on them, or whether the Russians were talking while they secretly mobilized. Sazonov's volatility and general unreliability did not help the situation.

When Saturday, Sunday, and Monday passed without an invasion of Serbia, Sazonov was visibly relieved. When he studied the Serbian answer on Monday, his spirits soared: he thought it offered Austria-Hungary "the fullest satisfaction."[20] After his promising talk with Szápáry on Sunday, he was confident that Austria would negotiate. Even when Pourtalès warned him that there was great danger in excessive Russian military measures, Sazonov replied that since Austria had said it would take no Serbian territory and since hostilities had not yet begun, he was sure that Russia could "build a golden bridge for Austria." Pourtalès warned Sazonov that Austria would not let itself be put off with lame excuses. "Serbia would have to swallow several bitter pills." Sazonov's answer was, "There must be a way of giving Serbia her deserved lesson while sparing her sovereign rights."[21]

On Tuesday Sazonov was down again. Berchtold still had not replied to his request for direct negotiations, and reports of Austria's mobilization against Serbia kept coming in. Buchanan asked Sazonov whether he would be satisfied with Austria's assurances of Serbian independence and territorial integrity. He emphasized that "it was important that we should know [the] real intentions of [the] Imperial Government." Buchanan wanted no surprises.

Sazonov was not entirely reassuring. With respect to Serbian independence and territorial integrity, he now said, "No engagement that Austria might take on these two points would satisfy Russia." As for Russian intentions, "on the day that Austria crossed [the] Servian frontier [the] order for mobilization against Austria would be issued." He repeated again that the only way to avert war was for Great Britain "to let it be clearly known that they would join France and Russia."[22]

By the time Buchanan left and Pourtalès came in, Sazonov had worked himself into a great state. He angrily told the German ambassador that Serbia's answer had given Austria "everything that Austria could demand" and that the whole crisis "was a well-laid scheme between us and the Vienna Cabinet." Pourtalès hotly denied the charge and observed, in turn, that in light of his information on Russian military preparations, Russia's military leaders were perhaps going "further than was intended here at St. Petersburg." Sazonov was dismissive: no mobilization orders had been given; there were just a few preparations. Offended by Sazonov's tone, Pourtalès replied that there was no point in continuing the conversation if the minister was going to speak in such a manner, and he walked out.[23]

When Szápáry saw Sazonov shortly afterward, Sazonov was calmer but still angry. He was disappointed that Berchtold had not authorized direct talks, and the two men rehearsed all the Austro-Russian differences. Predictably, they made no headway. Szápáry nonetheless told Berchtold that Sazonov desperately wanted peace and "was clutching at straws."[24]

In Paris, Bertie was increasingly annoyed with the Russian ambassador, Alexander Izvolsky, who had complained to Bertie's first counselor of the embassy that war was now inevitable and that it was all England's fault. The English had encouraged Austria by not declaring their solidarity with

France and Russia. Izvolsky had been Russian foreign minister during the 1909 annexation crisis, and he was still bitterly angry at the way he had been outwitted and humiliated by Vienna. He hated the Austrians, and he refused to accept the British argument that Serbia presented a serious problem to Austria-Hungary. Instead, Izvolsky insisted, "Austria's object is to extend Germanic influence and power towards Constantinople, which Russia cannot possibly permit." As foreign minister he had accepted Russia's humiliation in 1909 because he "had no choice then, as Russia was not in a position to fight, but things were different now."[25]

When Bertie heard about this conversation, he went to see Bienvenu-Martin to learn whether Izvolsky had used the same language with the French. The Russian ambassador had just returned from St. Petersburg, and if his language represented the view of the Russian government, "it was not promising for the preservation of peace." Bienvenu-Martin replied that Izvolsky had "spoken of the position as very serious but by no means hopeless." Bertie confided to his diary that Izvolsky "will do a good deal of mischief in fomenting a war spirit here." In the end, Britain might have to fight to save France, but he still did not think the Serbian question was one on which England should go to war.[26]

Meanwhile in Berlin, Jules Cambon, Goschen, and the Italian ambassador were comparing notes on Jagow's evasion of the British mediation proposal. Although they could not tell whether the Germans were acting in good faith, they all knew that the Austrians had not been happy with the 1912 ambassadors' conference. Cambon suggested that Grey should ask Jagow under what conditions Germany would enter into discussions with the other three mediating powers.

Goschen forwarded Cambon's proposal to London. Eyre Crowe liked the idea that Germany should show "what *she* proposes the Powers should do." Nicolson was irritated. "I am a little tired of these protestations and should like to see some practical action. If direct conversations are to take place between Vienna and St. Petersburg, we had better not confuse the matter by making any fresh proposals."[27] Grey agreed with Nicolson but said he would keep the suggestion in reserve "till we see how the conversations between Austria and Russia progress."[28] Berchtold, unfortunately, had just given Sazonov the impression that he rejected direct talks. Jules Cambon, who was working feverishly in Berlin to get some talks started, warned "that it is necessary to act fast if we are not to be overtaken by events."[29]

As Austro-Hungarian court officials were reviewing the declaration of war and a message to the Austro-Hungarian people for the emperor's signature, one of them remarked, "I will only say one thing: At the age of eighty-four one does not sign a war manifesto!"[30] He was wrong; Emperor Franz Joseph signed the papers. With Vienna eager and excited, with thousands of Berliners cheering and singing patriotic hymns in front of the Austrian embassy,[31] with German leaders impatient for the Austrian army to get rolling, and incoming reports that Russia was bluffing and unlikely to take military action, the Austro-Hungarian Empire, at eleven o'clock Tuesday morning, declared war on the Kingdom of Serbia.

The Austro-Hungarian government then found itself faced with a dilemma that today would be regarded as quaint. It had severed relations with Serbia; how, under the terms of the Hague Convention, would it deliver a declaration of war? After considering several alternatives and obtaining a legal opinion, the Austrians decided to send uncoded wires to the Serbian foreign ministry in Belgrade and in Nish. Another wire was sent to Serbian army headquarters. Since direct wires from Vienna to Belgrade had been cut, the messages had to be routed through Bucharest and a border town on the eastern frontier.

After the Belgrade government moved in, Nish was a crowded town, and the dining room of the Hotal Europa was packed. Between noon and 1:00 P.M. a messenger came into the room, looked for Pašić, and handed him a telegram—in French and uncoded. Everyone in the room watched as Pašić read. When he had finished, he paused, stood up, and announced, "Austria has declared war on us. Our cause is just. God will help us."[32]

A little later an identical telegram arrived at Serbian army headquarters. Pašić was baffled. No nation had ever declared war by sending out a series of uncoded telegrams. Was it a hoax? Or was it an Austrian trick to get Serbia to attack and therefore assume responsibility for the war?[33] Pašić grew even more suspicious when he spoke to the German minister, who, uninformed by Berlin, knew nothing about an Austrian declaration of war. Suspecting a hoax, Pašić wired St. Petersburg, Paris, and London: was it true that Austria had declared war on Serbia? Eventually, the answers came back. It was true; Austria and Serbia were at war.[34]

Spalajkovic sent a copy of the wire informing him that Austria and Serbia were at war to Sazonov with a cover note of his own. A Great Power had declared war on a "small Slav country" that had just come out of a series of "heroic but exhausting battles. In this moment, which is so grave for my country, I take the liberty of expressing the hope that this act, which disturbs the peace of Europe and revolts the conscience, will be condemned by the whole civilized world and be severely punished by Russia, protector of Serbia."[35]

21: The Tsar Decides Not to Decide

St. Petersburg, Early Morning to Late Night, 28 July

Sazonov had told everyone that Russia would not mobilize until Austrian troops actually crossed the Serbian frontier, but the shock of Austria's declaration of war changed his mind: Russia had to mobilize immediately. If Russia abandoned the Slav peoples, "she would be considered a decadent state and would henceforth have to take second place among the powers."[1] Sazonov had an appointment with the tsar at six o'clock, but before the meeting he had a talk with the army chief of staff, General Yanushkevich, from whom he received a second shock.

Russia's quartermaster general and mobilization expert, Gen. Yuri Danilov, had returned from his inspection tour late on Sunday, 26 July. When he reported to headquarters he found everything in confusion. The German foreign secretary had assured Entente ambassadors that Germany would not feel compelled to respond to a partial mobilization directed only against Austria-Hungary in the south. Sazonov had proposed just such a mobilization as a warning to Austria, and that decision had been approved by the Council of Ministers, the tsar, war minister General Sukhomlinov, and army chief of staff General Yanushkevich, who had ordered General Dobrolski to prepare the necessary orders.[2]

General Danilov knew that if Russia ordered a partial mobilization against Austria-Hungary, Vienna would respond with a full general mobilization and, under the terms of the Austro-German alliance, an Austrian mobilization provoked by a Russian threat would bring about a German mobilization, which almost certainly meant war with Germany. The Russian planners had never imagined that they could fight Austria without fighting Germany, and they had no plans for a partial mobilization aimed only against Austria. They were working on such a plan but it was not ready yet.

Wholly apart from the technical difficulties, there were Russia's military obligations to France. The Russians estimated that the Germans could mobilize and concentrate in ten days, the Austrians in fifteen days. Russia, with its enormous distances and weak rail net, required twenty to thirty days, depending on the theater. With recent improvements in the rail net and the institution of the Period Preparatory to War, two-thirds of the Russian forces could be in position within eighteen days of a formal mobilization order.[3] The Russians, heavily persuaded by French loans and fear of a French defeat, had promised to launch an offensive into East Prussia on the fifteenth day of mobilization, well before they were at full strength, so that the Germans could not throw their whole army against France. If the Russians sent units south to fight Austria in Galicia and later went to war with Germany, they might not be ready to attack in East Prussia within the required fifteen days. Finally, under the proposed partial mobilization, they could not mobilize in districts bordering Germany, so the men from those districts would be unavailable for units destined for the south—leaving Russia with only thirteen army corps mobilized against Austria-Hungary when the campaign plan required sixteen corps. A new campaign plan could not be improvised at the last minute!

From a military point of view, therefore, the real choice was between general mobilization and no mobilization at all. A partial mobilization would be suicidal.

General Danilov saw immediately that neither Sazonov nor the tsar nor the war minister nor the chief of staff understood the problem. The subordinate officers who did understand would not challenge their superiors. Danilov pleaded with Yanushkevich to reconsider, and Yanushkevich, who was beginning to worry about the partial mobilization, called a full staff conference to review the matter.[4] This conference, which was held on Monday, 27 July, convinced Yanushkevich that Danilov was right. When he saw Sazonov on Tuesday after the Austrian declaration of war, Yanushkevich told the foreign minister that a partial mobilization was impossible.

It was a terrible moment for Sazonov. By ordering a general mobilization, Russia would find itself at war with Germany. By ordering a partial mobilization, it would still find itself at war with Germany—but in a much more vulnerable posture. If Russia did nothing, it "would be abandoning Serbia to her tragic fate" and put the Dardanelles and Bosporus Straits at risk. This, Russia could not do.[5]

Sazonov and the Russian military never seem to have considered that they might win a military as well as a diplomatic advantage by just waiting until the Austrian army was fully engaged in Serbia. Once Conrad's B Group was engaged, there was no chance that its twelve divisions could reinforce A Group—assigned to the northern frontiers of Galicia—in time to defend against a Russian advance. The northeastern borders of the monarchy would be virtually undefended, and there would be no Austrian offensive in

Galicia to relieve the puny defensive forces the Germans planned to leave in East Prussia. Conrad and the German army chief of staff, General Moltke, worried about this scenario. They both needed to know what Russia intended to do. A silent, unmobilized Russia was too powerful to ignore. Studying the problem in 1912, the French general staff had concluded that Russia and France would gain a "decisive superiority" if Austria tied up the bulk of its forces in the Balkans.[6] No one in France seems to have recalled this memorandum or brought it to Russia's attention.

Of course, these insights are clear to the historian sitting with the maps and documents spread comfortably before him and with no enemy armies massing on his frontiers. But for those dealing with the crisis—tired, overworked, threatened, and not fully informed—the situation was far from clear. Sazonov did not know that the Period Preparatory to War was already creating a very high state of readiness. He did not know that Conrad would not attack Serbia for another two weeks. Too overwrought to coolly think through the possible advantages of not mobilizing at all, he excitedly told Yanushkevich that he would ask the tsar to sign the order for partial mobilization. He did not want a war with Germany; he did not want any war. He just wanted to warn Austria.

Yanushkevich asked Sazonov whether he could assure him that war with Germany could be avoided. Sazonov could not. He was almost certain that war was coming, but Buchanan had warned him over and over again against taking provocative measures if he ever expected British assistance. He simply could not ask for a general mobilization. Yanushkevich replied that Sazonov was obligated to point out to the tsar all the dangers of a partial mobilization.[7] Sazonov agreed, but, wavering a little, he asked Yanushkevich to have his staff prepare two different orders—one for partial mobilization and one for general mobilization.

French diplomacy at this stage of the crisis was not very helpful. The French were certain that they would be overrun by the Germans as they had been in 1870 unless the Russians launched an offensive into East Prussia as rapidly as possible, forcing the Germans to divide their armies. General Joseph Joffre, the French chief of staff, was always urging the Russians to concentrate on the Germans; Austria-Hungary would cease to be a threat once Germany was defeated.[8] The problem was that Russian field commanders, as opposed to the Russian staff officers who negotiated with the French, were much more interested in fighting Austria than in fighting Germany.

When Paris learned that Russia was considering a partial mobilization against Austria and that the Russian government wanted "to avoid any measure likely to be regarded as directed against Germany,"[9] the French military got nervous. General Joffre urged St. Petersburg "to immediately take the offensive in East Prussia" if hostilities broke out. Paléologue and General Laguiche were instructed to make clear "the great importance that we attach to their offensive taking place in conjunction with ours."[10] On 28 July the Russian military attaché reported that both War Minister Messimy and Joffre had assured him of France's complete readiness to fulfill its alliance obligations.[11] Bienvenu-Martin and Viviani, on the other hand, were instructing Paléologue to keep Russia in a negotiating posture.

Paléologue always took the position that Sazonov was doing his utmost for peace. When he was instructed to discuss Grey's mediation proposal with the English, German, and Italian ambassadors and to await further instructions before approaching Sazonov, Paléologue replied on the twenty-eighth, before he knew of the Austrian declaration of war, that Russia would agree to anything England and France might propose to keep the peace.[12]

Later in the day Paléologue received Viviani's instruction to tell Sazonov that France was ready to support any Russian action "in the interests of the general peace."[13] What he actually told Sazonov, just before Sazonov went off to see the tsar, was "that he could officially declare the complete readiness of France to fulfill her obligations as an ally in case of necessity."[14] Paléologue did not report that assurance to Paris. Instead, he wired that the Austrian and German ambassadors had left Sazonov with the impression that "Austria does not want to talk."[15] We do not know what Sazonov told Paléologue about a possible mobilization. Paléologue's reports do not mention it. What we do know is that Sazonov went off to see the tsar with Paléologue's assurances ringing in his ears.

Upon the unexpected death of his father in 1894, Nicholas Romanov, at the age of twenty-six, became Tsar Nicholas II, Autocrat of All Russia. Until that time he had been a royal playboy with a ballerina mistress, a commission in the horse guards, and unlimited wealth; then suddenly he was tsar. "What am I going to do, what is going to happen to me, to you, to Zenia [his sister], to Alix [his fiancee], to mother, to all of Russia?" he asked a cousin. "I am not prepared to be tsar. I never wanted to become one. I know nothing of the business of ruling. I have no idea of even how to talk to the ministers."[16]

Nicholas was rightly diffident about his abilities. He was not very intelligent, he was gullible, he was suspicious of change, and he was stubborn. He would not debate an issue with his ministers. If they grew too insistent, he would wrap himself in reverence for the past and resign himself to God's great design. Whereas German ministers suffered from the kaiser's delusions of grandeur, Russian ministers suffered from the tsar's remoteness from the realities of Russia and his unwillingness to make the slightest change.

When his ministers warned of revolutionary dangers, Tsar Nicholas and Tsaritsa Alexandra thought that the ministers were out of touch with the real Russia. They had complete faith in the loyalty and affection of the Russian peasant for his tsar. Court officials who served the tsar and his immediate family, as opposed to the ministers who ran the government, did nothing to disabuse the royal couple, and, unlike the ministers, they saw the tsar every single day. Gleb Botkin, whose father died with the imperial family in 1918, wrote bitterly after the war that "in the opinion of Tsarskoe Selo [the tsar's official residence] everything was always going well. The whole of Russia worshiped its 'Little Father the Czar,' and the danger of revolution, or even the slightest discontent existed only in the imagination of the alarmists and disheveled university students."[17]

The fact was that the tsar trusted neither his ministers nor anyone else outside his immediate family. He and his wife had withdrawn entirely from the society of St. Petersburg and deeply resented the pleasure that St. Petersburg took in slandering them. Nicholas had no intimates he could talk with and unburden himself; apart from official reports from his ministers, military reviews—which he enjoyed—and ceremonial occasions, he lived entirely within his small family circle in the imperial palaces of Tsarskoe Selo and Peterhof. He was very nearly as lonely as Austria-Hungary's Emperor Franz Joseph.

Even when ministers spoke to the tsar, they could not be sure they made a difference. When Nicholas did not agree with the speaker he would listen silently, talk pleasantly of something else, and go his own way. When officials, ministers, Duma leaders, his mother, even generals of the army screwed up the courage to warn Nicholas of the absolute necessity of making changes to save the dynasty, they received the tsar's habitual courtesy and things went on as before. "I suppose," his cousin reflected, "he was the politest man in Europe."[18] But he was also exasperating. Count Sergei Yulyevich Witte, a former prime minister and minister of finance, a man who worried French diplomats because he thought the alliance with France was dangerous, recalled one of the last occasions when he presented his views to the tsar. "We talked for two solid hours. He shook my hand. He embraced me. He wished me all the luck in the world. I returned home beside myself with happiness and found a written order for my dismissal lying on my desk."[19]

Nicholas detested personal confrontations. When two of his ministers began shouting at each other, he got up and left the room. When another disagreement erupted, he complained, "Why are you always quarreling? I always agree with everyone about everything and then do things my own way."[20] The result was that his ministers thought he was cowardly, shifty, and constantly changing his mind. They dogged his footsteps, even when he was away on vacation, to make sure no rival voice got his ear.

Nicholas was sustained by the unshakable belief that he and Russia were in the hands of God. In the midst of the 1905 revolution he told his foreign minister, Alexander Izvolsky: "I have the firm and absolute faith that the destiny of Russia, my own fate and that of my family, is in the hands of Almighty God, Who has placed me where I am. Whatever may happen, I shall bow to His will."[21] In a reign battered by disaster, the tsar needed all the help that God could give him.

More than thirteen hundred people were trampled to death when the crowd got out of control at his coronation. Two successive ministers of the interior were assassinated in 1903, another fell in 1904, his uncle was killed by a bomb the same year, and his prime minister was assassinated in 1911. He suffered a disastrous defeat at the hands of Japan in 1904–5, and a revolution in 1905 forced upon him the humiliation of a constitution. Assassinations, particularly of policemen, were endemic; right down to the outbreak of the war, they ran into the hundreds every year.[22] In the first six months of 1914, more than a million and a quarter workers went out on strike. In July, workers in St. Petersburg were tearing up the streets and using the stones to bombard the police from windows. When Poincaré arrived for the French state visit, four out of five trolley lines in St. Petersburg were out of service; fear and security men were everywhere.[23]

The tsar's personal life was not much better. When, after four daughters, he was finally given a son, Nicholas learned within months that the boy was an incurable hemophiliac, a "bleeder." Tsaritsa Alexandra, whom the tsar loved dearly, was timid, neurotic, and in chronic bad health. She had an elusive series of ailments, sometimes spending weeks at a time in bed or in a wheelchair. She suffered greatly from worry over her son, and Nicholas suffered equally for both son and wife. "She keeps to her bed most of the day," he wrote his mother, "does not receive anyone, does not come out to lunches and remains on the balcony day after day."[24]

God had one more cross for Nicholas to bear: his cousin by marriage, Kaiser Wilhelm. Wilhelm affected a condescending older-brother attitude toward Nicholas, who was nine years younger and who had come to the throne six years later. The kaiser gave advice freely. When Nicholas was beset by revolution, Wilhelm wrote, "The best way to relieve the cares and worries the situation at home causes you is, as you do, to occupy yourself with your fine Guard by inspecting them and speaking to them. It gives you pleasure and gratifies the troops," who will, therefore, prove "a loyal, trustworthy and keen weapon in the hand of the sovereign."[25] When they met on the unavoidable royal visits, Wilhelm would tap Nicholas on the shoulder and say, "My advice to you is more speeches and more parades."[26]

Nicholas was always glad when visits with the kaiser were over. First, there was Wilhelm himself. Second, his visits made the French nervous. Third, Nicholas's mother was a Danish princess and his wife was a Hessian princess. Wilhelm's grandfather had taken Schleswig-Holstein from Denmark in 1864 and incorporated a good part of Hesse into Prussia in 1866. Both women loathed cousin Willy. The kaiser, who pictured himself as forever straightening out the mess left by his diplomats, could not understand why his efforts with Nicholas did not bear greater fruit.

Events were moving very swiftly after the Austrian declaration of war, but the regular appointments with the tsar's ministers continued, and Tuesday was the day for the foreign minister. Sazonov took the forty-minute train ride to Tsarskoe Selo. He got off the train and was taken to the imperial enclave, where he passed through the line of constantly circling mounted cossacks; walked through the endless rooms, corridors, and antechambers, with police guards always visible; and finally arrived at the small office in which Tsar Nicholas II conducted his business.

Sazonov reported on the Austrian declaration of war and outlined the mobilization problem. After a considerable discussion, it was decided to announce immediately that Russia would declare partial mobilization the next day, Wednesday, 29 July. Nicholas also agreed that two mobilization decrees were to be prepared—one partial and one general—but declared that nothing was to be decided without a further order from him. Perhaps the announcement of partial mobilization would bring Austria to the negotiating table. Sazonov then walked out through the rooms and the corridors and the circling cossacks, went to the station, and rode another forty minutes back to St. Petersburg.

Nicholas was upset. His foreign minister, his war minister, his chief of staff, and his Council of Ministers had all approved a partial mobilization if the need arose. Now he learned that the army had no viable plan for a partial mobilization. Nicholas had promised the world that Russia would not be "indifferent" to Serbia's fate and had agreed with his Council of Ministers that Russia could not abandon Serbia, but he still dreaded war.

Nicholas rarely challenged anyone in a face-to-face talk, and even now he said he would wait and see what the announcement of a partial mobilization would bring. But he must have been angry; he told General Dobrolski afterward that "at the end of the present crisis, the mobilization plan shall be so revised that it affords the possibility of carrying out" a partial mobilization without wrecking a subsequent general mobilization.[27]

The Russian government announced Tuesday evening that "in consequence of Austria's declaration of war on Serbia, we shall declare mobilization in the military districts of Odessa, Kiev, Moscow and Kazan tomorrow [Wednesday, 29 July]." Ambassadors were instructed to "emphasize the absence of any intention of a Russian attack on Germany." To make clear that Russia was not contemplating immediate hostilities against Austria-Hungary, the instructions concluded that "our ambassador at Vienna is not being recalled from his post for the time being."[28]

Although the government spoke of partial mobilization, the army believed that if there were *any* mobilization, it would be general mobilization. A few minutes before midnight of the twenty-eighth, General Danilov asked the commander of the Warsaw military district—which bordered Germany as well as Austria—about arrangements for unloading two cavalry brigades there, something that was not included in the partial mobilization. He warned the commander not to let the troops get too close to the frontier, "for political reasons." An hour later, early on Wednesday morning, Danilov wired commanders that once mobilized they were not to open hostilities without a further express imperial order. Still later, at 7:20 A.M. on Wednesday, General Yanushkevich wired the commanding officers in all military districts: "For your information: 30 July will be proclaimed the first day of our *general mobilization.*"[29]

Sometime after he stormed out of Sazonov's office on Tuesday, Ambassador Pourtalès learned that Austria had declared war on Serbia and that Russia had announced it would declare partial mobilization the next day. He immediately called Sazonov's deputy and said that if Sazonov would make the slightest gesture of reconciliation, he would immediately go and see him. He could not break off contact when the government was threatening to mobilize! Pourtalès promptly received a telephone message telling him to come to the foreign ministry, and Sazonov greeted him "by flinging his arms around my neck and apologizing." Pourtalès agreed to regard the morning's incident as closed and promised not to report it to his government, but he repeated his warning that Russian military preparations were extremely dangerous.[30]

Paléologue, meanwhile, never directly informed Paris that Russia was about to order mobilization. He reported only, "It has been agreed that, in case of general mobilization, two [French] officers will be delegated to be sent to my Embassy."[31] Paléologue sent that message at 7:35 P.M. Tuesday. It was his only hint to Paris that mobilization was in the works; moreover, it was a general and not a partial mobilization.

22: THE KAISER SEES NO REASON FOR WAR

Berlin, Early Morning to Late Night, 28 July

The kaiser rose early to ride in the park with his aide, Gen. Hans von Plessen, who recorded their conversation in his diary. "I go riding with H. M. at 7:30 A.M. He tells me England thinks the Serbian answer to the Austrian ultimatum such that in essence all the demands are conceded and therewith all reason for war is gone. I said I thought Austria must at least lay hands on some pledge which would serve as guarantee for the carrying out of the concessions."[1] The general almost made history with that remark.

After his ride the kaiser breakfasted and sat down to read dispatches. Among them was Prince Lichnowsky's account of the previous day reporting that an irritated Grey thought the Serbian answer was a fair basis for negotiation. Grey had warned that if Austria attacked Serbia now, "the result would be the most frightful war that Europe had ever seen." Jagow had not been sure the kaiser should see such a forceful warning, but he was afraid to keep it from him, and Bethmann decided to send it on. So far, the kaiser had been very belligerent, rejecting every proposal for a German intervention in Vienna.[2]

The kaiser had appointed Lichnowsky over the objections of Bethmann and the foreign office, and he took his ambassador's reports seriously. He did not dismiss them as "just Lichnowsky." When he read the account of Lichnowsky's talk with Grey that Tuesday morning, and then studied the Serbian answer, he underwent a stunning about-face: "A brilliant performance for a time limit of only forty-eight hours. This is more than one could have expected. A great moral victory for Vienna; but with it every reason for war drops away, and Giesl might have remained quietly in Belgrade! On the strength of this *I* should never have ordered mobilization!"[3]

The kaiser immediately wrote Jagow that the Serbian answer was "a capitulation of the most humiliating kind, and as a result *every cause for war* falls to the ground." He underscored "every cause for war." With that statement, the kaiser flatly reversed the line taken by Bethmann and Jagow and adopted Grey's position: the Serbian answer was a fair basis for negotiation. The Serbs, however, were "orientals, therefore liars, tricksters, and masters of evasion. In order that these beautiful promises may be turned to truth and facts, *a bit of violence* must be exercised." He then took up General von Plessen's early-morning comment that the Austrian army should seize Belgrade and hold it until Serbia's promises were carried out.

Wilhelm instructed Jagow to prepare a proposal to Vienna along those lines. Serbia's promises could be guaranteed by an occupation of Belgrade just as Germany had occupied France after 1870 until the indemnity was paid. Such a solution would restore Austrian prestige and preserve the honor of the army, which had now "unnecessarily" mobilized for the third time in five years. Since there was to be no war, the kaiser must have assumed that Serbia would agree to an Austrian occupation of Belgrade.

Knowing that his fiery nationalists would again accuse him of backing down when real fighting threatened, the kaiser covered his retreat with bluster. He would ignore any proposals or protests to the contrary. Almost every power had appealed to him to maintain the peace—and he would do so, but "in my own way, as sparingly of Austria's *national feeling,* and the *honor of her arms* as possible." He assured Jagow that the army, including Moltke, was in complete agreement.[4]

The kaiser felt no sense of urgency. Neither Bethmann nor Jagow had told him that Vienna was about to declare war, or that they were telling the Austrians to hurry the opening of hostilities, or that Jagow had told Szögyény to ignore Grey's mediation proposals. Like Tsar Nicholas II and Emperor Franz Joseph, he was not in the habit of using the telephone. He sent his note to Jagow by messenger sometime before noon.[5]

Earlier, at two o'clock that morning, Bethmann had already wired Lichnowsky that it was impossible for Germany to tell Austria-Hungary to accept an answer it had just declared to be unsatisfactory. Germany was, however, prepared to do everything to cooperate with England to maintain the peace of Europe.[6]

Bethmann had also read Pourtalès's report of Monday's meeting with Sazonov, with its talk of "a golden bridge for Austria" and "bitter pills" for Serbia.[7] Sazonov seemed ready to make major concessions. Moreover, the favorable impression made by the Serbian answer was putting great pressure on Germany to intervene in Vienna. Later Tuesday morning, Bethmann and Jagow prepared a circular for the Associated Governments of the German Empire declaring that the Serbian answer was not made in good faith, that the Serbs would continue "their trouble-making," and that Austria-

Hungary had no choice "but to enforce its demands by the use of heavy pressure, or, if need be, by resort to military measures."[8]

The kaiser's letter to Jagow arrived in Berlin only after Bethmann and Jagow had prepared the circular and sent Lichnowsky his instruction rejecting negotiations on the basis of the Serbian answer. The kaiser now said there was no reason for war and the Serbian answer was a fair basis for negotiation. What were they supposed to do?

First, they waited until they were sure that Austria had declared war on Serbia, and they did not get word of that until 6:39 Tuesday evening.[9] When Bethmann talked with Moltke, he found the chief of staff calm. The general accepted the kaiser's mediation proposal; he had no objection to restraining Austria and was not pushing for a military confrontation. He did worry about the reports of Russia's premobilization activities but agreed with Bethmann that there was no need, just yet, for a really sharp warning to Russia. Perhaps Szápáry, the Austrian ambassador, could mention the danger of these actions at St. Petersburg, without any hint of a threat.[10]

Official Berlin was upset by Grey's conference proposal. After saying all along that he would stay out of an Austro-Serbian quarrel, he now wanted to mediate it. The foreign office blamed Lichnowsky for failing to control Grey,[11] but very few of these officials knew that the kaiser had just agreed with Grey.

Bethmann went to Potsdam late Tuesday afternoon to see what he could do. The conversation could not have been pleasant. There were reports that the kaiser told the chancellor, "You have got me into a fine mess."[12] In any event, Bethmann was clearly irritated when he got back to Berlin; it shows in the elaborate instruction he prepared for Tschirschky Tuesday evening.

Despite repeated queries, Bethmann said, the Austrian government had left Germany completely in the dark concerning its intentions. Conrad's long delay going into action was putting Germany in a very difficult position. Mediation and conference proposals were coming in from every direction. If the Germans continued to stand aloof from such proposals, they would "incur the odium of having been responsible for a world war."

Sazonov, Bethmann went on, seemed ready to agree that Serbia deserved a lesson. Would Tschirschky, therefore, suggest to Berchtold that he repeat to Russia that Austria-Hungary had no interest in acquiring Serbian territory? He should also state that Austria's military goal was limited to the occupation of Belgrade "and certain other localities on Serbian territory in order to force the Serbian Government" to comply with Austrian demands. As soon as their demands were met, the Austrians would evacuate just as Prussian troops had evacuated France after 1870 once the indemnity was paid. Tschirschky was instructed to "discuss the matter along these lines thoroughly and impressively to Count Berchtold, and instigate a move at St. Petersburg."

Bethmann's instruction did not ask the Austrians to negotiate on the basis of the Serbian answer as the kaiser wanted. He asked merely that they be less "uncompromising" and that they talk to St. Petersburg, but he still expected "the complete fulfillment" of their demands. Tschirschky, moreover, was "to avoid very carefully giving rise to the impression that we wish to hold Austria back. The case is solely one of finding a way to realize Austria's desired aim . . . without at the same time bringing on a world war." If Russia rejected the proposal, if war came nonetheless, they might then fight under better conditions—that is, Great Britain might not join France and Russia.[13]

This "urgent" telegram went to central telegraph at 10:15 Tuesday night. It embodied Bethmann's version of the kaiser's proposal and was widely referred to as "Stop-in-Belgrade." It thereafter became the great hope for peace, and its success depended on four conditions: (1) Russia's accepting an Austrian occupation of Belgrade; (2) Russia's persuading Serbia to accept such an occupation; (3) Austria's negotiating on the basis of the Serbian answer—no one outside Berlin seriously considered that Serbia would simply yield to the Austrian note; and (4) the suspension of hostilities while the details were worked out. These conditions were difficult enough, but Bethmann's telegram said nothing to change the message Jagow had given Szögyény the day before, which was that although the German government had to go through the motions, it did not seriously support mediation proposals.

Tschirschky did not get Bethmann's instruction until Wednesday morning. Throughout the day on Tuesday, therefore, Tschirschky was still operating under Bethmann's instruction of Monday, 27 July, which asked only for "Count Berchtold's opinion on the English suggestion, as likewise his views on Mr. Sazonov's desire to negotiate directly with Vienna."[14]

Tschirschky had waited until Tuesday evening, after war had been declared on Serbia, before delivering Bethmann's request. Berchtold said that he would let Tschirschky know his views "very soon," but he could already say that since Serbia had opened hostilities and war had been declared, he thought "that England's move was made too late."[15] Berchtold informed Szögyény in Berlin and Mensdorff in London of his talk with Tschirschky. He also asked Szögyény to thank Jagow for his message and to tell him that he fully understood why Germany had decided to pass on the English suggestion.[16]

In talks with Bunsen and Schebeko on Tuesday, Berchtold learned that both Britain and France wanted negotiations. He then instructed Mensdorff in London and Szécsen in Paris to make use of the critical analysis of the

Serbian answer that the foreign ministry had printed alongside the text of the Serbian answer, and of the dossier detailing the monarchy's case against Serbia, which had finally been mailed out on the twenty-fifth. All this material was intended to demonstrate Serbia's implacable hostility and lack of good faith.

Conrad, meanwhile, was very upset by the Russian announcement of a partial mobilization. Obsessed with obtaining a quick, crushing victory over Serbia, he had detached several divisions from A Group, which was supposed to defend Galicia against Russia, and sent them south with B Group. Conrad wanted to warn Russia as soon as possible that a partial mobilization against Austria would be met by general mobilization in both Austria and Germany. He could not advance into Serbia if Russian intentions were uncertain, and he had to know no later than 1 August. A few days earlier he had told Berchtold that he could wait until the third.[17]

At 11 P.M. Tuesday, Berchtold wired Szögyény that Conrad "considers it *positively* necessary to know whether we can march against Serbia with strong forces, or whether we must reserve our chief army, and use it against Russia."[18] The Germans, however, were prepared to wait in order to force Russia to confront a fait accompli. They were fairly certain that Russia would not opt for war—but they would have to wait. Conrad, having weakened his defensive screen in Galicia, was unwilling to wait. He could not risk a Russian attack that might overrun Galicia. He wanted the Germans to force a Russian decision now.

Bethmann in Berlin and Sazonov in St. Petersburg both knew that their monarchs were afraid of war. They therefore thought that a direct exchange between monarchs might help. Sazonov had the tsar wire the kaiser: "Am glad you are back. In this most serious moment I appeal to you to help me. An ignoble war has been declared on a weak country. The indignation of Russia, fully shared by me, is enormous. I foresee that very soon I shall be overwhelmed by the pressure brought upon me, and be forced to take extreme measures which will lead to war. To try and avoid such a calamity as a European war, I beg you in the name of our old friendship to do what you can to stop your allies from going too far." The wire went out at one o'clock Wednesday morning and was signed simply, "Nicky."

The kaiser's wire, which went out at 1:45 A.M., crossed the tsar's. The tsar spoke no German and the kaiser spoke neither Russian nor French, so the two monarchs always communicated in English—and the kaiser's English was not always quite right. After pointing out that the Serbs had murdered their own king and queen as well as the late archduke, the kaiser said, "I fully understand how difficult it is for you and your Government to face the drift of your public opinion. Therefore, with regard to the hearty and tender friendship which binds us both from long ago with firm ties, I am exerting my utmost influence to induce the Austrians to deal straightly to arrive to a satisfactory understanding with you. I confidently hope you will help me in my efforts to smooth over difficulties which may still arise. Your very sincere and devoted friend and cousin. Willy."[19]

PART VII: Is Russia Mobilizing?

23: THE CULT OF THE OFFENSIVE

"To take [the offensive spirit] to excess would
probably still not be far enough."

Colonel de Grandmaison, 1911

In 1898 Ivan S. (known also as Jean de) Bloch, a Russian financier, published a six-volume study entitled *La Guerre Future*. He argued that war in the modern age was impossible, or at least suicidal. The future of war was "not fighting, but famine, not the slaying of men but the bankruptcy of nations and the break-up of the whole social organization."[1] His book was widely studied, and its ideas were popularized in 1910 by Norman Angell's *The Great Illusion,* which became an international best-seller. War in the industrial era, argued Angell, even a victorious war, would never pay. Military power "is socially and economically futile, and can have no relation to the prosperity of the people exercising it."[2] Sir Edward Grey read Angell's book and often used its arguments. It became part of the accepted wisdom of the period that Great Power wars had no winners.

Nonetheless, the two books did not sweep all before them. All over Europe, otherwise reasonable men equated peace and pacifism with decadence and moral decline—the kaiser's naval aide Admiral Müller, for example. They believed war, or at least military service, would bring out the best in their people. For pan-German nationalists, war was almost a religion. Heinrich Class, a pan-German, a vicious anti-Semite, and a future Hitler supporter, wrote in 1912, "Politically, our nation is deadly ill. . . . Whoever, therefore . . . seeks to bring the crisis of our present illness to a head, must long for war as the inspiration for all the good, healthy power of our people."[3]

The demagogues made a lot of noise, but most of Europe's leaders were afraid of war. Aristocrats were sure that a great war would destroy what was left of their society. The tsar and his most conservative ministers, including three successive prime ministers, believed that war between Germany and Russia would mean a revolution for winner and loser alike.[4] Berchtold, Bethmann, Grey, Sazonov, and most of the diplomatic community agreed that war meant revolution. So did Emperor Franz Joseph and the kaiser.

Governments, however, insisted that peace was possible only through a balance of power. The difficulty was that no government wanted a true balance of power; each wanted clear military superiority so that the other side would not dare start a war. Indeed, to fall into a position of weakness by reducing arms or abandoning alliances would not preserve peace—it would only provoke war, since weakness invited aggression. In Paris, Ambassador Izvolsky regarded disarmament as "a craze of Jews, Socialists and hysterical women."[5] Paul Cambon believed that a weak and cowardly nation "is prey to the first who comes," but an armed country, "animated by a military spirit and ready to fight, is sure to command respect and to avoid the horrors of war."[6] The Austro-Hungarian memorandum that Hoyos brought to Berlin on 4 July concluded that only Austro-German military superiority sustained the peace of Europe. If they were to lose that superiority, they would encourage new Franco-Russian aggression in the Balkans.[7]

War was pointless; arms were not.

Europe's military establishments believed that war between modern industrial nations would be suicidal only if the war were prolonged. Future conflicts, therefore, must be short. After a brief, victorious war, men would soon be back at their jobs, production would resume, and society would be saved. In a short war, however, the opening battles were crucial. Victory or defeat would be decided within weeks, and victory could be assured only by launching an overwhelming offensive at the earliest possible moment. An army on the defensive could not win; at best it would face a long, drawn-out stalemate. A deputy explained to the French Chamber of Deputies, "The first great battle will decide the whole war, and wars will be short. The idea of offense must penetrate the spirit of our nation."[8]

This "cult of the offensive" became a kind of saving myth—a myth that defied the military experience of the past fifty years. Bloch's *La Guerre Future* had analyzed the deadly accuracy and range of modern rifles and artillery, but the great slaughters that resulted from frontal attacks in the American Civil War, the Franco-Prussian War, the Boer War, the Russo-Japanese War, and the two Balkan wars were all explained away. Most observers blamed bad training, bad leadership, and bad terrain. The analysis of modern firepower was dismissed as "simple ballistics." Military journals and infantry regulations insisted on "the decisive attack, head held high, unconcerned about casualties." Entrenched defenders were to be assaulted en masse, elbow to elbow, "to the sound of bugles and drums."[9]

One of the bizarre aspects of offensive doctrine was that the more overwhelming the evidence on the devastating effects of modern firepower, the more military journals emphasized morale, discipline, and esprit de corps. Noting that cossack cavalry charges had been defeated by relatively small bodies of Japanese infantry, Russian generals concluded that the cossacks had been cowardly and ordered them to give up their carbines so that they would be forced to charge with drawn sabers.[10] British staff manuals proclaimed that "the moral effect of the bayonet is out of all proportion to its material effect . . . it draws the attacking side on." If infantry and cavalry were deprived of bayonets and swords, "it would to some extent take away their desire to close."[11] This is the language of romance, not analysis.

There was a clear political agenda in the cult of the offensive. Military writers were calling for offensive operations requiring a heroic disregard of life, but cultural pessimists doubted whether modern man was capable of heroism. If modern, urban man was puny, gin-ridden, self-indulgent, and unreliable, one would have thought that defensive doctrines would prevail. Volunteers and short-term conscripts could fight from prepared defensive positions; only highly trained, disciplined troops, aglow with patriotism and martial ardor, could mount and sustain an attack on the modern battlefield. Defensive doctrine meant taking modern man as he is. Offensive doctrine required a new man, a man restored to the martial virtues of his ancestors.

In France, right-wing patriots insisted that at least three years were needed to transform the typical urban worker into a fearless, utterly obedient warrior who would charge the enemy regardless of casualties. The French army and the French right were prepared to defy German numbers and German discipline with French offensive ardor. Equally patriotic Frenchmen insisted that there was a less reactionary way to protect France: a defensive citizens' army made up of short-term conscripts.[12] This debate ravaged French politics in 1913 and 1914; meanwhile, Europe's military planners voted for the offensive.

If an offensive was more likely to bring victory than standing on the defensive, then a nation at war should immediately attack. To be caught on the defensive was to invite defeat. The Germans thought their only hope of victory lay in defeating France swiftly, then swinging east to fight Russia before it could launch an offensive. Jagow explained that "we are obliged to act as fast as possible before Russia has the time to mobilize her army."[13] The French and the Russians, on the other hand, felt they had to launch prompt and simultaneous attacks to split the German forces before they defeated France.

The end product of Europe's best military thinking was that within days of the Austro-Hungarian declaration of war on Serbia, the hair-trigger machinery of European mobilization was cocked and ready, awaiting only the order to launch.

Kaiser Wilhelm often referred to his army chief of staff as "sad Julius." General Helmuth von Moltke was one of the great pessimists in an age of pessimists. He had been tall and lanky as a young officer; in 1914, at sixty-six, he was flabby and not at all well[14]—and bad health did nothing to ease his dour melancholy.

Moltke worried about everything. He thought the kaiser was erratic and that Bethmann was neither firm nor able. He distrusted Roman Catholics, he wanted to lock up all the "anarchists," and he disliked the urban masses. Only the traditional rural population was truly loyal to the monarchy. Reflecting on the evils of industrialization, Moltke sometimes thought that the only solution lay in a huge continental expansion to create room for a new rural population outside the crowded cities.[15] In such troubled times as these, Moltke believed, the army and its officers must remain absolutely loyal.[16]

Moltke thought war was inevitable, but he did not look forward to it. On 29 July he described it to Bethmann as "the mutual butchery of the civilized nations of Europe."[17] But pessimist and Darwinian that he was, he was sure that when Russia and France felt strong enough, they would fall upon Germany.

In 1913, in the course of an intermittent correspondence with Conrad on strategic planning, Moltke explained that although Germany could not go to war to save Bulgaria, "I am of the persuasion that a European war must come sooner or later, and in the last resort it will be a war between *Germantum* and *Slaventum*. To prepare for this is the duty of all states that carry the banner of Germanic *Kultur*. The initial attack must come, however, from the Slavs." Conrad had to remind Moltke that if Austria-Hungary went to war under such a banner, "we can hardly rely upon our Slavs, who form 47 percent of the population."[18] Moltke never responded.[19]

When Moltke became chief of the army general staff in 1906, he had been a member of the kaiser's personal military entourage for years. Moltke was the namesake of his uncle, the famous Field Marshal Helmuth von Moltke, hero of Prussia's unification of Germany, the all-conquering general of the great Otto von Bismarck, and the architect of the defeat of France in 1870. The younger Moltke was also the successor to Field Marshal Count Alfred von Schlieffen, army chief of staff from 1891 through the end of 1905 and author of the famous—or infamous—Schlieffen Plan, which dominated German strategic thinking. Moltke inherited both his uncle's name and Schlieffen's plan. It was a daunting inheritance.

The elder Moltke had concluded that in a two-front war, a defensive strategy with limited offensives in the east to keep the Russians at bay would best serve the interests of the new German Empire. He believed that Germany could fight on the defensive almost indefinitely. This kind of thinking was regarded as dangerously old-fashioned by the new partisans of offensive doctrine.

Schlieffen believed that Germany could not survive a long war. In a two-front war, he called for a quick, annihilating victory over France. Such a victory was possible only with an overwhelming flanking assault through Belgium and Holland, turning the French left flank and crushing the French army from the rear. With the French army destroyed, the Germans would swing east to attack the Russians before they were fully mobilized. The younger Moltke, when he succeeded Schlieffen, came out for Schlieffen's strategy and against his uncle's. "A speedy decision," he wrote, "may be hoped for [against France], while an offensive against Russia would be an interminable affair."[20]

Schlieffen may have been a great strategic theorist, but he did not care for the nuts and bolts. He never had the manpower to carry out his great flanking maneuver and he never made the necessary logistical studies. Moltke was very different. He understood supply requirements and the need for railroads, transport, and meticulous planning. What Moltke lacked was imagination or, perhaps, the intellectual toughness and independence to follow an analysis to its logical conclusion. He was not, as Admiral Müller once put it, "consequent."

Moltke never solved the manpower problem, and his only significant change to the Schlieffen Plan was to limit the great flanking move to Belgium. Invading Holland, he thought, would leave a hostile country in his rear, whereas a neutral Holland would give Germany a "windpipe that enables us to breathe."[21] It is not clear why Moltke thought he needed a windpipe if the Schlieffen Plan was to bring about a short war, but once he dropped the swing through Holland, he denied his armies use of Holland's roads and railways; the massive German right wing would have to squeeze through the narrow Belgian funnel. This meant the Belgian city of Liège would have to be captured—with its four railway lines intact—in the first days of the war. Without those railways the German flanking maneuver would grind to a halt. Everything turned on the immediate capture of Liège and the uninterrupted use of Belgium's railroads.

Moltke's version of the Schlieffen Plan therefore called for an attack on Liège no later than the fourth day of mobilization, which meant going through Luxembourg on the second day. All through the prewar years, six brigades and supporting artillery were kept on a permanent war footing in the Aachen area, in easy reach of Liège. On 28 July, 29 July, and even as late as the morning of 30 July, Moltke resisted moving the attack group into position and revealing German intentions before they were certain of war. Once Germany mobilized, the Liège attack group would move through Luxembourg and invade Belgium. There would be no time for talk.

German officials and the foreign office knew, in a general way, that the army would attack France first and that the attack would go through Belgium. Jagow had warned Moltke in 1913 that an attack through Belgium would almost certainly bring Great Britain into the war. Could the plan be modified? Moltke promised to study the question. He arranged a staff study of the problem that concluded an attack through Belgium could not be avoided.[22] Jagow seems to have accepted this conclusion without further argument. The early attack on Liège, however, was a closely held secret. Bethmann did not learn about it until 31 July, and the German minister to Brussels did not know until 2 August.[23]

With Holland neutral, Moltke would have to move more than a million men and all their supplies over four railways through hostile Belgian territory. Moreover, he would have to move fast enough to take the French in the rear before they could swing north from the Franco-German frontier to face the Germans coming south. The maneuver would require packed trains moving at nineteen miles per hour at fixed intervals—180 trains per army corps—rolling steadily west around the clock. Once the attack was launched, the trains would have to keep rolling to supply the racing armies with food, replacements, and ammunition.[24] When France was defeated, the whole movement would have to be reversed to bring the Germans east in time to stop the Russians.

The general staff's planning was a model of technical proficiency and a tribute to the skills of its railway section. But it was madness to assume that such technical perfection could overcome the vagaries of war. Apart from its logistical flaws, Schlieffen's plan entailed enormous risks: Belgian resistance might disrupt rail traffic, the French might swing north in time, the Russians might overrun East Prussia, all Europe would be outraged by the violation of Belgian neutrality—and always there would be the unrelenting pressure of time. Germany had to mobilize the moment that war seemed likely; there could be no mistakes, and everything would have to go like clockwork.[25]

In 1913, despite Jagow's misgivings, the general staff dropped all plans for fighting a defensive war with limited aims on the model of the elder Moltke. When the crisis erupted in July 1914, Germany had only the Schlieffen Plan. For Germany, as for no other country, mobilization meant war.

A German army of some 87 divisions faced 62 French divisions in the west and more than 114 Russian divisions in the east, a combined total of 176 divisions. Even if Austria-Hungary put as many as 40 divisions into Galicia, Austro-German forces would still be outnumbered[26]—and the

Germans did not think much of the Austro-Hungarian divisions. Schlieffen had not even bothered to include them in his plans.

In Schlieffen's time, the Russian army was badly organized and badly equipped. Russia had a terrible railway system and was very slow to mobilize. When Moltke took over in 1906, war and revolution had decimated Russian military capability: it seemed reasonable to leave East Prussia virtually undefended while knocking France out of the war.

In the 1890s, Russian railways could barely move 200 trains per day to the frontier. Germany moved more than 650 trains a day over the Cologne bridges alone. By 1914, French money and French expertise had improved Russian carrying capacity to 360 trains a day, and the Russians planned to increase that number to 560 by 1917. A general mobilization still took thirty days in 1914, but thanks to improvements in the stationing of peacetime units and the new Period Preparatory to War, two-thirds of the Russian army would be in position by the eighteenth day. The Russians hoped to mobilize the entire army in eighteen days by 1917. The so-called Great Program also contemplated huge increases in Russian manpower; a 2 million strong peacetime army would almost equal Germany's total wartime effectives.

The German army had more than enough manpower to fight a war under the elder Moltke's defensive plans but not nearly enough for Schlieffen's great offensive concept. The army increases of 1911, 1912, and 1913 could not offset the growing Russian army and the increase in French effectives provided by France's three-year-service law. Moltke's right wing never had the three-to-one superiority over the French that military doctrine requires for offensive operations. Even if Moltke had the men, he could not increase the number of divisions on his right wing because fifty-four divisions were the maximum that could be deployed and supplied over the four Belgian railway lines. He used his new manpower to strengthen his left wing so that the French could not cut the line of communications of his circling right wing. He left only nine first-line and four reserve divisions to face thirty-eight Russian divisions in East Prussia. If Russian capabilities continued to improve, the Russians could be in Berlin before the Germans were in Paris.[27]

Nonetheless, Moltke and his staff spent eight years obsessively cementing every last detail of the plan. Chance, politics, enemy actions, changing power relations, Russian military reform, diplomatic damage—nothing was to affect even the most minute part of the Great Plan. If the Prussian general staff could not master the chaos of the modern world, it must be ready for the great fight to the finish: the Slavs against the Teutons.[28]

Moltke's uncle could have contemplated Russia's growing rail net and army with relative equanimity, confident of his own army's defensive capability. He could have adapted his military plans to Bethmann's July diplomacy, waiting out a Russian mobilization to see whether the Russians would incur the responsibility of attacking first. Under the Schlieffen Plan, East Prussia was stripped of troops in order to ensure the lightning-swift defeat of France, which made the growing size and speed of the Russian army a nightmare. If Russia ever mobilized, the German army could not afford to wait.[29]

Both Conrad and Moltke feared that the Austrian troops destined for Serbia (B Group) might be engaged in Serbia if Russia entered the war, leaving A Group to hold Galicia on its own. Moltke wanted A Group to launch an offensive to relieve East Prussia; Conrad wanted Moltke to launch an offensive south across the Narev to relieve A Group in Galicia. Each general had a defensive line that could not be held unless the other general launched a diversionary attack.

In 1909 Conrad had proposed that if Moltke would launch an offensive across the Narev River, he would attack with A Group in Galicia, whether B Group was back in time or not. Moltke knew that even with an Austrian offensive, a German offensive south across the Narev into Galicia would be suicidal. The attack would leave, at most, three or four divisions to face the entire Russian army at the Nieman River on the northeast frontier. Even if Moltke kept the entire German Eighth Army on the defensive along the Nieman, and even if he could defeat the French in six weeks, he would need a powerful Austrian offensive in Galicia to keep the Russians out of East Prussia.[30]

In the correspondence that followed, Moltke avoided answering Conrad's request for an East Prussian offensive, arguing that Austria's future would be settled in the west. Austria-Hungary should forget Serbia and concentrate on Russia until German forces were finished with France. Germany's Eighth Army, Romania's eight divisions, and the Austro-Hungarian forces could hold off the Russians; in any event, Germany would be finished with France in six weeks and come east in strength.[31]

Conrad would not be put off. He insisted that Moltke promise him an offensive in East Prussia. Finally, on 9 March 1909, Moltke gave in: "I will not hesitate to make the attack to support the simultaneous Austrian offensive. Your Excellency can count absolutely upon this assurance, which has been extensively considered."[32]

Moltke never intended to make this attack, but he had to be sure that the Austro-Hungarian army in Galicia would launch the offensive he needed to hold off the Russians. In every year that followed, Conrad got Moltke to reaffirm his commitment. After the Balkan wars of 1912 and 1913, Serbia was much stronger, Romania's eight divisions were no longer available, and Italy seemed less and less likely to fight alongside its allies. The correspondence between Conrad and Moltke ignored those developments; neither general was prepared to change his plans. Conrad wanted to crush Serbia, and Moltke wanted to crush France.

Moltke prayed that war would not come, but if it had to come, he hoped it would come while the Schlieffen Plan still had a chance. By 1914 he seems to have felt that Germany's situation, although not good, was probably better than it would be in the future.

24: The Russian Partial Mobilization

29 July

The Russian, German, and Austro-Hungarian governments were withdrawing reserves held in foreign banks. Gold and silver were in short supply, security prices fell, and the Berlin and the Brussels financial markets closed to prevent a complete collapse.[1] In some French and German cities there was a run on banks,[2] and the business community was demanding peace. Europe's press was edgy but not yet certain that a crisis was at hand.

Austro-Hungarian newspapers were beginning to perceive the growing Russian firmness, but that did not weaken their determination to make war on Serbia. The Budapest *Pester-Lloyd* said it all: "Austria-Hungary has burned her bridges, and no power on earth could change her course, not even her own will."[3]

British newspapers were dominated by the violence in Ireland. On Sunday morning, 26 July, a mixed force of police and English soldiers was returning to Dublin after trying to intercept an arms shipment when a crowd began throwing stones. Suddenly—and apparently without orders—the soldiers opened fire, leaving three dead and thirty-eight wounded. This was the main story in the English press on Monday and Tuesday. To the extent they covered the latest Balkan crisis, the English papers divided along party lines. The Conservative *Morning Post* asked on 30 July, "Must not England, if war is forced on Europe, stand by her friendships and play the game?" The Liberal *Manchester Guardian,* on the other hand, asked of Russia, "Is her national interest threatened? Is any substantial interest of hers at stake at all beyond the ambition to be regarded as the champion of the smaller Slav states?"[4] All shades of opinion, however, wanted to avoid war and supported Grey's mediation proposals.[5] This may have misled the Germans.

From 24 to 31 July, German newspaper reports from London carried headlines such as "English Press and Parliament Declare for Mediation," "English Press Favors Localization," and "Russia Hesitates–France Anxious–England disinterested." There were a few warnings—Grey had carefully

avoided promising neutrality, the British fleet had not dispersed after maneuvers—but they had little impact.[6] German papers continued to play the
loyal ally: "There is no better way to localize the war and to preserve the
peace of Europe than to show beyond the shadow of a doubt that the German army will mobilize at Russia's first move against Austria."[7]

The French press continued to be enthralled by the trial of Henriette
Caillaux, which ended on 28 July, the day Austria declared war on Serbia.
Afterward, it seemed to many Frenchmen that they had marched straight
from the courtroom to the trenches. Henriette Caillaux's lawyer, Maitre
Labori, pleaded temporary insanity and argued that there was no premedi-
tation, that she did not shoot to kill, and finally that Henriette did not kill
the unfortunate editor. It was the doctors, who could have saved Calmette,
who killed him by their incompetence. It was an emotionally charged trial
in which patriotic traditionalists bemoaned the divorce and adultery that
were destroying French population growth. They saw themselves defending France against immorality and decadence. As far as Joseph Caillaux
was concerned, the right was successful; he left the courtroom a ruined
man, and Poincaré and Viviani had no further worries about his return to
power. Henriette Caillaux was acquitted. Maitre Labori, a fierce warhorse
of the left, made a powerful and wholly illogical closing argument: "Let
us save our anger for the enemy outside . . . War is at our gates. . . .
Acquit Madame Caillaux."[8]

The Russians, annoyed that the French could be so preoccupied with a murder trial at a time of crisis, continued to prepare for the worst. On Wednesday morning, General Yanushkevich went to Tsarskoe Selo to get the
tsar's signature on two mobilization decrees—one partial, one general. At
9:30 A.M., Ambassador Pourtalès asked for an appointment with Sazonov,
saying he had an "agreeable communication." The foreign ministry official
who took the call remarked that Sazonov would be pleased to hear what the
ambassador had to say: "We have not been accustomed to hearing 'agreeable' news from Berlin lately."[9]

At 11:00 A.M. Pourtalès delivered his "agreeable communication." He
thanked Sazonov for offering "golden bridges" for Austria and reaffirmed
that Austria was not interested in Serbian territory. He also assured Sazonov
that Berlin was trying to persuade Vienna to speak frankly with the Russians
to demonstrate the "limited nature" of Austrian operations in Serbia. This
was Bethmann's way of implementing the kaiser's peace proposal.[10] The
primary goal of Pourtalès's communication was to persuade Sazonov that
there was no need to mobilize against Austria-Hungary.

*   *   *

Sazonov replied that although he was fully prepared to continue his talks with Vienna, there was no sign that Vienna was willing to talk. Reminding Pourtalès that Austria-Hungary had already mobilized, Sazonov said that Russia would be forced to mobilize the four military districts bordering on Austria-Hungary. The orders would go out that day.

Pourtalès begged Sazonov not to mobilize. The German and Austrian general staffs would not sacrifice their advantage in speed by letting Russia mobilize. Sazonov was all assurances: "Not the least thing" was to happen to Germany. Mobilization in Russia was far from meaning war, as it did in western European nations. Russian troops could remain under arms for weeks without crossing the frontier, but Russia had to be prepared for all eventualities, and he could not exclude an action against Austria. Pourtalès's final word was that though "the idea of a threat" was far from his mind, Sazonov had to be acquainted "with the obligations of our alliance with Austria."[11]

When he was done with Pourtalès, Sazonov met with his chief aides. Were the Germans really putting pressure on Vienna to negotiate, or were they only trying to get Russia to delay mobilization? The Russians concluded that even if Germany was sincere, it was not having much success in Vienna. They saw no reason to delay mobilization on the basis of German assurances.[12] Sazonov was confirmed in this view when he read Schebeko's report that Berchtold had refused to authorize further direct talks with St. Petersburg.[13] Schebeko, as we have seen, was mistaken. Berchtold had refused only to discuss the Serbian answer. But even if Schebeko had reported correctly, it might not have made much difference.

Pourtalès, meanwhile, was earnestly trying to persuade Buchanan that Russia was endangering the peace by mobilizing. When Buchanan reminded him of the harshness of the Austrian note, Pourtalès, following firm and repeated instructions from Berlin, said he could not discuss the Austro-Serbian problem. Buchanan then said that Germany could hardly expect Russia to accept the humiliation of an Austrian war on Serbia. If Russia did not mobilize, it would signal Austria that "she could go to any lengths and thus trade on Russia's desire for peace."[14] Buchanan conceded that further military measures by Russia would be dangerous and told Pourtalès that he had repeatedly given that warning to Sazonov.[15]

General Yanushkevich had returned from Tsarskoe Selo with the tsar's signature on both mobilization decrees. Nicholas had insisted, however, that the implementation of either decree would require "the fresh personal order of the tsar." He had also ordered Yanushkevich to tell Pourtalès that mobilization "did not constitute an act of hostility towards Germany" and that "Russia meant to maintain friendly relations with Germany."[16] Remembering

Pourtalès's agitation at the mere mention of a partial mobilization, Sazonov feared that the German ambassador might misunderstand such a message and alarm Berlin. He told Yanushkevich to deliver the tsar's message to Pourtalès's military attaché, Major Eggeling, instead.

Yanushkevich saw Major Eggeling at 3:00 P.M. Eggeling reported that Yanushkevich "gave me his word of honor in the most solemn manner and offered me written confirmation of the fact that up to the hour of 3 o'clock in the afternoon no mobilization had commenced anywhere, that is, the calling in of a single man or horse. He could give me no guarantees for the future, but could assure me most impressively that His Majesty, now as before, did not desire mobilization on the fronts along our borders." Eggeling did not believe Yanushkevich. He dismissed Russian assurances as "an attempt to mislead me as to the extent of the measures taken up to the present time." Pourtalès sent Eggeling's report to Berlin at 7:00 P.M.[17]

At about the time that Yanushkevich was talking to Eggeling, Sazonov saw Buchanan. Like most other diplomats, Buchanan knew that Russian military measures were extensive and that they were taking place along the German as well as the Austrian frontier. He therefore began by telling Sazonov "in confidence" that Jagow had assured Goschen in Berlin that Germany would not feel compelled to mobilize if Russia mobilized only against Austria. Sazonov replied that he was aware of that and it "was for this reason that it had been decided not to order the general mobilization which military authorities had strongly recommended."[18] There had been no such decision, but Sazonov had to be careful with the British, who were constantly warning him not to take provocative measures.

Buchanan then told Sazonov that Grey was prepared to wait with his four-power mediation to allow time for direct talks between St. Petersburg and Vienna. Sazonov responded that Berchtold had just rejected direct talks. Buchanan then mentioned a suggestion by San Giuliano in Rome that the four powers persuade Serbia to accept the Austro-Hungarian note in its entirety. A Serbian "agent" in Rome, according to reports, thought his government might accept Austrian demands unconditionally if certain points were explained.[19] The wily San Giuliano had also said that he did not expect Serbia to comply with its promises—the aim was to remove the threat of war—but Buchanan did not mention this detail. Sazonov said that although "he could not be more Servian than Servia," he thought the note would have to be toned down before Serbia could accept it.[20]

After this conversation with Buchanan, Sazonov called back Pourtalès to tell him that Austria had refused direct talks in St. Petersburg. Their only hope now was Grey's four-power mediation. They were not trying to subject Austria to a European court of arbitration, as Berlin feared, but Sazonov was "looking for a way out," and so "he was grasping at every straw." Pourtalès did not know Berlin's thoughts on Grey's proposal, but he did know that if Russia was hoping for a peaceful solution, mobilization would be a great mistake. Sazonov, he reported, "did not deny the imminence of mobilization, but stated that Russia was compelled by Austria to take this step." Mobilization, however, "was far from meaning war."[21]

If Russia was going to mobilize, Sazonov had to convince the Germans that they could safely permit it without declaring war. Pourtalès did his best to convince Sazonov that this was impossible for Germany. It is clear that Pourtalès thought they were talking only about a partial mobilization.

Sazonov saw Szápáry next. Vienna had become aware of their earlier misunderstanding, and Szápáry was instructed to tell Sazonov that although Berchtold was not prepared to discuss the Austro-Serbian quarrel with outside powers and was not prepared to negotiate on the basis of the Serbian answer, he would engage in the broadest possible exchange of views with Russia. Moreover, he was instructed to assure the Russian government that Vienna "had no wish to injure Russian interests, take Serbian territory or infringe Serbian sovereignty." Sazonov replied that even if Austria took no Serbian territory, a Serbian submission to the Austrian note "meant Serbian vassalage," which would "upset the balance of power in the Balkans and the latter was a Russian interest." When Szápáry insisted that Serbia was not a Russian question, Sazonov was blunt: "Russian interests were identical with those of Serbia."

Szápáry ignored this warning and turned to the question of mobilization, noting that "even a mere child in military matters could see that our southern corps constituted no threat to Russia." Sazonov replied that the tsar and the general staff were nonetheless alarmed and that the tsar was signing orders for "a mobilization on a considerable scale." Austria could be assured, however, that no attack was contemplated; the troops would stand in readiness in case Russian interests in the Balkans were threatened. Sazonov, of course, had just equated Russian interests with those of Serbia.[22]

The various ambassadors' reports of their talks with Sazonov during the course of Wednesday afternoon showed Sazonov edging toward the admission that the Russian mobilization might be general. With Buchanan he was precise: only a partial mobilization was in question. With Pourtalès he first mentioned a "mobilization on the Austrian frontier" and then spoke only of "mobilization," letting Pourtalès assume he meant a partial mobilization. With Szápáry, late in the day, Sazonov used the far more flexible phrase, "mobilization on a considerable scale."

During the night of 28–29 July, Austrian monitors on the Sava River fired on several defensive positions on the outskirts of Belgrade. The Serbians, thinking the Austrians were about to force a crossing and seize Belgrade, blew the bridge across the Sava. These were minor actions, but the report from Strandtmann, the Russian minister who was with the Serbian government in Nish, said, "The last hope is lost. Belgrade has been bombarded and the bridge over the Sava blown."[23] Spalajkovic, the Serbian minister in St. Petersburg, told the foreign ministry that the Austrian attack had already begun: they had blown the bridge and were bombarding Belgrade.[24]

Just as Sazonov was telling Szápáry that Russian mobilization did not mean war, Sazonov's telephone rang. He took the call and heard the news of the "bombardment of Belgrade." Hanging up, he turned furiously on Szápáry and told him, "You are only wanting to gain time by negotiations and are meanwhile advancing and bombarding an unprotected city. What else do you want to conquer when you are in possession of the capital?" When Szápáry replied that an attack on Serbia was the reverse of a move against Russia, Sazonov exploded, "What is the good of our continuing our conversation if you act in this manner?" Szápáry left. There was no hope for a calm discussion, he reported.[25]

Bethmann always knew that backing Austria was a gamble, but a gamble that could work: "A quick fait accompli, then a friendly gesture to the Entente," and they would make it. He was stimulated by the crisis and buoyed by the cheering crowds. "He is completely changed," wrote Bethmann's aide, "he does not have a minute's time to complain and is therefore alert, active, lively and without anxiety."[26] But the news on Wednesday was bad all day.

The Austrians were terribly slow to move and, late in the afternoon, Berlin received Major Eggeling's unsettling report that the Russians were deceiving them, as well as an equally unsettling wire from General Chelius saying that the tsar's entourage regarded war as inevitable. "They do not want any war," he wired, "and would like to be able to avoid it, and regret that no Power was successful in restraining Austria."[27] Eggeling had closed his report with a list of troop movements showing that several Russian divisions were moving to frontier assembly points.[28] The German general staff situation report of 29 July noted widespread mobilization measures, on both the German and the Austrian frontiers.[29]

Bethmann received a long memorandum from General von Moltke, noting that Russia was preparing to mobilize—not only in the four southern districts bordering Austria but in the north as well. Austria, he warned, "cannot enter upon a war with Serbia without securing herself against an attack by Russia. That means she will be forced to mobilize the other half of her army." Then "the collision between herself and Russia will become inevitable. But that, for Germany, is the *casus foederis* . . . she, too, must mobilize."

"Russia," Moltke continued, "assures Germany that she wishes to undertake nothing against her; but she knows perfectly well that Germany could not remain inactive in the event of a belligerent collision between her ally and Russia." France and Russia seemed to be "moving hand in hand as far as regards their preparations. . . . Thus the military situation is becoming from day to day more unfavorable for us, and can, if our prospective opponents prepare themselves further, unmolested, lead to fateful consequences for us."[30] Berchtold and Bethmann had hoped to keep Russia still, present the Russians with a fait accompli in Serbia, and force the tsar to make the decision for peace or war. Now Moltke was telling Bethmann that in light of Russian and French military preparations, Germany might not be able to wait. Time was running out.

Bethmann telegraphed Schoen in Paris, instructing him to warn the French that a continuation of their military activities would force Germany to declare the State of Imminent War, which, although not yet mobilization, "would nevertheless increase the tension."[31] His wire to Pourtalès in St. Petersburg was much more blunt: "Further continuation of Russian mobilization measures would force us to mobilize, and in that case a European war could scarcely be prevented."[32]

Pourtalès delivered this jolt to Sazonov at seven in the evening. Still angry over his shouting match with Szápáry and the news that Belgrade was being bombarded, Sazonov received the German ambassador for the third time that day. Pourtalès insisted that his communication "did not imply a threat" and was "simply a friendly communication," but its effect on Sazonov was electric. He thought that such a warning, so soon after he had informed Pourtalès that Russia was about to mobilize against Austria, was nothing less than an ultimatum. In great excitement, Sazonov repeated that a Russian mobilization did not mean Russia intended to go to war, "but that it intended only to enter upon a state of armed neutrality."[33] Sazonov said he would convey the message to the tsar immediately; once again the two men parted angrily.

After the war, Sazonov wrote that 29 July was a critical day. "On that day we learned for a fact that an armed conflict between Austria, Germany, Russia and France was inevitable. It would have been impossible to say it more plainly than the German Ambassador had done during his conversation with me. . . . Because we mobilized against Austria by way of precaution and in response to her mobilization, Germany threatened to mobilize her army against us, with the warning that this would mean war."[34]

As soon as Pourtalès left, Sazonov called in his chief aides. As they were arriving, the telephone rang; it was the tsar. He wanted to inform Sazonov of the reassuring wire he had just received from the kaiser, affirming his deep friendship and pledging to exert "my utmost influence to induce the Austrians to deal straightly" with Russia.[35] Sazonov then read the tsar his notes on his most recent talk with Pourtalès. Both men were baffled by the contrast between the kaiser's conciliatory tone and Pourtalès's sharp warning. The tsar declared that he would immediately ask the kaiser for an explanation. Meanwhile, he granted Sazonov permission to discuss the question of mobilization with General Sukhomlinov, the war minister, and the army chief of staff, General Yanushkevich.

The three men met in Yanushkevich's office while two staff officers and a foreign ministry official waited in an adjoining room. The tension was terrible. Everyone believed that Russian military readiness was critical and that a partial mobilization would cause a fatal delay. Given the likelihood that Russia would soon be at war with Germany, they concluded that "the risk could not be accepted of delaying a general mobilization later by effecting a partial mobilization now." At about 8:00 P.M., Sazonov called the tsar and obtained his permission to declare a general mobilization. That decision, wrote Sazonov's administrative chief, "was received with enthusiasm."[36]

Once the tsar signed the mobilization decree, it had to be countersigned by the ministers of the interior, war, and the navy. Only then could mobilization actually be ordered. General Dobrolski immediately went around to collect the necessary signatures. War Minister Sukhomlinov did not really want to mobilize, but his courage failed him and he signed. He was, he later wrote, only a soldier whose duty it was to obey orders, not "to warn the tsar against war." He would have been accused of cowardice.[37]

Dobrolski next obtained the signature of N. A. Maklakov, the minister of the interior, a devout man whose office was full of candles, holy pictures, and icons. As soon as Dobrolski explained his mission, Maklakov began to talk of revolution. "This war cannot be popular in the heart of the masses, and revolutionary ideas are more comprehensible to the people than the idea of victory over Germany." But there was the tsar's signature and there was Dobrolski. Maklakov crossed himself, made some room on a table full of candles and icons, and signed, saying, "One cannot avoid fate."

Admiral I. K. Grigorovitch, the minister of the navy, could not believe what he was being asked to do. "What? War with Germany? Our fleet is in no condition to take on the Germans." Grigorovitch insisted on calling Sukhomlinov for confirmation of the mobilization order. Sukhomlinov confirmed it and Grigorovitch signed. Dobrolski was at the St. Petersburg telegraph office with all three signatures by 9:00 P.M. The official in charge had earlier been notified that urgent state messages were to be transmitted; all the lines were clear. Taking the mobilization decree from the general, he gave copies to a bank of typists, who prepared the mobilization telegrams that would be simultaneously transmitted to every military district in Russia.

Dobrolski waited in the huge room full of transmitting machines while the typists tapped away. The telegrams were ready a little after 10:00 P.M. The operators were about to transmit them when a telephone call came from Yanushkevich. Dobrolski was to hold the transmissions. A captain from the general staff arrived and explained that he had been chasing Dobrolski all over St. Petersburg trying to deliver the tsar's order not to dispatch the general mobilization telegram. General mobilization, the captain said, was canceled. The tsar himself had issued the order to proceed instead with partial mobilization "on the lines previously laid down."

General Dobrolski had no choice. He collected the mobilization telegrams and ordered that new telegrams for partial mobilization be prepared. Those went out at midnight.[38]

After reading the Serbian answer to Vienna, the kaiser, in a burst of optimism, decided that war was not necessary. Then he learned that Austria-Hungary had already declared war and that he had the problem of persuading Russia to sit still while Austria-Hungary invaded Serbia. Now, on Wednesday morning, he got the tsar's telegram asking him to keep Austria from going too far. He had Jagow draft a reply, made a few corrections, and sent it in English and uncoded. He told the tsar that Austria planned only a very limited war—although he had no commitment from Austria on that score. Austrian actions, he argued, were designed solely to guarantee Serbia's compliance with the Austrian demands. He was doing all he could to facilitate a direct understanding between Russia and Austria-Hungary, but "military measures on the part of Russia which would be looked on by Austria as threatening would precipitate a calamity we both wish to avoid and jeopardize my position as mediator which I readily accepted on your appeal to my friendship and my help. Willy."[39]

When the tsar got the wire at 9:40 P.M., he immediately summoned Count Vladimir Fredericks, a court official. Fredericks wanted no war with Germany. After the war he wrote that it was Sazonov who persuaded the tsar to order general mobilization by arguing that it was the best way to save the peace. Sazonov, argued Fredericks, never understood that for the Germans a Russian mobilization meant war. Fredericks claims that he told Nicholas on Wednesday night that general mobilization was an irreparable act that would precipitate a war. The tsar replied that he did not want to be responsible for a slaughter and then remained silent for quite a while. Finally, he declared that he would cancel the general mobilization.

When the tsar's order came down, Sukhomlinov and Yanushkevich both warned that after a partial mobilization, any attempt at general mobilization would be much too slow. The tsar stubbornly resisted their pleas. He ordered Yanushkevich to suspend the general mobilization and to order a partial mobilization along the lines laid down by the 26 July Council of Ministers.[40] This was the order Dobrolski received sometime after 10:00 P.M.

The tsar's order is almost the only example one can find in July 1914 where the tsar exercised active leadership. Most of the time he was eerily remote, as if the crisis were happening somewhere else. He never went to the capital. He continued with the leisurely schedule of a country gentleman. When he was not in Tsarskoe Selo, he was at his summer residence at Peterhof, both nearly an hour away from St. Petersburg. He showed none of the emotional strain and excitement that is revealed in the kaiser's marginal comments, but then he never did. His ministers were always astounded at the remote calm with which he could receive the most calamitous news. His diary never rises beyond laconic detachment.

On 28 July, for example, when Austria declared war on Serbia, he wrote, "Received Sukhomlinov and Janushkevich with their reports. Lunch. Received reports of clerical congress at 2:30 P.M., then tennis. Tea with daughters at 5 P.M. Received Sazonov at 6 P.M. who told me that at noon today Austria declared war on Serbia."

The next day, as Sazonov and the military agonized over the mobilization decision, the tsar was annoyed that they kept bothering him: "Received Goremykin [the prime minister] in the morning. At palace at 12:15 where I promoted guards to ensign. Played tennis during the day; the weather was superb. But the day was extraordinarily busy, they calling me on the telephone all the time, now Sazonov, now Sukhomlinov or Janushkevich. Apart from that, I had urgent telegraphic correspondence with Wilhelm. In the evening I received Tatistchev, whom I will send to Berlin tomorrow."[41] General Ilja Tatistchev was the tsar's personal envoy to the kaiser, the Russian counterpart to General von Chelius. There is not a word about mobilization, not a hint of anxiety.

But neither is there a hint of his more personal anxieties. Nicholas's son had fallen and injured himself; he was bleeding and in great pain. The diary is silent on the boy's suffering. Nothing ever interrupted the flat, dry tone of its entries.

*   *   *

In Berlin, Theodor Wolff, owner and editor of the *Berliner Tageblatt,* thought his government was blind to the magnitude of the crisis. He was in the foreign office on Wilhelmstrasse almost every day now. The foreign office seemed to him like a great casino where players faced destruction gaily as they gambled away their last possessions. When he learned from Wilhelm von Stumm, the foreign office political director, on Tuesday, 28 July, that Germany would reject Grey's conference proposal because it was "impossible now, after [Austria] had begun to act, to force her to come to a stop," Wolff was beside himself. They were shutting off the only way out! Stumm sat silent as Wolff berated him, shrugging his shoulders and saying only that everything possible had been done.

Wolff saw Stumm again on Wednesday, after Austria had declared war on Serbia. Stumm thought the most serious problem was the continuing military activity in Russia. He hoped that Germany's own military would not lose its nerve and insist that Germany mobilize. English neutrality, Stumm said, depended on Russia attacking first. "What was appalling," recalled Wolff, "was simply the helplessness in the presence of the onward roll of events, the poverty of resource, the passiveness of these people, who had worked out a plan of strategy and now that it had gone awry did not know what to do. . . ."[42]

25: THE VIEW FROM PARIS
Poincaré and Viviani Return

France's ambassador to Russia, Maurice Paléologue, was a patriot of the right and proudly so. He could see no alternative to the Russian alliance; he thought three years of military service was critical to the survival of France; he adored aristocrats. His journal and his memoirs are full of the names and titles of the exalted personages with whom he wined and dined. Eager to be accepted by the Russian aristocracy, he identified completely with their Russian patriotism, their monarchical outlook, their distaste for Austria, and their fear of Germany. He believed that war with Germany was inevitable and imminent, and he told everyone who would listen that war was coming. France and Russia could not delay their military preparations; anything less than solidarity and firmness by England, France, and Russia would mean humiliation or defeat.

Paléologue was in Paris in June 1914 during the struggle over a new government and the battle for the three-year-service law. To everyone who mattered he urged three points: (1) war with Germany was inevitable and imminent—he gave peace no more than six months; (2) he had promised Tsar Nicholas that France would retain the three-year law and that he would resign if it was repealed; and (3) France would lose the Russian alliance if it repealed the three-year law.[1]

Paris newspapers headlined the scandal of a French ambassador threatening to resign over a piece of legislation, but Paléologue wrote proudly in his journal that important people congratulated him on his efforts. One politician told him that Viviani would have capitulated on the three-year law "but for my courageous intervention." "It is now a question," the admiring friend went on, "whether in several years there will still be a France."[2] It was a heady and self-dramatizing world in which Paléologue moved.

Paléologue had no great regard for Viviani, whose democratic and socialist mind could not comprehend the autocratic and military milieu that prevailed in Berlin, St. Petersburg, and Vienna.[3] Like Poincaré, he regarded

Viviani as a phrasemaker and a crowd pleaser—emotional, unstable, and not to be relied upon. Viviani did not understand international power politics. He had to be bludgeoned into supporting the three-year law, and God alone knew what he might do if he suddenly got word that Russia was ordering a general mobilization. Paléologue handled Viviani accordingly.

The full flavor of Paléologue's sense of himself comes in a passage in which he is explaining to Sazonov his unique position in Russia: "I do want you to realize that I am in a position which is unprecedented for an ambassador. The head of the State and the head of the Government are at sea. I can only communicate with them at intervals and through very uncertain channels; as their knowledge of the situation is incomplete, they cannot send me any instructions. The ministry in Paris is without its chief, and its means of communication with the President of the Republic and the President of the Council are as irregular and defective as mine. My responsibility is thus enormous." And so it was. Because of this responsibility, Paléologue claims, he urged Sazonov "to leave nothing undone to save the peace" and even got an astounded Sazonov to agree "to accept all the proposals France and England may make to you to save the peace."[4] Unfortunately, this was not the line that Paléologue took at the time.

As documents were published after the war, the evidence became overwhelming that Paléologue had done nothing to restrain Sazonov and that he had misled his own government on the timing and extent of Russian mobilization. Paléologue answered his critics with a virtual admission of the charges. He said that the French army general staff and the French government were in deadly fear of a German attack—which, in fact, very nearly succeeded. They were aware that Russia must begin its offensive in East Prussia as quickly as possible. "If," Paléologue argued, "in this situation, the responsible head of the government, Viviani, or I on my own initiative, had required the Russian general staff to alter the colossal machinery of mobilization, wouldn't we stand accused today of having had illusions in the face of an imminent German attack? Wouldn't they have said that we waited until the Germans were in Saint-Quentin before taking practical measures for France's salvation?"[5] "They" might well have said precisely that, given the nature of postwar recriminations, but in July 1914 Paléologue did not give his government the information necessary to make an informed decision.

In any event, Paléologue insisted that he was Poincaré's particular friend, and Sazonov had no reason to doubt that Paléologue's unqualified support was an official declaration of French policy.[6]

Poincaré and Viviani did not hear of Austria's declaration of war until Wednesday, 29 July, when the *La France* arrived off Dunkerque at eight in the morning. At nine o'clock they transferred to a small steam packet to go ashore. As they drew near, Poincaré could see that the shoreline and the quays were thick with people waving hats and handkerchiefs and shouting, *"Vive Poincaré!"* and *"Vive la France!"* Poincaré was stunned. The full extent of his isolation at sea suddenly became clear; he could not grasp that France was facing war with Germany.[7] The French public, on the other hand, released from the thrall of the Caillaux trial and shocked at the Austrian declaration of war, exploded with emotion, part relief at the return of the government, part patriotic defiance of the Germans, part national solidarity.

Poincaré was not ready for such emotion. In town and village during the whole of the three-hour train ride from Dunkerque to Paris, people ranged themselves along the tracks, waving flags, shouting, demonstrating. "[W]e saw the inhabitants massed on both sides of the way, shouting without ceasing the same greetings, the same cheers, the same vows of peace, the same promises of courage and resignation."[8] The nation felt itself facing the German menace once again. Poincaré did not. Some witnesses portray him as deeply skeptical of the war scare, others as saying that war was unavoidable; he himself probably did not know what he believed.

Abel Ferry, a young foreign ministry official, met Poincaré with the latest dispatches. Poincaré and Viviani had instructed Bienvenu-Martin to consult freely with his colleagues in the ministries of war, interior, and finance if a crisis should arise in their absence. It now appeared that the ministers had acted very vigorously indeed. On their special train to Paris, Ferry reviewed a long list of measures taken to prepare France for mobilization. Some 100,000 crack troops in Morocco had been ordered to assemble on the coast for shipment to France. French citizens and westerners were to abandon the interior of Morocco and go to the coastal cities, where they could be more easily protected.[9]

As the train rolled on and Ferry read aloud and commented on the dispatches, neither Poincaré nor Viviani wanted to accept that war was imminent. Was it not a little extreme to start bringing troops back from Morocco? Ferry explained that these things took time and planning; Poincaré and Viviani reluctantly agreed.[10]

At the Paris station they were greeted by a huge demonstration arranged by the ardent nationalist and eminent novelist Maurice Barrès, who led a delegation from the League of Patriots. All government ministers were on hand, and the crowd had been waiting for hours. War Minister Adolphe Messimy, carried away by the patriotic emotion that filled the streets, told Poincaré, "Mr. President, you are going to see Paris; it is magnificent." From the train station to the presidential palace, crowds lined the way and leaned from windows and balconies, shouting and cheering. Poincaré was deeply moved. "Many people had tears in their eyes and I could hardly hold back my own. From thousands of throats arose repeated shouts of: *Vive la France! Vive la Républic! Vive le President!* . . . The simplicity, the grandeur, the enthusiasm, the unity, the solemnity, all combined to make that reception something unforgettable." He could not help adding, "How far from all this is the Caillaux affair."[11]

The crowd's mood was infectious. Newspapers were full of patriotic determination, and *Echo de Paris* argued that "for every Serbian soldier killed on the Morava one more Prussian soldier can be sent to the Moselle. . . . It is for us to grasp this truth and draw the consequences from it before disaster overtakes Serbia."[12]

Bertie was annoyed by such patriotic excess, but he did not think that the French public would "allow itself to be worked up to warlike excitement." He closed his report by noting that the state of the financial market was causing anxiety.[13] In his diary that night he wrote, "The news to-night is less favourable than earlier in the day." The Austrians would not talk to the Russians, the Germans would not cooperate on mediation, and the Italian government was saying that only England could prevent war by announcing its solidarity with France and Russia. Bertie still did not think Serbia was worth fighting about.[14]

Poincaré and Viviani were on the train from Dunkerque when Ambassador Izvolsky delivered a note to the foreign ministry informing the French government that Russia would mobilize its four southern military districts against Austria. This announcement did not provoke undue alarm. The Russian government had declared its intention the day before, and Jagow had assured Jules Cambon that a partial mobilization not directed against Germany would not provoke a German mobilization.

Izvolsky's message also reported that direct talks with Vienna had been broken off. It was therefore necessary "that England bring its mediation into action as rapidly as possible and that Austrian military actions be stopped immediately." Otherwise, Austria would simply destroy Serbia while the Powers talked.[15] Once in Paris, Viviani immediately wired London supporting the Russian call for prompt English mediation.[16]

Poincaré called a council of ministers for 5:30 P.M. They met for two hours and agreed to meet every morning for the duration of the crisis. Poincaré felt he had to keep an eye on Viviani; he was afraid the ex-Socialist would be "hesitant and faint-hearted." His other ministers, he thought, were ready to do what was necessary.[17]

The ministers had no sooner seated themselves when a message arrived stating that the German ambassador had an urgent communication for Viviani. Excusing himself, Viviani went out to meet with Ambassador Schoen, who delivered the warning Bethmann had sent earlier in the day: France was of course at liberty to take whatever military measures it wished, but then Germany would have to declare a State of Imminent War—and of course the German government did not want to alarm the public.

As Viviani reported the talk, he replied only that "France is calm and resolute."[18] Schoen, however, reported a more extensive conversation. He claimed Viviani tried to convince him that French military precautions were very limited. Viviani also told him that France would have no objection if Germany did the same—although he, too, would regret the "alarming effect on public opinion." Viviani, according to Schoen, urged "the most speedy prosecution possible" of the English mediation proposal, which would be the surest way of decreasing tension.[19] If Schoen's report is correct, it looks as if Viviani was more anxious to reassure the Germans than he was prepared to admit to his fellow ministers and the formidable Poincaré.

By the end of the day, Izvolsky was very pleased with the French attitude. The government was firm and had wide support, and Viviani told him that he had informed Schoen that as much as France wanted peace, it was determined "to proceed in complete unity with its allies and friends." Izvolsky also noted that French newspapers were agreed that France "cannot remain indifferent." French solidarity with Russia, he said, "simply does not come under discussion."[20]

In assuring Izvolsky of French solidarity, neither Viviani nor anyone else in Paris had any idea that the Russians were about to order a general mobilization. Sazonov had never spoken of anything but a partial mobilization, and then only if Austria invaded Serbia. Viviani saw no reason to caution Izvolsky, although perhaps he should have. Like everyone else, he thought that if Russia mobilized only its southern military districts, talks could go on.

Paléologue sent a wire from St. Petersburg that arrived in Paris at 8:40 P.M. After reporting that Austria had rejected direct talks with Russia, Paléologue wrote, "Moreover, the Russian general staff confirms that Austria is accelerating its military preparations against Russia." This was not true. Conrad was far too obsessed with Serbia to deal with Russia—but then, every power exaggerated the threat to itself. Paléologue went on: "Consequently, the order to mobilize the thirteen army corps destined to operate against Austria will be dispatched tonight."[21] Paléologue filed his report at 6:14 P.M., St. Petersburg time, but the Russian government had not yet decided to mobilize. Sazonov did not get the tsar's permission to order mobilization until after 8 P.M., and that order was for a general—not a partial—mobilization.

The Russians had announced the previous evening that they would declare a partial mobilization the next day, and Izvolsky had reported this intention at eleven o'clock that morning. Why would Paléologue report a partial mobilization that had already been announced but not yet ordered? Perhaps he anticipated events in the general confusion of rumor and alarm, or perhaps, as Albertini believes, Paléologue tried to conceal the fact that a general mobilization was being considered because he feared that Paris would instruct him to warn Sazonov against it.[22]

On Wednesday, 29 July, it was widely known in St. Petersburg that general mobilization was under consideration. Baron R. R. Rosen, a conservative antiwar diplomat, remembered that he and his friends in and out of the government were concerned that the government might give such an order. Rosen expressed his fears to an imperial minister, who agreed: the only hope of avoiding war—and this a slender one—was to limit the Russian response to a partial mobilization against Austria.[23] If the scope of the impending mobilization was a matter of general discussion in St. Petersburg social and political circles, it is hard to believe that Paléologue knew nothing of it. On the other hand, Buchanan never knew.

Paléologue was perfectly capable of misleading Paris, and later that night and during the course of the following day he did withhold critical information on Russian mobilization. But it is also possible that Sazonov misled Paléologue just as he misled Buchanan, his own ambassadors, and other governments. Buchanan, who certainly cannot be suspected of attempting to deceive London, sent a report on his talk with Sazonov a few hours after Paléologue sent his telegram announcing a partial mobilization, by which time Buchanan could have known that the tsar had signed a mobilization decree. But he reported what Paléologue reported: "Order for partial mobilization was signed today."[24] Again, the problem is one of timing. What the tsar signed was an order for general mobilization, which was not rescinded in favor of partial mobilization until nearly midnight.

While it seems fairly clear that Sazonov lied to Buchanan, it is not clear what he told Paléologue. We know that when Paléologue wired Paris saying Russia was about to decree a partial mobilization, no decision had been made. Only after Pourtalès delivered his warning to Sazonov, and only after Sazonov had obtained the tsar's consent to mobilize, was general mobilization decreed.

Later Wednesday night, Sazonov sent Nicolai Alexandrovich Basili, a young foreign ministry official, to the French embassy to inform Paléologue that a general mobilization order would go out that night. Basili gave an account of this errand in his memoirs, and Raymond Recouly made a detailed reconstruction based on interviews in his 1922 book, *Les Heures Tragiques d'Avant-Guerre*. Basili told Paléologue that general mobilization was being ordered, and he reviewed all the technical difficulties that precluded partial mobilization.

Paléologue now had a problem. He would certainly have to inform Paris of the general mobilization, but he had already sent a wire announcing an impending partial mobilization when, in fact, no such decision had been made. He eased through this dilemma as best he could by drafting a telegram summarizing Pourtalès's warning to Sazonov and concluding, "The tone in which Count Pourtalès acquitted himself of the notification has decided the Russian government: 1. this very night to order the mobilization of thirteen corps destined to operate against Austria; 2. secretly to commence general mobilization."[25] "Secretly to commence" is not quite the same thing as "ordering," but Paléologue may have been reluctant to be too precise. There was, of course, no order for partial mobilization, and such an order would have made no sense if the Russians were secretly commencing a general mobilization.

When Paléologue had finished preparing his draft, Basili informed him that since the orders for general mobilization would not be posted in the streets until the next morning, the order must not be known in Berlin before it became public in Russia. Wire traffic from St. Petersburg was normally routed through Berlin, and a somewhat embarrassed Basili had to explain to the French ambassador that the French diplomatic code was no longer secure "and that there is every reason to believe that your message will be known immediately to the Germans." Paléologue was startled and probably not too happy to have a young diplomat tell him his diplomatic code was not secure. Basili insisted that the telegram be sent to Paris in a Russian code "of absolute security." The first secretary in Paléologue's embassy was an old friend of Basili's, and it was decided that the two men would go to Basili's office, where a Russian coding clerk would encode the wire with a Russian cipher.[26]

Paléologue's first secretary and the Russian code clerk were just finishing their work when Basili rushed in to announce that the tsar had canceled the general mobilization and was ordering partial mobilization instead. Immediately afterward, General Laguiche came racing from the French embassy with the same message: General mobilization had been canceled. It was now near midnight. Since Paléologue had ordered the first secretary to send the wire, the poor secretary was at a loss as to what to do. It is not clear why he did not call Paléologue directly, and it is one of the minor mysteries of this affair that in all accounts, Paléologue disappeared from the scene once the telegram left his embassy. In any event, Sazonov personally confirmed the cancellation, and the first secretary screwed up his courage and deleted the last six words: "and secretly to commence general mobilization."[27]

At some time after midnight, therefore, Paris got a second wire from Paléologue announcing a partial mobilization.[28] It must have been a little puzzling at the time, but it seems to have been forgotten in the rush of events. Paléologue, however, never notified Paris that on the night of Wednesday, 29 July, Russia had ordered a general mobilization without the "previous agreement" stipulated in their military convention. Paléologue blandly explained that omission in his memoir by saying that since the tsar had canceled the general mobilization, he "informed Paris of the mobilization only of the thirteen Russian corps destined for eventual operations against Austria." Paléologue's memoir also recounts that he told Basili, "I still think that your General Staff should take no step without previous discussion with the French General Staff."[29] Basili's memoir contains no such warning, and Paléologue's dispatches do not report it.

Before the tsar reversed his general mobilization order, Sazonov had to explain to Paris what he was doing. He instructed Izvolsky to say that since Russia could not comply with the German demand to stop arming, "it only remains for us to speed up our armaments and reckon with the probable inevitability of war." Sazonov may have hoped to slide by the need for a previous agreement by referring to his general mobilization as a "speed up" of armaments.

Sazonov also asked Izvolsky to convey "our sincere gratitude for the declaration, which the French ambassador made to me in his government's name, that we may count in full measure on the allied support of France."[30] That declaration was Paléologue's statement on Tuesday that he had been instructed to assure Sazonov "of the complete readiness of France to fulfill its alliance obligations in case of need."[31] Sazonov had no way of knowing that Paléologue had been instructed to say only that France would support Russia "in the interest of the general peace,"[32] which had quite a different thrust. Sazonov may also have hoped that Paléologue's declaration would constitute the necessary previous agreement. In any case, the message now arrived that Russia, faced with the "probable inevitability of war," was relying on Paléologue's assurance of support. Izvolsky received this wire an hour or so after midnight. He assumed that Sazonov was referring to a partial mobilization, but he nonetheless decided not to wait until morning.

War Minister Messimy was sound asleep in his Paris apartment at two o'clock Thursday morning when the war ministry telephoned to say that the Russian military attaché was urgently requesting to see him. Messimy recalled in his memoir that he had gone to bed only a few hours earlier and that he roused himself unwillingly, trying to shake off sleep and swearing at Russians "who never go to bed . . . and never get up." Lieutenant Colonel Alexei Ignatiev soon arrived in full dress uniform, very formal and grave and not at all his usual exuberant self. Excusing himself for rousing Messimy in the middle of the night, Ignatiev explained that he had an urgent message from Ambassador Izvolsky. The tsar had decided upon a partial mobilization of the four military districts bordering Galicia in the south, and Izvolsky wanted to know France's reaction to this decision. "I cannot return to the ambassador without an answer," said Ignatiev.

"My dear friend," said Messimy, "you know very well that I cannot give you an answer. The question is beyond my competence, it is a matter of government policy. The Ambassador should address himself to M. Viviani. . . ." Ignatiev then told the minister that "his Excellency is at the Quai d'Orsay at this very moment; but he told me to inform you officially at the same time."

Messimy was now thoroughly awake. "The ambassador is at Viviani's house! Give me time to telephone him!" Messimy went to another room and called Viviani, who had also just been awakened and was about to go to Poincaré. His aggravated nervousness, which according to Messimy became a permanent state in the month of August, exploded over the telephone.

"The damn Russians are sleepwalkers as well as boozers. . . . They just don't want to have to get up in the morning." Viviani was angry, and he was not prepared to give the Russians an immediate answer. They would discuss the matter in council in the morning. Meanwhile, Messimy was to tell Ignatiev that his government must "commit no stupidities and above all avoid any shooting! They will have to slow down the mobilization of the four districts. . . . Tell them to keep calm. Recommend sangfroid."

Returning to Ignatiev, Messimy raised the matter of the required previous agreement. "Do you think it conforms to the letter of our agreements to mobilize four army corps in the south, even with an Austrian declaration of war on Serbia, without giving us notice?" Without waiting for an answer, Messimy turned immediately to the main French concern: "Be careful! Germany is not only your principal enemy, it is your only one, absolutely the only one, just as it is our only one. Austria does not count; get that in your head. Don't, under the pretext that you are the defenders of the Slavs, fall into the trap the Germans have set for you." Whether Messimy spoke as bluntly to Ignatiev as he claims in his memoir may be doubted, but he was clear that he wanted the Russians in East Prussia, not in Galicia.

Messimy told Ignatiev that Russia must slow down the mobilization and begged him to urge his government to stay "calm, calm, calm!" Ignatiev said that he understood but added that mobilizations could not be speeded up or slowed down; once ordered, everything was automatic. Messimy replied that although this might be true for a full general mobilization, a partial mobilization was different. The French government was formally asking Russia to cease any mass transport of troops; better, the Russian government should formally announce the suspension of all troop movements to the Austrian frontier. "In any case," he concluded, "see me again this evening," then added, "if possible before two in the morning!"[33]

Viviani, meanwhile, had roused Poincaré. Viviani knew something was wrong. He had instructed Paléologue to say that France was prepared to do all in its power to support Russia in the interests of peace. Now Sazonov was saying that war was probably inevitable, that Russia was speeding up its armaments, and that he expected French support. Poincaré had barely gotten out of bed when Viviani arrived with Sazonov's wire, complaining that the Russian was putting "rather a wide meaning on any assurances which M. Paléologue may have given him." Whatever Paléologue said, it certainly did not correspond to the instruction Viviani had sent from the *La France* two days ago, and "it was important to lose no time in making things perfectly clear."[34]

Three hours later, at 7 A.M. Thursday, wires went out to the French ambassadors at St. Petersburg and London saying that Russia was going to "expedite her arming and considers war as imminent, that she counts on the help of France as an ally, and that she considers it desirable that England should join France and Russia without loss of time." "France," Viviani instructed them, "is resolved to fulfill all the obligations of her alliance," but, he added for Paléologue, "as I told you in my telegram of the 27th of this month, the Government of the Republic is determined to neglect no effort . . . in the interest of the general peace. . . . I therefore think it would be well that, in taking any precautionary measures of defense which Russia thinks must go on, she should not immediately take any step which may offer to Germany a pretext for a total or partial mobilization of her forces."[35] Izvolsky was given the substance of the telegram and promptly wired Sazonov.[36] Viviani had reacted exactly as Paléologue had feared.

Nobody got much sleep that night. General Joffre received reports that the Germans were cutting down trees and putting up barbed wire, strengthening patrols, moving covering forces to the frontier, and generally acting as if they were getting ready to mobilize. These reports were highly exaggerated. The Germans were not moving covering forces to the frontier; they had not even declared a state of readiness. Their measures were no different from French measures and were precautionary in exactly the way in which French measures were precautionary.

Joffre, however, was convinced that the Germans were preparing "in their methodical way" and that France must get ready "without a moment's delay." He saw Messimy at seven o'clock Thursday morning and asked permission to put French covering forces on the frontier at full wartime strength to prevent a sudden German incursion. Messimy promised to raise the matter at the council scheduled for 9:30 that morning.[37]

Ignatiev talked again with Messimy. Both Messimi and Viviani had insisted that massive troop movements be suspended; Ignatiev wanted to be sure that the French were not insisting on suspending the partial mobilization altogether. He asked Messimy what the French expected Russia to do.

At this point the French knew only that Russia was ordering a partial mobilization in the south and that it was "speeding up" its armaments. Because Paléologue was not keeping Paris properly informed, French civilian leaders—whatever Messimy and Joffre may have known—had no way of guessing that Russia was considering a general mobilization and was taking preparatory measures along the German frontier. Messimy repeated that Russia should announce a cessation of troop movements to the Austrian frontier, and he again suggested that they suspend the mobilization. Neither of these steps, he went on, would prevent Russia from continuing and even accelerating its military preparations. Messimy had been pushing French preparations without announcing a mobilization, and he may have thought that the Russian Period Preparatory to War provided for similar measures.[38]

Messimy also wanted the Russians to be ready in East Prussia if war broke out. "Through our military attaché, by the channel of the foreign ministry and our St. Petersburg ambassador, I urged with all my might that, in spite of the slowness of Russian mobilization, the tsar's armies should as soon as possible take the offensive in East Prussia."[39] Joffre, too, wanted to be sure that "if hostilities broke out, the Government of St. Petersburg would immediately take the offensive in East Prussia."[40] However, if the Russians were expected to "immediately take the offensive in East Prussia," they would have to prepare for general mobilization. There were limits, therefore, to the "slowdown" or "suspension" that Messimy had in mind. To a certain extent, he and Joffre may have undermined Viviani's words of caution.

Izvolsky reported to Sazonov that while the French did not want to interfere in Russian military preparations, they strongly recommended that such preparations "should be as little overt and provocative in character as possible." Messimy also suggested that Russia announce a slowdown of

mobilization measures. "This, of course, would not prevent us from deter-
mining our military measures or even speeding them up, so long as we refrain, as far as possible, from mass transport of troops." Izvolsky was not
sure what the French wanted, and he urgently asked for instructions.[41]

Having warned the Russians to be careful, Messimy and Viviani joined
Poincaré and the other ministers at a 9:30 A.M. meeting. According to a brief
note found in the papers of Abel Ferry, the Council of Ministers decided not
to ask the Russians to stop mobilizing. The council did ask that the partial
mobilization be slowed down and that massive troop movements and other
provocative measures be avoided. Viviani's 7:00 A.M. telegram to this effect
was read and approved.[42]

Messimy then presented General Joffre's request that French covering
forces be brought up to full strength and ordered to the frontier. This question took up the rest of the meeting and the rest of the day. The government
eventually agreed to send covering forces to the frontier, but with important
limitations: there was to be no call-up of reserves to bring covering forces
to full strength, no covering forces were to be moved by railway, and horses
and supplies could be purchased but not requisitioned. In short, anything
that might look like mobilization was prohibited.

Finally, to avoid an unforeseen border incident that might explode into
war—and to convince London that France was doing its utmost to avoid
provoking Germany—the covering forces were to be kept ten kilometers
(about six miles) from the frontier.[43] Joffre protested. He did not mind the
ten-kilometer withdrawal, but he did object to the bans on rail movements
and to the call-up of men for the covering units. Some units would never get
to the frontier on time, and others would be understrength. Messimy finally
agreed that covering forces requiring rail transport could be moved to their
embarkation points, but this was his only concession. These orders went out
at 5 P.M. on 30 July.

In a report to Berchtold, Ambassador Szécsen assessed the French mood
as follows: "In spite of chauvinistic national pride and justifiable patriotic
self-confidence, people here are with good reason apprehensive of war and
its unforeseeable consequences." But, the ambassador added, "Fear is a bad
counselor."[44]

26: THE VIEW FROM ROME

The Marchese di San Giuliano

The political rhetoric of patriotic Italy often displayed passages of breath-taking unreality: the recreation of the Roman Empire, the "greatness that was Rome," the Mediterranean as "mare nostrum." Italian diplomats were quick to argue that Italian interests in the ancient Mediterranean basin must be protected or that Italy must be compensated if Italian interests were diminished, but the harsh reality was that most governments were not prepared to listen. Italy was, at best, "the least of the Great Powers,"[1] and in 1914 Europe was not even sure that Italy ranked as the least of the great. This was the world in which an Italian foreign minister had to work.

The foreign minister of Italy in July 1914, and the man who controlled its foreign policy with only the most perfunctory deference to king, prime minister, parliament, army, navy, public opinion, or, indeed, anyone at all, was Antonino Paterno Castello di San Giuliano, aristocratic descendant of an ancient Sicilian family and "sixth Marchese Di San Giuliano, fourth Marchese Di Capizzi, fourth Signore Di Motta Camastra, sixth Barone Di Campopetro, third Barone Di Pollicarini . . ."—the list was very long.[2] He was the eldest son of an old and powerful family. From the time he was twenty years old he regularly suffered periods of intense pain that was attributed to gout but could have resulted from any number of illnesses. The pain was atrocious and never far away, and San Giuliano's youthful faith in progress gave way to a harsh and misanthropic cynicism.

San Giuliano was determined that Italy's just claims should not be ignored, as they had been when Austria annexed Bosnia-Herzegovina in 1908. The collapsing Ottoman Empire must not be taken over by the smaller powers, as had happened in the Turkish Balkans in 1912 and 1913; what was left was to go to the Great Powers, with Italy among them.[3] All Italy must be united by the recovery of the "Italian lands" of the Trentino, Trieste, and Dalmatia. Unfortunately the territories in question belonged to Italy's ally, the Hapsburg

Empire. During the Balkan wars, San Giuliano liked to hint to Hans von Flotow, the German ambassador, that if Austria demanded compensation because of Serbia's gains, Italy would be entitled to compensation: Trieste, the Trentino, and Dalmatia. As the contours of the Austrian blow against Serbia began to emerge during the course of July 1914, San Giuliano never lost sight of those "Italian lands," but he was playing the Great Game with the weakest hand in Europe.

San Giuliano knew that Italians had no desire to fight for the Hapsburgs and against the Serbian movement of national liberation. He also recognized the danger of breaking with the powerful Austrians and the even more powerful Germans. If the Austrians and the Germans won a diplomatic victory, the Austrian position in the Balkans would be enhanced and Italy would come away humiliated and empty-handed. If there was a war and Italy did not participate, and if Austria and Germany won—as seemed more than likely—how could Italy stand up to a resurgent and victorious Austria? What would become of Italy's dream of recovering Trieste, the Trentino, and Dalmatia? Moreover, San Giuliano knew that General Conrad had recommended a war with Italy in order to put an end to Italian irredentist claims. Therefore, unless he could be absolutely sure of French and English support—and equally sure that France and England would win—San Giuliano was not going to risk an open break with his allies. "Italy," he wrote, "cannot *break* with Austria and Germany if she does not have the certainty of victory. That is not heroic, but it is wise and patriotic."[4]

San Giuliano spent most of July at a spa in Fiuggi, trying to escape the Roman heat, to find some relief from his pain, and to keep out of the way of the obstinate and hostile Austro-Hungarian ambassador, Count Kajetan Mérey von Kapos-Mére. Both men were difficult and ill. San Giuliano would die in October and Mérey would return to Vienna in August for a major operation.

Mérey could barely hide his contempt for the Italians.When San Giuliano hinted at compensation for Italy, Mérey reported that "the common gesture of this country" was "the outstretched empty hand."[5] When San Giuliano assured him of Italy's support and friendship but warned that Italian public opinion would be hostile if Austrian demands on Serbia appeared unduly harsh or illegitimate, Mérey coolly replied that whatever his government's demands might be, they would be "carefully considered and absolutely necessary." Mérey came away from that interview with an impression of "many friendly phrases, but just as many mental reservations."[6]

Mérey believed that military action against Serbia was an absolute necessity. He had believed this in 1903; he continued to believe it in 1909, 1912, and 1913; and he still thought so in July 1914 when he wrote Berchtold, "I would regard it as a genuine stroke of luck if war with Serbia does come about."[7] He did not believe that the Italians were entitled to any compensation if Austria invaded Serbia, and he said they should be told so plainly and bluntly: "In the end, nothing impresses the Italians more than cool determination and ruthless energy." Mérey was sure that, in the end, Italy would fight on the side of Austria and Germany.[8] San Giuliano did not want to listen to all that.

On 14 July, San Giuliano made a lengthy analysis of the situation for Ambassador Bollati in Berlin: Austria had a long history of ignoring Italian interests. It regarded its quarrels with Serbia as none of Italy's business. Austrian expansion and Italy's dream of acquiring "Italian lands" within the Hapsburg Empire might one day force Italy to leave the Triple Alliance, but not yet. The Central Powers were too strong, and France could not be trusted. San Giuliano said on more than one occasion that if war did come, the best result for Italy would be if France and Austria were both beaten.[9]

Meanwhile, San Giuliano warned the German ambassador that if Austria took aggressive action against Serbia, Italy would not feel bound under the terms of the Triple Alliance to join Austria and Germany if Russia and France intervened. When Ambassador Flotow asked point-blank whether San Giuliano "would refuse to aid his ally in the event of serious European complications," San Giuliano backed off.[10] He wanted compensation, not an open break.

Article VII of the December 1912 version of the Treaty of Triple Alliance provided that Italy and Austria-Hungary would keep each other informed of their intentions in the Balkans, and that if "the maintenance of the status quo in the regions of the Balkans . . . should become impossible, and if . . . Austria-Hungary or Italy find themselves under the necessity of modifying it by a temporary or permanent occupation on their part, this occupation shall take place only after a prior agreement between the two Powers, based upon the principle of a reciprocal compensation for every advantage, territorial or other."[11] San Giuliano never let Austria or Germany forget Article VII—or that Austria-Hungary's failure to come to a prior agreement would relieve Italy of any obligation under the treaty. Moreover, if Austria-Hungary occupied Serbia, even temporarily, Italy was entitled to compensation.

Flotow vigorously contested the argument that Italy was not bound by the Triple Alliance treaty in the coming crisis. However, he knew that compensation was the heart of the matter, and he summarized the main points of

Italian policy: "first, the fear of public opinion in Italy, secondly, the con-
sciousness of military weakness, and thirdly, the desire to make use of this
occasion to get something for Italy, if possible, the Trentino."[12]

Flotow warned Berlin that "the active assistance of Italy in any European
conflict that may possibly arise can scarcely be counted on." However,
"the assumption of a directly hostile attitude to Austria by Italy might, as
far as can be foreseen today, be avoided by clever handling of the situation
by Austria."[13] "My task," he wired, "is made very difficult by the fact that
the Austrian Ambassador [is] sick in bed. [The] Counselor of Embassy incompetent."[14]

Pressed on all sides to clarify Italy's position, San Giuliano took himself
to a spa and avoided everyone. "Immediate decisions are not at all necessary, rather they would be extremely dangerous; for the moment, everybody,
at home and abroad, should be left in uncertainty . . . in order to try to get
some positive advantage. For the first time since the Kingdom of Italy has
existed, a German Minister of Foreign Affairs says that it is the right moment to have the Trentino." San Giuliano was reading a little too much into
German pressure on Vienna, but it was true that Berlin was prepared to have
Vienna promise anything. Whether Vienna would have to deliver was another matter. In any event, San Giuliano concluded, "we must work in silence, speak little, not be too hasty, and stay away from Rome as much as
possible." San Giuliano advised the king that it would be "very difficult,
perhaps impossible, certainly dangerous, to drag Italy into taking part in an·
eventual war caused by Austria, and made in the interests of Austria."[15]

On 25 July, San Giuliano asked the Serbian chargé d'affaires to advise
Belgrade "to yield to the Austrian demands in spite of all their monstrous-
ness." A Serbian capitulation would give Austria "only a shadow victory"
followed by a long period of negotiations.[16] On the twenty-seventh, San
Giuliano repeated this proposal to the Russian ambassador. When the Russian remarked that some of the Austrian demands would be impossible to
fulfill, San Giuliano put the matter plainly: the Serbs would have to accept
"even if they do not fulfill what they have accepted."[17] If Serbia yielded
all along the line and Austria suspended its invasion, Austria-Hungary
would be buried in international negotiations. Count Berchtold, of course,
saw that as well as San Giuliano and insisted that only military action
would bring results.

By then, both Luigi Albertini's newspaper *Corriere della Sera* and the
British ambassador were following San Giuliano's lead. The British ambassador wired that the Serbians "may be induced to accept note in its entirely
on advice of four Powers invited to conference. . . . This is also view of

Servian agent here, provided some explanation could be given as to how points 5 and 6 of conditions would be applied."[18] Points five and six dealt with the participation of Austrian officials both in the Serbian investigation of the assassination and in the apprehension and trial of those seeking to subvert the Hapsburg Empire. The suggestion that Serbia might swallow the Austrian note in its entirety was taken up by Sazonov and Grey, and San Giuliano might have had a promising trial balloon afloat—if Austria-Hungary had been willing to suspend its military operations, which it was not, and if Serbia had accepted the note in its entirety, which it would not.

When Austria declared war on Serbia on 28 July, San Giuliano's entire edifice of flimflam and assurance collapsed. Mérey warned Berchtold not to put too much faith in Italian protestations of loyalty and goodwill since Italy's primary concern was compensation. Furthermore, any "peaceful solution of the conflict" with Serbia would only worsen relations with Italy and cause a further decline "in our prestige and authority." Mérey was opposed to any discussion of compensation, and he was equally opposed to any pledge not to annex Serb territory. He assured Vienna that Italy "will not leave the Triple Alliance."[19] In a private letter to Berchtold he recommended that instead of discussion, San Giuliano be given an "outright, uncompromising rejection" of Italian claims for compensation.[20] It was little wonder that San Giuliano kept insisting that the Germans take a hand in the negotiations and that the negotiations take place in Vienna rather than in Rome.

San Giuliano's unsettling evasiveness had its effect on Berlin. The chief of the general staff, Moltke, insisted that it was "urgently necessary that Italy be held fast to the Triple Alliance." Bethmann and Jagow both wired Tschirschky that "it is necessary that Vienna and Rome should come to an agreement," and without further delay.[21] This was exactly the kind of German pressure San Giuliano was hoping for. He needed the Germans if he was going to get anything out of Austria-Hungary.

Berchtold replied that since the monarchy had no intention of taking Serbian territory, any discussion with Italy on compensation was premature. If this eventuality should arise, he would then be prepared to discuss compensation. San Giuliano responded on 28 July that there should be a *prior* agreement on compensation under Article VII; otherwise, "Italy cannot pursue a policy such as would now or later facilitate occupations by Austria-Hungary, whether temporary or permanent, and must, on the contrary, favour whatever would lessen the probability of such occupations."[22] This somewhat wordy circumlocution was as close as San Giuliano ever came to suggesting that Italy might oppose its allies. He never directly asked for

Trieste or the Trentino because he knew that all he had to offer was Italian neutrality; he certainly was not going to promise that Italy would go to war. It was a tough game, and the Germans knew what he was up to. But they pushed Berchtold anyway, because they wanted the Triple Alliance to show solidarity, and they did not want to lose Italy if it came to war.

An exasperated Berchtold told Tschirschky, "I see just what the situation is. I am Shylock, who insists on his pledge, and yet effects nothing." Tschirschky complained to Jagow that he was doing what he could, but "the Austrians will always remain Austrians. Pride and folly together are not easily or speedily overcome! I know them too well."[23] Berchtold insisted that a temporary occupation did not require compensation under Article VII. He also insisted that the term "the Balkan region" meant Balkan territories that had been under Turkish rule and not the territory that was Serbian before the Balkan wars.

The Germans kept hammering away until Berchtold finally agreed to a statement saying that if, "contrary to our intentions," Austria should "proceed to an occupation of Serbian territory that could not be regarded as purely temporary, we are prepared to enter upon an exchange of views with Italy on compensation in this case." In return, "we expect of Italy that the kingdom will not impede its ally in the action necessary to attain its ends, and will steadily maintain the anticipated friendly attitude toward us in accordance with the treaty."[24]

Berchtold explained to Mérey that he had agreed to the concession because the stakes were high and the difficulties all but insurmountable if the members of the Triple Alliance did not act together.[25] Mérey liked the agreement even less: "As things are, we have gained nothing while making gratis a concession of incalculable significance."[26]

If Berchtold and Mérey did not like the proposal, San Giuliano would not even consider it. The Austrians were promising only to hold talks if there was a permanent occupation, as if the treaty made no mention of temporary occupations. Moreover, there was no mention of the Trentino and no pledge not to take Serbian territory. When Mérey delivered the proposal to San Giuliano on 29 July, they had a nasty quarrel. San Giuliano said bluntly that he did not think much of Berchtold's proposal. Mérey said equally bluntly that he did not think that Italy should get even that much. "Things are pretty bad between Baron von Mérey and Marquis di San Giuliano," Flotow reported. "Both of them are sick and irritable."[27]

This was just one more problem for Bethmann, who regarded Berchtold's proposal as "absolutely unsatisfactory." He instructed Tschirschky to tell Berchtold that "the instructions sent to Baron Mérey can scarcely satisfy Italy."[28]

Reports of the Russian mobilization were now making a European war increasingly likely, and San Giuliano wanted a peaceful solution regardless of the longed-for Italian lands. Public opinion was irrelevant, except as a weapon against the Austrians and Germans, but most newspapers of the "parties of order"—the nationalists, clericals, and some liberals—favored going to war on the side of the Triple Alliance. The parties of the moderate left and the anticlericals favored war on the side of the Entente.[29] The military assumed that Italy would fight alongside Austria and Germany. None of this mattered. San Giuliano had already decided that neutrality would be Italy's high card.

27: The View from London
Prime Minister Asquith

The British prime minister was as determined as San Giuliano not to be dragged into a European war. On 24 July he wrote his daily letter to a young lady friend telling her how much he missed her, about the troubles in Ireland, and that "Austria has sent a bullying and humiliating Ultimatum to Serbia, who cannot possibly comply with it, and demanded an answer within 48 hours—failing which she will march." This would mean "almost inevitably" that Russia, then Germany, and then France would come in, "so that we are within measurable, or imaginable, distance of a real Armageddon, which would dwarf the Ulster & Nationalist Volunteers to their true proportion. Happily there seems to be no reason why we should be anything more than spectators. But that is a blood-curdling prospect—is it not?"[1]

Herbert Henry Asquith was a formidable man and sixty-one years old in 1914. He was quicker and brighter than most of the men he had to deal with and not inclined to take seriously views that differed from his own. He had been in Parliament for about thirty years, and almost from the day he won his first seat, Liberal Party leaders had treated him as one of the coming men. In 1908 Asquith became prime minister, which he accepted as no more than his due.

Asquith marked a break with the line of landed political families or immensely wealthy men who had traditionally held the office. He was from a middle-class family, but he was no democrat. "Opinion" for Asquith was not public opinion but rather the opinion of serious and talented people who knew what they were talking about, people whose company he found stimulating. Where he differed with the aristocracy was on the question of birth. For Asquith, the ticket of entry was talent, and talent alone. After Asquith became prime minister, a Conservative critic wrote: "No man in England ought to be Prime Minister except a man who either from wealth or from position does not depend on office for distinction." If Asquith were to lose his office, "he might soon be practically a nobody. In such a case, the temptation to retain office at all costs is too great."[2] Neither Edward VII nor George V were quite sure that Asquith was a gentleman,[3] but they respected his ability.

Asquith sailed imperturbably on, enjoying society, the ladies, his creature comforts, and the stimulus of interesting people. His exhausting social schedule led people to believe that he was neglecting his duties, which became a major political liability during the war. But Asquith could finish more work in casual snatches of time—after a round of golf, between dinner and bridge, or while talking with friends—than most men could complete in an entire day.

Asquith and Grey were far and away the most prestigious and well-known members of the cabinet and at the peak of their careers. Together with Richard Haldane they formed a close political triumverate. The older Haldane had guided both Grey and Asquith in their early election campaigns in the 1880s, and the three men remained close. Grey regularly stayed with Haldane when he was in London, and Prince Lichnowsky often approached Haldane when he could not get to Grey.

In July 1914, Asquith had been prime minister for more than six years —a long time for an English prime minister—and he had weathered an almost continuous series of crises while maneuvering adroitly between the two wings of his party. He, Grey, Haldane, and a very small minority in the cabinet believed that Great Britain's association with France and Russia was essential for the balance of power and for the protection of the British Empire. They faced an anti-Entente, anti-imperialist Liberal majority who worried about peace and social legislation. Such Liberals were suspicious of France, detested tsarist Russia, and were not under any circumstances prepared to see a British army fighting alongside France on the continent of Europe.

The overwhelmingly Conservative House of Lords had made a shambles of Liberal legislation in 1906, 1907, 1908, and 1909. In 1909, Asquith decided to challenge the lords with new taxes in Lloyd George's "People's Budget." The theory of the challenge was that traditionally the lords did not tamper with government finance bills. It never occurred to a man such as Asquith that the Conservative Party and the lords would shed their reason to such an extent that they would sabotage the very institutions to which they declared themselves devoted. But it happened: the lords rejected the budget and Asquith found himself leading a reform of the House of Lords, which he had never anticipated. The reformed House of Lords could now delay— but no longer veto—legislation, which brought Asquith and the lords face-to-face with Irish home rule, an issue even less open to rational argument than the powers of the House of Lords. By 1914 Asquith was referring to the Irish question as "the usual weekly 'crisis.' "[4]

In 1912, 1913, and 1914, violence became a part of British politics. Asquith was brilliant in parliamentary debate and political negotiation, but he could neither fathom nor handle the politics of the streets. He refused to accept that arson, bombings, strikes, demonstrations, arrests, hunger strikes, and all the paraphernalia of radical politics in any way reflected public "opinion." When coal strike negotiations failed in March 1912 and a minimum-wage bill was forced upon Parliament because of the threatening violence, Asquith broke down in the House of Commons and could not restrain his tears. Eighteen months later, when the far more serious Irish crisis was at its peak, he was once again his old, serene, commanding self and still one of the great masters of parliamentary debate.[5]

The rest of his cabinet, however, was exhausted. In the early months of 1914 there was considerable talk that a dissolution and a general election might "clear the air." Grey for one was strongly in favor of a general election as soon as Irish home rule was in operation; he was not at all averse to being voted out of office, or so he said. Asquith disagreed. His fellow ministers might be exhausted by eight years of crisis, but he was well into his romance with twenty-seven-year-old Venetia Stanley, the free-spirited and intelligent daughter of a prominent Liberal lord.

Asquith had begun seeing Venetia regularly in 1912, and she was thrilled to be the friend and companion of the great man of English politics. For his part, Asquith had been pursuing clever and attractive women all his life, sometimes several at a time. His wife, Margot, spoke bitterly of his "little harem" and complained in 1905 that "I ought to have my *own* husband and my *own* children in a home of my *own*. I have only been alone with Henry and my children three weeks in nineteen years."[6]

Asquith could not give up the young Venetia. He met her at parties and on country weekends, he took regular Friday drives with her, he saw or wrote her daily, and there were times when he saw *and* wrote her daily. By 1914 he was almost obsessively dependent upon her companionship.[7] They do not seem to have been lovers, although some contemporaries thought so. Asquith simply had a need for her company and solace and wrote her ardent letters—but he had written equally ardent letters to dozens of young women. By 1914, Venetia's mother was worrying about her daughter's reputation and pleaded with Margot Asquith to stop the romance. When the war came, the distraught mother was planning to take Venetia to India and Australia to put a little distance between her daughter and the ardent prime minister.[8]

*   *   *

Asquith was amused by the Caillaux trial, which he called "a masterpiece of irrelevence & indecency." He was particularly delighted by the news that two of the judges in the case had publicly quarreled and that one had challenged the other to a duel.[9]

Asquith wrote Venetia on Sunday, 26 July. After a paragraph of affectionate effusion and two paragraphs on the problems of Irish home rule, he turned to "the East of Europe." Asquith enclosed Buchanan's telegram of 24 July, which reported that Paléologue and Sazonov were trying to get a declaration of support from England. "Even at this stage," Asquith complained, "Russia is trying to drag us in." He went on to say that Serbia seemed to have capitulated on the main points of the Austrian note, but that Austria seemed to be "resolved upon a complete & final humiliation." Asquith's sympathies were not with Serbia. "The curious thing is that on many, if not most, of the points Austria has a good & Serbia a very bad case. But the Austrians are quite the stupidest people in Europe." There is, he went on, "a brutality about their mode of procedure which will make most people think it is a case of a big Power wantonly bullying a little one. Anyhow, it is the most dangerous situation of the last 40 years."[10]

That night while playing bridge, Asquith got word that British troops had fired on a crowd in Dublin. He was back in London at one o'clock Monday morning. He could not get over the stupidity of whoever had ordered the troops out in the first place, and he spent most of the day cleaning up the mess and making plans for the Amending Bill, which he hoped would finally settle the Irish question. Grey was scheduled to make a report to the House of Commons on the European situation and on his mediation proposals. Grey's report was to be followed by a debate on "the Dublin business."[11] The cabinet meeting that night, however, concentrated on Europe. It was worrisome that the Germans would not cooperate with Grey's four-power mediation proposal, and now the only real hope was that Austria and Russia might "come to a deal between themselves." But, he wrote Venetia, "things don't look well, & Winston's spirits are probably rising."[12]

He was referring to Winston Churchill, at that time a Liberal and first lord of the admiralty. A number of Liberal ministers, trapped in the morass of Irish religious differences, looked upon the crisis in Europe almost as a relief. Venetia had written Asquith that such an attitude was like "cutting off one's head to get rid of a headache" and Asquith quite agreed. "Winston, on the other hand is all for this way of escape from Irish troubles, and when things looked rather better last night, he exclaimed moodily that it looked after all as if we were in for a 'bloody peace'!"[13]

On Tuesday, 28 July, the day that Austria declared war on Serbia, Asquith again spent his time almost entirely on Ireland and the crisis created by the shootings in Dublin. The Irish Nationalists, who were an essential part of the Liberal majority, were furious that their people had been fired upon while the army closed its eyes to Protestant gunrunning. The day was filled with endless negotiations on the Amending Bill, a brutal debate on the Irish question, and a stream of visitors on almost every political issue, but in the evening Asquith scratched up an impromptu dinner party followed by a game of bridge. Afterward, toward midnight, he went across the street to Haldane's place to discuss the European situation with Grey and Haldane. They talked until one o'clock in the morning, "trying to discover bridges & outlets."

When the Russians announced a partial mobilization against Austria, Asquith thought that Ireland might be pushed into the background. He wrote Venetia on Wednesday, "The Amending Bill & the whole Irish business are of course put into the shade by the coming war—'coming' for it seems now as if nothing but a miracle cd. avert it."[14]

In the long and divisive cabinet meeting on Wednesday morning, Asquith and Grey faced a clear noninterventionist majority.[15] Churchill was certain, after the war, that if Grey had pressed for a firm commitment to defend France and Russia, "the Cabinet would have broken up, and it is also my belief that up till Wednesday or Thursday at least, the House of Commons would have repudiated his action."[16] According to John Morley, who bitterly opposed entry into the war, the noninterventionists were continuously encouraging one another to be firm and not be bullied. C. P. Scott, a stalwart Liberal and editor of the *Manchester Guardian,* wrote to a Liberal government official on Wednesday, "What a monstrous and truly hellish thing this war will be if it really brings the rest of Europe into it. It ought to sound the knell of all the autocracies—including that of our own Foreign Office."[17]

It was probably at the meeting on Wednesday that Grey first told the cabinet that if it decided on an unconditional declaration of neutrality, he would not be the man to carry out the policy. John Morley was delighted by this frank admission but was probably less pleased when Asquith said that if Grey went, he would go too. A clear declaration of neutrality would bring the government down. A clear declaration of support for France and Russia would also bring the government down. For the time being, the cabinet avoided both.

Morley and most Liberals thought that France and Russia were more than a match for Austria and Germany. "Have you ever thought what will happen if Russia wins?" Morley warned his colleagues. "If Germany is beaten and Austria is beaten, it is not England and France who will emerge pre-eminent in Europe. It will be Russia. . . . People will rub their eyes when they realize that cossacks are their victorious fellow-champions for Freedom, Equality of man (especially Jew man) and respect for treaties (in Persia for instance)." The government now realized that the split in the cabinet was serious. Morley wrote, "The Cabinet for the first time became seriously uneasy about the danger of these foreign affairs to our own cohesion."[18]

Asquith persuaded the cabinet that the government should be ready for all eventualities. Churchill had already arranged to keep the fleet concentrated after a trial mobilization, and Asquith, without consulting the cabinet, had ordered the First Fleet to its North Sea war station at Scapa Flow. Warning telegrams were sent to all naval, military, and colonial stations, ordering a state of readiness for the "precautionary period" that preceded mobilization. At two that afternoon, wires were sent to every government department ordering the implementation of the so-called War Book orders of the precautionary period.[19]

Although Asquith had said that he would not separate himself from Grey, he was far less certain than his foreign secretary that Great Britain ought to be "dragged in" to a continental war. Grey, therefore, was unable to take a very strong line in support of France, but knowing that any German invasion of France would go through Belgium, he forced the cabinet to review Britain's 1839 treaty obligations with regard to Belgian neutrality.

The 1839 treaty was brought out and the precedents and possibilities were examined, but the result was inconclusive. There was no ironclad treaty obligation to defend Belgian neutrality. A number of cabinet ministers, a large section of the Liberal Party, and most Liberal newspapers were ready to argue that if Germany took only a relatively narrow passage through Belgium—below the Sambre and Meuse Rivers, as opposed to occupying all Belgium and particularly its northern seaports—the Belgians would probably not even resist or would offer only token resistance. Britain could have no interest whatever in going to war over such a minimal violation of Belgian neutrality.[20] In the end, the cabinet decided that the question of Belgian neutrality "if it arises will be rather one of policy than of legal obligation."[21]

The noninterventionists were quite pleased with this vote. Asquith wrote Venetia, however, that "the acute point will arise if & when Germany proposes to invade France by way of Belgium . . . we having with other Powers guaranteed the neutrality of Belgian territory."[22] The cabinet had authorized Grey only "to inform the German and French Ambassadors that at this stage we were unable to pledge ourselves in advance, either under all conditions to stand aside or in any conditions to join in."[23] Asquith himself was not yet sure of his own position. "Of course we want to keep out of it," he wrote Venetia, "but the worst thing we could do would be to announce to the world at the present moment that in *no circumstances* would we intervene."[24]

Before tackling the French and German ambassadors, Grey had a long talk with the Austro-Hungarian ambassador, Count Mensdorff. Grey said he was very worried; direct talks between Austria and Russia had collapsed, and they were all on the verge of a European war. According to Mensdorff, Grey suggested that the European powers would be sympathetic if Austria "would be satisfied with the acceptance by Serbia of all our demands and in addition a guarantee from the Powers that these promises should be kept."

If those were Grey's words, he was probably basing them on reports from Rome, inspired by San Giuliano, to the effect that Serbia might be prepared to accept the entirety of the Austrian demands subject to certain "explanations." Mensdorff's answer reveals how fully his country was committed to a military operation against Serbia. He replied that in view of the declaration of war and the opening of hostilities, even if Serbia agreed to everything, the proposal was probably too late. Grey responded grimly, "Then it is perhaps too late also to avert a general war."

Mensdorff continued to insist that the Austro-Serbian quarrel had no connection with a European war and that Russia must be persuaded not to create one. Austria wanted no territory; it wanted only to preserve its interests, and he had just given Grey the large and long-awaited dossier that detailed the Austrian case against Serbia. Grey said he was not interested in the merits of Austria's differences with Serbia; the problem was that Russia also had a position in the Balkans. Like all Austrians, Mensdorff was exasperated by this argument. He reminded Grey that before the Balkan wars, "Serbia had always been regarded as being in the Austrian sphere of influence."

Grey was not interested in history; he wanted to prevent a war. As the ambassador left Grey's office, William Tyrrell, Grey's private secretary, gave Mensdorff a further warning: "Russian interests leave England cold but if French vital interests or the power position of France is at stake, no English government will be in a position to hold England back from taking part on the side of France."[25] This statement was much stronger than anything Grey was authorized to make, but in the last days of peace, Grey seems to have used Tyrrell to add a bit of unofficial muscle to his diplomacy. Mensdorff reported Tyrrell's warning and noted that Prince Lichnowsky had always warned that if the English ever suspected that Germany was pushing Austria in the Serbian conflict, they would undoubtedly side with their Entente partners. Mensdorff thought Lichnowsky was right.[26] The strategy of localization was beginning to look shaky.

Grey saw Paul Cambon next and flatly declared that England had no interest whatever in either the Austro-Serbian dispute or even in an Austro-Russian quarrel. It had always been British policy "to avoid being drawn into a war over a Balkan question." If Germany and then France became involved, Grey went on, "France would then have been drawn into a quarrel which was not hers, but in which, owing to her alliance, her honour and interest obliged her to engage. We were quite free from engagements, and we should have to decide what British interests required us to do." Cambon warned Grey what was going to happen: France would receive a demand from Germany that France remain neutral while Germany attacked Russia. France could give no such assurance.[27]

Only after talking with Mensdorff and Cambon did Grey address himself to Lichnowsky. He was very serious and told the German ambassador that the situation was becoming "more acute." Direct talks between Austria and Russia had been broken off, and Sazonov wanted mediation efforts to begin. Grey warned that mediation was now urgent "if a European catastrophe were not to result."

Having painted the blackest possible picture, Grey said he wanted to speak privately.

Grey, Lichnowsky reported, "did not want our warm personal relations and the intimacy of our talks on all political matters to lead me astray, and he would like to spare himself later the reproach of bad faith." Now as before, the British government wanted friendly relations with Germany and was prepared to stand aside so long as "the conflict remained confined to Austria and Russia." But if Germany and France came in, "the situation would immediately be altered, and the British Government would . . . find itself forced to make up its mind quickly." In short, if France and Germany went to war, Great Britain might find itself compelled to defend France. Grey assured Lichnowsky that he had no desire to make any kind of threat. He just did not want to mislead him and be accused of bad faith. Lichnowsky replied that he had been warning Berlin of the British position all along.[28]

It had been another long day. Asquith, Grey, and Haldane had been up until 1:00 A.M. the night before talking over the European crisis. The Irish question was unresolved, the Irish Nationalists were still angry over the Dublin shootings, Austria was preparing to invade Serbia, Russia was threatening war if Austrian troops crossed the Serbian frontier, direct talks were broken off, mediation was stalled, and the cabinet was hopelessly split. Margot Asquith, exhausted by the "strain of waiting for foreign telegrams with the fear of war haunting my brain," went to bed earlier than usual for her predinner nap but could not sleep.[29] Asquith consoled himself with Venetia, urging her to continue her daily letters. "You don't know what it means to me."[30] Lichnowsky's report of his latest talk with Grey was filed in London at 6:39 P.M. and reached the Berlin foreign office at 9:12 P.M. Given the time required for decoding and working its way through the foreign office, the report could not have reached Bethmann much before 11 P.M. Grey's warning was only the worst of an accumulating pile of bad news.

PART VIII: Stop-in-Belgrade!

28: THE VIEW FROM BERLIN
29 July

Berlin was not an island of calm on Wednesday. Newspapers were coming out with "Extras" all through the day, and the British chargé d'affaires thought "the situation was getting out of hand."[1] Nonetheless, Bethmann, Jagow, and Stumm still professed to believe that if no French territory were annexed, Great Britain would be neutral in a war. They knew of the antiwar mood in the Liberal Party and the London financial world,[2] and King George V was reported as saying that England would stay neutral, at least in the first instance.

Ambassador Goschen returned from London on Monday, 27 July, and devoted all his energies to getting Berlin to restrain Vienna. By Wednesday he was exhausted and thought that Jagow was too: depressed and not at all well. Jagow was worried "by reports of mobilisation in Russia, and of certain military measures, which he did not specify, being taken in France."[3] When Goschen urged him to restrain Vienna, Jagow again was less than honest. He said that "Austria was so determined to make war on Serbia and so frightened of being prevented from doing so, that any advice was likely to make her hurry to present a *fait accompli*." Goschen thought Jagow might be right, since Austria's declaration of war had followed "so close upon the heels of the suggestion that the Servian answer offered a basis for discussion."[4]

With his usual wooden earnestness, Bethmann told Goschen that "he was sincerely doing all in his power to prevent European complications," but he had to add that Austria-Hungary would not accept the Serbian answer as a basis for negotiation. Bethmann tried to soften the blow by saying that he had pressed Vienna to reassure Russia that Austria-Hungary was not interested in Serbian territory, that it wanted only guarantees for the future, and that "hostilities about to be undertaken against Serbia had [the] exclusive object of securing such guarantees." Bethmann concluded by telling Goschen that the kaiser and the tsar were in communication by telegram.

Eyre Crowe's comment on Bethmann's words was terse: "The one important point is the concluding sentence. It is difficult to attach much importance to the rest." Nicolson continued to worry. "I do not think that Berlin
quite understands that Russia cannot and will not stand quietly by while
Austria administers a severe chastisement to Servia."[5] Grey sent a quick
reply that same evening: "If [Bethmann] can succeed in getting Austria to
give assurances that will satisfy Russia and to abstain from going so far as
to come into collision with Russia we shall all join in gratitude for the preservation of peace in Europe."[6]

Sergei N. Sverbejev, the Russian ambassador, was also back in Berlin.
He went immediately to Jules Cambon to get his sense of the situation, and
Cambon declared that the chances for peace were almost zero. The French
ambassador added, however, that his brother Paul had wired from London
that with the Austrian rejection of the Serbian answer, England had assured
France and Russia of its support in the event of war. Sverbejev was
startled—this was not the way Buchanan was talking in St. Petersburg—and
Cambon showed him the telegram. Sverbejev did not think the wire was as
clear as Cambon believed, and he went to ask Goschen about the British
position. Goschen replied that he did not know what his government would
do in the event of war.[7]

Sverbejev finally saw Jagow at 5:00 P.M. He was instructed to inform
Jagow that Russia would that day order partial mobilization against Austria-
Hungary, but he never got to it. The two men, who had not talked since
6 July, went over all the issues: whether Austria had the right to blame
Serbia for the assassination, whether the Serbian answer should have been
accepted, whether Grey's four-power mediation should be tried, whether
Germany was doing enough to restrain Austria, whether Russia was entitled
to set itself up as Serbia's protector, and so on.

As they talked, there was a knock at the door; a messenger delivered a
wire from Pourtalès reporting that Russia was about to mobilize the four
military districts bordering on Austria-Hungary.[8] Jagow passed the wire to
Sverbejev and asked if it was true. Sverbejev confirmed that it was but
added that the mobilization was aimed only at Austria-Hungary, that there
was no hostile intention toward Germany. A frightened Jagow angrily declared that if Russia mobilized against Austria-Hungary, "Germany would
be obliged to mobilize as well. There was therefore nothing more to do:
from now on diplomats would have to let the cannons talk."

Sverbejev protested that Jagow had assured the French ambassador that
a partial mobilization against Austria-Hungary would not provoke a German
countermobilization. Jagow, flustered, changed his stance and insisted that

"after Germany had learned that Russia was readying troops along the German frontier it was necessary for Germany, on her side, to mobilize." Sverbejev denied that there was any military activity on the German frontier. Jagow denied that the Austrians were taking military action on the Russian frontier. Jagow argued that an Austrian invasion of Serbia was no threat to Russia; Sverbejev argued that a Russian mobilization against Austria-Hungary was no threat to Germany. Jagow finally asked whether the Russians had recalled their ambassador from Vienna, and Sverbejev replied that they had not; a Russian mobilization did not necessarily mean war. Jagow calmed down a little and said that he was not prepared to give an official response to the Russian mobilization; his remarks had been merely personal and private. There would, however, be a ministerial council that evening.[9]

The German failure to coordinate military and diplomatic planning was coming home to roost. Bethmann conferred with Chief of Staff von Moltke and Minister of War von Falkenhayn before the scheduled meeting. Like Moltke, Falkenhayn feared that if Germany did not act, its enemies would gain time and Germany would lose the advantage of speed. He had ordered railway officials to guard the railways, and he had authorized grain purchases. He had argued angrily with Bethmann the day before when, with the kaiser's support, he overruled Bethmann's objection and sent all troops on maneuvers back to their garrisons.[10] Bethmann did not want Germany engaging in visible and potentially provocative military preparations; Russia must appear as the aggressor. Falkenhayn wanted the government to declare the State of Imminent War, which, as all three men knew, led directly to mobilization and war. Bethmann insisted that his diplomacy be given a chance. Moltke, who had some understanding of what Bethmann was trying to do, limited his orders to military protection for important railway points.[11]

Bethmann, Falkenhayn, Moltke, and Gen. Moritz von Lyncker, chief of the kaiser's military secretariat, met with Kaiser Wilhelm at 4:40 P.M. to discuss the military position, and Bethmann again fended off the demand to proclaim a State of Imminent War.[12] He wanted to wait for Berchtold's response to his version of the kaiser's Stop-in-Belgrade proposal (Austria-Hungary would take no Serb territory; it would occupy only a few places temporarily until Serbia complied with its demands). If Berchtold agreed and Russia agreed, the danger of a Great Power war was almost nil, and Germany would not have to outrage world opinion with an invasion of Belgium. But if Russia was mobilizing, the German army could not afford to wait.

The situation was exactly what Stumm had feared when he talked with

Theodor Wolff the day before: Russian military measures were causing the
generals to push for mobilization before Bethmann's diplomacy had fully
worked itself out. Moreover, the Social Democrats had just told Bethmann
that they would vote war credits only for a defensive war in which Russia
was the aggressor. For the support of the Social Democrats and for a neutral
England, Russia had to make the first move; that meant waiting.

To gain time, Bethmann decided upon a step that largely contradicted the
policy of waiting for the Russians. He proposed that Germany make a bid
for English neutrality that would, he hoped, blunt the diplomatic shock of
the Schlieffen Plan: Germany would guarantee the territorial integrity of
France and offer England a naval agreement that would end the naval race.
In Bethmann's view, his offer would meet every legitimate British interest.
The kaiser angrily rejected any sacrifice by his beloved navy. After a heated
discussion, Bethmann agreed to make the proposal to the English ambassador with no mention of the navy.

Admiral Müller was waiting in the anteroom when Bethmann and the
army men came out. Müller recalled that Bethmann was red in the face, "but
otherwise they were in good spirits in the belief that England, at least at
first, would remain neutral, as the King of England had assured Prince
Henry by letter."[13]

At 6:10 P.M. the kaiser saw his brother, Prince Henry of Prussia, to review
Henry's talks with King George V of England. At 7:15 the kaiser's naval
chiefs joined them, and Wilhelm summarized what he regarded as King
George's assurance of English neutrality. Admiral Alfred von Tirpitz, the
head of the imperial naval office, saw foreign office dispatches and received
reports from the naval attaché in London. He remarked that Grey seemed to
be taking a somewhat different line. The kaiser would not hear of it. "I have
the word of a king, that is enough for me."

Wilhelm then told them of the proposal Bethmann would make to
Goschen that evening and reviewed his exchange of telegrams with Tsar
Nicholas. Wilhelm complained that the Serbs had yielded everything but a
few bagatelles, "but he still did not know what the Austrians wanted." He
could understand that the Austrian army required satisfaction after having
mobilized three times in vain against Serbia, but "holding some territory as
a pledge for performance should satisfy Austrian honor."

The kaiser became more and more agitated. Since the Austrians had delivered their memorandum four weeks earlier, they had said not a word of
their intentions. Wilhelm had thought they would take immediate steps.
Then they said it would take seventeen days, then there was another delay
so as not to disturb Poincaré's visit to Russia. Even after the Serbs failed to
satisfy their ultimatum, the Austrians had done nothing. Instead, they an-

nounced they could not go into action for another seventeen days. Wilhelm was beside himself, "I don't understand it."[14]

When Bethmann got back to Berlin he discussed Russia's mobilization with Jagow, Moltke, and Falkenhayn. Would Germany now be required to mobilize? Bethmann said no. Sazonov had told Pourtalès that a Russian mobilization did not mean war, and without a Russian attack on Austria, public opinion would not support warlike measures—either in Germany or in England. "England," Bethmann explained, "cannot stand alongside Russia if it unleashes the fury of a general war and assumes thereby the guilt for the great explosion." That was the heart of Bethmann's strategy and his only hope: if Russia attacked first by going after Austria, Grey would be unable to bring England into the war. Moltke protested mildly but went along.[15]

Bethmann had a quick supper and read a dispatch that Lichnowsky had filed at a little before 1:00 P.M. Lichnowsky complained that members of the Austrian embassy, including Count Mensdorff, had never made the least attempt to conceal the fact that their sole aim was to destroy Serbia, and that Mensdorff had told him only the day before that Serbia was to be "beaten to the earth." Austrian embassy officials were also saying that portions of Serbia would be presented to Bulgaria, and presumably also to Albania.[16]

Bethmann almost lost his composure. He had not noticed before that Austria was promising only that *it* would not take Serbian territory. Meanwhile, he had been promising all Europe that Serbia's territorial integrity would be preserved—and he had just finished explaining to his military leaders the importance of not provoking English public opinion. He fired off an angry wire to Tschirschky. "I regard the attitude of the Austrian Government . . . with increasing astonishment. At Petersburg it announces its territorial disinterestedness; us it leaves entirely at sea regarding its program; Rome is put off with meaningless phrases on the compensation question, at London Mensdorff is giving away portions of Serbia to Bulgaria and Albania, and placing himself in direct opposition to Vienna's solemn declarations at Petersburg." But Bethmann was not yet ready to force Austria's hand. Tschirschky was only to remind Berchtold "that it would be advisable to avoid suspicion . . . with regard to the integrity of Serbia."[17]

A little later, Bethmann read another report from Lichnowsky, this time on his talk with Grey that afternoon. Lichnowsky reported three items: (1) Grey was very upset that Berchtold had "flatly declined" to pursue talks with Sazonov on the Austrian note; (2) Grey had asked "whether it might not be possible to bring about an understanding as to the extension of Austria's military operations and as to the Monarchy's demands"—in other words, would Austria explain exactly what it wanted from Serbia? and (3) San Giuliano in Rome had been told by the Serbian chargé that if Austria would explain points five and six of the Austrian note, Serbia might "be inclined to swallow" the note.[18] Grey seemed to be backing down; maybe he would go along with a Stop-in-Belgrade settlement without insisting on the Serbian reply as a basis for negotiation.

It had been almost twenty-four hours since Bethmann had sent Tschirschky Telegram 174, based on the kaiser's desire for mediation. Telegram 174 urged Berchtold to be less "uncompromising" and asked him to tell Russia that Austrian military operations would be limited to holding a few pieces of Serbian territory as a guarantee. Bethmann still had no answer to that telegram. Now he wanted one, so he sent a wire to Tschirschky at 10:18 P.M. He was in such a hurry he did not even code the message: "Answer by wire immediately whether telegram 174 of yesterday has arrived there. Foreign Office." Twelve minutes later he added in code: "Expect immediate carrying out of dispatch 174."[19] Since coding took a while, the second wire did not get out until shortly before midnight. Having urged Austria to cooperate, Bethmann was ready for Goschen. He sent for the British ambassador just after 10:30 P.M.

Bethmann began by saying how tired he was. He had just come from Potsdam and still had to see Jagow, but he wanted to deliver an important message to Grey. Reading from typewritten notes, he said Germany was still working continuously to maintain peace, but if Russia attacked Austria, Germany's obligation as an ally might, to his great regret, "render a European conflagration inevitable, and in that case he hoped Great Britain would remain neutral." Bethmann then said that, as far as he could judge, the key to England's policy was that it would never allow France to be crushed. Germany had no such aim, and "the Imperial Government was ready to give every assurance to the British Government provided that Great Britain remained neutral that, in the event of a victorious war, Germany aimed at no territorial acquisitions at the expense of France."

The proposal revealed all of Bethmann's lack of diplomatic sensitivity. He had learned nothing from years of futile attempts to get a promise of English neutrality. To Bethmann and the rest of the German foreign ministry, the proposal was perfectly logical: Britain wished to preserve the balance of power, and Germany and Austria were barely in parity with France and Russia, and losing ground. The European balance would be maintained only if Austria-Hungary came out of the crisis with enhanced prestige. If Austria-Hungary collapsed or if Austria and Germany were defeated, the balance would tilt sharply in favor of Russia, which Britain could not possibly desire. It was precisely the argument John Morley had made to the British cabinet in London that morning.

Given those assumptions, the proposal had a certain logic, but it shocked Goschen. He asked a series of questions and learned that Germany was not prepared to guarantee France's colonies. However, Germany would respect Holland's integrity and neutrality if Germany's adversaries also did so. The treatment of Belgium would depend on what actions France forced Germany to take.

When Bethmann asked Goschen what he thought, the ambassador was frank. He did not think the proposal would be accepted. He would, however, send it exactly as Bethmann had read it to him.[20]

Almost immmediately afterward, Bethmann learned that his timing could not have been worse. Jagow told him that Grey had just warned Lichnowsky not to be misled by Great Britain's desire for friendly relations. If Germany and France were involved in the war, Great Britain would not be able "to stand aside and wait for any length of time."[21] Jules Cambon had warned Arthur Zimmermann earlier in the day "that England would without a doubt take her stand by us at the first shot." The Italian ambassador was telling Jagow the same thing, and Zimmermann, who had initially been confident that England would remain neutral, was beginning to have doubts.[22]

The kaiser had assumed that the Serbian answer could serve as a basis for negotiation, and Bethmann's Telegram 174 conceded that Serbia's answer had largely agreed to Austrian demands. Nonetheless, Bethmann never contested Vienna's refusal to negotiate on the basis of the Serbian answer. He merely insisted that Vienna tell Russia that the Austrians wanted no territory and would occupy Serbia only temporarily, leaving Berchtold free to insist on full compliance with the original note. Grey now appeared to believe that Serbia might yield to the Austrian note if the requirements of certain demands were spelled out. There was still hope.

Bethmann frantically fired off a series of telegrams during the night and early morning hours. The first, shortly before midnight, went to Pourtalès in St. Petersburg. If Russia mobilized and Austria responded, Sazonov's hopes for peace would "never be realized." In order to avoid such a catastrophe, he told Pourtalès, Germany was pressing Vienna to reaffirm its promise not to take Serbian territory and to assure Russia "that its military measures contemplate solely a temporary occupation, in order to force from Serbia a guarantee of future good behavior." If Austria made such a declaration, Bethmann went on, "Russia will have obtained all she desires." If Germany was successful in Vienna, "We expect . . . that . . . Russia will institute no belligerent conflict with Austria." Pourtalès was instructed to talk to Sazonov and to "wire report."[23]

*   *   *

Around midnight, after learning that the tsar had suspended general mobilization and ordered a partial mobilization, Sazonov called in Pourtalés. He pleaded with the ambassador to urge his government to participate in a four-power conference. There they might persuade Austria "to drop those demands which infringe on the sovereignty of Serbia." Sazonov observed that the kaiser's promise of friendly mediation was inconsistent with Pourtalés's warning that Russian military measures could lead to war.[24]

Pourtalés had barely returned from this meeting when he received Bethmann's new instruction. He immediately called the foreign ministry for another appointment, and Sazonov, who had just gone to bed, got up to talk with the German ambassador for the second time that night. Sazonov repeated that Austria's assurances of territorial disinterest were not enough; he could not abandon Serbia "without endangering the life of the Czar." Desperate for a way out, Pourtalés asked Sazonov to outline the conditions under which Russia would suspend military preparations. Sazonov wrote out the following formula: "If Austria declares that in recognition of the fact that its conflict with Serbia has assumed the character of a question of European interest, it declares itself ready to eliminate from its ultimatum those points which infringe on Serbia's sovereign rights, then Russia agrees to suspend all military preparations." It was a compromise Sazonov and Pourtalés had discussed as early as 26 July.

Wiring the new formula to Berlin, Pourtalés noted that it was "remarkable that Sazonov's document should not contain a word requiring the immediate suspension of Austria's punitive expedition."[25] Both men were exhausted, and military pressures were pushing them to the wall. Conrad wanted to force a clear statement of intention from the Russians; the German military was beginning to insist on a military response to Russian military measures; Russian generals wanted the tsar's partial mobilization replaced by full general mobilization; and Berchtold, despite the pressure from Bethmann, was in no mood for compromise.

At 12:20 A.M. Bethmann sent Tschirschky abstracts from Lichnowsky's talk with Grey in which Grey had proposed limits on Austrian military operations and mentioned the Italian report that Serbia might accept the Austrian note if points five and six were explained. Bethmann instructed Tschirschky to "kindly inform Count Berchtold at once of the foregoing and add that we consider such compliance on the part of Serbia an appropriate basis for negotiations. . . ."[26] Bethmann then sent Tschirschky a fourth telegram, informing him that Russia was mobilizing the four military districts bordering Austria and "urgently" requesting, "in order to prevent a general catastrophe, or at least to put Russia in the wrong, that Vienna inaugurate and continue with the conferences according to telegram 174."[27]

At this point, Bethmann must have reviewed the reports of Pourtalès and Tschirschky and realized that there had been a misunderstanding. According to Pourtalès, Sazonov believed that Vienna had refused to authorize any direct talks with Russia; according to Tschirschky, Vienna had only rejected "further discussion with Serbia."[28] At three in the morning, only minutes after his fourth telegram to Tschirschky, Bethmann sent a fifth: "Apparently there is some misunderstanding, which I beg to have cleared up. We cannot expect Austria to deal with Serbia, with whom she is at war. The refusal to hold any exchange of opinions with Petersburg, however, would be a serious error, as it would be a direct provocation of Russia's armed intervention, which Austria-Hungary is beyond all else interested to prevent." The wire ended on a note of desperation: "We . . . must decline to be drawn wantonly into a world conflagration by Vienna, without having any regard paid to our counsel. . . . Please talk to Count Berchtold at once with all impressiveness and great seriousness."[29]

More than three weeks after the meetings of 5 and 6 July, Berlin was making its first serious attempt to restrain its Austrian ally.

That task fell on Tschirschky, who had been taking a very hard line. The British, French, Italian, and Russian ambassadors were all convinced that an Austrian invasion of Serbia could not be prevented and that Tschirschky was "the most energetic supporter, if not the instigator of an aggressive action by Austria against Serbia."[30]

Sometime Wednesday morning Tschirschky read Bethmann's Telegram 174. The Entente ambassadors in Vienna had already learned from the indefatigable Jules Cambon in Berlin "that German Ambassador at Vienna is instructed to speak seriously to Austro-Hungarian Government against acting in a manner calculated to provoke European war."[31] They waited to see what Tschirschky would do.

Tschirschky was in a quandary. In the first days after the assassination, he had been reprimanded by the kaiser for urging moderation. He knew that Jagow had forwarded Grey's mediation proposals only to influence British opinion, not to put pressure on Vienna. For all he knew, this latest instruction had the same purpose and was leaked to Jules Cambon so that the British would hear that Germany was working for peace. Telegram 174, moreover, had warned Tschirschky "to avoid carefully giving rise to the impression that we wish to hold Austria back."[32]

Tschirschky himself believed that Austria-Hungary had no choice but to take military action against Serbia, and he had bluntly told the Austrians that Berlin would not understand any "weakness" in regard to Serbia.[33] He had been equally blunt with the Entente ambassadors: Serbia had to be punished. It would be extraordinarily difficult and personally embarrassing if now, at this late date, he had to tell the Austrians to explain their demands and to limit their military operations to a temporary occupation of Belgrade.

Tschirschky took his time executing Bethmann's new policy. Telegram 174 was in Vienna by 4:30 A.M. Wednesday, and he must have seen it as soon as he got to his desk. Bethmann waited all day for an answer, but Tschirschky reported only on Austrian talks with Bunsen and Schebeko in which Berchtold told both men that, given the mood in the monarchy, "further discussion with Serbia had become utterly impossible."[34] Neither Conrad's journal nor the Austrian documents nor Tschirschky's dispatches give any indication that Tschirschky took up the substance of the Stop-in-Belgrade proposal of Telegram 174 until late that evening, when he met with Berchtold to discuss the Russian partial mobilization.[35]

The ambassador does not appear to have tried very hard. He read aloud Bethmann's request that Austria consider mediation and that it offer to restrict its military operations to an occupation of Belgrade, but he also read Bethmann's warning that Tschirschky was not to "give rise to the impression that we wish to hold Austria back."[36] Berlin seemed merely to be going through the motions. Berchtold replied that he was ready to repeat his declaration of Austria's "territorial disinterestedness" to Russia, but he was not yet ready to limit Austro-Hungarian military operations.[37]

When Tschirschky left at one in the morning, Berchtold wired Szögyény instructions to notify the German government "that if the Russian mobilization is not suspended at once our general mobilization must ensue on military grounds." To avert a general war, Berchtold proposed that perhaps the Austrian and German representatives in St. Petersburg and in Paris could state "in a friendly spirit" that continuance of the Russian mobilization would lead to countermeasures in Germany and Austria-Hungary, which would "necessarily have serious consequences." Concerning Austria's planned military operations, "Will Your Excellency add that we shall of course not allow ourselves to be deflected from our military action against Serbia."[38]

29: The View from Nish

30 July

The status of Serbian interests as opposed to those of a European Great Power was made clear by Sir Edward Grey: "It was not a question of humiliating Austria. . . . There must, of course, be some humiliation of Servia, but Austria might press things so far as to involve the humiliation of Russia."[1] The Austrians, in short, could take any action against Serbia that was acceptable to Russia.

By Thursday, 30 July, England and Germany were urging Russia to accept an Austrian occupation of Belgrade as a guarantee that Serbia would do what the Great Powers agreed it must. Austria-Hungary would announce its terms, and the "four less interested powers"—Germany, Italy, France, and England—would mediate on precisely what these terms required while the Austro-Hungarian army sat in Belgrade. When Serbia had satisfactorily complied, the Austro-Hungarian army would leave. If Austria agreed to this arrangement, Russia would suspend its mobilization and Germany would not have to execute the Schlieffen Plan.

All of the proposals calling for a peaceful occupation of Belgrade assumed that a rapid Austro-Hungarian invasion would force the Serbian army to withdraw into the interior without defending Belgrade. Sazonov had suggested on 24 July that if Serbia found itself unable to defend Belgrade, it could withdraw the government and the army into the interior and appeal to the Powers.[2] Spalajkovic, Serbia's perennially angry minister to Russia, rejected such a withdrawal out of hand.

Strandtmann, Russia's acting minister to Serbia, approached the subject gingerly in the guise of exploring all of Serbia's options. He tried to make the Serbs realize that if the Austrians promptly seized Belgrade and northern Serbia, precluding even a "halfway successful resistance," a retreat without fighting was the only alternative.

The Serbs, who had been mobilizing since 25 July, had expected the Austrians to cross the border and seize Belgrade as soon as Giesl broke relations and headed north; they had therefore moved the government and the army south to Nish. When the invasion did not materialize, they were certain it would come when Austria declared war on 28 July. But on the thirtieth, except for the few shells fired around Belgrade, the Austrians still had not made a move. Pašić and his ministers began to feel easier about the future.

Spalajkovic, meanwhile, was all over St. Petersburg demanding that Russia defend Serbia. To stiffen the back of his government at Nish, he constantly assured it that Russia was ready to fight. On 29 July he told Sazonov that Austria was bombarding Belgrade. At midnight he reported to Nish that the Russian government had called an Imperial Council, which had decided to accept no compromise. The Russians would continue to negotiate with Berlin to gain time, but as soon as their forces were concentrated, they would declare war. An Austrian agreement to limit any occupation to Belgrade and a few border points could only help the Russian plan. "The die," he concluded, "is cast."[3]

The truth was that Sazonov and the tsar wanted a peaceful settlement. Nicholas had canceled his general mobilization order and directed only a partial mobilization because Wilhelm had assured him a settlement was possible. Tsarist diplomats regularly insisted that the Russian mobilization was only a precaution, a way to pressure Austria to negotiate. This was a detail the fiery Spalajkovic ignored.

In Nish on Thursday morning, Pasic was wiring his envoys abroad that Belgrade was under constant bombardment with many civilian casualties. The Russian, French, and British envoys all reported "fairly furious" shelling; Belgrade was being bombarded section by section.[4] However, on Friday, 31 July, the British minister had to confess that "Prime Minister's statement seems to have been exaggerated."[5] The Austrian cannonade was brief, did little damage, and was of no military value whatever. It was typical of the Austrian genius for outraging opinion to the point where the merits of the Austro-Hungarian case against Serbia all but disappeared.

On Wednesday Serbia's Prince Regent Alexander delivered a war manifesto that closed with the words, "Defend your homes, hearths, and Serbia with all your strength." The next day the legislature met in emergency session in Nish, and the prince regent's speech from the throne became a rousing call to battle. The Serbs had done all they could to avoid war, but their mighty neighbor to the north had fallen upon them. Now Serbia must resist, with tiny Montenegro by its side. When Alexander read the tsar's assurance "that Russia would in no case abandon Serbia," the house rocked with cheers. The legislators cheered at every mention of Russia and the tsar, they cheered at every mention of England and France.[6] The enthusiasm was enormous. Serbia was not alone; Austria-Hungary would be defeated.

Sazonov had informed Strandtmann that he was prepared to engage in direct talks with Vienna and, if these failed, to turn to four-power mediation. It might be best, he thought, if both went on simultaneously. Considering the concessions Serbia had already made, Sazonov thought a compromise on the remaining points should not be difficult if Austria showed goodwill.[7] When Strandtmann talked to Pašić along those lines on Thursday, Spalajkovic had already reported on the mediation proposals being circulated and on Vienna's rejection of direct talks with Russia.

Pašić had no great faith in Berlin's moderating influence on Vienna. He thought that Serbia had already yielded all it could in its answer of 25 July, and he no longer hoped for a peaceful outcome. But he thought that what he saw as a German effort to delay the outbreak of hostilities was of great advantage to Serbia and to Russia, giving them time to complete their mobilization and concentration. The Austrians' failure to launch an immediate attack and seize Belgrade was an enormous boon. A swift strike could easily have paralyzed the mobilization of at least three Serbian divisions. Now, instead of withdrawing to the south without fighting, the army would defend Belgrade.[8]

Serbia's decision to defend Belgrade caught Europe by surprise and removed the centerpiece of all Stop-in-Belgrade proposals. The French minister to Serbia reported that "everyone is protesting the decision to resist taken by the Serbian government, contrary to all assurances."[9] It was not simply that the Powers had left their legations in a war zone with their files and codebooks intact; the Serbs had overturned the basis of most diplomatic discussion.

The Serbs grew increasingly cocky. Since Russia was mobilizing in the Austro-Hungarian rear, they proposed an attack on Austrian forces on the Austrian side of the frontier! Strandtmann was a little worried by this news and asked his military attaché to look into it. The attaché reported that although the Serbian army suffered many deficiencies in material and weaponry, morale was high and the army was eager to fight. If the Serbs faced only six Austrian army corps, they might win. After the tsar's assurance of support, wrote Strandtmann, Prince Regent Alexander "faced the future quietly, convinced of the final triumph of his just cause."[10] The Great Powers, meanwhile, continued to explore a Stop-in-Belgrade solution that Serbia was not willing to accept.

30: RUSSIA MUST MOVE FIRST

Berlin, 30 July

Theodor Wolff was again at the foreign office on Thursday morning, 30 July, and spoke with Stumm. "So," he began, "there is no longer any chance of avoiding this terrible war?"

"It's a hundred to one there will be war," Stumm replied.

"And Britain?" asked Wolff. "Is there nothing from Lichnowsky?"

Stumm was not the man to ask about Lichnowsky. "Ach, Lichnowsky, of course he is in a devil of a stew, after telling us all the time that Britain wanted an understanding."

That was a half-truth at best. Lichnowsky had warned all along that Britain would defend France.

"Britain will go with France," Wolff insisted.

Stumm was not ready to admit the worst. "Nobody knows yet what Britain will do."

Wolff thought that "under his armour of outward self-possession," Stumm was worried and distracted. With Russia mobilizing, Generals von Moltke and von Falkenhayn were insisting that Germany also mobilize in order to be ready to execute the Schlieffen Plan. Control was slipping from the diplomats to the military. The great gamble was going wrong.[1]

On Thursday morning the kaiser received a wire from Tsar Nicholas telling him of his "military measures." Wilhelm also received a note from Bethmann reporting the Russian ambassador's assurance that mobilization did not mean war and that diplomatic relations with Austria-Hungary had not been broken off. Bethmann assured the kaiser that "no mobilization had in any way taken place against Germany."[2] These assurances were not enough to calm Wilhelm. He had been tricked by the tsar! If Russia was mobilizing against Austria-Hungary, "then I must mobilize too! . . . I regard my mediation action as brought to an end, as the Czar, instead of loyally awaiting its results, had already mobilized behind my back, without letting me know anything about it."[3]

Wilhelm had his brother, Prince Henry, telegrammed George V that Wilhelm was "trying his utmost to fulfill Nicky's appeal to him to work for peace," but Nicky "today confirms news that military measures have been ordered by him." France was taking military measures as well. Germany had taken none, "but may be forced to do so at any moment." Germany and England should work together "to prevent a terrible catastrophe." Henry begged King George to use his influence "on France and also Russia to keep neutral."[4]

The kaiser summoned Admiral Müller and his naval chief of staff, Adm. Hugo von Pohl, to the New Palace in Potsdam. He told them that he and Prince Henry had just drafted a telegram for the English king, who was the only possible mediator for peace with Russia. Pohl handed the kaiser a dispatch from the naval attaché in London, who reported Grey's warning to Lichnowsky with brutal directness: "England could not remain neutral in a war of Germany against France and would immediately go into action with its fleet." This, wrote Müller, "was the hardest blow of the day. . . ." No one had told the kaiser about Grey's warning.[5]

Wilhelm was convinced that he was the victim of a conspiracy. "The whole war is plainly arranged between England, France and Russia for the annihilation of Germany . . . the Austro-Serbian strife is only an excuse to fall upon us! God help us to fight for our existence, brought about by falseness, lies and poisonous envy!"[6]

War Minister Falkenhayn wanted to mobilize, but Moltke, though worried, was still not ready to declare the State of Imminent War, which would launch a German mobilization and the attack on Liège. He accepted Bethmann's argument that to keep England neutral and the German socialists loyal, Russia must be the first to mobilize and to attack. Moltke was prepared to wait, grudgingly, if he could obtain these political advantages. However, he told anyone who would listen that since neither France nor Russia was prepared for a major war, the present moment offered the best chance that Germany would ever have.[7]

By 11:00 A.M. the kaiser's excited comments had arrived in Berlin. Bethmann advised the kaiser that "Your Majesty do not—as long as Vienna's decision is still outstanding—express . . . the fact that Your Majesty's role as mediator is ended."[8] Rather, said Bethmann, Wilhelm should tell the tsar that his mediation would be endangered, if not made impossible, by Russian mobilization. The kaiser agreed and rewrote Bethmann's draft, which was sent uncoded to the tsar at 3:30 that afternoon.[9]

A few hours later, with still no word from Vienna, Bethmann had the kaiser wire Emperor Franz Joseph to "favor me with your decision as soon as possible."[10] The German line throughout the day was that although they were pressing for mediation in Vienna, they would not be able to continue their efforts much longer if Russia continued to mobilize. Jagow told Goschen that as soon as he learned of Grey's warning to Lichnowsky, "he asked the Austro-Hungarian Government whether they would be willing to accept mediation on the basis of the occupation by Austrian troops of Belgrade or some other point and issue their conditions from there." He still saw some chance of peace if Grey could convince Russia "to take no steps which might be regarded as an act of aggression against Austria."[11]

At a few minutes before noon, the German foreign office got a wire from Pourtalès confirming what they had suspected for days: Russia's mobilization was far more extensive than had been supposed and was going forward in every military district but Warsaw, Vilna, and St. Petersburg. Pourtalès's wire was immediately forwarded to the general staff, the admiralty staff, the naval office, and the war ministry.[12] Moltke and Falkenhayn thought the Russians were trying to carry out a secret general mobilization—in which case a Russian army would be soon gathering along the Nieman, facing East Prussia.

Bethmann met with Falkenhayn and Tirpitz at 1:00 P.M. Moltke, who had not been invited, attended anyway to be sure Bethmann understood the danger Germany now faced. Bethmann was worried but firm; neither Moltke nor Falkenhayn could get him to declare a State of Imminent War, or to suspend the pressure on Vienna to mediate.[13]

German intelligence estimated that fourteen Russian army corps were being mobilized.[14] Moltke showed the reports to Captain Fleischmann, the Austrian liaison officer to the general staff, and asked what Conrad was doing with his army.

When Fleischmann outlined the Austrian dispositions, Moltke realized that Conrad's Galician army was not nearly strong enough for an offensive and was, in fact, taking defensive positions well back from the frontier. Moltke panicked. He needed forty Austro-Hungarian divisions in Galicia ready to attack; what he was getting were twenty-five divisions standing on the defensive, facing fifty Russian divisions! The Russians were sneaking up on a general mobilization, and Conrad's B Group was still marching south! After that shock and the frightened kaiser's sudden insistence on mobilizing, Moltke gave up any thought of delay. He wanted Austrian and German armies in position in time to crush France and to stop Russia before East Prussia was overrun.

At about this time, the Austro-Hungarian military attaché came over from the foreign office to see Moltke, whom he found "more agitated than I have ever seen him before."[15] Moltke declared that the situation would be critical "if the Austro-Hungarian Monarchy does not mobilize immediately against Russia"—meaning that B Group and the divisions detached from A Group should turn around and head north. "Every hour's delay worsens the situation," he warned, "since the Russians will gain a head start." He also urged Austria to make concessions to the Italians to keep Italy in the Triple Alliance. "At all costs," Moltke urged, "leave not a man on the Italian border!" Nothing was to weaken the Austrian offensive in Galicia. Austria must, moreover, "reject renewed English *demarche* for maintenance of peace. Standing firm in a European war is the last chance of saving Austria-Hungary."[16] The military attaché immediately sent a wire to Conrad and informed Szögyény, who wired Vienna that evening that "Moltke urgently advises us to order immediate general mobilization."[17]

Given the structure of the German government, Moltke may not have exceeded his authority in urging Austria to mobilize, particularly since Bethmann and Jagow were almost certain that Austria would do so. But for Moltke, even unofficially, to tell an Austro-Hungarian official that Austria should reject English mediation proposals—when the imperial chancellor and the kaiser were still urging Vienna to make some show of accepting them—was, even by Prussian standards of military authority, outrageous. Moltke's actions can only be explained by the Prussian officer corps' general contempt for civilians and his own panic at the threat to East Prussia. A general staff officer explained after the war that the army was worried that if the Austrians saw a chance of an agreement with Russia, they would concentrate their army against Serbia.[18] Once Moltke learned that Russia was mobilizing extensively and that Conrad was going on the defensive in Galicia, he could think only of getting his armies in position before East Prussia was overwhelmed.

Berlin was by then full of rumors that "mobilization has been decided but not yet declared,"[19] and at two in the afternoon the Berlin *Lokal Anzeiger* came out with a special edition announcing that the kaiser had just ordered German mobilization.[20] Jagow immediately called Sverbejev and Cambon to assure them that the story was untrue.[21] Tension remained high.[22] Cambon reported the strengthening of garrisons at Metz on the Franco-German frontier, rumors of German troop movements, and reports by his military attaché of trainloads of troops and reservists. The attaché believed that German covering troops were already moving into position.[23] None of these reports was true.

Cambon asked Jagow whether Austria was already sending troops into Serbia. Jagow said he knew nothing about it; Cambon, who was a very nimble diplomat, observed that an Austrian invasion of Serbia would significantly change the situation. Austria would no longer have to worry about its prestige, and it could then accept the mediation of the "four less-interested powers," as Grey had suggested. Jagow, Stumm, and Bethmann were trying to get Austria to do precisely that, and Jagow replied that yes, he thought the situation would change after an Austrian invasion; mediation might then be possible.[24] Everyone was prepared to have Serbia pay for the peace of Europe by being invaded.

Shortly after the *Anzeiger* story broke, Bethmann got Pourtalès's report, and Sverbejev got Sazonov's report, outlining the formula that Sazonov had drafted for Pourtalès in the early hours of Thursday morning: if Austria would recognize the European character of its dispute with Serbia and would declare its readiness to eliminate those points in its note that would infringe upon Serbia's sovereignty, Russia would suspend its military preparations.[25]

Nothing so well illustrates the impact of a major crisis—as sleepless officials tried to keep up with a flood of dispatches and rumors and struggled to master their growing anxiety—as the German response to Sazonov's formula. Pourtalès's report must have worked its way to Bethmann by about 4:30 P.M. After reviewing the document, Bethmann queried, "What points of the Austrian ultimatum has Serbia refused anyway? To my knowledge, only the participation of Austrian officials in the judicial proceedings. Austria could abandon this participation on the condition that until the conclusion of the transaction she should occupy portions of Serbia with her troops."[26]

At the same time that Bethmann was considering the formula, Ambassador Sverbejev was asking Jagow what the German government thought about it. No one in Berlin had yet consulted Vienna, but Jagow answered for Austria without hesitation: "The proposal was unacceptable for Austria; it would be a humiliation that would lead to no result." Sverbejev remarked that "Austria, in my view, could be more forthcoming."[27] Apparently Bethmann was actively pursuing Sazonov's formula while Jagow was rejecting it. The sheer pace of the crisis was causing German policy to unravel.

Zimmermann told another ambassador, who again told Cambon, that "the military" was pressing very hard for general mobilization. Cambon sent a worried report to Paris. "Whatever the case, mobilization could be decided from one moment to the next." It was crucial, nonetheless, not to declare any mobilization measures in France until Germany had already taken similar steps, so that "English public opinion, which could play a great role in events, does not attribute to us any initiatives tending toward war."[28]

In a talk with Cambon late in the day, Jagow expressed surprise at Russia's partial mobilization after the tsar's appeal for the kaiser's help in

Vienna. Cambon did not see the problem; had not Jagow himself told Cambon that Germany would not have to mobilize unless Russia mobilized along the German frontier? That was clearly not the case. Jagow replied that the army wanted to mobilize; the generals insisted that any delay would be a loss of strength for Germany. Moreover, he said, his earlier comments did not constitute a firm commitment. Cambon recorded the conversation in his final dispatch for the day, which he sent at 1:30 in the morning on 31 July. "The chances of peace have decreased still more," he wrote wearily.[29]

At 5:00 P.M. on the thirtieth, Bethmann briefed the Prussian state ministers on the situation. At shortly before 9:00 P.M. he had another run-in with Falkenhayn and Moltke. Moltke insisted that it was suicidal to put off the State of Imminent War any longer. Both generals argued that the mediation attempts in Vienna would come to nothing; Bethmann was counting on a "miracle" if he thought they would. It was "unbearable" that Germany's national security should remain dependent upon Russian actions—on which intelligence was sparse—or upon Austrian decisions. Bethmann insisted that he needed time. If he was not going to be brutal and insist that the Austrians negotiate or Germany would abandon them, he had to wait for Vienna. It would be different if Russia acted first and ordered a general mobilization, which could only be aimed at Germany. Bethmann won another fifteen or sixteen hours by agreeing to make a final decision on declaring the State of Imminent War no later than noon the next day.[30]

Faced with this deadline, Bethmann sent Tschirschky an "urgent" telegram at nine o'clock Thursday night. "If England's efforts succeed, while Vienna declines everything, Vienna will be giving documentary evidence that it absolutely wants a war, into which we shall be drawn, while Russia remains free of responsibility. That would place us, in the eyes of our own people, in an untenable situation. Thus we can only urgently advise that Austria accept the Grey proposal." Tschirschky was instructed to immediately "express yourself most emphatically on this matter to Count Berchtold, perhaps also to Count Tisza."[31]

That was as close as Berlin ever came to issuing Vienna an ultimatum.

Eyre Crowe's initial comment on Bethmann's bid for British neutrality was that "these astounding proposals . . . reflect discredit on the statesman who makes them" and that "Germany is practically determined to go to war."[32] Crowe was wrong. Bethmann was determined to let Austria-Hungary deal with Serbia, even at the risk of a Great Power war, but he certainly did not want to fight such a war. What he wanted was some version of the Stop-in-Belgrade proposal that would be acceptable to both Austria and Russia.

*   *   *

At 3:30 Thursday afternoon, Grey wired Goschen that Bethmann's neutrality proposal "cannot for a moment be entertained." Great Britain could not permit France to lose its Great Power status and would not bargain away its interest in Belgian neutrality. The best way to maintain good Anglo-German relations would be "to continue to work together to preserve the peace of Europe." If they succeeded and if "this crisis be safely passed, my own endeavor would be to promote some arrangement to which Germany should be a party, by which she could be assured that no hostile or aggressive policy would be pursued against her or her allies by France, Russia, and ourselves, jointly or separately."[33]

This declaration from Grey was as much as Bethmann was ever going to get, but it was a great deal. Under the pressure of the July crisis, Grey had finally come to recognize that Germany regarded Great Britain's close association with France and Russia as a threatening disruption of the balance of power.

Lichnowsky spent all day Thursday trying to persuade Grey to pressure St. Petersburg.

Promising to do what he could, Grey assured Lichnowsky that France had taken no war measures beyond those already ordered by Germany. Grey also showed Lichnowsky the instruction he was sending Buchanan that evening, which began by reviewing the various Stop-in-Belgrade proposals, including Sazonov's early morning formula to Pourtalès requiring Austria to change its demands to respect Serbian sovereignty. The instruction declared that "if Austrian advance were stopped after occupation of Belgrade, I think Russian Minister for Foreign Affairs' formula might be changed to read that the Powers would examine how Servia could fully satisfy Austria without impairing Servian sovereign rights or independence. If Austria, having occupied Belgrade and neighboring Servian territory, declared herself ready, in the interest of European peace, to cease her advance and to discuss how a complete settlement can be arrived at, I hope that Russia would also consent to discussion and suspension of further military preparations, provided other powers did the same."[34]

This was now Grey's third formula. He had begun by proposing the Serbian answer as a basis for negotiation, then he had adopted what he thought was a Serbian proposal to accept the Austrian note subject to explanations, and now he was suggesting that Russia permit Austria to occupy Belgrade and then explain what it wanted.

Lichnowsky sent Grey's latest proposal to Berlin, noting that at his suggestion Grey had agreed to drop Sazonov's demand that Austria modify the language of its note. Serbia would accept the demands and then the Powers would discuss "the charges and obligations to be laid upon the Serbs."[35] San Giuliano's proposal—that Serbia accept and that the Powers then discuss just what it was that Serbia had accepted—was having a remarkable life.

Grey then called in Count Mensdorff to say that he could not intervene in Russia unless Vienna gave him something to offer. Mensdorff reported that Grey seemed to think that the only hope of avoiding a greater war would be if Austria contented itself with a limited occupation. He also noted that Grey was very careful not to make any suggestion himself. Grey apparently wanted to avoid getting ahead of Sazonov, who had yet to respond to the proposal Grey had sent Buchanan a little earlier.

Mensdorff also reported that he thought London would eagerly support any peace proposal and would seek to obtain "far-reaching satisfaction and guarantees with regard to future relations with Serbia if, although it may be too late for that now, we could give some assurance for the future existence of Serbia as an independent state that would be in any way acceptable to Russia."[36] This report did not arrive in Vienna until Friday afternoon—after the Imperial Council had already rejected Stop-in-Belgrade.

Wolff made another visit to the foreign ministry at about ten in the evening and again saw Stumm. The political director was very tired but, to Wolff's mind, strangely optimistic. Wolff asked whether there was any hope for a settlement based on a limited Austrian occupation of Serbia. Stumm replied that they were still trying. He acted like a man who was still in command of the situation: "Everything is being calculated down to the last detail, almost, one might say, mathematically—absolutely meticulously." What now mattered most, Stumm concluded, was the British attitude.[37] Unfortunately, that could not be calculated.

31: VIENNA DEFIES BERLIN

30 July

Berchtold and Conrad had learned on Wednesday evening, 29 July, that Russia was ordering a partial mobilization, but Vienna's Thursday morning papers made no mention of it, perhaps to avoid further panic in the financial markets.[1] Sazonov, however, insisted that a Russian mobilization, unlike mobilization in west European countries, did not necessarily mean war. A Russian field army could remain armed and mobilized for months without going to war.[2]

Conrad was intrigued by that. If the Russians mobilized and remained standing, he might still be able to crush Serbia without having to fight Russia. He had promised Moltke that he would reply to any Russian mobilization with a general mobilization, sending both A Group and B Group to Galicia to launch an attack on Russia. But what Conrad wanted above all else was to destroy Serbia. If he kept his promise to Moltke, he would have to cancel the invasion of Serbia, turn B Group around, and leave the eight divisions of Minimum Group Serbia to hold a defensive line. He had no intention of abandoning the invasion of Serbia.[3]

Conrad promptly went to see Berchtold. The two men agreed they had no choice but to order a general mobilization, but they would inform St. Petersburg that the monarchy had no "intention of attacking or threatening Russia." It would mobilize "merely as a precaution against a Russian attack, which Russia's mobilization seemed to indicate."[4]

By this time, Berchtold had received the first of Bethmann's messages through Tschirschky, and he told Conrad that the Germans wanted Vienna to continue direct talks with St. Petersburg so that if worse came to worst, Russia would be forced to assume "the odium of unleashing a great war." As far as Conrad was concerned, the diplomats could "talk all you want, just don't stop the operation against Serbia." Berchtold, who did not want a war with Russia, asked, "Can we make it financially? Stürgkh [the Austrian prime minister] thinks that we cannot afford a war with Russia as well as

226

one with Serbia." Conrad replied that it was too late to worry about money, adding, "Who knows, anyway, whether it will come to war with Russia? The Russians could just stand there hoping we will give up on Serbia."[5]

Throughout the day, Tschirschky delivered the telegrams sent by Bethmann during the course of the night. Berchtold was as charming and as courteous as ever. He agreed to instruct Szápáry to resume talks with Sazonov; it had all been a misunderstanding anyway. The monarchy was perfectly willing to explain its note to Sazonov, even though the note, "of course, had been superseded by war." Szápáry would also be instructed, and Berchtold himself would inform Ambassador Schebeko, "that the Monarchy had no idea of making any territorial requisitions in Serbia." Berchtold, however, would make no commitment on the scope of Austro-Hungarian military operations. He said only that Austria-Hungary would "occupy Serbian territory purely temporarily, in order to compel the Serbian Government to the complete fulfillment of its demands." Tschirschky filed this report at 2:30 P.M.[6]

Fifty minutes later, at 3:20 P.M., Tschirschky sent off another message. When the British ambassador, Bunsen, informed Berchtold that the Italians thought Serbia might accept the note in its entirety if one or two points were explained, Berchtold replied, "The integral acceptance of the demands of the note would have sufficed here, as long as a peaceful termination of the conflict between Serbia and the Monarchy was still possible. Now, since a state of war had supervened, Austria's conditions would naturally be different."[7] With or without explanations, an unconditional acceptance of the Austrian note would no longer be enough to stop the Austro-Hungarian invasion.

Tschirschky was lunching with Berchtold and Count Johann Forgách von Gymes und Gaes, Berchtold's chief of section, when he received the latest wire from Berlin, quoting Lichnowsky's account of Grey's Stop-in-Belgrade proposal and instructing the ambassador to "urgently and impressively suggest . . . acceptance of mediation on the above-mentioned honorable conditions."[8] Tschirschky waited until they had finished eating, then read them Bethmann's message.

Berchtold went pale as Forgách took notes. Tschirschky read the wire through twice and looked up. Berchtold said only that he would have to talk with Emperor Franz Joseph. Tschirschky, who now realized that Bethmann was serious, said that "a complete refusal of the mediation was out of the question." He argued that "the honor of Austrian arms would be satisfied by the occupation of Serbian territory" and that since the occupation would take place with Russian consent, it "unquestionably meant an important strengthening of Austrian influence with regard to Russia in the Balkans."

Tschirschky later assured Bethmann that "I begged both gentlemen to keep in mind the incalculable consequences of a refusal of the mediation."[9]

Those last wires from Berlin came as a terrible shock to Vienna. For three weeks, the Germans had been urging them to hurry up and attack. Now they suddenly wanted them to settle for the occupation of Belgrade. The news of Tschirschky's new instructions spread rapidly, but Bunsen, at least, was not sure that Tschirschky would be effective in a restraining role. "Unfortunately [the] German Ambassador is himself so identified with extreme anti-Serbian and anti-Russian feeling prevalent in Vienna that he is not likely to plead [the] cause of peace with entire sincerity."[10]

After Berchtold left to get ready for an audience with the emperor, Tschirschky continued talking with Forgách, appealing to the count's conscience. Forgách conceded that mediation might be necessary, but he did not see how military operations could be restricted.[11] Vienna wanted to destroy the Serbian army. Tschirschky talked by telephone with Stumm, who confirmed that Germany really did want an Austro-Russian negotiation on Serbia. Tschirschky had to tell Stumm that the Austrians, so far, were unwilling either to limit or to abandon their military action against Serbia.[12]

Stumm must have told Tschirschky that if Serbia would accept the Austrian note with explanations, Berlin wanted an agreement along the lines of Grey's proposal. Tschirschky went back to the foreign ministry and talked "very seriously" with Forgách and Hoyos, who told him that a formal commitment to limit military operations was out of the question. Given the serious nature of the German demands, however, they would have to consult Tisza before making any further reply—and Tisza would not be in Vienna until the next day, 31 July. Meanwhile, Berchtold and Conrad would talk with the emperor.[13] At 5:20 P.M., Tschirschky sent another wire to Berlin: "Instructions most emphatically carried out. Count Berchtold will forward full and complete answer after receiving commands of the Emperor Franz Joseph."[14]

While Tschirschky was talking with Berchtold, Forgách, and Hoyos, General Conrad was meeting with the head of his railway section. Conrad explained that a Russian mobilization was coming and he would have to mobilize the rest of the army, which was essentially A Group. Existing plans called for both A Group and B Group to go to Galicia together if general mobilization was ordered. Was it possible, Conrad inquired, to arrange for the simultaneous movement of A Group to Galicia while B Group continued on to Serbia? The section head replied that it would be difficult. His staff had never planned for B Group to act independently of A Group once general mobilization was ordered. They had always assumed that a general mobilization meant war with Russia. He would need a few days to work things out. A Group, therefore, could not be mobilized until the revisions were ready.[15] Conrad agreed, then went to talk with Berchtold before their audience with the emperor.

The original purpose of the audience had been to discuss a general mobilization. Now they would have to discuss the new German position. Forgách showed Conrad a four-page memorandum on the messages delivered by Tschirschky that morning. Conrad had just asked his railway expert to work out plans for a full-scale invasion of Serbia parallel with the mobilization of A Group. His reaction was predictable: the occupation of a few pieces of territory would only drive the Serbs to new heights of anger and terrorism; nothing short of the military destruction of Serbia would prevent further subversion and propaganda.[16] Conrad's real problem, however, was that he had no plans for an action limited to the seizure of Belgrade. He had always opposed what he called "half-measures," and his war plan called for the army to sweep west and south, around Belgrade, to pursue and destroy the Serbian army.

Berchtold had his own reasons for opposing a diplomatic solution. Grey's proposal "was not to be for the purpose simply of securing the fulfillment of our still unsatisfied demands on Serbia," but to arrange a four-power mediation in which only one of the four powers "stood politically on our side." Berchtold never regarded Italy as a friendly power. The results would be no better than those of the "so-called 'diplomatic triumphs'" of 1909 and 1913.[17] He remembered that on the eve of the First Balkan War in 1912, all the powers had agreed on maintaining the status quo in the Balkans, only to renege. After the fighting, Berchtold had forced them to recognize an independent Albania, and had wrung an agreement on Albania's borders from every nation involved, including Serbia. When Serbia nonetheless moved troops into Albania, no one made a move to enforce the agreements until Austria-Hungary threatened military action. Berchtold was not about to submit Austrian interests to another international conference. In this mood, Berchtold, Conrad, and War Minister Alexander von Krobatin went to see Franz Joseph.

By that time, they had all read the kaiser's wire to the emperor reporting the tsar's "personal plea" to "attempt mediation."[18] They also knew that Wilhelm had sent a series of proposals, among them that "Austria should announce her conditions after occupying Belgrade or other places." Wilhelm had asked Franz Joseph to "favor me with your decision as soon as possible."[19]

Both Bethmann and the kaiser were still maintaining the posture that they did not want to limit Austria's freedom of action; they were asking for a "decision," not demanding a change of policy. To the Austrians, however, Berlin seemed about to abandon them. Conrad recalled, "While H. M. Emperor Franz Joseph, in this no doubt gravest hour of his life, with deep earnestness and calm resolve took the step, the serious consequences of which were no less evident to him than its inevitability, it seemed at that moment as if Kaiser Wilhelm was meditating a retreat. . . ."[20]

Despite German pressure, the emperor and his advisers agreed that every single word of the demands of the 23 July note must be accepted. Until that happened, Vienna would continue mobilization and military operations, and Serbia would have to pay the costs. The Serbians had cost Austria millions by provoking mobilizations in 1909 and 1912; this time the Serbs would pick up the tab.

Conrad also wanted to annex Belgrade and other areas; the emperor and Berchtold said that was impossible.

Conrad moved to another topic. They must, he insisted, tell Germany that, "given the present mood of the army," military operations could not be halted. He added that "if Russia mobilizes, we must mobilize."

Berchtold objected. "That will cost millions."

"The Monarchy is at stake," Conrad declared.

Berchtold did not want general mobilization. "Once our army is in Galicia, it will mean war with Russia."

Conrad reassured him. "If the Russians do nothing, we don't have to do anything."[21]

After further discussion, the emperor agreed that Austria would order general mobilization and go forward with its invasion of Serbia. Tschirschky had thought that morning that the Austro-Hungarian government would "mobilize as soon as Berlin agrees to it";[22] now the decision was made to go ahead without Berlin, probably because they feared that if they asked for German agreement before mobilizing, the Germans would force them to accept the Stop-in-Belgrade scheme.

Not only was Vienna going to order general mobilization without conferring with Berlin, but Conrad was about to violate his solemn promise to Moltke to concentrate the bulk of his army against the Russians, in Galicia. Vienna also rejected Grey's mediation proposal insofar as it limited military operations. The rejection was to be veiled as diplomatically as possible. Mensdorff would thank Grey for his efforts and say that despite the Russian mobilization, Vienna was prepared to "go along" with Grey's mediation, but the invasion of Serbia would go forward. If Russia suspended its mobilization, Austria-Hungary would not order general mobilization.[23]

*   *   *

Berlin was informed that same afternoon.[24] There was one caveat: "Naturally, all declarations of our territorial disinterest are valid only if the war between ourselves and Serbia remains localized."[25] Berchtold—the infinitely courteous aristocrat, the dilettante, the connoisseur of art, of beautiful women, and of horses—was showing a steely stubbornness that most contemporaries, and subsequently most historians, attributed to the influence of the "militarists" and Tschirschky. But Berchtold was as determined as anyone to put an end to the Serbian troubles.

General mobilization would not be announced until 1 August. The Austrians had two reasons for that delay: (1) they first must talk with Tisza, and he would not be in Vienna until 31 July; and (2) given the urgency of Bethmann's telegrams, they did not want to embarrass German diplomatic efforts in London and St. Petersburg. They also agreed to Conrad's proposal that 4 August be designated as the first day of mobilization.[26] Conrad wanted this additional delay so that the railway section could work out a new schedule to keep B Group heading south while A Group headed north.[27]

Austrian policy was set: in Serbia they would keep fighting; in London and St. Petersburg they would keep talking. Bethmann could complain all he wanted, but they had a German commitment. Although they were a little shaken by Bethmann's latest telegrams, no one believed the Germans would renege.

After the audience with Franz Joseph, Berchtold called for Ambassador Schebeko. According to every report, the two men had a conciliatory and friendly talk. On Wednesday, when Schebeko had learned of his country's mobilization against Austria-Hungary, he had been thoroughly frightened. Berchtold had thought he was "chalk white" when they talked, although their conversation had been friendly enough.[28] Earlier in the day on Thursday, Schebeko had heard rumors "that Austria would declare war in reply to mobilisation," and he had begun packing his bags to leave.[29] It may have been sheer relief that war was not about to be declared that led him to find Berchtold so conciliatory.

Berchtold made it clear immediately that he had never intended breaking off direct talks with Russia; he had only refused to negotiate the demands on Serbia. Szápáry was instructed to give Sazonov whatever explanations he required on Austria's demands, and to explore fully with him all aspects of maintaining friendly Austro-Russian relations. Schebeko was delighted. He might have been less delighted if he had seen Szápáry's instructions; Szápáry was to limit his discussion of the Austrian note to "supplementary explanations, since it was never our intention to bargain on any point of the note."[30] Schebeko, in his relief at not being handed a declaration of war, may not have grasped the limits to Berchtold's remarks, or he may have believed that "explanations" could serve as a face-saving cover for negotiations.

Schebeko explained to Berchtold that the problem was that Russia had no idea what Austria-Hungary intended for Serbia: annex it, dismember it, limit its sovereignty, destroy it. Russia had not the slightest desire to diminish Austro-Hungarian prestige or to encourage Serbian provocations, but it could not stand by while Austria destroyed Serbia. The Russian mobilization was not an act of hostility to Austria-Hungary; its only purpose was to assure that the tsar be heard in any final settlement with Serbia.

Berchtold assured Schebeko that Austria-Hungary was not interested in territory and had no desire to limit Serbian sovereignty. What Vienna wanted was an end to the years of terrorism and subversion the monarchy had suffered at Serbia's hands. Serbia would never have undertaken such actions against a neighboring Great Power without assurances of Russian support. Schebeko replied that both he and Sazonov were opposed to the policy of supporting Serbian subversion of the monarchy—which by that time was probably true. The prospect of a European war had frightened everyone.

Schebeko came away with the impression that "Berchtold would really like to come to agreement with us, but nonetheless is of the opinion that it would be impossible for Austria to suspend its operations against Serbia without full satisfaction and guarantees for the future."[31] Schebeko was certainly correct that Berchtold and Conrad were prepared to accept Russia's partial mobilization without war. The Austrians would respond with a general mobilization in order to place covering troops along the Russian frontier. They would go forward with their invasion of Serbia, but if Russia did not attack them, they would not attack Russia. There was still time.

During the night of 30–31 July, London, Paris, and St. Petersburg were all informed of the interview. Schebeko went immediately to see the French ambassador, Alfred Dumaine, and found Bunsen with him. If Berchtold could be believed, it looked as if new direct talks might lead to a settlement along the lines of Grey's latest Stop-in-Belgrade proposal. All three ambassadors knew San Giuliano's theory that the Serbians could accept the note with explanations, and Szápáry was being authorized to explain the note to Sazonov. The ambassadors cautioned their governments against excessive optimism, but there might now be some hope; both Austria and Russia had given assurances that neither meant to attack the other, at least for the time being. Dumaine thought that "all chance of localizing the conflict was not lost."[32] When Eyre Crowe saw Bunsen's report late Thursday evening, he felt a flicker of optimism: "This looks at last as if some German pressure were making itself felt at Vienna."[33]

*   *   *

At a few minutes after 11:00 P.M., a wire from King George V arrived in Berlin. It contained Grey's latest proposal. "My Government is doing its utmost suggesting to Russia and France to suspend further military preparations, if Austria will consent to be satisfied with occupation of *Belgrade and neighboring* Serbian territory as a *hostage for satisfactory settlement* of her demands *other* countries meanwhile *suspending their war preparations.*" George V hoped Wilhelm would use his "great influence to induce Austria to *accept this proposal* thus proving that Germany and England are working together to prevent what would be an international catastrophe." Late that night the kaiser underlined the italicized passages and wrote, "Austria has this evening made the same proposals."[34] Austria had in fact just rejected them.

The first reports of a Russian general mobilization were just coming in when Bethmann saw King George's wire. The possibility of a Russian mobilization drove everything else from his mind. He promptly called Tschirschky and at 11:20 P.M. sent a wire ordering him to suspend his efforts on behalf of Grey's proposals. Bethmann then drafted a second telegram explaining that he had canceled the instruction to press for mediation because of Russian "military preparations." It is not clear why this news should cut off mediation efforts in Vienna instead of giving them more urgency. Bethmann simply said that "the military preparations of our neighbors, particularly in the east, will force us to a speedy decision if we do not wish to expose ourselves to a surprise."[35] This second wire was never sent.

Instead, Bethmann sent another message at 2:45 Friday morning, explaining that he had canceled the instruction in support of Grey's proposal "in consideration of the following telegram from the King of England," which urged the kaiser to get Austria to accept Grey's proposal. Tschirschky was instructed to communicate the king's wire to Berchtold "without delay." Berchtold, if he wished, could have a copy for Emperor Franz Joseph.[36]

It is hard to say just what was going on in Bethmann's mind. First he canceled the instruction to put pressure on Berchtold; then he explained the cancellation on military grounds but did not send the explanation; then he ordered Tschirschky to relay King George's urgent plea for acceptance. It is very baffling, but by Thursday evening Bethmann and his colleagues had been working for days with little or no sleep. Riezler had complained on Monday that "no one sleeps anymore" and later wrote that after the first news of Russian mobilization, they worked five days in a row until 5:00 or 6:00 A.M. He himself did not get a reasonable night's sleep until 14 August.[37] Given those conditions, no one was thinking—or writing—clearly.

No historian has made much sense of Bethmann's last telegram. His defenders say it was sent in good faith to support Grey's version of Stop-in-Belgrade.

Albertini rejects that argument. He thinks it makes more sense to say that Tschirschky was not supposed to obey the instruction, that there is no evidence that Tschirschky ever made use of the king's message, and that Bethmann sent it because he could neither ignore the British proposal nor tell Tschirschky to ignore it. The difficulty is that Bethmann goes out of his way to urge Tschirschky to communicate the wire to Berchtold and to make a copy for the emperor. Albertini's argument also ignores the last line of Bethmann's instruction, which reads, "A definite decision in Vienna during the course of today is urgently desired."[38] What else could that be but a demand that Vienna respond to Grey's proposals?

Perhaps Bethmann's last telegram should be read to mean exactly what it says: forget the original instruction, use King George's wire, and get a definite answer as soon as possible. Tschirschky may not have actually shown the king's wire to Berchtold, but Berchtold certainly believed that the Germans were insisting that Austria-Hungary agree to Stop-in-Belgrade.

PART IX: THE RUSSIAN GENERAL MOBILIZATION

32: Mobilization Does Not Mean War

30–31 July

Sazonov and the Russian generals were as nervous as Joffre and Moltke and were very unhappy with the tsar's decision to convert general mobilization to partial mobilization. It was typical of the way Nicholas governed that he never told Sazonov he had canceled general mobilization. He gave his orders directly to Yanushkevich, who later informed Sazonov.[1]

Sazonov wanted to keep Vienna talking, but he was equally determined to have Russian forces ready if war came—and he was by then almost certain that it would. Between nine and ten o'clock Thursday morning, 30 July, Sazonov had a long telephone conversation with Krivoshein, the powerful minister of agriculture whose speech to the Council of Ministers on 25 July had persuaded the ministers to stand by Serbia.[2] Both men worried that Russia would not be in a position to fight the Germans if partial mobilization went on too long. Moreover, Prime Minister Ivan L. Goremykin and at least one other minister were known to be doing their best to prevent the tsar from ordering a general mobilization. Goremykin, in fact, was seeing the tsar that morning.[3] Sazonov urged Krivoshein to ask for an audience to explain to the tsar the danger of partial mobilization. Krivoshein commanded great respect; the tsar would listen.

At around 11:00 A.M. Sazonov met with Minister of War Sukhomlinov and chief of the general staff Yanushkevich. Information received during the night indicated that Austria-Hungary was going to order general mobilization and that Germany's military preparations were far advanced. The Russians were right about Austria and wrong about Germany, but at that stage of the crisis almost any military activity by any potential opponent looked like the start of full mobilization. Sazonov and the generals agreed that they were facing a serious war; they could not delay general mobilization any longer.

Sukhomlinov and Yanushkevich telephoned the tsar, who was at his summer residence on the Baltic shore enjoying the sea and worrying about his son. The two generals tried to persuade Nicholas that there was no choice but to resume the general mobilization that he had ordered and then canceled the day before. The tsar, however, had twice received the kaiser's telegraphic assurance that an agreement between Russia and Austria-Hungary was possible. He had resisted his generals the night before and was in no mood to yield. "This conversation is at an end," he finally declared.

Yanushkevich could not let the matter drop. He said that the foreign minister wanted permission to say a few words to His Majesty. There was a long silence until the tsar finally agreed to listen. Sazonov then got on the telephone and asked the tsar to receive him so he could present "a report concerning the political situation which admitted of no delay." There was another long silence, then: "Is it all the same to you if I receive you at 3 o'clock at the same time as Tatistchev, as otherwise I have not a free minute today?" A very relieved Sazonov gave his thanks. He would be there at three.

Yanushkevich urged Sazonov to show the tsar the great danger of a German attack while Russia was still only partially mobilized. Moreover, the French ambassador was constantly urging them to be ready to attack in East Prussia. If the French and the Germans saw that Russia had compromised its commitment with a partial mobilization in the south, the Germans might well obtain a promise of neutrality from France![4] This reasoning, of course, was absurd. Szécsen was right: "Fear is a bad counselor."

The foreign minister was leaving when Yanushkevich said, only half jokingly, that when he received word that the tsar agreed, "I am going out; I will smash my telephone and see to it that I am totally unreachable in case someone wants to give me another order to call off general mobilization."[5]

Sazonov then saw Paléologue. Buchanan joined them a little later, and a three-way discussion ensued, during which Sazonov read aloud the formula he and Pourtalès had worked out at two that morning, stating the conditions under which Russia would halt its military preparations. Sazonov then said that "if Austria rejects this proposal preparations for a general mobilisation will be proceeded with and European war will be inevitable." At another point he said that "for strategical reasons Russia can hardly postpone converting partial into general mobilisation now that she knows that Germany is preparing." After telling them several times that general mobilization was likely, Sazonov informed the ambassadors that he was to see the tsar that afternoon. Buchanan's report to Grey warned that a Russian general mobilization was likely to come soon and confirmed that partial mobilization had been ordered the night before and that the Russians had begun "at the same time to commence preparations for general mobilisation."[6] Paléologue, however, made no such report to Paris.

When Paléologue got back to the embassy, he found the instruction from

Viviani to urge Sazonov to take "no immediate action that would offer to Germany a pretext for a partial or total mobilization of her forces."[7] Paléologue's response was to wire Viviani that "this very morning I have recommended to M. Sazonov to avoid all military measures that might furnish Germany with a pretext for general mobilization." He continued that in the course of the past night the Russian general staff had actually deferred certain secret precautions, the disclosure of which might have alarmed the German general staff.[8]

The "secret precautions" were, of course, the canceled order for general mobilization—but Paléologue did not bother to point that out. It was typical of the way he dealt with Viviani. He probably never warned Sazonov to avoid provoking the Germans as Viviani had instructed. Buchanan makes no mention of any warning by Paléologue, and he certainly would have reported something as remarkable as a warning from the French ambassador. In none of his Thursday telegrams does Paléologue report that Russia might be getting ready for a general mobilization. Throughout the day, the French government had no inkling that the Russians were contemplating such a move.

Krivoshein, meanwhile, had been told that the tsar was too busy to see him. This was not a good sign, and he begged Sazonov to do what he could to persuade the tsar that if they did not order general mobilization, "they were headed for certain catastrophe."[9]

At 2:00 P.M. Sazonov took the train for Peterhof along with Maj. Gen. Ilja Tatistchev, who was also scheduled to see the tsar. Receiving the two men in his office, Nicholas asked Sazonov whether he minded if Tatistchev was present while they talked. Sazonov, who found the tsar tired and anxious, said he would be pleased to have the general present, but he doubted that Tatistchev would be able to return to Berlin as a member of the kaiser's suite. The tsar was startled. "You think it is too late?" Sazonov said he did.[10] For almost an hour, from 3:10 to 4:00 P.M., Sazonov argued that if there was going to be war with Germany—and that seemed all but certain—they had to mobilize. Otherwise they would be unable either to defend themselves or to meet their obligations to the French.

It was a terrible hour for Sazonov and for the tsar and for the peace of Europe. Sazonov was convinced there was an Austro-German plot to march to the Bosporus and Dardanelles straits. He had not believed in Austrian moderation or German peace efforts since the Austrian declaration of war and the shelling of Belgrade. He was fully persuaded by the generals and by the French ambassador that Russia must be in East Prussia in time to split the German forces. The tsar listened and nodded, but he did not argue; that was the trouble—you never knew where you stood with him. Goremykin had already been at the tsar that morning and God alone knew how many pro-German or anti-French or antiwar members of the court had tried to make their influence felt.

Nicholas did not want to fight the Germans. No Russian in his right mind wanted that. But he had no use for the Austrians, and he could not abandon the Serbs. People kept telling him he would have a revolution and lose his throne if he abandoned the Serbs. They also told him that Russia could not stand a war, that millions would die and tsardom would collapse. Either way he faced a revolution.

Nicholas had listened stolidly to Goremykin's quiet insistence on peace, then his generals were after him on the telephone, and now his foreign minister was arguing passionately for a general mobilization that would almost certainly mean war. According to Paléologue's account of what Sazonov told him, the tsar was tense and pale. "Just think of the responsibility you're advising me to assume! Remember it's a question of sending thousands and thousands of men to their death!"[11] Sazonov replied, "Without blinking the fact that our preparations may bring on a war, it is nonetheless better to proceed carefully with them rather than be caught unprepared out of fear that they may offer a pretext for war."[12] The dilemma seemed inescapable.

General Tatistchev, who had been listening silently, interrupted to say, "Yes, it is difficult to decide." In a rare show of emotion, the tsar replied sharply, "I shall decide." The general held his tongue. Finally, as Sazonov talked and Nicholas listened, the tsar conceded that the most dangerous situation was to remain unprepared in the face of an apparently unavoidable war. Sazonov argued, and apparently believed, that Russia could order general mobilization without necessarily provoking a war with Germany. He asked for permission to authorize general mobilization. The tsar reluctantly consented.

Sazonov did not waste time. He asked to use a palace telephone to call the army chief of staff. The tsar agreed, and Sazonov left the tsar's quarters and hurried downstairs to call Yanushkevich, who was waiting anxiously for instructions. Sazonov told the general that the tsar had agreed to general mobilization, then added, "Now you can smash your telephone"[13] and "disappear for the rest of the day."[14]

Once again Yanushkevich summoned Dobrolski and once again Dobrolski went about collecting the necessary signatures. This time it was easy, as all the ministers were gathered for a council meeting. By five that afternoon, Dobrolski was again at the telegraph office, and by six the lines were cleared. The operators waited for copies of the mobilization telegram. Except for the rustle of papers and the shifting of bodies, silence reigned; then the machines began to tap out the decree. Dobrolski waited until about 7:00 P.M. for every military district to confirm receipt of the telegram. That night, bright red mobilization notices were posted all over Russia. General mobilization had begun.[15]

Russia was the first of the Great Powers to order general mobilization. Emotionally and politically, Russia's leaders felt they could not do otherwise. A 1912 Russian staff conference had concluded that Russia could not stand by while Austria-Hungary attacked Serbia. Russian mobilization was so slow that if it did not begin promptly, Serbia would be crushed and the Austrian armies would be back in Galicia before Russia was ready.[16] Neither Sazonov nor the generals were prepared to suffer another humiliation such as Bosnia and Herzegovina at the hands of Austria.

Russian generals, moreover, shared the general faith in offensive doctrine. Waiting, allowing the enemy to gain the initiative, was thought to be fatal. In the case of an Austrian attack on Serbia, it was also unbearable. It would have meant appearing weak before the Russian people. It would have meant appearing weak before their French ally. It would have meant ignoring the frantic French calls that Russia be ready to invade East Prussia the moment war broke out.

Militarily, however, Russia would have been better off waiting. Austria had no plans to attack Russia. Neither did Germany—and if Russia did not mobilize, Germany would not mobilize. War with Germany was not inevitable unless Russia mobilized or attacked Austria, a decision that Russia could well afford to delay. A Russian delay was just what Conrad and Moltke most feared. If Russia mobilized after Conrad was in Serbia, B Group would never get back to Galicia in time to support A Group, and the Germans, who would first have to conquer France, might not get back to the east in time to help.[17]

Sazonov refused to believe that a Russian mobilization would necessarily provoke a war. He also believed that mobilization could go forward in secret. He had no idea that red mobilization notices would be plastered all over St. Petersburg, so he was in no hurry to inform the major ambassadors of the mobilization order. Once the news was out, he continued to insist that mobilization did not mean war. Russian armies would engage in no hostile actions unless attacked; there was still time to negotiate.

Bethmann clearly wanted to negotiate. Between two and three o'clock Thursday morning he sent two telegrams asking Pourtalès to clear up the misunderstanding between Austria and Russia on the question of direct talks. Pourtalès did not get to see Sazonov until early in the evening, after the foreign minister had returned from his fateful audience with the tsar.

Pourtalès was instructed to tell Sazonov that Berlin would "continue to mediate; but only on the assumption that no hostilities are for the time being undertaken by Russia against Austria."[18] Pourtalès's other message was that Berlin was urging Vienna to resume direct talks but did not yet have a response.[19]

Sazonov agreed that talks with Austria should resume and that "Russia would refrain for the time being from hostilities, in case she receives no provocation from Austria." He insisted, however, that he would be risking the tsar's life if he suspended defensive measures before Austria made a declaration along the lines of his 2:00 A.M. formula: Austria must concede the European nature of its quarrel with Serbia and eliminate those demands that infringed upon Serbian sovereignty.[20] Pourtalès assumed that Sazonov's reference to defensive measures meant a partial mobilization against Austria-Hungary, and Sazonov did not tell him otherwise.

Sazonov was not much more forthcoming with Buchanan. He apparently did not bother seeing him that evening, and the published British documents do not have Buchanan reporting the fact of general mobilization until 6:40 P.M. Friday, almost twenty-four hours after the event. The editors of the British documents argue that since red mobilization notices were posted all over St. Petersburg on Friday morning, it was "most improbable" that Buchanan would wire the news so late. Either the date was a mistake or transmission was delayed. Maybe, but none of Buchanan's other transmissions were delayed. Buchanan, who was as convinced as Nicolson and Crowe that England must not stand aside in a European war, knew that English intervention would be all but impossible if Russia appeared as the aggressor by mobilizing first. Buchanan's memoir, which came out a few years before the published British documents brought the delay to light, says nothing about it.[21] Nonetheless, Buchanan was never a man to move fast; there is nothing to show that he did more than act with his usual lackadaisical nonchalance.

Paléologue was another matter entirely. The Franco-Russian military agreement expressly required "previous agreement" for a general mobilization unless Germany had already ordered general mobilization or engaged in acts of war—and neither of these conditions had been met. The French had repeatedly warned that since they would bear the brunt of the initial German attack, they were entitled to be kept informed of Russia's actions. When the tsar first decided on general mobilization on Wednesday night, Sazonov immediately informed Paléologue; and there was no reason for him not to do the same on Thursday evening. Paléologue's memoir entry for 30 July fully describes the tsar's decision to consent to general mobilization, which he almost certainly got from Sazonov that same evening. On the other hand, Sazonov did not tell Buchanan or his own ambassador in Paris, Izvolsky, who, as late as the evening of the thirty-first, still did not believe that Russia had ordered general mobilization.[22]

Sazonov and Paléologue were both patriots and they were both frightened. They dreaded above all that the Russian army would not be ready in East Prussia. They both distrusted the pacifists, radicals, and Socialists in Paris, and Paléologue, at least, counted Viviani among them. It is almost certain that Sazonov was frank with Paléologue, particularly when deception meant risking the French commitment. But if Paléologue had decided not to tell Viviani that Russia was mobilizing because he feared that Viviani might raise objections and disrupt the alliance, then Sazonov certainly could not tell Izvolsky. The ambassador to France was much too excitable to carry out that kind of deception.[23]

Paléologue covered all his bases in the wire he sent to Paris on Thursday evening. It reads like a brief for the defense rather than a diplomatic report. He began by saying that after his talk with Pourtalès, "Sazonov was obliged to come to the conviction that Germany will not speak the decisive word at Vienna which would safeguard the peace." In a paragraph headed "Secret," Paléologue went on to say that the tsar came away with the same suspicions in his exchange of telegrams with the kaiser. Perhaps, but the tsar's last telegram from the kaiser was the one he received the evening before, causing him to cancel general mobilization. The kaiser's 30 July telegram, in which he warned that his mediation efforts would be endangered by further Russian armaments, did not reach the tsar until hours after he had agreed to order general mobilization.[24]

Only after these preliminaries did Paléologue announce that "the Russian general staff and admiralty have received disquieting information concerning the preparations of the German army and navy. In consequence the Russian government has decided to proceed secretly to the first measures of general mobilization." This is hardly the language of a professional diplomat. Had Russia ordered mobilization or not? Was it about to do so? Was it trying to carry out a secret mobilization? What about Viviani's request that Russia take no provocative action? Paléologue ignored such details and concluded with a word of comfort: "In giving me this information M. Sazonov added that the Russian government is nonetheless continuing its efforts toward conciliation. He repeated to me, 'I shall negotiate until the last moment.'"[25]

On Friday morning, however, Paléologue wired Viviani, "The general mobilization of the Russian army has been ordered."[26] Paléologue, like Sazonov, had forgotten—if he ever knew—that St. Petersburg would be covered with red notices bearing the heading: "Imperial *ukaze* of general

mobilization." Once he realized that the mobilization was a matter of public notice, he probably decided he had no choice but to notify Viviani. But,
for reasons that are still a matter of controversy, Paris did not get
Paléologue's wire until 8:30 P.M. Friday.[27]

Neither Paris nor London, therefore, had direct reports of the Russian
general mobilization from their ambassadors until twenty-four hours after
the event. Until then, German reports of Russia's mobilization were treated
as a ploy to get Paris and London to put pressure on St. Petersburg, or as an
attempt to provoke a premature French declaration of war. In this way, St.
Petersburg and Paris were able to hide from London that Russia had precipitously launched the first general mobilization just as Vienna was agreeing to
resume talks with St. Petersburg. By the time London heard from Buchanan
that Russia was in fact mobilizing its entire army, Germany had already sent
ultimatums to France and Russia.

33: "WHAT IS THE POINT OF WAR?"

31 July

Neither Buchanan nor Paléologue responded to the news of Russia's general mobilization with anything remotely resembling Pourtalès's urgency. Pourtalès was about to leave for the foreign ministry on Friday morning, 31 July, when Major Eggeling came in to tell him that red mobilization notices were posted on every corner in St. Petersburg. Pourtalès was horrified and raced to the foreign ministry. Time, now, was everything.

Sazonov was attending a Council of Ministers with the tsar at Peterhof, so Pourtalès exploded instead at Anatoli Neratov, Sazonov's undersecretary. How could Russia do it? Vienna had just agreed to resume direct negotiations with St. Petersburg. And just two days before his government had been assured that the Russians would take no military steps aimed at Germany. Neratov was taken aback by Pourtalès's vehemence. Like Sazonov and the tsar, Neratov hoped that Russia and Germany could mobilize and wait while negotiations continued. He assured the ambassador that he would give his message to the foreign minister.

Pourtalès did not wait; he rushed back to the embassy and called Peterhof. He got Sazonov out of his meeting and repeated what he had just told Neratov: Berlin would regard the Russian mobilization as a hostile act. Sazonov responded stiffly that "the decision taken by the Imperial Government merely constituted a precautionary measure. . . . Russia for her part would do nothing that was irrevocable . . . despite her mobilization, peace could be maintained if Germany would . . . exercise a moderating influence upon her ally."[1] Pourtalès dismissed such assurances. Germany would never sit still while Russia mobilized. Sazonov said he would deliver the ambassador's warning to the tsar. Again Pourtalès did not wait but instead called directly for an appointment with the tsar. He was told to come to Peterhof by the next train.

Nicholas II received Pourtalès in the small workroom of the Alexandra Palace at Peterhof and listened intently as the ambassador explained "that

the mobilization was a threat and a challenge to Germany, and, as it occurred at the moment when our kaiser was endeavoring to mediate between
Russia and Austria, must be regarded as an insult to His Majesty." The tsar
was surprised. *"Vous croyez vraiment?"* (You really think so?) Pourtalès
repeated emphatically that only "a withdrawal of the mobilization order"
could prevent war. Nicholas replied that Pourtalès, "as a former officer,
must realize that on technical grounds a recall of the order issued was no
longer possible."

Pourtalès "then attempted to call the tsar's attention to the dangers that
this war represents for the monarchic principle." Nicholas agreed and said
he hoped things would turn out right after all. When Pourtalès remarked that
he did not think a peaceful solution was possible if Russian mobilization
continued, "the tsar pointed heavenwards: 'Then there is only One who still
can help.'"[2] The tsar showed Pourtalès the wire he was about to send the
kaiser, which pledged his solemn word that as long as Austria continued to
negotiate with regard to Serbia, "my troops shall not take any *provocative*
action." The wire concluded with another declaration of faith: "I put my
trust in God's mercy."[3] Pourtalès was not comforted. When he got back to
St. Petersburg he again talked to Sazonov and got the same answer: Russia
would not attack if Austria kept negotiating, but it would not demobilize.[4]

Paléologue and Sazonov both described a tsar choked with emotion at
the prospect of war. Pourtalès found him so remote, so calm, that he thought
Nicholas did not understand the gravity of the situation. The tsar's diary
reflects the same detached placidity. In his entry for Thursday, 30 July,
when he finally consented to general mobilization, Nicholas listed the
people he saw during the day and closed with: "Bathed in the sea with pleasure. Olga ate with us and spent evening with us." For Friday, 31 July, when
Pourtalès warned him that the Russian mobilization would bring their two
countries to the brink of war, Nicholas barely hinted at his feelings: "The
day was grey, which matched the state of my mind. Had meeting of Council of Ministers at 11:00 A.M. Returned home for an hour. After lunch received the German ambassador. Took a walk with my daughters. Worked
until dinner in the evening."[5]

Nonetheless, the strain of the crisis was beginning to tell. Pierre Gilliard,
his son's tutor, was struck by the tsar's exhausted appearance: "The features
of his face had changed, and the small bags which appeared under his eyes
when he was tired seemed far bigger."[6] The tsar was remote but not inhuman.

Berchtold wanted to keep Russia talking while Conrad destroyed the
Serbian army. Berchtold told Schebeko on Thursday that he was perfectly
ready to have Szápáry talk with Sazonov. At the same time, Grey was

discussing his latest formula with the Russian ambassador, Benckendorff. Count Benckendorff was skeptical, given Austria-Hungary's declaration of war on Serbia, its shelling of Belgrade, and Germany's threat to mobilize if Russia kept arming. Russia could not stand by and let Serbia be destroyed. Grey, who believed that Austrian troops were already in Belgrade and who was faced with a cabinet that opposed any intervention in a continental war, insisted that they had to try something.[7] He wired his new formula, which accepted an Austrian occupation of Belgrade, to Buchanan in St. Petersburg.[8]

Sazonov accepted one part of Grey's new formula: Russia would no longer insist that Austria-Hungary amend its note. Sazonov hoped to get what he wanted from the ambassadors' conference in London. He said in his memoir that he did not like the formula, and that the tsar was "unpleasantly surprised" at Grey's intervention and only reluctantly agreed to the new formula.[9]

Sazonov had originally drafted his formula when Pourtalès asked what it would take to halt mobilization. Sazonov promised that if Austria accepted the formula, "then Russia agrees to suspend all military preparations."[10] Grey and Lichnowsky therefore proposed their revisions assuming that a Russian acceptance would mean a halt to mobilization. But Sazonov was by then convinced that Russia had to mobilize, and his modification of Grey's newest proposal said, "If Austria agrees to halt the advance (marche) of its troops into Serbian territory," and agreed to a four-power inquiry "into the satisfaction which Serbia might give," then "Russia engages to maintain her waiting attitude." There was no longer any promise "to suspend all military preparations."

Sazonov sent out these modifications on Friday morning,[11] leaving the precise status of an occupation of Belgrade up in the air. About the only positive sign was that Vienna and St. Petersburg were willing to keep talking. The Austrians persisted in believing that Russia had no reason to intervene in their war with a nation that threatened the very survival of the Hapsburg Empire, particularly when the assassination of royalty was involved. If Russia did intervene, it meant Russia was determined upon war with Austria-Hungary. When Berchtold and Szápáry insisted that Austria-Hungary's survival depended upon the containment of the Great Serb threat, and when the kaiser, Bethmann, and Pourtalès insisted that Germany's position in Europe depended upon Austria's survival, the Russians saw only the threat of a new humiliation and the collapse of tsardom.

Count Friedrich Szápáry was not inclined to obey Berchtold's instruction to resume talks with Sazonov. He was a hard-line anti-Serb who believed that the annexation of Bosnia-Herzegovina in 1908–9 had restored the monarchy as "a powerful factor in European politics,"[12] and he meant to keep it that way. Szápáry also agreed with those foreign ministry officials who believed that Berchtold had been much too passive with the Serbs during the Balkan wars. Berchtold, in fact, had appointed Szápáry ambassador to Russia in 1913 to replace an ambassador who seemed too ready to accept Sazonov's peaceful assurances at face value.

It was late Thursday evening when Szápáry received the instruction to resume talks with Sazonov. The next morning, he wired Berchtold that he had already talked with Sazonov on his own authority on Wednesday, and Sazonov had terminated the conversation when news came that Belgrade was being bombarded. The mood in St. Petersburg was hostile. Sazonov had told Pourtalès that Russia would not be satisfied with an Austrian declaration that it "would neither diminish (!) Serbian territory, nor encroach on Serbian sovereignty, nor injure Russia's Balkan or other interests"—all points that Berchtold had stressed in his talk with Schebeko. In the meantime, Russia had mobilized against Austria and then ordered a general mobilization. There did not seem much point in having another conversation, and Szápáry therefore thought he would wait "pending further express orders from Your Excellency."[13]

Szápáry, who felt strongly that something had to be done about Serbia, apparently put the exclamation point after the word *diminish* because it did not track the Austrian formula of "territorial disinterest," which would not preclude diminishing Serbia for the benefit of Bulgaria or Albania. After sending Berchtold his reasons for not making an appointment with Sazonov on Friday morning, Szápáry changed his mind. He concluded from Pourtalès's account of his talks with Neratov, Sazonov, and the tsar, and from the fact that the anti-Austrian demonstrations in front of the embassy had suddenly stopped, that St. Petersburg had not yet decided what its policy ought to be.[14] He also noted that the tsar had promised the kaiser that "the army will not undertake any action if Austria-Hungary is inclined to negotiate with Russia." Although he expected no great result, Szápáry decided to give Sazonov another try. It could do no harm; it would confirm the kaiser's declaration that Vienna was always ready to talk, and at the same time it would put Russia in the wrong for mobilizing while Austria was still negotiating.[15] Great aristocrats were not easy ambassadors.

When Szápáry met with Sazonov on Friday afternoon, he began by warning that he spoke without knowing whether the Russian general mobilization had created a new attitude in Vienna. Sazonov was all nerves, drained by the growing tension and the enormity of the general mobilization. He had just been warned by the German ambassador that if Russia continued to mobilize, Germany would follow suit, which would bring their nations to the verge of war. A very shaken Sazonov broke in with great emotion to assure Szápáry "that the mobilization had no significance and that Tsar Nicholas had pledged his word to Kaiser Wilhelm that the army would not budge so long as a conversation tending towards an agreement was still going on with Vienna." The two men briefly argued over who had mobilized first until Sazonov ended it by telling Szápáry to forget chronology: "There was no fear that the guns would go off by themselves."

Szápáry then explained that there had been a misunderstanding. Berchtold "was not only ready to negotiate with Russia on a broad basis," but was even ready "to discuss the text of our Note, as far as interpretation was concerned." Szápáry warned Sazonov that whereas Russia wanted the note modified, Berchtold was willing only to elucidate its meaning. Sazonov thought that "this was good news," and told Szápáry that he still hoped that matters could be resolved. Sazonov was obviously eager to maintain a friendly atmosphere, and Szápáry had to warn him several times that he was not sure how the Russian mobilization would affect Vienna's attitude.

The ambassador noted that Sazonov "seemed greatly relieved by my information and to attribute excessive importance to it, so that I again and again had to point to the changed situation [mobilization], the discrepancy between our initial points of departure, etc." Szápáry warned Berchtold that "two main points were entirely evaded: on my side, the partly retrospective and theoretical character of a conversation on the text of the note . . . on his side, what should happen as regards military operations during the eventual negotiations." The latter was probably deliberate on Sazonov's part. His reply to Grey's formula had been pointedly vague on whether or not Austria-Hungary would be permitted to occupy Belgrade during the negotiations.

Szápáry may have misled Sazonov with regard to the Austrian note. After pointing out that he was authorized only to explain the note whereas Sazonov wanted to modify it, Szápáry remarked that "on the whole it seemed to me that it came to the same thing."[16] After such a comment, Sazonov was entitled to believe that perhaps the talks would lead to substantive negotiations on the demands of the note. Or he might have let the remark go, believing that he would get substantive negotiations if Serbian compliance was to be reviewed by the four ambassadors in London. The two men parted on the best of terms. It was virtually a replay of their love feast of the twenty-sixth, and the mood matched that of Berchtold's friendly talk with Schebeko the day before. Szápáry thought their talk had not advanced matters much; Sazonov thought they had made progress; and Berchtold continued to believe that he could keep Russia talking while Conrad crushed Serbia.

*   *   *

The Russians were unaccountably relieved. When Berchtold and Szápáry insisted that Austria would not attack Russia and that they wanted to talk, Sazonov and Schebeko acted as if there had been a major breakthrough. They seemed to think they could not possibly be at war with Germany if they were not at war with Austria-Hungary. After the meeting with Szápáry, Sazonov told his ambassadors that Vienna would "consent to enter upon a discussion of the substance of the ultimatum sent to Serbia"—which was precisely what Berchtold was not prepared to do. Sazonov added "that it would be preferable that the negotiations should be carried out in London with the participation of the Great Powers." Once again, Sazonov was de-railing a promising negotiation by trying to involve London, a forum that Vienna would never accept. The tsar saw the problem right away: "The one thing does not rule out the other. Continue conversations with the Austrian ambassador." As to Austria's military operations, Sazonov was firmer with his ambassadors than with England and Austria, informing them that it "would be very important that Austria should suspend her military operations on Serbian territory."[17] Important, perhaps, but presumably not essential.

Schebeko was greatly encouraged by Sazonov's report, particularly the statement that Count Szápáry "had at last conceded the main point at issue by announcing to M. Sazonov that Austria would consent to submit to me-diation the points in the note to Servia which seemed incompatible with the maintenance of Servian independence." Sazonov told his ambassador that any agreement must be "on condition that Austria would refrain from the actual invasion of Servia," but both Bunsen and Schebeko agreed that "it was too much for Russia to expect that Austria would hold back her armies." Bunsen thought, however, that "this matter could probably have been settled by negotiation, and M. Schebeko repeatedly told me he was prepared to accept any reasonable compromise, such as an arrangement that Austria should occupy Belgrade . . . provided only that Russia should have a voice in the final settlement of affairs with Servia." Those hopes were destroyed, according to Bunsen, "by the transfer of the dispute to the more dangerous ground of a direct conflict between Germany and Russia."[18]

Bethmann, meanwhile, was transfixed by the Russian mobilization. When Goschen tried to read him Grey's reply to the German neutrality pro-posal on Friday morning, Bethmann would not listen. Instead, he informed Goschen that Russia was "taking military measures along the German frontier. . . . He was now going to see [the kaiser] and he wished me to tell you [Grey] that it is quite possible that in a very short time, perhaps even to-day, they would have to take some very serious steps."[19] In vain, Goschen tried to direct Bethmann's attention to Grey's answer: France could not be abandoned, but if the present crisis "was safely passed," Anglo-German friendship would be assured, and Grey would make every effort to obtain some arrangement that would secure Germany against aggression by France, Russia, and Great Britain.[20] Bethmann, however, was so shaken by Russia's actions "that he made no remarks whatever upon your communication." He asked, instead, for a written paraphrase that he could study later, "as his mind was so full of grave matters that he could not be certain of remembering all I had said."[21]

On Wednesday the twenty-ninth the Liberal cabinet had refused Grey's request to give France strong support during the crisis. When Grey asked for a discussion of Belgian neutrality, the cabinet refused to acknowledge any treaty obligation and put off a discussion of Belgium until the next meeting—which was not until Friday. Grey therefore had to tell Prince Lichnowsky and Paul Cambon on Wednesday that he could not yet say what position the government would take in the event of war.[22] On Thursday, Cambon went to Grey to point out that in an exchange of letters in November 1912, the two governments had agreed that "if the peace of Europe was seriously threatened, we would discuss what we were prepared to do." Handing Grey a paper listing German military preparations along the French frontier, Cambon asked for that discussion now. He told Grey that he expected Germany to demand that France either cease making its own preparations or declare French neutrality in the event of a Russo-German war. He did not ask for a commitment but inquired as to what England would do if Germany attacked France. Grey could only say that he would raise the point with the cabinet the next day.[23]

Lichnowsky spent all day Thursday trying to get Berlin to force Vienna to accept some form of Grey's Stop-in-Belgrade proposal. He knew that his life's dream of Anglo-German friendship would be realized only if the stubborn Hapsburg leaders could be brought to reason. He had instructions to warn Grey that Russia's partial mobilization and French military measures were imperiling German mediation efforts. Grey replied reassuringly on both points and promised British support for German mediation in St. Petersburg. Lichnowsky added that Grey had told "a confidential friend . . . that if German-English cooperation was successful this time in preserving peace, our relations would be firmly established for all time."[24] That was exactly what Goschen had told Bethmann, but Bethmann was not listening.

Lichnowsky went to bed Thursday night racked by the Austrian problem and Russia's partial mobilization. When he woke up on Friday morning he wired Bethmann to suggest that the kaiser telegraph the tsar and ask if Russia would suspend its mobilization if Austria suspended its operations against Serbia.[25] Lichnowsky then went to see Grey to deliver Jagow's message of the previous day, which asked Grey to use his influence in Petersburg now that Berchtold had instructed Szápáry to resume his talks with Vienna.[26]

Grey was delighted by the news that talks between Vienna and St. Petersburg were on again. He instructed Buchanan to tell Sazonov that "I earnestly hope he will encourage them."[27] Neither Grey nor Lichnowsky yet knew that Russia had ordered a general mobilization, but Grey knew that the majority of his cabinet opposed aiding the French if France went to war in aid of Russia. He desperately wanted a negotiated settlement.

In fact, Grey offered Lichnowsky a virtual guarantee of English neutrality if only Berlin could get a reasonable agreement out of Vienna. "Everything depended on Austria's conceding so far as to put Russia in the wrong, and if the latter should then still refuse, he would be in a position where he could use pressure in Paris and Petersburg." For England to refuse to participate in a war with France and Russia, there must be "some palpable injustice on the part of Russia." Bethmann, of course, was hoping that the Russian mobilization would constitute just that "palpable injustice."

Lichnowsky seized eagerly on Grey's suggestion and urged Berlin to persuade Vienna to limit its military operations. But, he cautioned, "From my knowledge of conditions in Vienna, nothing less than very energetic pressure exercised from Berlin will succeed in bringing Vienna" to agree to anything that might affect "England's attitude in the war."[28]

Lichnowsky was suddenly hopeful. The cabinet split, the antiwar attitude of the financial community, Grey's constant assurances of friendship, and his virtual offer of neutrality if Vienna would concede enough to put Russia in the wrong all had their effect: "I have today for the first time the impression that the improved relations with Germany of late years and perhaps also some friendly feeling for Germany in the cabinet makes it appear possible that, in case of war, England will probably adopt an attitude of watchful waiting." That, for Lichnowsky, was an uncharacteristic burst of optimism, but he warned that Germany must not be perceived as giving Austria unconditional support.[29]

Friday turned out to be a bad day for Sir Edward Grey. After his talk with Lichnowsky, he attended a cabinet meeting. Bethmann's neutrality bid had made it all but certain that Germany would invade Belgium in a war with France, but the Liberal cabinet gave little comfort. "British opinion would not now enable us to support France—a violation of Belgium might alter public opinion, but we could say nothing to commit ourselves."[30] One of the leaders of the anti-interventionist group penciled a triumphant note to a colleague: "It is now clear that *this* Cabinet will not join in the War."[31]

Asquith was particularly disappointed; the crisis was probably going to ruin his weekend with Venetia. He wrote her that evening complaining that "the general opinion at present—particularly strong in the City—is to keep out at all costs. . . . Things look almost as bad as they can be, & I fear much about tomorrow, to which I have looked forward day by day as the one oasis in my desert pilgrimage."[32] He wrote his wife that the City's leaders were "the greatest ninnies . . . all in a state of funk, like old women chattering over tea cups."[33]

Right after the meeting, Grey instructed Goschen to urge Jagow to accept his latest version of Stop-in-Belgrade, in which the four powers would assure Austria of satisfaction and assure Russia that Austria would respect Serbian sovereignty and territory. Grey said that he would work on St. Petersburg, and "if Germany could get any reasonable proposal put forward which made it clear that Germany and Austria were striving to preserve European peace, and that Russia and France would be unreasonable if they rejected it, I would support it at St. Petersburg and Paris and go the length of saying that if Russia and France would not accept it His Majesty's Government would have nothing more to do with the consequences."[34] Grey, faced with a cabinet determined to stay out of a continental war, was offering Germany a tremendous diplomatic victory in return for an Austrian agreement to submit to four-power mediation.

Grey, however, still had Paul Cambon to deal with, and that was a painful encounter. Their conversations were slow and awkward in any event. Grey understood some French but could not speak it; Cambon understood some English but could not speak it. Grey therefore spoke slowly in English, and Cambon would reply, equally slowly, in French. If Grey was making an important statement, Cambon would repeat it in French to make sure he got it right.[35] Their painstaking dialogues were made worse by Grey's embarrassment over his inability to promise more for France.

Grey began by denying the French charge that England was encouraging Austria and Germany: he had told Lichnowsky that morning that if France and Germany were involved in war, "we should be drawn into it." He assured Cambon that "we had not left Germany under the impression that we would stand aside." Perhaps, but he had not convinced Lichnowsky, who thought that England might, after all, just watch and wait. When Cambon asked what the cabinet had to say about the 1912 exchange of letters, Grey had to answer "that we could not give any pledge at the present time."[36] The majority had decided that the time was not ripe for asking Parliament for authorization to intervene. Belgian neutrality would be important, and he planned to ask France and Germany for assurances. Cambon then asked if the British government intended to wait until France was invaded, adding that "help would then be too late."[37] Grey was evasive: they would have to await further developments.

Cambon argued that German military measures along the French frontier were just such further developments. Could Grey at least give him the same assurance he had given Lichnowsky, that England would not remain neutral if France were drawn in? Grey replied that he could not do so. When he had spoken to Lichnowsky, he was just trying to warn Germany.[38] By that time, moreover, Grey had learned of the Russian mobilization, and he told the Frenchman that this "would make it appear that German mobilisation was being forced by Russia."[39] That was exactly how Bethmann hoped it would look.

Cambon was now seriously worried about the English. The keystone of French policy was about to fail. He went to his friend Nicolson to unburden himself. Nicolson comforted the ambassador as best he could, then went to Grey and urged him to have the fleet and the army mobilized as a precautionary measure. Grey said the cabinet would consider the question when it met on Saturday. Meanwhile, Grey sent wires to Goschen in Berlin and to Bertie in Paris: in view of the existing treaties on Belgian neutrality, he wanted pledges from France and Germany "to respect the neutrality of Belgium so long as no other Power violates it." He wanted an early answer.[40] If Berlin would not bring Vienna to the bargaining table, he could at least play the Belgian card.

It had been a terrible day, and Grey was exhausted. He left the foreign office to relax over a late dinner in the company of his parliamentary private secretary. Afterward they played billiards at Grey's club. He needed a few quiet hours.[41]

For most of Friday, Sazonov and the tsar continued to believe that peace negotiations would continue despite their mobilization. So did Vienna. Since London and Paris did not hear of the Russian mobilization until late Friday afternoon, those two capitals also thought there was still time to negotiate. In Berlin, however, news of the Russian mobilization unleashed a telegraphic whirlwind that included ultimatums to France and to Russia that all but guaranteed that war would follow.

The situation created by the Russian mobilization without a declaration of war had not been foreseen on 5 and 6 July. Bethmann, Moltke, and Falkenhayn had agreed on Thursday night that if the Austrians accepted Grey's proposal by Friday morning, the Austrian agreement would be telegraphed directly to the tsar, bypassing Sazonov. The Germans had a much clearer insight than the English into how the Russian government worked;

in emergencies, they went straight to the tsar. The agreement, however, would be accompanied by a German ultimatum "concerning the suspension of mobilization."[42] The Grey proposal assumed that an Austro-Russian agreement would automatically bring the Russian mobilization to a halt. An ultimatum would underscore the importance of that aspect of the agreement.

The decision to send an ultimatum was nonetheless a mistake. It was not necessary if Austria and Russia agreed on a Stop-in-Belgrade proposal, and Russia would certainly not back down before a German ultimatum as it had in 1909. But the fear of the Russian hordes, the terrible time pressure of the Schlieffen Plan, Moltke's wafer-thin defenses in East Prussia, and Conrad's decision to stand on the defensive in Galicia would not permit Bethmann or Moltke the luxury of waiting while Russia's mobilization gained time on that of Germany. At the time, the decision to accompany the news of an Austrian acceptance with a demand to halt mobilization seemed sensible.

But the Austrian acceptance never came. Instead, at 10:20 Friday morning, Pourtalès wired that general mobilization had been ordered in Russia. "First day of mobilization, July 31."[43] That wire arrived in Berlin twenty minutes before Bethmann's noon deadline for deciding on the State of Imminent War. Russia had not yet attacked and was insisting that it would not attack. Berlin, however, could now argue that Russia had made the first belligerent move, and Bethmann capitulated: the State of Imminent War would be declared. Worse, the ultimatum would go to St. Petersburg without Austria's acceptance of Grey's plan.

Moltke did not even want to wait for the ultimatum. According to the quartermaster general, Moltke "just wanted to get to mobilization, then the war would begin of itself, a prior ultimatum could only hurt us." As Bethmann remembered it after the war, Moltke wanted not only an immediate mobilization but an immediate opening of hostilities and declaration of war on Russia. Moltke was a rigid and fearful man whose only hope of victory rested on the Schlieffen Plan, which presupposed a war with Russia to justify the attack on France. As far as Moltke was concerned, the war had begun once Russia mobilized. He did not share Bethmann's hopes for English neutrality, and he no longer cared about the political damage from being the first to declare war. He would not risk the failure of the Great Plan with even the smallest delay.

Bethmann won one last victory over the chief of the general staff: the Germans would not order mobilization or open hostilities; they would send the ultimatum first. The State of Imminent War was declared shortly after noon on Friday, and at 3:30 P.M. the ultimatum was telegraphed to Pourtalès. "For the security of the Empire," it read, "we have been compelled by these Russian measures to declare a . . . [State of Imminent War], which does not yet mean mobilization. Mobilization must follow, however, in case Russia does not suspend every war measure against Austria-Hungary and ourselves within twelve hours and make us a distinct declaration to that effect."[44] The German ultimatum demanded not only that Russia suspend its general mobilization, but "every war measure against Austria-Hungary" as well. This last demand was undoubtedly Moltke's doing; he could not have a Russian army marching into Austria while Conrad marched into Serbia.

Wires went off to London, Paris, and Rome announcing that "in spite of the still pending and apparently not hopeless mediation, and although we ourselves had taken no mobilization measure of any kind, Russia has today ordered the mobilization of her entire army and navy, thus against us also. We have had to declare a . . . [State of Imminent War], which must be followed by mobilization, in case Russia does not suspend all war measures against Austria and ourselves within twelve hours."[45] Flotow, in Rome, was given the wildly unrealistic additional instruction that "we are counting with assurance upon the fact that Italy will live up to the obligations she has assumed."[46]

German military planning assumed that in any war with Russia, France would never resist the opportunity to take Germany in the rear. When the ultimatum went off to Russia, the army insisted that the German government demand a pledge of neutrality from France, a demand the army was certain France would refuse. A French refusal would then justify the preliminary attack on France. In the unlikely event that France pledged neutrality, Moltke would insist that German forces occupy key French border positions to secure the German rear.

Ambassador Schoen was therefore instructed to "please ask the French Government if it intends to remain neutral in a Russo-German war. Answer must be given within eighteen hours. . . . Utmost haste necessary." If France agreed to remain neutral, Schoen was further instructed "to demand the turning over of the fortresses of Toul and Verdun as a pledge of neutrality." They would be returned "after the completion of the war with Russia."[47] Moltke had no plans for fighting Russia without a prior attack on France. Realism was not the order of the day in Berlin that Friday afternoon.

When the kaiser learned on Thursday of Grey's warning to Lichnowsky that Great Britain could not abandon France in a war with Germany, he remembered Prince Henry's report that George V had said England would remain neutral. "Grey," the kaiser wrote, "proves the King a liar." Grey "knows perfectly well that, if he were to say one single, serious, sharp and warning word at Paris and St. Petersburg . . . both would become quiet at once." But, he "threatens us instead! Common Cur! England *alone* bears the responsibility for peace and war, not we any longer! That must be made clear to the world."[48]

That evening the kaiser read a wire from Pourtalès reporting Sazonov's request that Germany persuade Austria to participate in a four-power conference, and Sazonov's explanation that Russia's partial mobilization "could no longer possibly be retracted, and that the Austrian mobilization [Austria's partial mobilization against Serbia] was to blame for it." The kaiser could barely contain himself. Either Germany would shamefully betray its Austrian ally, or "we are to be attacked in common by the Triple Entente." The whole thing had been planned by his uncle, the late King Edward VII, and was now coming to fruition. "The net has been suddenly thrown over our head. . . . Edward VII is stronger after his death than am I who am still alive!" Wilhelm ordered that German consuls be instructed to foment rebellion throughout the entire Muslim world, "for if we are to be bled to death, England shall at least lose India."[49]

On Friday the kaiser learned that Russia had ordered general mobilization. He wired King George: "Your proposals coincide with my ideas and with the statements I got this night from Vienna which I have had forwarded to London." The "statements" from Vienna were Berchtold's agreement to resume talks with Sazonov, not an agreement to consider Stop-in-Belgrade. But, the kaiser went on, "Nicky has ordered the mobilization of his whole army and fleet. He has not even awaited the results of the mediation I am working at and has left me without any news." The kaiser, who was in Potsdam, closed ominously: "I am off for Berlin to take measures for ensuring safety of my eastern frontiers where strong Russian troops already posted."[50]

Wilhelm also wired the tsar that despite the Russian mobilization he was continuing to mediate in Vienna, but that "responsibility for the safety of my Empire forces preventive measures of defense upon me. . . . The responsibility for the disaster which is now threatening the whole civilized world will not be laid at my door. . . . The peace of Europe may still be maintained by you, if Russia will agree to stop the military measures which must threaten Germany and Austria-Hungary."[51]

Wilhelm's wire went out at 2:00 P.M. and crossed with another wire from Nicholas declaring that mediation efforts "give one hope that all may yet end peacefully." But, the tsar continued, "it is *technically* impossible to stop our military preparations which were obligatory owing to Austria's mobilization [against Serbia]. We are far from wishing war. So long as the negotiations with Austria on Serbia's account are taking place my troops shall not take any *provocative* action. I give you my solemn word for this."[52]

When Nicholas received the kaiser's telegram saying that the peace depended on the tsar canceling his mobilization, Nicholas replied on Saturday,

1 August, that he understood that his mobilization required Germany to mobilize as well. However, he wanted "the same guaranty from you as I gave you, that these measures DO NOT mean war and that we shall continue negotiating for the benefit of our countries and universal peace dear to all our hearts."[53]

The tsar's promise to mobilize and wait, combined with acceptance of Grey's Stop-in-Belgrade proposal, would have given the Germans an extremely favorable negotiating position if they, too, could have mobilized and waited. Austria would have had no choice but eventually to accept some form of Stop-in-Belgrade, and negotiations would have proceeded with an Austrian army in full possession of Belgrade. The German general staff, however, had no plan for a mobilization that would leave its armies waiting on the defensive, and neither Bethmann nor the kaiser had the strength of character to force the general staff to improvise one.

Admiral Alfred von Tirpitz was not happy with the way things were going. Russia was mobilizing, the State of Imminent War had been declared, and Germany seemed to be heading for a war with England. He did not want a war and he did not trust the army. Admiral Tirpitz was the creator and presiding genius of the German High Seas Fleet. He had sold his huge naval program to the kaiser and to the nation by arguing that if the German navy were strong enough, Great Britain would be unwilling to risk war with Germany. Bethmann detested Tirpitz because his political propaganda for the navy alienated the English. Tirpitz detested Bethmann because he opposed new naval construction. Tirpitz usually won their battles because the kaiser loved his navy.

Early Friday afternoon, Admirals Müller and Tirpitz received an "Absolutely Secret" memorandum from the kaiser "For the Guidance of Imperial Naval Office and Admiralty Staff." The kaiser's memorandum blamed England and Russia for the crisis. It also enclosed King George's letter outlining Grey's latest Stop-in-Belgrade proposal. The kaiser claimed that George's proposals "are similar to mine," and that he had sent such proposals to Vienna, but that Vienna "has left us six days without an answer." Still, talks "have at last commenced between Vienna and Peterhof, and Peterhof has also begged London for mediation" because the Russians were suffering revolutionary disturbances and "are getting scared about what they have done . . . with their premature mobilization."[54]

When Müller and Tirpitz discussed the documents, they concluded that the Russian and Austrian positions were close enough to hope for a settlement. Tirpitz asked, "What is the point of a war?" He decided to talk to Bethmann about the situation, and Müller encouraged him to do so.[55]

Showing Bethmann the kaiser's memorandum and King George's answer to Prince Henry, Tirpitz asked how such a promising situation could be reconciled with the declaration of the State of Imminent War. Bethmann replied that the kaiser was mixing up two different matters—the state of mediation talks and the Russian mobilization. The critical issue was the Russian mobilization, which was "such an unheard-of procedure against us that we could not put up with it; if Russia went on with it, we should have to mobilize too and an ultimatum ought to have been dispatched to the tsar so as not to let our mobilization fall too much in arrears."

Tirpitz was not convinced. Any ultimatum to Russia should at least point out that there was substantial agreement on all sides and that a favorable mediation was in progress. "The Chancellor," according to Tirpitz, "replied testily that this had been said all along and Russia had just answered by mobilizing."[56]The two men did not like each other; the discussion was not fruitful; and in any event the ultimatum had already been sent.

34: The German Ultimatum
31 July

While Bethmann and Tschirschky were urging Vienna to accept some form of mediation along the lines of Stop-in-Belgrade, Moltke was wiring Conrad to "stand firm against Russian mobilization . . . mobilize at once against Russia. Germany will mobilize." At about the same time, the Austro-Hungarian military attaché in Berlin was wiring that Moltke says, "Reject renewed English demarche for maintenance of peace."[1]

Conrad took the messages to the war minister and together they went to the foreign ministry, where the imperial ministers were gathered for a critical meeting. Conrad read the two wires to the assembled ministers. Berchtold could not help enjoying the confusion in Berlin. "That is something! Who's in charge there, Moltke or Bethmann?" Berchtold then read the kaiser's telegram to the emperor, urging Franz Joseph to consider limiting military operations to the seizure of Belgrade as a pledge for the satisfaction of Austro-Hungarian demands.[2] After these preliminaries, he convened a formal meeting of the Imperial Council of Ministers to review the Austro-Hungarian position.

When Berchtold opened the meeting he knew (1) that Russia had decreed general mobilization, (2) that Germany had decreed the State of Imminent War, (3) that the German general staff expected the Austrians to mobilize against Russia as soon as possible, (4) that Bethmann intended to send Russia an ultimatum demanding that it cease mobilizing,[3] and (5) that the Italians in St. Petersburg were telling "anyone who will listen that Italy will not march with Austria."[4]

Schebeko, the Russian ambassador in Vienna, was insisting that Russia wanted friendly relations with Austria-Hungary. Ambassador Szápáry was reporting that although Sazonov did not want war any more than the tsar, he was determined to prevent the destruction of Serbia, and that the "military circle" in Russia was ready "to precipitate matters as soon as a certain war readiness is arrived at," if the circumstances were favorable.[5] The Imperial

Council had to assess the probable German and Russian response to Austro-Hungarian actions.

Berchtold opened the meeting by summarizing the status of Grey's proposals and reporting Grey's warning that England "could not remain inactive" if Germany and France went to war. England was prepared to lead a four-power mediation while Austria occupied Belgrade and the surrounding area until it was satisfied that its demands were met. If Austria agreed, Grey would urge the solution upon the Russian government. The Germans backed the proposal but did not insist upon it. Looking back today, the Grey proposals appear to have offered a great victory for Austria-Hungary and a considerable humiliation for Russia. The Austro-Hungarian ministers saw it differently.[6]

In the first place, the ministers were all of the view that their diplomatic "victories" of 1909, 1912, and 1913 had not done a bit of good. Berchtold informed the ministers that he had immediately told the German ambassador that a cessation of hostilities against Serbia was impossible. The emperor had made the same declaration, and the council unanimously supported it.

With respect to the German request that Austria-Hungary consider the English mediation proposal, Berchtold said that any consideration of the proposals would be subject to three principles: (1) the war against Serbia would continue; (2) Vienna would not negotiate on the English mediation until the Russian mobilization had been stopped; and (3) "our demands must be accepted integrally and we cannot negotiate about them in any way." As Berchtold explained after the war, the English proposal was not designed to force the Serbs to accept the Austrian note unconditionally. True, the latest English formulation would not require Austria to amend its demands. Instead, the powers in London would decide what constituted a Serbian compliance—which as far as Berchtold was concerned was virtually the same thing as a conference on the Austrian demands.[7] Moreover, a four-power conference in London was not a favorable forum. England, France, and Italy would take the Russian side, and "anything might sooner be expected from Prince Lichnowsky than that he would warmly represent our interests."

Finally, a "mere occupation of Belgrade would be of no good to us; even if Russia would allow it. All this was moonshine," said Berchtold. Russia would pose as the savior of Serbia and especially of the Serbian army. The Serbian army would remain intact, and "in two or three years we could expect a renewed attack of Serbia under far more unfavourable conditions." Here was the heart of the matter: Vienna wanted an immediate and final end to the Serbian threat, which meant the destruction of the Serbian army and the division of Serbia among its neighbors. Given these aims, the Austrians could not seriously consider mediation by an ambassadors' conference.

The ministers were vehement and unanimous that they would not under any circumstances agree to another conference in London. Moreover, mobilization had created an entirely new situation. "Proposals which might have been acceptable at an earlier date, are no longer acceptable now." As Berchtold had already told Tschirschky, the Austrian note of 23 July was "overtaken by events." But no one was prepared to offend Germany by brusquely rejecting Grey's proposal.

Tisza took the floor. He had been a reluctant warrior from the start. On 7 July he had argued for a settlement without war, and in the ensuing weeks he had fought for a note that could be accepted by the Serbian government. But he had been isolated even within Hungary. The Germans had wanted action, and he had yielded step-by-step until he finally approved a note that was virtually a forty-eight hour ultimatum. One minister bragged later that "the only one against the war was Tisza, but we finally dragged him along."[8]

Tisza was concerned that England and Germany not be needlessly offended. He recommended that the Austro-Hungarians reply that they were ready to accept mediation in principle "but only on the condition that our operations in Serbia be continued and the Russian mobilization stopped." Tisza's recommendation was unanimously adopted.[9]

The discussion on Italian compensation took almost as long as that on the English mediation, and once again the Germans were pressing for a position that the Austrians were reluctant to take. In the end, Berchtold was authorized "in principle to promise Italy a compensation in the eventuality of a lasting occupation of Serbian territories on our part . . . if circumstances should demand it and Italy actually fulfills its duties as an ally." In other words, Italy should fight alongside its allies, and if the Austrians actually stayed in Serbia, they would discuss compensation. The Germans had already informed Vienna that Italy regarded such an offer as inadequate, but in Vienna the necessities of war went only so far.

Immediately after the meeting Emperor Franz Joseph replied to the kaiser's wire asking for a decision on Grey's proposal.[10] The emperor told the kaiser that the proposed mediation was too late. The Russian mobilization would force the "mobilization of my *entire* armed forces."[11] The invasion of Serbia would continue, because "a rescue of Serbia by means of Russian intervention at the present time would bring about the most serious consequences for my territories, and therefore it is impossible for me to permit such an intervention."[12] This was the end of Stop-in-Belgrade.

The Austrians simply did not take the threat of Russian intervention seriously; a European war over Serbia was unthinkable. A high Austro-Hungarian civil servant told of meeting Berchtold outside his office in late July. When Berchtold asked him why he was looking so unhappy, the civil servant replied, "I beg your pardon, Excellency, but when a man stands on the eve of a world war, he has every reason to be serious and sad." Berchtold was astounded. "In heaven's name, where did you get that nonsense about a world war?"[13]

No one expected the four-year slaughter that ensued, or the collapse of the monarchy.[14]

Once Russia ordered general mobilization, the Germans dropped the pressure on Vienna to mediate. The kaiser told the Austro-Hungarian military attaché that Vienna's rejection of the British proposal was "understandable" and declared that the main Austro-Hungarian action must be aimed at Russia in Galicia.[15]

Berlin's distrust of Vienna was patent throughout the day. In an early draft of a message to Emperor Franz Joseph, Wilhelm argued that the Russian mobilization had made mediation efforts "futile" and would force Germany to mobilize. If the tsar did not come to his senses, then "I trust that, shoulder to shoulder, we may win victory."[16] When Berlin realized that Austria-Hungary was not going to give up its invasion of Serbia, this draft was scrapped and a more vigorous and precise demand was prepared. Wilhelm reminded Franz Joseph that "in fulfillment of the obligations of my alliance," he was going to war with France and Russia. It was therefore "of the utmost importance in this grave struggle that Austria oppose her principal forces to Russia, and not fritter away her strength by a simultaneous offensive against Serbia."[17]

Moltke was angered by Conrad's obvious reluctance to give up the invasion of Serbia. Conrad had wired that "we are still not clear that Russia is not bluffing, therefore we cannot let ourselves be diverted from proceeding against Serbia."[18] Moltke replied that "Germany has sent ultimatum to Russia and France. . . . if reply unsatisfactory, mobilization will be ordered tomorrow." After more excuses from Conrad, Moltke insisted that Austria concentrate on Russia and check Serbia only with "limited forces."[19] The entire exchange made Moltke very edgy; he was tense and more anxious than ever to get mobilization started as soon as possible.

Goschen saw Jagow late Friday evening and talked for more than an hour trying to convince him to "make another effort to prevent [the] terrible catastrophe of a European war" by having Vienna make a concession that would put Russia and France in the wrong if they refused it.[20] Jagow said the German government could not consider any proposal until Russia stopped mobilizing. If that happened, "He thought personally that [Grey's] proposal merited favourable consideration." Berlin had been urging Austria to continue discussions with Russia, and the talks had taken a promising turn, "but Russia's mobilisation had spoilt everything."[21]

Goschen then turned to Belgium. Would the German government be prepared to respect Belgian neutrality in the event of war? Goschen's query was acutely uncomfortable for Jagow. His answer, Goschen reported, "gave me to understand that he rather doubted whether they could answer at all," since any answer would reveal their war plans. Jagow foolishly added that Belgium had already committed certain hostile acts. When Goschen asked for details, the only instance Jagow could cite was that Belgium had embargoed a consignment of grain destined for Germany.[22]

While Goschen and Jagow were talking, Bethmann sent a long telegram to Lichnowsky explaining that Russia's general mobilization "cut short Austria's pending reply to our mediation proposal. . . . We can not stand idly by as spectators and watch Russian mobilization on our borders. We have told Russia we should have to mobilize, which would mean war, unless, within twelve hours, the military preparations against Austria-Hungary and ourselves were suspended. . . . Please use every means to insure this course of events is duly recognized in the English press."[23]

That line of argument had no effect whatever on the settled suspicion of Germany by men such as Eyre Crowe and Arthur Nicolson. Crowe thought "this is an endeavour to throw the blame for military preparations on Russia. All our information shows that short of the issue of actual 'mobilization orders' in set terms, German mobilization has for some time been proceeding actively on all three German frontiers." That information was largely of French origin and completely false, but among the fearful in all powers, the enemy was on the verge of attack. Nicolson was protective of the Russians as always: "Russia is taking very reasonable and sensible precautions, which should in no wise be interpreted as provocative. Germany, of course, who has been steadily preparing now wishes to throw the blame on Russia— a very thin pretext."[24]

Bethmann's instruction ordering Pourtalès to deliver the German ultimatum arrived at the St. Petersburg embassy at 11:10 on Friday night. By the time the message was decoded and in Pourtalès's hands, it was close to midnight. Pourtalès immediately got an appointment with Sazonov and read him Bethmann's wire: Germany would mobilize if Russia did not "suspend every war measure against Austria-Hungary and ourselves within twelve hours and make us a distinct declaration to that effect."[25] An answer was due by noon Saturday.

Sazonov went over the same arguments he had been rehearsing for the past twenty-four hours: for a country as huge as Russia, to reverse mobilization was technically impossible. A Russian mobilization did not have the significance of a German mobilization, and there was no reason that negotiations could not continue. The tsar had given the kaiser his word of honor that Russian troops would not move so long as Austria continued to negotiate on Serbia. Pourtalès asked if Sazonov could "give me a guaranty that Russia intended to keep the peace, even in the event that an agreement with Austria was not reached?" Sazonov could not. Pourtalès said that then Germany could not be blamed "if our Supreme Command refused to wait until Russia had assembled her mighty army masses on our frontier."

Sazonov asked whether Germany could not mobilize without going to war. Bethmann's instructions to Schoen in Paris and to Flotow in Rome had stated that "mobilization will mean war,"[26] but there was no such statement in the instruction to Pourtalès. Therefore, Pourtalès replied that if Russia did not stop mobilizing and Germany had to mobilize, they would be "on the brink of war."[27] Sazonov, as he had all along, took Pourtalès's response to mean that although the situation was very dangerous, both countries could mobilize without fighting. He did not call the tsar that night to tell him about Pourtalès's message, which he certainly would have done if he thought Russia was being threatened with a German declaration of war. Instead, he sent a note to the head of the foreign ministry chancellery, Schilling, the next morning that stated, "I think one ought to send the tsar a report of my nocturnal conversation with Pourtalès. This should be done at once and it ought to be added that at 2:00 P.M. a council of ministers will be held which I must in all circumstances attend." He also wired his ambassadors advising, "Upon my asking whether [mobilization] was equivalent to war, the ambassador answered that such was not the case, but that we should be extraordinarily near war."[28] Thus on Saturday morning, Sazonov and the tsar saw themselves facing a German general mobilization, but not necessarily a declaration of war.

Even though the public did not know exactly what was going on, it was evident there was a crisis. When Berlin declared the State of Imminent War, long lines appeared outside the banks as Germans tried to withdraw their savings. There was a run on food in the stores, prices climbed dizzily, and the government had to announce that there were ample supplies; there was no cause for alarm.[29] Europe's financial markets were all but shut down.

The English bank rate went from 4 to 8 percent on 31 July, and it would increase to 10 percent the next day. The governor of the Bank of England was waiting for the government to consent to the suspension of gold payments for the first time in nearly a hundred years.[30] "The city has simply broken into chaos," Winston Churchill wrote to his wife. "The world's credit system is virtually suspended. You cannot sell stocks & shares. You cannot borrow. Quite soon it will not perhaps be possible to cash a cheque. Prices of goods are rising to panic levels."[31]

Europe's newspapers continued to support their governments. Serbian papers assured their readers that Russia and Europe would support the Serbian people against the Hapsburg oppressor. Austrian papers were equally sure that Europe would support the government's punishment of the murderous Serbs. German papers never wavered in their support for Austria; some may have been irritated by the harshness of the Austrian note, by Austria's inept handling of the Serbian answer, and by its slowness to act, but only the socialist *Vorwärts* doubted that Germany should back its ally to the bitter end. With the news of Russia's partial and then general mobilization, even moderate papers became anxious that the government mobilize before it was too late.[32] Very few wanted war. With varying degrees of resignation or enthusiasm, the overriding mood was that Germany must be true to its Austrian ally and come to its aid if it were attacked by Russia.[33]

Russian newspapers were equally sure of Russia's duty to defend Serbia. They were outraged by Austria-Hungary's declaration of war on 28 July and by the news of Austria's bombardment of Belgrade on the twenty-ninth, which was ferociously reported the following day. Though Sazonov was undoubtedly sincere, he was probably wrong when he argued that a tsarist government that abandoned the Serbs would be swept away by revolution.[34]

Until the German invasion of Belgium, the English press continued to be split and was not unanimous even then. Many British papers were either advising the Serbs to yield to the Austrian ultimatum, or insisting that Austria and Serbia be left to fight out their quarrels alone. They were unanimous only in supporting Grey's mediation proposals. The major concern of all British papers was to preserve the peace. On the Conservative side, there was an almost equal concern about the danger to the empire if war came and Great Britain stood aside. The *Times* insisted on 30 and 31 July that London make it clear to Germany that in a general war England would back the Entente. A number of papers had come to a similar view by 1 August, when the German ultimatums to France and Russia became known. But even then, a large segment of the press was opposed to any British participation in a general war.[35]

The situation in France was unique. The press virtually ignored the crisis until Wednesday, 29 July, when the Caillaux trial ended. On Thursday, when French newspapers finally turned their attention to Europe, Austria had already declared war on Serbia, Russia had ordered a partial mobilization, Germany had warned Russia that further military preparations would require Germany to mobilize—which could mean war—and Russia, despite that warning, was about to change the partial to a general mobilization.

When the French press did deal with the European crisis, Russia had their full support; the Austro-German assault on Serbia was regarded as an attack on Russia. French newspapers also asserted that Russia was acting with moderation.[36] The *Temps* on 30 July perfectly expressed the French consensus: "One thing that is certain for France and for England is that Russia has done everything and continues to do everything not to precipitate the crisis."[37] This was not only what the French public believed, it was what the English had to believe as well.

But the Russia that was doing everything not to precipitate the crisis had been the first to mobilize. It had ordered partial mobilization on Wednesday and general mobilization the next evening. The Austrians did not order general mobilization until 12:30 P.M. on Friday. The Germans did not declare the State of Imminent War until half an hour later—almost twenty hours after the Russian mobilization—and did not order general mobilization until Saturday. How would that look to the English?

35: FRANCE MUST NOT FACE GERMANY ALONE

Friday, 31 July, to Saturday Morning, 1 August

On Friday, 31 July, Viviani explained to his major ambassadors that France and Germany "each want to leave to the other the responsibility of having ordered the first mobilization." But "neither France nor Germany want to be surprised by an opposing mobilization and each continues to make preparations without engaging in acts of mobilization proper. That fatal competition, to which that of Russia was about to be added, remains profoundly dangerous."[1]

At 12:30 P.M. an increasingly nervous Viviani wired Paul Cambon the completely unfounded rumor that "tens of thousands" of German reservists were being called up and that German troops were advancing to the frontier. French covering forces, on the other hand, were pulling back, and at least two German patrols had penetrated territory evacuated by the French. Viviani urged Cambon to make clear to the English government the pacific intentions of France and the aggressive intentions of Germany.[2]

At around two o'clock that afternoon, General Joffre learned of Pourtalès's warning to Sazonov that continued Russian military action would require Germany to mobilize. Believing that a German attack was imminent, Joffre handed War Minister Messimy a note warning that if Germany continued mobilizing without actually declaring a general mobilization, then "starting with this evening, every delay of twenty-four hours in calling up our reservists and issuing orders prescribing covering operations will have as a result the withdrawal of our concentration points by from ten to twelve miles for each day of delay; in other words, the initial abandonment of just that much of our territory. The Commander-in-Chief must decline to accept this responsibility."[3] Messimy and Viviani now found themselves under the same kind of military pressure that Bethmann faced in Berlin.

General Joffre professed to believe that the Germans were secretly mobilizing by using individual notifications to reservists instead of public notices.[4] He must have known better, but French nervousness was aggravated by the need to be ready for the German onslaught, the fear that Russia would not be ready in East Prussia, and the growing concern that England might not join the war against Germany. The English must be convinced that French and Russian actions were in response to a German aggression.

Paris knew by late Thursday night that "the Russian government has decided to proceed secretly to the first measures of general mobilization."[5] Viviani, who had warned Paléologue only that morning that the Russians should do nothing to provoke the Germans, sent no wire to Paléologue on Friday morning. He neither asked his ambassador what the Russians were going to do nor demanded to know what was being done about his request that Russia avoid provoking a German mobilization.

Poincaré, Viviani, and French official historians took the position during the day on Friday and for years afterward that France had no official word of the Russian mobilization until Friday night, and therefore had no reason to ask Russia to stop; in any event, they insisted, Russia had ordered general mobilization only in response to a *prior* Austrian general mobilization.

The French almost had to take this position. On Friday morning Bertie told Viviani how pleased Grey was that Viviani had urged Russia not to precipitate a crisis.[6] When Bertie asked whether there was any news, Viviani replied that "he has no recent information except that there are conversations in a friendly tone at Vienna between the Russian ambassador and the Austrian Government."[7] He had nothing to say about a possible Russian mobilization.

At that point, Viviani was running to Poincaré on almost every question, and Poincaré saw himself faced with an excitable, uncertain, and inexperienced prime minister, a parliament suspicious of his foreign policy, and a number of ministers and deputies who did not like the alliance with Russia. Had Caillaux's wife not shot the editor Calmette, Caillaux might well be the head of the government and might long since have made overtures to the Germans and warned the Russians against anything remotely resembling mobilization. But Caillaux was on the sidelines. It was Jean Jaurès and other Socialist leaders who insisted that the government restrain Russia.

Jean Jaurès was a formidable figure. A deputy in the chamber and the editor of the Socialist *l'Humanite,* he was a powerful orator, one of the leaders of the Radical-Socialist coalition that had triumphed in the June elections, an ally of Caillaux, and a major figure in the French and European Socialist movement. Juarès was passionately committed to Socialist opposition to any war. He was afraid that the government was not really trying to restrain the Russians and was saying so every chance he got.[8]

"Are we going to unleash a world war because Isvolsky is still furious over . . . the Bosnian affair?"[9]

On Friday morning, Paris papers carried stories that Russia had ordered general mobilization. If Viviani and Poincaré were not prepared to challenge the general mobilization and the lack of prior agreement, they had to take the position—which they did—that there was no official word of a Russian mobilization. The story was probably a German trick to maneuver France into an early mobilization. *Le Matin,* the warhorse of official French policy, was still reporting on Saturday, 1 August, that news of a Russian mobilization was a "tendentious German report."[10]

At 3:30 P.M. Friday, the foreign ministry received a "Very Urgent" telegram from Jules Cambon in Berlin reporting that "the German ambassador at St. Petersburg seems to have telegraphed that Russia had just decided on total mobilization in reply to Austrian total mobilization. In these conditions the almost immediate publication is to be expected of the German order of general mobilization."[11] Even Jules Cambon was caught up in the myth that the Austrian general mobilization had preceded and provoked the Russian general mobilization.

Viviani probably had Jules Cambon's wire in his hands by 4:00 P.M. or shortly thereafter, when it would have been delivered to him during the cabinet meeting. He does not appear to have laid the wire before the ministers for discussion. The cabinet had already decided not to ask the Russians to suspend their partial mobilization, and Viviani may not have wanted to raise the question again. If he had, he might have had to answer some difficult questions. Why was Russia ordering a total mobilization? Had the French government any notice of Russian intentions? If so, what had it done about it? The discussion could have been very uncomfortable.

Instead, Messimy demanded that he be permitted to speak first on a matter of urgency. He read Joffre's note with its warning that every twenty-four hours of delay in moving covering forces into position would mean giving up ten to twelve miles of French territory. The ministers responded by lifting most of the restrictions they had imposed the day before and agreed that covering forces could move to their positions. But they insisted that these troops be maintained at peacetime strength; no reserves were to be called up. The orders went out at 5:40 P.M.[12]

After the meeting, Viviani and Poincaré discussed Cambon's original wire and a second telegram reporting that Germany had declared the State of Imminent War. The declaration would enable German authorities to declare martial law, suspend certain public services, and close the frontiers. Berlin was demanding that Russia suspend its mobilization or Germany would have to mobilize. Schoen had been instructed to ask the French government what attitude it would adopt in the light of these decisions.[13]

There it was. The Russian mobilization was going to provoke a German mobilization, which meant an all-out attack on France. The Russians had not consulted France. It was just what Viviani had been afraid of when he had asked Sazonov to do nothing to provoke the Germans. Ambassador Schoen had a seven o'clock appointment, and Viviani consulted with Poincaré about what he should say. They agreed that he would put off any answer until the next day, and then would say only that France would regard its own interests. Viviani then went off to meet the German ambassador.

Jean Jaurès was upset by the stories of a Russian mobilization. When he learned on Friday evening that Germany had declared the State of Imminent War, he was thoroughly alarmed and led a Socialist delegation to the foreign ministry to see Viviani.

The prime minister could not see them; he was with the German ambassador. Jaurès and his colleagues instead went charging off to Abel Ferry, the undersecretary for foreign affairs. The foreign ministry had Jules Cambon's two telegrams but no word from Paléologue about what was going on in Russia. The hapless Ferry had no information and less comfort. "Everything is finished," he said. "There is nothing left to do."

The Socialist leader "looked as though he had been hit with a sledge hammer" and roared with anguish and frustration, "You are victims of Izvolski and of a Russian intrigue, we shall denounce you, dimwits (*ministres a la tête légerè*), you ought to be shot."[14] As he left, Jaurès again turned on Abel and said, "To the very end, we will continue to struggle against war." Ferry, although sympathetic, was brutally frank. "No, you won't be able to continue. You will be assassinated on the nearest street corner."[15]

Viviani had the foreign ministry political director, Bruno Jaequin de Margerie, with him when he received Ambassador Schoen for his seven o'clock appointment. Until Schoen received Bethmann's instruction, the ambassador had still hoped for a peaceful settlement, but he knew now that France and Germany were headed for war. He delivered Bethmann's warning that Germany would mobilize "in case Russia does not suspend every war measure against Austria and ourselves within twelve hours. Mobilization will inevitably mean war."[16] Viviani replied that he had heard nothing about a Russian mobilization either from Paléologue or from Izvolsky. Schoen then asked what the French government would do "in a Russo-

German conflict." Viviani told him, as he and Poincaré had just agreed, that he could not yet give an answer. Schoen pressed him. When would he be able to answer? "Tomorrow at 1 o'clock," Viviani replied.[17]

Both Schoen's report and that of the French foreign ministry are very laconic. According to Poincaré's diary and his postwar memoir, there was a more extended discussion. As Schoen was about to leave, he said to Viviani, "If I am obliged to leave Paris, I count on your being good enough to facilitate my departure. . . . Will you kindly present my respects to the President of the Republic and hand me my passports." Viviani replied, "I won't do that, Mr. Ambassador. . . . Why leave? M. de Pourtalès is still at his post in St. Petersburg, the Austrian ambassador is here. Why give the signal of departure and without orders shoulder such a responsibility?" Schoen nodded and said he would return the next day, 1 August, for an answer.[18]

If Schoen indeed carried out the letter of Bethmann's instructions and warned Margerie and Viviani that a German mobilization meant war, he presented the French government with a serious dilemma. If Paris knew that a Russian mobilization was pushing the Germans to mobilization and war, why wasn't Paris on the wire to Paléologue to warn the Russians, to try to gain time, to find out what was going on? Because, Poincaré explained after the war, Schoen did not carry out his instructions. They were too brutal, and he could not bring himself to do it. The French government, therefore, not only had no word from its ambassador or from Izvolsky that Russia was mobilizing but was not told that a German mobilization meant war.[19]

It is a truly astounding argument, but Poincaré was eager to show that he had no reason to interfere in St. Petersburg. His invincible self-righteousness led him to forget that he himself had sketched the story of Schoen asking for his passports. Why would the German ambassador have made such a request if he had not warned that mobilization meant war? Schoen himself, when he read Poincaré's postwar account, said it was nonsense. If he wanted to force the French government to declare itself and to restrain St. Petersburg, he had to make it clear that if Germany mobilized, it would go to war. He would have no motive for hiding those facts.[20]

In fact, Viviani was in no doubt as to Schoen's message. Just after his talk with Schoen, Lord Bertie arrived at the foreign ministry to discuss the new Stop-in-Belgrade formulas proposed by Grey and Sazonov, but Schoen's warning had driven all thought of mediation proposals from Viviani's mind. Bertie wrote, "Naturally from the character of the communication which M. Viviani had just received he was in a highly nervous state and forgot all about the object for which he had sent for me." Bertie's closing sentence read: "M. de Schoen sent a message of good-bye to the

President of the Republic"[21]—which could only mean that Schoen had made his message clear.

The interview with Schoen took place between 7:00 and 7:30 P.M. on Friday. At 9:00 and 9:20 P.M., Viviani sent two messages to Paléologue. The first summarized the talk with Schoen but did not warn that Germany was threatening war, only that "Germany will mobilize in her turn." There was no word of Schoen's asking about arrangements for his passports. There was nothing, really, that would dispel Sazonov's illusions about negotiating while he mobilized, and certainly nothing to warn him of the imminence of war.

The second wire asked Paléologue to report Schoen's message to Sazonov "immediately and to report to me, as a matter of urgency, as to the reality of the alleged general mobilization in Russia." Paris had known a Russian mobilization was coming since Thursday night and had reports that it had already taken place on Friday afternoon, but not until after nine o'clock Friday night did anyone ask Paléologue what was going on. Viviani concluded by repeating what he had been saying since Thursday morning: "As I have already told you, I do not doubt that the Imperial Government, in the overriding interests of peace, will on its side avoid anything that might open up the crisis."[22]

The French cabinet met again at 9:00 P.M. on Friday, while diplomatic information was flooding in. Ambassador Camille Barrère in Rome was reporting that San Giuliano thought Italy would remain neutral. San Giuliano was insisting that Russia not act imprudently and stop uselessly asking Austria to modify its note.[23] Grey was insisting that France support England in urging Sazonov to continue talking with Vienna. Ambassador Dumaine reported that Austria-Hungary was about to order general mobilization—but only as a defensive measure because of the Russian mobilization along Austria's borders—and that Berchtold wanted to keep talking with Sazonov.[24] The Germans had told the Russians to demobilize within twelve hours or face a German mobilization, which would mean war, and the German ambassador had asked about the French attitude in a Russo-German conflict. Dozens of reports had the Germans secretly mobilizing already. Between 8:30, when it came in, and sometime after nine, when it was decoded, a wire from Paléologue finally acknowledged that Russia had ordered general mobilization.[25] Jaurès and his Socialists demanded that the government restrain Russia, and General Joffre countered that the government lose no time in ordering general mobilization.

At a little before ten o'clock the prefect of police interrupted the meeting to inform the ministers that Jean Jaurès had just been assassinated while sitting at a cafe with a friend. Poor Abel Ferry had become an inadvertent prophet. The assassin was a mentally disturbed man who believed that Jaurès was a traitor to his country. The French nationalist press had been calling Jaurès a traitor for years. The more violent right-wing papers accused him of wanting "to give Paris to the Prussians"; in July 1914 two separate journals suggested, although they had "no wish to incite anyone to political assassination," that the country would be better off if Jaurès were dead.[26] For the past two days Jaurès had become increasingly and visibly vocal in his suspicion that the government was not doing enough to hold Russia back.

The assassin could not have struck at a worse time. There were several long moments of panic and disarray. The minister of the interior left the room. When he returned he announced that "the prefect of police telephoned me saying there will be a revolution in Paris in three hours. The *faubourgs* will descend upon us." Another minister wailed, "Then what, a foreign war and a civil war?" After a great deal of agitated discussion, the ministers ordered a reluctant General Joffre to hold two cavalry regiments that were on their way to the frontier in Paris, just in case. Messimy objected; the troops were needed at the frontier. But the majority insisted, and Joffre had to countermand their orders and keep the two regiments in Paris. The order was totally unnecessary; Paris remained calm.[27]

When the cabinet settled down, it turned to consider Joffre's demand for immediate mobilization. Since it was already too late to begin mobilizing the next day, the cabinet decided to wait a little longer. If there was no improvement on Saturday, mobilization would be ordered at 4:00 P.M., which was the latest possible hour if it was to begin on Sunday. Joffre promptly wired his corps commanders to get ready.[28] Poincaré signed a series of decrees on the import and export of essential materials. He wrote letters of condolence to the widow and brother of Jaurès. Viviani drafted a poster urging Parisians to be calm. The French government was preparing for war; it gave little thought to restraining Russia.

At 10:30 P.M., Viviani was called out of the meeting to talk to Bertie, who had been instructed to ask "whether the French Government [was] prepared to engage to respect neutrality of Belgium so long as no other Power violates it." Grey wanted an early answer, and Bertie had gone directly to the presidential palace where the ministers were meeting.[29] Viviani took note of the request but gave no immediate answer. He inquired instead what England was going to do in view of recent developments and asked for an answer as soon as possible. He also told Bertie that "the German Embassy is packing up."[30]

What was in the forefront of French thought was the anticipated German attack, and France was not about to take chances with England. At one o'clock Saturday morning Bertie was able to report that the "French Government are resolved to respect the neutrality of Belgium."[31]

In those last hours of peace, virtually every official in Europe was looking for a way out. Men on the periphery of power and representatives of minor powers hurried from one private talk to another. They saw influential ministers whenever they could, and they asked endlessly: Have you tried this? Or that? Why don't you talk to Vienna? Or to Belgrade? What if? Virtually all of the proposals turned on some version of Stop-in-Belgrade, and none of them was very promising. Austria was not willing to stop in Belgrade and Serbia would not surrender its capital. In any event, Russia was no longer prepared to stop mobilizing, which meant that Germany would soon begin. Although the French would have liked a negotiated settlement, nothing seemed promising enough to risk a sharp warning to Russia—no matter how hard the English pressed them.

The English *were* a problem. They wanted the French to encourage talks between St. Petersburg and Vienna and to keep Russia from acting precipitously. This required a certain amount of play-acting in Paris. Between 11:00 and 11:20 A.M. Saturday, the foreign ministry drafted a series of dispatches for Viviani's signature. They were addressed to the Cambon brothers in London and Berlin, to Paléologue in St. Petersburg, to Dumaine in Vienna, and to Barrère in Rome. The dispatches declared that the hopes raised by talks between Austria and Russia had been dashed by the German ultimatum to Russia to demobilize within twelve hours, which would expire at noon that day. The ultimatum "is not justified, for Russia has accepted the British proposal which implies a cessation of military preparations by all the Powers. The attitude of Germany proves that she wishes for war. And she wishes for it against France."[32]

It was not true that Sazonov had agreed to "a cessation of military preparations"; what he promised was a "waiting attitude." The French dispatches charged that the German will to war, as evidenced by its ultimatum, was endangering the peace; there was no mention of the Russian mobilization that had provoked the ultimatum. By Saturday, 1 August, the French were convinced that war was unavoidable. They wanted a united Entente to meet the challenge at full strength. Margerie told Izvolsky that Viviani regarded Schoen's message "as a trick to put the blame for the declaration of war on France."[33] Messimy assured Izvolsky late Friday night of France's "firm resolve to fight," and begged that "all our efforts will be directed against Germany and that Austria will be regarded as a negligible quantity."[34] Maybe the French should have tried harder to slow down the Russian military response; maybe they should have pushed harder for direct Austro-Russian talks. But they no longer felt they had a choice.

According to the official French position at the time, Germany sent its ultimatum before Russia had mobilized and just as Russia and Austria were on the verge of agreeing to Grey's latest Stop-in-Belgrade proposal. When it became known that Russia had mobilized first, the French maintained that they had known nothing of the Russian mobilization at the time. The charade went on for years. According to Poincaré, France had never approved the mobilization, had learned about it only at a very late date, and then had continued to advise against it. Besides, Germany had begun mobilizing when it declared the State of Imminent War, "which permits Germans to recall their reservists immediately."[35]

Most of the arguments for putting the primary blame for the outbreak of war on France and Russia are based on the Russian mobilization, the French failure to object to their mobilization, and the subsequent lies to cover up that failure.[36] But, whatever the French lack of candor, it makes no sense to portray France and Russia as deliberately provoking war. It is more important to understand the emotional atmosphere in which French and Russian leaders worked.

Paléologue's journal recounts his talks with various French leaders in June 1914, when he was predicting that Europe would almost certainly be at war within a very short time. These men, as Paléologue describes them, all feared a German attack and were desperate for a Russian offensive into East Prussia at the earliest possible date.[37]

Poincaré explained the French dilemma in his 1927 memoir. French policy was based on two considerations that had to be carefully balanced: "not to break up an alliance on which French policy had been based for a quarter of a century and the breakup of which would leave us in isolation at the mercy of our rivals; and nevertheless to do what lay in our power to induce our ally to exercise moderation in matters in which we are much less directly concerned than herself."[38] This is a perfectly clear statement of French policy—and it is a sensible policy, except that the restraint of Russia seemed to fade as the fear of Germany rose.

On the morning of 1 August, *Le Matin* declared, "We well know that never has war offered itself under aspects more favourable to us." Austria was throwing its best units against Serbia, the Russian army had gone through a huge buildup, and France's three-year-service law had just come into full force. "In truth," *Le Matin* went on, "if we were inclined to war, if we were not deeply attached to the cause of civilization and peace, would we not feel the strong temptation of war?" Of course, France would never yield to such a temptation and could not be held responsible for the war if it came. But if it did come, "we are convinced that it will bring us the reparations which are our due."[39]

On 31 July, therefore, the precise conditions for victory outlined in the October 1912 general staff memorandum were unfolding.[40] Then came news of a major hitch: instead of Austria and Germany mobilizing first and casting themselves in the role of aggressors, Russia had mobilized first. If the French government was unwilling to risk its alliance to stop Russia, it had to create a scenario in which Russia was responding to German and Austrian aggression, and be sure that Russia was ready in East Prussia. That is exactly what the French did.

Finally, in Paris as in every other major capital, the nation's leaders were exhausted. Poincaré, Viviani, and Margerie had been back in France only a little more than forty-eight hours. On Friday, after a night of virtually no sleep, they were overwhelmed with news of the Russian mobilization and the German declaration of the State of Imminent War. In the published French documents for 31 July, there are thirty-six separate incoming reports assessing German military actions.[41] Things were happening so fast and under such tension, and men were in such a state of exhaustion, that historians who later attempt their meticulous reconstruction and analysis often miss the critical element: there simply was no time for meticulous analysis.

36: FRANCE MOBILIZES

1 August

As far as Bertie was concerned, it was nonsense to fight a war over an Austro-Serbian quarrel, and "rubbish" for Russia to bring on such a war in order to sustain its role as protector of the Serbs.[1] He was a lot more blunt with the French than the French were with the Russians—probably more blunt than Grey would have liked.

Bertie did not trust Russian policy and could not stand Alexander Izvolsky, the Russian ambassador to France, who had been foreign minister when Austria-Hungary annexed Bosnia and Herzegovina. Izvolsky was not blessed with Bertie's certainties. He was poor and Bertie was rich. Bertie, heir to generations of privilege, went his way caring little what the mass of men might say or think. Not so Izvolsky. Nervous, vain, and insecure, he worried constantly about money, his reputation, what the press was saying about him, Sazonov's unpredictable angers, French prickliness, and his success or lack of it in society. Berchtold, while ambassador to Russia, had dismissed him as a "prickly parvenu" and an "arrogant hysteric." Poincaré complained that instead of concealing his thoughts in diplomatic silence, Izvolsky "drowned them in a flood of words."[2]

A cooler and less burdened man might have done more to calm French anxieties, but Izvolsky had to make sure of French support and at the same time assure the touchy French that Russia would not go off half-cocked. Moreover, it was difficult for a man as insecure as Izvolsky to forward French requests for restraint to Sazonov. When Izvolsky reported that Bienvenu-Martin appeared to agree that moderating advice should be given at St. Petersburg as well as at Vienna, Sazonov erupted, and the chastened ambassador had to explain that Bienvenu-Martin "did not for one moment" consider restraining St. Petersburg, and that Bienvenu-Martin meant that it was Vienna, much more than St. Petersburg, that needed a moderating influence.[3] Under the circumstances, this was not very helpful, but it was typical of the kind of thing Izvolsky felt he had to do.

When news of Russia's general mobilization came to Paris on Friday, 31 July, Izvolsky was baffled. This was a major escalation of the crisis, and he had not received a word about it from St. Petersburg. Perhaps the report was a German trick to provoke France into a premature mobilization.[4] Late that evening, when Paléologue finally confirmed Russia's general mobilization, Izvolsky reported that Messimy "told me with a tone of enthusiastic sincerity" of France's firm decision for war. Messimy also asked him to confirm that Russia's efforts would be concentrated against Germany and that "Austria would be considered a *'quantité négligeable.'*"[5]

On Saturday, Izvolsky reported that the French continued to worry about the extent of German military preparations but were reluctant to order general mobilization because "for political reasons relating both to Italy and still more to England, it is very important for France that her mobilization shall not precede that of Germany but be the answer to it."[6]

Bertie observed all this with a baleful eye. On 30 July he wrote Grey that Poincaré was "convinced that preservation of peace between Powers is in hands of England" and "that if there were a general war on the continent England would inevitably be involved in the course of it, for protection of her vital interests," but a declaration to that effect now might save the peace.[7] Bertie did not like that kind of talk. Neither did Grey, who vehemently rejected Poincaré's charge that British policy was a decisive factor in the situation. "Germany does not expect our neutrality. . . . France is being drawn into a dispute which is not hers. . . . We cannot undertake a definite pledge to intervene in a war."[8]

Bertie complained privately to Grey that "the French instead of putting pressure on the Russian Government to moderate their zeal expect us to give the Germans to understand that we mean fighting if war break out. If we gave an assurance of armed assistance to France and Russia now, Russia would become more exacting and France would follow in her wake."[9] And all this, Bertie wrote disgustedly in his diary, "in a question involving Austro-Serb quarrel."[10]

On 31 July, Bertie was again upset by Izvolsky, who "goes about declaring that Russia is ready and war inevitable. What a fool, even if it be the truth!" Izvolsky thought the French papers were "firm." Bertie thought they were "bellicose," but he did not think the same of the French people. "The populace—for French people—is very calm," he wrote on 1 August.[11]

Paul Cambon was twenty-five years old when France went to war with Prussia in 1870. His younger brother Jules fought under the walls of Paris while Paul worked as a secretary to Jules Ferry when the latter became mayor of Paris. Paul's subsequent career never faltered. By 1891 he was

France's ambassador to the Ottoman Empire in Constantinople, and in his first audience with the sultan he announced that France had recovered her old power and influence in Europe. The sultan would be making a serious error if he did not consider French interests in making policy.[12] In 1898 Paul became France's ambassador to the Court of St. James. By 1914, at the ages of sixty-nine and seventy-one, respectively, Jules and Paul Cambon were France's most experienced and influential ambassadors.

Apart from their age, their experience, and their devotion to France, no two brothers could be more different. Jules was a man of geniality and wit who always looked a little rumpled. Paul arrayed himself in perfectly tailored clothes and assumed the calm, self-conscious dignity that befitted France's senior diplomat. Paul's son recalled that few men changed as little during the course of their lives as did his father.[13] Paul Cambon was, and always had been, a devoted servant of the French government. Even as a young boy, he would say, "When I am a minister . . .";[14] as a grown man he never let anyone forget that he was the ambassador of the Republic of France.

Cambon disliked modern times. In 1911, when Monte Carlo was swarming with well-to-do Germans instead of the usual English gentlemen, he mourned the decline of gentility and complained that even in Paris, "one no longer sees the elegance of yesteryear. At the opera, people do not seek boxes as before."[15] He had little good to say about democracy or "progress," and in a 1912 letter to a colleague he lamented "the collapse of everything that we have seen and loved."[16]

Private tragedy may have saddened him early. In 1875, after only three years of marriage, his wife suffered an accident that left her a semiinvalid for the rest of her life. Just two years after his wife's accident he broke his leg in a riding mishap that left the leg permanently shortened. The doctors advised his wife to spend her winters in mild climates, which meant long periods of separation. When she died in 1898, Paul could finally accept the embassy in London and the cold, damp English winters.

Paul Cambon's precisely tailored aura of calm dignity was accentuated by an almost unvarying routine,[17] which included daily visits to the foreign office at Whitehall to see his friend Nicolson. The two men had been friends for more than thirty years. Their paths had crossed regularly in the course of their careers, and they shared a common outlook on the Germans and the modern era. In the four years since Nicolson had become Grey's permanent undersecretary for foreign affairs, they saw each other almost every day. For Cambon, one of Nicolson's great attributes was that he spoke French, whereas Grey did not. The two old friends—Nicolson angry, feeling isolated in a Liberal government, and prematurely bent with age, Cambon neat and grave and determined to save France—regarded themselves as fellow warriors in the long struggle against German aggression.

Cambon would enter Nicolson's office slowly, place his gray top hat carefully upon its accustomed table, settle himself comfortably upon his accustomed chair and declare—in French, of course—as he carefully drew off one kid glove and then the other: "Here I am again, my friend, your daily bread."[18] After a talk with Nicolson, and perhaps with Grey, he would return to his embassy to report on what was said and deal with correspondence. After supper, if the weather was good and if there was no official function, he would go for a stroll. He would finish the evening with more work or a game of chess with one of the embassy staff. It was a calm, orderly, lonely life—made even lonelier by Cambon's inability, or unwillingness, to master English.

Richard von Kühlmann, Prince Lichnowsky's embassy first secretary, thought it was typically French to be totally ignorant of the language. Jules Cambon could not even read the German newspapers, and Paul's inability to speak English put him at an enormous disadvantage on the English social scene, where the popular Lichnowsky and his brilliant wife carried all before them. Cambon sensed this and confided sadly to a friend in May 1914 that in the duel for English friendship, "I have lost the match."[19]

When Grey became foreign secretary in 1905, France was confronting Germany in the first Moroccan crisis. One of Cambon's first questions to Grey was whether France could count on English armed aid in the event of German aggression. Grey put him off, promising no more than diplomatic support on the Moroccan issue. This exchange established the pattern of their talks for the next nine years, with Cambon seeking precise assurances and Grey replying that no English government could give them. Then Cambon would nibble away: joint talks between the army chiefs of staff, the 1912 exchange of letters recording the disposition of the French and English navies, an agreement to consult in the event of a crisis threatening the peace of Europe. Each time Grey would insist that the English government remained uncommitted, and each time Cambon and the French government would convince themselves that they had enmeshed England in a web of honor.

Like Paléologue in St. Petersburg, Paul Cambon thought a war with Austria and Germany was sooner or later inevitable. At the end of the First Balkan War, when Austria announced its opposition to all further Serbian expansion, he wrote that Austria had been expanding to the southeast for six centuries; the 1908–9 annexation of Bosnia-Herzegovina showed that Germany was now a partner in that drive, with the goal of extending the two German states from the North Sea and the Baltic in the north to the Aegean in the south. France, England, and Russia had no choice but to oppose this design, for "if the government of Vienna, by its actions, forces us into avowed opposition to its views, the French Republic will find itself once again taking up the struggle engaged in by the French monarchy against the House of Austria."[20]

Cambon did his best to turn the 1912–13 London Ambassadors' Conference into a solid front of the Entente against Austria and Germany, and he was almost too successful. Grey, Benckendorff, and Cambon met almost daily before each conference session and cooperated in every respect.[21] The memory of those days lingered so painfully in Vienna and Berlin that both governments determined not to walk into such a forum again. They would have nothing to do with four-power mediation in London. Paul Cambon's conference colleagues found him adamant in opposing every Austro-German claim, reluctant to yield even when the Russians were willing. Mensdorff complained that Cambon was always standing in the way of a favorable settlement and thought the Frenchman's "self-conceit" was involved.[22] Count Benckendorff came away with the impression that of all the European powers, France was most ready to face a war.

Surprisingly, Cambon did not expect trouble when the archduke was assassinated. He dismissed Grey's fears on 8 July and did not send a report on the Austro-Serbian crisis until the twenty-second. Only after Austria had rejected Serbia's answer on the twenty-fifth and declared war on the twenty-eighth did he begin to consider the possibility of a European war. On Wednesday, 29 July, Grey had informed Lichnowsky and Cambon that he could not yet make any commitment on the government's position in the event of war. On Thursday and Friday he still insisted that England was uncommitted, but he did tell Lichnowsky on Friday morning that if Berlin could get a reasonable offer out of Vienna, he would be prepared to tell France and Russia that if they did not accept it, England would stand aside. As late as Friday afternoon, Grey still did not have a cabinet majority for supporting France.

British imperialists such as Asquith and Grey regarded a continental war with Great Britain on the sidelines as an unspeakable calamity. However, Asquith had to admit on Friday that "the general opinion at present . . . is to keep out at all costs."[23] Nicolson dropped a note to Grey that evening with the warning, "It is useless to shut our eyes to the fact that possibly within the next 24 hours Germany will be moving across the French frontier."[24]

The situation had looked moderately hopeful earlier in the day. Russia and Austria were talking again, Lichnowsky had said that Berlin was trying to induce Vienna to accept a halt in Belgrade while the talks went on, and

Grey hoped that Sazonov would drop his insistence that Austria amend its note and agree to the Austrian occupation of Belgrade. "It is a slender chance of preserving peace," he wired Buchanan, "but the only one I can suggest if Russian Minister for Foreign Affairs can come to no agreement at Berlin."[25]

While Grey was finding solace at his club that Friday evening, Lichnowsky received Bethmann's wire informing him of the Russian general mobilization and Germany's ultimatum. Lichnowsky gave the wire to Tyrrell. Grey being unavailable, Tyrrell brought it to Asquith. Bethmann's telegram emphasized that Berlin was still trying to mediate in Vienna when Russia mobilized,[26] which Asquith took to mean that the Russian mobilization was frustrating Germany's efforts for peace.

Asquith moved quickly. The Russians had to ease German apprehensions and delay hostilities while Russia and Austria talked. Asquith, Tyrrell, and several others worked on a draft of a wire from King George V to Tsar Nicholas II. They called ahead to Buckingham Palace to have the king awakened and drove there at about 1:30 in the morning. The king received them with a brown gown over his nightshirt and read both Bethmann's wire on the German response to Russian mobilization and the proposed message to the tsar. George said he wanted the tone to be more intimate, addressed to "My dear Nicky" and signed "Georgie." The draft was revised accordingly and at 3:30 A.M. a wire went out asking "Nicky" to "leave still open grounds for negotiation and possible peace." Unlike the kaiser's telegrams, which went directly to the tsar, King George's wire was sent to Buchanan, who was instructed to apply for an audience with the tsar "at once" to deliver the king's message.[27]

On Saturday morning Grey addressed the German side of the problem. So long as the public perceived the crisis as an Austro-Serbian quarrel in which Germany might have to protect Austria from Russia, there was no hope for English intervention. Nor was there much enthusiasm for coming to the aid of France. Grey was in precisely the bind that Bethmann had anticipated.

Still, the Russians and the Austrians were talking, and Russia said it would not attack so long as the talks continued. Hostilities might not break out for days. Austria had declared war on Serbia on Tuesday, and there still had been no major engagement. It was common knowledge that in a two-front war, Germany would take advantage of its speed and interior lines to knock France out of the war before Russian mobilization was completed. The immediate danger, therefore, lay in the west.

Grey tackled the problem directly. What if the Germans were assured that France would not attack them while Germany and Russia mobilized? He sent Tyrrell to talk to Lichnowsky while he met with Asquith and Haldane

prior to the noon cabinet meeting. Tyrrell told Lichnowsky that Grey hoped
to make a proposal that might keep both Germany and England out of a war.
Would Germany remain neutral if France did not attack? What he and Grey
meant was, if France promised not to attack Germany, would Germany refrain from attacking Russia or France? Unfortunately, Tyrrell asked only
whether Germany would remain neutral if France did not attack, and
Lichnowsky took "neutral" to mean neutral with respect to France. It was a
gift from heaven. Without checking with Berlin and on his own authority, he
said yes—if France remained neutral, Germany would too.[28]

Tyrrell hurried back to report to Grey, who was still talking with Asquith
and Haldane. Grey immediately telephoned Lichnowsky and repeated the
question. Would Germany be prepared to remain neutral if France did? The
misunderstanding continued. Grey meant neutrality to Russia as well as to
France, whereas Lichnowsky thought that only France was involved. Grey
said he would present this proposal to the cabinet that day in hopes it might
prevent the outbreak of hostilities. Lichnowsky said he would be prepared
to take personal responsibility for such an assurance. Much relieved, Grey
went back to his meeting, and Lichnowsky immediately cabled Berlin that
if Germany "did not attack France, England would remain neutral and
would guarantee France's neutrality." Tyrrell reinforced the misunderstanding by warning Lichnowsky that German troops must not cross the French
border. "Everything would depend upon that." Lichnowsky passed that
warning on to Berlin.[29]

After Lichnowsky's wire was on its way, Grey must have realized that
war might be declared on all sides before everything was worked out—
which did not necessarily mean immediate hostilities. War could be declared while the armies stood still. Grey sent Tyrrell back to Lichnowsky,
but again Tyrrell was not entirely precise and Lichnowsky thought more was
being offered than Grey intended. Lichnowsky's next telegram read: "Sir
William Tyrrell has just called on me to tell me that Sir E. Grey wanted to
make proposals to me this afternoon regarding England's neutrality even in
the event that we should have war with France as well as Russia. I am to see
Sir. E Grey at three-thirty and will report at once."[30]

This discussion took place on Saturday morning. The previous afternoon,
Wilhelm II von Hohenzollern, German kaiser and All-Highest Warlord,
moved from Potsdam to Berlin to take charge of the crisis. The kaiser and
the kaiserin rode in an open car along Unter den Linden and the crown
prince and his wife and the kaiser's other sons and their wives followed in
a cavalcade of cars as the crowds along the avenue cheered. The kaiser was
not his usual exuberant public self. He sat staring straight ahead, occasion-

ally acknowledging the crowd by touching his hand to the brim of his helmet. It was, the Russian ambassador wrote, a "solemn entry into Berlin."

That evening, Berliners gathered at the palace and the kaiser appeared on a balcony. He told the crowd that he was doing all he could for peace, but if his efforts should fail, "we will show our enemies what it means to challenge Germany. And now I commend you all to God. Go to church, kneel down before Him and beg His help for our brave army." The crowd cheered wildly.

By eleven that night, extra editions were announcing the ultimatum to Russia and the query to France about its neutrality in the event of a Russo-German war. Admiral Müller thought the papers were fairly belligerent, but he was pleased that they accepted the official view: the kaiser had agreed to the tsar's request to mediate at Vienna and had been doing his best to bring about an agreement while the tsar, contrary to all loyalty and trust, secretly armed.[31]

During the course of Saturday morning, Berlin learned that Pourtalès had delivered the twelve-hour ultimatum to Sazonov at midnight, and that both the tsar and Sazonov, without expressly rejecting the ultimatum, had said that canceling the general mobilization was a "technical impossibility." However, they could see no reason why negotiations could not continue while Germany and Russia mobilized.[32] Neither the tsar nor Sazonov made any further response to the German ultimatum. Pourtalès, meanwhile, continued doing his professional best to persuade the Russians to halt mobilization.

As the ambassador was leaving Peterhof after his audience with the tsar on Friday afternoon, he received a message from Count Vladimir Fredericks, a court official who was in daily attendance upon the tsar and his family, asking Pourtalès to call upon him. Pourtalès went to the count's residence, where Fredericks offered to do all he could to help avoid a war. War, the count said, would be a disaster for Russia, and he offered to convey to the tsar any communication that Pourtalès might care to make.[33] For a court official to intervene in high policy was a serious breach of protocol, but it was an unusual opportunity for Pourtalès. After his midnight interview with Sazonov and a few hours of sleep, he wrote the count at 7:30 A.M. that he wished to "take advantage of the friendly permission you were so kind as to grant me."

He wrote that he had been instructed to tell Sazonov that if Russia did not declare positively that it was suspending all mobilization measures by noon, Germany would mobilize. "You know what that means in our country. We cannot conceal from ourselves that in such an event we are but a finger's breadth from war." The count got the letter at 10:30 A.M. and presumably transmitted it or its contents to the tsar. At 2:00 P.M., Fredericks telephoned Pourtalès to read him the tsar's latest message to the kaiser, in which the tsar assured the kaiser that in Russia mobilization did not mean war, and that his troops would take no "provocative action" so long as negotiations with Austria were taking place. Nicholas asked Wilhelm to give him a similar guarantee.[34]

The pace in St. Petersburg was leisurely. Suspicious as they were of Austrian and German intentions, the Russians still thought that negotiations could continue while both sides mobilized. Even Pourtalès may have clung to this straw, because noon came and went without the German ambassador giving Berlin any word of a Russian response or even trying to see Sazonov again.

Berlin therefore spent most of Saturday not knowing what was happening in Russia. Moltke no longer cared. He wanted to declare war and order general mobilization as soon as the twelve-hour ultimatum expired so that he could start his campaign in the west while the Russians were still mobilizing and finish with France before Russia attacked.[35] Bethmann did not like being the first to declare war, but he did not see how he could justify an attack on Luxembourg, Belgium, and France to the German people—particularly the Social Democrats—if Germany was not at war with Russia. Moltke talked at length with Bethmann late Friday night and finally convinced him. The kaiser agreed the next morning. Officials in the foreign office worked on the declaration of war through Friday night and Saturday morning.[36]

There was no difficulty with the general tenor of the declaration. Russia had interrupted the German mediation effort with a general mobilization, and the German government "felt itself compelled" to ask the Russians to suspend "said military activities." The problem arose in expressing the precise reason for declaring war, since Russia was not attacking Austria or Germany. After several drafts, the final declaration said simply, "His Majesty the Emperor, my August Sovereign, accepts the challenge in the name of the Empire, and considers himself as being in a state of war with Russia."[37] The Germans were in such a hurry to send the declaration that they did not wait for the approval of the Federal Council of the Associated Governments, as required by the constitution.

The declaration of war went to Pourtalès shortly after 1:00 P.M. Saturday. Not only was it sent without constitutional approval, but Moltke changed his mind about it just as it was being sent. War minister Falkenhayn, who was as sure as Moltke that war was imminent—and with England as well as France and Russia—was more sensitive than Moltke to the international consequences if Germany was the first to declare war. Moreover, he could see no reason for a declaration if there were not going to be hostilities in the east for the next several days. Falkenhayn said he "went to Moltke and persuaded him to . . . delay the foolishly premature declaration of war." Moltke agreed, and the two men went to Bethmann, who also agreed.

Later, however, either Bethmann or Jagow told the generals it was too late. The instruction for Pourtalès had already been sent.[38] This was a little strange, since a countermanding wire could easily have been sent to Pourtalès, who was not to deliver the declaration of war until five that afternoon. Bethmann and Jagow may have preferred to leave things as they were.

Bethmann then addressed the Federal Council, made up of representatives of the German states who voted under instruction from their governments. Bethmann reviewed the events since the assassination and argued that German and British mediation efforts in Vienna were just beginning to bear fruit when "Russia mobilized her entire military forces on land and sea," threatening "the safety of our fatherland."

Bethmann explained that Berlin had sent an ultimatum to Russia and asked for a French declaration of neutrality. "I do not know what the replies will be. . . . If the Russian reply should prove unsatisfactory and France does not make a plain and unconditional declaration of neutrality . . . the Emperor will declare to the Russian Government that he is forced to consider himself in a state of war with Russia." Germany did not know the exact terms of the Franco-Russian alliance, but the kaiser would say to France "that we are at war with Russia, and, as France will not guarantee her neutrality, he must assume that we are at war with France also."

Today, far from that hot August afternoon, the whole proceeding seems devoid of sense. Germany had no plans to invade Russia, and Russia was insisting that it would not attack Austria so long as negotiations continued. Germany had no quarrel of any kind with France.

The situation looked different to the Germans. Why would Russia mobilize if it was not planning to crush Germany while France struck them in the rear? Bethmann received unanimous approval for declarations of war if Germany did not receive "satisfactory" responses to the ultimatums. He concluded with his usual fatalism, "If the iron dice are now to be rolled, may God help us."[39]

By Saturday, the French government in Paris knew beyond denial that Russia had ordered a general mobilization that would in all probability provoke a German attack on France. Joffre, filled to the ears with the doctrine of the invincible offensive, wanted his army in position to attack before the Germans robbed him of the initiative and forced him on the defensive.

At eight that morning Joffre caught Messimy on his way to a cabinet meeting and gave him a note declaring that the German army would be completely mobilized by 4 August without ever publicly declaring mobilization. Germany would then have a lead of forty-eight to seventy-two hours, and it was "imperative" that the French immediately order mobilization. They could not conduct a mobilization in secret, step-by-step, the way the Germans were. The French mobilization had to be public and everything had to happen at once. Berlin's demand that Russia and France cease military preparations was not serious; Germany wanted to continue talking and secretly mobilize while France and Russia remained on a peacetime footing.[40]

Joffre's analysis was pure fantasy. If a secret mobilization was not possible in France, it was equally impossible in Germany. But French diplomatic and military reports were full of warnings about a "secret" German mobilization. Poincaré and French officials believed, or professed to believe, that Russia had ordered general mobilization because "she has learned that Germany has already commenced its mobilization."[41] If it is true that the Russians mobilized because they thought Germany was secretly mobilizing, then one must conclude that the final, precipitating event of the July crisis was based on a sheer misapprehension of what was happening.

Joffre, however, believed it, and as army chief of staff he convinced his government. He insisted that mobilization be ordered for Sunday, 2 August. If it were not, he warned, "I cannot possibly continue to bear the crushing responsibility of the high office which is entrusted to me."[42] To begin mobilization on Sunday, orders would have to go out no later than 4:00 P.M. Saturday.[43] Messimy took Joffre to explain the situation to Poincaré and to insist that the general accompany them to the cabinet meeting to repeat his arguments to the ministers. Poincaré agreed. The chief of staff painted a grim picture: France, he feared, "outstripped by German mobilization, the most rapid of them all, might speedily find herself in an irreparable state of inferiority."[44]

The cabinet discussion was still going on when Viviani was called away to see Schoen at the foreign ministry. Schoen had arrived an hour earlier than his appointment to get an answer to his question on France's neutrality in a Russo-German war. Viviani seemed hesitant; Schoen had to repeat his question several times until Viviani finally delivered the noncommittal reply he and Poincaré had agreed upon: "France will have regard to her own interests." Schoen, according to Viviani, thought about this for a moment and then said, "I confess that my question is rather ingenuous. But, after all, have you not got a treaty of alliance?"

"Exactly," replied Viviani.[45]

The two men knew precisely where they stood. Viviani could no longer deny that Russia was mobilizing, nor could he say that France was going to try to do anything about it. He developed another argument instead. He explained that the situation had changed, that "it is officially reported here that Sir E. Grey's proposal of a general suspension of military preparations has been accepted in principle by Russia, and that Austria-Hungary has declared that she will not infringe on Serbia's territory or sovereignty." Schoen knew about Austria's assurances, but a Russian agreement in principle to a suspension of its mobilization was a major revelation that could alter the whole situation. He was, however, baffled that he had not heard about so momentous a development.

Reading Schoen's report that evening, the kaiser was equally puzzled. "Do not know of any [reports of a Russian agreement]," he wrote. "I have received none."[46]

Viviani and French diplomats drew a picture that entirely ignored the Russian mobilization. When reporting his talk with Schoen to his ambassadors, Viviani stressed that Germany had handed Russia an ultimatum "at the very moment when this Power had just accepted the British formula (which implies the cessation of military preparations by all the countries which have mobilized)." Germany now "regarded a diplomatic rupture with France as imminent." Going even further, he said that Austria had agreed to submit its dispute with Serbia to a discussion of the powers at London.[47]

Both propositions were untrue, and it is hard to believe that Viviani actually told Schoen that Austria agreed to put its dispute with Serbia before the powers. Schoen did not mention it in his report; up to that point, all he had heard was that the Austrians agreed to nothing. He would at least have asked Berlin if such a startling change of position had really taken place. Of course, the conversations that took place in the chancelleries of Europe on Saturday, 1 August, were almost certainly not as logical and calm as the diplomatic reports make them. Exhaustion, anxiety, and uncertainty left plenty of room for misunderstanding.

Viviani desperately wanted peace. He may well have exaggerated the possibilities in the Austro-Russian conversations. Schoen's report indicates as much. Viviani told his ambassadors that Schoen left without making "any fresh request for an answer to his question concerning the attitude of France," and did not repeat his request for arrangements for his passports.[48] But after talking to Schoen, Viviani had to go back to the cabinet and face hard-nosed and skeptical men such as Poincaré, Messimy, and Joffre, who were absolutely certain that war was coming.

Poincaré did not trust Viviani. He had never wanted as prime minister a former Socialist, an opponent of the three-year-service law, and a man who did not understand the German danger. He wrote contemptuously that Viviani returned from his talk with Schoen "with an air of relief *(le front moins soucieux)*." Even before Viviani could report his meeting, a skeptical

Poincaré warned his colleagues, "Not too much optimism; if Schoen has been friendly, it is because matters are becoming more serious." Viviani reported that Schoen "has said nothing more about leaving and that everything, perhaps, was on the point of being settled." According to Poincaré, Messimy and Joffre had everything ready for ordering general mobilization that afternoon, but when Viviani came into the meeting with his "radiant air, I could see the moment when, after the visit from Schoen, yesterday's decision would be abandoned." But Joffre had warned of the dangers of delay, and "I was therefore very firm in council that we not go back on yesterday's decision in principle to order mobilization today, and in the end everyone agreed."[49]

In order to hold open the possibility of a settlement as long as possible, Viviani asked Messimy not to issue the order until the last moment. This request was probably what so annoyed Poincaré, but Messimy agreed and Joffre did not object. If there was no improvement, the order would go out at 4:00 P.M. that day for mobilization to begin at 12:01 A.M. on Sunday.[50]

While Viviani was out talking to Schoen, Poincaré met with Bertie, who showed him the wire that Asquith had drafted for King George, asking the tsar "to leave still open grounds for negotiation and possible peace." The English king promised to do whatever he could to help the tsar reopen conversations with Austria and Germany.[51] Poincaré saw immediately that the Russian mobilization could jeopardize French hopes for an English intervention, and he told Bertie that the German government was trying to put the blame for the crisis on Russia; "the Emperor of Russia did not order a general mobilisation until after a decree of general mobilisation had been issued in Austria." Poincaré added that measures already taken by the German government, "though not designated a general mobilisation, are so in effect" and that "France is already forty-eight hours behindhand as regards German preparations." German troops, he said, had already made incursions on the frontier while the French had withdrawn six miles.[52] None of this was true, but Poincaré had to convince the British that Germany, not Russia, was the aggressor, and he successfully imposed this line on the whole of French diplomacy.

Paléologue, who also did not trust Viviani, continued to fear that the prime minister would interfere with Russia's mobilization. Instead of reporting that Germany would not mobilize if Russia canceled its call-up, he merely wired, "The German ambassador has just declared to the Russian government that the general mobilization of the German army will be ordered tomorrow morning, 1 August."[53] It did not matter; Viviani had already been informed of the true situation by Bertie, Jules Cambon, Izvolsky, and Schoen. A few hours later, Paléologue abandoned his portrait of a cautiously pacific Russia and wired enthusiastically, "General mobilization continues with precision and activity. Even among the working class, war with Germany evokes keen enthusiasm."[54]

Telegrams informing the French nation that "the first day of mobilization would be Sunday, 2 August" were prepared and delivered to the Paris central telegraph office at 3:45 P.M. and went out a few minutes before 4:00 P.M.[55] The Germans had still not ordered a general mobilization, which worried Viviani. He prepared a public manifesto, which Poincaré and the entire cabinet approved: "Countries whose constitutional and military legislation do not resemble our own have, without a previous decree of mobilization, begun and continued preparations equivalent in reality to actual mobilization and in fact effecting it in advance of France." But, the statement continued, "mobilization is not war." Although taking necessary precautions, the government still hoped for peace. Viviani's manifesto to the French people closed with one of his better efforts: "At this hour there are no longer parties. There is only eternal France, pacific and resolute France."[56]

Immediately after the cabinet meeting, Poincaré urged Messimy to remind the troops that they were strictly forbidden to enter the six-mile neutral zone.[57] If there were going to be hostilities along the frontier, Germany must appear as the invader.

PART X: THE LOGIC OF MADNESS: THE SCHLIEFFEN PLAN

37: THE BRITISH ARE NOT COMING IN!

1 August

Theodor Wolff was at the foreign office again on Saturday morning, 1 August, talking with Arthur Zimmermann, the under state secretary. The telephone rang; Zimmermann picked it up and, covering the mouthpiece, whispered, "Moltke is on the phone." Zimmermann listened, then said, "No, nothing yet, Your Excellency." After a pause, Zimmermann said, "Yes, I think so too—but I suppose we must wait a bit longer—no, not very much longer."[1] Moltke wanted to get started.

Bethmann began the day assuming Germany would declare war if Russia continued to mobilize. At noon he still did not know whether or not Russia would stop mobilizing, or whether Germany would be at war with Russia. He therefore wired Schoen, authorizing him to give the French another two hours—from 1:00 until 3:00 P.M. Paris time, which would have been four o'clock in Berlin—to declare whether they would be neutral in a Russo-German war.[2]

At 4:00 P.M., four hours after the German ultimatum had expired, there was still no word from St. Petersburg. War minister Falkenhayn drove to Bethmann's office to tell him that they had to get the kaiser's consent for general mobilization. Bethmann hesitated. He wanted time for the impact of Russia's actions to influence England, and he certainly did not want to start an invasion of Luxembourg and Belgium any sooner than was necessary. Falkenhayn warned that the military situation was becoming untenable, and Bethmann reluctantly agreed to summon Moltke and Tirpitz and go to the kaiser with them to get the mobilization order. The meeting with the kaiser produced the first real discussion of the political and diplomatic consequences of the Schlieffen Plan.

Bethmann, Moltke, Falkenhayn, Tirpitz, and Admiral Müller gathered in the kaiser's office in his Berlin palace for the formal signing of the order for general mobilization. Also present were General Lyncker, the head of the

kaiser's personal military secretariat, and General Plessen, the head of the
kaiser's personal military headquarters. The kaiser sat on his saddle-chair at
a table made from the timbers of Nelson's *Victory*. Falkenhayn remembered
the scene. "As he signed, I said: 'God Bless Your Majesty and your arms,
God protect the beloved Fatherland.' The Kaiser gave me a long handshake
and we both had tears in our eyes."[3] It was a moment of great emotion.
Everyone in the room recognized the danger if the huge Russian army was
mobilizing. But mobilization was not the problem. The problem was the
Schlieffen Plan; it left Germany no choice but to launch an attack.

Pourtalès had been instructed to deliver the declaration of war at 5:00 P.M.
Berlin time if Russia did not demobilize; that hour had passed and there
was still no word from Pourtalès. Were they at war with Russia or not?
Tirpitz had been bothered all along by the problem of declaring war on
Russia.[4] He asked whether Germany would open hostilities even if the
Russian government refused to accept the declaration of war and insisted
that negotiations continue. After all, Tirpitz pointed out, Germany would
be on the defensive in the east, and with very meager forces there, why
hasten hostilities?

Moltke, who was tense and nervous and worried about the disposition of
the Austrian army, was irritated by the admiral's cross-examination. "We
have to start right away," he insisted, thinking of Belgium and its rail net.

But Tirpitz was thinking about Russia. "Will our troops cross the border?"

Moltke, thinking the admiral meant the French border, replied, "No, that
won't happen for at least a few days."

"Then," Tirpitz responded, "a declaration of war is certainly not necessary." They were not talking about a major military operation, he continued.
There would be patrols, maneuvers, and minor skirmishes—but no invasion
until France was defeated in the west. So why the hurry to declare war on
Russia? Why not wait until Russia had clearly opened hostilities?

Bethmann, who had been listening without comment, had a different
worry: how could the Germans invade Luxembourg, Belgium, and France if
they were not at war with Russia?

While this argument was going on, Wolff was still at the foreign office
waiting for news. As he glanced down a corridor, he saw Jagow hurrying
out of the building, a sheet of paper in his hand and a smile on his face. A
minute or two later, Wolff looked out the window and saw Jagow get into a
car and drive toward the palace. Jagow was plainly in good spirits. A hot
and perspiring Zimmermann came next. "I have to go to the War Minister,"
he told Wolff.

"Have you had good news?" Wolff asked.

Zimmermann answered, "May be—it seems the British are not coming in."[5]

* * *

At the palace, the discussion of Germany's military options was rapidly becoming a shouting match when Jagow burst into the room to announce the first of Lichnowsky's wires. It was an important message and would be brought in as soon as it was decoded. Tirpitz was more convinced than ever that Germany should wait, not only with the declaration of war but with mobilization as well. What would an hour or two matter?

Moltke would have none of that. Whatever he thought about a declaration of war, he would not delay mobilization. The kaiser agreed with Tirpitz, and so did Admiral Müller and General Lyncker. Moltke and Falkenhayn were adamant. After endless hours of delay, they finally had the kaiser's signature on a mobilization order; they did not want him changing his mind because of some wire from Lichnowsky. Tirpitz thought they should wait at least until they heard the British message. The generals cut off further talk by simply leaving, taking the signed mobilization order with them. Wilhelm II, All-Highest Warlord, did not order his generals to wait.[6]

Moltke and Falkenhayn wasted no time. The order for general mobilization began going out shortly after 5:00 P.M. Saturday—4:00 P.M. Paris time and therefore just minutes after the French ordered their own mobilization. Wolff saw Moltke after the general left the meeting. "His face was bathed in perspiration, and he was as excited as a youngster—so much so that his helmet was not on quite straight. He had brought with him the order for mobilization." In the streets, extra editions were already announcing that Germany was mobilizing. Officers drove along the avenues in open cars waving handkerchiefs and swords.[7]

After a confused ten minutes at the palace, the decoded dispatch from London was delivered. The English had insisted all along that they could not stand aside and allow Germany to crush France. Now Lichnowsky wired that Grey was going to propose to the cabinet "that in case we did not attack France, England would remain neutral and would guarantee France's neutrality."[8]

To all appearances, England was about to hand Berlin a huge diplomatic victory, allowing Germany to go to war with Russia while holding France back. Instead of three opponents, Germany would have only one— and even Social Democrats thought a war with Russia was justified. The kaiser, Bethmann, and Jagow were overjoyed. They had done it; they had split the Entente! It was unbelievable—and it should have been, but no one looked twice. Moltke and Falkenhayn were immediately ordered to return. While they waited, a jubilant kaiser told Tirpitz that the matter was simple: the Entente had not believed that Germany had the nerve to go to war.

When Moltke and Falkenhayn got back, they heard Lichnowsky's message. The kaiser, bubbling with triumph and excitement, told Moltke, "We shall simply march the whole army east!"

The chief of staff was stunned. They were going to wreck years of careful planning! When he recovered himself, Moltke delivered a lecture on basic logistics. "I assured His Majesty that this was not possible. The deployment of an army of a million men was not a matter of improvisation. It was the product of a whole heavy year's work and, once worked out, could not be changed. If His Majesty insisted on leading the whole army eastwards, he would not have an army ready to strike, he would have a confused mass of disorderly armed men without commissariat."

Moltke was right on the logistic chaos that would result from such an abrupt change of plan,[9] but according to Admiral Müller, Moltke then added: "Now all we need is that Russia calls it off, too."[10] The general seemed to despair of ever seeing Schlieffen's strategic masterpiece in action.

The kaiser had no such feelings. "Your uncle would have given me a different answer!" Moltke was deeply hurt by the comparison with his famous uncle. "I have never claimed," he wrote later, "to be the equal of the field marshal." He was even more upset that no one respected his professional judgment. "Nobody seemed to reflect that it would bring disaster upon us if we were to invade Russia with our entire army, leaving a mobilized France in our rear."[11] How could the English stop France from attacking?

A terrific argument ensued. Moltke declared that he "could not take the responsibility if changes were made in the concentration as laid down under mobilization." Bethmann replied that he "could not take the political responsibility" of rejecting Grey's proposal. After the first angry outbursts, Tirpitz pointed out that whether or not there was any substance to the Grey proposal, Berlin could not afford to turn it down, "because, when Grey's dispatch was published, we should be put flagrantly in the wrong." Everyone, including the kaiser, suddenly realized that Grey had them: it was politically impossible to turn down the proposal; the invasion of France would have to be stopped. Moltke all but lost his self-control.

Falkenhayn asked permission to talk privately with Moltke, and the two generals went into another room. He assured Moltke that he was right: sending the army east was nonsense, but they could not politically afford to reject the Grey proposal. Moltke's feelings should not be hurt by the temporary postponement of the invasion while the army completed its concentration in the west. The kaiser was right to avoid war, or at least a two-front war, if he could. Falkenhayn himself did not "for one moment believe that [Lichnowsky's] telegram will change anything." When the two generals returned to the kaiser's office, Moltke persuaded Wilhelm to let the bulk of the German army continue moving to the French frontier and then halt. The Eighth

Army would continue its defensive buildup in East Prussia. If the English proposal worked out, they would simply move the army from west to east without fighting France, "but the concentration itself must proceed unchanged, or else I could not be responsible for things."

Moltke could not believe that the kaiser still hoped for peace after a Russian mobilization. He wrote afterward that he was all but broken by this experience and "nearly fell into despair. I regarded these diplomatic moves, which threatened to interfere with the carrying out of our mobilization, as the greatest disaster for the impending war. . . . Years earlier the foreign ministry had told me that France might possibly remain neutral in a war between Germany and Russia. I had so little faith in this possibility that I said even then that, if Russia declared war on us, we should have to declare war on France at once if there was the least doubt about her attitude."[12]

Moltke was a truly rigid man. Haunted by the lurking dangers of the modern world and the numerical superiority of Germany's enemies, he had placed all hope of salvation on the meticulous execution of the Schlieffen Plan. By 1914 his commitment to the Great Plan was beyond all reason. Any war with Russia would have to begin with an attack on France unless the French gave an absolute guarantee not to strike the Germans in the rear—but he had no plans for such a contingency. Clearly, the work of the Prussian general staff involved more than technical proficiency. These were men drained by years of anxiety. They wanted to strike, to put an end to it, to settle matters once and for all. Only the Schlieffen Plan could accomplish that.

When the decision was made to continue the concentration but delay the invasion, tempers cooled. There was still no formal British proposal, just a suggestion that a proposal might be made. But Bethmann and the kaiser, excited and relieved, decided to accept in advance. Bethmann, Jagow, Falkenhayn, and Moltke went to an adjoining room to draft the official response. As they were working, Lichnowsky's second wire came in: England might be neutral "even in the event that we should have war with France as well as Russia."[13] Astounding! England was going to back out altogether! The kaiser, unable to contain his happiness, ordered champagne. Tirpitz exulted. His navy had done it—"The risk theory worked." Müller had his doubts; England had no reason to fear the German fleet.[14]

The atmosphere was euphoric, but they decided to reply on the basis of Lichnowsky's first telegram, which assumed that France would remain neutral. They could wait on the rest. The formal response from Bethmann read, "Germany is willing to agree to the English proposal, provided England will pledge security with all her armed forces for the unconditional neutrality of France in a German-Russian conflict, and, moreover, for a neutrality to last until the final completion of this conflict. Germany alone would have to decide when that completion had been reached." Germany had already mobilized in "response to the Russian challenge," and the concentration on the French frontier could not be halted, but Berlin was prepared to guarantee that no troops would cross the French border before 7:00 P.M. on 3 August, and would not cross it at all if there was an agreement in the meantime.[15]

At Tirpitz's suggestion, the kaiser drafted a wire to George V. Wilhelm repeated the German acceptance of a proposal that had yet to be made, and explained that his army would continue concentrating on the French frontier but would not cross it. "I hope that France will not become nervous," he added.[16] Jagow at the same time asked Lichnowsky to give Grey "our best thanks for his proposal."[17]

The wires left Berlin at 7:02, 7:15, and 7:20 P.M.—just as Viviani and his cabinet were working out a long instruction to Paul Cambon outlining how to handle the awkward fact that France and Russia had mobilized first. France, Viviani wrote, had never ceased to cooperate with England in urging moderation on Russia, and Sazonov had urged Serbia to accept everything in the Austrian note compatible with its sovereignty. Sazonov was still engaged in direct talks with Austria, and he was ready to have the four less interested powers mediate. He had even modified his formula for settlement to conform more closely to the latest English formula. "It would therefore seem that an accommodation between the suggestion of Sir Ed. Grey, the formula of M. Sazonoff and the declarations of Austria should be readily attainable. . . . But, while negotiations were going on . . . Austria was the first to proceed to general mobilization. Russia believed itself forced to follow suit in order not to be in an inferior position." Beginning with Poincaré's talk with Bertie that Saturday morning, French diplomacy consistently argued that a prior Austro-Hungarian mobilization had forced Russia to mobilize in self-defense.

The tsar had given his word, Viviani noted, that his army would not attack so long as the talks between St. Petersburg and Vienna continued. France and Russia would continue to work for peace, but "the attitude of Germany has put us under the absolute necessity of ordering mobilization today." Viviani made clever use of Paléologue's distorted report of the German ultimatum: "Today, M. Paléologue has telegraphed that Count Pourtalès has informed the Russian government of the German mobilization." Viviani conveniently ignored the fact that the Germans had actually said that if Russia did not stop mobilizing, Germany would have to mobilize. The French chose to maintain the fiction that Germany had been secretly mobilizing since 29 July. The document closed by repeating that "mobilization is not war . . . it is the best means for France safeguarding the peace; the government of the Republic will redouble its efforts to bring the negotiations to a conclusion."[18]

Schoen, meanwhile, got Bethmann's wire offering the French a two-hour extension on the German ultimatum. Schoen concluded that the ultimatum was still in effect and that Berlin did not know of any new concessions such as Viviani had suggested, either from Russia or from Austria. He could not see Viviani until 5:30 P.M., and then could not get him to move beyond his earlier reply that "France would act in accordance with her interests." Viviani reiterated what was by then the common Franco-Russian line: he could not abandon his hope for peace; mobilization did not mean war; there was still time for negotiations; French troops would withdraw from the frontier to avoid accidental skirmishes.[19]

The deadline for the ultimatum to Russia had come and gone. The deadline for the ultimatum to France had also come and gone, and the French had ordered general mobilization.[20] Schoen wired this news almost immediately, but Berlin did not hear about it until after 9:00 P.M.[21] At about 6:10 P.M., Berlin received the wire that Schoen had sent from Paris at 1:05 in the afternoon, reporting that in response to his definite and repeated requests, Viviani had "stated to me, hesitatingly, that France would act in accordance with her interests" and that Viviani thought the Russians would agree to suspend military measures.[22] Jagow did not want to have to deal with the French just yet. Not knowing that France had just mobilized, he sent a wire at 8:45 P.M. discreetly advising Schoen that Grey might propose an English guarantee of French neutrality if Germany did not attack France, and that Berlin would agree if certain conditions were met. "Please keep the French quiet for the time being. On our part, no hostile action against France is contemplated, despite [our] mobilization, which had already been ordered before arrival of London proposal."[23]

All the messages from Berlin that evening repeated that German mobilization had already been ordered when the London proposal arrived. But the German mobilization order only went out shortly after 5:00 P.M., so nothing irrevocable had yet taken place. Lichnowsky's wire had not arrived too late to stop mobilization; it was Moltke who insisted that it go forward, and since there was no other plan of concentration, neither Bethmann nor the kaiser was prepared to stop him. The German army had to be at the French frontier as soon as possible, either to attack France or to be ready, if England kept France neutral, to turn around and deal with Russia.

Moltke's version of the Schlieffen Plan required that Germany invade Luxembourg on the first day of mobilization—Sunday, 2 August—to seize the Luxembourg railroads before the French did. Cavalry patrols had already crossed into Luxembourg, and the 16th Division from Trier was about to follow.[24] Moltke had agreed to halt at the French frontier, but he saw no reason not to invade Luxembourg and Belgium. When Bethmann realized Moltke's intentions, he insisted that the army must not on any account invade Luxembourg, as that would be a direct threat to France and would jeopardize negotiations with England. The kaiser, peremptory as always, turned to his aide-de-camp and, without consulting Moltke, who was right there, ordered that the 16th Division be halted at the border.

After the violent argument over the deployment of the army, this slight was almost more than Moltke could bear. "I thought my heart would break," he wrote. The men around him did not seem to understand the confusion that could result in making last-minute changes to the mobilization plan. Moltke tried "in vain to convince His Majesty that we needed and must secure the Luxemburg railways," but the kaiser cut him off. "Use other railways instead."[25] The kaiser almost never took such a tone with his beloved Moltke, but he did not want to hear about railroads when a diplomatic triumph seemed almost in hand. He sent Moltke home.

There was one last problem: they had not heard from Pourtalès. The German government still did not know whether it was at war with Russia, and there was now considerable doubt whether war should be declared at all. Meanwhile, there was the wire from the tsar, which had arrived during the course of the afternoon, asking the kaiser to give the same assurance as Nicholas—that mobilization did not mean war and that their governments would continue negotiating for the sake of peace.[26] Bethmann did not want to leave the tsar's message unanswered; he wanted the record to show that Germany was still striving for peace. But he did not know whether or not Germany was at war with Russia. After the meeting he decided to ignore the problem and draft a response for the kaiser. The only way for Russia to avoid war was to demobilize: "Immediate, affirmative, clear and unmistakable answer from your Government is the only way to avoid endless misery. Until I have received this answer, alas, I am unable to discuss the subject of your telegram." That wire went out at 10:45 P.M.[27] and arrived in St. Petersburg early Sunday morning.

Wolff maintained his vigil at the foreign ministry. At 9:00 P.M., Stumm returned from his club in formal dress. A little put off by Stumm's elegance during a time of crisis, Wolff unburdened himself, saying, "Now war is upon us. I have long been afraid that would be the end of it." Stumm was not ready to concede as much. He replied a little hoarsely, "It is not yet certain."

Wolff was doubtful. "Not yet certain? But is not mobilization under way?"

Stumm began, "Nonetheless—" but Wolff cut him off.

"You think there is still a chance?"

"Yes. Yes," said Stumm, "it is possible, we may yet come through."

Wolff pressed him. "Without war?"

"Yes, and without war."[28]

Wolff would have liked to believe him, but he thought Stumm was clutching at straws. Still, if England was really not coming in, anything was possible.

It was a great moment for the kaiser: the proud English were about to capitulate. At a little after 10:00 P.M., Ambassador Szögyény arrived at the palace to deliver a wire from Emperor Franz Joseph. The emperor assured Wilhelm that as soon as he had heard that Germany was "determined to commence war against Russia . . . we here came to the firm determination, too, to assemble our principal forces against Russia."[29]

Szögyény found the kaiser in excellent humor, surrounded by his family in a little palace garden. The kaiser excitedly told him all that had happened, exulting in his role of All-Highest Warlord. "In these conditions it was a matter of persevering calmly but with great firmness in the path pursued up to the present; that above all [the kaiser] was determined to settle accounts with France in which he hoped to be completely successful."[30] Despite the pledge of neutrality, the kaiser apparently thought he would be free to "settle" with France when he was done with Russia. It was a typical outburst of imperial euphoria. It did not last.

Moltke was in a terrible state after the kaiser dismissed him. When the order to halt the 16th Division was handed to him for signature, he slammed his pen on the desk and said, "I will not sign it." The troops would regard it as a sign of indecision if he revoked the precise sequence of his carefully planned mobilization. "Do as you like with the telegram," he told the officer who brought the order. "I am not going to sign it." Moltke sat, brooding and hurt, until 11:00 P.M., when he was ordered back to the palace.

The kaiser had obviously been awakened after having gone to bed. He stood before Moltke with a coat over his nightclothes and handed him a telegram from King George V. The king informed Wilhelm that there must have been some misunderstanding. Grey's proposal had been to discuss only "how actual fighting between German and French armies might be avoided while there is still a chance of some agreement between Austria and Russia."[31] The kaiser had seen his dreams of glory vanish in the night. Angry and once again full of anxiety, he told Moltke, "Now you can do what you want." Grey had warned that Germany's respect for Belgian neutrality "would play a very important role" in England's ultimate decision,[32] but the kaiser was finished. In a moment of triumph, he had screwed himself up to defy his chief of staff; now, stung by humiliation and defeat, he could not do it again.

With the kaiser's new orders in hand, Moltke immediately wired the 16th Division to go ahead with the invasion of Luxembourg. Still anxious not to appear indecisive, he thought he should explain this sudden renewal of the division's original orders: "It has just been learned that France has ordered mobilization." The Great Plan was on again, but Moltke wrote that he "never got over the effects of this experience. It destroyed something in me that could not be built up again; confidence and trust were shattered." After the war, Moltke's widow claimed that her husband had been in perfect health until that 1 August conference with the kaiser.[33] Moltke had in fact been ailing for months, but it is true that he was deeply shaken by the initial order to abandon his meticulously organized Schlieffen Plan.

Grey had no idea that his trial balloon was causing such turmoil in Berlin. After he and Tyrrell had spoken with Lichnowsky on Saturday morning, the cabinet met for more than two hours and remained badly split. "We came, every now & again," Asquith wrote Venetia, "near to the parting of the ways." There were those who took what Asquith called the "Manchester Guardian tack"—that the government should declare "at once that in no circumstances will we take a hand. This is no doubt the view for the moment of the bulk of the party."

Grey warned that if such a policy were announced, he would resign; Asquith said that he would go, too. Both men knew that most of the cabinet would make every possible concession rather than see a Liberal government collapse. Churchill, who had been sounding out Conservative leaders, read a letter from a Conservative member of Parliament that assured the cabinet of Conservative support, particularly if Germany invaded Belgium.[34] Now the noninterventionists knew that if they brought down the government, it would immediately be replaced by a Conservative government or a wartime coalition. After that meeting, Asquith concluded that "the main controversy pivots upon Belgium & its neutrality."[35]

Despite the threats from Asquith, Grey, and Churchill, the antiwar group won a great victory. It had always been an article of faith among good Liberals that no British army should ever be sent across the Channel to be devoured by the conscript masses of the Continent. The cabinet, including Asquith and Grey, agreed that even if Britain were drawn into the war, the British Expeditionary Force (BEF) would not immediately cross the Channel. This was a remarkable decision. Since 1905, the strategic planning of the British army general staff had assumed that in a continental war, the BEF would fight on the left wing of the French army and, moreover, that its presence there would be critical to averting French defeat. The army general staff had planned this move down to the last detail; as in Germany, there was no other plan. But Asquith had never believed that a British army ought to go to the Continent, and Grey for a long while doubted whether it should go right away.[36] General Henry H. Wilson, the director of military operations, was outraged when he learned that the government had no intention of sending the army to France and that Asquith had stated formally "the Govt had never promised the French the E.F. [Expeditionary Force]!!"[37]

The critical British debates of 2 and 3 August therefore assumed that if war came, Britain would fight a naval war and the British army would remain at home. Grey and Churchill may not have been entirely candid with their colleagues.[38] Churchill had fought hard to get the navy to support a continental strategy, but when he wanted to persuade Lloyd George not to resign on the war issue and to await events, he assured him that "the naval war will be cheap."[39] It is equally possible that, as with the Russian government and partial mobilization and the German government and the Schlieffen Plan, Great Britain's civilian leaders were ignorant of the logic of the war their army had planned. Perhaps with reason; even Gen. Douglas Haig, the future commander of the BEF, thought they could delay sending the army to the Continent for a few months, and Asquith wrote Venetia on Sunday morning that "the despatch of the Expeditionary force to help France at this moment is out of the question & wd. serve no object."[40] The nonintervention group thought they had won. John Morley, the most articulate of them, told Churchill after the vote, "We have beaten you after all." John Burns, another nonintervention stalwart, was not so sure. He thought there still had been "no decision."[41]

When Grey made his proposal for British neutrality to Lichnowsky that morning, he believed that the cabinet would be adamantly opposed to going to war for France. During the course of the cabinet's discussion, he realized that the almost certain German invasion of Belgium might change everything. Asquith, as usual, played for time. He wanted to avoid resignations that would force the Liberal government out of power. The Germans might remove the problem with a naval attack on the French coast or an invasion of Belgium.[42] Grey therefore saw no need to inform his colleagues of his idea for keeping Germany and France neutral.[43] Instead, he reported that France had agreed to respect Belgian neutrality if Germany did, and that Germany had given an evasive answer. Grey asked for and received unanimous approval to warn Lichnowsky that "it would be hard to restrain English feeling on any violation of Belgian neutrality by either combatant."[44]

Sometime between their morning conversation and their 3:30 P.M. meeting, Grey and Lichnowsky became aware that they had misunderstood each other; Lichnowsky had to explain to Tyrrell that although he could guarantee that

Germany would not attack France, he could make no such assurance regarding Russia.[45] Lichnowsky expected, nonetheless, to discuss the conditions of English neutrality when he met Grey that afternoon. Instead, Grey told him that Germany's evasive answer on the question of Belgian neutrality "is a matter of very great regret . . . if there were a violation of the neutrality of Belgium by one combatant while the other respected it, it would be extremely difficult to restrain public feeling in this country." Lichnowsky, though taken aback, immediately asked whether Grey "could give me a definite declaration on the neutrality of Great Britain on the condition that we respected Belgian neutrality." Grey replied that such an assurance was not possible. He could say, however, that if Germany violated Belgian neutrality, "a reversal of public feeling would take place that would make it difficult for the Government here to adopt an attitude of friendly neutrality."

Grey was still not sure how the cabinet would go, and he did not want Germany to attack France, so he came back to his proposal as Lichnowsky had originally understood it. He wondered whether Germany and France could not "remain facing each other under arms, without attacking each other, in the event of a Russian war." Lichnowsky asked Grey "if he were in a position to say whether France would agree to a pact of that sort. Since we intended neither to ruin France nor to conquer any territory, I could imagine that we might enter upon that sort of an agreement."

Lichnowsky had hit upon the weak point in Grey's proposal. Would France accept? Grey replied that he did not know; "he would inform himself." Lichnowsky realized at once that an English guarantee of French neutrality was dead. France would never agree to such a betrayal of Russia. But he reported to Berlin that "if it is possible in any way, they want to keep out of the war, but that the reply . . . concerning Belgian neutrality has caused an unfavorable impression."[46] Lichnowsky's report got to Berlin at 10:02 P.M. Saturday. Even if it would have made a difference—which seems unlikely—by the time it was decoded the kaiser had already told Moltke to go ahead with his invasion of Luxembourg.

Grey's next conversation was with Paul Cambon, who insisted that England had to help France. For the sake of public opinion in England, France had withdrawn its troops from the frontier and could therefore "take only the defensive, and not the offensive, against Germany." This was not true; according to Joffre the withdrawal meant only that the offensive would start from inside the frontier instead of at the frontier. France, Cambon went on, in accordance with the 1912 exchange of letters, had concentrated its fleet in the Mediterranean, leaving its northern coasts exposed to the German fleet. Grey dismissed the idea that the German fleet would risk an English attack by coming down the Channel to bombard the French coast.

There was, moreover, no British obligation to defend France. Grey reminded Cambon that he "had assured Parliament again and again that our hands were free." It had been different in the Moroccan incidents of 1905 and 1911, when England had undertaken specific obligations. "Now," Grey said, "the position was that Germany would agree not to attack France if France remained neutral in the event of war between Russia and Germany. If France could not take advantage of this position, it was because she was bound by an alliance," and Britain was not a party to that alliance. Grey warned that, for the moment, France must make her decision without reckoning on British assistance.

Cambon was ashen; his career and French policy were about to fall in ruin. He said he could not transmit Grey's reply to his government and begged that Grey "authorise him to say that the British Cabinet had not yet taken any decision." Grey insisted that the decision *had* been made. "We could not propose to Parliament at this moment to send an expeditionary military force to the continent. Such a step had always been regarded here as very dangerous and doubtful." Grey added, however, that a German naval attack on the coast of France or a German invasion of Belgium might alter public feeling. Cambon could tell his government that the English were "already considering the Belgian point," and that Grey would "ask the Cabinet to consider the point about the French coasts."[47] Cambon could get no more.

Cambon went from Grey to Nicolson and staggered into the latter's office, sheet white, speechless, and trembling. Nicolson immediately got up to help his old friend to a chair. Cambon was muttering, "They are going to abandon us. They are going to abandon us."

When Cambon was somewhat calmed, Nicolson went upstairs to Grey's office, where he found the foreign secretary pacing, troubled, and biting his lips. Nicolson could not help himself. "Is it true that we are going to refuse to support France at the moment of her greatest danger?"

Grey shrugged helplessly and confirmed they would not be sending the BEF to France.

Like Cambon, Nicolson saw his life's work collapsing. "But that is impossible, you have over & over again promised M. Cambon that if Germany was the aggressor you would stand by France."

Grey, the moralist, replied, "Yes, but he has nothing in writing!"[48]

"You will render us a by-word among nations,"[49] Nicolson retorted and stalked out of the office.

When Nicolson returned, Cambon had pulled himself together. Despite his talk with Grey, he continued to take his stand on the 1912 exchange of letters. Holding copies, he said that perhaps the time had come for his "little piece of paper." France, he insisted, had sent its entire fleet to the Mediterranean on the understanding that Great Britain would protect the northern and western coasts of France. Of course, Cambon knew there was no such understanding. Grey had just denied it, and Churchill had warned against precisely this argument when the letters were exchanged in 1912. Moreover, the cabinet had agreed to the exchange of letters only after the insertion of language to the effect that the arrangements in no way implied any kind of commitment to cooperate in war.

Nicolson, however, regarded Cambon's argument as a "happy inspiration" to which "there could be but one answer."[50] He advised Cambon not to send an official note in view of the tension surrounding the whole issue of neutrality. He would inform Grey instead. Nicolson then wrote Grey, "M. Cambon pointed out to me this afternoon that it was at our request that France had moved her fleets to the Mediterranean, on the understanding that we undertook the protection of her Northern and Western coasts . . . it would be well to remind the Cabinet of the above fact." Grey was not prepared to concede either that Britain had asked the French fleet to concentrate in the Mediterranean or that there was any obligation to defend the French Channel coast, but he was prepared to ask the cabinet what it would do if the German fleet steamed into the Channel. He therefore told Nicolson, "I have spoken to the [Prime Minister], and attach great importance to the point being settled tomorrow."[51]

When he sent his report, Cambon was his old self again; despite Grey's objection, he told Viviani that the British had not yet made a decision. The British government had also rejected a German request for neutrality and at the moment was keeping its hands free. Grey would ask the cabinet for permission to declare to Parliament on Monday that the British government would not permit a violation of Belgian neutrality. Cambon also said that Grey had agreed to ask the cabinet to consider authorizing the British fleet to defend the French coasts.[52] Since Germany would almost certainly invade Belgium, and since it was very nearly an act of war for Britain to tell Germany to keep its fleet out of the English Channel, Cambon had reason to hope.

Grey, however, was still toying with the idea of Franco-German neutrality. He wired Bertie: "German Ambassador here seemed to think it not impossible, when I suggested it, that after mobilisation on western frontier French and German armies should remain, neither crossing the frontier as long as the other did not do so. I cannot say whether this would be consistent with French obligations under her alliance. If it were so consistent, I suppose French Government would not object to our engaging to be neutral as long as German army remained on frontier on the defensive."[53]

Bertie could not believe what he was reading. He fired back at 1:15 A.M.:

> Do you desire me to state to the French Government that . . . we propose to remain neutral so long as German troops remain on the defensive and do not cross French frontier, and French abstain from crossing German frontier? I cannot imagine that in the event of Russia being at war with Austria and being attacked by Germany it would be consistent with French obligations towards Russia for French to remain quiescent. If French undertook to remain so, the Germans would first attack Russians and, if they defeated them, they would then turn round on the French.
>
> Am I to enquire precisely what are the obligations of the French under the Franco-Russian Alliance?[54]

A chastened Grey replied a few hours later, "No action required now."[55]

Long before Bertie fired his projectile, Grey had given it all up. Lichnowsky never delivered Bethmann's and Jagow's wires accepting Grey's proposals because after his afternoon talk with Grey, he knew that no proposal was likely to come. But King George V received the wire from the kaiser, and Grey was summoned to Buckingham Palace to answer the kaiser's acceptance, which had come in at 8:00 P.M. Grey now had to avoid the embarrassment of not having reported his talks with Lichnowsky to the cabinet. Using a pencil and a scrap of paper, he drafted a reply for the king, saying that "there must be some misunderstanding as to a suggestion that passed in friendly conversation between Prince Lichnowsky and Sir Edward Grey this afternoon when they were discussing how actual fighting between German and French armies might be avoided while there is still chance of some agreement between Austria and Russia. Sir Edward Grey will arrange to see Prince Lichnowsky early tomorrow to ascertain whether there is a misapprehension on his part."[56]

There was no misapprehension. Grey had launched a trial balloon for English, French, and German neutrality in the west and then abandoned it.

38: Germany Declares War on Russia

1–2 August

Ambassador Buchanan continued to display a singular lack of urgency. The wire from "Georgie" asking "Nicky" to keep open the possibility of further negotiations was sent at 3:30 A.M. Saturday, 1 August. Normally, a 3:30 A.M. transmission from London would have been in Buchanan's hands no later than noon or 1:00 P.M. local time. Buchanan always insisted that he did not receive the wire until 5:00 P.M. Saturday evening.

Moreover, the kaiser's wires always went directly to the tsar and were promptly answered, whereas the British sent royal messages through their ambassador. When Pourtalès asked for an appointment with the tsar on Friday, he called directly and was able to go to Peterhof by the next train. Buchanan called Sazonov, who made an appointment for 10:00 P.M. But Buchanan arrived late and therefore did not deliver King George's plea for restraint until long after Pourtalès had delivered the German declaration of war. The tsar did not respond to King George until 3:10 P.M. Sunday, almost thirty-six hours after the King's wire left London.[1]

Buchanan personally believed that if war came, Great Britain would have to fight on the side of France and Russia, and by 1 August he was almost certain that war would come. But he infinitely preferred no war at all, and from the beginning he had warned Sazonov that Russia should not "precipitate matters by mobilizing."[2] Russia had mobilized anyway, and now Buchanan had a royal message for the tsar that he knew had been drafted by Asquith or Grey and Asquith.

The wire from "Georgie" declared that since the stated positions of Austria and Russia were so close, there must be some misunderstanding. The king asked the tsar "to remove the misapprehension" and "to leave still open grounds for negotiation and possible peace."[3] King George and the Liberal government were apparently saying that the Russian mobilization must be based upon a "misapprehension," which they were asking the tsar to clear up. If there was no satisfactory Russian explanation, the prospect of English intervention would be dim. Furthermore, the time limit on the German ultimatum had expired hours earlier, at noon.

Buchanan, Paléologue, and Sazonov met to discuss an answer sometime before 7:00 P.M. It was a little unusual to call Paléologue into the discussion. Buchanan had no instructions to show the wire to the French ambassador, and neither his reports nor his memoir ever mentioned doing so.

However, Paléologue says he was there and described the meeting in a report that went out at 8:30 P.M. He said he urged that the tsar tell King George that mobilization did not mean war and that Russia was ready to continue negotiations. "I particularly pointed out," Paléologue wired, "that the tsar's reply must leave no doubt as to his will to save the peace still, for this reply will perhaps decide whether England will or will not take sides against Germany."[4] If Paléologue is to be believed, the thrust of the conference was not how to restrain Russia, but to make the Russian mobilization palatable to the British government.

Germany solved this problem by declaring war on Russia. Pourtalès had been instructed to deliver Germany's declaration of war at 5:00 P.M. Berlin time—six in St. Petersburg—if Russia did not give a satisfactory answer to the demand for demobilization. He called the foreign ministry and asked to see Sazonov "at once." Baron Schilling, who took the call, told the ambassador that he would inform Sazonov as soon as he returned from the ministers' meeting. Sazonov got back at about 6:00 P.M. and received the message. The foreign minister was not optimistic. "He will probably bring me a declaration of war."

After talking with Buchanan and Paléologue about King George's wire, Sazonov excused himself at 7:00 P.M. to see Pourtalès.

When Pourtalès entered Sazonov's office, he was barely able to contain his emotion. He immediately asked whether the Russian government was "ready to give a favourable answer to the ultimatum presented the day before." Sazonov replied that though the mobilization could not be canceled, Russia was ready to continue negotiations for a peaceful outcome. Pourtalès could not accept this answer. Shakily, he took a piece of paper from his pocket and once more, formally, read out the German demand for demobilization, telling Sazonov that a negative answer would have serious consequences. Sazonov, according to Schilling, "firmly and calmly again confirmed the reply he had just given." Almost tearfully, Pourtalès asked a third time, and Sazonov could only answer, "I have no other reply to give you."

Pourtalès then drew another piece of paper from his pocket and said, "In that case, sir, I am instructed by my Government to hand you this note." Pourtalès was so upset that he handed Sazonov the declaration of war with two alternative formulations, one to be delivered if the Russians gave no reply at all, the other if they gave an outright refusal. Neither man noticed; what did it matter? Both Sazonov and Schilling say that at this point, Pourtalès lost all self-control. He leaned his head against a window and burst into tears, saying, "Who could have thought that I should be leaving St. Petersburg under such circumstances!"[5] Sazonov admitted that he, too, was in a state of great emotion, which, however, "I managed to overcome, I felt sincerely sorry for him. We embraced each other and with tottering steps he walked out of the room."[6]

Pourtalès remembered the moment somewhat differently. According to him, it was Sazonov who was overcome by emotion, throwing his arms around his neck and saying, "Believe me, we shall see you again." The two men exchanged accusations. Sazonov thought that Tschirschky in Vienna had brought on the war. Pourtalès said no, it was the men around the tsar who had talked him into mobilization. Sazonov, wrote Pourtalès, denied all responsibility, saying, "What could I as Foreign Minister do when the War Minister [Sukhomlinov] told the Tsar that the mobilization was necessary?" Pourtalès replied that he must have known what would happen if Russia mobilized, and that Sazonov as foreign minister was the one most competent to restrain the tsar "from this fatal step." Sazonov, wrote Pourtalès, "gave me an impression of utter helplessness, which confirmed my view that in the final phase of the crisis he just allowed himself to drift with the current, letting himself be the passive tool of the warmongers."[7]

Who knows where the truth lies in these postwar accounts? At the time, both men were overcome with emotion. They probably both broke down and wept and engaged in recriminations, but by the time they wrote it all down the business of assessing blame dominated their recollections.

Pourtalès's terse wire gives no hint of the high emotion of the meeting: "I asked Mr. Sazonoff three successive times whether he could make me the declaration . . . concerning the suspension of hostile measures against Austria and us. After my question had been answered in the negative three times, I handed over the note as instructed."[8]

In the early hours of Sunday morning, therefore, the Germans were mobilizing for a two-front war while Russia and France were mobilizing along Germany's eastern and western frontiers. France, which had no intention of being the first to declare war, had pulled its forces back six miles from the frontier and was carefully avoiding any hint to Germany of its plans. So far as Berlin knew, Germany was not at war with anyone, and Russia was insisting that it wished negotiations to continue.

As soon as Pourtalès left, Sazonov wired his ambassadors that Germany had just declared war. He then went to join Buchanan and Paléologue for dinner before Buchanan's 10:00 P.M. audience with the tsar. When Buchanan retired to his embassy and was getting ready to leave for Peterhof, a foreign ministry messenger brought him a draft answer for the tsar's approval. Buchanan went by car and arrived some forty-five minutes late, but the tsar saw him at once and Buchanan handed him the foreign ministry draft. When Nicholas asked him what he thought of it, Buchanan replied that he thought the message was too formal. He suggested that the tsar should try writing it in his own words. Nicholas agreed and asked Buchanan to help him. Buchanan then "virtually had to dictate the telegram to him on the lines of the draft which Sazonov had given me and on what His Majesty had told me." Writing this privately to Nicolson a few days later, Buchanan seemed not at all embarrassed about admitting that he had ignored his government's plea for Russian restraint; of course, Germany by then had declared war.[9] It was 2:00 A.M. Sunday morning when Buchanan got back to St. Petersburg. He did not send the tsar's reply to London until 3:15 Sunday afternoon.

The tsar's answer—the joint work of Buchanan, Paléologue, Sazonov, and Nicholas—began by saying, "I would gladly have accepted your proposals had not German Ambassador this afternoon presented a note to my Government declaring war"; this response pretty well ended any hopes for demobilization and effectively transferred the blame to Germany. The rest of the note outlined all the conciliatory steps by Russia to find some means of mediation, but "I was eventually compelled to [mobilize] in consequence of complete Austrian mobilisation, of the bombardment of Belgrade, of concentration of Austrian troops in Galicia, and of secret military preparations made by Germany. . . . I have done all in my power to avert war. Now that it has been forced upon me, I trust your country will not fail to support France and Russia in fighting to maintain balance of power in Europe."

Buchanan added as his personal opinion that "if we do not respond to [the tsar's] appeal for our support, we shall at [the] end of the war, whatever be the issue, find ourselves without a friend in Europe, while our Indian Empire will no longer be secure from attack by Russia. If we defer intervention till France is in danger of being crushed, sacrifices we shall then be called upon to make will be much greater. . . ."[10] Here was the heart of the interventionist case: the empire had to be protected; France could not be crushed. Buchanan did not mention Belgium.

A truly bizarre situation now developed. Although Sazonov wired all his other ambassadors that Germany had just declared war, he wired Schebeko in Vienna that "up to the present we continue to be in diplomatic relations with Austria."[11] Schebeko himself was reporting his talk with Berchtold, who, although declining to give up an invasion of Serbia, gave the impression that he would not be opposed to a proposal that would ease the Austrians out of the present situation "without damage to their self-esteem or prestige." From Nish, Strandtmann reported that the Serbian minister in Paris thought Szécsen, the Austrian ambassador, was proposing mediation of the Austro-Serbian dispute.[12] How could Russia be at war with Germany if relations with Austria-Hungary were intact and Austria was looking for a way out?

Russia and Germany had been at war for several hours when Nicholas received a final message from "Willy" that peace could be saved if Russia stopped mobilizing and that on no account must Russian troops cross the German frontier.[13] This was the wire Bethmann had suggested to the kaiser earlier that evening, when the Germans were not certain whether or not they were at war with Russia. Sazonov called Pourtalès at four o'clock in the morning, getting him out of bed. What did the wire mean? Weren't they at war? Pourtalès could give no explanation; perhaps it was sent before the decision to declare war. As instructed, Pourtalès had asked for his passports and was about to leave. He therefore wired Berlin, "If there is anything further to communicate or to be cleared up here, I suggest that it be attended to direct, or perhaps through the medium of the Italian Ambassador, since I leave by way of Stockholm in three hours."[14]

Paléologue also took his time informing his government. He must have known at 8:00 P.M. Saturday, when he dined with Buchanan and Sazonov, that Pourtalès had just delivered a German declaration of war. However, he did not send the information to Paris until 1:19 Sunday morning, and Paris did not get the wire until 2:00 P.M.[15] Izvolsky, who got the news much earlier from Sazonov, went to the presidential palace at 11:30 Saturday night urgently insisting that he see Poincaré.

The two men met in Poincaré's office. Izvolsky, Poincaré later wrote, was a thoroughly frightened man with only one question: "What is France going to do?"[16] Poincaré told him that although France was determined to carry out the obligations of its alliance with Russia, it would not immediately declare war on Germany. Under the French constitution, a declaration of war required the approval of the Chamber of Deputies, and although he was confident about the vote, he preferred to avoid a public debate—which, of course, made perfect sense: why would Poincaré want a debate on the Russian mobilization, on whether France had prior notice, on what had been done to prevent it? Concerning England, Poincaré explained that it would be much better if Germany rather than France declared war.

Poincaré's answer upset Izvolsky, and the president of France had to reassure him: "Today is the first French mobilization day and it would be more advantageous for both allies if France did not begin military operations until mobilization had gone further." Poincaré was also afraid, Izvolsky wired Sazonov, "that Germany will not wait for France to declare war on her and will attack France without warning in order to interfere with the completion of her mobilization."[17]

Poincaré then called his ministers to the presidential palace. The French ministers met from midnight until almost 3:00 A.M. and authorized Viviani to inform Izvolsky, who was waiting in a nearby room, that France would fulfill its alliance obligations but wanted to complete its mobilization before "the opening of military operations, and this will take ten days. At that moment the Houses [of the French legislature] will be summmoned."[18] The frightened Izvolsky wanted a more definite public announcement of French support, but he had to make do with what he could get and left, Poincaré wrote, "with a lugubrious air."[19]

At first, Bethmann had expected a Russian attack on Austria, which everyone knew would force Germany to come to Austria's defense. What he got was a Russian mobilization and an offer to negotiate. He then hoped that Russia would open hostilities so that Germany could declare war in response to warlike acts; in the best of all possible worlds, Russia would pressure France into declaring war before Germany had to go into Belgium. By Sunday, 2 August, Bethmann was so absorbed by the need for a proper legal and political basis for an invasion through Belgium that he all but lost sight of his original strategy of forcing Russia and France into the role of aggressors.

Everything was ready for declaring war on France when the argument broke out over the declaration of war on Russia. Lichnowsky's wire that England might guarantee French neutrality had further delayed the declaration of war on France. Then came King George's wire claiming that Lichnowsky must have misunderstood Grey. At 2:30 Sunday morning, as the French government was affirming its support for Russia, Bethmann called in Tirpitz, Moltke, and Falkenhayn for another discussion about declaring war on France. Tirpitz arrived first to find an array of foreign ministry officials: Jagow, Stumm, Zimmermann, Otto Hammann—the press officer—and Johannes Kriege, head of the legal section. They were arguing wildly over Russia—were they at war or not?—and the declaration of war on France, which, they said, had to be made that day (2 August), since the army intended to march into Luxembourg immediately and into Belgium on 4 August.

Tirpitz said that he still did not understand why Germany had declared war on Russia even before ordering mobilization, and similarly could "see no use in launching the declaration of war on France before we actually marched into France." The army was exasperated by the debate. As far as it was concerned, Germany was at war as soon as it mobilized, which meant getting the troops through Luxembourg and Belgium and into France as rapidly as possible. All the rest was nonsense. When Falkenhayn arrived, he brusquely broke into the discussion to say that "the war is here and the question of a declaration of war on France is a matter of indifference."

Moltke arrived next and made the same point. "The war was there and that was that," he declared. The generals were harsh and contemptuous, and Bethmann was at his didactic, know-it-all worst, insisting that international law required some formal confirmation of a state of war. Both men lost their tempers but soon recovered, apologized, and got back to the business at hand. Moltke tried to deal with the question of formalities by saying that the Russians had already fired across the frontier. Bethmann seized on that assertion, saying, "Then of course the case is clear; the Russians have been the first to start and I shall have the declaration of war handed over the frontier to the nearest general." He still did not know whether Pourtalès had delivered a declaration of war.

Belgium was next. Tirpitz pointed out that according to the latest report from Lichnowsky, a march through Belgium would bring England into the war. Was it possible for the army to postpone the march through Belgium? Was it essential that they do so? Moltke, irritated at this constant interference with his plans, stiffly replied that there was no other way; they had to go through Belgium. Tirpitz now learned for the first time that Moltke and the general staff had only one plan of concentration and attack; there was no transport or provision for anything else. "In that event," said Tirpitz, "we must at once reckon on a war with England." With every day of mobilization Germany was that much ahead, "therefore make the demand on Belgium as late as possible." Tirpitz wanted time to protect his fleet from an English attack.

Moltke did not object. The army did not need the demand on Belgium until 3 August. Kriege, the legal officer, tried to point out the requirements of international law and was rudely cut off by Moltke.

Tirpitz was horrified by the Schlieffen Plan and thought the army was completely blind to its political and diplomatic consequences. He also had the impression that Bethmann had not known about the march through Belgium and was now trying to prevent it. Tirpitz was mistaken; Bethmann had known about the march through Belgium, but now he faced the reality. As Falkenhayn, Moltke, and Tirpitz left, they complained to one another that the civilian leadership had completely lost its head—which was more than likely, since the Schlieffen Plan was making a shambles of German diplomacy. Moltke, who could barely control his own anxieties and who would collapse when his huge right wing was stopped at the Marne River, declared that "he thought he would have to take the political conduct of affairs in hand."[20]

As the military buildup developed along the eastern and western fronts, there were a number of minor clashes as men lost their way and crossed the frontier or eager unit commanders exceeded their orders to challenge the enemy on his own territory. All governments wildly exaggerated the number and extent of these incidents and took the position that for all practical purposes, the war had begun.

For Germany, the question of declaring war on France was still open, and another stormy meeting took place in the kaiser's palace later that Sunday morning. Moltke and Bethmann argued angrily, with Moltke insisting that a declaration of war was not necessary and Bethmann insisting it was. Moltke recited a whole series of hostile acts by the French and repeated that "we are already at war; there is no going back. A declaration of war does not mean a thing." Tirpitz concurred, adding, "The army has to go through Belgium, but I can't see why a declaration of war is necessary at all—it always has an aggressive flavor." An unannounced invasion of Belgium, apparently, did not.

Bethmann was beginning to realize how the Schlieffen Plan would look to the German people. Berlin could not simply announce the invasion of Luxembourg and Belgium. There had to be a good reason for such a violation of international law: Germany would have to be at war with France as well as with Russia. "Without a declaration of war on France," Bethmann insisted, "I cannot make the demand on Belgium." Tirpitz did not understand the chancellor's reasoning at all.[21]

After bitter recriminations and finger pointing, it was finally agreed that Bethmann would wire England and explain that a French concentration along the Belgian border forced Germany to march through Belgium to avoid a surprise attack, but that the integrity of Belgium would, under all conditions, be respected. For the time being, Germany would not declare war on France.

When Bethmann left the meeting, Moltke and Tirpitz could no longer restrain themselves. Moltke asked the kaiser to inform his civilian leadership that Germany was already at war, a fact that the politicians still did not seem to believe. Moltke was convinced that Germany was in need of his political wisdom and told the kaiser that he had sent a detailed memorandum to Bethmann outlining Germany's position with respect to each nation, a memorandum that Tirpitz caustically called Moltke's "political recipe for the foreign ministry."

Moltke was now in full cry. The situation in the foreign ministry was "deplorable; they had made no preparations for the present situation." That was true. On the other hand, no one on the military side had made clear to the diplomats that, in the event of war, the army had but one campaign plan: an immediate attack through Luxembourg and Belgium. "They simply do not want to believe," Moltke went on, "that a tremendous avalanche such as the one now underway is no longer to be halted; they think that diplomatic notes can still achieve something."

Tirpitz said he felt the same way. The foreign ministry "had been working badly for years." Why not replace Jagow? Tirpitz suggested one of his admirals as a replacement. The kaiser, as usual, did not defend his civilian ministers; he said only that "We cannot make changes at a moment like this."[22]

Tirpitz detested Bethmann because Bethmann had opposed his fleet. The generals detested Bethmann because with his notes from Lichnowsky he had almost caused the cancellation of the entire mobilization plan. Now the chancellor was complicating matters with senseless arguments over formal declarations of war. After the war, generals and nationalists endlessly accused Bethmann of weakness and diplomatic failure: the agonizing, indecisive "philosopher of Hohenfinow"[23] had forced Germany to fight the whole world alone.

But it was the generals who destroyed Imperial Germany. Suppose that Moltke had not dropped his uncle's plan for a defensive posture in the west. A Russian mobilization would not then have forced Germany to attack France, and the difficulties for France and Russia would have been enormous. Even if Austria-Hungary had gone forward with its invasion of Serbia, as it almost certainly would have done, what could Russia do—attack Austria-Hungary and risk a war with Germany? War with Germany was the last thing any Russian wanted. Even assuming that Russia was willing to risk a German war to defend Serbia, Germany would then be defending Austria against a Russian attack, and France, however reluctantly, would have to attack Germany. Under those conditions, Britain would not have come into the war for months, if at all. That was the sequence Bethmann and the kaiser had assumed would follow when they told Austria to go ahead on 5 and 6 July. They were reasonable assumptions by the Great Power standards of the day, but the Schlieffen Plan robbed them of all hope of success.

39: Belgium and Britain

2 August

In 1839 Britain, France, Prussia, Austria, and Russia ratified a treaty that not only required Belgium to maintain its neutrality in European conflicts, but also guaranteed Belgium's "perpetual neutrality."[1] That treaty had been reconfirmed by all signatories on numerous occasions and was still in force in 1914. There was not, however, general agreement on what the treaty entailed.

Britain, France, and Germany believed that each of them could independently enforce Belgian neutrality against an invader or against the Belgians themselves, whether or not Belgium requested this protection. But Brussels insisted that no power had the right to protect Belgian neutrality unless asked to do so. Belgium would resist not only the invader, but any uninvited protector: "If the Germans enter first we shall put up a strong resistance. If, after the Germans, come the French, we shall turn against them equally. Our interest is to make common cause with nobody."[2]

If anything, the Belgian government was more suspicious of the French and British than of the Germans. Belgium had traditionally relied upon British neutrality and British protection to deter France and Germany. After France and Great Britain signed the Entente agreements in 1904 and Europe was divided between the Triple Entente and the Triple Alliance, the Belgian government took the position that Britain, having abandoned its "splendid isolation," was no longer a neutral guarantor. Belgium would have to rely upon its own resources[3] because the British would resist an invasion of Belgium "only in her own interest or in that of the French."[4] The Belgians were absolutely correct.

Sir Charles Hardinge, Nicolson's predecessor as permanent undersecretary, had pointed out that if "France violated the neutrality of Belgium in a war against Germany, it is, under present circumstances, doubtful whether England or Russia would move a finger to maintain Belgian neutrality, while if the neutrality of Belgium were violated by Germany, the converse would be the case." Grey thought Hardinge's observation was "to the

319

point."[5] In his postwar memoir, he wrote that under the 1839 neutrality treaty Great Britain would be obliged to defend Belgium if Germany invaded.[6] He did not discuss the position if France invaded.

French and British military men worried whether, under the 1839 treaty, they could march through Belgium to meet a threatened German invasion. Both armies pressed their governments on this point, and French and British inquiries in Brussels, however delicately phrased, only raised Belgian suspicions. The British naval attaché in Brussels reported that the Belgian army chief of staff "made it quite clear that in his opinion the danger of a breach of Belgian security lay more with England than anywhere else."[7] The Belgians were afraid that in a Franco-German war, the British would land troops in Belgium with or without Belgian consent. In 1914, therefore, despite years of reports and rumors on the nature of the Schlieffen Plan, the Belgian government would not credit reports that Germany would violate its neutrality.

British and French diplomats were afraid that the Belgians would not resist a German invasion, thereby speeding the German advance and keeping Britain from aiding France on the ground that it was defending Belgian neutrality. Both the French minister to Belgium and the French military attaché reported over and over again that although the Belgian population, particularly in the Walloon areas, was sympathetic to France, upper class, clerical, and government circles were strongly pro-German and suspicious of French intentions. The Catholic press was openly pro-Austrian.[8] The Spanish minister in Brussels was struck by the enormous gap between the Belgian government, which "largely out of fear" tended to "go with Germany," and "public opinion, which is inclined . . . to France."[9]

A. W. Klobukowski, the French minister, struggled endlessly and in vain with the Belgian foreign minister, J. Davignon, whose distrust of France was intense. Klobukowski described Davignon as a man of "imperturbable placidity. . . . In his room the sounds of the outside world seemed to arrive hushed and muted like distant echoes shorn of the urgency they had conveyed before entering. . . . In the anxious period we were passing through, which shook him somewhat out of his usual habits, his final remark invariably was: 'Let us hope it will turn out all right in the end.'"[10]

At seven o'clock on Saturday evening, 1 August, a German infantry company seized the railway station and telegraph office just across the border in Luxembourg. When the kaiser forced Moltke to call off the attack, a second detachment arrived at 7:30 P.M. to declare that the invasion had been a mistake. At 11:00 P.M. the kaiser again changed his mind and told Moltke he could do what he liked, and by midnight the railway station and the telegraph office were in German hands. The rest of Luxembourg was occupied by German forces during the course of Sunday, 2 August.

The neutrality of Luxembourg was guaranteed by the 1867 Treaty of London. On Sunday morning the Luxembourg government wired Grey that Luxembourg was being invaded in violation of that treaty. Luxembourg had "energetically protested"[11] but had offered no armed resistance. If Belgium took the same course, Grey would have a problem.

Early Sunday morning, Paul Cambon received an uncoded telegram from Viviani announcing the German violation of Luxembourg's neutrality.[12] Cambon immediately asked to see Grey, who offered to meet with him at 3:00 P.M. Cambon insisted that he see Grey at once, and Grey, who had had a long night and faced a difficult cabinet meeting at 11:00 A.M., reluctantly agreed. Cambon brought with him a copy of the 1867 Treaty of London, in which the European powers—including Prussia and Great Britain—guaranteed the neutrality of Luxembourg.[13] Cambon believed that the British government would have to act on this commitment. Grey, however, believed that the 1867 guarantee of Luxembourg's neutrality, unlike the 1839 treaty on Belgium, was collective and did not oblige the signatory powers to aid Luxembourg unless all the signators agreed to do so. Therefore, the violation of Luxembourg's neutrality might give Britain a reason to go to war with Germany but did not oblige it to do so. When Grey told Cambon that Great Britain was under no obligation to defend Luxembourg, the French ambassador warned that Belgium would be next.[14]

Cambon was bitterly disappointed and complained angrily to the journalist Wickham Steed that "I do not know whether this evening the word 'honour' will not have to be struck out of the British vocabulary."[15] Lichnowsky, meanwhile, was wiring Berlin that war with England would be unavoidable if they invaded Belgium.[16]

Baron Napoléon Eugene Louis Beyens, the Belgian minister to Germany, was a good deal more worried about German intentions than was his government, and Zimmermann at the foreign office was not very reassuring. On Friday, 31 July, Beyens asked Zimmermann why the Germans had responded so quickly to the news of the Russian mobilization when negotiations were still going on. Zimmermann insisted that Germany wanted peace, but France and Russia had to stop arming. Berlin had sent ultimatums to both countries asking them to stop, and if the answers were unfavorable, the State of Imminent War would be followed by general mobilization. "Russia wants war," Zimmermann concluded. "The responsibility falls upon her."[17]

Belgium began mobilizing on Saturday, 1 August. Brussels had instructed its ambassadors to inform all signatory governments that Belgium had "scrupulously observed the duties of a neutral state," that it "confidently expects that her territory will remain free from any attack," and that the Belgian government had taken "all necessary steps to ensure respect of Belgian neutrality."[18] Ambassador Goschen had already told Beyens that when Great Britain had asked France and Germany to respect Belgium's neutrality, France had given the necessary assurances and Jagow had refused to answer.[19] Beyens went to the German foreign office on Sunday morning to read Zimmermann his government's statement.[20] Zimmermann listened but said nothing. What could he say?

When Beyens returned to his ministry, the military attaché told him that a German infantry division had invaded Luxembourg that morning. The attaché had heard the news from an officer in the kaiser's military entourage, who assumed that Belgium would welcome the Germans with open arms. Beyens promptly wired Brussels: "Pessimistic rumors concerning us. I believe Belgian army should be ready immediately for all eventualities."

The Belgian government, however, gave no sign that it shared Beyens's concern. On Friday, Grey had instructed his minister in Brussels to tell Davignon, "I assume that Belgium will to the utmost of her power maintain her neutrality and desire and expect other Powers to observe and uphold it. You should ask for an early reply."[21] Grey's position in the cabinet would be much stronger if Belgium were to ask Great Britain for assistance. On Saturday the British minister in Brussels had to reply, "Minister for Foreign Affairs states that Belgian Government have no reason whatever to suspect Germany of an intention to violate neutrality. He says that Belgian Government have not considered idea of appeal to other guarantee Powers, nor of intervention should a violation occur; they would rely upon their own armed force as sufficient to resist aggression from whatever quarter it might come." London got this wire at 1:25 P.M., just as the morning cabinet session was ending.[22] Grey was not comforted.

Sunday was hot and muggy in London. Although many Englishmen were upset and frightened by the unexpected German declaration of war on Russia, they still did not expect England to be involved. That expectation began to fade with the invasion of Luxembourg.

Grey remained the austere and lonely figure he had always been. He was intensely angry at the Austrians and the Germans, and he would have no part in any policy of neutrality if France were involved. But he was deeply and passionately a man of peace, and he took Norman Angell's *The Great Illusion* to heart: a Great Power war would mean the collapse of society.

By the end of July, the strain was beginning to tell.[23] Grey avoided Lichnowsky and used William Tyrrell to communicate with him. He would disappear to his club in the evenings for dinner, billiards, and the company of his parliamentary secretary, Arthur Murray. He slept, when he did sleep, at the home of Richard Haldane, who tried to give what counsel he could; but Grey, wrote Haldane, "was splendidly self-reliant." When dispatches were brought to Haldane's house, "I had a servant sitting up with instructions to bring them to my bedroom and waken me so that I might open the boxes with my Cabinet key and decide whether it was necessary to break in upon Grey's rest."[24]

Grey never talked freely to the cabinet because he was afraid the neutralists would force a vote that would bring down the government. He was more than usually short with questioners in the House of Commons. He no longer consulted with Nicolson or Crowe because Nicolson wanted a statement of support for Russia and Crowe wanted a declaration of solidarity with the Entente powers, neither of which the cabinet would permit Grey to give. Asquith was no help; he was waiting for matters to sort themselves out. Neither Grey nor Asquith consulted with the military chiefs, who were eager to get the BEF ready for dispatch to France. No meeting of the Committee of Imperial Defense was called and no military opinion was solicited, either before or after the 1 August vote to keep the BEF at home.

Grey's memoir describes a conversation with an active Liberal Member of Parliament (MP) in the lobby of the House of Commons. The MP told Grey that under no circumstances whatever should the country take part in the coming war. "It did not seem to occur to him that if men like himself were feeling the strain of the situation, the Secretary for Foreign Affairs might be feeling it as much, or more, and the strain was very great. . . ." Grey answered sharply, "It was nonsense to say that there were no circumstances conceivable in which we ought to go to war."

"Under no circumstances whatever," the MP insisted.

"Suppose Germany violates the neutrality of Belgium?" asked Grey.

The MP paused—Belgian neutrality was sensitive ground—but he pushed the problem aside, saying, "She won't do it."

Grey pressed him. "I don't say she will, but supposing she does."

"She won't do it," the MP stubbornly repeated.[25]

Grey felt he could spare himself conversations of that nature.

Within the cabinet, there seems to have been a tacit conspiracy of reticence: "One side did not press the other to authorize a pledge of support to France; the other side did not press for an intimation to France that we would stand aside. . . . Between the two groups were no doubt members of the Cabinet who reserved decision. . . . Such were the conditions in which, inside the Foreign Office, the demand from France and Russia to know whether they could count on British support in war had to be received and could not be answered."[26]

Like the rest of the government, the antiwar left was totally immersed in the Irish question. When the European crisis burst upon them on 1 and 2 August, they had barely begun to get their bearings on events on the Continent. Most Liberal MPs assumed that the government would stay out of an Austro-Russian war; not until 30 July were they told that German mobilization was a distinct possibility. Even then, neither Asquith nor Grey in their remarks to the House of Commons offered any hard information except that the government's hands were free and the government was working for peace. Most MPs trusted those assurances.

Moreover, the noninterventionist majority won the early skirmishes. On 29 July they rejected Churchill's request to mobilize the fleet. On 1 August they forced Grey to tell Cambon not only that France should make its decisions without regard to British assistance, but that even if Britain came in, the BEF would not "immediately" go to the Continent. Arthur Ponsonby, a Liberal MP who claimed to speak for seventy noninterventionist members, sent Grey a resolution declaring that "Great Britain in no conceivable circumstances should depart from a position of strict neutrality."

Grey immediately called in Ponsonby and said he would make no such declaration; in the interest of peace it was useful that British intentions be uncertain. He and Churchill pleaded with the noninterventionists to remain silent over the weekend. "It [would] be wrong," Churchill warned Ponsonby, "at this moment to pronounce finally one way or another as to our duty or our interests."[27] What the Liberal imperialists—Asquith, Grey, Haldane, Churchill—wanted above all was that there should be no split in the cabinet until the almost inevitable German invasion of Belgium gave them an unassailable position.

On Saturday, 1 August, the Liberal government was still intact and the noninterventionists were losing ground. There were as yet no resignations, and Asquith was beginning to think there might be no serious ones. Without further cabinet consultation, he allowed Churchill to mobilize the fleet on the night of 1 August, despite the cabinet's rejection of that move on 29 July. Noninterventionists, fearful of endangering the peace, remained quiet during a weekend of frustrating futility. "We felt," one of them later wrote, "as helpless as rats in a trap."[28]

Nonetheless, the possibility of an antiwar rebellion in the cabinet was still real. Churchill thought a majority would resign if the government committed Britain to war. The Liberal press—the *Manchester Guardian,* the *Daily News,* and the *Westminster Gazette*—were insisting on British neutrality. One of the middle group of waverers in the cabinet, Herbert Samuel, wrote his wife that if a clear-cut vote on intervention or nonintervention were taken that Sunday, "Asquith would have stood by Grey in any event, and three others would have remained. I think all the rest of us would have resigned."[29]

Asquith also thought on Sunday afternooon that there was a "strong party . . . against any intervention in any event," which amounted to a majority of the cabinet. He thought these numbers might change. Germany had declared war on Russia and invaded Luxembourg; Jagow had refused to guarantee Belgian neutrality. Austria and Russia were talking, but there was no sign that they were getting anywhere. The prime minister could afford to wait.

The cabinet was bitterly divided over the weekend of 31 July–2 August. Eight members (Lord Haldane, Augustine Birrell, Lord Crewe, Reginald McKenna, Winston Churchill, Charles Masterman, Grey, and Asquith) were ready to come to the aid of France, particularly if the German fleet came into the Channel or the German army into Belgium. Eleven members (Lord John Morley, John Burns, David Lloyd George, Lewis Harcourt, Lord Beauchamp, Sir John Simon, J. A. Pease, Walter Runciman, Herbert Samuel, Thomas McKinnon Wood, and Charles Hobhouse) were opposed to fighting a war for France and Russia. But only Burns and Morley were adamant. Burns's position was clear: "Splendid isolation. No balance of Power. No Incorporation in the Continental System."[30] Radical Liberals had been making that speech for years, but Burns understood it and meant it.

Until that Friday, opposition leaders had believed that the Liberal government shared their view that England had an obligation to defend France against German aggression. But Churchill, General Wilson—the director of Military Operations—and leaks from the French embassy made them nervous. Asquith and Grey were facing stiff opposition from radical noninterventionists, and Tyrrell was warned by the editor of the right-wing *Morning Post* that "we have been led by the [foreign office] under your chief's guidance to be prepared for [Anglo-French naval and military cooperation]. We have worked hard to prepare public opinion for it and now when we get to the jump, as it were, we are refusing it."[31] Tyrrell passed these comments on to Grey.

General Wilson, meanwhile, was in despair because the government would not let him prepare to mobilize the army. A fierce Ulster Protestant and a Liberal-Unionist (Liberals who split from the party because of their opposition to Irish home rule), he hated "Squiff [Asquith] and his filthy cabinet." He believed that Great Britain was obligated to support France, and he intrigued constantly against the carefully noncommittal policy of the government. After seeing Grey and Nicolson on the morning of 1 August, he was so upset by the cabinet's lack of commitment that he ran off to consult with those opposition leaders who were still in London over the weekend. Wickham Steed recalled meeting with a young Conservative MP who told him, "It's all up. The Government are going to 'rat.'"

"What are the Opposition leaders doing?" Steed asked.

"They are going into the country to play lawn tennis," the MP replied. "Balfour, Bonar Law, the whole set of them . . ."

"Can't you go and gather them?" Steed suggested.

They agreed that the opposition leadership should be called back to London.

After considering a variety of alternatives, the opposition leaders finally decided that Lord Lansdowne, the leader in the Lords, and Bonar Law, the leader in the Commons, would send a joint letter to Asquith. The letter declared that "it would be fatal to the honour and security of the United Kingdom to hesitate in supporting France and Russia at this juncture; and we offer our unconditional support to the Government in any measures they may consider necessary for this object." Asquith and Grey had this note in hand when they met with the cabinet on Sunday morning.[32]

The noninterventionists in the cabinet were as anxious as the Conservatives. They sensed that events were moving against neutrality, and six of them—Runciman, Lloyd George, Harcourt, Beauchamp, Simon, and Pease—met on Sunday morning to review their position before the eleven o'clock cabinet meeting. By then they knew that Germany had invaded Luxembourg and would probably invade Belgium. They knew that Asquith and Grey would bring down the government by resigning if the cabinet voted for neutrality. They knew that they could bring down the government even without a majority, if enough of them resigned. But where would resignation get them, except out of employment?

Moreover, for all their complaints about Grey and the ententes, they were not fundamentally opposed to Grey's conception of a European balance of power. They simply never believed that the German threat was as great as Grey made it out to be.

These were men who had built their public careers on peace, on the reduction of armaments, on the advance of social welfare for the common man, and on the rejection of any commitment to fight a European war on behalf of France and Russia. How could they vote for war without shamefully abandoning the loudly proclaimed principles of a lifetime?[33] On the other hand, if the Germans were behaving abominably—and German power was awesome—how would they fare if France were crushed and Russia defeated? The voters would blame them for not standing up to the menace.

How would they look if England fought a war that was short, victorious, and glorious without Liberal support? They finally declared that "we are not prepared to go into war now, but . . . in certain events we might reconsider [the] position such as the invasion wholesale of Belgium."[34] Note the word *wholesale*—a German invasion limited to the south of Belgium might still not mean war. Burns and Morley did not attend the meeting; they had already decided that the issue was war, not Belgium. If Britain went to war, they would resign.

Although Lichnowsky knew that an invasion of Belgium would bring Great Britain into the war against Germany, he kept pleading for British understanding of Germany's strategic dilemma.[35] He breakfasted with Asquith on Sunday morning.

Asquith described the prince as "very *emotionné*." He "implored me not to side with France. He said that Germany, with her army cut in two between France & Russia, was far more likely to be 'crushed' than France. He was very agitated poor man & wept. I told him that we had no desire to intervene, and it rested largely with Germany to make intervention impossible, if she would (1) not invade Belgium, and (2) not send her fleet into the Channel to attack the unprotected North Coast of France. He was bitter about the policy of his Government in not restraining Austria, & seemed quite heartbroken."[36]

Lichnowsky, however, described Asquith as the one overcome with emotion. "Tears repeatedly stood in the eyes of the old gentleman," Lichnowsky wrote, "and he said to me: 'A war between our two countries is quite unthinkable.'" Lichnowsky also saw Grey before the cabinet meeting and reported that neither Grey nor Asquith wanted to intervene in a war, but whatever goodwill and pro-German feeling there might be would be severely tested by a German invasion of Belgium.[37]

Grey had predicted that Sunday's cabinet would be a "tussle."[38] It sat contentiously from 11:00 A.M. to about 2:00 P.M., and Herbert Samuel wrote his wife that it "almost resulted in a political crisis to be super-imposed on the international and the financial crisis." He added that Grey's position was "unacceptable to most of us. He is outraged by the way in which Germany and Austria have played with the most vital interests of civilisation, have put aside all attempts at accommodation made by himself and others, and, while continuing to negotiate, have marched steadily to war."[39] Early in the discussion, Asquith read aloud the letter from Conservative leaders declaring their support for any assistance the government might give to France and Russia. The noninterventionists were now sure there would be a war cabinet no matter what they did. Grey was no longer prepared to continue a noncommittal line: "I believe war will come [and] it is due to France they shall have our support."[40] The cabinet, however, was not prepared to fight a war simply to support France.

Grey reminded the members of the 1912 exchange of letters with France. These letters confirmed that the British fleet had concentrated in the Channel and the North Sea while the French fleet had concentrated in the Mediterranean. Both nations had done so independently, but Cambon had suggested that it would be well simply to record what had been done. Grey now told the cabinet that with the French fleet concentrated in the Mediterranean the northern French coasts were open to attack by the German High Seas Fleet. The neutralists were appalled. When Grey had submitted the letters for approval in 1912, they had forced Grey to insert a passage in his letter to Cambon that said that neither the military talks nor the fleet dispositions were "based on any agreement to cooperate in war."[41] The cabinet had assumed that this language completely assured their freedom of action; now the disclaimer appeared to be worthless. "What a singularly thin and deceptive document it was turning out," wrote Morley bitterly.[42]

For two years the cabinet had silently acquiesced in the concentration of the French fleet in the Mediterranean. Now it was faced with the argument that the French, having relied on British friendship, were defenseless before a German naval attack. Even Morley believed that the cabinet could not permit a "Franco-German naval conflict in the narrow seas on our doorstep, so to say." Harcourt slipped a note to Pease that read, "I can't decline this."[43] The neutralists twisted and turned. McKenna suggested that the Channel should be neutralized for both sides. Grey, Walter Runciman wrote, was adamant: "If the Channel is closed against Germany, it *is* in favour of France, & we cannot take half measures—either we must declare ourselves neutral, or in it. If we are to be neutral he [Grey] will go, but he cannot blame the Cabinet if they disagree with him. He therefore asks for a sharp decision."[44]

Still wavering, Herbert Samuel proposed a series of compromise formulas. Britain "should be justified in joining in the war either for the protection of the northern coasts of France, which we could not afford to see bombarded by the German fleet and occupied by the German army, or for the maintenance of the independence of Belgium, which we are bound by treaty to protect and which again we could not afford to see subordinated to Germany." Samuel's proposal had several advantages. First, it reassured the noninterventionists that Britain would not go to war "for the sake of our goodwill for France or for the sake of maintaining the strength of France and Russia against that of Germany and Austria." Second, it enabled the government to say that if war came, "it will be an action of Germany's, and not ours which will cause the failure."[45] Third, the proposal spoke of the "independence" of Belgium, not neutrality or a German invasion, permitting some noninterventionists to believe they were not yet committing themselves to war.

It took three grueling hours to move the radical noninterventionists that far. Grey again agreed that imperial defense would not permit sending the BEF to France, and he may himself have thought so. Satisfied that they were only considering the possibility of a naval war, the noninterventionists agreed that Grey propose to Parliament on Monday that "we should take action if the German fleet came down the Channel to attack France. (Almost the whole of the French fleet is in the Mediterranean.)" Typical of the neutralist dreamworld was the hopeful scenario Herbert Samuel drew for his wife: if Germany attacked neither the Channel nor Belgium, England could stay out of the war "while rendering to France the greatest of all services— the protection of her northern coasts from the sea and the protection of her 150 miles of frontier with Belgium. If we can achieve this, without firing a shot, we shall have accomplished a brilliant stroke of policy."[46]

Neither Burns nor Morley was so foolish. Declaring that closing the Channel to the German fleet was equivalent to declaring war on Germany, Burns immediately announced that he would resign. Morley declined to resign over a warning to Germany to respect the Channel, but he warned Asquith that he would resign if it came to war. Other noninterventionists were acutely uncomfortable with the way that Grey was forcing them, step-by-step, to war with Germany, but they did not threaten to resign. At Asquith's suggestion, the cabinet agreed to meet again that evening to deal with Belgium. Asquith also persuaded Burns to wait until then before resigning. Sometime later, Runciman penciled across the top of his summary of the Sunday morning meeting, "The Cabinet which decided that war with Germany was inevitable."[47] Runciman, Morley, and Burns, at least, understood the meaning of the morning's decisions.

40: THE GERMAN INVASION OF BELGIUM

2–4 August

Europe was astonished by the German invasion of Luxembourg. Grand Duchess Marie Adelheid of Luxembourg addressed herself directly to Kaiser Wilhelm: "I beg Your Majesty to hasten [an] explanation and to respect the country's rights."[1] By treaty, the Luxembourg railways were under the management of the German railway system. Bethmann and Stumm therefore replied that "military measures in Luxemburg indicate no hostile action against Luxemburg, but are solely measures for the protection of the Luxemburg railroads under our management there, against attack by the French. Luxemburg will receive full compensation for any possible damages."[2] A similar explanation was sent to Lichnowsky[3] and was posted in placards by the German commander in Luxembourg. Luxembourg's prime minister fired back: "There is absolutely not a single French soldier in Luxemburg territory, nor is there the least indication of a threat to her neutrality on the part of France." On the contrary, the French had torn up the railway tracks running into Luxembourg on the French side of the border.[4]

The invasion was a diplomatic catastrophe, but the implacable machinery of the Schlieffen Plan rolled on. Bethmann, Jagow, and the kaiser continued to believe that England might remain neutral, and Moltke proposed that if England offered neutrality in return for a promise of "moderation" in the case of a victory over France, Germany should give that assurance. He included this wild hope in a staff memorandum he submitted to the German foreign office on Sunday. His other recommendations were: "Turkey ought to declare war on Russia as soon as possible"; "Attempts must be made to instigate an uprising in India, if England takes a stand as our opponent"; ditto for Egypt and South Africa; and Sweden should be urged to mobilize and advance on the Finnish border, followed by mobilization in Denmark and Norway as well. Japan and Persia were also to be encouraged to participate in the war. Italy must "declare immediately whether or not she is willing to take an active part in the approaching war." A declaration of war on Russia was of no consequence; Russia was already invading.

There was no connection, Moltke wrote, between the invasion of Belgium and a declaration of war on France. "I do not consider it necessary yet to deliver the declaration of war on France; on the other hand, I am counting on the likelihood that, if it is held back at present, France, on her part, will be forced by public opinion to organize warlike measures against Germany, even if a formal declaration of war has not been presented." The French six-mile withdrawal had made absolutely no impression on Moltke. He assumed that "France will move into Belgium in the role of the protector of Belgian neutrality, just as soon as the step taken by Germany in Belgium becomes known in Paris."[5]

In London, the invasion of Luxembourg continued to undermine the non-interventionists. The Sunday morning cabinet meeting had been exhausting and left Asquith with the impression that there was a "strong party" against intervention under any circumstances. In the House of Commons, he thought, three-quarters of his party was "for absolute non-interference at any price."[6]

Burns and Morley were clear on where they stood; the other noninterventionists were not. They conceded that Britain had to fight if British interests were involved; but then they could not escape the logic of Eyre Crowe's analysis. First, Crowe argued, a declaration that "England cannot in any circumstances go to war" would be "an act of political suicide." Second, although it was true there was no actual written commitment to support France, "the whole policy of the *Entente* can have no meaning if it does not signify that in a just quarrel England would stand by her friends. This honourable expectation has been raised. We cannot repudiate it without exposing our good name to grave criticism." Crowe's argument was precisely why noninterventionists had opposed the Entente policy over the years; now they were faced with its consequences.[7]

The noninterventionists met throughout Sunday afternoon, agonizing over the German invasion of Luxembourg, looking for some way out of their dilemma, blowing off steam, complaining of Grey's repeated threats of resignation, and wringing their hands because the cabinet was being "rather artfully drawn on step by step to war for the benefit of France and Russia." Morley later lamented, "If I, or anybody else, could only have brought home to them that the compound and mixed argument of French liability and Belgian liability must end in expeditionary force, and active part in vast and long-continued European war, the Cabinet would undoubtedly have perished that very evening."[8]

Grey continued to keep to himself. He spent an hour at the zoo watching birds.[9] When he returned, he met with Cambon and told him that he had been authorized to ask Parliament on Monday "to give an assurance that if the German fleet comes into the Channel or through the North Sea to undertake hostile operations against French coasts or shipping the British fleet will give all the protection in its power." Grey had to add, however, that because of the dangers Great Britain faced in Egypt and India, they could not reduce their available land forces by sending the BEF to France. "Does that mean you never will?" asked Cambon. Grey replied that the question would be reconsidered if and when hostilities actually broke out.[10]

Grey had wired Brussels the French and German replies to his request for assurances on Belgian neutrality. While he was talking with Cambon, he was handed the Belgian response indicating the Belgians could take care of themselves without outside help.[11] Cambon wrote that "this strange answer . . . gave us the idea that there was perhaps some secret arrangement between Germany and Belgium." Grey, however, pointed out "that the neutrality of [Belgian] territory is not more a Belgian than an English interest, and that England is bound to see that it is respected."[12] The Belgians knew that this was the English view and insisted that they could take care of themselves.

By the evening cabinet meeting on Sunday, almost all the noninterventionists were ready to accept Herbert Samuel's compromise language, which, Samuel wrote his wife, made the situation easier. "The point of contention [a British obligation to support France] was not pressed, and with the exception of the two I have mentioned [Burns and Morley], we remained solid."[13] Lord Crewe, a firm interventionist, reported to King George that the evening cabinet meeting, "without any attempt to state a formula," had agreed that "a substantial violation" of Belgian neutrality would "compel us to take action." Morley promptly informed Asquith that he, too, would resign.[14]

Burns was gone, Morley was going, and others might go. After the evening cabinet meeting, the waverers were still agonizing. Lloyd George, who complained that he had been working for eighteen straight hours, worried about future problems if the Entente won and Russia dominated the Continent. When he was told to let the future take care of itself, that Germany would overrun France, Lloyd George replied, "How will you feel if you see Germany overrun and annihilated by Russia?" Simon had similar concerns: "The Triple Entente was a terrible mistake. Why should we support a country like Russia?" No one was sure the cabinet would hold together. At one point, Lloyd George said, "We intend," then stopped, paused a moment, and said, "that is, if we are governing the country tomorrow, which is very doubtful."[15]

Churchill perfectly summarized the noninterventionist retreat: "The Cabinet was overwhelmingly pacific. At least three-quarters of its members were determined not to be drawn into a European quarrel, unless Great Britain were herself to be attacked, which was not likely. Those who were in this mood were inclined to believe first of all Austria and Serbia would not come to blows; secondly, that if they did, Russia would not intervene; thirdly, if Russia intervened, that Germany would not strike; fourthly, they hoped that if Germany struck at Russia, it ought to be possible for France and Germany to neutralize each other without fighting. They did not believe that if Germany attacked France, she would attack through Belgium or that if she did the Belgians would forcibly resist. . . ."[16] But agonize and complain as they might, even the staunchest noninterventionists knew they were going to war.

Liberal ministers could not tell their constituents that Britain had entered the war to uphold the balance of power; they needed a German invasion of Belgium. If the Germans had not gone through Belgium, a large number of Liberals would have resigned rather than vote for war. The last danger to the unity of the cabinet, therefore, was whether or not Belgium would resist.[17] On Sunday night no one yet knew whether Belgium would (a) acquiesce, (b) offer only formal resistance, or (c) offer vigorous resistance. Herbert Samuel thought vigorous resistance the most likely and wrote later, "It is certainly not the case that the whole Cabinet expected (a) or (b)."[18]

Earlier on Sunday, Prime Minister René Viviani had wired London that when he addressed the French Chamber of Deputies on Monday, he would be asked about England's position. What should he say?[19] Grey told Cambon that the answer would depend on what the Germans did and on what the situation was when he himself addressed the House of Commons on Monday. He suggested that Viviani tell the Chamber of Deputies that the two governments were in agreement on a number of points, but that a more precise response would have to wait until the British foreign secretary's address to the House of Commons.

Paul Cambon reported to Paris that public opinion was moving in their favor. The English were very upset by the German invasion of Luxembourg and by reports of German violations of French territory without a declaration of war. A Socialist peace rally at Trafalgar Square, he wrote, was a total failure.[20] Viviani decided to put off his address to the Chamber of Deputies until Tuesday. The way things were going, he could afford to wait.

Grey did not want to talk to Lichnowsky until after he had spoken to Parliament. Lichnowsky, therefore, was unable to report the results of either of the Sunday cabinet meetings except to note that the British fleet was being mobilized, that defensive measures were being taken along the coast, and that the Straits of Dover were occupied by torpedo boats. He thought, however, that the English had not yet decided on war. "I believe that the attitude will be one of waiting for the present."[21]

*   *   *

On 26 July, Moltke had given the German foreign office a draft ultima-tum to Belgium: Belgium was to permit the passage of German troops to the French frontier because on its own it would be unable to resist a French and an English invasion. Germany would guarantee Belgium's sovereignty and integrity, pay cash for all requisitions, make good any damage done by German troops, and support any territorial claims Belgium might entertain against France. If Belgium refused, future relations between the two nations would be governed by "the decision of arms." Brussels had twenty-four hours to reply. Moltke's draft was as blunt as it could be and was not toned down in the foreign office. It was revised by Stumm to eliminate any refer-ence to the English joining a French invasion, and Zimmermann and Bethmann made a few minor alterations. It was signed by Jagow.[22] On 29 July, the final draft was sent, sealed, to the German minister at Brussels with instructions not to open the enclosure until instructed to do so.[23]

On Sunday, 2 August, Klaus von Below-Saleski, the German minister in Brussels, received instructions to open the enclosure. Jagow also instructed him to delete the reference to supporting Belgian claims to French territory, to give the Belgian government twelve hours rather than twenty-four hours to reply—this was at Moltke's insistence—and to deliver the demand at 8:00 P.M. that night, Berlin time, which would be seven in Brussels. Below was also instructed to give the Belgian government the impression that he had received his instruction just that afternoon. The Belgian reply was to be in Berlin by 2:00 P.M. local time on Monday, 3 August.[24]

Even the German invasion of Luxembourg had not shaken the invincible optimism of the Belgian government. During the war, an official in the for-eign office argued that the reasons given for occupying the duchy did not necessarily apply to Belgium.[25] Whenever the Belgian government asked Klaus von Below whether Germany would respect its neutrality, Below replied that "up to the present he had not been instructed to make us an of-ficial communication, but that we knew his personal opinion as to the feel-ings of security which we had the right to entertain towards our eastern neighbours."[26]

The unfortunate Below cannot have been a happy man when he finally unsealed his instructions on Sunday afternoon. "The Imperial Government is in receipt of reliable information," the message began, "relating to the advance of French armed forces along the Meuse. . . . They leave no doubt as to France's intention to advance against Germany through Belgian terri-tory."[27] Below was further instructed to "please assure the Belgian Govern-ment most earnestly that there is absolutely no doubt of the accuracy of our information as to the French plans, despite the promise made at Paris."[28]

Below screwed up his courage and at 6:30 P.M. telephoned for an appoint-ment to deliver an important communication. At a little after seven o'clock, he arrived at Davignon's office, pale and shaky.

"What is the matter?" Davignon asked. "Are you not well?"

Below said, "I came up the stair too quickly, it is nothing. I have a most confidential communication to make to you on behalf of my Government." He took an envelope from his pocket and handed it to Davignon. Davignon was now genuinely apprehensive. He opened the envelope, read the ultima-tum quickly, then read it again. He, too, was pale and trembling. "No, surely? . . . No, it is not possible!" He dropped the note and it fell between the two diplomats.

Below recovered sufficiently to give a verbal summary of the ultimatum, insisting that Germany wanted peace and that France was preparing an of-fensive through the Meuse River valley. Davignon grew angrier as he lis-tened. He had trusted the Germans. He had assured the French and British ministers over and over again that Belgium had nothing to fear from Ger-many. He was outraged at the suggestion that Belgium would not be truly neutral, and by the sheer unlikelihood of the charge that France was prepar-ing an attack. He assured Below that the German note would be discussed without delay, and Below took his leave.[29]

The Belgian cabinet was immediately assembled. At least one of the twelve precious hours had been spent on a translation. When it was ready, it was read aloud. After a short silence, the prime minister turned to the minister of war and said, "Well, M. le Ministre. Are we ready?"

"Yes," the minister replied, "we are ready. . . . But, there is a but; we have no heavy guns."

Guns were the least of the Belgian problems. The ministers informed the king, who called a Crown Council at the palace. They worked through a night of acrimonious argument—not on whether to reject the German ul-timatum, on which there was unanimity. Even the right-wing pro-Ger-mans, sympathetic to Catholic Austria and trusting in German friendship, agreed that Belgium had to resist. The argument turned mainly on the best way to do so.

The army was not sure whether Germany would occupy all of Belgium or stay south and east of the Meuse River. Should they try to defend the terri-tory on the far side of the river? Should they fight at the frontier or with-draw into the interior? Should they call on the Guaranteeing Powers? The king first wanted pledges safeguarding Belgian independence and the autonomy of its army. Belgian troops were not to fight under French or En-glish command. A minister objected that "when one is drowning one does not ask one's rescuer to show his credentials." The ministers finally agreed on a compromise. Belgium would immediately ask the Guaranteeing Powers for diplomatic support but would not ask for military support until an invasion actually began. There was then a long debate on how to reject the German ultimatum. Many of the ministers still hoped that once the Germans realized that Belgium would resist and that Europe was outraged, they might change their minds about invading Belgium.[30]

Jagow, meanwhile, sent Below a series of wires enumerating alleged French border violations and arguing that a French invasion of Belgium was imminent. Below replied that he did not think such arguments would have any effect in Brussels.[31] But orders were orders, and at one o'clock Monday morning he went to the foreign ministry to deliver his message. Davignon was at the Crown Council, so Below had to see his deputy, Baron van der Elst. When Below had finished his recitation, van der Elst asked where the incidents had taken place. Below replied, "In Germany."

"In that case," replied van der Elst, "I do not understand the object of your call."

An intensely embarrassed Below had to explain that his government wished to show France's aggressive intentions. Van der Elst's angry reply could be heard all the way down the hall, where the ministers were meeting.[32]

By 10:55 Monday morning, Below could wire that Belgium would reject the German demand "and will oppose by force any violation of her neutrality."[33] No subsequent German action so outraged Europe as the invasions of Luxembourg and Belgium. Whatever merit there may have been in the Austrian case for a war on Serbia, or in Germany's claim that it was only responding to a Russian general mobilization, was buried by the two invasions. The German diplomatic position never recovered.

As Bethmann and Jagow gradually realized the full magnitude of the diplomatic disaster that the Schlieffen Plan had imposed upon them, they lost all sense of reality. Jagow sent a stream of wires to Brussels, London, Rome, and the capitals of the smaller neutrals claiming the usual military transgressions—French cavalry patrols were crossing the frontier, eighty French officers in Prussian uniforms had tried to cross the German frontier, French infantry had fired across the frontier at Alsace, French aircraft had dropped bombs on German territory, a French airman had been shot out of the sky.[34] Moreover, Jagow charged, a French doctor and two Frenchmen had tried to poison wells in Metz, and a French flour dealer was poisoning flour to be sent to Germany.[35]

London was also receiving reports on German border violations. Prince Lichnowsky relayed Eyre Crowe's warning that these reports "would make a bad impression upon the Cabinet."[36] Jagow wired back that such reports were "wholly imaginary."[37] The allegations kept flowing into London, and by Monday morning Lichnowsky was beside himself. "Advance into France," he wired, "has had an ominous effect here and has seriously offended English sense of justice. Urgently request explanation I can use."[38] Jagow and Bethmann both sent wires Monday afternoon: "Up to the present time no single German soldier has crossed French frontier."[39]

In Brussels, King Albert and Davignon still hoped that if Belgium were not too openly aligned with France and England, Germany might change its mind. The king and his ministers therefore decided that the Entente ministers should be told as little as possible. Davignon wired only brief summaries of the German note and the Belgian reply to his ministers abroad. A. W. Klobukowski and Sir Francis Villiers, the French and English ministers in Brussels, were never officially informed of the German ultimatum. Klobukowski learned of it at eight o'clock Monday morning from a foreign ministry official with whom he had served in Cairo, who read him the ultimatum and said, "I am not leaving a copy. . . . I have not even my Minister's authority to communicate it to you."[40] Klobukowski wired the news to Paris, adding that Belgium intended "vigorously to defend its neutrality."[41] Villiers wired the same news to London an hour or so later, at 9:31 A.M. Later that afternoon, he succeeded in getting copies of the German ultimatum and the Belgian answer, and he wired summaries to London.[42]

During the course of Monday, Klobukowski, on his own authority and after consulting with the British and the Russian ministers, delivered a declaration to Davignon, who promised to submit it to the cabinet: the French government, in its capacity as a Guaranteeing Power, would respond to any Belgian appeal for aid, but if Belgium made no appeal, France, unless driven to act otherwise by "the needs of self-defence . . . would refrain from intervening until Belgium had carried out some effective measure of resistance." After a further cabinet meeting, Davignon thanked Klobukowski and replied that there would be no appeal at the present time. "Later the Royal Government will judge what is needful to do." King Albert wired King George in similar terms, asking for diplomatic, but not military, assistance.[43]

Belgian caution made the Entente powers very nervous. They were afraid that the Belgians would offer only token resistance and then let the Germans through.[44] As the hours passed on Monday without news of an actual German invasion of Belgium, Klobukowski began to suspect that the German ultimatum was merely a maneuver to induce France "to be the first to intervene in Belgium, thus causing an initial conflict between the Belgian army and our own."[45] Villiers, the English minister, was also not sure what the Belgians would do. They had refused a French offer of aid and they were vague about their ultimate response. The French military attaché had been assured that if Germany actually invaded Belgium, the Belgians would appeal to France and England for military aid, but not "so long as Belgian soil is not violated by formidable bodies of German troops." So far, only German patrols had appeared on Belgian soil.[46]

All doubt disappeared on Tuesday morning, 4 August, when Brussels learned that German troops had entered Belgium at 8:00 A.M. Even before the news reached Brussels, the Belgian parliament had voted unanimously to resist. The decision was wildly popular. "If we had been weak enough to yield, tomorrow in the streets of Brussels the people would have hanged us," King Albert said.[47] Klaus von Below reported, "Feeling against Germany strong."[48] Klobukowski was sure that it was public opinion that had forced the government to resist and to ask the Guaranteeing Powers for help.[49]

Bethmann, meanwhile, was trying to plead the German case in London. Between noon and 1:00 P.M. on Sunday, he sent two wires to Lichnowsky. The first listed French border violations and asked the prince "to present seriously to Grey the dangerous situation in which Germany is placed . . . driven by her opponent to adopt the role of an injured party who must make up arms, for the preservation of her very existence."[50] The second wire reviewed once again how the Russian mobilization had forced Germany to declare war. "The indignation of the German public at the Russian mobilization was so great that the refusal to demobilize had to be accepted as a hostile act affording ground for war, were we not prepared to sacrifice our national honor."[51] The British foreign office, however, had long since stopped listening to German allegations. When a secretary of the German embassy delivered the report that eighty French soldiers in Prussian uniforms had violated the territory of Germany, Crowe almost laughed, asking "whether he meant me to take this statement seriously."[52]

While the Great Powers slid into war, the lesser powers were doing what they could to stand clear of the collision. Bulgaria was ready to ally with Germany and Austria if Germany would promise to help it recover territory lost in the Second Balkan War. But Belgium, Denmark, Holland, Italy, Luxembourg, Norway, and Romania all announced their determination to remain neutral, and Sweden was about to do so. It galled the Italian leadership to be lumped with the minor powers in this way, but San Giuliano was absolutely clear that neutrality, at least in the early stages of the war, was Italy's safest path, regardless of the shame.

Jagow refused to give up on Italy. He wired Rome that it was bound by the terms of the alliance to fight alongside Austria and Germany. "French aviators are dropping bombs in the distant neighborhood of Nuremburg," and "French patrols have crossed the frontier. These hostile acts before a declaration of war constitute an attack on us by France. As a result, a *casus foederis* is afforded."[53] Like Bethmann's wires to London, these fabrications were an exercise in futility.

Austria's Ambassador Szögyény was told by an official in the German foreign office on Monday that the German army's decision to attack France through Belgium was unshakable. When Szögyény pointed out that an invasion of Belgium would almost certainly place England among their enemies, the official replied that "the military have taken over and there was no talking with them."[54] The Bavarian minister in Berlin reported Moltke as saying that English neutrality would come too high if it could be bought only by respecting Belgian neutrality.[55] "It is clear," he warned Munich, "that in the coming war, Germany and Austria will be facing the entire world."[56]

In Paris the French ministers were meeting continuously on Sunday. Messimy complained that with so much talking he had no time to think or to make decisions.[57] With the Germans in Luxembourg, General Joffre thought the situation was sufficiently clear to move his troops into the six-mile buffer zone, but with accusations of border violations flying back and forth and London still undecided, Messimy wanted to avoid any semblance of French aggression. During the early afternoon, however, reports of border crossings by German troops were too numerous and too serious to ignore. At about 2:00 P.M., Messimy phoned Joffre and gave him "full liberty of action for the execution of his plans, even if these should lead to crossing the German frontier." Despite this freedom of action, Joffre claimed that in order to leave the Germans entirely responsibe for hostilities, French forces would limit themselves to driving attacking forces back across the frontier without carrying the pursuit into enemy territory.[58]

Viviani protested to Schoen about German frontier violations. Schoen protested to Viviani about French frontier violations. Both governments protested their innocence in London while marshaling reports of ever new transgressions by the other.

Poincaré had other problems. He spent several days finding a replacement for the minister of the navy, whom he regarded as incompetent. He wanted to replace Viviani as foreign minister as well, and Viviani, who was not comfortable in the job, was willing to give up the post and remain as prime minister without portfolio. The problem was that Poincaré wanted to bring in one of two fiery nationalist hard-liners who were unacceptable to the left. Finally, on 3 August, after days of maneuvering and to Poincare's great relief, Gaston Doumerge, a former foreign minister under Poincaré, came back to replace Viviani.[59]

PART XI: GREAT BRITAIN AND AUSTRIA-HUNGARY ENTER THE GREAT WAR

41: RINGING BELLS AND WRINGING HANDS

2–4 August

At three o'clock on Sunday afternoon, 2 August, the entire tsarist court, high government officials, and officers of the guard attended a solemn mass in the huge St. George's gallery of the Winter Palace. An altar was set up in the center of the room, bearing an icon before which Field Marshal Prince Kutusov was said to have prayed before facing Napoleon in 1812. Tsar Nicholas had Ambassador Paléologue stand directly opposite him during the service, "to do public homage in this way to the loyalty of the French ally."

After the final prayer, the court chaplain read the tsar's manifesto to his people, declaring that the actions of Russia's enemies had made war inevitable. The tsar then went up to the altar, raised his right hand toward the Bible that was held out to him, and in a low, slow voice repeated the vow made by Tsar Alexander I in 1812: "Officers of my guard here present, I greet in you my whole army and give it my blessing. I solemnly swear that I will never make peace so long as one of the enemy is on the soil of the fatherland." When he finished, the hushed, religious solemnity of the ritual exploded into cheering. The uproar, made chaotic by the huge crush of people, went on for more than ten minutes and spread to the crowds waiting outside. It was, Paléologue recalled, a "grandiose spectacle."[1]

The announcement of war in Russia was a court ceremony; in England, France, and Germany it was a parliamentary event.

When Bonar Law and Lord Lansdowne promised the government the support of the Conservative Party on Sunday, 2 August, they made no mention of Belgium. Asquith, in reply, had been careful to point out that Britain's long-standing friendship with France did not "impose upon us the obligation at this moment of active intervention either by sea or by land." As to Belgium, British policy would depend on "the circumstances and conditions of any German interference with Belgian territory." When Law and Lansdowne saw Asquith again on Monday morning, they "laid great stress upon Belgian neutrality."[2]

By Monday, Asquith had four resignations in hand. Burns had resigned the day before. Letters of resignation came from Morley and Simon that morning, and Beauchamp announced at the cabinet meeting that he would follow them. In ordinary circumstances, wrote Morley, the government would have to resign after four such resignations. But the situation was not ordinary, and when the cabinet met that morning, Asquith warned that resignations would only bring about a coalition government, and coalitions "have hardly ever turned out well in our history."[3] The fiercely neutralist C. P. Scott of the *Manchester Guardian* warned Lloyd George by wire, "Feeling of intense exasperation among leading Liberals here at prospect of Government embarking on war. No man who is responsible can lead us again."[4]

Asquith described the Monday morning cabinet meeting to Venetia as "a rather moving scene." There were four resignations and a great deal of uneasiness, but in the end the cabinet approved Churchill's unauthorized mobilization of the navy and ordered mobilization of the army. Grey was authorized to tell the House of Commons that the British navy would defend the northern and western coasts of France against the German fleet, and that Great Britain would "take action" if Germany invaded Belgium. Lloyd George made a powerful plea to his fellow noninterventionists not to leave, or at least to say nothing that day and to sit in their accustomed places in the House. The dissidents agreed.[5] It was an important concession. When Grey made his speech to the House that afternoon, the Liberal government would sit united, implying full support for Grey.

The cabinet was far from certain what its reception in the House would be, but as the members left the meeting and read the headlines and saw the crowds on the streets, it was clear that public opinion was moving much faster than the government. Newspaper opinion had divided along party lines since Austria-Hungary had declared war on Serbia, but Luxembourg and the threat to Belgium swept all argument away, and patriotic crowds filled the streets.[6]

There were crowds before the House of Commons, before Downing Street, before the war office. Young men sang "La Marseillaise," hundreds of Union Jacks were waving, and crowds cheered Asquith "with extraordinary fervour" whenever they saw him.[7] Asquith observed that "war or anything that seems likely to lead to war is always popular with the London mob. You remember Sir R. Walpole's remark: 'Now they were ringing their bells; in a few weeks they'll be wringing their hands.'"[8] Nonetheless, any Liberal who was thinking of voting against the government knew that he would have to face an angry public—and a Conservative or a coalition war government.

The House of Commons was "crowded to the roof and tense with doubt and dreadful expectation." The scene was described by George Trevelyan, then a junior minister in the government and an angry opponent of Grey's Entente policy, although he changed his mind during the war. Grey, he wrote, was "gaunt from weeks of ceaseless toil and deepening misery, pressed every moment on every side by fresh imperious tasks, harrowed by those painful interviews with Cambon. . . ." As Grey sat waiting to speak, he remembered himself as an obscure young bridegroom waiting in a similarly packed house for the great Gladstone to introduce his first Irish home rule bill. He was engulfed by the sense of passing years, the death of his wife, and the world's descent into "universal darkness." He almost cried but recovered himself as he rose to speak.[9]

Grey knew that a great many members, perhaps a majority, were opposed to any war for the sake of France or for the sake of the European balance of power. He was absolutely convinced that Great Britain had to fight and knew it would be disastrous to fight if the nation was divided on the necessity of war. He therefore had to make two points: that he had kept his oft-repeated pledge to leave Great Britain free of binding engagements, and that nonetheless Great Britain had to fight.[10]

He began by saying that he wished to speak strictly "from the point of view of British interests." On this simple point there could be no dissent. He then reviewed a series of occasions leading up to the present crisis, at each of which he and the prime minister had been able to assure the House that "it was free to decide what the British attitude should be." In 1906, during the first Moroccan crisis, when Britain had interests guaranteed by treaty in Morocco, he had told the French that he could promise nothing, but he thought that if war were forced on France because of the Moroccan agreement, public opinion would rally to France. When the French pointed out that such support would be worthless without prior military planning, he agreed that military talks could take place, "but on the distinct understanding" that nothing in the talks should "bind either Government or restrict in any way their freedom to make a decision."

In 1912, after the talks had been going on for some time, "it was decided that we ought to have a definite understanding in writing . . . that these conversations . . . were not binding upon the freedom of either Government." Grey then read the House the letter to Paul Cambon of 22 November 1912, including the sentence that read, "The disposition, for instance, of the French and British Fleets respectively at the present moment is not based on an engagement to co-operate in war." The government, in short, "remained perfectly free."

Grey gave a third of his speech to establishing the government's complete freedom of action. He now entered upon dangerous ground, saying that "for many years we have had a long-standing friendship with France." This was met with a shouted interruption—"and with Germany"—which

Grey ignored. Cambon reported that Grey was vigorously applauded whenever he referred to England's "obligations of honor and friendship" to
France.[11] Grey plunged ahead: "How far that friendship entails obligations
[Grey paused], how far that entails an obligation let every man look into his
own heart, and his own feelings, and construe the extent of the obligation
for himself." Lord Hugh Cecil, who was no admirer of Grey, later commented on the "extraordinary dexterity" with which Grey "dealt with the
weak spot in his argument," the fact that there was no obligation to France.
"With wonderful skill," Lord Cecil wrote, "he did not argue the point, but
he changed to a note of appeal to the individual conscience, thereby disarming criticism . . . without any departure real or apparent from perfect sincerity." It was a remarkable performance.

Grey argued that because of its long-standing and trusting reliance on
British friendship, "the French Fleet is now in the Mediterranean, and the
Northern and Western coasts of France are absolutely undefended." Of
course the 1912 letter had assured the government's freedom of action, but
what if a German fleet sailed into the Channel and "bombarded and battered
the undefended coasts of France" and Britain did nothing? Either the English would have to watch France be bombarded, or the French fleet would
leave the Mediterranean—and what would happen if British interests were
threatened there? The British fleet was no longer in the Mediterranean in
strength. Therefore, Grey continued, the cabinet had assured France that if
the German fleet undertook hostile operations on its northern coast, the
British fleet would, subject to the approval of the House of Commons, oppose it. He assured the House that this was no declaration of war or promise of immediate aggressive action, but only a commitment to undertake
"aggressive action should that contingency arise."

Grey hurried on. He had just heard that Germany would agree not to attack the northern coast of France "if we pledge ourselves to neutrality." But
"there is the more serious consideration—becoming more serious every
hour—there is the question of the neutrality of Belgium." Grey had reached
the halfway point in his speech; he devoted the rest of it to Belgium. According to every account, from the time he put Belgium on the table he had
the House with him. He reviewed the history of the treaties of guarantee, his
demand that Belgian neutrality be respected, France's assurances, and
Germany's evasions. "It now appears, from the news I have received today—which has come quite recently, and I am not yet quite sure how far it
has reached me in an accurate form—that an ultimatum has been given to
Belgium by Germany, the object of which was to offer Belgium friendly
relations with Germany on the condition that she would facilitate the passage of German troops through Belgium."

Grey then read a wire from King Albert of Belgium: "I make a supreme appeal to the diplomatic intervention of your Majesty's Government to safeguard the integrity of Belgium." Bethmann, Jagow, and Lichnowsky had all repeatedly assured Grey that Belgian integrity would be respected, but Grey feared "not so much that their integrity but that their independence should be interfered with. . . . If her independence goes, the independence of Holland will follow," and then that of Denmark, and what would be the consequences if France were beaten to its knees? Grey jumbled all this together in a wonderfully muddled passage, then said that if the British ran away "from those obligations of honor," they would not, in the end, "be in a position . . . to exert superior strength" to force a settlement of the war consistent with British interests. "For us, with a powerful fleet, which we believe able to protect our commerce, to protect our shores, and to protect our interests, if we are to engage in war, we shall suffer but little more than we shall suffer if we stand aside." This last passage has often been cited as one of appalling ignorance or appalling dishonesty, but what Grey was trying to say was that even if Great Britain were to stand aside in a European war, it would suffer terribly from the collapse of commerce. "Foreign trade is going to stop, not because our trade routes are closed, but because there is no trade at the other end."

This argument, nonetheless, reinforced the widely held belief that for Britain, the war in question would be a naval war. Grey himself appears to have believed it. Given the far-flung interests of the empire, "we must take very carefully into consideration the use which we make of sending an Expeditionary Force out of the country until we know how we stand." He concluded by saying that Ireland would not be a problem, that the army and the navy had never been stronger, and that Britain had done all in its power to preserve the peace and now was faced with terrible decisions. He sat down amid cheers while Bonar Law and John Redmond pledged the support of the Conservatives and the Irish Nationalists, and Ramsay MacDonald declared the opposition of the irreconcilable neutralists in the Labor Party. Grey rose again to read a note he had just received from the Belgian legation. It declared that Brussels had rejected the German proposal and that "Belgium is firmly resolved to repel aggression by all possible means." Grey's final words were: "Of course, I can only say that the Government are prepared to take into grave consideration the information which it has received. I make no further comment upon it."

The House then approved Grey's offer to protect the French coast and authorized him to warn Germany that Great Britain would take action if Belgium were invaded. Conservative and Liberal interventionists were delighted, but Liberal noninterventionists were appalled. Trevelyan wrote that he "was prepared for bad news, but in no way the barefaced, deliberate appeal to passion. He gave not a single argument why we should support France."[12] After the session, twenty-eight despondent Liberals resolved that there was no sufficient reason for British intervention and that negotiations should continue,[13] but their opposition no longer mattered. Asquith was pleased. "Grey made a most remarkable speech—about an hour long—for the most part almost conversational in tone & with some of his usual ragged ends; but extraordinarily well reasoned & tactful & really *cogent*—so much so that our extreme peace-lovers were for the moment reduced to silence."[14]

Cambon reported that public opinion "was moving more and more in our favor" and that war credits might be voted that evening.[15] As he left the House, he asked Grey what Doumerge, the new foreign minister, could tell the French Chamber of Deputies on Tuesday. Grey replied that Doumerge could say that the British fleet would defend the French Channel coasts from German attack, "that the British government cannot disinterest itself in the neutrality of Belgium," that the fleet was already mobilized, and that orders had already gone out to mobilize the army. Grey added confidentially that he would instruct Goschen on Tuesday to ask the Germans to withdraw their demand on Belgium. If they refused, it would be war. The danger of a split in the cabinet, Grey thought, was virtually over.[16]

The cabinet met again at 6:00 P.M. that Monday to formulate a response to the German ultimatum to Belgium. The members decided, however, to put off any reply until the next day rather than give Germany a pretext for a surprise attack on Britain. In any event, the House was to reassemble in a little while to vote war credits and other preparatory measures. Asquith wrote a strong letter asking Simon to reconsider his resignation, while his colleagues worked on Morley, Beauchamp, and other waverers. That evening Grey was alone with a friend, who apparently told Trevelyan about a scene that has become a staple in all accounts of Great Britain's entry into the war: "That night, as the lamps were being lit in the summer dusk, Grey, standing in the windows of his room in the Foreign Office overlooking St. James Park, said to a friend: 'The lamps are going out all over Europe; we shall not see them lit again in our lifetime.'"[17]

In Paris, meanwhile, Schoen received instructions to deliver Germany's declaration of war at 6:00 P.M. Monday.[18] A large part of the text received by Schoen was undecipherable, but Jagow had wired him that morning that as a result of continued border violations by French troops and aircraft, "a rupture of diplomatic relations is imminent,"[19] and Schoen reconstituted the declaration of war as best he could. As a result, the declaration as presented by Schoen stressed alleged French aerial attacks, all reports of which turned out to be false, instead of border violations by French troops, some of which were true.[20] Schoen was bitterly angry after the war that his government had put him and the nation in the posture of declaring war over events that had never occurred.

According to Schoen, Viviani received the declaration of war "without any sign of emotion" and with "icy composure" but stated emphatically that "it was out of the question that any of the air attacks spoken of could actually have taken place." The interview, Schoen wrote, was carried out with perfect courtesy. He asked for his passports, discussed the details of his journey home, asked Viviani to do what he could for the thousands of Germans stranded in France, and left.[21] There was nothing more to say. France and Germany were at war.

For Baron Beyens, the Belgian minister in Berlin, Monday and Tuesday were terrible. Berlin was quiet on Sunday, and the French and Russian embassies were guarded by police, but the Monday papers reported that crowds had gathered in Munich before the French and Russian legations, shouting and smashing windows. Worse, the official press was running articles explaining that the invasion of Luxembourg was necessary to prevent the French from seizing its railways. Beyens hurried to the foreign ministry to see whether he could confirm this information.[22]

Unable to see any official in the foreign office, he spent the rest of the day worrying. His only comfort was that his family was safe with relatives in England. That evening at the legation, he decoded a message informing him of the German ultimatum and Belgium's determination to fight. In his memoir, Beyens professed to be astounded, but then the entire Belgian government had been living with its head in the sand for weeks. During a sleepless night, he made up his mind to see Jagow first thing Tuesday morning. He had no instructions, but he had to do something.

When Beyens called at the foreign office at 8:00 A.M. Tuesday, German troops were already entering Belgium. Jagow agreed to see him immediately, and Beyens had the impression that Jagow was as eager to see him as he was to see Jagow. When Beyens got there, the foreign office was still deserted except for cleaning women and Jagow, a man who was not ordinarily at his desk that early in the morning. Jagow got right to business. "You have something to say to me?"

"I would like an explanation for the ultimatum which the German minister submitted to my government Sunday night," said Beyens. "I assume that you have something to add, some reason for such an act."

"An absolute necessity forced us to make that demand on you." Jagow stuck doggedly to the official line. "The Kaiser and the government were sick at heart at having to do it. For myself, it was the most painful decision, the most cruel that I have had to take in my entire career. But a passage through Belgium is for Germany a matter of life and death."

Beyens was caustic: the Germans had a 120-mile border with France; they had to detour through Belgium? Jagow replied that the French frontier was too heavily fortified for a quick victory; Germany had to defeat France quickly, before Russia was fully mobilized.

The argument went on at pointless length. At the end, Jagow wearily conceded that he understood Beyens's anger. "As a private person, I understand it. But, as secretary of state, I have no opinion to express."

"You will not take Liège as easily as you think," Beyens warned him, "and you will have England to deal with."

Jagow shrugged. He knew as well as anyone what the invasion of Belgium meant.

Beyens concluded by saying that he was ready to leave Berlin with all his personnel, and he asked Jagow to make the necessary arrangements. This seemed to catch Jagow by surprise. "But I do not wish to break relations with you in that way," he cried. "We shall perhaps have occasion to talk again."

"It is for my government to make that decision," Beyens replied. "It does not depend on either you or me. I shall wait for its order to ask for my passports."

Jagow was so visibly upset that Beyens left with the distinct impression that he had not expected Beyens to greet him with angry recriminations. Perhaps, like Moltke, Jagow hoped that the Belgians would agree to a German passage after token resistance.[23]

Germany was at war with France and Russia, but Vienna and St. Petersburg were still talking. On 2 August, General Conrad asked Count Berchtold whether Germany had declared war on Russia yet. Berchtold replied that it had done so the evening before. Conrad then asked, "Would Your Excellency tell Germany that we will go with them through thick and thin, but it would be to our interest to delay a Russian attack so long as possible, so that we can complete our concentration in peace, and then attack. . . . I would prefer that our declaration of war be delayed somewhat." In succeeding days Conrad asked that declarations of war on both Russia and France be delayed as long as possible. He claimed that he needed time to get ready, but it is clear that he did not want to fight anyone but Serbia.[24]

Schebeko kept on talking with Austrian foreign ministry officials. He knew that Vienna was postponing a declaration of war, "apparently to gain time to complete their military preparations,"[25] but on Tuesday he still believed that Austria-Hungary would be happy to find a way out: "They do not want a war with us; they are very much afraid of it and are angry at Germany's clumsy provocation, which has made a general war unavoidable. The mood is unquestionably depressed."[26] Bunsen and Dumaine were equally in doubt as to whether Austria would necessarily be at war with France.[27]

Meanwhile, in Paris, Count Szécsen found himself acutely uncomfortable. German and Austrian shops were being plundered by street gangs, and Austro-Hungarian nationals were being thrown out of their homes. Embassy personnel no longer dared to go out, and the situation was even worse at the German embassy. Szécsen complained to Viviani, who in turn complained of German frontier violations. Szécsen pointed out that these did not involve Austria and that their two countries were still at peace. In any event, even in wartime, diplomatic personnel—not to mention innocent women and children—were entitled to protection. The French colony in Vienna was suffering no such indignities. Viviani retreated, offering his regrets and promising to do what he could.[28] On Monday evening, Szécsen reported that Schoen had just delivered the German declaration of war and was leaving Paris with his embassy personnel by special train that night. He closed with an urgent plea for instructions.[29]

In Berlin Tuesday morning, Bethmann was annoyed and embarrassed to find Austria still making no move to fight Russia or to assist the German diplomatic program. That afternoon he was to address the Reichstag to explain that Germany was forced to go to war to defend its Austro-Hungarian ally. At 11:40 A.M. he wired Vienna: "We have been compelled to go to war on account of Austria's procedure, and have a right to expect that Austria should not seek to hide this fact, but will openly announce that the threat of interference (mobilization against Austria) in the Serbian conflict is forcing Austria to go to war."[30] This was the opening salvo in a bickering quarrel that was to go on for years.

At 3:00 P.M., twenty-four hours after Grey's triumph in the House of Commons, Bethmann went to the podium of the Reichstag to ask for war credits. He had already secured the agreement of all party leaders and did not, like Grey, have to face an uncertain audience. "All the Ministers were in their places," wrote Theodor Wolff. "The dignitaries of the realm were present in great numbers, and many members of the right-wing parties appeared in the uniform of the cuirassiers of the Guards, or of the Hussars, or in other officer's uniform."[31] It was a tremendous spectacle, and as always in moments of great crisis, Bethmann gave himself up to the forces of destiny. "A momentous fate is breaking over Europe," he lamented. "In the forty-four years since we created the German Empire and gained the respect of Europe in war, we have lived in peace and guarded the peace of Europe."

Now, "Russia has put the torch to our house. We have been forced into war with Russia and France." Bethmann's opening words were greeted with thunderous enthusiasm, and his speech was repeatedly interrupted by applause, shouts of assent, and "Bravo."[32]

Bethmann recapitulated the events since 28 June and was careful, since England's intentions were not yet certain, to point out that England and Germany had worked together to localize the war and bring about a settlement. Every capital in Europe had sought to limit the conflict to Austria and Serbia; only Russia had claimed a right to interfere. At the tsar's personal request, the kaiser had attempted to mediate in Vienna, and he had barely begun when Russia mobilized all its forces bordering on Austria-Hungary, although Austria had mobilized only its southern armies against Serbia, far from the Russian border.

Berlin had warned the Russian government repeatedly, in a friendly way, that its mobilization would force Germany to respond in kind. Nonetheless, without warning and without explanation, Russia had mobilized. "Only on the afternoon of [31 July] did a wire arrive from the Tsar promising that his army would take no provocative action against us. But the mobilization along our frontier had been going on since the night of 30 July . . . along our long, virtually open frontier. France, to be sure, had not yet mobilized, but it was taking preparatory military measures, as it admits. And we?—We had at that point, for the sake of European peace, deliberately not called up a single recruit!" Was Germany now to wait between two arming powers and let them choose the time to strike? "It would have been treason to expose Germany to such danger." Therefore the Russians were told that only demobilization could save the European peace; if they refused, war must follow. "How Russia replied to our demand for demobilization we do not know to this day."

The German government waited hours after the deadline before ordering mobilization, Bethmann continued. At the same time, Germany asked France whether it would remain neutral. France replied that it would act as its interests required—for all practical purposes a negative reply. Nevertheless, the kaiser gave strict orders to respect the French frontier. France announced that it would withdraw its forces six miles from the frontier. "And what happened?" Bombs from aircraft, cavalry patrols, company-sized incursions. "With those actions, although war had not been declared, France broke the peace by attacking us." Bethmann did not mention that Schoen was about to deliver a declaration of war. On the German side, he continued, only one patrol had entered French territory, and that contrary to orders. He read Moltke's report: "Probably it was shot to pieces. Only one man returned."[33]

Bethmann turned to Luxembourg and Belgium. "Gentlemen, we must defend ourselves; and necessity knows no law! Our troops have occupied Luxembourg and may already be on Belgian territory. Gentlemen, that is a violation of international law." But despite French assurances, the government knew that France was about to go through Belgium to fall on the German flank, which could be fatal. "We were therefore forced to ignore the justified protests of Luxembourg and Belgium. The wrong—I say it openly— the wrong we thereby do, we shall make good again as soon as our military objective is achieved." Suddenly, in the middle of the argument, without introduction or explanation, Bethmann declared, "Gentlemen, we stand shoulder to shoulder with Austria-Hungary." He then dropped the Austrians and explained that Germany had assured the English that the fleet would not attack the French coast so long as England remained neutral, and that the integrity and independence of Belgium would remain untouched. Bethmann concluded by saying, "I repeat the words of the Kaiser: 'Germany goes into battle with a clear conscience!' . . . The great hour of testing for our people has struck. But we meet it with complete confidence. Our army is in the field, our fleet is battle-ready—and behind them stands the entire German nation! The entire German nation down to the last man." Cheers, shouts, and thunderous applause accompanied his peroration.

Bethmann's final word was to ask the Reichstag to vote war credits without further discussion. Amid wild enthusiasm, party leader after party leader rose to declare his party's patriotic support—even Hugo Haas, chairman of the Social Democratic delegation in the Reichstag and leader of the radical and bitterly antiwar minority in the party. Ever since the German declaration of war on Russia, Haas had been arguing against a favorable vote on war credits, but Bethmann and high Prussian officials had been working on the party's moderates for more than a week. Bethmann knew he had the votes; Haas's radical group had been defeated in caucus, 78 to 14, the majority arguing that a vote against war credits was a useless gesture that could only injure the party. Haas had then said that although it was his duty as party chairman, he could not rise to announce the party's support. In the end, his colleagues and party discipline prevailed, and a sad and angry Haas rose to read his party's statement, which concluded with the declaration, "In this we are doing what we always said we should do—we are not leaving our Fatherland in the lurch in the hour of danger."[34] Germany's Socialists would talk only of war with Russia; France went unmentioned.

Europe's governments had been worrying about their Socialists for decades. When the hour of testing came, they proved to be men like other men. They marched.

Wolff described the final vote:

The war credits were voted unanimously. It was really an extraordinary scene when the whole assembly rose to its feet in token of its unanimous determination, amid a hurricane of applause from the spectators. Nobody at that sitting offered any objection to the invasion of Belgium . . . not a hint of regret was mingled with the spontaneous applause. . . . The world was out of joint, the clearest heads were liable at that moment to be unable to see clearly, the coolest lost their coolness, and many who generally stood firm were swept off their feet by the first rush of emotion. . . . Once escaped from mass suggestion, they recognized that here, in addition to the catastrophe of war, was a tragic denial of right.[35]

Wolff wrote that passage in the bitterness of defeat, of a war he hated, fought for a policy he opposed.

Poincaré was very pleased to see that Great Britain was almost certain to come in, but it worried him that Grey's speech made no commitment to send the BEF. With the consent of his ministers, he immediately wrote King George. After thanking the king for an earlier letter, Poincaré requested the earliest possible embarkation of British troops to cover the French left flank if the Germans should make a sweep through Belgium. Such a measure, Poincaré argued, would have a good effect in France and Belgium.[36]

At three o'clock Tuesday afternoon, while German forces rolled into Belgium, the upper and lower houses of the French Parliament met in special session. Poincaré had carefully composed an address to each house, and they were read to roaring shouts of "*Vive la France! Vive la République!*" In the Chamber of Deputies, Viviani mounted to the podium to read Poincaré's presidential message, "barely able," according to Poincaré, "to contain that excess of emotion from which he so frequently suffered." The entire chamber got to its feet to cheer Poincaré's words. "Gentlemen," Viviani read, "France has been subjected to a brutal and premeditated aggression in arrogant defiance of international law. Before any declaration was delivered to us, even before the German ambassador asked for his passports, our territory was violated. It was not until yesterday evening that the Emperor of Germany belatedly gave the true name for the condition which he had already created." There was no reason for such aggression. "For forty years, the French, in their sincere love of peace, had buried their legitimate desire for reparation deep in their hearts." He of course meant France's longing for the return of Alsace and Lorraine.

After reading the presidential message, Viviani—like Bethmann in Berlin—gave a rousing account of the events that had led from the assassination to the present moment and closed amid thunderous applause with a paean to French courage and French innocence: "We are without reproach. We are without fear. France has often proved, under less favorable circumstances, that it is a most redoubtable adversary when it fights, as is the case today for liberty and justice." Thereupon, without further discussion and by unanimous votes, war credits and emergency measures were adopted. Deputies poured over to the presidential palace after the session to share their enthusiasm with Poincaré. "Never," they declared, "had there been a spectacle as magnificent as that in which they had just participated. Why," they asked over and over again, "couldn't you be there? In the memory of man, there has never been anything more beautiful in France."[37]

42: GREAT BRITAIN GOES TO WAR

4 August

The kaiser learned Sunday night, 2 August, that England was prepared to defend the French Channel coasts from the German fleet. He wrote angrily to Admiral Tirpitz that this was an act of war: "My fleet must have complete freedom of action." Tirpitz was ordered to be at the palace at ten o'clock Monday morning, where he argued that declaring war on England was not "opportune—particularly since the navy had no plans to sail down the Channel to attack the French coast."

Jagow and Bethmann, who knew nothing of the kaiser's reaction, wired Lichnowsky at 9:30 A.M., advising him "that there will be no threatening of the northern coast of France on our part so long as England remains neutral."[1] On Monday afternoon, Bethmann and Jagow were still hoping to keep England neutral, and in his address to the Reichstag on Tuesday, Bethmann was very careful to keep open the possibility of English neutrality.

Moltke continued to usurp political authority and sent Jagow a series of directives. If Italy was not going to fight, it should at least facilitate imports for Germany. The foreign office should wire London that Germany had no intention of annexing Belgian territory. England must understand that Germany was fighting for German "*Kultur* . . . against uncivilized Slavdom. Germany is unable to believe that England will be willing to assist . . . in destroying a civilization—a civilization in which English spiritual culture has for ages had so large a share."

Moltke suggested that the note be sent to Lichnowsky uncoded. "It will not do us any harm if this note . . . should also become known elsewhere." Moltke could not believe that the Belgian government, traditionally so friendly, would oppose German forces. The government must insist that it "is ready at any moment to hold out to Belgium the hand of a brother, and is even willing to enter upon negotiations concerning an acceptable *modus vivendi,* subject to the prosecution of the war forced upon us by France's procedure."[2]

Jagow promptly followed Moltke's suggestions. He wired Flotow in Rome to urge Italy to facilitate the importations of foodstuffs; he wired Below in Brussels offering to negotiate an acceptable modus vivendi; and he wired Lichnowsky, uncoded, that clearly Germany would not annex Belgian territory after the war.[3] No one in Berlin seems to have realized that Belgium was a political necessity for British entry into the war; once the Schlieffen Plan gave Grey and Asquith Belgium, they were not interested in German guarantees.

In London, the government was moving slowly—Cambon and Poincaré thought much too slowly—but no one doubted where it was going. Grey learned during the night that Germany had declared war on France. On Tuesday morning, before he had any word that Germany had actually invaded Belgium, he wired Goschen: "His Majesty's Government . . . must request an assurance that the demand made upon Belgium will not be proceeded with, and that her neutrality will be respected by Germany. You should ask for an immediate reply."[4] He also wired Villiers in Brussels: "His Majesty's Government expect that [the Belgians] will resist by any means in their power . . . His Majesty's Government will support them in offering such resistance" and was prepared to cooperate with France and Russia to that end.[5]

Asquith had not been able to see Venetia over the weekend, and he hoped against hope that he might find time to be with her the following Friday, or Saturday, or Sunday. He was, however, "rather alarmed at the family curiosity as to the contents of my letters, & I am sure you were judicious in what you read to them (& didn't read)." Asquith then moved on to political matters. "You will be relieved to hear that there is a slump in resignations." Beauchamp and Simon had both returned. Burns and Morley were staying out, as was Trevelyan. "Happily," Asquith wrote sarcastically, no one is indispensable—"*il n'y a pas d'homme nécessaire*."

The cabinet had met again Tuesday morning just as news came in that Germany had invaded Belgium. "We had an interesting Cabinet, as we got the news that the Germans had entered Belgium, & had announced to '*les braves Belges*' [Asquith rarely took his own propaganda very seriously] that if necessary they wd. push their way through by force of arms. This simplifies matters, so we sent the Germans an ultimatum to expire at midnight. . . . We are on the eve of horrible things," he added, then told her, "I wish you were nearer my darling; wouldn't it be a joy if we could spend Sunday together. I love you more than I can say."[6] The incautious prime minister had reason to worry if Venetia's family was curious about his letters.

*   *   *

Goschen caught Jagow right after Bethmann's speech to the Reichstag and handed him Grey's wire asking for an immediate reply to his request "that the demand made upon Belgium will not be proceeded with." Jagow, who had already had a painful talk with Beyens, had to say that he could give no such assurance because German troops had crossed the Belgian frontier that morning. The advance through Belgium was a "military necessity," a "matter of life and death for the Empire." He had explained all this to London and given London every assurance with respect to the integrity and independence of Belgium. He could not go further.[7] Goschen kept trying. "I asked him whether there was not still time to draw back and avoid possible consequences which both he and I would deplore." Jagow replied that it was impossible.[8]

As this conversation was taking place, Grey sent the ultimatum mentioned by Asquith. Goschen received it late Tuesday afternoon and read it to Jagow at about 7:00 P.M. "Unless Imperial Government could give assurance by 12 o'clock that night that they would proceed no further with their violation of Belgian frontier and stop their advance, I had been instructed to demand my passports and inform the Imperial Government that His Majesty's Government would have to take all steps in their power to uphold neutrality of Belgium." Regretfully, Jagow replied that he could give no answer other than the one he had already given. Goschen handed Jagow a paraphrase of the ultimatum and pointed out that it did not expire until midnight. Jagow said that even if he had twenty-four hours, his answer would still be the same. "In that case," Goschen replied, "I shall have to demand my passports."

Faced by a war with England, Jagow almost broke down. He and Bethmann had worked hard for a policy of friendship with the English. Goschen refused to give up. Could he see Bethmann? Under the circumstances, this might be his last opportunity to do so. Jagow eagerly agreed. Indeed, he "begged" Goschen to do so.

Goschen found the chancellor completely distraught. He began by asking whether Bethmann could not give him an answer other than Jagow's. Bethmann, according to Goschen, delivered a twenty-minute harangue in English: Great Britain was taking a terrible step, and just for a word—*neutrality*—a word that was often disregarded in wartime. "Just for a scrap of paper, Great Britain was going to make war on a kindred nation who desired nothing better than to be friends with her." England's step would bring his efforts at Anglo-German friendship down like a house of cards. "What we had done was unthinkable; it was like striking a man from behind while he was fighting for his life against two assailants." Goschen angrily objected.

Bethmann and Jagow argued that going through Belgium was a matter of life and death for Germany, but for Great Britain "it was, so to speak, a matter of 'life and death' for the honour of Great Britain." Bethmann interrupted: "But at what price. . . . Has the British Government thought of that?" Goschen gave no further answer. Bethmann, he wrote, "was so excited, so evidently overcome by the news of our action and so little disposed to hear reason, that I refrained from adding fuel to the flame."[9]

From these interviews, all but unbearable in their emotional intensity and dealing with events entirely out of their everyday experience, each man drew different recollections. According to Bethmann, it was Sir Edward Goschen who was overwrought and who kept repeating over and over, "Oh, this is too terrible."[10] Bethmann did not deny using the fateful phrase "a scrap of paper." He explained that he was goaded beyond endurance by Goschen's insistence upon English honor and Belgian neutrality, which he knew were not the considerations that had driven Great Britain to war. It was fear of Germany and fear for its empire. He had worked for years for Anglo-German friendship, and now England was going to destroy it all, and for what? "Because of Belgian neutrality. . . . Compared to the disaster of a world war, did not the significance of this neutrality dwindle into a scrap of paper?"[11] After the war, Bethmann angrily contended that if he did use the phrase "scrap of paper," it had slipped out in the anger and excitement of the moment during a private, not an official, conversation that Goschen himself had requested. Since Goschen saw fit, nonetheless, to expose Bethmann's agitation, the ambassador could at least have reported that he himself had left in tears, and had begged the chancellor to permit him to wait in an anteroom while he composed himself before stepping out among the chancery personnel.[12]

On the street, meanwhile, Wolff ran into Wilhelm von Stumm. Before Wolff could say a word, Stumm blurted out, "Now it is done—England has just declared war on us." Wolff asked whether he could publish an extra edition that night and Stumm agreed. The news would have to come out, whether sooner or later could make little difference. Wolff hurried to the *Tageblatt* offices to get out his "extra."

At about nine o'clock, Zimmermann went to see Goschen to say how very sorry he was that their "very friendly official and personal relations . . . were about to cease." Zimmermann then asked if Goschen's request for passports amounted to a declaration of war. Goschen referred to his instructions: His Majesty's government expected an answer by midnight, and in default of a satisfactory answer, Great Britain "would take such steps as their engagements required." Zimmermann agreed that since the imperial government "could not possibly give the assurance required either that night or any other night," such language was indeed a declaration of war.

Zimmermann left. Within hours, Wolff's *Berliner Tageblatt* was on the streets, headlining that Great Britain had declared war on Germany. Almost immediately, an angry mob gathered before the embassy. At first they only shouted insults. Then the crowd overpowered the small police guard; before long, cobblestones were shattering the windows and crashing on the floors. Stumm's careless permission to publish had caught the government off guard; the police protection was completely inadequate. Goschen called the foreign office to report what was happening. Jagow called the police, who sent a mounted unit to disperse the crowd. Jagow himself went the next morning to apologize.

The kaiser also apologized but in his own inimitable style. He sent an aide-de-camp to express his regrets for the night's occurrences, adding, however, that the incident should give "an idea of the feelings of his people respecting the action of Great Britain in joining with other nations against her old allies of Waterloo." The kaiser, the aide went on, "also begs that you will tell the King that he has been proud of the titles of British Field-Marshal and British Admiral but that in consequence of what has occurred he must now, at once, divest himself of those titles." Goschen wrote that "the above message lost none of its petulant acerbity by the manner of its delivery."[13]

London received no news from Goschen, whose reports of his talks with Jagow, Bethmann, and Zimmermann never arrived. Grey and Asquith therefore had to wait for the midnight time limit. Grey had assumed that "midnight" meant London time, whereas Goschen thought it meant Berlin time. Thus, Germany and England were technically at war at 11:00 P.M. London time—an hour earlier than Grey had expected. That, however, was the least of anybody's worries.

On Tuesday, diplomats were overwhelmed. Counts Mensdorff in London, Szécsen in Paris, and Szápáry in St. Petersburg were struggling with the anomaly that Germany was at war with England, France, and Russia, while Austria-Hungary was still at peace with all of them. Grey told Mensdorff that so long as Austria-Hungary was not at war with France, he saw no reason for their two nations to be at war.[14]

The truly tragic figures in London on that day were the German ambassador and his wife. Asquith wrote to Venetia on Wednesday, saying, "I am truly sorry for the poor Lichnowskys: they are broken-hearted, and she spends her days in tears."[15] Walter Page, the American ambassador, wrote President Wilson a few days later that he had to see Lichnowsky on

Wednesday afternoon to settle details on taking over the German embassy. "I went to see the German Ambassador at three o'clock in the afternoon. He came down in his pajamas, a crazy man. I feared he might literally go mad. He is of the anti-war party and he had done his best and utterly failed. This interview was one of the most pathetic experiences of my life. The poor man has not slept for several nights."[16] Mensdorff wrote in his diary that "Prince Lichnowsky has exerted himself so yeomanly and had been completely frustrated. He of course spoke ill of the military influences in Berlin and of us as well—particularly that we were not more conciliatory and didn't accept the responsibility of discussing the Serbian reply with the Powers. That was of course scarcely possible—but now, the *pity of it.*"[17]

The emotional strain on diplomats was enormous. Sazonov, Pourtalès, Goschen, Bethmann, Asquith, Grey, Mensdorff, and Lichnowsky all, at one time or another, broke down and cried. French diplomats appear to have remained dry eyed.

The scene in London was one of chaos and sheer wretchedness. Walter Page described frightened Germans mobbing the American and German embassies because they were afraid of being arrested. "Howling women come and say their innocent German husbands have been arrested as spies. English, Germans, Americans—everybody has daughters and wives and invalid grandmothers alone in Germany. In God's name, they ask, what can I do for them?" Page found himself confronted by one wrenching scene after another: "I shall never forget Sir Edward Grey's telling me of the ultimatum—while he wept; nor the poor German ambassador who has lost his high game—almost a demented man; nor the King as he declaimed at me for half-an-hour and threw up his hands and said, 'My God, Mr. Page, what else could we do?' Nor the Austrian Ambassador's wringing his hands and weeping and crying out, 'My dear Colleague, my dear Colleague.' . . . Everybody has forgotten what war means—forgotten that folks get hurt. But they are coming around to it now."[18]

Paul Cambon was relieved of his main concern. By Tuesday evening he knew that England would be at war with Germany, but he still did not know what British involvement would mean as a practical matter. "How will you fight the war?" he asked Grey. "Will you send your Expeditionary Force?"

"No," Grey replied. "We shall blockade the German ports. We have not yet considered sending a military force to the Continent."

Grey repeated British worries about the empire and the reluctance of the British public to denude the British islands of troops. On a map, Cambon showed Grey the exposed French left flank if the Germans came through Belgium; they needed British forces there. Cambon begged Grey to bring these considerations to the attention of Asquith and the cabinet. Grey said he would.[19]

Since the 1 August decision to keep the BEF at home, the assumption had been that if Great Britain went to war, it would fight a naval war and blockade the German ports. This assumption had made it very much easier to bring the cabinet and the House of Commons to support a commitment to protect Belgian neutrality. Asquith soon learned, however, that the army's only plan for war, worked out in agreement with the French military, was to mobilize the BEF and have it fall in on the left flank of the French army. Moreover, the army's plan assumed that the BEF would be mobilized as soon as the French mobilized and would immediately be sent to the Franco-Belgian frontier. On 4 August, France had been mobilized for three days, and British mobilization was only just beginning. All through the days of 4 and 5 August, a debate raged over whether to keep the BEF at home or send it to the Continent. On the sixth the cabinet finally agreed to send British troops to the Continent.

The decision was made "with much less demur than I expected," Asquith wrote Venetia,[20] but by then everyone realized that the army had no other plans. Once the decision was made to send the BEF abroad, the question arose as to whether it should not go to Antwerp to threaten the German rear, rather than to the Franco-Belgian border. Again, the decision was all but forced because the only detailed preparations were for sending the BEF to France. Then a further argument arose: given the long delay and the clear German head start, should the BEF follow its original plan and proceed to Maubeuge—in the middle of the Franco-Belgian border, where it would meet the full brunt of a German advance if the Germans made a wide sweep through Belgium—or would it not be more prudent to send it to Amiens— north of Paris and near the coast, where it could easily be extricated if things went badly? General Wilson was adamant: the French would be furious if they did not receive immediate British support. On 12 August the general carried the day: the BEF would go to Maubeuge.

Through all this, the French waited. The BEF was almost fifteen days late when it finally began to form its battle line. It could easily have been overrun before it was fully deployed, but the stiff Belgian resistance delayed the Germans just long enough to let British forces get into position.

43: FINALLY, AUSTRIA

3–12 August

Austria-Hungary declared war on Serbia on 28 July. On 29 July, Russia ordered partial mobilization against Austria. On 30 July, the Russians ordered general mobilization. On 31 July, the Germans gave Russia twelve hours to revoke the mobilization or Germany would mobilize. The Russians rejected the German demand, and on 1 August, Germany declared war on Russia. On 2 August, Germany invaded Luxembourg. On 3 August, Germany declared war on France and demanded passage for its armies through Belgium. Belgium refused. On 4 August, Germany invaded Belgium, and Great Britain declared war on Germany. None of this was what the Austrians had expected.

Until 1 August, they had believed that Germany would go to war only if Russia attacked Austria. By Sunday morning, 2 August, Berchtold had learned that Berlin was at war with Russia and that Berlin expected Austria to go to war with Russia. Berchtold claimed after the war that he was completely surprised when Count Tschirschky told him that Germany and Russia were at war and that Germany expected an immediate Austrian attack on Russia. He was even more upset by the German invasion of Belgium; he had always assumed that England would remain neutral.[1] By then, however, it was too late for second thoughts.

Ambassadors Schebeko and Dumaine both told Berchtold on Sunday that they regretted Germany's sudden declaration of war, and both suggested that Austria and Russia could come to some agreement on Serbia. A Russian embassy official asked an Austrian foreign ministry official "whether Austria was really bound to stand by Germany against Russia." Reporting these developments in the early hours of Monday, 3 August, Tschirschky added that the Russians had withdrawn their troops about a mile and a half from the Galician frontier of Austria-Hungary to demonstrate that they had no hostile intentions. "It is beyond doubt," he concluded, "that the Russians are attempting . . . to drive a wedge between Austria and us."[2]

On Monday afternoon, Berchtold sadly asked Emperor Franz Joseph to authorize a declaration of war on Russia. The declaration was difficult to draft, since the Austro-German alliance was a defensive alliance and Germany had declared war. But they managed: "In view of the threatening attitude adopted by Russia in the conflict between the Austro-Hungarian Monarchy and Serbia" and because "Russia has seen fit . . . to open hostilities against Germany . . . Austria-Hungary considers herself also at war with Russia from the present moment." Depending on the political or military situation, the declaration was to be delivered the next day or on one of the following days.[3] The Austrians were in no hurry.

General Conrad was still obsessed by Serbia. When Austria ordered general mobilization on 30 July, he had kept B Group heading south toward Serbia instead of ordering it north to Galicia. Worse, A Group was being deployed defensively, well back from the Russian frontier. Moltke, the kaiser, Bethmann, and Jagow all sent messages urging Vienna to concentrate its forces against Russia.

On 1 August, Emperor Franz Joseph wired the kaiser that Austria had decided to "concentrate the great majority of our forces against Russia." But B Group kept rolling south, and Conrad was making no effort to turn it around.[4] Tisza warned Conrad that if Austrian forces were not in Galicia in strength, the Russians would win the early battles. If the Romanians saw Russia winning, they would be encouraged to invade and seize Transylvania. Only an early Austro-Hungarian victory in Galicia would keep the Romanians out.[5]

Conrad listened but told his southern commanders that instructions "with regard to Case 'B', and especially the transport arrangements for Case 'B', are to remain in force." On Monday, 3 August, the commander of the Balkan campaign began developing a plan of attack on Serbia that assumed the continued presence of B Group. On Tuesday he reviewed this plan in a private letter to Conrad. That same day, three days after Germany had declared war on Russia and one day after Emperor Franz Joseph had approved a declaration of war on Russia—at a time, therefore, when war with Russia was virtually certain—the southern armies, including B Group, began their final preparations for the campaign against Serbia.

On 5 August, Conrad learned that he would get no offensive from Moltke in East Prussia and that the Bulgarians would not join Austria and Germany until the Germans had a decisive success against France. Conrad had always known that A Group could not meet the Russians in Galicia on its own unless Moltke went on the offensive in East Prussia. Once he realized that Moltke was not going to deliver that offensive, Conrad had to break off the invasion of Serbia and, at long last, send B Group back to Galicia.[6] B Group was finally ordered north on 6 August.

*   *   *

Conrad had been able to hold out as long as he did because Berchtold did not want a war with Russia any more than he did. On 3 August, Ambassador Bunsen wrote Grey that Dumaine, the French ambassador, was not sure whether a Franco-German war "necessarily entails a state of war between France and Austria." Bunsen also doubted "whether possible contingency of war between England and Germany would cause me to be immediately withdrawn from Vienna."[7] Bunsen and his wife had been in Vienna for only eight months and were very comfortable there. Schebeko thought they were much too sympathetic to Austria.[8]

Dumaine wrote later that the Bunsens were so pleased with their assignment in Vienna that they dreaded "the eventuality of a rupture with Austria-Hungary." Dumaine also thought that Schebeko, whose wife was ill, was not anxious to make the long trip back to Russia. Schebeko and Bunsen, he wrote, worked with particular zeal to avoid war with Austria.[9] So did Dumaine. He "tried everything" to convince a senior foreign ministry official that the Austro-Hungarian government had been duped by Berlin. "Without the ruthless German intrusion, satisfactory arrangements might yet have been concluded with Russia, thus sparing Austria a fearful war," Dumaine wrote. "I even hinted that, as the situation did not oblige one to leave Vienna immediately, I might stay on unless relations were to be entirely broken off."[10]

The situation was not very different in London. England had no hostile feelings toward Austria-Hungary, and Mensdorff was personally very popular. Mensdorff hoped to the very end that his country might avoid a war with England. On the evening of 4 August, when it was clear that England would soon be at war with Germany, he talked with Grey. The English foreign minister repeatedly expressed his despair at the war and was, Mensdorff reported, completely broken up. Mensdorff said it was unthinkable that their two countries should go to war. Why, he wondered, should England wish to bring about a Russian preponderance in Europe and the east? Grey replied that a war between Austria and Serbia or even between Austria and Russia faded to inconsequence compared to German preponderance in the west. "If Belgium were to be crushed by Germany, that would be the end of Belgian, Dutch, Danish, and perhaps Swedish and Norwegian independence, which was of the most vital interest to England."

Grey added, however, that "we have no quarrel with Austria; I am not recalling Bunsen. If you went to war with France, it would be different. We could not well collaborate with France in the Atlantic and not in the Mediterranean. But anyhow we shall not begin if you do not attack us; I trust you will do nothing without observing the formality of a declaration of war."

Grey instructed Bunsen immediately afterward that since Austria was not at war with Russia or with France, "I do not therefore contemplate instructing you to ask for your passports or to address any communication to the Austrian Government."[11]

But all through Wednesday, 5 August, Berlin kept insisting that Austria-Hungary "send declaration of war not only to Russia and France but immediately to England." Germany's position was ridiculous if Austria-Hungary was still at peace, and Berlin was anxious to have the Austrian fleet assist two German battle cruisers, the *Goebben* and the *Breslau,* which were being chased through the Mediterranean by French and English warships.[12]

Berchtold replied through Szögyény that Austria-Hungary was ready to fulfill its alliance obligations with regard to Russia, and was even prepared to declare war on England if Berlin insisted. But the navy was not ready, and Vienna did not want uselessly to offer it up to destruction by a premature declaration of war on France and England. Moreover, if England and France were to land on the Dalmatian coast, Austria's Balkan operations would be disrupted and their own South Slav population might be seriously affected. Austria-Hungary, therefore, would like to delay its declaration of war on those two powers until "our navy has completed its preparations."[13]

Berlin would not yield, and Berchtold reluctantly reported to the emperor later on Wednesday that with Germany at war with France and England, Austria could no longer stay out. Bethmann was pressing him, he said, and the German public must never doubt Austria's loyalty to the alliance.[14] The emperor agreed.

Even then, Berchtold was not ready for war with France and England; instead he tried to calm Berlin by declaring war on Russia. The emperor had already approved a declaration of war on Russia, and Conrad was about to send B Group back to Galicia. Berchtold told Schebeko on Wednesday evening that their two countries would be at war, and he instructed Szápáry in St. Petersburg that he was to deliver the Austrian declaration of war on Thursday, 6 August.

Having thus demonstrated Austrian loyalty and willingness to fight, Berchtold again wired Szögyény on Thursday that they were ready to declare war on France and England if Germany insisted, but a declaration of war would immediately bring a French flotilla into the Adriatic—which would only result in the useless destruction of the Austrian navy. If Bethmann could wait a few more days, the Austrian navy might be in a position to achieve some success in the Mediterranean.[15] Jagow said he would check with the military authorities, and a few hours later he agreed to the delay, on the distinct understanding that Vienna would declare war on France and England no later than 12 August.[16]

*   *   *

In Paris, Count Szécsen's difficulties mounted. He complained to Bertie that he was insulted in restaurants and in the streets. Tradesmen refused to supply his embassy, and thousands of Austrians were ordered to leave Paris but were given no means to do so. "They were to be directed to the west of France where work was to be found for them."[17] Szécsen wired Berchtold that "there was not much use in dragging out the present situation much longer."[18]

Mensdorff's position in London was also deteriorating. Since Austria was a German ally, its embassy was considered a security risk by British military authorities, who insisted that the Austrians could neither send nor receive coded messages. Mensdorff asked Tyrrell if Grey's friendly assurances still held good. Tyrrell said they did, "but things are moving so rapidly." Mensdorff insisted on seeing Grey; after trying to put him off, Tyrrell suggested they meet at 3:00 P.M. Thursday. When Mensdorff arrived for his appointment, Austria was already at war with Russia, and he was told that Grey was engaged in Parliament and that the rest of his night would be taken up by the defense committee. Tyrrell suggested he see Nicolson. Mensdorff knew that would be a waste of time, but he went—and learned nothing.

Mensdorff then sent Grey a note, insisting that he see him. Tyrrell replied, assuring Mensdorff that he could see Grey the next day. "At the moment," Mensdorff concluded, "my situation is laughable; I am the ambassador here but with the prohibition of coded messages I am completely cut off from my government. Bunsen is still in Vienna and can, it appears, still send in code."[19]

On Friday, 7 August, Mensdorff finally had his talk with Grey, who again said that Bunsen would remain in Vienna unless Austria wanted to "precipitate matters." Mensdorff assured him that Vienna had no such desire; he even tried to argue that their two countries might remain at peace to provide a channel of communication between the two warring groups. Grey declined to discuss such a prospect. Mensdorff was sure in any case that if Austria went to war with France, it would soon be at war with England.

Grey was very bitter at the way the military had taken control in Berlin. He said over and over again, with respect to the war, "I hate it, I hate it." He also told Mensdorff that he would have been prepared to abandon France and Russia if Germany and Austria had come up with any reasonably acceptable settlement. "I believe," Mensdorff went on, "that the attack on the neutrality of Belgium ruined everything, as well as [Bethmann's 29 July offer to Goschen] for English neutrality which [Grey] has published in his Blue Book[20] and which made him very angry." Grey told Mensdorff that the war "is the greatest step towards Socialism that could possibly have been made. . . . We shall have labour Governments in every country after this."

Mensdorff reported that despite the onset of war, everyone was very friendly, and one and all assured him that they had no hostile feelings for Austria. Lord Rosebery, the old Liberal leader, a former foreign minister, and a former prime minister, came especially to offer his sympathies and to complain that "we fight for a balance of power without seeming to see that we are going to establish the supremacy of Russia all over the world." Some of the Conservative papers, however, were not so friendly and wanted to know why Mensdorff was still in London, seeing that Austria was at war with Russia and England was at war with Germany. When Mensdorff mentioned it, Grey said, "I hope you will not mind it."[21] It was a curious limbo in which Austrian ambassadors found themselves.

The French expected to be at war with Austria-Hungary eventually and wanted the British Mediterranean squadron to help them against the Austrian navy, but France did not want war with Austria until it had completed the transfer of troops from Morocco. When the transfer was completed, however, Paris would need a reason for war compelling enough to bring Great Britain in against Austria.

Paris begin laying the groundwork on Monday, 3 August. Doumerge astonished Szécsen by asking about rumors that Austrian troops were crossing Germany and heading for Alsace. Szécsen replied that he knew nothing about such troop movements but would check with Vienna. Dumaine then asked an equally surprised Berchtold about the troop movements. Berchtold told Dumaine that there was no chance whatever that French and Austrian troops would meet in combat.

The conversations between Dumaine and Berchtold were not pleasant. Berchtold resented the French refusal to accept Austrian assurances, and Dumaine did not like the Austrians, did not like Vienna, and did not like Berchtold. Alfred Dumaine was a good republican and an ardent patriot who believed strongly in the Russian alliance and identified completely with the Great Serb cause. In his reports the Serbs were always the "brave Serbs," and the Bosnian Serbs lived under a reign of terror. He referred to the Austrian determination to put a stop to terrorism and subversion as "the implacable and absurd combat of Austria against Serbia."[22]

It did not help that Dumaine felt snubbed in Vienna. Society there was very gracious but very aristocratic, he wrote, and the oldest nobility did not tolerate strangers and "excelled at haughty impertinences that recalled the distance between them and others."[23] He found Berchtold's aristocratic mien and easy assurance intolerable: "With a nonchalant and amiable air, that

handsome man, a little pale, sought to give the impression of a grand courteous seigneur who interrupts his pleasures to give a few moments to questions he finds boring."[24]

Dumaine reported to Doumerge on Wednesday, 5 August, that there was
"hardly any doubt" that an Austrian army corps was heading for Alsace-
Lorraine,[25] and on Thursday, Doumerge duly told Szécsen that the French
government was certain that Austrian troops were in Alsace. There was, in
fact, not a single Austrian soldier heading west; Serbia and Russia were
more than enough for Conrad. On Sunday, 9 August, Berchtold wired
Szécsen: "The news of participation of our troops in the Franco-German
war is invented from beginning to end."[26]

When Szécsen delivered this assurance to Doumerge on Monday, Doumerge asserted that he had positive information that an Austrian army corps
was in Germany and that its presence permitted the Germans to transfer
additional troops to the French frontier. Szécsen protested that this was simply not the case. Doumerge refused to accept his assurances. He told
Szécsen to leave by special train that night and wired Dumaine to ask for
his passports.[27]

The next day, Tuesday, 11 August, Jagow suddenly announced that
Vienna could decide when to declare war on France and England—but if the
French fleet appeared in the North Sea, Berlin expected Austria to declare
war and to send its fleet into the Mediterranean. Berlin had been worried
that Austria's delay might affect German public opinion, but war enthusiasm was so great and so sustained, the Germans no longer felt the need to
press Austria.[28] Moreover, the two German battle cruisers were hopelessly
trapped; there was nothing the Austrian fleet could do. By then it no longer
mattered; France had broken relations with Austria, and Dumaine was asking for his passports.[29]

By Wednesday, 12 August, Mensdorff's situation in London was bewildering. France had broken relations with Austria but had not declared war.
When he asked Tyrrell about the British position, Tyrrell told him that "naval considerations" would be the decisive factor for war or peace. In the
rigid manner peculiar to him, Sir Eyre Crowe told Mensdorff's first secretary that it was "illogical and unthinkable to maintain the fiction of peace
between the Monarchy and England." Nonetheless, wrote Mensdorff, "I am
still here and Bunsen is still in Vienna."[30]

Paul Cambon was about to put an end to that. After consulting with
Doumerge, the French ambassador presented Grey with a note on 12 August
stating that Austrian troop movements had created a state of war with
France. Grey promptly sent for Mensdorff and told him that "the Austro-
Hungarian Government, after declaring war on Serbia . . . has, without any

provocation on the part of the Government of the French Republic, extended the war to France" by sending troops to the French frontier. Therefore, "the rupture with France having been brought about in that manner, the Government of His Britannic Majesty is obliged to announce that a state of war exists between Great Britain and Austria-Hungary after midnight that night."[31]

It was a sad, stiff interview. The alleged Austro-Hungarian troop movements were pure fiction, and Grey probably knew it. But Austria was not invading Belgium and had not attacked France, and Paris and London needed a reason for declaring war on Austria, with whom they had no quarrel of any kind.

Grey wired Ambassador Bunsen in Vienna that he should ask for his passports because England would be at war with Austria after midnight that night.[32] Bunsen went immediately to Berchtold and said that since France and Austria were at war, his government would consider itself at war with Austria as of midnight. Berchtold had heard nothing from Mensdorff. He protested that France and Austria were not at war, the French had only severed relations. Bunsen, however, was bound by his instructions. He asked for his passports, and Berchtold had to comply.

It was another scene of great poignancy: Berchtold was frustrated and angry; he had no news from Mensdorff, the French were breaking relations over nonexistent troop movements, and now England was declaring war. He could not understand how Austria-Hungary's completely justified act of self-defense against Serbia could bring on a European war that no one wanted.

Bunsen sympathized with him. "So just was the cause of Austria held to be that it seemed to her people inconceivable that any country should place itself in her path, or that questions of mere policy or prestige should be regarded anywhere as superseding the necessity which had arisen to exact summary vengeance for the crime of Serajevo."[33]

Bunsen and his wife adored Vienna. Austria and Great Britain had been friendly powers for more than a century and allies in the wars against Napoleonic France; they had, time and again, stood shoulder to shoulder against Russia and the Turks. Bunsen told Berchtold how sad he was to see his mission end so tragically. There was no reason for it, he wrote: "There was no difference between England and the Monarchy that could in the remotest way justify such a war." As the two men commiserated, Bunsen said he hoped the war would not last for long—a futile hope that was being voiced in every capital in Europe. Berchtold sadly agreed: there were no differences between their two countries; on the contrary, their relations had traditionally been close and friendly.[34]

The atmosphere was very different when Dumaine came to ask for his passports. Berchtold bluntly told him that the story of Austrian troop movements against France was an invention from beginning to end. Dumaine reported later that he thought Berchtold was lying and that Berchtold's habitual courtliness did nothing to dissuade him; it was merely a facade for a timid man who had a horror of confrontation and was quite prepared to hide behind a lie. Even at that tragic hour, Dumaine wrote, when the destiny of the monarchy was at stake, Berchtold "did not once, in my presence, indicate that he was aware of his enormous responsibility."[35]

After midnight on 12 August, fifteen days after Austria-Hungary declared war on the Kingdom of Serbia, every European Great Power except Italy was at war, and Italy would abandon its former allies to join the Entente powers in May 1915. No one seemed able to keep out, but only Bulgaria and Turkey fought with Austria and Germany, Turkey coming in on 2 November 1914 and Bulgaria finally declaring war on Serbia on 14 October 1915. The Entente powers gained steadily. Tiny Montenegro declared war on Austria on 5 August 1914. Japan, which was anxious to obtain Germany's Far Eastern colonies, declared war on Germany on 23 August 1914. Romania jettisoned its secret alliances with Austria and Germany and declared war on Austria in 1916. After the United States entered the war against Germany in April 1917, almost every country in the world, from Siam to Haiti, lined up against Austria and Germany—to be in at the kill and to have a place at the peace conference. Once the Bolsheviks gained control of the Russian revolution in November 1917, Russia was out of the war, signing a separate peace in March 1918. All hostilities ceased on 11 November 1918: Germany and Austria were defeated, and monarchical, aristocratic Europe was dead, just as the great aristocrats had feared it would be.

PART XII: Retrospect

44: WE HAD NO CHOICE

Only Serbia and Romania came out of the slaughter having achieved anything like their war aims. Romania acquired the Romanian-speaking parts of Hungarian Transylvania and Serbia finally acquired Bosnia-Herzegovina and emerged as the United Kingdom of the Serbs, Croates, and Slovenes, which, with the inclusion of Montenegro and a sizable Albanian minority, became Yugoslavia. But the cost to the South Slavs who eventually made up the new state, between the First Balkan War of 1912 and the armistice of 1918, was a staggering 1.9 million dead, almost 16 percent of the South Slav population.[1] Pašić survived, ancient and indomitable, but the new Yugoslavia led a tormented existence and in the 1990s is being torn apart by ethnic conflict, fueled by the same Great Serb dream that drove the Hapsburg Empire to take the fatal step toward war.

The Austrian Hapsburg, the German Hohenzollern, and the Russian Romanov dynasties disappeared. Austria-Hungary dissolved into the so-called successor states: Austria, Czechoslovakia, Hungary, and Poland. Germany lost its colonies, its navy, and its merchant fleet and was saddled with a huge reparations bill. It lost Alsace and Lorraine to France; Danzig in East Prussia became a free city; and Silesia and a huge corridor through East Prussia went to a newly restored Poland. Russia suffered a revolution, surrendered to Germany, lost huge pieces of its western territories, and slid into the Leninist-Stalinist dictatorship.

The victors had only the consolation of winning. Italy was lured into the war by promises of substantial Austrian territories. At the peace conference it obtained most of the Italian-speaking areas of what had been Austria-Hungary and several Adriatic islands, but it received nothing of what it had been promised in Slavic Dalmatia, which went to the new Yugoslavia. The "mutilated victory" and the social dislocations of the war disrupted Italian politics for years. In 1922 the Italian monarchy delivered itself into the hands of Mussolini's Fascists.

France suffered a demographic and strategic collapse. After more than 1.3 million dead, it still faced a Germany that, relative to France, was as strong as ever. France's former Russian ally had become the Bolshevik enemy, and Great Britain and the United States would soon withdraw from the Continent. Great Britain suffered enormous casualties and an all but irremediable loss of national wealth. Its decline as a world empire and a European Great Power accelerated. The United States suffered relatively few casualties and enjoyed substantial economic growth, but it was disillusioned by the peace and came to believe that it had been lured into the war by international arms dealers and devious Old World diplomacy.

With so little to show after such a bloody slaughter, no one was prepared to assume responsibility for the Great War.

The Marchese di San Giuliano died in October 1914. Count Szögyény was replaced before the end of the year and died before the war was over. General Moltke, Count Tschirschky, and Emperor Franz Joseph all died in 1916. Tsar Nicholas II, his wife, his son, and his four daughters were executed by a Bolshevik unit in October 1917. Count Tisza was shot down in his home by disaffected soldiers in July 1918. Those who survived the war had to defend their actions.

In Austria the all but universal enthusiasm for the attack on Serbia was soon forgotten, but Count Berchtold steadfastly maintained that he could not have acted differently. Serbia was implacable, Russia was organizing a Balkan League against Austria-Hungary, and France was financing them both and had adopted the three-year-service law. "Would it not have been suicide to wait for one's opponents to choose their moment?" It was exactly the argument Berchtold had made to Count Mérey, his ambassador in Rome, on 21 July 1914.[2] Berchtold suffered terrible bouts of depression in his last years and destroyed his diary entries for 1914 during one of those attacks. He died in 1942 at the age of eighty-six, still believing that he had no choice but to attack Serbia if he was going to save the monarchy, and that the Great War need never have occurred if Russia had not mobilized and Germany had not declared war.[3]

General Conrad continued to believe that the monarchy should have destroyed Serbia when Serbia objected to the annexation of Bosnia-Herzegovina in 1908–9, and he blamed Berchtold and the civilians for holding him back. He never did understand why Russia should care if Austria destroyed a disturber of the peace such as Serbia—unless Russia was already determined to make war on the monarchy.[4]

One theme is common to all Austro-Hungarian apologists: they had no choice. If the monarchy were not to be overrun by a Russian-Serbian assault, or simply disintegrate under the pressure of Great Serb and pan-Slav subversion, Austria had to do something about Serbia, come what may. This was the opinion of every responsible Austro-Hungarian leader in 1914, even Tisza, who asked only that they wait for a more favorable opportunity.

Sergei Sazonov and most of his officials and ambassadors ended their days in exile, explaining the fall of tsarist Russia. Sazonov wrote that the Austrian ultimatum to Serbia was the opening gun of an Austro-German drive to push Russia out of the Balkans. Russia, whose mobilization was terribly slow, had no choice but to "prepare for a general mobilization" when Austria declared war on Serbia. But Russia's mobilization did not justify Germany's declaration of war; Russia was perfectly prepared to have its mobilized armies stand and wait. It wanted only to warn Austria and Germany that it would be prepared if war came.[5]

Sazonov may have been sincere in making this argument, but the whole point of the Franco-Russian alliance was to force Germany to face two armies simultaneously,[6] and both general staffs knew that the Germans would never let that happen. If Russia mobilized, Germany would go to war immediately in order to defeat France before Russia was ready. It was for this reason that President Poincaré insisted to Sazonov in 1912 that Russia must consult with France before undertaking any dangerous initiatives.

Nonetheless, very few Russian memoirs suggest that mobilization should have been canceled or never attempted. If Russia had backed down, its "prestige in the Slav world and in the Balkans would perish never to return."[7] Even after the collapse of tsardom and the defeat of Russia, the diplomat Basili concluded that "there was no other way out."[8]

Germany became a republic and Kaiser Wilhelm was forced to abdicate on 9 November 1918. President Wilson refused to negotiate "with the military masters and monarchical autocrats of Germany," and the army said it could no longer guarantee the kaiser's safety in revolutionary Germany. Wilhelm fled to exile in Holland, where he lived to see Nazi troops saluting him in his courtyard. Until his death in 1942, he remained what he had always been: a child. In his 1922 memoir, Wilhelm was a man without fault, betrayed by his ministers despite the brilliant victories of his army.[9] In 1931 his adjutant in exile wrote, "I have now almost finished reading the second volume of Bülow's [Bethmann's predecessor] memoirs and am struck over and over again by how little the Kaiser has changed since those times. Almost everything that occurred then still happens now, the only difference being that his actions, which then had grave significance and practical consequences, now do no damage."[10]

Most German memoirists remained convinced that Austria-Hungary could not let the assassination go unpunished. If the Hapsburg monarchy collapsed, an isolated Germany would be crushed between the Russian hordes and the vengeful French. They had not expected Russia to intervene in an Austro-Serbian quarrel; Russia's decision to mobilize came as a great surprise. The Russian mobilization was the true cause of World War I.

Foreign secretary Gottlieb von Jagow reiterated the constant German query: "Were we supposed to wait until the entire Russian army had marched to our frontier, ready to overrun our country? Until our very existence was simultaneously threatened from east and west by an annihilating superiority of power?"[11] Chancellor Bethmann-Hollweg thought the Russians would shrink back before "making the terrible last step."[12] That terrible last step, however, was not an attack on Austria or even a declaration of war, but mobilization—and a Russian mobilization was critical only because of the Schlieffen Plan.

Bethmann lost his oldest son in the war and was pilloried until the day he died as the agonizing, indecisive "philospher of Hohenfinow" who was unable to provide the leadership the nation needed. The question of his responsibility never ceased to torment him. In July 1917 a coalition of army generals, right-wing parties, and the extreme left forced Bethmann to retire—the generals and the right because they believed that Bethmann wanted a negotiated peace rather than victory, the left because they believed that Bethmann wanted victory rather than peace. His reputation never recovered—not because he got Germany into the war, but because he did not win it.

Bethmann was consistent to the end: neither individual men nor singular events were responsible for the war, but fate. "This world cataclysm was conjured up, not only through the collective guilt of nations but also through the collective guilt of men and parties within them," he wrote. War could have been avoided only "by a rapprochement with England. . . . But after we had decided for a [common] policy with Austria, we could not desert her in that crisis."

He died of pneumonia in the closing days of 1920 at the age of sixty-four, just as he was beginning to hope that life might once again be bearable.[13]

Wilhelm von Stumm brooded for years over the advice he had given Bethmann and blurted out to a friend, in 1921, "I was in error in 1914 and advised Bethmann wrongly."[14] Unfortunately, he never went public with his confession, and he left Bethmann and Lichnowsky to fend for themselves.

German anger at the English "betrayal" of their cultural and racial brothers was epic, and Lichnowsky was the scapegoat: the naive prince had been taken in by Grey's assurances and allowed his government to be trapped into a war with Great Britain. The kaiser, Bethmann, Jagow, and virtually every journalist in Germany, with the exception of Theodor Wolff and one or two others, all turned on Lichnowsky. Bethmann threatened him with prosecution if he used official documents to defend himself.

The prince spent the years until his death in 1928 vainly trying to clear his name. He wrote that Bethmann and Stumm did not listen to him because they disliked him; they could not accept the advice of a man they regarded as a rival.[15] "Only he who knows the truly fabulous incompetence of our leading statesmen will understand that such a policy was indeed possible *without* their desiring war!"[16]

For French postwar polemics, the case, at first, was easy. Germany had declared war on Russia, invaded Luxembourg, invaded Belgium, and declared war on France while France was still trying to obtain a negotiated settlement. When it became clear that the Russian general mobilization was ordered long before Austria's general mobilization, and that the German declarations of war had been in response to the Russian general mobilization, the French case became more complicated. Poincaré made the position worse by lying and then being caught lying. Pompous, self-righteous, and irritatingly legalistic, Poincaré was not prepared to concede even the slightest degree of responsibility. As president of the republic, he had no power to do anything on his own. He could make no decision without the countersignature of a minister, and he could not impose his will upon the government—which in any case was perfectly peace loving. Alexander Izvolsky, the Russian ambassador, moreover, was a liar. Foreign ministry political director Bruno de Margerie and war minister Adolphe Messimy never suggested, as Izvolsky reported, that Russia could go forward with a secret mobilization: "Izvolsky, once again, spoke of people as it suited him."[17]

Unfortunately for Poincaré, it was easy to show that Ambassador Paléologue was running amuck in St. Petersburg and not informing his government. It was easy to show that Paris had done remarkably little to inform itself of Russian actions or to exercise some control. It was easy to show that Margerie and Messimy were careful not to let the Russians think they wanted a halt to military preparations. It was easy to show that the wartime collection of French documents had falsified the sequence of mobilizations. But it was, and is, impossible to show that the French government wanted a war and encouraged Russia's mobilization to provoke it. What one can say is that French governments had invested a quarter of a century and billions of francs in an alliance that would produce an immediate Russian mobilization that would force Germany to fight a war on two fronts. It would have taken a Frenchman of extraordinary courage and cool nerves to risk all that in July 1914.

Paléologue was unrepentant. In a 1935 book, responding to charges that he had encouraged Russian military preparations and done little or nothing to prevent the Russian general mobilization, he defended himself pugnaciously: in the face of an imminent German attack, would it not have been illusory to slow down the Russian mobilization?[18]

David Lloyd George replaced Herbert Asquith in 1916 and became leader of a wartime coalition government. After the war he had to explain how a leader of the former antiwar radicals had agreed to go to war. Lloyd George replied by echoing Herbert Samuel's hopeful rationale for guaranteeing Belgian neutrality: if Germany could not go through Belgium, an attack on France would have enabled Great Britain to remain neutral, at least for a while. France would be defending a heavily fortified 250-mile frontier instead of the 500 miles of French *and* Belgian frontier. In the former case, France would have had no difficulty holding off the Germans, and Great Britain would have had time to build up its land forces. Then, with its fleet mobilized and a million men under arms, it would have been able to force a peaceful settlement. But the "invasion of Belgium put an end to all these possibilities. Then our Treaty obligations were involved." Once Belgium was invaded, the war became immensely popular: "Never was there a war so universally acclaimed as that into which Britain entered on the 4th of August, 1914."[19]

Asquith too asserted that it was the invasion of Belgium that brought Great Britain into the war.[20] Neither Asquith nor Sir Edward Grey were prepared to argue publicly that British interests required Britain to defend France against Germany. Asquith stressed that "we are fighting to fulfill a solemn international obligation" and "to vindicate the principle that small nationalities are not to be crushed."[21] Their real concern, however, was that Germany would "dominate Europe."[22] This was a legitimate concern, but Asquith and Grey were accused of being so anti-German and so committed to France and Russia that they helped to bring on the crisis and were unable to act effectively to force a negotiated settlement.

Asquith and Grey always replied that the ententes with France and Russia were never aimed at Germany and that they left Great Britain "at full liberty to determine whether or not to intervene."[23] Asquith was frank about Britain's imperial concerns: "It is not too much to say that [the Russian entente] put an end, once and for all, to the 'Russian Menace to India' which had haunted the minds of British statesmen and diplomatists—for generations." It was never "aimed in any way at the 'isolation' of Germany."[24]

But the ententes undermined Great Britain's traditional support of Austria-Hungary when the Hapsburgs came into conflict with Russia in the Balkans and in the Near East. Austria-Hungary and Great Britain had always been friendly powers; now Austro-Hungarian diplomats saw every effort to stabilize the Balkans frustrated by Entente support for Serbia, and by Germany as well because Bethmann wanted better relations with England. Austria found itself isolated, no longer respected as a Great Power, facing disintegration and decline. On 28 July 1914, "Austria decided not to die quietly"[25] and declared war on Serbia.

The most striking feature of these postwar apologia is their consistency. Before, during, and after the war the same arguments were made. After the war they all came to the same conclusion: what else could we do? Such consistency almost forces one to conclude—with all due allowance for postwar protective coloration—that the arguments expressed the actors' deepest convictions. If that is true, then one must also conclude that, apart from the Austro-Hungarian determination to punish Serbia, these men did not want to go to war. Even the Austrians believed that the strike against Serbia had been forced upon them as the only way to bring Great Serb terrorism and subversion to a halt.

There are many historians who argue that one side or the other deliberately launched or provoked a war of aggression. Fritz Fischer, Immanuel Geiss, and J. C. G. Röhl claim that Germany was a deliberate aggressor. Early revisionists such as Harry Elmer Barnes and Jules Isaac say that France and Russia deliberately provoked the war. These extreme positions are not supported by the documents. Fritz Fischer's entire case, for example, rests on the hugely expansionist war aims developed by the Germans during the war, and on the equally wild ambitions of the German nationalist press. One could as well argue that France was longing for war because there were French nationalists who would have nothing to do with a "German peace" that surrendered Alsace and Lorraine, and because French negotiators at the peace conference demanded not only the recovery of Alsace and Lorraine, but the west bank of the Rhine, the dismemberment of Germany, and a reparations bill so huge that Germany would be economically enfeebled for a century.

Other historians, perhaps most, take a more nuanced position. Sidney B. Fay, Luigi Albertini, and, more recently, David Kaiser and Paul Schroeder place much of the immediate blame on Austria and Germany—but in a long-term context that recognizes a great deal of shortsightedness on all sides. Georges Michon in 1929 and George Kennan in 1984, for example, have both argued that the Franco-Russian alliance "was endlessly unfortunate" because it caused a 1914 Balkan quarrel to grow into a general European war.[26] They do not slight the mad dynamics of the Schlieffen Plan, but without the Franco-Russian alliance there might not have been a Schlieffen

Plan. This third group of historians has far more support in the documents than the first two, but the so-called war guilt controversy does not raise the most important questions.

It is more important to remember that the international arena is a dangerous place. Peace is always precarious; forty years without a major war is a long time. Since 1945 the United States alone has fought North Korea, China (in North Korea), North Vietnam, Grenada, Panama, and Iraq, and supplied troops to several United Nations peacekeeping missions, to say nothing of the decades of Cold War confrontation with the Soviet Union that followed World War II. To keep the peace, everything has to go right— and usually a lot goes wrong. Students of disaster—wars, plane crashes, train crashes, the collapse of a dam or a building, Chernobyl—almost always remark on the number of separate and independent failures that contribute to a major catastrophe. July 1914 was no exception.

In the forty-five days from the archduke's assassination to the British declaration of war on Austria-Hungary, no fewer than thirty-four men in eight capitals dealt with the crisis at different levels of intensity, from different points of view and with different solutions in mind; and this number represents only kings, presidents, prime ministers, foreign ministers, military chiefs of staff, and major ambassadors. If we include influential advisers and important groups such as staff officers, foreign office staffs, the British cabinet, the French cabinet, the Russian Council of Ministers, the Austro-Hungarian Imperial Council, the Serbian ministers, the kaiser's entourage, and major party leaders, we have well over a hundred men working in dozens of different institutional environments. There was no decisive center for negotiation and exchange of information; different men learned different things at different times; some were wholly misinformed. The machinery for dealing with a major crisis was slow, cumbersome, unfocused—and certainly not up to the peculiar structure of the July crisis.

Earlier crises were immediately recognized as dangerous. The assassination of the Austro-Hungarian heir apparent was not immediately perceived as a likely cause for war. In France and England this perception came very late. The French public and the country's political establishment were engrossed with the Caillaux trial until 29 July. The European crisis did not come close to replacing the Irish question in the British cabinet until the meetings of 30 and 31 July. For most Europeans, the assassination exploded into war almost before they knew what was happening.

It is one of the ironies of that age of offensive doctrine that the war was brought about in part by the methodical slowness of Austria's military concentration. General Conrad was completely oblivious to Berchtold's demand for speed. Had he been prepared to strike quickly and seize Belgrade, as every diplomat and general expected that he would, some version of Stop-in-Belgrade might have been negotiated.

Conrad's delay also enabled the Austrian and the German leadership to make decisions without fully facing the risk of war. Once the Russian mobilization made the risk clear, a retreat from those decisions was difficult. A sharp German demand—virtually an ultimatum—that Austria negotiate seriously might have facilitated Stop-in-Belgrade. The kaiser was ready to make such a demand after he had read the Serbian answer, but he gave it up when Austria declared war and Russia mobilized. Bethmann made belated attempts to get Vienna to deal seriously with English mediation, but he needed time. For him to hold up the Schlieffen Plan while he put pressure on Austria would also have required extraordinary courage and strength of will. He did not do it.

Time is always critical in a crisis. When Europe's statesmen finally recognized the danger, they fought desperately for time, but time was the one thing their military planners could not give them. Once faced with the probability of war, every general but Conrad was obsessed by the necessity for speed.

Finally, a crisis by definition involves threat and fear. The crisis in 1914 was disastrous because of the rigidity of Europe's leaders. Why weren't more options considered? Why wasn't there more flexibility, more discussion?

Why did Vienna reject every version of Stop-in-Belgrade? Why didn't the Russians see the advantages of waiting, unmobilized, while Conrad became enmeshed in Serbia? Why were the Germans so convinced that France and Russia would sooner or later attack? Why were they driven to the all-or-nothing risks of the Schlieffen Plan? Why were Poincaré and the French government so afraid of Germany that they neglected the dangers of the Russian alliance? Why were Grey, Asquith, Nicolson, and Crowe so afraid of losing the friendship of France and Russia that they abandoned England's centuries-old mediating role in the European balance of power?

"Fear has created more history than it is usually given credit for." These words were written in 1927,[27] and one still cannot begin to explain the outbreak of war in 1914 without considering the overwhelming force of fear, particularly the fear of losing Great Power status. Grey explained that "the real reason for going into the war was that, if we did not stand by France and stand up for Belgium against this aggression, we should be isolated, discredited, and hated; and there would be before us nothing but a miserable and ignoble future."[28] Bethmann wrote that if Germany had failed to support Austria-Hungary in 1914, it would have become the "pliant vassal" of the Slavic world, and "a disobedient Germany could then be obliterated from the ranks of the Great Powers at any time its oppressors chose to do so."[29] Sazonov wrote that Russia "had either to unsheath the sword for the defence of our vital interests and to wait, fully armed, for the enemy's attack . . . or to refuse to fight, surrender to the enemy's mercy and perish in the end covering ourselves with everlasting shame."[30]

"A miserable and ignoble future," "pliant vassal of the Slavs," "obliterated from the ranks of the Great Powers," "perish . . . covering ourselves with everlasting shame"—what was the source of such apocalyptic fear? European nations had been at war with one another, or threatening war with one another, for centuries. Why were Europe's leaders so afraid?

It was not only that they had gone through a series of international crises going back to the Russo-Japanese war of 1904–5, or even that they were beset by sharp domestic crises. The anxiety that embedded and exacerbated all the particular anxieties seems to have been an intense awareness that traditional Europe was being replaced by a new and ominous industrial order.

The cult of the offensive was born of this anxiety. The vague apprehension of a dreadful future focused on fear of the enemy without. Joffre's Plan XVII, which provided only for an all-out assault on the enemy whenever the opportunity arose; the Schlieffen Plan; Plan B (Balkans); and the theory of the all-out offensive—all were designed to crush that enemy once and for all. When India was indefensible, when Austria-Hungary was about to disintegrate, when Germany was a colossus, when Russia was raising huge armies, when a belligerent France was undergoing a national revival, and traditional Europe was collapsing all around them—to ask the leaders of Europe to face these dangers calmly and to consider consequences and alternatives would have been asking the impossible.

At a 1965 North Atlantic Treaty Organization (NATO) symposium, it was pointed out that there were two kinds of reactions to threat: that of the rabbit, to flee, and that of the lion, to fight.[31] In 1914, Europe was full of lions.

Appendix

Calendar: 28 June to 12 August 1914

Sunday	Monday	Tuesday	Wednesday	Thursday	Friday	Saturday

JUNE

Sunday	Monday	Tuesday	Wednesday	Thursday	Friday	Saturday
28	29	30				

JULY

Sunday	Monday	Tuesday	Wednesday	Thursday	Friday	Saturday
			1	2	3	4
5	6	7	8	9	10	11
12	13	14	15	16	17	18
19	20	21	22	23	24	25
26	27	28	29	30	31	

AUGUST

Sunday	Monday	Tuesday	Wednesday	Thursday	Friday	Saturday
						1
2	3	4	5	6	7	8
9	10	11	12			

Notes

Preface

1. Harry F. Young, *Prince Lichnowsky and the Great War* (Athens, Ga.: Univ. of Georgia Press, 1977), 167–68 n.27.

Chapter 1: Assassination Sunday

1. Hugo Hantsch, *Leopold Graf Berchtold: Grandseigneur und Staatsmann*, 2 vols. (Graz; Vienna: Verlag Styria, 1963), 2:551.

2. Soloman Wank, "The Appointment of Berchtold as Austro-Hungarian Foreign Minister," *Journal of Central European Affairs*, 23, no. 2 (July 1963): 150 n.45. Hantsch, *Graf Berchtold*, is the great work on Berchtold.

3. Heinrich Lützow, *Im diplomatischen Dienst der k.u.k. Monarchie*, ed. P. Hohenbaken (Vienna: Verlag für Geschichte und Politik, 1971), 193.

4. Joseph Redlich, *Schicksaljahre Österreichs: Das politische Tagebuch Joseph Redlichs*, ed. Fritz Fellner, 2 vols. (Graz: Verlag Hermann Böhlhaus Nachf., 1953), 1:138.

5. Joachim Remak, *Sarajevo* (New York: Criterion Books, 1959), 155.

6. Vladimir Dedijer, *The Road to Sarajevo* (London: MacGibbon & Kee, 1960), 371–81; Remak, *Sarajevo*, 43–49.

7. Quoted by the Austrian military attaché in Belgrade, *Österreich-Ungarns Aussenpolitik von der Bosnischen Krise 1908 bis zum Kriegsausbruch 1914*, eds. Ludwig Bittner, et al., 8 vols. (Vienna: Ministerium des Aussern, 1930) (Hereinafter cited as *OUA*), 7:874. Reports on Serbian statements and attitudes in Ibid., 871–74, and doc. no. 9597, vol. 8, doc. no. 9805.

8. Redlich, *Politische Tagebuch*, 1:155; Hantsch, *Graf Berchtold*, 2:500, 520–21; *Die Grosse Politik der Europäischen Kabinette 1871–1914*, eds. Joh. Lepsius, A. Mendelssohn-Bartholdy, and Fr. Thimme, 39 vols. (Berlin: Auswärtigen Amtes, 1922–27) (Hereinafter cited as *GP*), vol. 39, docs. nos. 15716, 15842; vol. 35, docs. nos. 13508, and 13564 at 147n.

9. Redlich, *Politische Tagebuch*, 1:233–35.

Chapter 2: Belgrade and Vienna

1. These events were extensively reported by resident diplomats in Belgrade, *Documents Diplomatiques Français (1871–1914)*, 3d series, 11 vols. (Paris: Ministère des Affaires Etrangères, 1936) (Hereinafter cited as *DDF*), vol. 10, docs. nos. 285, 331, 363, 394, 451, and 461 at 662; *OUA*, vol. 8, docs. nos. 9673, 9734, 9809, 9919.

2. Dedijer, *Road to Sarajevo*, 389–91; Luigi Albertini, *The Origins of the War of 1914*, 3 vols., trans. Isabella M. Massey (London: Oxford Univ. Press, 1952), 2:90.

3. Quoted in Friedrich Würthle, *Die Spur Führt Nach Belgrad. Sarajevo 1914* (Vienna: Molden Verlag, 1975), 95–96.

4. On whether Pasic did all he could, compare Dedijer, *Road to Sarajevo,* 393–95, and Würthle, *Die Spur,* 95–96.

5. *OUA,* vol. 8, doc. no. 8763; Albertini, *Origins of the War,* 2:99–100 n.5. On Pašić generally, see Alex N. Dragnich, *Serbia, Nikolas Pašić, and Yugoslavia* (New Brunswick, N.J.: Rutgers Univ. Press, 1974).

6. Remak, *Sarajevo,* 155.

7. *OUA,* vol. 8, doc. no. 9943.

8. Remak, *Sarajevo,* 146–49.

9. *British Documents on the Origins of the War (1898–1914),* ed. G. P. Gooch and Harold Temperley, 11 vols. (London: Foreign Office, 1926–38) (Hereinafter cited as *BD*), vol. 11, doc. no. 29.

10. Serbian Blue Book, doc. no. 8, in *Collected Diplomatic Documents Relating to the Outbreak of the European War* (London, 1915) (Hereinafter cited as *CDD*), 372–73; *OUA,* vol. 8, doc. no. 10122.

11. Karl Kautsky, ed., *Outbreak of the World War: German Documents Collected by Karl Kautsky,* trans. Carnegie Foundation for International Peace (New York: Oxford Univ. Press, 1924), doc. no. 14A.

12. Otto Hoetzsch, ed., *Die Internationalen Beziehungen im Zeitalter des Imperialismus,* German ed., 1st series, vols. 4 and 5 (Berlin: Oxford Univ. Press, 1931–34), vol. 4, doc. no. 148.

Chapter 3: Are We Covered by the Germans?

1. Albertini, *Origins of the War,* 1:1–119; Dedijer, *Road to Sarajevo;* Würthle, *Die Spur;* and Remak, *Sarajevo,* have detailed accounts of the assassination and the assassins.

2. Kurt Peball, "Briefe an eine Freundin," *Mitteilungen des Österreichischen Staatsarchivs,* 25 (1972): 499–500; Oskar Regele, *Feldmarschall Conrad. Auftrag und Erfüllung 1906–1918* (Vienna: Verlag Herold, 1955), 57.

3. Franz Conrad von Hötzendorf, *Aus Meiner Dienstzeit, 1906–1918,* 5 vols. (Vienna: Rikola, 1922–25), 3:52, 119, 129, 144.

4. Ibid., 4:17–18.

5. Kautsky, *German Documents,* doc. no. 7.

6. Conrad, *Dienstzeit,* 4:33–34.

7. Gustav Erenyi, *Graf Stefan Tisza, ein Staatsmann und Märtyrer* (Vienna; Leipzig: E. P. Tal, 1935), and Gabor Vermes, *Istvan Tisza,* East European Monographs, No. 184 (New York: Columbia Univ. Press, 1985), have written biographies of Tisza.

8. Vermes, *Istvan Tisza,* 133.

9. Joseph M. Baernreither, *Fragmente Eines Politischen Tagebuches,* ed. Joseph Redlich (Berlin: Verlag für Kulturpolitik, 1928), 178–79,195–96.

10. 15 March memorandum and 24 June memorandum, *OUA,* vol. 7, doc. no. 9482, vol. 8, doc. no. 9918.

11. *OUA,* vol. 8, doc. no. 9902 at 174–75.

12. *DDF,* vol. 10, doc. no. 456 at 655.

13. R. A. Kann, *Kaiser Franz Joseph und der Ausbruch des Weltkriegs* (Vienna: Böhlau in Komm., 1971), 11.

14. Hantsch, *Graf Berchtold,* 2:560–61.

15. *OUA,* vol. 8, doc. no. 9966.

16. Ibid., doc. no. 10038.

17. Ibid., doc. no. 10006.

18. Kautsky, *German Documents,* docs. nos. 9, 11.

19. Ottokar Czernin, *Im Weltkrieg* (Berlin; Vienna: Ullstein Verlag, 1919), 16.

20. Alfred Dumaine, *La Derniére Ambassade de France en Autriche* (Paris: Plon, 1921), 131–33.

21. *BD,* vol. 10, part 2, doc. no. 494, part 1, doc. no. 106.

22. *GP,* vol. 39, doc. no. 15374 at 361.

23. Hantsch, *Graf Berchtold,* 2:562–63.

24. *OUA,* vol. 8, doc. no. 10037; Ernest U. Cormons, *Schicksale und Schatten* (Salzburg: Müller Verlag, 1951), 161–62; Hantsch, *Graf Berchtold,* 2:567; Albertini, *Origins of the War,* 2:133–50; Fritz Fellner, "Die 'Mission Hoyos,'" in *Deutschlands Sonderung von Europa,* ed. Wilhelm Alff (Frankfurt a/M; New York: P. Lang, 1984), 387–418.

25. For a comparison of the preassassination and postassassination memoranda, see H. Bertil Peterson, "Das österreichisch-hungarische Memorandum an Deutschland vom 5. Juli 1914," *Scandia,* 30 (1964):138–90; Roderich Gooss, *Das Wiener Kabinett und die Entstehung des Weltkrieges* (Vienna: L. W. Seidel, 1919), 18–25, 25 n.1; Hantsch, *Graf Berchtold,* 2:572–73; *OUA,* vol. 8, doc. no. 9984; Kautsky, *German Documents,* docs. nos. 13, 14.

26. Hantsch, *Graf Berchtold,* 2:567–68, 573; Fellner, "Die 'Mission Hoyos,'" 295.

Chapter 4: The Emperor and the Field Marshal

1. Regele, *Feldmarschall Conrad,* 68, 150, 172, 180; Norman Stone, *The Eastern Front 1914–1917* (New York: Scribner, 1975), 34–35, 71–72; S. L. A. Marshall, *World War I* (1964; reprint, New York: American Heritage, 1971), 91–92.

2. H. Hantsch, "Kaiser Franz Joseph und die Aussenpolitik," in *Probleme der Franzisko-Josephinishen Zeit 1848–1916,* ed. Engel-Janosi and Helmut Rumpler (Vienna: Verlag für Geschichte und Politik, 1967), 31.

3. Egon Caesar Corti and Hans Sokol, *Der Alte Kaiser,* 3d ed. (Graz; Vienna: Styria Verlag, 1956), 382.

4. Joseph Redlich, *Emperor Francis Joseph of Austria* (London: Macmillan, 1929), 483.

5. Albert von Margutti, *Kaiser Franz Joseph: Persönliche Erinnerungen* (Vienna; Leipzig: Rhombus, 1924), ix, 24, 207.

6. Redlich, *Emperor Francis Joseph,* 222–26.

7. Corti and Sokol, *Der Alte Kaiser,* 196.

8. Ibid., 394.

9. Ibid., 234, 266, 358.

10. Conrad, *Aus Meiner Dienstzeit,* 4:36–37.

11. Ibid., 40.

Chapter 5: Kaiser Wilhelm II

1. Richard Kühlmann, *Erinnerungen* (Heidelberg: Schneider, 1948), 382–85; August Bach, ed., *Deutsche Gesandtschaftsberichte zum Kriegsausbruch* (Berlin: Auswärtiges Amtes, 1937), 60–62, 63; Immanuel Geiss, ed., *Julikrise und Kriegsausbruch 1914. Eine Dokumentsammlung,* 2 vols. (Hannover: Verlag für Literatur und Zeitgeschehen, 1963–64), vol. 1, doc. no. 15.

2. Georg Alexander Müller, *Regierte der Kaiser?* 2d ed., ed. Walter Görlitz (Göttingen; Berlin: Musterschmidt, 1959), 31.

3. Prince Karl Max Lichnowsky, *Heading for the Abyss* (New York: Payson and Clarke, 1928), 4–6, quoted in Young, *Prince Lichnowsky,* 98; Theodor Wolff, *The Eve of 1914,* trans. E. W. Dickes (New York: Knopf, 1936), 433ff.

4. Lichnowsky, *The Abyss,* 71–73.

5. Kautsky, *German Documents,* doc. no. 7; Geiss, *Julikrise,* vol. 1, doc. no. 3.

6. Lichnowsky, *The Abyss,* 72; Albertini, *Origins of the War,* 2:151–53.

7. Quoted in Wolff, *The Eve of 1914,* 146–47.

8. *OUA,* vol. 8, doc. no. 4290, p.783.

9. *Das Tagebuch der Baronin Spitzemberg,* ed. Rudolf Vierhaus (Göttingen: Vanderhoeck & Ruprecht, 1960), 543.

10. John C. G. Röhl, *Kaiser Hoff und Staat. Wilhelm II und die deutsche Politik* (Munich: C. H. Beck, 1987), 29–30.

11. Georg Alexander Müller, *Der Kaiser: Aus den Tagebüchern des Chefs des Marinekabinetts Admiral George Alexander von Müller,* ed. Walter Görlitz (Göttingen; Berlin: Musterschmidt, 1965), 109; John C. G. Röhl, "Admiral von Müller and the Approach of War, 1911–1914," *The Historical Journal,* 12, no. 4 (1969), 656.

12. M. D. Elizabeth Radziwill, ed., *Lettres de la Princesse Radziwill au Général de Robilant 1889–1914,* 4 vols. (Bologna: Zanichelli, 1934), 1:47.

13. Quoted in Robert Zedlitz-Trützschler, *Zwölf Jahre am deutschen Kaiserhof* (Berlin; Leipzig: Deutsche Verlag, 1924), 187.

14. *The Diary of Edward Goschen 1900–1914,* ed. Christopher H. D. Goschen (London: Royal Historical Society, 1980), 54.

15. *Tagebuch der Baronin Spitzemberg,* 515; John C. G. Röhl, "The emperor's new clothes: a character sketch of Kaiser Wilhelm II, " in John

C. G. Röhl and Nicolaus Sombart, eds., *Kaiser Wilhelm II. New Interpretations. The Corfu Papers* (New York: Cambridge Univ. Press, 1982), 47–48; Röhl, *Kaiser Hoff und Staat,* 23–28; Isabell V. Hull, *The Entourage of Kaiser Wilhelm II, 1888–1918* (Cambridge: Cambridge Univ. Press, 1985), 17, 20.

16. Quoted in Röhl, "The emperor's new clothes," 47–48.

17. Wolff, *The Eve of 1914,* 60.

18. Paul Cambon, *Correspondance 1870–1924,* 3 vols. (Paris: Grasset, 1940–46), 2:341–42.

19. Quoted in Wolff, *The Eve of 1914,* 369.

20. Quoted in Malcolm Carroll, *Germany and the Great Powers 1866–1914* (New York: Octagon Books, 1975), 767.

Chapter 6: The Blank Check

1. *OUA,* vol. 8, docs. nos. 9984, 9987. English translation in Kautsky, *German Documents,* docs. nos. 13, 14.

2. *OUA,* vol. 8, doc. no. 10058; Geiss, *Julikrise,* vol. 1, doc. no. 21.

3. *OUA,* vol. 8, doc. no. 10058.

4. Quoted in Konrad H. Jarausch, *The Enigmatic Chancellor: Bethman Hollweg and the Hubris of Imperial Germany* (New Haven: Yale Univ. Press, 1973), 154. See ibid., 148–59, for Jarausch's account of German thinking at this time.

5. Hoyos memoir in Fellner, "Die 'Mission Hoyos,'" 311; Alexander Hoyos, *Der deutsch-englische Gegensatz und sein Einfluss auf die Balkanpolitik Österreich-Ungarns* (Berlin: de Gruyter, 1922), 9, 12, 20–21, 66, 93–95; Redlich, *Tagebuch,* 1:214–15, 215 n.1, 245–46.

6. Konrad H. Jarausch, "The Illusion of Limited War: Chancellor Bethmann Hollweg's Calculated Risk, July 1914," *Central European History,* 2, no. 1 (March 1969): 57 n.30; ———, *The Enigmatic Chancellor,* 468 n.9.

7. Werner von Rheinbaben, *Kaiser Kanzler Präsidenten* (Mainz: Hase & Koehler, 1968), 108.

8. Hoyos memoir in Fellner, "Die 'Mission Hoyos,'" 311–12; Jan Opocénsky, "A War-Time Discussion of Responsibility for the War," *The Journal of Modern History,* 4, no. 3 (September 1932): 415–29; Albertini, *Origins of the War,* 2:143–45.

9. Geiss, *Julikrise,* vol. 1, docs. nos. 22, 23a, 23b, 24a, 24b.

10. Rheinbaben, *Kaiser Kanzler Präsidenten,* 96; Wolff, *The Eve of 1914,* 265, 354–55.

11. Jarausch, *The Enigmatic Chancellor,* 155; Albertini, *Origins of the War,* 2:141.

12. Jarausch, *The Enigmatic Chancellor,* 99, 102, 105, 107, 453 n.2; Theodor von Bethmann-Hollweg, *Betrachtungen zum Weltkrieg,* 2 vols. (Berlin: Hobbing, 1919–21), 1:234ff.

13. Geiss, *Julikrise,* vol. 1, docs. nos. 32a, 32b, 33.

14. Quoted in Fritz Fischer, *Krieg der Illusionen* (Düsseldorf: Droste, 1969), 692.

15. Hoyos memoir in Fellner, "Die 'Mission Hoyos,'" 312–13; Bethmann's report, Kautsky, *German Documents,* doc. no. 15; Szögyény's report (drafted by Hoyos), *OUA,* vol. 8, doc. no. 10076.

16. Geiss, *Julikrise,* vol. 1, doc. no. 23a.

17. See the analysis in Sebastian Haffner, *The Ailing Empire. Germany from Bismarck to Hitler,* trans. Jean Steinberg (New York: Fromm International, 1989), 87–93.

Chapter 7: Second Thoughts

1. Quoted in Jarausch, "The Illusion of Limited War," 53; ————, *The Enigmatic Chancellor,* 148–59; Kurt Riezler, *Tagebücher-Aufsätze-Dokumente,* ed. Karl Dietrich Erdmann, Deutsche Geschichtsquellen des 19. und 20. Jahrhunderts, vol. 48 (Göttingen: Vandenhoeck & Ruprecht, 1972), 183. There is a controversy over Erdmann's editing of the Riezler diary, particularly the entries from 7 July through 14 August 1914, ibid., 181–95, the so-called Blockblätter or Hohenfinow entries. Kurt Riezler instructed his family to destroy his diary, but the Riezler family destroyed only the prewar portion of the diary after selected sections were copied for publication. Some German scholars now argue that the 7 July through 14 August entries were revised by Riezler to hide the fact that Bethmann and the German government actively wanted a continental war in 1914, Bernd Sösemann, "Die Tagebücher Kurt Riezlers. Untersuchungen zu ihrer Echtheit und Edition," *Historische Zeitschrift* 236, no. 2 (April, 1983): 327–69. Erdmann replied in the same issue, "Zur Echtheit der Tagebücher Kurt Riezlers. Eine Antikritik," ibid., 371–402. The controversy was investigated by Bernd F. Schulte, *Die Verfälschung der Riezler Tagebücher* (Frankfurt a/M; Bern; New York: Peter Lang, 1985). Schulte concludes that the entries were rewritten after the war but that he cannot discover to what extent the rewritten entries differ from the originals. Friends of Riezler's who read, or heard Riezler read from, his diary in the 1930s, remembered after World War II that the diary made Bethmann sound like he wanted war. But one witness, who had extensive conversations with Riezler, and who made memoranda of most of them, said Riezler described Bethmann as being afraid of a world war—although he was prepared to risk it to save Austria—and as utterly opposed to annexing more land in the event of victory, which is the portrait which comes through in the diary as published by Erdmann, and in the published German documents on the war, and which is adopted in this book. Since Bethmann's private papers and Riezler's original prewar diary entries have been lost or destroyed, the controversy has probably gone as far as it can go.

2. Quoted in Hull, *The Entourage of Kaiser Wilhelm II,* 198.

3. Jarausch, *The Enigmatic Chancellor,* 70.

4. See the portrait of Bethmann in David E. Kaiser, "Germany and the Origins of the First World War," *Journal of Modern History,* 55, no. 3 (September 1983): 442–74, particularly 445, 448, 450.

5. Ibid., 472; Paul Kennedy, "The Kaiser and German *Weltpolitik,*" in Röhl and Sombart, *Kaiser Wilhelm II,* 144–45; Arno J. Mayer, *The Persistance of the Old Regime: Europe to the Great War* (New York: Pantheon, 1981), 45.

6. *DDF,* vol. 7, doc. no. 177, pp. 210–11.

7. Müller, *Der Kaiser,* 105; Kaiser, "Germany and the Origins of the First World War," 463.

8. Riezler, *Tagebücher,* 182 n.2; Lichnowsky, *The Abyss,* 94–96.

9. Egmont Zechlin, "Deutschland Zwischen Kabinettskrieg und Wirtschaftskrieg: Politik und Kriegsführung in den ersten Monaten des Weltkrieges 1914," *Historische Zeitschrift,* 199, no. 2 (October 1964), 347–458, which I find more convincing than the argument that Bethmann wanted war to attain hegemony in Europe, Harmut Pogge von Strandmann, "Germany and the Coming War, " in J. W. Evans and Harmut Pogge von Strandmann, eds., *The Coming of the First World War* (Oxford: Clarendon, 1988), 87–123.

10. Radziwill, *Lettres de la Princess,* 4:232.

11. Willibald Gutsche, *Aufsteig und Fall eines Reichskanzlers* (Berlin: Akademie Verlag, 1973), 107. For the strain on Bethmann generally, see Jarausch, *The Enigmatic Chancellor,* 98–107; Wolff, *The Eve of 1914,* 356.

12. Pius Dirr, ed., *Bayerische Dokumente zum Kriegsausbruch und zum Versailler Schuldspruch,* 3d ed. (Munich, 1925), doc. no. 1.

13. Jarausch, *The Enigmatic Chancellor,* 152.

14. Riezler, *Tagebücher,* 181–84, 7–8 July.

15. Ibid.

Chapter 8: A Note with a Time Limit

1. Protocol, *OUA,* vol. 8, doc. no. 10118.

2. Wladimir Giesl, *Zwei Jahrzehnte im Nahen Orient,* ed. R. von Steinitz (Berlin: Verlag für Kulturpolitik, 1927), 256.

3. Kautsky, *German Documents,* doc. no. 29; Giesl, *Zwei Jahrzehnte,* 255–56.

4. *OUA,* vol. 8, doc. no. 10215 at 407.

5. Kautsky, *German Documents,* doc. no. 40; Geiss, *Julikrise,* vol. 1, doc. no. 82.

6. Lützow, *Im diplomatischen Dienst,* 218–20; Hantsch, *Graf Berchtold,* 2:595.

7. Kautsky, *German Documents,* doc. no. 50.

8. Hantsch, *Graf Berchtold,* 2:588–90.

9. *OUA,* vol. 8, doc. no. 10395 and *Beilage.* The note was delivered in French; there is an English translation in Kautsky, *German Documents,* Supplement I, 603–6.

10. Protocol, *OUA,* vol. 8, doc. no. 10393 at 511.

11. Quoted in Hantsch, *Graf Berchtold,* 2:605.

Chapter 9: Lichnowsky and Grey

1. Michael Brock and Eleanor Brock, eds., *H. H. Asquith Letters to Venetia Stanley* (Oxford: Oxford Univ. Press, 1982), letter of 14 June, notes 1 and 2.

2. Harold Nicolson, *Sir Arthur Nicolson, Bart., First Lord Carnock* (London: Constable, 1930), 391.

3. Young, *Prince Lichnowsky,* 31.

4. Ibid., 55.

5. Quoted in George Macaulay Trevelyan, *Grey of Fallodon* (Boston: Houghton Mifflin, 1937), 200.

6. Kühlmann, *Erinnerungen,* 377.

7. Quoted in Zara S. Steiner, *Britain and the Origins of the First World War* (New York: St. Martin's, 1977), 186. On Grey's eyesight and work, ibid., 153, 266; Keith Robbins, *Sir Edward Grey* (London: Cassell, 1971), 278–85.

8. Kühlmann, *Erinnerungen,* 312.

9. Viscount Grey of Fallodon, *Twenty-Five Years,* 2 vols. (New York: Frederick A. Stokes, 1925), 1:167, 188.

10. *Graf Benckendorffs Diplomatischer Schriftswechsel,* ed. Benno von Siebert, 3 vols. (Berlin; Leipzig: de Gruyter, 1928), 3:293–94; Grey, *Twenty-Five Years,* 1:278–79.

11. M. K. Ekstein, "Great Britain and the Triple Entente on the eve of the Sarajevo Crisis," in F. H. Hinsley, ed., *British Foreign Policy Under Sir Edward Grey* (London: Cambridge Univ. Press, 1977), 344.

12. Quoted in Zara S. Steiner, "The Foreign Office, 1905–1914," in Hinsley, *British Foreign Policy,* 56.

13. Wolff, *On the Eve of 1914,* 379–85; Lamar Cecil, *Albert Ballin: Business and Politics in Imperial Germany* (Princeton, N.J.: Princeton Univ. Press, 1967), 201–2; M. Ekstein, "Great Britain and the Triple Entente," 345–58.

14. Grey, *Twenty-Five Years,* 1:278–79.

15. Kautsky, *German Documents,* doc. no. 5.

16. Ibid., doc. no. 6.

17. D. C. Watt, "The British Reactions to the Assassination at Sarajevo," *European Studies Review,* 1, no. 3 (1971): 237, 239; Herbert Butterfield, "Sir Edward Grey in July 1914," *Historical Studies,* 5 (1965): 7–8.

18. Nicolson, *First Lord Carnock,* 410.

19. Kautsky, *German Documents,* doc. no. 20; Geiss, *Julikrise,* vol. 1, doc. no. 36; *BD,* vol. 11, doc. no. 32.

20. Hoetzsch, *Imperialismus,* vol. 4, doc. no. 146.
21. *BD,* vol. 11, docs. nos. 38, 39; *DDF,* vol. 10, doc. no. 483.
22. *BD,* vol. 11, doc. no. 41; Kautsky, *German Documents,* doc. no. 30.

Chapter 10: Jagow

1. *Memoirs of Prince von Bülow,* trans. Geoffrey Dunlop, 4 vols. (Boston: Little, Brown), 3:38–42, 72–73, 93; Lamar Cecil, *The German Diplomatic Service, 1871–1914* (Princeton, N.J.: Princeton Univ. Press, 1976), 154–58, 317–19; Radziwill, *Lettres de la Princess,* 4:217, letter of 8 January 1913; *Tagebuch der Baronin Spitzemberg,* 554, 9 January 1913; Wilhelm Eduard von Schoen, *The Memoirs of an Ambassador,* trans. Constance Vesey (New York: Brentano's, 1923), 54–55.
2. *Diary of Edward Goschen,* 37–38.
3. Quoted in C. J. Lowe and M. L. Dockrill, *The Mirage of Power,* 3 vols. (London; Boston: Routledge & Kegan Paul, 1972), 1:119.
4. *BD,* vol. 10, part 2, docs. nos. 454, 532.
5. Quoted in Jarausch, *The Enigmatic Chancellor,* 137.
6. Bach, *Deutsche Gesandtschaftsberichte,* doc. no. 4; Geiss, *Julikrise,* vol. 1, doc. no. 125.
7. Riezler, *Tagebücher,* 185.
8. Kautsky, *German Documents,* Supplement IV, doc. no. 2 at 616–17.
9. Kautsky, *German Documents,* doc. no. 62.
10. Wolff, *On the Eve of 1914,* 265, 354–55; Rheinbaben, *Kaiser Kanzler Präsidenten,* 96.
11. Kautsky, *German Documents,* doc. no. 72.
12. Hoetzsch, *Imperialismus,* vol. 4, doc. no. 328.
13. Kautsky, *German Documents,* doc. no. 85.
14. Ibid., doc. no. 42; James Joll, *The Origins of the First World War,* 2d ed. (London; New York: Longman, 1992), 32–35.
15. Quoted in R. J. B. Bosworth, *Italy, the Least of the Great Powers: Italian Foreign Policy before the First World War* (Cambridge: Cambridge Univ. Press, 1979), 382.
16. Kautsky, *German Documents,* doc. no. 33.
17. R. J. B. Bosworth, *Italy and the Approach of the First World War* (New York: St. Martin's, 1983), 384–86.
18. *OUA,* vol. 8, doc. no. 10364, and note (b).
19. Hoetzsch, *Imperialismus,* vol. 4, doc. no. 245; Albertini, *Origins of the War,* 2:184.
20. Hoetzsch, *Imperialismus,* vol. 4, doc. no. 247; Albertini, *Origins of the War,* 2:184–85.
21. *BD,* vol. 11, docs. nos. 50, 55, 56, p. 45.
22. *BD,* vol. 11, doc. no. 77.

23. V. R. Berghahn and Wilhelm Diest, "Kaiserliche Marine und Kriegsausbruch, 1914. Neue Dokumente zur Juli-Krise," *Militärgeschichtliche Mitteilungen,* 7 (1/1970): 37–58, docs. nos. 10, 11.

Chapter 11: Poincaré and the Russians

1. Quoted in Pierre Miquel, *Poincaré* (1961. Paris: Fogard, 1984), 34, 28–38.
2. Quoted in Albertini, *Origins of the War,* 1:333.
3. Quoted in Jean-Denis Bredin, *Joseph Caillaux* (Paris: Hachette littâerature, 1980), 152.
4. *DDF,* vol. 3, doc. no. 359.
5. Ibid., vol. 5, doc. no. 22.
6. *Un Livre Noir. Diplomatie d'avant guerre d'après les documents des Archives Russes,* 3 vols. (Paris: Librairi du Travail, 1923–32) (Hereinafter cited as *LN*), 1:340–43, letter from Izvolsky dated 25 October/7 November 1912; translation in Sidney B. Fay, *The Origins of the World War,* 2 vols. (Reprint, New York: Free Press, 1966), 1:339–40.
7. Stone, *Eastern Front,* 39–40; Gerhard Ritter, *The Sword and Scepter,* trans. Heinz Norden (Coral Gables, Fla.: Univ. of Miami Press, 1965), vol. 2, *The European Powers and the Wilhelminian Empire,* 225, 23, and 279 n. 15; L. C. F. Turner, *The Origins of the First World War* (New York: Norton, 1970), 29, 51, 52; Erich Ludendorff, *The General Staff and Its Problems,* trans. F. A. Holt (London: Hutchinson, 1921), 66–67.
8. Radziwill, *Lettres de la Princesse,* 4:188, 230.
9. Quoted in Miquel, *Poincaré,* 326.
10. Bredin, *Joseph Caillaux,* 169–73.
11. Poincaré Diary, 15 May. This diary is in the Bibliotheque Nationale: Papiers Poincaré, vol. 36, Notes Journaliéres, Mars Août 1914. Fonds: Nouvelles Acquisition Francaises, No. 16027. I worked from a typewritten transcript generously lent to me by Professor Arno Mayer of Princeton University.
12. Quoted in John F. Keiger, *France and the Origins of the First World War* (New York: St. Martin's, 1983), 138.
13. Jean-Jacques Becker, *1914: Comment les Francais son entrès dans la guerre* (Paris: Fondation nationale des sciences politiques, 1977), 137; Bredin, *Joseph Caillaux,* 185–86.
14. Maurice Paléologue, *Au Quai d'Orsay a la Vielle de la Tourmente: Journal 1913–1914* (Paris: Plon, 1947), 317–18.
15. *DDF,* vol. 10, docs. nos. 36, 92, vol. 9, docs. nos. 168, 186, 262, 263, 378, 411.
16. Ibid., vol. 10, docs. nos. 23, 24, 25, 26, 58, 82, 101, 111.
17. Ibid., vol. 10, doc. no. 404.
18. Poincaré Diary, 26 March.
19. Ibid., 16, 17, 18 July; Keiger, *France and the Origins,* 149–50.

20. Quote from C. M. Andrew, "France and the German Menace," in Ernest R. May, ed., *Knowing One's Enemies* (Princeton, N.J.: Princeton Univ. Press, 1984), 143; Poincaré Diary, 18 July.

21. Paléologue memorandum in Poincaré Diary, 134.

22. Poincaré Diary, 21 July; Maurice Paléologue, *An Ambassador's Memoirs,* trans. F. A. Holt, 3 vols. (1923. New York: Octagon, 1972), 1:20.

23. Ibid., 18–19.

24. *OUA,* vol. 8, doc. no. 10461.

25. Poincaré Diary, 22 July.

26. Hoetzsch, *Imperialismus,* vol. 4, doc. no. 322.

27. *BD,* vol. 11, docs. nos. 76, 84, 97 and minutes.

28. Paléologue, *Memoirs,* 1:24–25; Raymond Poincaré, *Au Service de la France* (Paris: Plon, 1926–33), 4:279.

29. *BD,* vol. 10, doc. no. 101 at 80.

Chapter 12: No Serious Complications Are to Be Feared

1. Poincaré, *Au Service,* 4:202–4; *DDF,* vol. 10, docs. nos. 483, 484, 493; *BD,* vol. 11, doc. no. 59.

2. *DDF,* vol. 10, doc. no. 558.

3. *OUA,* vol. 8, doc. no. 10491; *DDF,* vol. 10, docs. nos. 554, 555, 563.

4. *BD,* vol. 11, doc. no. 62; *OUA,* vol. 8, doc. no. 10274.

5. *BD,* vol. 11, docs. nos. 65, 81, 82; Hoetzsch, *Imperialismus,* vol. 4, doc. no. 249.

6. Hoetzsch, *Imperialismus,* vol. 4, doc. no. 286.

7. M. Boghitschewitsch, ed., *Die auswärtige Politik Serbiens 1903–1914,* 3 vols. (Berlin: Brückenverlag, 1928–31), vol. 1, doc. no. 408.

8. Hoetzsch, *Imperialismus,* vol. 4, doc. no. 247; *OUA,* vol. 8, doc. no. 10365; *BD,* vol. 11, doc. no. 60.

9. Lowe and Dockrill, *The Mirage of Power,* vol. 3, doc. no. 74 at 488.

10. *DDF,* vol. 10, doc. no. 559, and p. 739 n.1.

11. *BD,* vol. 11, minute to doc. no. 77 at 63.

12. *BD,* vol. 11, docs. nos. 50, 56.

13. Ibid., docs. nos. 73, 77

14. Kautsky, *German Documents,* doc. no. 38.

Chapter 13: Belgrade

1. *OUA,* vol. 8, docs. nos. 10435, 10518, 10519, 10521.

2. Giesl, *Zwei Jahrzehnte,* 289–91.

3. *OUA,* vol. 8, doc. no. 10437 at 549, 550.

4. Giesl, *Zwei Jahrzehnte,* 266–67; Albertini, *Origins of the War,* 2:284–85; *OUA,* vol. 8, docs. nos. 10395 at 517, 10396 at 518–19.

5. *BD,* vol. 11, doc. no. 102.

6. *OUA,* vol. 8, docs. nos. 10606, 10608; Kautsky, *German Documents,* doc. no. 154.

7. Hoetzsch, *Imperialismus,* vol. 5, doc. no. 37; Albertini, *Origins of the War,* 2:349–50.

8. *BD,* vol. 11, doc. no. 114; *DDF,* vol. 11, doc. no. 63.

9. Dirr, *Bayerische Dokumente,* doc. no. 18; Geiss, *Julikrise,* vol. 1, doc. no. 240.

10. Geiss, *Julikrise,* vol. 1, doc. no. 241.

11. *OUA,* vol. 8, doc. no. 10294; *DDF,* vol. 11, p. 11 n.1.

12. *OUA,* vol. 8, doc. no. 10537.

13. English press quotations in Carroll, *Germany and the Great Powers,* 206–45.

14. *BD,* vol. 11, docs. nos. 91, 98.

15. Kautsky, *German Documents,* doc. no. 157; *BD,* vol. 11, docs. nos. 98, 99; *OUA,* vol. 8, doc. no. 10537.

16. David Lloyd George, *War Memoirs,* 2d ed., 2 vols. (London: Odhams Press, 1938), 1:33.

17. Grey, *Twenty-Five Years,* 1:305.

18. *OUA,* vol. 8, doc. no. 10519.

19. Ibid., doc. no. 10599; *BD,* vol. 11, docs. nos. 104, 105.

Chapter 14: What Do the Russians Think?

1. D. C. B. Lieven, *Nicholas II Twilight of the Empire* (New York: St. Martin's, 1993), 199–200.

2. *OUA,* vol. 8, docs. nos. 10616, 10617, 10619; Albertini, *Origins of the War,* 2:291–92.

3. Stone, *Eastern Front,* 26; L. C. F. Turner, "The Russian Mobilization in 1914," in Paul M. Kennedy, ed., *The War Plans of the Great Powers* (London: Allen & Unwin, 1979), 252–68; ———, "The Russian Mobilization in 1914," *Journal of Contemporary History,* 3, no. 1 (January 1968): 65–88.

4. Sergei Dobrolski, *Die Mobilmachung der russischen Armee 1914,* Beiträge zur Schuldfrage, vol. 1 (Berlin, 1922), 17–18; Albertini, *Origins of the War,* 2:292–93; Fay, *The Origins of the World War,* 2:292–94.

5. George Buchanan, *My Mission to Russia and Other Diplomatic Memories* (Boston: Little, Brown, 1923), 139, 180, 192.

6. Albertini, *Origins of the War,* 1:554.

7. Keiger, *France and the Origins,* 50 n.18; *OUA,* vol. 8, doc. no. 9201.

8. Hoetzsch, *Imperialismus,* vol. 1, doc. no. 13 at 15 n.1, 19–20; *LN,* 2:130–35, letter of Izvolsky dated 1/14 August 1913, 132.

9. Paléologue, *Memoirs,* 1:27–28, 31; *DDF,* vol. 11, doc. no. 322.

10. *BD,* vol. ll, doc. no. 101; Paléologue, *Memoirs* 1:31–32; Albertini, *Origins of the War,* 2:294–96.

11. A. V. Krivoshein, minister of agriculture, quoted in D. C. B. Lieven, *Russia and the Origins of the First World War* (New York: St. Martin's, 1983), 142–43.

12. This paragraph follows D. W. Spring, "Russia and the Coming of War," in Evans and Strandmann, *The Coming of the First World War,* 57–86.

13. Lieven, *Russia,* 141–44, has a detailed account of the meeting. The final recommendations are summarized in Hoetzsch, *Imperialismus,* vol. 5, docs. nos. 19, 25.

14. Albertini, *Origins of the War,* 2:354.

15. Hoetzsch, *Imperialismus,* vol. 5, doc. no. 22; comment in Gale Stokes, "The Serbian Documents from 1914: A Preview," 71–72, available as an on-demand-supplement to *Journal of Modern History,* 48, no. 3 (September 1976). Order through: Microfilm International, 300 North Zeeb Road, Ann Arbor, Michigan 48106. Order No. IJ–00011.

16. Stokes, "The Serbian Documents from 1914," 70–71.

17. Serbian Blue Book, doc. no. 36, in *CDD.*

18. Kautsky, *German Documents,* doc. no. 160 at 186.

19. Ibid., docs. nos. 160, 204; Hoetzsch, *Imperialismus,* vol. 5, doc. no. 25 at 33.

20. Paléologue, *Memoirs,* 1:33–34. Albertini, *Origins of the War,* 2:303, is very skeptical that such a conversation ever took place.

21. *DDF,* vol. 11, docs. nos. 21, 34.

Chapter 15: What Is Going On?

1. Becker, *1914,* 131–35.

2. *OUA,* vol. 8, doc. no. 10400(3); Kautsky, *German Documents,* doc. no. 100.

3. *DDF,* vol. 11, doc. no. 7; *OUA,* vol. 8, doc. no. 10606; Albertini, *Origins of the War,* 2:323.

4. *DDF,* vol. 11, doc. no. 20; *OUA,* vol. 8, doc. no. 10608.

5. Hoetzsch, *Imperialismus,* vol. 5, doc. no. 26; *DDF,* vol. 11, doc. no. 20.

6. Quoted in Carroll, *Germany and the Great Powers,* 798.

7. *BD,* vol. 11, doc. no. 123.

8. Kautsky, *German Documents,* docs. nos. 169, 170.

9. *DDF,* vol. 11, doc. no. 8.

10. Ibid., docs. nos. 19, 21, 34; *BD,* vol. 11, doc. no. 101.

11. *DDF,* vol. 11, doc. no. 51; Albertini, *Origins of the War,* 2:326–27.

12. Genevieve Tabouis, *The Life of Jules Cambon,* trans. C. F. Atkinson (London: J. Cape, 1938), 20–21.

13. *The Diary of Edward Goschen,* 28.

14. *DDF,* vol. 3, doc. no. 216, vol. 8, doc. no. 659 at 831, vol. 9, doc. no. 178 at 213.

15. Ibid., vol. 7, doc. no. 317 at 351–53, vol. 8, doc. no. 659, vol. 9, doc. no. 272.

16. Ibid., vol. 10, doc. no. 194.

17. Quoted in Keiger, *France and the Origins,* 132.

18. *DDF,* vol. 8, doc. no. 522 at 661.

19. Ibid., vol. 11, doc. no. 33. Cambon told the British and the Russian chargés about his talk with Jagow, *BD,* vol. 11, docs. nos. 103, 160; Hoetzsch, *Imperialismus,* vol. 5, doc. no. 29.

20. *DDF,* vol. 11, docs. nos. 18, 29.

21. *BD,* vol. 11, doc. no. 101; minutes of 25 July, ibid. at 81–82.

22. *BD,* vol. 11, docs. nos. 106, 107, 109, 110.

23. Ibid., doc. no. 112.

24. Quoted in Nicolson, *First Lord Carnock,* 305; Zara S. Steiner, *The Foreign Office and Foreign Policy, 1898–1914* (New York: Cambridge Univ. Press, 1969), 129 n.4.

25. *BD,* vol. 11, doc. no. 101, minute at 82.

26. Robert Vansittart, *The Mist Procession* (London: Hutchinson, 1959), 99, 120.

27. Quoted in Steiner, "The Foreign Office, 1905–1914," in Hinsley, *British Foreign Policy,* 52.

28. Ibid., 53.

29. D. W. Sweet and R. T. B. Langhorne, "Great Britain and Russia, 1907–1914," in Hinsley, *British Foreign Policy,* 253–54.

30. Lowe and Dockrill, *The Mirage of Power,* 1:133, 134.

31. *BD,* vol. 11, docs. nos. 129, 134.

32. Quoted in Keith M. Wilson, *The Policy of the Entente* (Cambridge; New York: Cambridge Univ. Press, 1985), 15.

33. Quoted in ibid., 76.

34. Quoted in ibid., 5, 93.

35. Quoted in A. J. Anthony Morris, "C. P. Trevelyan's Road to Resignation 1906–1914: The Odyssey of an Antiwar Liberal," in Soloman Wank, ed., *Doves and Diplomats: Foreign Offices and Peace Movements in Europe and America in the Twentieth Century* (Westport, Conn.: Greenwood, 1978), 93.

36. Quoted in George Monger, *The End of Isolation: British Foreign Policy 1900–1907* (London: T. Nelson, 1963), 299.

37. Quoted in Wilson, *Policy of the Entente,* 91, 95–96.

38. Kautsky, *German Documents,* doc. no. 153.

39. Ibid., doc. no. 163.

40. *BD,* vol. 11, doc. no. 122.

41. Kautsky, *German Documents,* doc. no. 171.

42. Ibid., doc. no. 172; Hoetzsch, *Imperialismus,* vol. 5, doc. no. 3.

Chapter 16: The Serbian Answer Is Unacceptable

1. Hoetzsch, *Imperialismus,* vol. 5, doc. no. 47 at 46.
2. Stokes, "The Serbian Documents from 1914," 71.
3. Kautsky, *German Documents,* doc. no. 291 at 270.
4. Ibid., doc. no. 194.
5. Giesl, *Zwei Jahrzehnte,* 267–68, whose account is translated in Albertini, *Origins of the War,* 2:357.
6. Quoted in Albertini, *Origins of the War,* 2:363–64. Albertini's analysis of the Serbian reply together with the Austrian comments on the reply, ibid., 364–67.
7. Giesl, *Zwei Jahrzehnte,* 268–69.
8. Serbian Blue Book, docs. nos. 40, 41, in *CDD,* 390–91.
9. *OUA,* vol. 8, doc. no. 10571.
10. Quoted in Giesl, *Zwei Jahrzehnte,* 269.
11. Margutti, *Kaiser Franz Joseph,* 413–15; Hantsch, *Graf Berchtold,* 2:25.
12. Serbian Blue Book, doc. no. 42, in *CDD,* 391.
13. Redlich, *Politische Tagebuch,* 1:239–40.
14. Giesl and Berchtold both confirmed this to Albertini after the war, Albertini, *Origins of the War,* 2:379–80.
15. English text of Austrian note, Kautsky, *German Documents,* Supplement I. English text of Serbian answer together with Austrian comments, Albertini, *Origins of the War,* 2:364–71. French texts in *OUA,* vol. 8, docs. nos. 10395, 10648.
16. Albertini, *Origins of the War,* 2:372.
17. Wolff, *The Eve of 1914,* 460–61; *DDF,* vol. 11, docs. nos. 111, 69, 72, 100, 169; Baron Beyens, *Deux Années A Berlin 1912–1914,* 2 vols. (Paris: Plon, 1931), 2:243.
18. Bach, *Deutsche Gesandtschaftsberichte,* doc. no. 17; Geiss, *Julikrise,* vol. 2, doc. no. 444.
19. Kautsky, *German Documents,* Supplement IV, doc. no. 9 at 623.
20. Newspaper quotations from Jonathan F. Scott, *Five Weeks: The Surge of Public Opinion on the Eve of the Great War* (New York: John Day, 1927), 163–64, 166–67.
21. Ibid., 188; Kautsky, *German Documents,* doc. no. 166.
22. English press summaries and quotations from Carroll, *Germany and the Great Powers,* 206–45.

Chapter 17: The View from the *Hohenzollern*

1. Müller, *Regierte der Kaiser?* 32.
2. The following comments on the kaiser's military entourage follow the fine analysis in Hull, *The Entourage of Kaiser Wilhelm II.*

3. Ibid., 245–47; Görlitz, "Einleitung des Herausgebers," in Müller, *Regierte der Kaiser?* 26.
4. Kautsky, *German Documents,* doc. no. 76 n.7.
5. Ibid., doc. no. 157 at 183 n.5.
6. Ibid., doc. no. 29.
7. Ibid., doc. no. 53.
8. Ibid., doc. no. 117.
9. Ibid., doc. no. 121.
10. Müller, *Regierte der Kaiser?* 33.
11. Kautsky, *German Documents,* doc. no. 154.
12. Ibid., doc. no. 155.
13. Ibid., doc. no. 159.
14. Müller, *Regierte der Kaiser?* 34–35.
15. Ibid., 35; Kautsky, *German Documents,* docs. nos. 182, 221.
16. Poincaré Diary, 25, 26 July.
17. *DDF,* vol. 11, docs. nos. 88, 91, 83, 128.

Chapter 18: There Must Be a Way

1. Conrad, *Dienstzeit,* 3:466. For instances of similar discussions, see ibid., 106, 177, 238, 312–13, 443–44; Albertini, *Origins of the War,* 2:454–55. So far as I know, the only scholar who has noted this peculiarity of Conrad's is Soloman Wank, "Some Reflections on Conrad von Hötzendorff and His Memoirs based on Old and New Sources," *Austrian History Yearbook,* 1 (1965): 143–51.
2. Friedrich von Pourtalès, *Am Scheidewege zwischen Krieg und Frieden* (Charlottenburg: Deutsche Verlagsgesellschaft für Politik und Geschichte, 1919), 19–20; Kautsky, *German Documents,* doc. no. 217.
3. As reported by Paléologue, *DDF,* vol. 11, doc. no. 103.
4. *OUA,* vol. 8, doc. no.10835.
5. Turner, "The Russian Mobilisation in 1914," in Kennedy, *War Plans,* 260–61; Stone, *Eastern Front,* 41.
6. Kautsky, *German Documents,* doc. no. 219.
7. Pourtalès, *Am Scheidewege,* 24–25.
8. Kautsky, *German Documents,* doc. no. 230.
9. Ibid., docs. nos. 230, 242.
10. Ibid., doc. no. 238.
11. Hoetzsch, *Imperialismus,* vol. 5, doc. no. 86. See *OUA,* vol. 8, docs. nos. 10835, 10837.
12. *DDF,* vol. 11, doc. no.103.
13. *OUA,* vol. 8, doc. no. 10758.
14. Kautsky, *German Documents,* doc. no. 238; Pourtalès, *Am Scheidewege,* 23.

15. Kautsky, *German Documents,* doc. no. 222.

16. Ibid., docs. nos. 240, 241.

17. Ibid., doc. no. 245.

18. Bach, *Deutsche Gesandtschaftsberichte,* 22, cited in Albertini, *Origins of the War,* 2:438.

19. Dirr, *Bayerische Dokumente,* 148, doc. no. 35; Bach, *Deutsche Gesandtschaftsberichte,* 79–81, docs. nos. 24–28.

20. Müller, *Regierte der Kaiser?* 35–36.

21. *OUA,* vol. 8, docs. nos. 10678, 10736, 10443, 10658, 10679, 10788, 10790.

22. Ibid., doc. no. 10684.

23. *BD,* vol. 11, doc. no. 135.

24. Ibid., doc. no. 128.

25. Ibid., doc. no. 125.

26. Ibid., docs. nos. 139, 140, 141, 144.

27. Kautsky, *German Documents,* doc. no. 274.

28. Ibid., docs. nos. 201, 207.

29. Ibid., doc. no. 192.

30. Ibid., doc. no. 199.

31. *BD,* vol. 11, doc. no. 145.

32. Young, *Prince Lichnowsky,* 103, 223 n.30.

33. Riezler, *Tagebücher,* 192.

34. *BD,* vol. 11, doc. no. 146.

35. Ibid.

36. Ibid., doc. no. 125 at 94.

37. Ibid., doc. no. 146

38. Kautsky, *German Documents,* docs. nos. 218, 236.

39. Ibid., doc. no. 192.

40. Ibid., doc. no. 248.

41. *DDF,* vol. 11, docs. nos. 8, 54.

42. *BD,* vol. 11, doc. no. 125.

43. Hoetzsch, *Imperialismus,* vol. 5, docs. nos. 89, 91; Albertini, *Origins of the War,* 2:414.

Chapter 19: The English Mediation Proposal
1. *DDF,* vol. 11, docs. nos. 50, 89.

2. Ibid., doc. no. 138 and note (3); Albertini, *Origins of the War,* 2:593.

3. Poincaré Diary, 27 July; Poincaré, *Au Service,* 4:337.

4. *BD,* vol. 11, doc. no. 170 and minutes at 120–21.

5. Ibid., doc. no. 170.

6. Ibid., doc. no. 179; Hoetzsch, *Imperialismus,* vol. 5, doc. no. 86.

7. *BD,* vol. 11, docs. nos. 198, 206; Hoetzsch, *Imperialismus,* vol. 5, doc. no. 116; Albertini, *Origins of the War,* 2:407–8.

8. *BD,* vol. 11, docs. nos. 198, 203.

9. Ibid., doc. no. 179 and minute at 126.

10. Kautsky, *German Documents,* doc. no. 258; *BD,* vol. 11, doc. no. 188; *OUA,* vol. 8, docs. nos. 10812, 10813.

11. Hoetzsch, *Imperialismus,* vol. 5, docs. nos. 122, 123, 124.

12. Kautsky, *German Documents,* doc. no. 72 at 132.

13. Francis Leverson Bertie of Thame, *Diary 1914–1918,* ed. Lady Algernon Gordon Lennox, vol. 1 (London: Hodder & Stoughton, 1924), 1, 26 July.

14. Paléologue, *Journal 1913–1914,* 148, 5 June 1913.

15. Bertie, *Diary 1914–1918,* 2, 27 July; *BD,* vol. 11, docs. nos. 192, 184.

16. *BD,* vol. 11, doc. no. 183.

17. Ibid., docs. nos. 192, 184.

18. Hoetzsch, *Imperialismus,* vol. 5, doc. no. 129; Albertini, *Origins of the War,* 2:401.

19. *DDF.* vol. 11, doc. no. 134.

20. *BD,* vol. 11, doc. no. 185; *DDF,* vol. 11, doc. no. 167.

21. *DDF,* vol. 11, doc. no. 184; *BD,* vol. 11, doc. no. 185.

22. *BD,* vol. 11, doc. no. 129 and minute to doc. no. 185.

23. Hoetzsh, *Imperialismus,* vol. 5, doc. no. 134.

24. Kautsky, *German Documents,* doc. 238 n.5.

25. *DDF,* vol. 11, doc. no. 168, p.141.

26. *BD,* vol. 11, doc. no. 185; *DDF,* vol. 11, doc. no. 134 at 116.

27. *DDF,* vol. 11, doc. no. 168.

28. *BD,* vol. 11, doc. no. 190.

29. Kautsky, *German Documents,* doc. no. 257.

30. Ibid., doc. no. 258.

31. Ibid., doc. no. 265. Zechlin, "Deutschland Zwischen Kabinettskrieg und Wirtschaftskrieg," discusses the differences in British and German views on the balance of power, as does Albertini, *Origins of the War,* 2:442–46.

32. Kautsky, *German Documents,* doc. no. 266.

33. Ibid., doc. no. 277.

34. Ibid., doc. no. 277.

35. *BD,* vol. 11, doc. no. 115.

36. Ibid., doc. no. 149 and minutes.

37. *OUA,* vol. 8, doc. no. 10793.

38. Hoetzsch, *Imperialismus,* vol. 5, doc. no. 149.

Chapter 20: Austria-Hungary Declares War on Serbia

1. *OUA,* vol. 8, docs. nos. 10656, 10599.

2. Conrad, *Dienstzeit*, 4:109–10, 122; Norman Stone, "Die Mobilmachung der österreichisch-ungarischen Armee 1914," *Militärgeschichtliche Mitteilungen*, 16 (2/1974) (1974): 67–95.

3. Conrad, *Dienstzeit*, 4:53–54, 131–32.

4. *OUA*, vol. 8, doc. no. 10459.

5. Ibid., doc. no. 10991 at 890.

6. *BD*, vol. 11, doc. no. 188.

7. Ibid., docs. nos. 227, 230; *OUA*, vol. 8, doc. no. 10892.

8. *BD*, vol. 11, doc. no. 199; Hoetzsch, *Imperialismus*, vol. 5, doc. no. 139.

9. Hoetzsch, *Imperialismus*, vol. 5, doc. no. 188.

10. *OUA*, vol. 8, doc. no. 10915; Albertini, *Origins of the War*, 2:464.

11. *BD*, vol. 11, doc. no. 248; Kautsky, *German Documents*, doc. no. 356; Albertini, *Origins of the War*, 2:463–65.

12. Albertini, *Origins of the War*, 2:349.

13. Stokes, "The Serbian Documents from 1914," 76–77.

14. Russian Orange Book, doc. no. 40, in *CDD*, 280–81.

15. Hoetzsch, *Imperialismus*, vol. 5, doc. no. 120 n.3, and doc. no. 8 of the "Beilagen" at 356; Boghitschewitsch, *Auswärtige Politik Serbiens*, vol. 1, doc. no. 413. I have combined Strandtmann's reports of 29 July and 6 August.

16. Kautsky, *German Documents*, docs. nos. 216, 230, 442.

17. Turner, "The Russian Mobilization," 5–88. Turner returned to the subject again in "The Russian Mobilization in 1914" in Kennedy, *War Plans*, 262.

18. *DDF*, vol. 11, docs. nos. 89, 185.

19. George F. Kennan, *The Fateful Alliance* (New York: Pantheon, 1984), 249 ff., Appendix III, 271; Georges Michon, *The Franco-Russian Alliance 1891–1917*, trans. Norman Thomas (1919. New York: Howard Fertig, 1969), 50–53.

20. Hoetzsch, *Imperialismus*, vol. 5, doc. no. 119.

21. Kautsky, *German Documents*, docs. nos. 282, 339.

22. *BD*, vol. 11, doc. no. 247.

23. Kautsky, *German Documents*, doc. no. 338; Pourtalès, *Am Scheidewege*, 31–35; Albertini, *Origins of the War*, 2:532–33. Pourtalès's memoir states that Sazonov was upset by the Austrian declaration of war, but Albertini shows that Sazonov did not learn of it until after his talks with Pourtalès.

24. *OUA*, vol. 8, doc. no. 10999.

25. *BD*, vol. 11, doc. no. 216.

26. Ibid., docs. nos. 229, 232; Bertie, *Diary 1914–1918*, 3, 28 July.

27. *BD*, vol. 11, doc. no. 215 and minutes.

28. Ibid., doc. no. 223.

29. *DDF*, vol. 11, doc. no. 203.

30. Margutti, *Kaiser Franz Joseph*, 424.
31. *OUA*, vol. 8, doc. no. 10660.
32. Würthle, *Die Spur*, 238.
33. Hoetzsch, *Imperialismus*, vol. 5, docs. nos. 201, 202.
34. Albertini, *Origins of the War*, 2:461.
35. Boghitschevitch, *Auswärtige Politik Serbiens*, vol. 1, doc. no. 412; Serbian Red Book, doc. no. 47, in *CDD*, 397.

Chapter 21: The Tsar Decides Not to Decide

1. Quoted in Lieven, *Russia*, 142.
2. Turner, "The Russian Mobilization in 1914," in Kennedy, *War Plans*, 261.
3. Stone, *Eastern Front*, 41.
4. Youri Danilov, *La Russie dans la Guerre Mondiale* (Paris: Payot, 1927), 37–38; Albertini, *Origins of the War*, 2:541–45.
5. Danilov, *La Russie dans la Guerre*, 37–38.
6. *DDF*, vol. 3, doc. no. 359.
7. Maurice Fabian Schilling, *How the War Began in 1914*, trans. W. Cyprian Bridge (London: Allen and Unwin, 1925), 16–17.
8. Turner, "The Russian Mobilization in 1914," in Kennedy, *War Plans*, 257–58.
9. *DDF*, vol. 11, docs. nos. 50, 89.
10. *The Personal Memoirs of Joffre, Field Marshal of the French Army*, trans. Col. T. Bentley Mott, 2 vols. (New York; London: Harper & Bros., 1932), 1:211; Raymond Recouly, *Les Heures Tragiques d'Avant-Guerre* (Paris: La Renaissance du livre, 1929), 69–70.
11. Hoetzsch, *Imperialismus*, vol. 5, docs. nos. 180, 181, 182.
12. *DDF*, vol. 11, docs. nos. 123, 145, 192.
13. Ibid., doc. no. 138.
14. Schilling, *How the War Began*, 43; Hoetzsch, *Imperialismus*, vol. 5, doc. no. 172.
15. *DDF*, vol. 11, doc. no. 208.
16. Alexander, Grand Duke of Russia, *Once a Grand Duke* (Garden City, N.Y.: Farrar & Rinehart, 1932), 168–69.
17. Gleb Botkin, *The Real Romanovs* (New York: Fleming H. Revell, 1931), 61.
18. Alexander, *Once a Grand Duke*, 178.
19. Ibid., 179.
20. Lieven, *Nicholas II*, 106.
21. Quoted in ibid., 64; Alexander Izvolsky, *Recollections of a Foreign Minister* (New York: Doubleday, 1921), 206.
22. G. Vernadsky and Ralph T. Fisher, Jr., eds. *A Source Book for Russian History from Early Times to 1917*, vol. 3, *Alexander II to the February Revolution* (New Haven; London: Yale Univ. Press, 1972), 750, 784.

23. Nicholas V. Riasanovsky, *A History of Russia,* 3d ed. (Oxford: Oxford Univ. Press, 1977), 476; S. S. Oldenburg, *The Last Tsar,* trans. L. I. Milhalap, vol. 3 (Gulf Breeze, Fla., 1977), 139, 177; Lieven, *Russia,* 15.

24. Edward J. Bing, ed., *The Secret Letters of the Last Tsar: The Confidential Correspondence between Nicholas II and His Mother, Dowager Empress Marie Fedorovina* (New York: Longmans, Green, 1938), 248.

25. Lieven, *Russia,* 211.

26. Robert K. Massie, *Nicholas and Alexandra* (1967. Reprint. New York: Dell, 1971), 88.

27. Letter of General Dobrolski to Albertini, *Origins of the War,* 2:544 n.1.

28. Hoetzsch, *Imperialismus,* vol. 5, doc. no. 168.

29. Ibid., doc. no. 210 (my emphasis); Gunther Frantz, *Russlands Eintritt in den Weltkrieg* (Berlin: Deutsche Verlagsgesellschaft für Politik und Geschichte, 1924), 241, 245; Fay, *Origins of the War,* 2:452–53.

30. Pourtalès, *Am Schediewege,* 31–35.

31. *DDF,* vol. 11, doc. no. 216.

Chapter 22: The Kaiser Sees No Reason for War

1. Quoted in Bach, *Deutsche Gesandtschaftsberichte,* 23.

2. Kautsky, *German Documents,* docs. nos. 258, 283 n.3.

3. Ibid., doc. no. 271 at 254.

4. Ibid., doc. no. 293. Here and above, the kaiser underlined the passages indicated.

5. Albertini, *Origins of the War,* 2:470–71.

6. Kautsky, *German Documents,* doc. no. 279.

7. Ibid., doc. no. 282.

8. Ibid., doc. no. 307.

9. Ibid., doc. no. 176.

10. Ibid., doc. no. 299.

11. Dirr, *Bayerische Dokumente,* doc. no. 40 at 153–54.

12. Wolff, *On the Eve of 1914,* 472.

13. Kautsky, *German Documents,* doc. no. 323.

14. Ibid., doc. no. 277; *OUA,* vol. 8, doc. no. 10871.

15. Kautsky, *German Documents,* doc. no. 313.

16. *OUA,* vol. 8, docs. nos. 10864, 10865.

17. Conrad, *Dienstzeit,* 4:134–37.

18. *OUA,* vol. 8, doc. no. 108631.

19. Kautsky, *German Documents,* docs. nos. 322, 335.

Chapter 23: The Cult of the Offensive

1. Quoted in Michael Howard, "Men Against Fire: Expectations of War in 1914," in Steven E. Miller, Sean M. Lynn–Jones, and Stephan Van Evera,

eds., *Military Strategy and the Origins of the First World War* (Princeton, N.J.: Princeton Univ. Press, 1991), 43. T. H. E. Travers, "Technology, Tactics and Morale: Jean Bloch, the Boer War, and British Military Theory, 1900–1914," *Journal of Modern History,* 51, no. 2 (June 1979): 264–86, is excellent on Bloch's impact.

2. Norman Angell, *The Great Illusion* (New York: G. P. Putnam's Sons, 1913), viii.

3. Heinrich Class, *Wenn Ich der Kaiser War' politisches Wahrheiten und Notwendigkeiten,* 5th enl. ed. (Leipzig: Dietrich, 1914), 53; Friedrich von Bernhardi, *Germany and the Next War,* trans. Allen H. Powles (New York: Longmans, Green, 1914), 9.

4. Robbins, *Sir Edward Grey,* 249; Radziwill, *Lettres de la Princess,* 4:207; Reginald Esher, *The Captains and the Kings Depart,* ed. Oliver Esher (New York: Scribner's, 1938), 25; Vernadsky and Fisher, *Source Book,* 793, 797.

5. Quoted in Barbara W. Tuchman, *The Proud Tower* (Reprint. New York: Bantam, 1972), 324.

6. Cambon, *Correspondance,* 2:285, 12 May 1909.

7. *OUA,* vol. 8, doc. no. 9918.

8. Quoted in Cairns, "International Politics and the Military Mind: The Case of the French Republic," *Journal of Modern History,* 25, no. 3 (September 1953), 282. See Stephan van Evera, "The Cult of the Offensive and the Origins of the First World War," in Miller, *Military Strategy,* 59–107, 61.

9. Quoted in Howard, "Men Against Fire," in Miller, *Military Strategy,* 12. See Travers, "Technology, Tactics and Morale," 266, 267, 268, 272, 280.

10. Stone, *Eastern Front,* 17.

11. Michael Howard, "Men Against Fire," in Miller, *Military Strategy,* 11. The argument in the foregoing paragraphs draws heavily on the articles by Michael Howard and Stephan van Evera in Miller, *Military Strategy.*

12. Andrew, "France and the German Menace," in May, *Knowing One's Enemies,* 127–49, particularly 138–39; Travers, "Technology, Tactics and Morale," 274–75.

13. Quoted in van Evera, "The Cult of the Offensive," in Miller, *Military Strategy,* 94.

14. Correlli Barnett, *The Sword Bearers* (London: Eyre & Spottiswood, 1963), 45–46.

15. Hull, *The Entourage of Kaiser Wilhelm II,* 241–42; Müller, *Der Kaiser,* 186.

16. Helmuth von Moltke, *Erinnerungen, Briefe und Dokumente 1877–1916* (Stuttgart: Der kommende Tag, 1922), 313–16, letters of 1 February and 4 February 1905.

17. Kautsky, *German Documents,* doc. no. 349 at 307.
18. Conrad, *Dienstzeit,* 3:147–51.
19. Müller, *Der Kaiser,* 185–86.
20. van Evera, "The Cult of the Offensive," in Miller, *Military Strategy,* 92.
21. L. C. F. Turner, "The Significance of the Schlieffen Plan," in Kennedy, *War Plans,* 199–221, 212.
22. Ritter, *The European Powers,* 219.
23. Kautsky, *German Documents,* doc. no. 648.
24. Barnett, *Sword Bearers,* 35.
25. Gerhard Ritter, *The Schlieffen Plan: Critique of a Myth,* trans. Andrew and Eva Wilson (London: O. Wolff, 1958), 57–68.
26. Marshall, *World War I,* 43–45; Stone, *Eastern Front,* 18; Ritter, *European Powers,* 226, 306 nn. 50, 51, 52. No two authors agree on precise numbers, but they all agree that the Entente powers had a sizable numerical advantage.
27. Stone, *Eastern Front,* 40–43.
28. Hull, *The Entourage of Kaiser Wilhelm II,* 200–201, 241, 249–56. I am very much indebted to Professor Hull's analysis of German strategic rigidity.
29. See the analysis in Snyder, "Civil-Military Relations and the Cult of the Offensive, 1914 and 1984," in Miller, *Military Strategy,* 108–46.
30. Turner, "The Significance of the Schlieffen Plan," in Kennedy, *War Plans,* 222, 226.
31. Norman Stone, "Conrad and Moltke: Relations between the Austro-Hungarian and German General Staffs, 1909–1914," in Kennedy, *War Plans,* 227–28.
32. Quoted in ibid., 229.

Chapter 24: The Russian Partial Mobilization

1. *DDF,* vol. 11, doc. no. 229.
2. Ibid., doc. no. 230.
3. Scott, *Five Weeks,* 98.
4. Ibid., 233–35.
5. O. J. Hale, *Publicity and Diplomacy With Special Reference to England and Germany 1890–1914* (New York; London: D. Appleton-Century, 1940), 461.
6. Scott, *Five Weeks,* 128–40; Hale, *Publicity and Diplomacy,* 453–54; Carroll, *Germany and the Great Powers,* 791–99.
7. The National Liberal *Magdeburgische Zeitung* in Carroll, *Germany and the Great Powers,* 793.
8. Quoted in Bredin, *Joseph Caillaux,* 195.

9. Foreign ministry journal for 29 July, Hoetzsch, *Imperialismus,* vol. 5, doc. no. 224.

10. Kautsky, *German Documents,* docs. nos. 300, 315.

11. There are several reports of this conversation, ibid., doc. no. 343; Hoetzsch, *Imperialismus,* vol. 5, docs. nos. 218, 224 at 161; Pourtalès, *Am Scheidewege,* 40–41.

12. Hoetzsch, *Imperialismus,* vol. 5, doc. no. 224 at 161.

13. Ibid., doc. no. 188.

14. *BD,* vol. 11, doc. no. 276 at 177.

15. Pourtalès, *Am Scheidewege,* 43–44.

16. Quoted in Albertini, *Origins of the War,* 2:547–48; Fay, *The Origins of the World War,* 2:464, n.44.

17. Kautsky, *German Documents,* doc. no. 370; Albertini, *Origins of the War,* 2:457.

18. *BD,* vol. 11, doc. no. 276.

19. Ibid., doc. no. 202.

20. Ibid., doc. no. 276.

21. Kautsky, *German Documents,* doc. no. 365.

22. *OUA,* vol. 8, docs. nos. 11003, 11094.

23. Hoetzsch, *Imperialismus,* vol. 5, doc. no. 257 and doc. no. 8 in the "Beilagen" at 356.

24. Würthle, *Die Spur,* 239.

25. *OUA,* vol. 8, docs. nos. 11003, 11094.

26. Riezler, *Tagebücher,* 185, 192, 193.

27. Kautsky, *German Documents,* doc. no. 344.

28. Ibid., doc. no. 370.

29. Ibid., doc. no. 372 at 327.

30. Ibid., doc. no. 349.

31. Ibid., doc. no. 341.

32. Ibid., doc. no. 342.

33. Ibid., docs. nos. 342, 378; *OUA,* vol. 8, doc. no. 11003 at 900.

34. Serge Sazonov, *Fateful Years 1909–1916* (New York: Frederick A. Stokes, 1928), 195–96.

35. Kautsky, *German Documents,* doc. no. 335.

36. Hoetzsch, *Imperialismus,* vol. 5, doc. no. 224 at 162.

37. W. A. Sukhomlinov, *Erinnerungen* (Berlin: R. Hobbing, 1924), 359–64.

38. Dobrolski, *Die Mobilmachung,* 25–26; Albertini, *Origins of the War,* 2:557.

39. Kautsky, *German Documents,* doc. no. 359.

40. Sukhomlinov, *Erinnerungen,* 364–65; Albertini, *Origins of the War,* 2:558–59.

41. M. Benouville and A. Kaznakov, eds. *Journal Intime de Nicolas II (Juillet 1914–Juillet 1918)* (Paris: Payot, 1934), 15.

42. Wolff, *The Eve of 1914*, 467–70.

Chapter 25: The View from Paris

1. Paléologue, *Journal*, 298–99, 9 June.

2. Ibid., 294–95, 7 June.

3. Ibid., 310–11, 18 June.

4. Paléologue, *Memoirs*, 1:36–37, 40–41.

5. Maurice Paléologue, *Guillaume II et Nicolas II* (Paris: Plon, 1935), 213–14. See comment by Mario Toscano, *The History of Treaties and International Politics*, vol. 1, *The Documentary and Memoir Sources* (Baltimore: John Hopkins Press, 1966), 366–67.

6. Keiger, *France and the Origins*, 159.

7. Becker, *1914*, 136–39.

8. Poincaré Diary, 29 July; Poincaré, *Au Service*, 4:366.

9. Poincaré, *Au Service*, 4:366; *DDF*, vol. 11, docs. nos. 130, 163.

10. Abel Ferry, *Les Carnets Secrets (1914–1918)* (Paris: Grasset, 1957), 24; Becker, *1914*, 136.

11. Poincaré Diary, 29 July; Poincaré, *Au Service*, 4:367–69.

12. Quoted in Albertini, *Origins of the War*, 2:596.

13. *BD*, vol. 11, doc. no. 270.

14. Bertie, *Diary 1914–1918*, 4, 29 July.

15. *DDF*, vol. 11, doc. no. 243; Hoetzsch, *Imperialismus*, vol. 5, docs. nos. 167, 168.

16. *DDF*, vol. 11, doc. no. 260.

17. Poincaré Diary, 29 July.

18. *DDF*, vol. 11, doc. no. 258.

19. Kautsky, *German Documents*, doc. no. 367.

20. Hoetzsch, *Imperialismus*, vol. 5, docs. nos. 232, 233, 234.

21. *DDF*, vol. 11, doc. no. 274.

22. Albertini, *Origins of the War*, 2:583, 582–89.

23. Romanovic Rosen, *Forty Years of Diplomacy*, 2 vols. (London: Allen and Unwin, 1922), 2:163–64, 29 July.

24. *BD*, vol. 11, doc. no. 276.

25. *DDF*, vol. 11, doc. no. 283; Paléologue, *Memoirs*, 1:42.

26. Nicolas de Basiley (Nicolai Basili), *Diplomat of Imperial Russia 1903–1917* (Stanford: Hoover Institution, 1973), 95–96.

27. Recouly, *Heures Tragiques*, 160–61; Albertini, *Origins of the War*, 2:582–89.

28. *DDF*, vol. 11, doc. no. 283.

29. Paléologue, *Memoirs,* 1:42–43.

30. Hoetzsch, *Imperialismus,* vol. 5, doc. no. 221.

31. Ibid., doc. no. 172.

32. *DDF,* vol. 11, doc. no. 138.

33. Adolphe Messimy, *Mes Souvenirs* (Paris: Plon, 1937), 181–84.

34. Poincaré Diary, 29 July; Poincaré, *Au Service,* 4:384–85; Hoetzsch, *Imperialismus,* vol. 5, docs. nos. 221, 289; Albertini, *Origins of the War,* 2:601–3.

35. *DDF,* vol. 11, doc. no. 305.

36. Hoetzsch, *Imperialismus,* vol. 5, doc. no. 289.

37. *Personal Memoirs of Joffre,* 2:122.

38. *DDF,* vol. 11, note (2) to doc. no. 305 at 262–63; Albertini, *Origins of the War,* 2:606–8.

39. Quoted in Recouly, *Heures Tragiques,* 69–70.

40. *Personal Memoirs of Joffre,* 1:117.

41. Hoetzsch, *Imperialismus,* vol. 5, doc. no. 291; Poincaré, *Au Service,* 4:386–87.

42. *DDF,* vol. 11, note (2) to doc. no. 305; Albertini, *Origins of the War,* 2:609.

43. Messimy, *Mes Souvenirs,* 140–41.

44. *OUA,* vol. 8, doc. no. 11082.

Chapter 26: The View from Rome

1. That is the title of R. J. B. Bosworth's book, *Italy, The Least of the Great Powers.*

2. Ibid., 69.

3. Ibid., 339–40, 350–52, 366–67.

4. Quoted in ibid., 402. Emphasis in the original.

5. *OUA,* vol. 8, doc. 10989 at 888. Quoted in Albertini, *Origins of the War,* 3:316; Joll, *The First World War,* 35.

6. *OUA,* vol. 8, doc. no. 10460.

7. Ibid, doc. no. 10991 at 890.

8. Ibid, doc. no. 10989 at 887.

9. Bosworth, *The Least of the Great Powers,* 393.

10. Kautsky, *German Documents,* doc. no. 64 at 126.

11. Albert Francis Pribram, ed., *The Secret Treaties of Austria-Hungary 1879–1914,* vol. 1, *Texts of the Treaties and Agreements* (London: Harvard Univ. Press, 1920), doc. no. 25, Article VII, 249–50.

12. Kautsky, *German Documents,* docs. nos. 156, 168, 244.

13. Ibid., doc. no. 244.

14. Ibid., doc. no. 156.

15. Quoted in Bosworth, *The Least of the Great Powers,* 389.

16. Hoetzsch, *Imperialismus,* vol. 5, doc. no. 95 at 91.

17. Ibid., doc. no. 131.

18. Albertini, *Origins of the War,* 3:269; *BD,* vol. 11, doc. no. 202.

19. *OUA,* vol. 8, doc. no. 10989.

20. Ibid., doc. no. 10991 at 892.

21. Kautsky, *German Documents,* docs. nos. 202, 267, 269.

22. *OUA,* vol. 8, doc. no. 10988, translation of full note in Albertini, *Origins of the War,* 3:276.

23. Kautsky, *German Documents,* doc. no. 326.

24. *OUA,* vol. 8, doc. no. 10909.

25. Ibid., doc. no. 10909 at 847.

26. Ibid., docs. nos. 10987, 10991.

27. Kautsky, *German Documents,* doc. no. 363 at 318, doc. no. 419.

28. Ibid., docs. nos. 340, 361, p.317.

29. Bosworth, *The Least of the Great Powers,* 393.

Chapter 27: The View from London

1. Brock, *Asquith Letters,* letter no. 103.

2. A. V. Dicey quoted in Stephan Koss, *Asquith* (London: A. Lane, 1976), 94.

3. Roy Jenkins, *Asquith. Portrait of a Man and an Era* (New York: E. P. Dutton, 1966), 186–87.

4. Brock, *Asquith Letters,* letter no. 104.

5. Ibid., 7–8.

6. Quoted in ibid., 13. Emphasis in original.

7. Koss, *Asquith,* 140.

8. Brock, *Asquith Letters,* 119.

9. Ibid., 126 n.6.

10. Ibid., letter no. 105 and n. 4.

11. Ibid., letter no. 106.

12. Ibid., letter no. 107 at 129.

13. Ibid.

14. Ibid., letters nos. 108, 109 at 132.

15. Koss, *Asquith,* 157.

16. Winston S. Churchill, *The World Crisis,* abridged and rev. ed. (New York: Thornton Butterworth, 1932), 118.

17. *The Political Diaries of C. P. Scott 1911–1918,* ed. Trevor Wilson (Ithaca, N.Y.: Cornell Univ. Press, 1970), 93, 29 July.

18. John Morley, *Memorandum on Resignation August 1914* (New York: Macmillan, 1928), 3–7.

19. Jenkins, *Asquith,* 325.

20. Michael Brock, "Britain Enters the War," in Evans and Strandmann, *Coming of the First World War,* 145–78, 150.

21. Wilson, *Policy of the Entente,* 136.

22. Brock, *Asquith Letters,* letter no. 109 at 132.

23. Jenkins, *Asquith,* 325.

24. Brock, *Asquith Letters,* letter no. 109 at 133 (Asquith's emphasis).

25. *BD,* vol. 11, doc. no. 282; *OUA,* vol. 8, doc. no. 10973; Albertini, *Origins of the War,* 2:511–12.

26. *OUA,* vol. 8, doc. no. 10974 at 879.

27. *BD,* vol. 11, doc. no. 283; *DDF,* vol. 11, docs. nos. 266, 281.

28. Kautsky, *German Documents,* doc. no. 368; *BD,* vol. 11, doc. no. 286.

29. Margot Asquith, *An Autobiography,* vol. 1 (New York: George H. Doran, 1922), 15, 29 July.

30. Brock, *Asquith Letters,* letter 109.

Chapter 28: The View from Berlin

1. Quoted in Martin Gilbert, *Sir Horace Rumbold* (London: Heinemann, 1973), 113–14.

2. Cecil, *Albert Ballin,* 208–9.

3. *BD,* vol. 11, doc. no. 281.

4. Ibid., doc. no. 677 at 361–62, doc. no. 281.

5. Ibid., doc. no. 264 and minutes.

6. Ibid., doc. no. 266.

7. Hoetzsch, *Imperialismus,* vol. 5, Beilage no. 6 at 333–34.

8. Kautsky, *German Documents,* doc. no. 343.

9. Hoetzsch, *Imperialismus,* vol. 5, doc. no. 241, Beilage no. 6 at 333–36.

10. Albertini, *Origins of the War,* 2:490.

11. Ibid., 491.

12. Ibid., 496–97.

13. Müller, *Regierte?* 36; Geiss, *Julikrise,* vol. 2, doc. no. 675(b).

14. Geiss, *Julikrise,* vol. 2, doc. no. 675(a) at 275; Alfred von Tirpitz, *Erinnerungen* (Leipzig: Koehler, 1919), 237–38.

15. Geiss, *Julikrise,* vol. 2, doc. no. 676.

16. Kautsky, *German Documents,* doc. no. 301.

17. Ibid., doc. no. 361.

18. Ibid., doc. no. 357.

19. Ibid., doc. no. 377, n.3; Albertini, *Origins of the War,* 2:504.

20. *BD,* vol. 11, docs. nos. 293, 677 at 362.

21. Kautsky, *German Documents,* doc. no. 368 at 322.

22. *OUA,* vol. 8, doc. no. 10950.

23. Kautsky, *German Documents,* doc. no. 380.

24. Ibid., docs. nos. 401, 412.

25. Ibid., doc. no. 421. Pourtalès and Sazonov had a whole series of conferences during the night of 29–30 July and the morning of 30 July, and the various accounts of these meetings are not always consistent. But there is no dispute on the substance of what happened and that the talks were held sometime during the night and morning of 29–30 July. See Albertini, *Origins of the War,* 2:561–64.

26. Kautsky, *German Documents,* doc. no. 384, referring to doc. no. 357.

27. Ibid., doc. no. 385.

28. Ibid., docs. nos. 356, 365.

29. Ibid., doc. no. 396.

30. Hoetzsch, *Imperialismus,* vol. 5, doc. no. 243; *BD,* vol. 11, doc. no. 307.

31. *BD,* vol. 11, docs. nos. 295, 307; *DDF,* vol. 11, doc. no. 284; Hoetzsch, *Imperialismus,* vol. 5, doc. no. 243.

32. Kautsky, *German Documents,* doc. no. 323.

33. *OUA,* vol. 8, doc. no. 10145.

34. Kautsky, *German Documents,* doc. no. 356.

35. Ibid., doc. no. 386.

36. Ibid., doc. no. 323 at 289; *OUA,* vol. 8, doc. no. 10939.

37. Kautsky, *German Documents,* doc. no. 388.

38. *OUA,* vol. 8, doc. no. 10937.

Chapter 29: The View from Nish

1. *BD,* vol. 11, doc. no. 284.

2. Hoetzsch, *Imperialismus,* vol. 5, doc. no. 22.

3. Würthle, *Die Spur,* 238–39.

4. Hoetzsch, *Imperialismus,* vol. 5, doc. no. 257; *DDF,* vol. 11, doc. no. 368; *BD,* vol. 11, docs. nos. 332, 388(a), 389.

5. *BD,* vol. 11, doc. no. 485.

6. Hoetzsch, *Imperialismus,* vol. 5, doc. no. 320; *DDF,* vol. 8, doc. no. 367.

7. Hoetzsch, *Imperialismus,* vol. 5, doc. no. 218.

8. Ibid., doc. no. 321.

9. *DDF,* vol. 11, doc. no. 366.

10. Hoetzsch, *Imperialismus,* vol. 5, doc. no. 322.

Chapter 30: Russia Must Move First

1. Wolff, *The Eve of 1914,* 479–80. On the growing military pressure, see Bach, *Deutsche Gesandtschaftsberichte,* docs. nos. 40, 41, cited in Jarausch, *Enigmatic Chancellor,* 171 n.33.

2. Kautsky, *German Documents,* doc. no. 399.

3. Ibid., doc. no. 399, marginalia.

4. Ibid., doc. no. 417.

5. Müller, *Regierte?* 37.

6. Kautsky, *German Documents,* doc. no. 402.

7. Jarausch, *Enigmatic Chancellor,* 169, n.30; Albertini, *Origins of the War,* 3:6; Report of von Leuckart, 29 July, Bach, *Deutsche Gesandtschaftsberichte,* 93.

8. Kautsky, *German Documents,* doc. no. 408.

9. Ibid., doc. no. 420.

10. Ibid., doc. no. 437.

11. *BD,* vol. 11, doc. no. 305.

12. Kautsky, *German Documents,* doc. no. 410; Ritter, *European Powers,* 256–57.

13. *DDF,* vol. 11, docs. nos. 339, 380; Albertini, *Origins of the War,* 3:7, 13.

14. Ritter, *European Powers,* 313, n.32.

15. Quoted in Ritter, *European Powers,* 257; Albertini, *Origins of the War,* 3:11. The Austrian attaché's postwar recollection puts the talk at "about 2:00 P.M.," but Szögyény's report, which did not go out until 7:40 P.M., says that the attaché "had just now" talked with Moltke (*OUA,* vol. 8, doc. no. 11033), so they probably talked much later in the afternoon.

16. Quoted in Fay, *Origins of the World War,* 2:509–10; Albertini, *Origins of the War,* 3:11; Ritter, *European Powers,* 257–58.

17. *OUA,* vol. 8, doc. no. 11033.

18. Albertini, *Origins of the War,* 3:11.

19. Hoetzsch, *Imperialismus,* vol. 5, docs. nos. 301, 302, 303; Geiss, *Julikrise,* vol. 2, docs. nos. 817, 818, 819.

20. Albertini, *Origins of the War,* 3:9–10.

21. *DDF,* vol. 11, doc. no. 330.

22. Ibid., doc. no. 322.

23. Ibid., docs. nos. 317, 322, 377.

24. Ibid., doc. no. 319.

25. Kautsky, *German Documents,* doc. no. 421; Hoetzsch, *Imperialismus,* vol. 5, doc. no. 305.

26. Kautsky, *German Documents,* doc. no. 421 n.5.

27. Hoetzsch, *Imperialismus,* vol. 5, doc. no. 305; Geiss, *Julikrise,* vol. 2, doc. no. 820.

28. *DDF,* vol. 11, doc. no. 339.

29. *DDF,* vol. 11, docs. 334, 380; Geiss, *Julikrise,* vol. 2, doc. no. 841.

30. Geiss, *Julikrise,* vol. 2, doc. no. 801. It is typical of Fritz Fischer's determination to show Germany bent upon war that in his *Krieg der Illusionen,* 716, he insists that the decision was made to "declare" the State of Imminent War by noon, 31 July, when in fact Bethmann forced the generals to wait and promised only to make his "decision" then.

31. Kautsky, *German Documents,* doc. no. 441.

32. *BD,* vol. 11, doc. no. 293, minute at 186.

33. Ibid., doc. no. 303.

34. Ibid., doc. no. 309.

35. Kautsky, *German Documents,* doc. no. 439.

36. *OUA,* vol. 8, doc. no. 11064.

37. Wolff, *The Eve of 1914,* 488.

Chapter 31: Vienna Defies Berlin

1. *BD,* vol. 11, doc. no. 307 at 195.

2. Conrad, *Dienstzeit,* 4:146–47.

3. Conrad, *Dienstzeit,* 4:122–23; Stone, *Eastern Front,* 71–72; Ritter, *European Powers,* 253.

4. Conrad, *Dienstzeit,* 4:147.

5. Conrad, *Dienstzeit,* 4:147–48

6. Kautsky, *German Documents,* doc. no. 433.

7. Ibid., doc. no. 432.

8. Ibid., doc. no. 395.

9. Ibid., doc. no. 465.

10. *BD,* vol. 11, doc. no. 307 at 196.

11. Kautsky, *German Documents,* doc. no. 465.

12. See ibid., doc. no. 441 at 372.

13. Ibid., doc. no. 465.

14. Ibid., doc. no. 434.

15. Stone, *Eastern Front,* 75.

16. Conrad, *Dienstzeit,* 4:148.

17. Quoted in Albertini, *Origins of the War,* 2:656.

18. The kaiser undoubtedly meant the tsar's wires of 29 July, Kautsky, *German Documents,* docs. nos. 332, 366.

19. Ibid., doc. no. 437.

20. Conrad, *Dienstzeit,* 4:151.

21. Conrad, *Dienstzeit,* 4:150–51; Albertini, *Origins of the War,* 2:669–70.

22. Quoted in Albertini, *Origins of the War,* 2:655.

23. *OUA,* vol. 8, doc. no. 11155.

24. Kautsky, *German Documents,* docs. nos. 427, 429.

25. *OUA,* vol. 8, doc. no. 11121.

26. Conrad, *Dienstzeit,* 4:150–51; Albertini, *Origins of the War,* 2:670.

27. Stone, *Eastern Front,* 75–76; Stone, "Moltke and Conrad," in Kennedy, *War Plans,* 234–35; Ritter, *European Powers,* 260.

28. Kautsky, *German Documents,* doc. no. 356.

29. *BD,* vol. 11, doc. no. 311.

30. *OUA,* vol. 8, doc. no. 11093 at 933, translation in Albertini, *Origins of the War,* 2:662.

31. *OUA,* vol. 8, doc. no. 11093; Hoetzsch, *Imperialismus,* vol. 5, doc. no. 307.

32. *DDF,* vol. 11, doc. no. 364 at 302; *BD,* vol. 11, doc. no. 311.

33. *BD,* vol. 11, doc. no. 311, minute at 198.

34. Kautsky, *German Documents,* doc. no. 452.

35. Ibid., doc. no. 451.

36. Ibid., doc. no. 464.

37. Riezler, *Tagebücher,* 193, 194, 27 July, 15 August.

38. Kautsky, *German Documents,* doc. no. 464. See Albertini, *Origins of the War,* 3:28; Fischer, *Krieg,* 716 n.121.

Chapter 32: Mobilization Does Not Mean War

1. Kautsky, *German Documents,* doc. no. 421; Hoetzsch, *Imperialismus,* vol. 5, doc. no. 728; Albertini, *Origins of the War,* 2:562–63.

2. The account that follows accepts the chronology as recorded in Schilling's foreign ministry journal, Hoetzsch, *Imperialismus,* vol. 5, doc. no. 284. There are substantial variations in timing and chronology between it and Pourtalès's diary and reports, Buchanan's reports, and Paléologue's journal, but Schilling's is a contemporary record and is consistent with most of the evidence. See the discussion in Albertini, *Origins of the War,* 2:563–64 n.2. Albertini has an English translation of Schilling's account, ibid., 565.

3. Rosen, *Forty Years of Diplomacy,* 164–65, 169–71.

4. Dobrolski, *Die Mobilmachung,* 28, attributes this argument to Yanushkevich.

5. Hoetzsch, *Imperialismus,* vol. 5, doc. no. 284 at 197; Sazonov, *Fateful Years,* 200–201. Albertini, *Origins of the War,* 2:565–68, where he is very hard on Sazonov.

6. *BD,* vol. 11, doc. no. 302(a).

7. *DDF,* vol. 11, doc. no. 305.

8. Ibid., doc. no. 342.

9. Hoetzsch, *Imperialismus,* vol. 5, doc. no. 284 at 197.

10. Sazonov, *Fateful Years,* 202.

11. Paléologue, *Memoirs,* 1:45.

12. Hoetzsch, *Imperialismus,* vol. 5, doc. no. 284 at 198.

13. Ibid.

14. Dobrolski, *Die Mobilmachung,* 28. Sazonov, *Fateful Years,* 196–205, has a highly partisan account of his interview with Nicholas.

15. Dobrolski, *Die Mobilmachung,* 28–29.

16. Lieven, *Russia,* 148–49.

17. Dirr, *Bayerische Dokumente*, doc. no. 49 at 160; Kautsky, *German Documents*, doc. no. 349 at 307.

18. Albertini, *Origins of the War*, 2:620, where the translation is somewhat clearer than that in Kautsky, *German Documents*, doc. no. 392.

19. Kautsky, *German Documents*, doc. no. 397.

20. Ibid., docs. nos. 221, 449, Supplement V, 645–46; Pourtalès, *Am Scheidewege*, 49, 50–54.

21. *BD*, vol. 11, doc. no. 347 and "NOTE."

22. Hoetzsch, *Imperialismus*, vol. 5, doc. no. 354; *BD*, vol. 11, doc. no. 357.

23. Albertini, *Origins of the War*, 2:613–27, examines this question in detail, including the views of other historians.

24. Kautsky, *German Documents*, doc. no. 420; Albertini, *Origins of the War*, 2:621.

25. *DDF*, vol. 11, doc. no. 359.

26. Ibid., doc. no. 432.

27. See Albertini, *Origins of the War*, 2:622.

Chapter 33: "What Is the Point of War?"

1. Hoetzsch, *Imperialismus*, vol. 5, doc. no. 349.

2. Pourtalès, *Am Scheidewege*, 57–64, abstracts quoted and translated in Albertini, *Origins of the War*, 3:55–56.

3. Kautsky, *German Documents*, doc. no. 487.

4. Reported by Szápáry, *OUA*, vol. 8, doc. no. 11174. Emphasis in original.

5. Benouville and Kaznakov, *Journal Intime*, 16–18.

6. Pierre Gilliard, *Treize Années A La Cour de Russie* (Paris: Payot, 1921), 85.

7. Hoetzsch, *Imperialismus*, vol. 5, doc. no. 286.

8. *BD*, vol. 11, doc. no. 309.

9. Sazonov, *Fateful Years*, 210.

10. Kautsky, *German Documents*, doc. no. 421.

11. Hoetzsch, *Imperialismus*, vol. 5, docs. nos. 342, 346; *BD*, vol. 11, doc. no. 417.

12. Quoted in Albertini, *Origins of the War*, 1:294.

13. *OUA*, vol. 8, doc. no. 11177.

14. Ibid., doc. no. 11174.

15. Ibid., doc. no. 11179.

16. *Diplomatische Aktenstücke zur Vorgeschichte des Krieges 1914*, 3 vols. (Vienna: Deutsche Verlagsgesellschaft für Politik und Geschichte in Berlin, 1919) (Hereafter cited as *DAV*), vol. 3, doc. no. 97 at 95, translated in Albertini, *Origins of the War*, 2:682–83.

17. Hoetzsch, *Imperialismus*, vol. 5, doc. no. 348.

18. Report of Bunsen dated September 9, *BD,* vol. 11, doc. no. 676 at 358.

19. Ibid., doc. no. 337.

20. Ibid., doc. no. 303.

21. Ibid., doc. no. 336.

22. *DDF,* vol 11, docs. nos. 281, 298.

23. *BD,* vol. 11, doc. no. 319.

24. Kautsky, *German Documents,* doc. no. 435.

25. Ibid., doc. no. 469.

26. *BD,* vol. 11, doc. no. 444.

27. Ibid., doc. no. 335.

28. Kautsky, *German Documents,* doc. no. 489.

29. Ibid., doc. no. 484.

30. Pease Diary, quoted in Cameron Hazlehurst, *Politicians At War* (New York: Knopf, 1971), 84.

31. Quoted in Hazlehurst, *Politicians At War,* 85. Emphasis in the original.

32. Brock, *Asquith Letters,* 138–39, letter of 31 July.

33. Quoted in Brock, *Asquith Letters,* 138–39 n.3.

34. *BD,* vol. 11, doc. no. 340; Kautsky, *German Documents,* doc. no. 496; Geiss, *Julikrise,* vol. 2, doc. 910.

35. Keith Eubank, *Paul Cambon Master Diplomatist* (Norman, Okla.: Univ. of Oklahoma Press, 1960), Appendix B, 209 ff.

36. *BD,* vol. 11, doc. no. 367 at 226.

37. *DDF,* vol. 11, docs. nos. 445, 459.

38. Ibid., doc. 445.

39. *BD,* vol. 11, doc. no. 367 at 227. I reconstructed this conversation from the reports cited in this and the preceding three footnotes.

40. Ibid., doc. no. 348.

41. Arthur Murray's Diary, 31 July, cited in Hazlehurst, *Politicians At War,* 86.

42. Count Hugo von Lerchenfeld-Köfering, Bavarian minister to Berlin, to Munich, 31 July; Kautsky, *German Documents,* Supplement IV, doc. no. 21; Albertini, *Origins of the War,* 3:27–31; Jarausch, *Enigmatic Chancellor,* 172–74.

43. Kautsky, *German Documents,* doc. no. 473.

44. Ibid., doc. no. 490.

45. Ibid., doc. no. 488.

46. Ibid., doc. no. 492 at 406.

47. Ibid., doc. no. 491.

48. Ibid., doc. no. 368. Kaiser's emphasis.

49. Ibid., doc. no. 401.

50. Ibid., doc. no. 477.

51. Ibid., doc. no. 480.

52. Ibid., doc. no. 487. Emphasis in original.

53. Ibid., doc. no. 546. Capitalized in original.

54. Ibid., doc. no. 474.

55. Müller, *Regierte?* 38–39; Geiss, *Julikrise,* vol. 2, doc. no. 909; Kautsky, *German Documents,* docs. nos. 474, 417, 452.

56. Alfred von Tirptitz, *Politische Dokumente,* vol. 2, *Deutsche Ohnmacht-spolitik im Weltkrieg* (Hamburg: Hanseatische Verlagsanstalt, 1926), 10; Geiss, *Julikrise,* vol. 2, doc. no. 895; Albertini, *Origins of the War,* 3:191.

Chapter 34: The German Ultimatum

1. Conrad, *Dienstzeit,* 4:152.

2. Kautsky, *German Documents,* doc. no. 437.

3. *OUA,* vol. 8, doc. no. 11201.

4. Ibid., doc. no. 11000.

5. Ibid., doc. no. 11094.

6. The protocol of the conference in ibid., doc. no. 11203, translation in Immanual Geiss, *July 1914* (New York: Norton, 1967), doc. no. 154.

7. Berchtold's 1927 letter quoted in Albertini, *Origins of the War,* 2:656.

8. Rudolf Sieghart, *Die Letzte Jahrzehnte einer Grossmacht* (Berlin, 1932), 173.

9. Protocol, *OUA,* vol. 8, doc. no. 11203.

10. Kautsky, *German Documents,* doc. no. 437; *OUA,* vol. 8, doc. no. 11026.

11. Author's emphasis. Austria-Hungary had already partially mobilized.

12. *OUA,* vol. 8, doc. no. 11118; Kautsky, *German Documents,* doc. no. 482.

13. Lützow, *Im diplomatischen Dienst,* 234.

14. Sieghart, *Die Letzte Jahrzehnte,* 169.

15. *OUA,* vol. 8, docs. nos. 11133, 11134.

16. Kautsky, *German Documents,* doc. no. 502.

17. Ibid., doc. no. 503.

18. Conrad, *Dienstzeit,* 4:152.

19. This exchange of messages is conveniently collected at Albertini, *Origins of the War,* 3:46–50.

20. *BD,* vol. 11, doc. no. 340.

21. Ibid., doc. no. 385.

22. Ibid., doc. no. 383.

23. Kautsky, *German Documents,* docs. nos. 513, 540.

24. *BD,* vol. 11, doc. no. 337, minutes.

25. Kautsky, *German Documents,* doc. no. 490.

26. Ibid., docs. nos. 491, 492.

27. Pourtalès, *Am Scheidewege,* 74–75; Kautsky, *German Documents,* doc. no. 536.

28. Hoetzsch, *Imperialismus,* vol. 5, doc. no. 385.

29. Wolff, *The Eve of 1914,* 496.

30. Brock, *Asquith Letters,* letter of 31 July, n.4.

31. Randolph S. Churchill, *Winston S. Churchill,* vol. 2, *Young Statesman 1901–1914* (Boston: Houghton Mifflin, 1967), 698–99.

32. Fischer, *Krieg,* 719–20.

33. Scott, *Five Weeks,* 143–52.

34. Ibid., 170–78.

35. Ibid., 233–39.

36. Becker, *1914,* 217–18.

37. Scott, *Five Weeks,* 204.

Chapter 35: France Must Not Face Germany Alone

1. *DDF,* vol. 11, doc. no. 388 at 327.

2. Ibid., doc. no. 390.

3. *Personal Memoirs of Joffre,* 1:125.

4. Ibid., 1:119, 120, 125; Albertini, *Origins of the War,* 3:66–67.

5. *DDF,* vol. 11, doc. no. 359.

6. *BD,* vol. 11, doc. no. 310.

7. Ibid., doc. no. 342.

8. Becker, *1914,* 231.

9. Harvey Goldberg, *The Life of Jean Jaurès* (Madison, Wis.: Univ. Wisconsin Press, 1968), 470.

10. Becker, *1914,* 230.

11. *DDF,* vol. 11, doc. no. 402.

12. *Personal Memoirs of Joffre,* 1:126; Messimy, *Mes Souvenirs,* 145–46.

13. *DDF,* vol. 1, doc. no. 403.

14. Ferry, *Carnets Secrets,* 26–27.

15. Goldberg, *Jean Jaurès,* 471.

16. Kautsky, *German Documents,* doc. no. 491.

17. *DDF,* vol. 11, doc. no. 417; Kautsky, *German Documents,* doc. no. 528.

18. Poincaré Diary, 31 July; Poincaré, *Au Service,* 4:449–50.

19. Poincaré, *Au Service,* 4:448–49.

20. Albertini, *Origins of the War,* 3:75.

21. *BD,* vol. 11, doc. no. 374.

22. *DDF,* vol. 11, doc. no. 438.

23. Ibid., doc. no. 411.

24. Ibid., docs. nos. 419, 428, 431.

25. Ibid., doc. no. 432.

26. Albertini, *Origins of the War,* 3:86–87.

27. *Personal Memoirs of Joffre,* 1:126–27; Poincaré, *Au Service,* 4:474–75; Albertini, *Origins of the War,* 3:85–88.

28. *Personal Memoirs of Joffre,* 1:127.

29. *BD,* vol. 11, doc. no. 348.

30. Ibid., doc. no. 380.

31. Ibid., doc. no. 382.

32. *DDF,* vol. 11, docs. nos. 481, 484.

33. Hoetzsch, *Imperialismus,* vol. 5, doc. no. 355.

34. Ibid., doc. no. 356.

35. Poincaré Diary, 31 July; Poincaré, *Au Service,* 4:454–55.

36. See Albertini, *Origins of the War,* vol. 3, chapter 2. A good discussion but maybe a little hard on the French.

37. Paléologue, *Journal,* 318, 196–99, 304, 23 June and 8, 9, and 13 June.

38. Poincaré, *Au Service,* 4:412.

39. Quoted and translated in Albertini, *Origins of the War,* 3:81–82.

40. The general staff memorandum is discussed at p. 62–3 above.

41. *DDF,* vol. 11, docs. nos. 379, 446, 449.

Chapter 36: France Mobilizes

1. Bertie, *Diary 1914–1918,* 1.

2. Poincaré, *Au Service,* 1:301. See the portraits by Berchtold, *OUA,* vol. 1, doc. no. 629 at 492, vol. 2, 88; Hantsch, *Graf Berchtold,* 1:227; Paléologue, *Journal,* 305, 15 June,1914.

3. *LN,* 2:283–84, wire from Izvolsky dated 15/28 July 1914.

4. Hoetzsch, *Imperialismus,* vol. 5, doc. no. 354.

5. Ibid., doc. no. 356.

6. Ibid., vol. 5, doc. no. 405.

7. *BD,* vol. 11, docs. nos. 318, 373.

8. Ibid., doc. no. 352.

9. Ibid., doc. no. 320(a), (b).

10. Bertie, *Diary 1914–1918,* 4–5.

11. Ibid., 7.

12. Eubank, *Paul Cambon,* 41.

13. H. Cambon, *Un Diplomate, Paul Cambon Ambassadeur de France 1843–1924* (Paris: Plon, 1937), 3.

14. Tabouis, *Jules Cambon,* 14.

15. Cambon, *Correspondance,* 2:313, letter of 23 May.

16. Ibid., 3:30–31, letter of 6 December.

17. H. Cambon, *Paul Cambon,* 4–5.

18. Nicolson, *First Lord Carnock,* 302; Eubank, *Paul Cambon,* 63.

19. Kühlmann, *Erinnerungen,* 325–26.

20. *DDF,* vol. 4, doc. no. 627.

21. Eubank, *Paul Cambon,* 162–63.

22. *OUA,* vol. 6, docs. nos. 6971, 7230, 7231, 7292 at 608, 7441.

23. Brock, *Asquith Letters,* 138, letter of 31 July.

24. *BD,* vol. 11, doc. no. 368.

25. Ibid., doc. no. 309.

26. Kautsky, *German Documents,* doc. no. 488; *BD,* vol. 11, doc. no. 372.

27. *BD,* vol. 11, doc. no. 384.

28. Harry F. Young, "The Misunderstanding of August 1," *The Journal of Modern History,* 48, no. 4 (December 1976): 663, 665.

29. Kautsky, *German Documents,* doc. no. 562.

30. Ibid., doc. no. 570.

31. Müller, *Regierte?* 37–38; Lyncker Diary in Geiss, *Julikrise,* vol. 2, docs. nos. 889, 909, 1000(d), p.560 n.1a; Theodor Wolff, *Tagebücher 1914–1919,* ed. Bernd Soesemann, vol. 1 (Boppard am Rhein: H. Boldt, 1984), 496–97; Schilling, *How the War Began,* 76.

32. Kautsky, *German Documents,* docs. nos. 535, 536.

33. Pourtalès, *Am Scheidewege,* 70–71.

34. Kautsky, *German Documents,* docs. nos. 546, 487; Albertini, *Origins of the War,* 3:64.

35. Bethman, *Betrachtungen,* 1:156.

36. Ritter, *European Powers,* 267.

37. All of this is detailed in Kautsky, *German Documents,* doc. no. 542, nn. 5 and 6 at p.432 and nn. 3 and 4 at p.433. All the drafts are printed in the original French and in English. See Albertini, *Origins of the War,* 3:169 n.1.

38. Ritter, *European Powers,* 268; Geiss, *Julikrise,* vol. 2, doc. no. 1000(a) at 555.

39. Kautsky, *German Documents,* doc. no. 553, Supplement IV, doc. no. 28.

40. Poincaré Diary, 1 August.

41. Ibid.

42. Messimy quoted the general to that effect after the war, Recouly, *Heures Tragiques,* 84.

43. *Personal Memoirs of Joffre,* 1:124–25; Recouly, *Heures Tragiques,* 83; Albertini, *Origins of the War,* 3:99–100.

44. Poincaré, *Au Service,* 4:479.

45. René Viviani, *As We See It: France and the Truth About the War,* trans. Thomas R. Ybarra (London: Hodder and Stoughton, 1923), 184–85.

46. Kautsky, *German Documents,* doc. no. 571.

47. *DDF,* vol. 11, doc. no. 505.

48. Ibid.

49. Poincaré, *Au Service*, 4:579; Poincaré Diary, 1 August.

50. *Personal Memoirs of Joffre*, 1:127–28.

51. *BD*, vol. 11, doc. no. 384.

52. Ibid., doc. no. 403.

53. *DDF*, vol. 11, doc. no. 490.

54. Ibid., doc. no. 506.

55. *Personal Memoirs of Joffre*, 1:128.

56. Poincaré, *Au Service*, 4:483–86.

57. Recouly, *Heures Tragiques*, 86; Albertini, *Origins of the War*, 3:108.

Chapter 37: The British Are Not Coming In!

1. Wolff, *The Eve of 1914*, 503–4.

2. Kautsky, *German Documents*, doc. no. 543.

3. Falkenhayn diary quoted in Albertini, *Origins of the War*, 3:169. Five accounts of this series of Saturday meetings are collected in Geiss, *Julikrise*, vol. 2, docs..nos. 1000(a)–(e).

4. Tirpitz, *Erinnerungen*, 276–77; Albertini, *Origins of the War*, 3:192; Tirpitz, *Ohnmachtspolitik*, 16.

5. Wolff, *The Eve of 1914*, 504.

6. Tirpitz, *Ohnmachtspolitik*, 16–17; Geiss, *Julikrise*, vol. 2, doc. no. 1000(e); Albertini, *Origins of the War*, 3:171.

7. Wolff, *The Eve of 1914*, 504.

8. Kautsky, *German Documents*, doc. no. 562.

9. See the comment of Marshall, *World War I*, 49.

10. Müller, *Regierte?* 38–39.

11. Moltke, *Erinnerungen*, 21; Albertini, *Origins of the War*, 3:172–74.

12. Moltke, *Erinnerungen*, 21; Geiss, *Julikrise*, vol. 2, doc. no. 1000(a); Tirpitz, *Ohnmachtspolitik*, 17–19; Albertini, *Origins of the War*, 3:171–74.

13. Kautsky, *German Documents*, doc. no. 570.

14. Müller, *Regierte?* 39; Geiss, *Julikrise*, vol. 2, doc. no. 1000(d).

15. Kautsky, *German Documents*, doc. no. 578.

16. Ibid., doc. no. 575.

17. Ibid., doc. no. 579.

18. *DDF*, vol. 11, doc. no. 523.

19. Kautsky, *German Documents*, docs. nos. 598, 571, 543.

20. *DDF*, vol. 11, doc. no. 507.

21. Kautsky, *German Documents*, doc. no. 590; Tirpitz, *Ohnmachtspolitik*, 20.

22. Kautsky, *German Documents*, doc. no. 571.

23. Ibid., doc. no. 587.

24. Müller, *Regierte?* 38–39.

25. Moltke, *Erinnerungen,* 21–22.

26. Kautsky, *German Documents,* doc. no. 546.

27. Ibid., docs. nos. 599, 600.

28. Wolff, *The Eve of 1914,* 506–7.

29. Kautsky, *German Documents,* doc. no. 601.

30. *DAV,* vol. 3, doc. no. 105, quoted in Albertini, *Origins of the War,* 3:176–77.

31. Kautsky, *German Documents,* doc. no. 612.

32. Ibid., doc. no. 596.

33. Moltke, *Erinnerungen,* 23, x–xi.

34. Wilson, *Policy of the Entente,* 140–41.

35. Brock, *Asquith Letters,* 40, letter of 1 August.

36. Grey, *Twenty-Five Years,* 2:66–68.

37. Quoted in Hazlehurst, *Politicians At War,* 90. The whole issue is discussed in ibid., 87–91.

38. Ibid., 90–91.

39. R. S. Churchill, *Young Statesman,* 703.

40. Brock, *Asquith Letters,* 146, letter of 2 August.

41. Wilson, *Policy of the Entente,* 136–37.

42. Brock, *Asquith Letters,* 139–41, letter of 1 August.

43. Young, "The Misunderstanding of August 1," 650 n.26; Hazlehurst, *Politicians At War,* 82 n.1.

44. Morley, *Memorandum on Resignation,* 13.

45. Young, "The Misunderstanding of August 1," 663; ———, *Prince Lichnowsky,* 115.

46. Kautsky, *German Documents,* doc. no. 596.

47. *BD,* vol. 11, docs. nos. 426, 447.

48. Quoted from Gen. Sir H. H. Wilson's diary in Hazlehurst, *Politicians At War,* 88.

49. Nicolson, *First Lord Carnock,* 304.

50. Nicolson to Hardinge, 5 September 1914, Lowe and Dockrill, *The Mirage of Power,* vol. 3, doc. no. 76 at 492.

51. Nicolson, *First Lord Carnock,* 304–5; *BD,* vol. 11, doc. no. 424.

52. *DDF,* vol. 11, doc. no. 532.

53. *BD,* vol. 11, doc. no. 419.

54. Ibid., doc. no. 453.

55. Ibid., doc. no. 460.

56. Kautsky, *German Documents,* doc. no. 612; Harold Nicolson, *King George the Fifth: His Life and Reign,* (London: Constable, 1952), 328–29.

Chapter 38: Germany Declares War on Russia

1. Buchanan, *My Mission to Russia,* 205; *BD,* vol. 11, doc. no. 665 at 345. See the discussion in Albertini, *Origins of the War,* 3:128–38.

2. Buchanan, *My Mission to Russia,* 195 (25 July), 196 (26 July), 197 (28 July).

3. *BD,* vol. 11, doc. no. 384.

4. *DDF,* vol. 11, doc. no. 536.

5. Schilling, *How the War Began,* 77; Sazonov, *Fateful Years,* 212–13.

6. Sazonov, *Fateful Years,* 212–13.

7. Pourtalès, *Am Scheidewege,* 86–88.

8. Kautsky, *German Documents,* doc. no. 588 n.5. This wire never arrived in Berlin.

9. *BD,* vol. 11, doc. no. 665 at 345–46.

10. Ibid., doc. no. 490.

11. Schilling, *How the War Began,* 80.

12. Hoetzsch, *Imperialismus,* vol. 5, docs. nos. 418, 433; Geiss, *Julikrise,* vol. 2, doc. no. 1033.

13. Kautsky, *German Documents,* doc. no. 600.

14. Ibid., doc. no. 666.

15. *DDF,* vol. 11, doc. no. 582.

16. Poincaré, *Au Service,* 4:495.

17. Hoetzsch, *Imperialismus,* vol. 5, doc. no. 409; Geiss, *Julikrise,* vol. 2, doc. no. 1031.

18. Hoetzsch, *Imperialismus,* vol. 5, doc. no. 412.

19. Poincaré, *Au Service,,* 4:496.

20. This account of the meeting is based on a memorandum Tirpitz claims to have written immediately afterward, Tirpitz, *Ohnmachtspolitik,* 20–21.

21. Ibid., 14; Bülow, *Memoirs,* 3:162–63; Albertini, *Origins of the War,* 3:201.

22. Tirpitz, *Ohnmachtspolitik,* 21–22.

23. Bethmann's critics often taxed him with this label, Jarausch, *Enigmatic Chancellor,* 150.

Chapter 39: Belgium and Britain

1. Albertini, *Origins of the War,* 3:413.

2. *DDF,* vol. 11, doc. no. 551.

3. Ibid., doc. no. 178.

4. *BD,* vol. 8, doc. no. 326.

5. Ibid., doc. no. 311.

6. Grey, *Twenty-Five Years,* 2:3–7.

7. *BD,* vol. 8, doc. no. 324.

8. *DDF,* vol. 11, doc. no. 229 at 191, doc. no. 373 at 310.

9. Ibid., doc. no. 372 at 308–9.

10. Quoted in Albertini, *Origins of the War,* 3:445.

11. *BD,* vol. 11, doc. no. 466.

12. *DDF,* vol. 11, doc. 563.

13. Ibid., doc. no. 579.

14. Ibid.

15. Quoted in Albertini, *Origins of the War,* 3:401.

16. Kautsky, *German Documents,* docs. nos. 641, 669.

17. Beyens, *Deux Années,* 257–60, 31 July.

18. Belgian Grey Book, doc. no. 2, in *CDD,* 300–301.

19. Beyens, *Deux Années,* 260–62, 1 August.

20. Kautsky, *German Documents,* doc. no. 656.

21. *BD,* vol. 11, doc. no. 351.

22. Ibid., doc. no. 476.

23. The following portrait of Grey during the last days of the July crisis follows Steiner, *Britain and the Origins,* 227–41.

24. *Richard Burdon Haldane: An Autobiography* (New York: Doubleday, Doran, 1929), 292.

25. Grey, *Twenty-Five Years,* 1:327–28.

26. Ibid., 328.

27. Quotes in Hazlehurst, *Politicians At War,* 35–39.

28. Quoted in ibid., 39.

29. Lowe and Dockrill, *Mirage of Power,* vol. 3, doc. no. 77 at 490.

30. Quoted in Hazlehurst, *Politicians At War,* 58–59.

31. Quoted in Wilson, *Policy of the Entente,* 144.

32. M. G. Ekstein and Z. Steiner, "The Sarajevo Crisis," in Hinsley, *British Foreign Policy,* 405; Albertini, *Origins of the War,* 3:396–99.

33. See, particularly, Wilson, *Policy of the Entente,* chapter 8; Hazlehurst, *Politicians At War,* 66–117.

34. Pease diary, 2 August 1914, in Hazlehurst, *Politicians At War,* 66.

35. Kautsky, *German Documents,* doc. no. 641.

36. Brock, *Asquith Letters,* 146, letter of 2 August.

37. Kautsky, *German Documents,* docs. nos. 676, 641.

38. Hazlehurst, *Politicians At War,* 91.

39. There are a number of accounts of the meeting: Samuel in Lowe and Dockrill, *Mirage of Power,* vol. 3, doc. no. 77; Runciman and Pease in Hazlehurst, *Politicians At War,* 92–94; Morley, *Memorandum on Resignation,* 10–14; Asquith in Brock, *Asquith Letters,* 145–47, letter of 2 August.

40. Pease diary, in Hazlehurst, *Politicians At War,* 95.

41. *BD,* vol. 10, part II, doc. no. 416.

42. Morley, *Memorandum on Resignation,* 18.

43. Hazlehurst, *Politicians At War,* 95.

44. Runciman's emphasis, ibid., 93.

45. Samuel, in Lowe and Dockrill, *Mirage of Power,* vol. 3, doc. no. 77.

46. Ibid., 489–91.

47. Hazlehurst, *Politicians At War,* 93, 94–96.

Chapter 40: The German Invasion of Belgium

1. Kautsky, *German Documents,* docs. nos. 637, 638.

2. Ibid., doc. no. 640.

3. Ibid., doc. no. 643.

4. Ibid., doc. no. 730.

5. Ibid., doc. no. 662.

6. Brock, *Asquith Letters,* 146, letter of 2 August.

7. *BD,* vol. 11, doc. no. 369.

8. Morley, *Memorandum on Resignation,* 14–16, 17; Hazlehurst, *Politicians At War,* 67.

9. Hazlehurst, *Politicians At War,* 96.

10. *BD,* vol. 11, docs. nos. 487 at 275, 488, 495; *DDF,* vol. 11, doc. no. 612 at 469.

11. *BD,* vol. 11, doc. no. 395.

12. *DDF,* vol. 11, doc. no. 612.

13. Letter of 2 August, Lowe and Dockrill, *Mirage of Power,* vol. 3, doc. no. 77 at 490; Hazlehurst, *Politicians At War,* 97–98.

14. Quotes in Hazlehurst, *Politicians At War,* 98.

15. *The Riddell Diaries* ed. J. M. McEwan (London: Athlone Press, 1986), 87, entry for 2 August.

16. W. S. Churchill, *World Crisis,* 114–15. There are slight variations in the text in the many editions of this work.

17. Steiner, *Britain and the Origins,* 237.

18. Quoted in Hazlehurst, *Politicians At War,* 100.

19. *DDF,* vol. 11, doc. no. 596.

20. Ibid., doc. no. 638.

21. Kautsky, *German Documents,* docs. nos. 691, 706, 707.

22. Ibid., doc. no. 376.

23. Ibid., doc. no. 375.

24. Ibid., doc. no. 648.

25. Albertini, *Origins of the War,* 3:453.

26. Quoted in ibid., 450.

27. Kautsky, *German Documents,* doc. no. 376.

28. Ibid., doc. no. 648.

29. This paragraph follows the accounts quoted in Albertini, *Origins of the War,* 3:456.

30. Ibid., 455–63, has an excellent account of the Belgian response.

31. Kautsky, *German Documents,* doc. no. 709.

32. Albertini, *Origins of the War,* 3:464.

33. Kautsky, *German Documents,* docs. nos. 735, 779.

34. Ibid., docs. nos. 677, 682, 693.

35. Ibid., docs. nos. 690, 710.

36. Ibid., doc. no. 689.

37. Ibid., doc. no. 713.

38. Ibid., doc. no. 731.

39. Ibid., docs. nos. 742, 744.

40. Albertini, *Origins of the War,* 3:466.

41. *DDF,* vol. 11, doc. no. 644.

42. *BD,* vol. 11, docs. nos. 521, 561.

43. Ibid., doc. no. 551; *DDF,* vol. 11, docs. nos. 664, 676; Albertini, *Origins of the War,* 3:467.

44. Hoetzsch, *Imperialismus,* vol. 5, doc. no. 498.

45. *DDF,* vol. 11, docs. nos. 680, 687.

46. *BD,* vol. 11, doc. no. 562.

47. Quoted in Albertini, *Origins of the War,* 3:464.

48. Kautsky, *German Documents,* doc. no. 779 at 554.

49. *DDF,* vol. 11, doc. no. 773 at 565.

50. Kautsky, *German Documents,* doc. no. 693.

51. Ibid., doc. no. 696.

52. *BD,* vol. 11, doc. no. 471.

53. Kautsky, *German Documents,* doc. no. 664.

54. *DAV,* vol. 3, doc. no. 114; Geiss, *Julikrise,* vol. 2, doc. no. 1105.

55. Dirr, *Bayerische Dokumente,* doc. no. 80.

56. Ibid., doc. no. 78; Geiss, *Julikrise,* vol. 2, doc. no. 1090.

57. Messimy, *Mes Souvenirs,* 151–52.

58. *Personal Memoirs of Joffre,* 1:132–33.

59. Poincaré Diary, 1 August.

Chapter 41: Ringing Bells and Wringing Hands

1. Paléologue, *Memoirs,* 1:51–52; *DDF,* vol. 11, doc. no. 623.

2. Scott, *Five Weeks,* 93–94; Brock, *Asquith Letters,* 144, 148, letter of 1 August.

3. Morley, *Memorandum on Resignation,* 25; Hazlehurst, *Politicians At War,* 114–15.

4. *Diaries of C. P. Scott,* 94, telegram of 3 August.

5. Brock, *Asquith Letters,* 148, letter of 3 August.

6. Watt, "The British Reactions to the Assassination at Sarajevo," 246–47.

7. The London *Daily News* quoted in Lloyd George, *War Memoirs,* 1:41.

8. Brock, *Asquith Letters,* 148, letter of 3 August.

9. Trevelyan, *Grey,* 298–99.

10. Grey's speech is given verbatim in Grey, *Twenty-Five Years,* Appendix D, 2:308–26, and Sir Edward Grey, *Speeches on Foreign Affairs 1904–1914,* ed. Paul Knaplund (London: Allen & Unwin, 1931), 297–313. It is analyzed at length in Trevelyan, *Grey,* 299–303; Hazlehurst, *Politicians At War,* 43–48.

11. *DDF,* vol. 11, doc. no. 711.

12. Quoted in Hazlehurst, *Politicians At War,* 44.

13. Ibid., 46.

14. Brock, *Asquith Letters,* 148, letter of 3 August. Emphasis in original.

15. *DDF,* vol. 11, doc. no. 690.

16. Ibid., doc. no. 712.

17. Trevelyan, *Grey,* 302.

18. Kautsky, *German Documents,* doc. no. 734.

19. Ibid., doc. no. 716.

20. Ibid., docs. nos. 734A, B, C.

21. Schoen, *Memoirs of an Ambassador,* 201–4; Poincaré, *Au Service,* 4:521–22.

22. Beyens, *Deux Années,* 267.

23. Ibid., 266–73.

24. Conrad, *Dienstzeit,* 4:166–74.

25. Hoetzsch, *Imperialismus,* vol. 5, doc. no. 496.

26. Ibid., doc. no. 495.

27. *BD,* vol. 11, doc. no. 582.

28. *DAV,* vol. 3, doc. no. 119.

29. Ibid., doc. no. 154.

30. Kautsky, *German Documents,* doc. no. 814.

31. Wolff, *The Eve of 1914,* 514.

32. Jarausch, *Enigmatic Chancellor,* 179. The full text of Bethmann's 4 August address is in Geiss, *Julikrise,* vol. 2, doc. no. 1146.

33. Kautsky, *German Documents,* doc. no. 869.

34. Quoted in Wolff, *The Eve of 1914,* 516; Jarausch, *Enigmatic Chancellor*, 178.

35. Wolff, *The Eve of 1914,* 516.

36. Poincaré, *Au Service,* 4:534–35.

37. Ibid., 542–48.

Chapter 42: Great Britain Goes To War

1. Tirpitz, *Ohnmachtspolitik,* 25; Kautsky, *German Documents,* doc. no. 714.

2. Kautsky, *German Documents,* docs. nos. 788, 804, 807.

3. Ibid., docs. nos. 805, 806, 810.

4. *BD,* vol. 11, doc. no. 573.

5. Ibid., doc. no. 580.

6. Brock, *Asquith Letters,* 150, 151, letter of 4 August.

7. *BD,* vol. 11, doc. no. 666; Kautsky, *German Documents,* doc. no. 823 n.2; Wolff, *The Eve of 1914,* 517.

8. *BD,* vol. 11, doc. no. 671 at 350–51; Gottlieb von Jagow, *Ursachen und Ausbruch des Weltkrieges* (Berlin: Hobbing, 1919), 172.

9. *BD,* vol. 11, doc. no. 671 at 351–52.

10. Quoted in Jarausch, *Enigmatic Chancellor,* 176.

11. Ibid.

12. Bethmann, *Betrachtungen,* 1:179–80 n.1.

13. *BD,* vol. 11, doc. no. 671 at 352–53.

14. *DAV,* vol. 3, doc. no. 131.

15. Brock, *Asquith Letters,* 157, letter of 5 August.

16. Burton J. Hendrick, *The Life and Letters of Walter H. Page,* 3 vols. (New York: Doubleday, 1924), 1:306.

17. Quoted in Young, *Prince Lichnowsky,* 126–27. Emphasis in the original.

18. Hendrick, *Walter H. Page,* 1:306–9.

19. *DDF,* vol. 11, doc. no. 754.

20. Brock, *Asquith Letters,* 158, letter of 6 August.

Chapter 43: Finally, Austria

1. Albertini, *Origins of the War,* 3:529–30.

2. Kautsky, *German Documents,* doc. no. 704.

3. *DAV,* vol. 3, doc. no. 124; Albertini, *Origins of the War,* 3:532.

4. *OUA,* vol. 8, doc. no. 11204; Norman Stone, "Moltke and Conrad," in Kennedy, *War Plans,* 235.

5. Stone, *Eastern Front,* 76; ———, "Die Mobilmachung der österreich-ungarischen Armee 1914," 67–95.

6. Stone, "Moltke and Conrad," in Kennedy, *War Plans,* 240–41.

7. *BD,* vol. 11, doc. no. 582.

8. Hoetzsch, *Imperialismus,* vol. 5, doc. no. 419 at 263.

9. *DDF,* vol. 11, doc. no. 795 at 597.

10. Ibid., doc. no. 747.

11. *BD,* vol. 11, doc. no. 618; *DAV,* vol. 3, docs. nos. 131, 132, 156.

12. Kautsky, *German Documents,* docs. nos. 870, 874; *DAV,* vol. 3, doc. no. 138.

13. *DAV,* vol. 3, doc. no. 135; Kautsky, *German Documents,* docs. nos. 877, 878; Conrad, *Dienstzeit,* 4:174.

14. *DAV,* vol. 3, doc. no. 147.

15. Ibid., doc. no. 151.

16. Ibid., docs. nos. 152, 153.

17. *BD,* vol. 11, doc. no. 659.

18. *DAV,* vol. 3, doc. no. 143.

19. *DAV,* vol. 3, doc. no. 156.

20. Blue Books were official reports from the government to Parliament. The British foreign office put out a Blue Book on the July crisis immediately after the declaration of war on 4 August.

21. *DAV,* vol. 3, doc. no. 159.

22. *DDF,* vol. 10, doc. no. 462 at 663; Dumaine, *La Derniére Ambassade,* 108, 226–28.

23. Dumaine, *La Derniére Ambassade,* 29.

24. Ibid., 21–22.

25. *DDF,* vol. 11, docs. nos. 701, 756, 772.

26. *DAV,* vol. 3, docs. nos. 163, 165; *DDF,* vol. 11, doc. no. 780.

27. *DAV,* vol. 3, docs. nos. 168, 169, 170.

28. Ibid., docs. nos. 171, 172.

29. Ibid., doc. no. 173.

30. Ibid., doc. no. 174.

31. *DDF,* vol. 11, doc. no. 792; *DAV,* vol. 3, doc. no. 175.

32. *BD,* vol. 11, doc. no. 672.

33. Ibid., doc. no. 676 at 357.

34. *DAV,* vol. 3, doc. no. 176; Albertini, *Origins of the War,* 3:544.

35. *DDF,* vol. 11, doc. no. 791.

Chapter 44: We Had No Choice

1. Dedijer, *Road to Sarajevo,* 446.

2. Berchtold diary, 4 and 10 September 1914, in Hantsch, *Graf Berchtold,* 2:828–29; *OUA,* vol. 8, doc. no. 10459.

3. Hantsch, *Graf Berchtold,* 2:826–41, describes Berchtold's last years.

4. Conrad, *Dienstzeit,* 4:118.

5. Sazonov, *Fateful Years,* 175, 182, 196.

6. Kennan, *Fateful Alliance,* 39.

7. Quoted in Lieven, *Russia,* 147.

8. Basiley, *Diplomat of Imperial Russia,* 99.

9. William II *The Kaiser's Memoirs,* Thomas R. Ybarra, trans. (1922, Reprint. New York: Harper, 1976), 289.

10. Quoted in John C. G. Röhl, "The emperor's new clothes: a character sketch of Kaiser Wilhelm II," in Röhl and Sombart, *Kaiser Wilhelm II,* 29.

11. Jagow, *Ursachen,* 146.

12. Bethmann, *Betrachtungen,* 1:13.

13. Quotes from Jarausch, *Enigmatic Chancellor,* 148–49.

14. Rheinbaben, *Kaiser Kanzler Presidenten,* 96.

15. Young, *Prince Lichnowski,* 186.

16. Quoted in ibid., viii. Emphasis in the original.

17. Poincaré, *Au Service,* 4:408, 532–33; Hoetzsch, *Imperialismus,* vol. 5, docs. nos. 289–91.

18. Paléologue, *Guillame et Nicolas II,* 213–14.

19. Lloyd George, *War Memoirs,* 1:42–44.

20. Herbert Henry Asquith, *The Genesis of the War* (London: Cassell, 1923), 311.

21. Ibid., 315.

22. Grey, talking to Ambassador Page, Hendrick, *Walter H. Page,* 1:313–14.

23. Asquith, *Genesis of the War,* 104–5.

24. Ibid., 93; Grey, *Twenty-Five Years,* 1:154, 160, 245.

25. Paul W. Schroeder, "World War I as Galloping Gertie," *Journal of Modern History,* 44, no. 3 (September 1972): 335, 345.

26. Kennan, *Fateful Alliance,* xiii–xiv.

27. Scott, *Five Weeks,* 12.

28. Grey, *Twenty-Five Years,* 2:15–16.

29. Bethmann, *Betrachtungen,* 1:133.

30. Sazonov, *Fateful Years,* 204.

31. Leonard Levi, ed. *Emotional Stress.* Paper delivered at Proceedings of an International Symposium arranged by the Swedish Delegation for Applied Medical Defense Research, Stockholm, 5–6 February 1965 (New York: American Elsevier Publishing Co., 1967), 23.

Bibliography

Toscano, Mario. *The History of Treaties and International Politics.* vol. 1, *The Documentary and Memoir Sources.* Baltimore: John Hopkins Press, 1966. A useful guide to the published document and memoir sources up to 1965.

I. Published Document Collections
Bach, August, ed. *Deutsche Gesandtschaftsberichte zum Kriegsausbruch.* Berlin: Commissioned by the Auswärtiges Amtes, 1937.

Benckendorff, Count Alexander von. *Graf Benckendorffs Diplomatischer Schriftswechsel.* 3 vols. Benno von Siebert, ed., Berlin; Leipzig: De Gruyter, 1928.

Berghahn, V. R., and Wilhelm Diest. "Kaiserliche Marine und Kriegsausbruch, 1914. Neue Dokumente zur Juli-Krise." *Militärgeschictthliche Mitteilungen* 7 (1/1970): 37–58.

British Documents on the Origins of the War (1898–1914). 11 vols. G. P. Gooch and Harold Temperley, eds. London: Foreign Office, 1926–38. *(BD)*

Collected Diplomatic Documents Relating to the Outbreak of the European War. London, 1915. A collection of the so-called color books. *(CDD)*

Grosse Politik der Europäischen Kabinette, Die 1871–1914 39 vols. Sammlung der diplomatischen Akten des Auswärtigen Amtes. Joh. Lepsius, A. Mendel-ssohn-Bartholdy, and Fr. Thimme, eds. Berlin, 1922–27. *(GP)*

Diplomatische Aktenstücke zur Vorgeschichte des Krieges 1914. 3 vols. Vienna: Deutsche Verlagsgesellschaft für Politik und Geschichte in Berlin, 1919. *(DAV)*

Dirr, Pius, ed. *Bayerische Dokumente zum Kriegsausbruch und zum Versailler Schuldspruch.* 3d ed. Munich, 1925.

Documents Diplomatiques Francais (1871–1914). 11 vols. Ministère des Affaires Etrangères. Commission de Publication des Documents Relatifs aux Origins de la Guerre de 1914, 3d series. Paris, 1936. *(DDF)*

Geiss, Immanuel, ed. *Julikrise und Kriegsausbruch 1914. Eine Dokumentsammlung.* 2 vols. Hannover: Verlag für Literatur und Zeitgeschehen, 1963–64.

———. *July 1914.* New York: Norton, 1967. English translations of documents selected from Geiss's *Julikrise.*

Hoetzsch, Otto, ed. *Die Internationalen Beziehungen im Zeitalter des Imperialismus.* Dokumente aus den Archiven der Zarischen und der

Provisorischen Regierung. 1st series, vols. 4, 5. German ed. Berlin: Oxford Univ. Press, 1931–34.

Kautsky, Karl, ed. *Outbreak of the World War: German Documents Collected by Karl Kautsky*. Translated by Carnegie Foundation for International Peace. New York: Oxford Univ. Press, 1924. This is a one-volume English translation of *Die Deutschen Dokumente zum Kriegsausbruch*. Karl Kautsky, Walter Schücking, and Max Montegelas, eds. 3 vols. Berlin, 1919.

Un Livre Noir. Diplomatie d'avant guerre d'après les documents des Archives Russes. 3 vols. Paris: Librairi du Travail, 1923–32. (*LN*)

Official German Documents Relating to the War. Translated by Carnegie Foundation for International Peace. New York: Carnegie Foundation, 1923.

Österreich-Ungarns Aussenpolitik von der Bosnischen Krise 1908 bis zum Kriegsausbruch 1914. 8 vols. Diplomatische Aktenstücke des Österreichisch-Ungarischen Ministerium des Aussern. Ludwig Bittner, Alfred Pribram, Heinrich Srbik, and Hans Übersberger, eds. Vienna, 1930. (*OUA*)

Pribram, Albert Francis, ed. *The Secret Treaties of Austria-Hungary 1879–1914*. Vol. 1, *Texts of the Treaties and Agreements*. London: Harvard Univ. Press, 1920.

Vernadsky, G., and Ralph T. Fisher, Jr., eds. *A Source Book for Russian History from Early Times to 1917*. Vol. 3, *Alexander II to the February Revolution*. New Haven and London: Yale Univ. Press, 1972.

II. Letters, Diaries, Memoirs

Alexander. *Once A Grand Duke*. New York, Garden City: Farrar & Rinehart, 1932.

Asquith, Herbert Henry. *The Genesis of the War*. London: Cassell, 1923.

Asquith, Margot. *An Autobiography*. Vol. 1. New York: George H. Doran, 1922.

Baernreither, Joseph M. *Fragmente Eines Politischen Tagebuches*. Joseph Redlich, ed. Berlin: Verlag für Kulturpolitik, 1928.

Basiley, Nicolas de (Nicolai Basili). *Diplomat of Imperial Russia 1903–1917*. Stanford: Hoover Institution, 1973.

Benouville, M., and A. Kaznakov, eds. *Journal Intime de Nicolas II (Juillet 1914–Juillet 1918)*. Paris: Payot, 1934.

Bertie of Thame, Francis Leverson. *Diary 1914–1918*. Vol. 1. Lady Algernon Gordon Lennox, ed. London: Hodder & Stoughton, 1924.

Bethmann-Hollweg, Theodor von. *Betrachtungen zum Weltkrieg*. 2 vols. Berlin: Hobbing, 1919–21.

Beyens, Baron. *Deux Années A Berlin 1912–1914*. 2 vols. Paris: Plon, 1931.

Bing, Edward J., ed. *The Secret Letters of the Last Tsar: The Confidential*

Correspondence between Nicholas II and His Mother, Dowager Empress Marie Fedorovina. New York: Longmans, Green, 1938.

Boghitschewitsch, M., ed. *Die Auswärtige Politik Serbiens 1903–1914.* 3 vols. Berlin: Brückenverlag, 1928–31.

Botkin, Gleb. *The Real Romanovs.* New York: Fleming H. Revell, 1931.

Brock, Michael, and Eleanor Brock, eds. *H. H. Asquith Letters to Venetia Stanley.* Oxford: Oxford Univ. Press, 1982.

Buchanan, George. *My Mission to Russia and Other Diplomatic Memories.* Boston: Little, Brown, 1923.

Bülow, Bernhard von. *Memoirs of Prince von Bülow.* 4 vols. Translated by Geoffrey Dunlop. Boston: Little, Brown, 1931.

Cambon, Paul. *Correspondance 1870–1924.* 3 vols. Paris: Grasset, 1940–46.

Class, Heinrich. *Wider den Strom.* Leipzig: Koehler, 1932.

Conrad, Franz von Hötzendorff. *Aus Meiner Dienstzeit, 19061918.* 5 vols. Vienna: Rikola, 1922–25.

Cormons, Ernest U. *Schicksale und Schatten.* Salzburg: Müller Verlag, 1951.

Czernin, Ottokar. *Im Weltkrieg.* Berlin; Vienna: Ullstein Verlag, 1919.

Danilov, Youri. *La Russie dans la Guerre Mondiale (1914–1917).* Paris: Payot, 1927.

Dobrolski, Sergei. *Die Mobilmachung der russischen Armee 1914.* Beiträge zur Schuldfrage, vol. 1. Berlin, 1922.

Dumaine, Alfred. *La Derniére Ambassade de France en Autriche.* Paris: Plon, 1921.

Esher, Reginald. *The Captains and the Kings Depart.* Oliver, Viscount Esher, ed. New York: Scribner's, 1938.

Ferry, Abel. *Les Carnets Secrets (1914–1918).* Paris: Grasset, 1957.

Giesl, Wladimir. *Zwei Jahrzehnte im Nahen Orient.* R. von Steinitz, ed. Berlin: Verlag für Kulturpolitik, 1927.

Gilliard, Pierre. *Treize Années A La Cour de Russie.* Paris: Payot, 1921.

Goschen, Edward. *The Diary of Edward Goschen 1900–1914.* Christopher H. D. Goschen, ed. London: Royal Historical Society, 1980.

Grey, Sir Edward. *Speeches on Foreign Affairs 1904–1914.* Paul Knaplund, ed. London: Allen & Unwin, 1931.

Grey of Fallodon, Viscount. *Twenty-Five Years.* 2 vols. New York: Frederick A. Stokes, 1925.

Haldane, Richard Burdon. *Richard Burdon Haldane: An Autobiography.* New York: Doubleday, Doran, 1929.

Hoyos, Alexander. *Der deutsch-englische Gegensatz und sein Einfluss auf die Balkanpolitik Österreich-Ungarns.* Berlin: de Gruyter, 1922.

Izvolsky, Alexander. *Recollections of a Foreign Minister.* New York: Doubleday, 1921.

Jagow, Gottlieb von. *Ursachen und Ausbruch des Weltkrieges*. Berlin: Hobbing, 1919.

Joffre, Joseph L. *The Personal Memoirs of Joffre Field Marshal of the French Army*. Translated by Col. T. Bentley Mott. 2 vols. New York; London: Harper & Bros., 1932.

Kühlmann, Richard. *Erinnerungen*. Heidelberg: Schneider, 1948.

Lichnowsky, Prince Karl Max. *Heading for the Abyss*. New York: Payson and Clarke, 1928.

Lloyd George, David. *War Memoirs*. 2d ed. 2 vols. London: Odhams Press, 1938.

Ludendorff, Erich. *The General Staff and Its Problems*. Translated by F. A. Holt. London: Hutchinson, 1921.

Lützow, Heinrich. *Im diplomatischen Dienst der k.u.k. Monarchie*. P. Hohenbaken, ed. Vienna: Verlag für Geschichte und Politik, 1971.

Margutti, Albert von. *Kaiser Franz Joseph: Persönliche Erinnerungen*. Vienna; Leipzig: Rhombus, 1924. Margutti wrote an earlier English edition, *The Emperor Francis Joseph and His Time*. London: Hutchinson, 1921. This has minor variations in the description of incidents.

Messimy, Adolphe. *Mes Souvenirs*. Paris: Plon, 1937.

Moltke, Helmuth von. *Erinnerungen, Briefe und Dokumente 1877–1916*. Eliza von Moltke, ed. Stuttgart: Der kommende Tag, 1922.

Morley, John. *Memorandum on Resignation August 1914*. New York: Macmillan, 1928.

Müller, Georg Alexander. *Der Kaiser: Aus den Tagebüchern des Chefs des Marinekabinetts Admiral Georg Alexander von Müller*. Walter Görlitz, ed. Göttingen; Berlin: Musterschmidt, 1965.

———. *Regierte der Kaiser?* 2d ed. Walter Görlitz, ed. Göttingen; Berlin: Musterschmidt, 1959.

Paléologue, Maurice. *An Ambassador's Memoirs*. 3 vols. Translated by F. A. Holt. 1923. New York: Octagon, 1972.

———. *Au Quai d'Orsay a la Veille de la Tourmente: Journal 1913–1914*. Paris: Plon, 1947.

———. *Guillaume II et Nicolas II*. Paris: Plon, 1935.

Peball, Kurt. "Briefe an eine Freundin." *Mitteilungen des Österreichischen Staatsarchivs*, 25 (1972): 492–503.

Poincaré, Raymond. *Au Service de la France*. 10 vols. Paris: Plon, 1926–33.

Poincaré Diary. Bibliotheque Nationale: Papiers Poincaré, Volume XXXVI, Notes Journaliéres, Mars–Août 1914. Fonds: Nouvelles Acquisition Francaises, No. 16027. I worked from a typewritten transcript that was generously lent to me by Professor Arno Mayer of Princeton University.

Pourtalès, Friedrich von. *Am Scheidewege zwischen Krieg und Frieden*. Charlottenberg: Deutsche Verlagsgesellschaft für Politik und Geschichte, 1919.

Radziwill, M. D. Elizabeth, ed. *Lettres de la Princesse Radziwill au Général de Robilant 1889–1914.* 4 vols. Bologna: Zanichelli, 1934.

Redlich, Joseph. *Schicksaljahre Österreichs: Das politische Tagebuch Joseph Redlichs.* 2 vols. Fritz Fellner, ed. Graz: Verlag Hermann Böhlhaus Nachf., 1953.

Rheinbaben, Werner von. *Kaiser Kanzler Präsidenten.* Mainz: Hase & Koehler, 1968.

Riddell, Sir George. *The Riddell Diaries.* J. M. McEwan, ed. London: Athlone Press, 1986.

Riezler, Kurt. *Tagebücher-Aufsätze-Dokumente.* Karl Dietrich Erdmann, ed. Deutsche Geschichtsquellen des 19. und 20. Jahrhunderts, vol. 48. Göttingen: Vandenhoeck & Ruprecht, 1972.

Rosen, Romanovic. *Forty Years of Diplomacy.* 2 vols. London: Allen and Unwin, 1922.

Rumbold, Sir Horace. *The War Crisis in Berlin July–August 1914.* London: Constable, 1940.

Sazonov, Serge. *Fateful Years 1909–1916.* New York: Frederick A. Stokes, 1928.

Schilling, Maurice Fabian. *How the War Began in 1914.* (Diary.) Translated by W. Cyprian Bridge. London: Allen and Unwin, 1925. Much of this diary is duplicated in Hoetzsch, *Imperialismus.*

Schoen, Wilhelm Eduard von. *The Memoirs of an Ambassador.* Translated by Constance Vesey. New York: Brentano's, 1923.

Scott, C. P. *The Political Diaries of C. P. Scott 1911–1918.* Trevor Wilson, ed. Ithaca, N.Y.: Cornell Univ. Press, 1970.

Sieghart, Rudolf. *Die Letzte Jahrzehnte einer Grossmacht.* Berlin: Ullstein Verlag, 1932.

Spitzemberg, Baroness. *Das Tagebuch der Baronin Spitzemberg.* Rudolf Vierhaus, ed. Göttingen: Vanderhoeck & Ruprecht, 1960.

Sukhomlinov, W. A. *Erinnerungen.* Berlin: R. Hobbing, 1924.

Tirpitz, Alfred von. *Erinnerungen.* Leipzig: Koehler, 1919.

———. *Politische Dokumente.* Vol. 2, *Deutsche Ohnmachtspolitik im Weltkriege.* Hamburg: Hanseatische Verlagsanstalt, 1926.

Vansittart, Robert. *The Mist Procession.* London: Hutchinson, 1959.

Viviani, René. *As We See It. France and the Truth About the War.* Translated by Thomas R. Ybarra. London: Hodder and Stoughton, 1923.

William II. *The Kaiser's Memoirs.* Translated by Thomas R. Ybarra. 1922. Reprint. New York: Harper, 1976.

Wolff, Theodor. *The Eve of 1914,* Translated by E. W. Dickes. New York: Knopf, 1936.

———. *Tagebücher 1914–1919.* Vol. 1. Bernd Soesemann, ed. Boppard am Rhein: H. Boldt, 1984.

Zedlitz-Trützschler, Robert. *Zwölf Jahre am deutschen Kaiserhof.* Berlin; Leipzig: Deutsche Verlag, 1924.

III. Secondary Literature

Albertini, Luigi. *The Origins of the War of 1914.* 3 vols. Translated by Isabella M. Massey. 1952. London: Oxford Univ. Press, 1967.

Allain, Jean-Claude. *Joseph Caillaux: le defi victorieux 1863–1914.* Paris: Imprimerie nationale, 1978.

Angell, Norman. *The Great Illusion.* New York: G. P. Putnam's Sons, 1913.

Balfour, Michael. *The Kaiser and His Times.* Boston: Houghton Mifflin, 1964.

Barnett, Correlli. *The Sword Bearers.* London: Eyre & Spottiswood, 1963.

Becker, Jean–Jacques. *1914: Comment les Francais son entrés dans la guerre.* Paris: Fondation nationale des sciences politiques, 1977.

Bernhardi, Friedrich von. *Germany and the Next War.* Translated by Allen H. Powles. New York: Longmans, Green, 1914.

Bosworth, Richard J. B. *Italy, the Least of the Great Powers: Italian Foreign Policy before the First World War.* Cambridge: Cambridge Univ. Press, 1979.

———. *Italy and the Approach of the First World War.* New York: St. Martin's Press, 1983.

Bredin, Jean-Denis. *Joseph Caillaux.* Paris: Hachette littâerature, 1980.

Butterfield, Herbert. "Sir Edward Grey in July 1914." *Historical Studies,* 5 (1965): 1–25.

Cairns, John C. "International Politics and the Military Mind: The Case of the French Republic." *Journal of Modern History,* 25, no. 3 (September 1953): 273–86.

Cambon, H. *Un Diplomate, Paul Cambon Ambassadeur de France 1843– 1924.* Paris: Plon, 1937.

Carroll, Malcolm. *Germany and the Great Powers 1866–1914.* New York: Octagon Books, 1975.

Cecil, Lamar. *Albert Ballin: Business and Politics in Imperial Germany.* Princeton, N.J.: Princeton Univ. Press, 1967.

———. *The German Diplomatic Service, 1871–1914.* Princeton, N.J.: Princeton Univ. Press, 1976.

Churchill, Randolph S. *Winston S. Churchill,* vol. 2: *Young Statesman 1901– 1914.* Boston: Houghton Mifflin, 1967.

Churchill, Winston S. *The World Crisis.* Abridged and revised ed. New York: Thornton Butterworth, 1932.

Class, Heinrich [Daniel Frymann, pseud.]. *Wenn Ich der Kaiser War' politisches Wahrheiten und Notwendigkeiten.* 5th enl. ed. Leipzig: Dietrich, 1914.

Corti, Egon Caesar, and Hans Sokol. *Der Alte Kaiser.* 3d ed. Graz; Vienna: Styria Verlag, 1956.

Dedijer, Vladimir. *The Road to Sarajevo.* London: MacGibbon & Kee, 1960.

Dragnich, Alex N. *Serbia, Nikola Pasic and Yugoslavia.* New Brunswick, N.J.: Rutgers Univ. Press, 1974.

Engel-Janosi and Helmut Rumpler, eds. *Probleme der Franzisko-Josephinishen Zeit 1848–1916.* Vienna: Verlag für Geschichte und Politik, 1967.

Erenyi, Gustav. *Graf Stefan Tisza, ein Staatsmann und Märtyrer.* Vienna; Leipzig: E. P. Tal, 1935.

Eubank, Keith. *Paul Cambon Master Diplomatist.* Norman, Okla.: Univ. of Oklahoma Press, 1960.

Evans, J. W., and Harmut Pogge von Strandmann, eds. *The Coming of the First World War.* Oxford: Clarendon, 1988.

Fay, Sidney B. *The Origins of the World War.* 2 vols. 1930. Reprint. New York: Free Press, 1966.

Fellner, Fritz. "Die 'Mission Hoyos.' " In *Deutschlands Sonderung von Europa 1862–1945.* Wilhelm Alff, ed. 283–316. Frankfurt a/M; New York: P. Lang, 1984.

Fischer, Fritz. *Krieg der Illusionen.* Düsseldorf: Droste, 1969.

Frantz, Gunther. *Russlands Eintritt in den Weltgrieg.* Berlin: Deutsche Verlagsgesellschaft für Politik und Geschichte, 1924.

Gilbert, Martin. *Sir Horace Rumbold.* London: Heinemann, 1973.

Goldberg, Harvey. *The Life of Jean Jaurès.* Madison, Wis.: Univ. of Wisconsin Press, 1968.

Gooss, Roderich. *Das Wiener Kabinett und die Entstehung des Weltkrieges.* Vienna: L. W. Seidel, 1919.

Gutsche, Willibald. *Aufsteig und Fall eines Reichskanzlers.* Berlin: Akademie Verlag, 1973.

Haffner, Sebastian. *The Ailing Empire. Germany from Bismarck to Hitler.* Translated by Jean Steinberg. New York: Fromm International, 1989.

Hale, O. J. *Publicity and Diplomacy With Special Reference to England and Germany 1890–1914.* New York; London: D. Appleton-Century, 1940.

Hantsch, Hugo. *Leopold Graf Berchtold: Grandseigneur und Staatsmann.* 2 vols. Graz; Vienna; Cologne: Verlag Styria, 1963.

Hazlehurst, Cameron. *Politicians At War.* New York: Knopf, 1971.

Hendrick, Burton J. *The Life and Letters of Walter H. Page.* Vol. 1. New York: Doubleday, 1924.

Hinsley, F. H., ed. *British Foreign Policy Under Sir Edward Grey.* London: Cambridge Univ. Press, 1977.

Hull, Isabell V. *The Entourage of Kaiser Wilhelm II, 1888–1918.* Cambridge: Cambridge Univ. Press, 1985.

Jarausch, Konrad H. *The Enigmatic Chancellor: Bethmann Hollweg and the Hubris of Imperial Germany.* New Haven: Yale Univ. Press, 1973.
———. "The Illusion of Limited War: Chancellor Bethmann Hollweg's Calculated Risk, July 1914." *Central European History,* 2, no. 1 (March 1969): 48–76.
Jászi, Oscar. *The Dissolution of the Habsburg Monarchy.* 1929. Reprint. Chicago: Univ. of Chicago Press, 1964.
Jenkins, Roy. *Asquith. Portrait of a Man and an Era.* New York: E. P. Dutton, 1966.
Joll, James. *The Origins of the First World War.* 2d ed. London; New York: Longman, 1992.
Kaiser, David E. "Germany and the Origins of the First World War." *The Journal of Modern History,* 55, no. 3 (September 1983): 442–74.
Kann, R. A. *Kaiser Franz Joseph und der Ausbruch des Weltkriegs.* Vienna: Böhlau in Komm, 1971.
Keiger, John F. *France and the Origins of the First World War.* New York: St. Martin's, 1983.
Kennan, George F. *The Fateful Alliance.* New York: Pantheon, 1984.
Kennedy, Paul M., ed. *The War Plans of the Great Powers.* London: Allen & Unwin, 1979.
Koss, Stephan. *Asquith.* London: A. Lane, 1976.
Levi, Leonard, ed. *Emotional Stress.* Proceedings of an International Symposium arranged by the Swedish Delegation for Applied Medical Defense Research, Stockholm, 5–6 February 1965. New York: American Elsevier Publishing Co., 1967.
Lieven, D. C. B. *Russia and the Origins of the First World War.* New York: St. Martin's, 1983.
———. *Nicholas II Twilight of the Empire.* New York: St. Martin's, 1993.
Lowe, C. J., and M. L. Dockrill, eds. *The Mirage of Power.* 3 vols. London; Boston: Routledge & Kegan Paul, 1972.
Marshall, S. L. A. *World War I.* 1964. Reprint. New York: American Heritage, 1971.
Massie, Robert K. *Nicholas and Alexandra.* 1967. Reprint. New York: Dell, 1971.
May, Ernest R., ed. *Knowing One's Enemies.* Princeton, N.J.: Princeton Univ. Press, 1984.
Mayer, Arno J. *The Persistance of the Old Regime: Europe to the Great War.* New York: Pantheon, 1981.
Michon, Georges. *The Franco-Russian Alliance 1891–1917.* Translated by Norman Thomas. 1919. New York: Howard Fertig, 1969.
Miller, Steven E., Sean M. Lynn-Jones, and Stephan Van Evera, eds. *Mili-*

tary Strategy and the Origins of the First World War. Revised and expanded ed. Princeton, N.J.: Princeton Univ. Press, 1991.

Miquel, Pierre. *Poincaré.* 1961. Paris: Fogard, 1984.

Monger, George. *The End of Isolation: British Foreign Policy 1900–1907.* London: T. Nelson, 1963.

Nicolson, Harold. *Sir Arthur Nicolson, Bart., First Lord Carnock.* London: Constable, 1930.

———. *King George the Fifth: His Life and Reign.* London: Constable, 1952.

Oldenberg, S. S. *The Last Tsar.* Translated by L. I. Milhalap. Vol. 3. Gulf Breeze, Fla., 1977.

Opocénsky, Jan. "A War-Time Discussion of Responsibility for the War." *Journal of Modern History,* 4, no. 3 (September 1932): 415–29.

Peterson, H. Bertil. "Das österreichisch-hungarische Memorandum an Deutschland vom 5. Juli 1914." *Scandia,* 30 (1964): 138–90.

Recouly, Raymond. *Les Heures Tragiques d'Avant-Guerre.* Paris: La Renaissance du livre, 1929.

Redlich, Joseph. *Emperor Francis Joseph of Austria.* London: Macmillan, 1929.

Regele, Oskar. *Feldmarschall Conrad. Auftrag und Erfüllung 1906–1918.* Vienna: Verlag Herold, 1955.

Remak, Joachim. *Sarajevo.* New York: Criterion Books, 1959.

Riasanovsky, Nicholas V. *A History of Russia.* 3d ed. Oxford: Oxford Univ. Press, 1977.

Ritter, Gerhard. *The Sword and Scepter.* Vol. 2, *The European Powers and the Wilhelminian Empire, 1890–1914.* Translated by Heinz Norden. Coral Gables, Fla.: Univ. of Miami Press, 1965.

———. *The Schlieffen Plan: Critique of a Myth.* Translated by Andrew and Eva Wilson. London: O. Wolff, 1958.

Robbins, Keith. *Sir Edward Grey.* London: Cassell, 1971.

Röhl, John C. G. *Kaiser Hoff und Staat. Wilhelm II und die deutsche Politik.* Munich: C. H. Beck, 1987. This has recently been translated as *The Kaiser and his court: Wilhelm II and the government of Germany.* Translated by Terrence F. Cole. New York: Cambridge Univ. Press, 1995.

———. "Admiral von Müller and the Approach of War, 1911–1914." *The Historical Journal,* 12, no. 4 (1969): 651–73.

Röhl, John C. G. and Nicolaus Sombart, eds. *Kaiser Wilhelm II. New Interpretations. The Corfu Papers.* New York: Cambridge Univ. Press, 1982.

Schroeder, Paul W. "World War I as Galloping Gertie." *Journal of Modern History,* 44, no. 3 (September 1972): 319–45.

Scott, Jonathan F. *Five Weeks: The Surge of Public Opinion on the Eve of the Great War.* New York: John Day, 1927.

Steiner, Zara S. *The Foreign Office and Foreign Policy, 1898–1914.* New York: Cambridge Univ. Press, 1969.

———. *Britain and the Origins of the First World War.* New York: St. Martin's, 1977.

Stokes, Gale. "The Serbian Documents From 1914: A Preview." Available as an on-demand-supplement to *Journal of Modern History,* 48, no. 3 (September 1976). Order through: Microfilm International, 300 North Zeeb Road, Ann Arbor, Mich. 48106. Order no. IJ-00011.

Stone, Norman. "Die Mobilmachung der österreichisch-ungarischen Armee 1914." *Militärgeschichtliche Mitteilungen* 16 (2/1974): 67–95.

———. *The Eastern Front 1914–1917.* New York: Scribner, 1975.

Tabouis, Genevieve. *The Life of Jules Cambon.* Translated by C. F. Atkinson. London: J. Cape, 1938.

Travers, T. H. E. "Technology, Tactics and Morale: Jean Bloch, the Boer War, and British Military Theory, 1900–1914." *Journal of Modern History,* 51, no. 2 (June 1979): 264–86.

Trevelyan, George Macaulay. *Grey of Fallodon.* Boston: Houghton Mifflin, 1937.

Tuchman, Barbara W. *The Proud Tower.* 1966. Reprint. New York: Bantam, 1972.

Turner, L. C. F. *The Origins of the First World War.* New York: Norton, 1970.

———. "The Russian Mobilization in 1914." *Journal of Contemporary History,* 3, no. 1 (January 1968): 65–88.

Vermes, Gabor. *Istvan Tisza.* East European Monographs, No. 184. New York: Columbia Univ. Press, 1985.

Wank, Soloman. "The Appointment of Berchtold as Austro-Hungarian Foreign Minister." *Journal of Central European Affairs,* 23, no. 2 (July 1963): 143–51.

———. "Some Reflections on Conrad von Hötzendorff and His Memoirs based on Old and New Sources." *Austrian History Yearbook,* 1 (1965): 74–89.

Wank, Soloman, ed. *Doves and Diplomats: Foreign Offices and Peace Movements in Europe and America in the Twentieth Century.* Westport, Conn.: Greenwood, 1978.

Watt, D. C. "The British Reactions to the Assassination at Sarajevo." *European Studies Review,* 1, no. 3 (1971): 233–47.

Wilson, Keith M. *The Policy of the Entente.* Cambridge; New York: Cambridge Univ. Press, 1985.

Würthle, Friedrich. *Die Spur Führt Nach Belgrad. Sarajevo 1914.* Vienna: Molden Verlag, 1975.

Young, Harry F. *Prince Lichnowsky and the Great War.* Athens, Ga.: Univ. of Georgia Press, 1977.

————. "The Misunderstanding of August 1," *The Journal of Modern History,* 48, no. 4 (December 1976): 644–65.

Zechlin, Egmont. "Deutschland Zwischen Kabinettskrieg und Wirtschaftskrieg: Politik und Kriegsführung in den ersten Monaten des Weltkrieges 1914." *Historische Zeitschrift,* 199, no. 2 (October 1964): 347–458.

Index